(Continued on back endsheets)

Seventeenth-Century British Nondramatic Poets

Third Series

Seventeenth-Century British Nondramatic Poets

Third Series

Edited by
M. Thomas Hester
North Carolina State University

A Bruccoli Clark Layman Book
Gale Research Inc.
Detroit, Washington, D.C., London

Advisory Board for
DICTIONARY OF LITERARY BIOGRAPHY

John Baker
William Cagle
Jane Christensen
Patrick O'Connor
Peter S. Prescott

Matthew J. Bruccoli and Richard Layman, Editorial Directors
C. E. Frazer Clark, Jr., Managing Editor
Karen L. Rood, Senior Editor

Printed in the United States of America

Published simultaneously in the United Kingdom
by Gale Research International Limited
(An affiliated company of Gale Research Inc.)

The paper used in this publication meets the minimum requirements
of American National Standard for Information Sciences—Permanence
Paper for Printed Library Materials, ANSI Z39.48-1984. ∞ ™

Library of Congress Catalog Card Number 93-8481
ISBN 0-8103-5390-3

I(T)P™

The trademark ITP is used under license.

10 9 8 7 6 5 4 3 2 1

Contents

Plan of the Series

The advisory board, the editors, and the publisher of the *Dictionary of Literary Biography* are joined in endorsing Mark Twain's declaration. The literature of a nation provides an inexhaustible resource of permanent worth. We intend to make literature and its creators better understood and more accessible to students and the reading public, while satisfying the standards of teachers and scholars.

To meet these requirements, *literary biography* has been construed in terms of the author's achievement. The most important thing about a writer is his writing. Accordingly, the entries in *DLB* are career biographies, tracing the development of the author's canon and the evolution of his reputation.

The purpose of *DLB* is not only to provide reliable information in a convenient format but also to place the figures in the larger perspective of literary history and to offer appraisals of their accomplishments by qualified scholars.

The publication plan for *DLB* resulted from two years of preparation. The project was proposed to Bruccoli Clark by Frederick C. Ruffner, president of the Gale Research Company, in November 1975. After specimen entries were prepared and typeset, an advisory board was formed to refine the entry format and develop the series rationale. In meetings held during 1976, the publisher, series editors, and advisory board approved the scheme for a comprehensive biographical dictionary of persons who contributed to North American literature. Editorial work on the first volume began in January 1977, and it was published in 1978. In order to make *DLB* more than a reference tool and to compile volumes that individually have claim to status as literary history, it was decided to organize volumes by topic, period, or genre. Each of these free-standing volumes provides a biographical-bibliographical guide and overview for a particular area of literature. We are convinced that this organization – as opposed to a single alphabet method – constitutes a valuable innovation in the presentation of reference material. The volume plan necessarily requires many decisions for the placement and treatment of authors who might properly be included in two or three volumes. In some instances a major figure will be included in separate volumes, but with different entries emphasizing the aspect of his career appropriate to each volume. Ernest Hemingway, for example, is represented in *American Writers in Paris, 1920–1939* by an entry focusing on his expatriate apprenticeship; he is also in *American Novelists, 1910–1945* with an entry surveying his entire career. Each volume includes a cumulative index of the subject authors and articles. Comprehensive indexes to the entire series are planned.

With volume ten in 1982 it was decided to enlarge the scope of *DLB*. By the end of 1986 twenty-one volumes treating British literature had been published, and volumes for Commonwealth and Modern European literature were in progress. The series has been further augmented by the *DLB Year-books* (since 1981) which update published entries and add new entries to keep the *DLB* current with contemporary activity. There have also been *DLB Documentary Series* volumes which provide biographical and critical source materials for figures whose work is judged to have particular interest for students. One of these companion volumes is entirely devoted to Tennessee Williams.

We define literature as the *intellectual commerce of a nation:* not merely as belles lettres but as that ample and complex process by which ideas are generated, shaped, and transmitted. *DLB* entries are not limited to "creative writers" but extend to other figures who in their time and in their way influenced the mind of a people. Thus the series encompasses historians, journalists, publishers, and screenwriters. By this means readers of *DLB* may be aided to perceive literature not as cult scripture in the keeping of intellectual high priests but firmly positioned at the center of a nation's life.

   DLB includes the major writers appropriate to each volume and those standing in the ranks immediately behind them. Scholarly and critical counsel has been sought in deciding which minor figures to include and how full their entries should be. Wherever possible, useful references are made to figures who do not warrant separate entries.

   Each *DLB* volume has a volume editor responsible for planning the volume, selecting the figures for inclusion, and assigning the entries. Volume editors are also responsible for preparing, where appropriate, appendices surveying the major periodicals and literary and intellectual movements for their volumes, as well as lists of further readings. Work on the series as a whole is coordinated at the Bruccoli Clark Layman editorial center in Columbia, South Carolina, where the editorial staff is responsible for accuracy of the published volumes.

   One feature that distinguishes *DLB* is the illustration policy — its concern with the iconography of literature. Just as an author is influenced by his surroundings, so is the reader's understanding of the author enhanced by a knowledge of his environment. Therefore *DLB* volumes include not only drawings, paintings, and photographs of authors, often depicting them at various stages in their careers, but also illustrations of their families and places where they lived. Title pages are regularly reproduced in facsimile along with dust jackets for modern authors. The dust jackets are a special feature of *DLB* because they often document better than anything else the way in which an author's work was perceived in its own time. Specimens of the writers' manuscripts are included when feasible.

   Samuel Johnson rightly decreed that "The chief glory of every people arises from its authors." The purpose of the *Dictionary of Literary Biography* is to compile literary history in the surest way available to us — by accurate and comprehensive treatment of the lives and work of those who contributed to it.

The *DLB* Advisory Board

Introduction

"So we beat on, boats against the current, borne back ceaselessly into the past."

F. Scott Fitzgerald, *The Great Gatsby* (1925)

This volume of the *Dictionary of Literary Biography* comprises the literary biographies of the third generation of seventeenth-century British nondramatic poets: those born after the start of the Thirty Years' War in 1618 and before the Restoration of the Stuart monarchy in 1660. The sole exception – John Milton (1608-1674) – is included because his most significant poems (*Paradise Lost,* 1667, and *Paradise Regained* and *Samson Agonistes,* both 1671) were publications comtemporaneous in spirit as well as printing to the other poetry discussed in this volume, poetry on which they had significant influence also. Like Milton, most of this generation of poets began to compose poems during the Stuart reign of Charles I (1625-1649) and during the Commonwealth period when, after the victory of the Puritan-parliamentary forces over the Royalist army in the civil wars (and the subsequent legal execution of the king, 30 January 1649), the nation was ruled by the military Council of State (1649-1653) and then by (the Puritan lord protector) Oliver Cromwell (1653-1658) and his son Richard Cromwell (1658-1659). All of these poets except Richard Lovelace and Patrick Cary lived to see the restoration of the Stuarts to the throne with the return from French exile and reigns of Charles II (1660-1685) and his brother James II (1685-1688). Most were still alive and writing when James II was exiled and deposed by the Glorious ("Bloodless") Revolution, which brought William III and Mary II to rule (1689-1702); a few of these poets lived to see the reign of Queen Anne (1702-1714); and Jane Barker and Sir Richard Blackmore lived even to see the start of the reign of the House of Hanover by George I (1714-1727) and George II (1727-1760). As a group, then, this generation of poets lived during one of the most tumultuous periods of change in the history of England – a period during which it moved from a "medieval" to a "modern" state and culture; theirs was "a warlike, various, and a tragical age," said Abraham Cowley, "best to *write of,* but worst to *write in.*" Thus, it is not surprising that these poets would in-

cline repeatedly to writing *public, historical poetry,* or that the modes of private verse they would use primarily to assess the power of "Time's winged chariot," or that their sole successful example of *the* genre of national appraisal would be a *meditative* justification of seeking "a Paradise *within.*"

Most of the poetry of this generation of British poets was composed during the final stages of a century-long cultural movement away from a largely hierarchical, autocratic code of aristocratic *honour* in which the "medieval" authority of church and state controlled in large degree the stability of the Elizabethan "Settlement" that had held in tense suspense the potentially disruptive effects of the threat posed by the Reformation to ancient and traditional definitions of authority. Inheritors of the Renaissance tradition of Christian humanist learning, with its Ciceronian emphasis on "eloquent" service to church and state, and of an essentially medieval political theology that seemed to have been successfully stabilized by the national and international successes of Queen Elizabeth I, these poets were all firm believers in the Christocentric universe of Providential order and benevolence. To a large degree, the central literary conflicts of the age arose from their differing interpretations of the *means* by which His Providence "tried" mankind's confessional positions – to use but the most significant examples, whether King Charles I or Oliver Cromwell was God's Providential "minister," or the satanic prefiguration/embodiment of His "scourge" announcing the Millennium, or merely an agent of "Time" caught like everyone else in the atomistic whirl of political and cultural motions, either divine or natural. The cultural tradition inherited by this generation asserted certain basic principles, by which man was the central creature in God's Creation, like the sun at the center of the elemental macrocosm that man mirrored in shape and form; man maintained vestiges of the *imago dei* (image of God) in the tripartite (memory-understanding-will) structure of his rational soul, despite the adamant proclivities of his libidinous and rebellious "fallen will" that had brought his expulsion from Paradise; and he could be saved and "regain" Paradise through the free gift of God's Grace, which alone could save man from the damnation he naturally deserved. These poets inherited, in other words, with little modification, the divine cosmos and Christian economy of the Middle Ages, a system of divinely ordained analogies in which the cosmological, the social, the political, and the religious spheres of thought and action rigorously corresponded. As the Metaphysical poet John Donne phrased it in his "Satire III," despite the differing confessional choices across the broad spectrum of Anglo-Catholic belief, this "medieval" tradition insisted that everyman "Of force must one / And forc'd but one [confession] allow; / And the right"; the "cure" for the "worne maladies" of the fallen world was to "Seeke true religion":

> on a huge hill
> Cragged and steep, Truth stands, and hee that will
> Reach her, about must, and about must goe;
> And what the'hills suddenes resists, winne so;
> Yet strive so, that before age, deaths twilight,
> Thy Soule rest, for none can worke in that night.
> . . . .
> So perish Soules, which more chuse mens unjust
> Power from God claym'd, then God himselfe to trust.

In this sense, then, it is likely that Donne's warning about imminent chaos in *An Anatomy of the World* (1611), with its reliance on the medieval typology of Christ as the Phoenix and its alarm at the privileging of the subjective self, is less a frightened recoil from the innovations of Copernicus's heliocentric universe than it is the traditional *contemptus mundi* (contempt for the world) response to man's inevitable failures in moral and intellectual insight:

> new Philosophy cals all in doubt,
> . . . .
> 'Tis all in pieces, all cohærence gone;
> All just supply, and all Relation:
> Prince, Subject, Father, Sonne, are things forgot,
> For euery man alone thinkes he hath got
> To be a Phoenix, and that there can bee
> None of that kinde, of which he is, but hee.

Donne's "intellectual curiosity in scientific speculation provided him with convenient illustrations in *An Anatomy of the World* of the decay and disorder of the world and in *The Second Anniversary* (1612) of the soul's ignorance," F. P. Wilson suggests in *Elizabethan and Jacobean* (1945); but the novelty or "wit" of these poems that is representative of the philosophical meditations of Donne's contemporaries does not lie in their quite conventional and medieval meditations on habitual failures of mankind to maintain the *imago dei* within. Thus, even in its reliance on the planes of correspondence between the micro-

cosm and macrocosm to indict an age in which "art is lost, and correspondence too," Donne's tense anatomy of man's plight is generally continuous with the final warnings of the Doctor in *Everyman,* the sermons on order and obedience in the official *Book of Homilies,* or Ulysses' speech on "degree" in William Shakespeare's *Troilus and Cressida* (1609):

> The heavens themselves, the planets, and this centre
> Observe degree, priority, and place,
> Insisture, course, proportion, season, form,
> Office, and custom in all line of order;
> And therefore is the glorious planet Sol
> In noble eminence enthron'd and spher'd
> Amidst the other; whose med'cinable eye
> Corrects the ill aspects of planets evil,
> And posts like the commandment of a king,
> Sans check, to good and bad. . . .
>   O, when degree is shak'd
> Which is the ladder of all high designs,
> The enterprise is sick. . . .
> . . . .
> Take but degree away, untune that string,
> And hark what discord follows. Each thing meets
> In mere oppugnancy: the bounded waters
> Should lift their bosoms higher than the shores,
> And make a sop of all this solid globe;
> Strength should be lord of imbecility,
> And the rude son should strike his father dead;
> Force should be right, or rather, right and wrong
> (Between whose endless jar justice resides)
> Should lose their names, and so should justice too!
> Then every thing include itself in power,
> Power into will, will into appetite,
> And appetite, an universal wolf
> (So doubly seconded with will and power),
> Must make perforce an universal prey,
> And last eat up himself.

The resilience of this organic view of the universe is attested by its survival amid Milton's parodies of "heroic" models in *Paradise Lost,* when his archangel Raphael describes the vertical scale of God's design for mankind:

> So from the root
> Springs higher the green stalk, from thence the leaves
> More aerie, last the bright consummate floure
> Spirits odorous breathes: flours and thir fruit,
> Mans nourishment, by gradual scale sublim'd
> To vital Spirits aspire, to animal,
> To intellectual, give both life and sense,
> Fansie and understanding, whence the soule
> Reason receives, and reason is her being.

In fact, Milton's organic scheme allows the possibility of a human spiritual development (through Grace) that recalls the original optimistic bases of the Renaissance humanist vision of man's dignity:

Your bodies may at last turn all to Spirit,
Improv'd by tract of time, and wingd ascend
Ethereal, as wee, or may at choice
Here and in Heav'nly Paradises dwell;
If ye be found obedient.

The character of "epic" virtue has been radically redefined by Milton, of course (as denoted in the last line above), but the power of the organic concept to explain God's "Cov'nant" to the Puritan reader – by which "one just Man" renews the divine promise by which

> Day and Night
> Seed time and Harvest, Heat and hoary Frost
> Shall hold their course, till fire purge things new,
> Both Heav'n and Earth, wherein the just shall dwell

– survives even Milton's appraisal of the *decay* of the English national mission. However, that Milton's Puritan contemporary Andrew Marvell in 1650 could make the subject of a commendatory "Horatian Ode" a "forward youth" who "could not cease / In the inglorious arts of peace, / But through advent'rous war / Urged his active star" in order to overthrow a divine king and who, as "the Wars' and Fortune's son," was urged to remember *above all* that "The same arts that did gain / A *power* must it maintain" (however equivocal or ambiguous the poet's own opinion of Oliver Cromwell) is a revealing indication of how far from the world of Shakespeare's *Troilus and Cressida* and how deeply into the world of Thomas Hobbes's *Leviathan* (1651) England had come by the time of the maturity of this third generation of seventeenth-century poets.

From one perspective, the crisis of cultural revolution which these poets confronted (or which confronted them) was merely the culmination of a general and specific assault on nonsecular society which can be traced back (at least) to King Henry VIII's placing of his own dynastic and amatory/sexual desires before the demands of the spiritual courts, perhaps even back – if one notes the Civil War as an inevitable consequence of the strains that the Reformation placed on the medieval hegemony – to the culmination on English soil of a general secularizing movement whose origins one could find in Martin Luther's posting of his personal demands for the reform of the church (generated in large measure by his own search for a creed of *personal assurance*) on the *outside* of the cathedral at Wittenberg in 1517. This is not to suggest, of course, that the sort of personal manipulation of "the divine rights of king" theology of James I and Charles I, or the immorality of their courts, or the failures of the later Stuart monarchs to maintain the balance of the Elizabethan Settlement or to provide a celebratory model for the nation were not instrumental to the general assault on "Authority" in England during the century. The Stuart kings, for instance, seemed not to understand that their authority could not be formalized by rigorous defenses of a theory of "the divine rights of kings" or maintained by the insistent performance of a sort of daily royal "masque" that obtained only the illusion of medieval political theology. Neither James I nor Charles I was able to inspire the personal confidence and devotion that had helped Elizabeth I shape England – through the genius of her chosen counselors and advisers, of course – into a confident, international state proud of its traditions and image. The offensive absolutism of James I's divine-right theory, which lacked any basis in English custom and any appeal to the increasingly restless gentry and commercial classes – much less to the Puritans whom he had threatened to "harry out of the country" or to the radical sectarians who had engineered the Gunpowder Plot not long after the king's accession – was muted by the muddling moderation of his policies, the endless befuddlements of the "Spanish Match," and his own controversial personal conduct. After the failures and melancholic results of James's rule, the efforts of Charles to make the divine-right theory into a reality on the Gallic model was simply a recipe for disaster – especially when the king's court became more and more aloof from the changes the society was undergoing, and specifically when it was apparent that the king's only significant "change" of policy was his self-indulgent movement from the questionable influence of George Villiers, first Duke of Buckingham, to the objectionable influence of his Roman Catholic queen, Henrietta Maria, and his Arminian religious adviser, Archbishop William Laud.

The formal, efficient, and civil instrument of change that this generation of poets witnessed was, of course, the Revolution that resulted in the *legalized* execution of Charles I and the (momentary) military dictatorship of the Puritan-parliamentary forces, literally and emblematically embodied in the rise of Oliver Cromwell to the authority of "protector" of a British "Commonwealth." Cromwell made significant advances in the state of England in the world. Not only did he unite the whole island into a commonwealth through his subjection of the Irish and the Scots, but he revived and brought to world status the navy, managed to maintain a formidable force against the French attempt to subject the Continent to the authority of Louis XIV, and began the movement toward a broad religious toleration by subjecting ecclesiastical authority to the Parliament. But then, on his death, the weakness of his son and the assumption of actual power by Gen. George Monck only hastened the call for a restoration of the monarchy.

Charles II arrived confident of a return of royal authority, but when confronted by a strong Parliament he began to engage in a series of secret negotiations and treaties with King Louis XIV aimed at restoring Catholicism to England. Despite the wisdom and advice of Edward Hyde, Lord Clarendon, who was soon replaced by the pro-Catholic "Cabal," Charles seemed unable to learn from the example of his father's mistakes. On coming to power, his brother openly engaged in an even stronger Catholic allegiance; and, after Louis XIV's revocation of the Edict of Nantes that had granted religious tolerance in France, when James II refused to give shelter to the Huguenots or to heed the call for an English response to such an assault on international Protestantism, the stage was set for the Glorious Revolution by which the sole successful opponent of the French forces in Europe, William of Orange, was "invited" to join with the daughter of King James II to rule the country.

Complementary to this political movement from royal autocracy to constitutional pluralism during the century was the movement to a largely "modern" worldview, by which a materialistic, pluralistic, mechanistic, republican code of individual and class *politics,* in which future "monarchs" could claim only limited authority and little power, was endorsed by a largely sectarian and individualistic religious creed and by a new social "settlement" that was largely based on contracts between secular social units. In response, the poets of this "new" dispensation remain committed to the defense of Providence – Cowley, for instance, can support the "new science" of Sir Francis Bacon's inductive methodology to a large degree because Bacon had successfully defended it as a means to discern the complexity of the Providential design; Marvell strives throughout his career to accommodate the history of Cromwell and the Revolution to that divine design; and even two poets as far apart politically and ideologically as Milton and John Dryden maintain a singular focus of attention on how the successes and failures of the Revolution or the Restoration reveal "the ways of God to men." But those literary forms and modes associated with the (Tudor-Stuart) court system of patronage and privilege – the sonnet, the pastoral allegory, the masque and madrigal, and blank verse (with the notable ex-

ceptions of the poetic genius by which a Milton and a Dryden found new life and uses in them) – were largely displaced by "new" codes of decorum or by the revival of genres more adept at addressing the pressing political issues of a pluralistic society with a wider readership than the court coterie.

The lyric, for instance – the masterpiece and centerpiece of Tudor-Stuart achievement, the genre that Petrarch and Sir Thomas Wyatt and Henry Howard, Earl of Surrey, had used to justify the excellence of their native languages, which Shakespeare, Donne, Ben Jonson, Christopher Marlowe, Samuel Daniel, and the host of court poets had taken to new heights of excellence and experimental diversity – lost its position of prominence in the poetry of this generation. The lyric was largely replaced by the vehicles of *public* justification, *political* history, *personal* praise and blame: the epic, the ode, and the verse satire, all three frequently addressed in the "more scientific" and (in Dryden's terms) the "newer" *rational*istic cadences of the rhymed couplet. The first generation of seventeenth-century poets (as exemplified by Donne, Jonson, and Michael Drayton) had turned from the general failures of the court to provide a celebratory model to the *private* modes, but thus rendering their subversion of the hierarchy in private rather than public form. The second generation (as exemplified by Thomas Carew, Robert Herrick, and George Herbert) had exhibited a range of responses to cultural change, from a strained attempt to justify the excesses of the court, to an equivocal response to the onslaught of "*Times transhifting,*" through a retreat to the pastoral critique of imminent Puritan literalism seemingly effaced only by the "Pillar" of poetry, to a meditative retreat from the aristocratic and urban, modern world altogether. The third generation (given the caveat that any generalization about a generation is only a useful metaphor of general features) seemed to have engrafted the personal, meditative voice with the public, political voice by which, to iterate the paradox of modernity, the public spirit and the private perspective maintain or achieve the status of the religious confession even while asserting the separation of the spheres of the secular and the sacred. The "new" authority of the rhymed couplet, then, became increasingly popular for its discursive power; satire gained a popularity never before attained in British literature; and the epic, through the profound achievement of Milton and the aptness of the genre as a vehicle for reflection on the travails of the civilization itself in the civil wars, reached a prominence and perfection surpassing even the most "English" epic model for the age, Edmund Spenser's *Faerie Queene* (1589, 1596). The poets of this third generation, then, searched through the models of the ancient and modern poets in order to express a new "settlement" with the "new" world of the "modern" age and its emphasis on the privilege of the individual reader rather than the courtly hierarchy. Perhaps that is why Milton's is indeed the *last* English epic; for his transformation of this vehicle of aristocratic aesthetics into a defense of the individualistic Protestant *inner voice* (that "Paradise within thee happier farre") through the reliance on Ovidian parody (as explained by Louis Martz in *Poet of Exile,* 1980) of those "old" codes of heroic action and virtue is so successful and so "new" that it radically redefines (and, in a sense, therein erases the hierarchical substructures of) the genre. As Alastair Fowler phrases it, Milton "had a new myth of virtue to offer – a morality of individual responsibility to God [that] he believed to be superior to the aristocratic honour of hierarchy" (*A History of English Literature,* 1987). Once the epic has been so powerfully *internalized* – as a literary complement of the movement toward a "modern" pluralistic, individualistic concept of the self – it becomes a vehicle only the Romantics will strive to reenact. For the post-Restoration poets (especially those such as Milton, Marvell, and Dryden who, for different reasons, were equally disenchanted by the attempts to solve spiritual problems by political means, and who in a most significant sense shared Milton's eventual disillusionment with the attempts to "restore" or "regain" Paradise through secular-political instruments) the epic became the mock-epic; and when even satire proved an insufficient recoil from the world of spiritual dunces and failed political experiments, then the *return* to classical translations emerged as an ultimate attempt to discover some model worthy of imitation and action. It is not surprising, then, that on the death of Charles II and the ascendancy of the hapless James II even those most radically hedonistic poets of Charles's "ministry of pleasure" would turn to Whig Parliamentarianism in their desperate search for some form of stability; it is revealing, in fact, that Dryden, the poet of the *new* age (who identified himself as *Neander* ["the new man"] in his *Of Dramatick Poesie: An Essay* [1667] in defense of the Moderns), would conclude his poetic career with *translations* of the classics.

It is not simply the radical changes of the social and political landscape alone that endorsed or brought about these major shifts of generic interest. The novel, of course, might well be exemplary of the transfer of reading authority from the upper to the middle class; and Milton may well have spoken prophetically when he described his audience for an epic to be "few." Other pressures than the political, for instance, explain equally well the general demise of the lyric in the century; foremost is the general "decay" of the lyric itself, at least in the hands of the male poets of the Stuart courts. For female poets, the "new" voices of the age – new in the sense of their growing number of *publications,* their growing *recognition* by the largely male audience, and their *confidence* of expression and assertion – the lyric remained a powerful and useful vehicle of expression. Indeed, the transference of her skills in the lyric of female friendship to the "heroic" drama of the popular stage (as well as her translation of its content to the new prose of the protonovel) was instrumental to the success of Aphra Behn as the first Englishwoman to earn a living by writing. And the accommodations of the genre by poets such as Katherine Philips and Anne Killigrew to the themes of female friendship and love (along with Behn, of course), as well as the voluminous "similizing" by which Margaret Cavendish adapted and compressed the Donnean conceit into a vehicle for expression of philosophical speculation, scientific skepticism, and materialistic atomism – underscored by their readiness and ability to adapt lyrical themes and strictures to other revived "new" forms such as the Pindaric ode and the poem of advice – attest to the ways in which the lyric could be adapted to suit the voices of a "progressive" culture. Philips, for instance, goes beyond the conventions of the poetry of friendship to "rework the conventions, giving them new meanings that express a particularly female perspective" (as in Philips's revision of Donne's compass conceit in her "To my dearest Lucasia"), and thus manages to "negotiate a space of autonomy for herself and her female friends [and] to produce an image of female solidarity" (as Elaine Hobby explains in her *Virtue of Necessity: English Women's Writing 1649-88* [1989]). And Behn, while adept at the conventional love airs and songs, also finds a revisionist vein in the love poem. Turning the commonplace complaints about infidelity on the male lover while daring to discuss the rapacious capability of male desire in order to evoke a critique of men equal to the satiric lyrics of John Wilmot, Earl of Rochester, she dares in many poems to elicit a clarion call for women to reject that "faithless wanderer" ("To Alexis, in Answer to his poem") with his self-serving code of "honour." In that *translation* of a French source which expresses (in Hobby's terms) her "precise sentiments," Behn goes *outside* the English lyric to subvert its ideological underpinning: "Oh cursed honour! thou who first didst damn / A woman to the sin of shame / Honour that robst us of our gust, / . . . / Be gone!" ("The Golden Age," in Hobby).

Among the male lyrical poets, on the other hand, it is sometimes difficult to distinguish the lyric from the satire. Unlike those female poets using the genre to express a progressive ethos through which they might assert and define (that is, redefine) their selfhood and significance, the male court poets inevitably or eventually found the lyric's focus of attention on the authority of the self only a means to explore their personal and political instability. Lovelace's search for a way to maintain the aristocratic code of honor amid what he saw as the wilderness of the Interregnum, for instance, manages to discover in the amatory vows of the lyric a courtly system of *gesture* in which the unstable world of romantic love can offer no relief from the terrors of the "new" world surrounding him; he opts to retreat from his mistress and the imperative of the lyric into the desperate bows toward an equally hopeless (and politically doomed) authority: "I could not love thee, dear, loved I not honour *more.*" Certainly, the precise elegance and demeanor of his poems of devotional captivity work graceful variations on the central amatory theme of the genre, but they seldom revive the vigor or transcendence that Donne and Jonson had brought to it. And the lyrics of the hedonistic "ministry of pleasure" of the Restoration court manage only to carry this sense of entrapment native to the genre to its most cynical and skeptically desperate conclusion. In the lyrics of Charles Sackville, Lord Buckhurst and Earl of Dorset, for instance, the clever play with mock blasphemy and witty pornography familiar to Donne's inventive "monarchy of wit" becomes an anatomy of the scatological; in Sir Charles Sedley the humorous sophistry of "Nature's" amatory "idiots" is treated as the object of a scathing satire in which "concatenated Beasts" manage only to "deprave their Noble kind, / While sordid Avarice corrupts the mind" ("The Happy Pair"). Even the nobility of the "heroic" gesture is lost, in fact, when Rochester sets loose within the lyric the naturalistic brutalities of "Imperfect Enjoyment" and the atomistic indirections of relentless lust. From the self-conscious inclination to nihilism and the disenchanted mockery of any human pretension to transcendence in Rochester's lyrics there emerges, as Graham Roebuck phrases it, "a world without traces of a sense of larger ordering"; in Rochester's "Tunbridge Wells" the lyric proves a vehicle only to *parody* Hamlet's fleeting faith in human dignity:

"what thing is man, that thus / In all his shapes, he is ridiculous." Whether the general "failure of love" (A. J. Smith, *The Metaphysics of Love,* 1985) in the lyrics of the Stuart court poets reflects their understanding of the instability of the Restoration, or their attempt to test the ultimate limits to which this genre could take the secularism of their post-Revolution world (and its "constitutional" instead of "divine" monarch), or their fears that Hobbes's cynical reading of the new "Nature" was sound, it remains clear that – unable like Philips, Cavendish, and Killigrew to use the lyric as a vehicle of self-presentation and "new" definition – these poets managed finally only to turn the lyric into its generic opposite, the Juvenalian satire. Thus, Rochester's brilliant "Satyr against Reason and Mankind" – his ultimate parody (Roebuck points out) of Donne's dramatic meditation on love and religion as the pursuit of "our Mistresse Truth" / "our Mistresse, faire Religion" – in its Hobbesian mockery and worldweary ridicule of human amatory aspiration, best expresses "the true vein of Satyre" into which the court poets moved the lyric, and which they would bequeath to the neoclassical satirists, Alexander Pope and Jonathan Swift. Rochester describes all those deep "designs" underpinning the genre – "wisdom, power, and glory" – as arising "all from fear, . . . / Merely for safety":

Which is the basest creature, man or beast?
....
Man undoes man to do himself no good.
....
With voluntary pains works his distress,
Not through necessity, but wantonness.
....
Most men are cowards, all men should be knaves.
....
　　　　　　　　　　　　grant me this at least:
Man differs more from man, than man from beast.

Rather than teach "Honour, Love and Friendship to this Age," that is, the court poets turned the amatory lyric into a satiric expression of the *absence* of certainty and design in their world; the "genital urge" dominant in their lyrics, by which man becomes the creature of heartless time and indifferent nature, on the one hand is instrumental to their "search for the condition of the Eden" they had lost (Smith, *The Metaphysics of Love*), but on the other hand it also expresses the fear and trepidation with which they approached the "new" world of their culture. Their fervent search for new genres to express that world and their testing to their limits the old genres they inherited are signs of the intensity of their responses to the cultural revolution of the century.

(One should also note that the movement of the lyric into the satiric mode was accompanied by a scarcity of religious lyrics – or by the absence of strong religious lyricists – after Herbert and Henry Vaughan. As George Parfitt concludes in his *English Poetry of the Seventeenth Century* [1985], in this "new" age "the religious impulse . . . is diverted" to other genres, "into the serious doubts of the best of Rochester or into the secularized religion of Dryden.")

As for the specific content and shape of this "brave new world," the British cultural revolution of the century was not just a series of social, economic, religious, or political changes; it "embraced the whole of life. Two conceptions of civilization were in conflict," and its effects are demonstrable in every aspect of English life and culture (Christopher Hill, *The Century of Revolution*, 1961). The effects are most obvious, of course, in changes of the "source" of royal authority. James I came to the throne by hereditary right and could claim without impunity, even though without universal consent, to be the "divine" choice of Authority. After the Interregnum (which might well have led to the coronation of Cromwell had he not died and left his authority to his feeble son), King Charles II was "invited" by Parliament to return from exile in Holland and France; but when James II, in violation of the Test Act excluding Catholics from the throne, tried to restore the pro-Catholic policies that had been incremental to the fall of Charles I and had nearly cost Charles II his throne, Parliament "invited" William of Orange to inaugurate the last successful "invasion" of England and to accept the throne; and after the death of Queen Anne it was only by an act of Parliament, which in fact ignored several candidates with stronger hereditary claims, that the Hanoverians came to "power" (to serve mainly at the pleasure of a constitutional prerogative as interpreted in large degree by Parliament). This movement from Tudor-Stuart autocracy to a sort of loosely defined constitutional "monarchy" was underscored by the loss of real authority by the rulers as well. The most important choice of royal ministers was also moved from selection by the monarch to approval by the majority vote of Parliament; the financial and administrative authoritative independence enjoyed by James I (although he had to go to Parliament for war funds) became the Parliament's responsibility for national finances, customs, foreign policy, price controls, and monopolies.

Internationally, Hill reminds us, the status of England in the world community also changed drastically during the century. Due in large measure to the building of the Royal Navy under the leadership of Robert Blake, the nation became a first-rate world power with a growing colonial empire on three continents. The East India Company became the most powerful corporation in the world. English dress, tableware, diet, and manners changed with the surplus of booty from the colonies that displaced leather with more-comfortable clothes and expanded the menu with the new (Continental) custom of three meals a day. Even the major urban threat of the English Renaissance – the plague – largely disappeared by the end of the century. New institutions and groups accompanied these new habits and changes in national status. Under the leadership primarily of Thomas Osborne, Earl of Danby, and Anthony Ashley Cooper, Earl of Shaftesbury, the first two political parties of England were founded: the Tory party composed primarily of High Churchmen and landowners, inclining toward Royalism and support of monarchist causes, and the Whig party with its Puritan roots and its support of the rationalism and latitudinarianism of the Royal Society and the middle-class Dissenters. And after the rapid and violent shifts of ecclesiastical power and authority, the attitude toward religious difference and dissent by the end of the century had changed from statutory offense to tolerated "difference of opinion." To a large degree, then, as these selected examples outlined by Hill indicate, the national condition at which Donne scoffed in 1601 as most antithetical to the pursuit of "Truth" – a world in which, he warned in "Metempsychosis,"

Ther's nothing simply good, nor ill alone,
Of every quality comparison,
     The onely measure is, and judge, opinion

– had in many ways become the "new" England of the "modern" world. For Cowley, of course, Donne's fears and doubts had proven unfounded; for him, as exemplified in the founding of the Royal Society, the "new" nation stood as tall as Hercules, now embodied in someone like Thomas Sprat, who would

from all Old Errors free
And purge the Body of Philosophy;
     So from all Modern Folies He
Has vindicated Eloquence and Wit.

Driven by the example of that "mighty Man," Bacon, the Royal Society under Sprat continued the battle against "Authority" – "that Monstrous God which stood / In midst of th' Orchard, and the whole did claim [and] made / Children and superstitious Men afraid" ("To the Royal Society").

These radically opposed definitions of "Authority" are not just the differences of two opinions. Throughout all fields of inquiry and endeavor there was indeed a "new Philosophy." Most obviously, there was a "new" heliocentric universe, discovered by Copernicus and confirmed by Galileo and Johannes Kepler. There was even a new "microcosm," discovered by William Harvey, in which the "sensual" heart of man became a mechanical pump regulating the motions of the blood and segregated from the fluctuations of the emotions. There was even a "new" brand of metaphysical rationalism, invented by René Descartes, in which the subjective self assumed the status of self-creator by which man "thinks" and "therefore is." Thus, Donne's early warning that the "new Philosophy" only "cals" all in doubt focuses attention on the essential *nominalism* at the heart of the "new Philosophy" (as seen in its claim that abstract concepts or universals exist as names only) and on the kind of verbal and ontological *separations* of the spiritual and the material that were to characterize the "new learning." From this perspective, recollection of Donne's definition of "Power" as thoroughly divine in origin and effect (in "Satyre III" most prominently) throws in broad relief the thoroughly *modern* dimensions of Marvell's view of the mind's ostentatiously *non*-sacramental "Annihilating all that's made / To a green Thought in a green shade" ("The Garden"). In the same "new" vein is Marvell's curious figuration of the Pilgrims as trapped "all the way" in a "time" they can embrace only through the mechanical rhythms of their "falling Oars" ("Bermudas"). Equally "modern" are the tense and resolute ambiguities by which the execution of the last truly authoritative English monarch (or despot) is figured by Marvell as the motions of a "*Royal Actor*" who "nothing did or mean / Upon that memorable Scene" (with its possible suggestion that Charles I did "mean . . . nothing" during the "memorable Hour" of his brief strut across the stage of history) and by which the triumph of Cromwell is figured as the timely authority of one "fit for highest Trust" by Providence who presents his tithes to "the *Commons Feet* " and justifies his role as "the Wars' and Fortune's Son" by his understanding that "the last effect" of rule is the ability to "gain / A Pow'r" and "maintain" it ("An Horatian Ode upon Cromwell's Return from Ireland"). Even Marvell's lyrics, as Robert V. Young phrases it, exhibit an "acute, sensitive mind

confronting the myriad implications of that transformation" of medieval into modern England – but without a consistent (medieval-like) devotional impulse to see Providence as something more than "political." Fears about the political future of the nation and the integrity of man's own rational processes, it seems, come close to displacing Donne's fear about how "Soules perish" in Marvell's exquisite "modern" meditations.

Only Hobbes's description of the pluralistic and mechanistic character of the new universe or Bacon's pleas for the separation of the world of religious belief from the world of the "new learning" offers fuller description of the "new Philosophy" of the "modern" age. Written in response to the chaos of the Civil War, based on the traditional description of Providential history as a cyclic pattern alternating between peace and war, Hobbes's *Leviathan* recommends a plan to bring about a social *progress* and to prevent the repeated return to endless war by society's going outside Nature to accept the oppression of a secular and powerful "monster" that could regulate the biological shape of human conflict; this move – a sort of "abolition of man" (to recall C. S. Lewis's 1947 essay) that would eradicate or at least control the natural brutality of fallen man – was founded, of course, on a new meaning of Nature by which it is devoid essentially of spirit. "Nature, the art whereby God has made and governs the world," Hobbes explains,

is by the *art* of man, as in many things, so in this also imitated, that it can make an artificial animal. For seeing life is but a motion of limbs, the beginning whereof is in some principal part within; why may we not say, that all *automata* (engines that move themselves by springs and wheels as doth a watch) have an artificial life? For what is the heart but a spring; and the nerves but so many strings, and the joints, but so many wheels, giving motion to the whole body, such as was intended by the artificer?

The mechanization of the macrocosm works also to refigure microcosmic man's mind:

All fancies are motions within us, relics of those made in the sense: and those motions that immediately succeeded one another in the sense, continue also altogether after sense: in so much as the former coming again to take place, and be predominant, the latter follows, by coherence of the matter moved, in such manner, as water upon a plain table is drawn which way any one part of it is guided by the finger. . . . [O]nly this is certain, [whatever we think next] shall be something that succeeded the same before, at one time or another.

Thus, he observes or "induces,"

> the felicity of this life, consists not in the repose of a mind satisfied. For there is no such *finis ultimus,* (utmost aim) nor *summum bonum,* (greatest good), as is spoken of in the books of the old moral philosophers. . . . Felicity is a continual progress of the desire, from one object to another; the attaining of the former, being still but the way to the latter. The cause whereof is, that the object of man's desire, is not to enjoy once only, and only for one instant of time; but to assure forever, the way of his future desire. . . .

Hobbes presents this mechanistic model as a solution to the cycles of disharmony and war – a view more amenable to the market-oriented economy of the century, Carolyn Merchant points out (*The Death of Nature,* 1980), than the old organic hierarchy. Hobbes's erasure of the animistic universe in the name of stability and order differs little, then, from Kepler's claim that his "aim [was] to show that the celestial machine is to be likened not to a divine organism but to a clock work." (It is not insignificant that Hobbes's program, although he himself was a Royalist, was read in the age as a defense of the rule of Cromwell.) Driven by a similar post-Revolution anxiety to make the disorderly atoms of nature and society run on time, it is not surprising that the newly founded Royal Society would engage in a similar campaign – although to offset the "fantastical terms [of] our *Religion Sects*" (Sprat, *History of the Royal Society,* 1667) – to regularize along "scientific" guidelines those most fanciful integers, the rhythms of poetic metrical expression.

Hobbes and the Royal Society were, in a sense, merely following the lead of the most influential propagandist for the "new Philosophy" – Bacon, another scientific "theodicean" intent on regularizing the glory of God's Creation by excising it from the dangerous demesne of the "old" theologians. Following the strictures of his family Calvinism and its utilitarian soteriology by which John Calvin had defended the sacraments as valuable primarily because of their usefulness, Bacon followed his claim that "Truth therefore and utility are here the very same thing" with a program for *The Advancement of Learning* (1605) by which a "Great Instauration" (a grand restoration) of Nature and Learning was to be achieved. Identifying the three "vanities" blighting man's intellectual "progress" to be that of "zealous Divines," "severe" politicians, and the "imperfections and errors of learned men themselves," he offered a *novum organum,* or new method, by which "the end ought to be . . . to separate and reject [such] vain speculations":

> God hath framed the mind of man as a mirror or glass, capable of the image of the universal world, and joyful to receive the impression thereof, as the eye joyeth to the light; and not only delighted in beholding the variety of things and vicissitudes of times, but raised also to find out and discern the ordinances and decrees, which throughout all those changes are infallibly observed.

Just as the members of the Royal Society, in the words of Sprat, "would bring [the] volubility of *Tongue*" to a purity "as near the Mathematicall plainness as they can," so Bacon's scientist would rely on the instruments of the new pragmatics and mechanics to control and interrogate Dame Nature, treating her not "as a bond-woman, to acquire and gain to her master's use; but as a spouse, for generation, fruit, and comfort." (Some hierarchies are more equal than other hierarchies from the perspective of Bacon's legalistic natural colonizer, Aphra Behn might well have noted.)

The "cultural revolution" of this generation of British poets, then, was positively cataclysmal in its scope and depth, confronting these writers with two antithetical visions of reality/Reality. Representative of the poles or perspectives that this revolution brought about was the first of a seemingly endless number of disputes in the century between the Ancients and the Moderns: the debate about the significances of the *pattern* of change in nature by Godfrey Goodman (1583–1656) and George Hakewill (1578–1649), a controversy whose essence, as in so many areas of thought and feeling, had been best dramatized by Shakespeare:

> These late eclipses in the sun and moon portend no good to us. Though the wisdom of nature can reason it thus and thus, yet nature finds itself scourg'd by the sequent events. Love cools, friendship falls off, brothers divide: in cities, mutinies; in countries, discord; in palaces, treason; and the bond is crack'd 'twixt son and father. . . . there's son against father: the King falls from bias of nature; there's father against child. We have seen the best of our time.
>
> (*King Lear,* 1608)

The earl of Gloucester's lines might well forecast not only the horrors of the Civil War at the middle of the century, but the "eclipses" of the old, medieval organic universe as well, its fall before the rationalistic "bias of nature." Goodman asserts such in his *Fall of Man* (1616):

> nature . . . is corrupted and much declined from her first perfection, which certainly was intended by the Founder

and by all probable conjecture was imparted to her in her first institution. . . . Hence began a great alteration in nature, and all things were changed to the worst, [so that] in this general confusion, . . . even the whole world and all the several kinds of creatures, tend to confusion. . . . the time of the end cannot be long absent.

Hakewill agreed that the "world shall have an end . . . in its due time" but urged that the universe of man and the "heavenly bodies are not at all . . . impaired or subject to any impairing or decay":

> Seeds of decay were not infused into the world before the Fall, nor after it, and consequently not at all. . . . There is, it seems, both in wit and arts, as in all things besides, a kind of circular progress.

Hakewill's *Apology or Declaration of the Power and Providence of God in the Government of the World* (1653) insists, then, that the melancholic anatomy of the Ancients must and should be countered by the enthusiastic zeal of the Moderns. The appraisals of the "ways of God to men" indicate the poles between which the third generation of seventeenth-century British poets moved in their own readings of the "hand-writing" of God as discernible in the cultural revolution they were experiencing.

Twentieth-century responses to the monumental changes of the seventeenth century, in fact, also replicate in significant ways those of the seventeenth-century writers themselves. Alan Sinfield's outline of the Reformation bases for a secular worldview – by which Calvin's assertion of the total impotence of human learning and endeavor to the spiritual realm led him to grant that human learning should therefore "extend not merely to the learning of the art, but to the devising of something new" (*Institutes*, 1535) – concludes that the "beginning of secularism" in the century amounted to "a disbelief or disregard for a spiritual or supernatural dimension. Since 1600 ever-increasing areas of thought have *gained independence* from the *domination* of religious attitudes" (*Literature in Reformation England 1560–1600* [1983]). Herbert Butterfield would concur that science was able to "*free* men from the *necessity* of regarding spirits as the source of some of the motions . . . of the physical universe" ("The Establishment of a Christian Historiography," in *The Origins of History*, edited by Adam Watson, 1981). As indicated by my italics, this interpretation of the century as a *progressive* movement of *liberation* accords not only with Bacon's insistence that his *Novum Organum* could be the means by which the "commerce between the mind of man and the nature of things . . . might be restored to its perfect

and original condition" (*Advancement of Learning*) but was a reading endorsed with similar enthusiasm by poets such as Milton, Cowley, Behn, Cavendish, and Dryden during the age. On the other hand, following T. S. Eliot's discovery of a "dissociation of sensibility" in the century, S. L. Bethell speaks of "the *lost* universe" of an age of "violent contrasts" during which there was a "gradual *ousting* of 'metaphysical' writing by neoclassicism"; "the 'old' reason that was so *much more than* merely rational," he concludes, "*vanished* along with the organic universe, the multifold complexity, divine, human and natural, that it had existed to apprehend and manipulate," and even "the mind itself *suffered* fragmentation; its means of deepest experience and understanding had been discarded . . . : mundane affairs were *lost* to religion – in the world a secular philosophy *prevailed*" (*The Cultural Revolution of the Seventeenth Century*, 1951). Such a reading of the *loss* of Paradise and the *degeneration* endemic to such a devastating *absence* replicates another prevalent reading of Time in the age by authors such as Henry Vaughan, Thomas Traherne, Hobbes, Goodman, and Robert Burton and in the later works of Milton and Dryden. Whether the revolutionary changes across the entire spectrum of human thought and conduct in the century indicated the irremediable *loss* of "Paradise" or signaled the means by which it might be *regained* is central to the poetry of this third generation of seventeenth-century, British, nondramatic poets. "Truth," all of them would have agreed, "is the Daughter of Time." Whether Time had proven to be degenerative or progressive is the major concern of their melancholic or enthusiastic, meditative or public readings of the Providence of "change." Vaughan (an "ancient" alienated by the "modern" age), Milton (a radical "ancient-modern" who transformed ancient forms into "modern" vehicles of a vision "unattempted yet in Prose or Rhyme"), and Dryden (a "modern" who became steadily and progressively more "ancient") offer a representative variety of such readings.

* * * * * * * *

One of the severest responses to the "new learning" of Baconian induction in the century came from the author who had translated *The Advancement of Learning* into Latin for his old family friend – the second generation meditative poet Herbert. His wry critique of the "mechanics" of the new learning in his re-creation of the Creation story in "The Pulley" is only one of his many poems focusing attention on the "restlessness" of fallen man's search for his Creator. Such verses mock Bacon's claims that a universal "Sabboth" will be obtained through the success of his scientific "priests" armed with his *novum organum*. Herbert's "Vanitie" (I) relies on the specific language of Bacon's propaganda for the "new method," in fact, in order to attack the destructiveness of the separation of matter and spirit, nature and religion that was integral to the ideology and methodology of Bacon's "New Atlantis" (1626) of scientific induction. "The fleet astronomer" of this "new" intellectual world, Herbert urges, "can bore / And thread the spheres" but actually only "Surveys" the universe "as if he had designed / To make a purchase there"; "The nimble diver" "Cuts through the working waves" of mere natural motions only "That he might save his life" but brings only "destruction" and "danger" to Dame Nature; and "The subtle chymic" (the alchemist) aims to "divest / And strip the creature naked" only to be "Admitted to [Nature's] bed-chamber." The ultimate result of this material/sexual assault on Nature – and on her "principles" that would unite the world of man and the mind of God through man's response to the Spirit of his Creator in the "Book of Nature" (as described by Shakespeare earlier) – is figured by Herbert as a parody of divine creativity that would bring "death" to man and nature. The sum of the scientific assault on Nature through the astronomer's parody of the Father's "design," the diver's parody of the Son's "bearing" of the "pearl" of sacrifice for man's salvation, and the alchemist's parody of the loving Spirit of God, Herbert concludes, is a world of "death" and absence by which Bacon's New Man inverts mankind's duty (*imitatio christi* = "to imitate Christ") and his spiritual status as an *imago dei*. Herbert's critique of "the new learning," that is, directly contradicts Bacon's own claim that the separation of theology and science would "bring the mind back again to Religion" (*Advancement of Learning*) and even overcome the ravages of the Fall as long as man ceases to "mingle" "the realms of knowledge [so] that knowledge may not be, as a curtesan, for pleasure and vanity only, or as a bond-woman, to acquire and gain to her master's use." For Herbert "a curtesan" is exactly what a deallegorized, unemblematic Nature would be: "Poor man, thou searchest round / To find out death, but missest life at hand." From Herbert's perspective, then, Bacon was the point man in the assault on the "medieval" world by the middle-class Calvinistic mercantile ideology; Herbert would have agreed with Merchant that Bacon's "description of nature and his metaphorical style . . . were instrumental in his transformation of the earth as a

nurturing mother and womb of life into a source of secrets to be extracted for economic advance" (*Death of Nature,* 1980) – a wild creature who has to be "molded" by the mechanics of Bacon's "searchers and spies of nature" (*Advancement of Learning*), even tortured like one of James I's "witches" in order to yield her bounty. Herbert's plaintive cry at the end of "Vanitie" (I) – "Where's this command?" by which God's "glorious law [that] Embosomes in us, mellowing the ground / With showres and frosts, with love and law," is displaced by the new "search" – smartly voices his alarm at the "command" of a new class of legalistic scientists in British church, state, and learning. But also, in his view of how it confounds "glorious law" by secular "command," adroitly encapsulates the *separation* of Law and law, Religion and science, medieval theologies of monarchy and Hobbesian systems of power which would characterize the "new learning." As he reiterates in his companion poem, "Vanitie" (II), the "Poore silly soul, whose hope and head lies low; / Whose flat delights on earth do creep and grow," whose "false embroyderies" of induction "purchase" only "earthly joy," "Is but a bubble, and makes thee a boy." Herbert's view of the "new learning" as a "process" that would un-create man and his divinely ordered Book of Nature, turning life into a "bubble" (recalling ironically Bacon's own despairing poem "The World is but a bubble") and mankind into a "boy" (into a ridiculous version of the Christian aim to "become as a little child"), is reiterated in the third generation of poets by the self-proclaimed "son of Herbert," Henry Vaughan. In those volumes published shortly after the defeat of the conservative Royalist forces and the execution of "God's king" by the "command" of the new Parliamentarian forces of Puritan ideology – *Silex Scintillans* (1650, 1655) – Vaughan converts Herbert's critique to an even more anxious and alienated reading of the "new learning."

A rejoinder to Bacon's claim that the present state of learning is "but like the boyhood of knowledge, and has the characteristic property of boys: it can talk, but it cannot generate" (preface to *Instauratio Magna*), Vaughan's *Silex Scintillans* is framed by its author as a "retreat" from the "modern" world of Puritan "noise" ("Distraction") and "*idle books*" (preface to *Silex* II) to the rewriting of the "effectual success [of] that blessed man, Mr. *George Herbert,* whose holy *life* and *lines* gained many pious *Converts* (of whom I am the least)." The central imperative of this project of rewriting (as intimated in the profusion of *Re-* titles in *Silex:* "Recovery," "Regeneration," "Relapse," "Religion," "Repentance," "Request," "Resolve," "Resurrection and Immortality," "Retirement" [I], "Retirement" [II], "Revival") is indicated by Vaughan's best-known poem, "The Retreate":

> Happy those early dayes! when I
> Shin'd in my Angell-infancy.
> Before I understood this place
> Appointed for my second race,
> Or taught my soul to fancy ought
> But a white, Celestial thought,
> When yet I had not walkt above
> A mile, or two, from my first love,
> And looking back (at that short space)
> Could see a glimpse of his bright-face;
> When on some *gilded Cloud*, or *flowre*
> My gazing soul would dwell an houre,
> And in those weaker glories spy
> Some shadows of eternity;
> Before I taught my tongue to wound
> My Conscience with a sinfull sound,
> Or had the black art to dispence
> A sev'rall sinne to ev'ry sence,
> But felt through all this fleshly dresse
> Bright *shootes* of everlastingnesse.
>   O how I long to travell back
> And tread again that ancient track!
> That I might once more reach that plaine,
> Where first I left my glorious traine,
> From whence th'Inlightened spirit sees
> That shady City of Palme trees;
> But (ah!) my soul with too much stay
> Is drunk, and staggers in the way.
> Some men a forward motion love,
> But I by backward steps would move,
> And when this dust falls to the urn
> In that state I came return.

This poem is typical of the central childhood motif of *Silex Scintillans* (see M. Thomas Hester, " 'broken letters scarce remembred': Herbert's *Childhood* in Vaughan," *Christianity and Literature,* Spring 1991), which was published one year after the beginning of the military dictatorship by the Parliamentarian Council of State and republished two years after the rule of the Puritan "Protector" of the "Commonwealth." Aptly termed "a poet of darkness" by Jonathan F. S. Post (*Henry Vaughan,* 1982), Vaughan "longs," in one sense, to return to that "ancient track" of his own childhood in Wales; but in a more significant sense he engages in a meditative "search" for the Life of the Spirit he once experienced before "that state" was erased by the new learning of Puritan and scientific literalism. "[T]hat state" was most "effectually" figured forth for him in Herbert's *The Temple* (1633), the sacramental presence and liturgical frames of which Vaughan strives to imitate, to

revive, or to "recall" in nearly every poem of the two editions of *Silex Scintillans.* As John N. Wall points out, any reading of Vaughan must recall that the "community where . . . Herbert found [his] understanding of God through participation in the tradition of liturgical enactment enabled by the Book of Common Prayer was now absent. . . . Vaughan is the chronicler of the experience of that community when its source of Christian identity was no longer available" (*Transformations of the Word,* 1988). *Silex Scintillans* records his memory of that worship and the vestiges of that world before the "forward motion[s]" of the Puritan hegemony forbade the rites, rituals, and readings Herbert's *Temple* recorded. Ousted from what Richard Hooker called the "mutuall participation [in the] heavenlie ceremonies, which God hath sanctified and ordained, . . . as meanes conditionally which God requireth" (*Of the Laws of Ecclesiastical Politie,* 1594–1597), Vaughan's displaced "child" must continually strive to recall the lost light of his innocence and election. Thus Vaughan, re-writing in "The Retreate" Herbert's two Holy Baptism poems, sees only absence and loss as his lot; "shadows," "sinfull sound," and "the black art to dispence / A sev'rall sinne to ev'ry sence" overwhelm the recollection of his "Angell-infancy." Separated from the liturgical re-enactment of God's dispensation as figured forth in Herbert's poems on the rite of baptism, Vaughan's exiled "soul" hears not the Word but only his own fallen words, which affirm only the "longing" for the world he has lost. As he wrote in "Childe-hood," an oblique re-vision of Herbert's "The Collar":

> I cannot reach it; and my striving eye
> Dazles at it, as at eternity.
>   Were now that Chronicle alive,
> Those white designs which children drive,
> And the thoughts of each harmless hour,
> With their content too in my pow'r,
> Quickly would I make my path even,
> And by meer playing go to Heaven.

For when he does "study now, and scan," he can "onely see through a long night" the "edges" and "bordering light" of the lost world. He searches for Presence in what he sees as an essentially *profane* world (*pro* = outside, *fanus* = the temple).

    Both Ishmael and Nicodemus, forced literally and figuratively from the participation in the "*life and lines*" of significant existence recalled in Herbert, Vaughan begins *Silex Scintillans,* in fact, with a largely affirmative attempt to read God's Book of Nature as a sacred temple. Framed as the closest he can come to the experience of communal-eucharistic Presence described in "The Collar" (in which Herbert's wayfaring rebellious heart "struck the board, and cried no more" before finally experiencing the eternal conversation with God within the temple), Vaughan's "Regeneration" begins in imitation of Herbert – "one day / I stole abroad" – and does manage to record the presence of God's voice: "I heard / A rushing wind / . . . / It whisper'd, *Where I please*." But unlike Herbert's speaker, who receives a *call* directed to him that identifies him generically and who discovers the appropriate response in his own words, Vaughan's pilgrim hears only a general call that may or may not be directed at him, and in response he turns to paraphrase and allusion, borrowing the terms of Herbert's "The Temper" and 3 John in a complex allusiveness that hints at several of Herbert's poems. The mysterious and not entirely reassuring words of the Caller leads Vaughan, it seems, to doubt the efficacy of his own words, to defer to the words of others (and the Other). Indeed, he concludes "Regeneration" by citing the Canticles, hoping that the expansive typology of the biblical covenant includes him. "Storm'd" by sudden voices, emblematic vistas, and rushing noises, when Vaughan descends into his self he cannot find sufficient terms for any clarifying response. Certainly the final plea of the poem – "*let me dye before my death!*" – connotes his desire for a return to the clarity and surety of childhood evoked in Herbert's conclusion ("I heard one calling, *Child!* / And I reply'd *My Lord!*"); but Vaughan's pilgrim is unable to engage in or to voice that exchange directly. At best he is only a "Ward . . . still in bonds," unable to attain the liberation of the child's vision. Perhaps the most notable point about Vaughan's poem is the absence of the reference to the Communion table of "The Collar." Herbert's repeated misspelling ("I will *abroad*") of that *board* in his (former) rebellious denial – as he warned in "The Flower," man cannot "spell" "all" – is all that remains for Vaughan's alienated believer when he "stole abroad." The absent *board* of "Regeneration" forces the speaker into another divine book for a site of remembrance – and eventually, of course, back into the only books with which he is left, the book of his own childhood memory and the Book of Nature. But such "steps" are increasingly and continuously more unstable than Herbert's presence within the Temple.

Thus Vaughan's attempts to re-create the poem in which Herbert affirms or remembers the validity of the childhood trope are characterized above all by the *absence* of the child and the *Child* in his imitations. Whereas Herbert's speaker, standing at the moment of the poem at "the board" of remembrance, evokes the Presence of the Word "At every word," Vaughan's troubled speaker, forced "abroad," discovers no *call* that clarifies his relationship to the divine Caller. Separated from the forms through which God speaks to His children – the rites, sacraments, and liturgy of the Anglican church – Vaughan hears "At every word" only the babble of pride, arrogance, and confusion (what he called the "noise" of Puritan victory in "Distraction"). As he explains in "The Brittish Church," "He is fled"; Christ the mediator – the Incarnation of the Word who has always already redeemed fallen man and his words, the "*Child*" who re-creates the conversation between God and His created words – has been eradicated from the national church, the ritual vehicles ("the board") of Grace banished ("abroad") from the community. From this perspective it is understandable that Vaughan's focus and "fright" fall more emphatically on the absence of meaning in human words, on the unredeemed nature of human communication: man and words without God are "noise." Within the context of a ceremonial dialogue Herbert (re)discovered the divine simplicity of the eternal conversation of man and God – *In principio erat sermo* (In the beginning was the conversation): "I reply'd." Denied that context, that communal conversation, Vaughan confronts the insufficiency of human words on their own. Such, *King Lear* would reiterate, is the nature of "bare, unaccommodated," and unmediated words in the natural world of the Fall.

Vaughan's poems offer, then, what might be called a "deconstructionist" reading of Herbert – although this would be actually to "miscall" Vaughan's poem, if by "deconstructionist" we mean the monolithic atheism of Derridean postmodernist readings in which the Christian acceptance of words as mediators spoken/written to recall their origins in the Word is turned into a gospel of mere absence and verbal meaninglessness. The desperate deferences to the words of "holy *Herbert*" and the Bible with which Vaughan's poems conclude, in fact, would stand as his affirmation of the possibility of devotional conversation even in a "modern" world in which the sacramental vehicles of such conversation have been erased. In this sense it might be more accurate to call Vaughan's poems his attempts to rewrite the Herbert text after it had been "modernized" by the Puritan victory, after the liturgical and sacramental vehicles of human participation in the Word (from his perspective, that is) had been erased.

When Vaughan does attempt a Herbertian emblematic reading of the spiritual form of nature, in fact, his lack of enthusiasm for the "new learning" is considerable, as evident in his own companion to Herbert's "Vanitie" poems, "Vanity of Spirit":

> Quite spent with thoughts I left my Cell, and lay
> Where a shrill spring tun'd to the early day.
> I beg'd here long, and groan'd to know
> Who gave the Clouds so brave a bow,
> Who bent the spheres, and circled in
> Corruption with this glorious Ring,
> What is his name, and how I might
> Descry some part of his great light.
> I summon'd nature: peirc'd through all her store,
> Broke up some seales, which none had touch'd before,
> Her wombe, her bosome, and her head
> Where all her secrets lay abed
> I rifled quite, and having passed
> Through all the Creatures, came at last
> To search my selfe, where I did find
> Traces, and sounds of a strange kind.
> Here of this mighty spring, I found some drills,
> With Ecchoes beaten from th' eternall hills;
> Weake beames, and fires flash'd to my sight,
> Like a young East, or Moone-shine night,
> Which shew'd me in a nook cast by
> A peece of much antiquity,
> With Hyerogliphics quite dismembred,
> And broken letters scarce remembred.
> I tooke them up, and (much Joy'd) went about
> T' unite those peeces, hoping to find out
> The mystery; but this neer done,
> That little light I had was gone:
> It griev'd me much. At last, said I,
> *Since in these veyls my Ecclips'd Eye*
> *May not approach thee, (for at night*
> *Who can have commerce with the light?)*
> *I'le disapparell, and to buy*
> *But one half glaunce, most gladly dye.*

This attempt to rewrite Herbert's poem as well as the traditional Christian language of "purchase" — to "re-deem" the traditional import that Bacon has used to "strip" Nature of her allegorical dress — manages only the "Traces, and sounds of a strange kind" in the natural and religious landscape of English worship after the Puritan conquest. Vaughan discovers only "Hyerogliphics quite dismembred" and "broken letters scarce remembred." The "new Philosophy" calls "all in doubt" for him, too; the Puritan literalism makes it impossible for him "T'unite those peeces" that his childhood poems hope to revive. Forced to rely on his own words to respond to the divine call that he cannot always hear amid the noise and babble of the Puritan sectaries and denied access to the sacramental and liturgical forms that symbolize and convey God's grace, he finds his own words incapable of re-creating the conversation that Herbert called *Childhood*. Thus, for Vaughan, the childhood trope is an emblem only of his loss, a "Trace" that denotes his absences, a "broken letter" he can recall only in negatives, a sign that only emphasizes the experience that much postmodernist criticism has called *différance* (itself ironically a misspelling that aims to erase the All from human experience).

In that first poem of *Silex Scintillans,* "Regeneration," as Ted-Larry Pebworth and Claude Summers have pointed out ("Vaughan's Temple in Nature and the Context of 'Regeneration,' " *JEGP,* July 1975), Vaughan strains to "see" the precise architecture of a High Anglican church in the "pinacle" of Nature; by the conclusion of *Silex Scintillans,* however, even the "Traces" have largely disappeared, as he prays that God "shalt restore trees, beasts and men" and "make all new again" ("The Book"); and in the last poem of the collection (called "L'Envoy," like the last poem of *The Temple*), he finds solace only in the call for "The new worlds new" of the Apocalypse — the ultimate and final "return" to "A state for which thy creatures all / Travel and groan, and look and call," when "the curse" shall reign no more and "Grace" shall "Descend, and hallow all the place." Countering the principle of utility and "rest" central to the promise of the new learning and the new (Puritan) Protestants, he prays:

> So shall we know in war and peace
> Thy service to be our sole ease,
> With prostrate souls adoring thee,
> Who turn'd our sad captivity!

The only "progress" Vaughan can see in the "new" is through movement back to the original unity of time and eternity, nature and spirit, promised in the regeneration of the End. As he phrases it in "Man in Darkness, or A Discourse of Death," for Vaughan the "*new way* [by which] We have seen Princes brought to their graves, . . . the highest order of humane honours trampled upon by the lowest, . . . and Ministers [such as his twin brother Thomas] cast out of the Sanctuary, & barbarous persons without light or perfection, usurping holy orders" was but another *banishment* of man from the Light, an "eclipsing" of the mind ("Regeneration"). As Donne had said of the "new" religiopolitical ideologies of the age, "this light too much blindnesse breeds" ("Satyre III"); or, as Vaughan phrases it in his best poem: "There is in God (some say) / A Deep, but dazling darkness; /. . . / O for that night! where I in him / Might live invisible and dim" ("The Night"). For Vaughan, the "new way" brings only "Heathens rule": "Thus is the solemn temple [of church, state, and nature] sunk agen / Into a Pillar, and conceal'd from men" ("Jacobs Pillow, and Pillar"). The return to that state of childhood, unity, and harmony promised by the mediation of the divine Child is a memory and a promise that he can read and write only as "broken letters scarce remembred" – anything but the "Great Instauration" promised by the new learning, new order, and new men gaining power during the middle decades of the century. *Silex Scintillans,* then, is profitably read as the book of memory of the exiled Anglo-Catholic Royalist poet after the Civil War, "stand[ing] alone amidst the natural creation, seeking his own rehabilitation in the order of Love," the alienated "survivor . . . isolated from the ruinous world he saw around him" (Smith, *The Metaphysics of Love*); but Vaughan's meditative record also represents all those seventeenth-century "anatomies of melancholy" – from Donne, John Webster, Burton, and Goodman to Rochester – which voice a longing to reverse what they saw as the degenerative pattern of civilization in their age. The perpetual unevenness of Vaughan's poetry, in fact – its flashes of memorable lines that fade into less successful expressions, the very unevenness of his canon overall – might best reflect the truth of the human condition as he saw and lived it, as a medieval poet striving against "the dying of the light" in a modern age.

* * * * * * * *

The views opposite Vaughan's "medieval," meditative response to the "new" age come from a stylish public poet who had served the Caroline court in exile and praised Cromwell during the Interregnum and from a Puritan poet who offered a response to the failure of the Commonwealth government similar to Vaughan's response to its success – Cowley and Milton. During and after his exile (along with Hobbes and Edmund Waller), Cowley proffered one of the most enthusiastic endorsements of Bacon and his "Project for Experiments," finding in them a model and stimulus for his own "progressive" projects in the realm of poetry. In fact, unlike Herbert's and Vaughan's uses of Bacon's specific language to criticize the spiritual dangers of the new learning, as Achsah Guibbory has shown, Cowley finds in those same terms a rich source for his own attempts to reenact the *novum organum* in verse. And Milton, as Martz has shown,

while assimilating, like Herbert and Vaughan, the rhetoric and structure of the Augustinian meditation, in his case to the rigors of a new national epic, offers a response to the "new" definition and conditions of worship in England that is directly opposite that of the High Church Metaphysical religious lyricists. Whether Milton's emphasis on Paradise being *lost* reflects his own recoil from the euphoria of the Restoration or indicates his disappointment with the failure of the Commonwealth government to realize a sacred politics able to sustain his own radical republicanism, his concluding counsel that mankind might "regain" at best only "a Paradise within" is diametrically opposed to the search for an "old" liturgy and Anglican *via media* in Vaughan. Both Cowley and Milton, in fact, exemplify in different ways the aim of the Moderns to achieve *new* "Things unattempted yet."

Like William Davenant's *Gondibert* (1651), Cowley's two attempts at the genre illustrate the difficulties of composing "the native epic" in the age, as Parfitt has noted (*English Poetry of the Seventeenth Century*), especially for someone who is primarily a poet of the panegyric, comfortable in trying out new genres such as the Pindaric ode but not greatly adept at managing the scope and tensions essential to epic. Perhaps, despite the Royalist enthusiasm of his unfinished *Civil War,* Cowley knew all along the insufficiency of the Caroline cause to satisfy epic standards, as indicated by his eventual rejection of his Royalism during the Interregnum, when he wrote his three most successful odes. His second attempt at epic, this time in praise of the Protectorate – the *Davideis* – does not measure up to the achievement of the final panegyric to Lucius Cary, Lord Falkland, with which *The Civil War* concludes, nor to the compelling intelligence of the praise in his Restoration *Ode* (1660) of the "practical man" who in effect brought about the Restoration – General Monck. Indeed, as Nicholas Jose points out (*Ideas of the Restoration in English Literature,* 1984), just as Cowley could not "identify the Protector with God's messianic plan [in his] conception of restoration [that] is far above politics," so his praises of Charles II's return comprehends "a large and mysterious act of God's will working in time through the sufferings of his people." The *Ode* begins, for instance, with the sort of doubts unacceptable to the Stuart mythology – "Will ever *Religion* appear / In these deformed Ruins? . . . / Will *Justice* hazard to be seen?" – with doubts that would well explain why Cowley never regained the favor he sought from the restored court. It is not just that Cowley (in Parfitt's terms) "seems to lack loyalty . . . to self and his art" as well as to his rulers but that he found the political tumults of his age insufficient for the idealism of his proposed panegyric. Thus, the failures of the Restoration to fulfill its avowedly idealistic *return* to the "Golden Age" that poets such as Dryden forecast for it, and the failure of the Protectorate to achieve the broad republican project with which Cowley had identified it in his odes, inevitably led Cowley not to a Vaughanian retreat into an allegorical reading of the "medieval" Book of Nature in search of his lost Community but to a pursuit of the goals enunciated by what he and many others (of various political allegiances) saw as the truly *new* kingdom of the mind, the Royal Society.

In his last work, "To the Royal Society" (1667) – following the lead of Bacon's defense of the "new learning" in terms compatible with the sort of liberal "Puritan" republicanism Cowley came to avow – this poet, who proved mostly "tedious" and "uncompelling" in his attempts at epic praise, seems to have found his metrical métier. His 1656 ode "To Mr. Hobbes" had announced his "modern" perspective in its Baconian celebration of the overthrow of the authority of Aristotle:

> Long did the mighty Stagirite retain
> The universal intellectual reign
> . . . .
> So did this noble empire waste,
> Sunk by degrees from glories past,
> And in the school-men's hands, it perished quite at last.

Like Bacon's attack on the "vanities" of ancient learning, Cowley's praise of Hobbes's project figures the "new" philosopher as the "great Columbus of the golden lands of new philosophies [whose] eloquence and wit / Has planted, peopled, built, and civilized / . . . / Thy learned America." In "To the Royal Society" Bacon himself is the "divinely inspired" rebel against "Authority" who liberated British learning and civilization; and his "religion," natural philosophy, not the king, is "the great and only heir / . . . / Unforfeited by man's rebellious sin," now come "to put an end of the authority [of] Some negligent and some ambitious men":

> 'twas Rebellion called to fight
> For such a long-oppressed Right.
> Bacon at last, a mighty Man, arose
> Whom a wise king and Nature chose
> Lord Chancellor of both their Laws,
> And boldly undertook the injured pupil's cause.

In the same year that Dryden composed his *Annus Mirabilis* to show how the millenarian fears associated with the year 1666 (666 is the number of the Antichrist in Revelations) should be stilled by recognition of the Providential return to a "Golden Age" under Charles II, Cowley asserts that the Royal Society, by endorsing the nominalism ("words . . . are but pictures of the thought") and "the mechanic way" of the New Science, fulfills Bacon's liberating rebellion against the old "Authority." "The orchard's open now and free" through "the liberty [of] true reason's light": "Bacon, like Moses . . . Did on the very border stand / Of the blessed promised land," and now God's new Elect, the members of the society, whom "God with design has picked . . . / To do these noble wonders by a few," will bring about the true Restoration:

> Io! Sound too the trumpets here!
> Already your victorious lights appear;
> New scenes of heaven already we espy,
> And crowds of golden worlds on high.
> . . . .
> So virtuous and so noble a design,
> So human for its use, for knowledge so divine,
> . . . .
> You from all old errors free
> And purge the body of philosophy.

The design of Providence is completed, Cowley concludes, by the composition of *a history,* Sprat's *History of the Royal Society* – by an account of how the "noble," divinely inspired, utilitarian, materialistic, mechanistic, rebellious, "judicious" *method* of the Society will erase and exile "all old errors" and "all modern follies." Unable to compose a sacred epic that "justified" unequivocally either the king or the protector, Cowley in his final work finds a national project commensurate to his limited poetic capacity in his characterization of the "sacred" similitudes of the *history* of the *new, secular* science. Bacon had cited Scripture in order to assert that history "commands" man to "look forward to that part of the race which is still to be run," to define poetic invention as the wit "to discover that which we know not, not to recover or resummon that which we already know," and to call incessantly for things "new in substance," "new works," "new sciences," "new creations," and "new matter" (as noted by Guibbory in "Imitation and Originality: Cowley and Bacon's Vision of Progress," *Studies in English Literature,* Winter 1989); so, too, Cowley, in the best of his "new" Pindaric odes, accommodates the book on which Vaughan had relied (the Bible) in his "medieval" reading of the Book of Nature in order to affirm finally the "progressive" reading of natural history central to the "modern" worldview.

For Milton the attempt to achieve the "unattempted" in English literature – to write the "modern" sacred epic – was infinitely more successful poetically, although personally (and "politically") more disheartening. For him, the "new" age calls not for a progress into the world of scientific nature in pursuit of a New Atlantis of "true reason" but for a "new" definition of epic heroism and virtue that takes into account the recent disasters of political solutions to spiritual problems. The new Eden for Milton's "modern" reader is to be "within thee." Milton's post-Restoration triptych – *Paradise Lost, Paradise Regained, Samson Agonistes* – returns to (what Martz has aptly termed) a "poetry of exile" that is thematically similar to Vaughan's in its meditative search for an exemplary worship, but its decidedly "modern" privileging of *the self* bases its survey of human history and divine Providence on an adamant faith in the *progress* of society rather than on the return to the "old." Like Vaughan, Milton searches in the night (the darkness of the Royalist victory and Restoration) for a "return" to "Paradise"; but his liberal republicanism posits the mastery of the self (which sounds much like the "obedience" to the rational imperatives of the self as "guided" by inner promptings thought to be Providential in the Elect) to be the means for mankind (and for England, if it can throw off the self-enslavement to monarchy to which it had returned in 1660) to achieve a "Paradise within" that is, in fact, "*happier* farre" than that which Adam and Eve lost. In many ways an analysis of the present situation in which England found itself after the failure of the Commonwealth, an analysis in the spirit of Renaissance Ciceronian eloquence by which the *vatic* poet realizes poesy as the best *teacher* of fallen man, Milton's revolutionary Christian humanist triptych explains the origins of man's adamant incompetence (*Paradise Lost*) that lay at the heart of the nation's failure to achieve a sacred politics and then turns to a reading of the example of the Bible and the exemplary meditation of Christ in the wilderness (*Paradise Regained*) and the dramatic story of Samson's regeneration of mind (*Samson Agonistes*) in order to show his readers how and why the Protestant political mission failed and how and why it can be redeemed by a revolutionary restoration of the divine image of man through his subjugation of his worldly dreams to faith in the ultimate power of Providence.

As *political* poems, these three works might well be considered a tripartite meditation on the history of England. The first (which appeared the same year as Sprat's history and Cowley's ode prefacing it) *remembers* the *origins* of the self-enslavement and exile from liberty under which the Elect suffer since the Restoration through the nation's cyclic *return* to subjugation to the enemies of human liberty. The second poem briefly *reasons* how this present condition might be overcome, how this time in the desert of Royalist bondage can be rationally countered by the example of Christ's self-mastery so that man might "gain" a "*fairer* Paradise" through "deeds / *Above* Heroic." The third – appropriately a *closet drama* reflecting the movement of the actions of the self to the *internal theatre* – dramatizes the possibility of meaningful action that God's Elect can attain, toward which they should aspire, or which God will fulfill in the Apocalypse. The accommodation of the goals of the Sidneian poetic to the directives of the religious meditation thus adapts classical and Christian materials to the strictures of the essential Puritan code by which the reading of the biblical truths that the three poems re-present directly criticizes the crypto-Catholic propaganda of Stuart idolatry. As exemplified by Dryden's 1660 figuration of the Restoration in *Astraea Redux* ("Justice Returned") as a return to "times like those alone / By fate reserved for great Augustus' throne," by which a "returning prince [whose] goodness only is *above the law*" will silence "The rabble [who] such freedom did enjoy" ("They owned a lawless savage *liberty*"), the demise of the Commonwealth was acclaimed by Milton's enemies to be a new "Golden Age" in which England "shall no limits know, / But like the sea *in boundless circles* flow" (italics added). For Dryden the "just circle," by which the Restoration of the Stuarts "Redeemed from error" the English nation, was validated even by the advancement of learning by Bacon; Dryden announced in his panegyric for Dr. Walter Charleton's "discovery" that Stonehenge (where King Charles II had "sheltered once his sacred head" from the Puritan army) was a temple built by the Danes. Another admirer of Bacon (for his intellectual "progress"), Milton counters the circular ("crown") imagery of the Stuart ethos and propaganda by figuring Satan and his followers in *Paradise Lost* as exempla of "wand'ring" error, caught endlessly (like the "vain" false teachers in Bacon's attacks on the authority of medieval theology and Aristotelianism) in *circles* of perpetual *restlessness*. Milton's Satan, as Guibbory points out, is the perpetual "conservative or reactionary, . . . essentially against change" – a parody of the "new" Law and its recommendation of a pedagogy that would "teach mankind by progressive revelations disclosed in various ages" (*The Map of Time*, 1986). "We know no time when we were not as now," says

Satan, the mock-royal enemy of human freedom, and thus must oppose all "new Laws . . . impos'd" because "New Laws from him who reigns . . . new minds may raise" and "New counsels" might lead to (parliamentary) "debate" about "what may ensue." Thus, just like Charles II's erasure of the Commonwealth on his Restoration, which he dated 30 January 1649, so "The apostate" Lucifer dates his origin – his rebellion – as the *ridicula imitatio* (parody) of the divine circle:

> Know none before us, self-begot, self-raised
> By our quickening power, when fatal course
> Had circled his full orb, the birth mature
> Of this our native heaven, ethereal sons.

Milton uses the same cyclic image to discover the Fall of Adam:

> Earth trembled from her entrails, as *again*
> In pangs, and Nature gave a *second groan*
> . . . at *completing* of the mortal sin
> Original; while Adam took no thought
> Eating his fill, nor Eve to iterate
> Her *former* trespass feared, the more to soothe
> Him with her loved society.

The fullest rebuke in *Paradise Lost* to the cyclic pattern of history central to the Stuart myth is provided by the *linear* narrative of Providential history as recounted by God's schoolmaster-poets, Michael and Raphael, with its implicit indictment of the Royalist overthrow of church and state as a *return* to the circles of error told and retold in this (mock-heroic, antiaristocratic, libertarian) epic. Thus, when the original pupils of Providence are allowed "to walk" "the race of Time" that is life's linear journey, having been "Greatly instructed" that "the sum / Of wisdom" is "to obey," they are told that they must

> only add
> Deeds to thy knowledge answerable, add faith,
> Add virtue, patience, temperance, add love,
> By name to come called Charity, the soul
> Of all the rest: then wilt thou be loath
> To leave this Paradise, but shalt possess
> A Paradise within thee, happier far.

So instructed, Adam and Eve on their way into history look *backward* only momentarily and then move forward "hand in hand" toward Milton's audience – instructive examples of the *natural* inclination of fallen man to subject the race to false kings but yet some "occasion" for hope in the *linear* pattern of intellectual "knowledge" they have achieved. In the words of Martz, the last scene of

Paradise Lost "with its sad and bitter story of the *cycles* of mankind's growth and decay, nevertheless *moves toward* the day when the just will receive immortal joy and time will cease" (*Poet of Exile,* italics added).

The meditative recollection of the origins of the circles of error in *Paradise Lost* led Milton to an attempt to understand (or to teach his pupils to understand) how that "inner" Paradise is a progress over the lost pastoral world elegized at the center of the epic:

> I who erewhile the happy garden sung,
> By one man's disobedience lost, now sing
> Recovered Paradise to all mankind,
> By one man's obedience fully tried.

Like the epic, the "comic" brief epic *Paradise Regained* reveals that for Milton "true and substantial liberty . . . must be sought, not without, but within, and . . . is best achieved, not by the sword, but by a life rightly undertaken and rightly conducted" (*Defensio Secunda,* cited in John T. Shawcross, *Paradise Regain'd: "worthy t'have not remain'd so long unsung,"* 1988). For Milton, that is, "The real political arena is the self, where duty must be understood and managed[:] Self-mastery" (Arnold Stein, *Heroic Knowledge,* 1957); or, as Shawcross points out, in *Paradise Regained* Milton not only turns to the Bible to offer mankind an exemplary model of self-mastery by which one comes to terms with one's "election," but he offers the "comic" education of Christ's "human" example as a guide for "how to live one's life, with achievement of independence from others through independence from the lures of the self. The rite of passage from dependence whether from parents, relatives, friends, or even from one's god to independence is the only means" to realize one's "election" (*Paradise Regain'd: "worthy t'have not remain'd so long unsung"*). This phrases precisely the essence of Milton's *modernity,* political and philosophical, which counteracts the "new" (Royalist) Hobbesian view of the need for the state machinery to control fallen man's brutality but does so by advocating a radical republicanism and essential individualism and pluralism wholly in the spirit of Bacon's "new learning," by which the "separation" of the religious and the material would be actualized by a separation of the private and the public, and by which the *private* self, rightly read, becomes the authority for public action.

In some ways *Paradise Regained* confirms Milton's deepest disillusionment at the Restoration, as expressed in Christ's retort to Satan's advice that he seek glory instead of sacrifice:

For what is glory but the blaze of fame,
The people's praise, if always praise unmixt?
And what the people but a herd confus'd,
A miscellaneous rabble, who extol
Things vulgar, and well weigh'd, scarce worth the
    praise?
They praise and they admire they know not what;
And know not whom, but as one leads the other;
And what delight to be by such extoll'd,
To live upon thir tongues and be thir talk,
Of whom to be disprais'd were no small praise? –
His lot who dares be singularly good.
Th' intelligent among them and the wise
Are few, and glory scarce of few is rais'd.
This is true glory and renown, when God
Looking on th' Earth, with approbation marks
The just man, and divulges him through Heav'n
To all his Angels, who with true applause
Recount his praises. . . .

After all, Christ surmises (in lines that seem posed to address the 1660s in England and its "choice" to recall Charles II), to grant "liberty" to such a crowd would only lead them to more "Heathen round [and] heathenish crimes." But, at the same time, Milton's own personal example of the "firm obedience" of "one man," whose faith in Providence must have been severely and "fully tried" by the "waste wilderness" of the Restoration, provides circumstantial evidence (in the composition of the poem itself) that the "exiled" poet had not lost all faith in the power of Christ's example to move England to virtue. And in this composition his "True image of the Father . . . enshrined / In fleshly tabernacle, and human form, / Wandering the wilderness," not only "hast regained lost Paradise" but has made available "A fairer Paradise . . . For Adam and his chosen sons" such as Milton. Christ "foundes" a progressive revelation when he refuses to reenact the errors of the past, rejecting Satan's challenge for him to fulfill only the figures of the Old Testament types (seen here once again as the "restless" circles of human fallibility and "historical" inevitability). Whether the example of a Christ "refreshed" by progress in self-knowledge and understanding of the mission he has "come down to install" can lead mankind beyond the repetitions of idolatry that Adam and Eve "renewed" and which the recent history of England ironically restored in its return to Stuart rule – whether Milton's poetic meditation can move mankind beyond memory and understanding to resubmission of the will to the King of Kings – those are the subjects of the third of Milton's post-Restoration poems, *Samson Agonistes*.

On the morning after his fall from Grace, at the moment of his discovery of his loss of "honour"

after a night of "unrest," Adam is compared by Milton in *Paradise Lost* to "the Danite strong / Herculean Samson [who] from the harlot-lap / Of Philistean Dalilah . . . waked / Shorn of his strength [and] virtue." *Samson Agonistes* – "a Dramatic Poem which is called Tragedy . . . not ancient only but modern" ("Preface") – opens with the "restless thoughts" of the blind, imprisoned biblical figure "in Gaza *at the mill*," literally (re)enacting the *circle* of error the disobedient angels and Adam and Eve initiated. This closet drama, or private play, about how the fallen hero of God achieves a spiritual restoration by which he destroys the worldly stage or theater of the worshipers of Dagon once again frames this account of how Samson overcomes his past errors as an exemplum for post-Restoration England. Here God's Elect (and Milton's alter ego) is encircled by an "authority" intent "that to the public good / Private respects must yield"; like the Stuart court (which had reintroduced the play into England and which continued to foster its court myth by masque and play, and which served a king himself dominated sexually by the actress Nell Gwyn), Samson's oppressors are

an impious crew
Of men conspiring to uphold thir state
By worse then hostile deeds, violating the ends
For which our countrey is a name so dear.

In fact, as Jose points out, the description of the Philistines' court as "inauthentically imperial, outwardly showy, theatrical, martial, and, most importantly, false and transient" aims specifically to subvert the hyperbole of Stuart panegyric; and the figure of Dalila as the "royal" actress arriving on the stage of history registers the immediacy and depth of the poet's contempt for the Restoration regime as "superficial, secular, imperial, greedily mercantile, crypto-Catholic, absolutist, and hence evil." And the characterization of the English Independents in the biblical typology of the poem does not sound a more encouraging note; as Samson tells the Chorus, he offered the enslaved people freedom but, "seeing those great acts which God had done, [they] Acknowledged not, or not at all considered / Deliverance offered." Samson, however, does avoid repeating again the cycle of human self-betrayal himself, growing from "dragon" to "eagle" to "phoenix" in the religious emblems of the poem, until he "begin[s] to feel / Some rousing motions in [himself] which dispose / To something extraordinary [his] thoughts." Samson's "Paradise" again is a "calm of mind all passion spent" – a "*new* acquist / Of true experience" "happier farre" than the false promises of power and idolatry proffered him – and it may foretell Milton's faith in the possibility of political reform through obedience to and patient faith in God's "uncontrollable intent" that "unexpectedly returns" to "his faithful champion[s]." "They also serve who only stand and wait," Milton had concluded in his sonnet on his own blindness; and the last Renaissance humanist, even in his final poem on the public role of God's Elect, turns *inward* to affirm his faith that the psychic history of mankind could progress beyond the circles of political failure he had patiently endured. He becomes, in effect, the ultimate radical "modern" of his age, outgoing even Bacon's claim that the new learning could restore Adam's condition before the Fall in order to assert his belief in the power of the virtuous to restore within the mind a paradise even "happier" than Eden, discouraged by English history but seemingly resolute until the end in his faith in man's ability to liberate himself and to achieve "Things unattempted yet."

* * * * * * * *

Milton, needless to say, would have been delighted when the Stuart regime collapsed in 1688 without a shot being fired, in some ways as a result of its own monarchist arrogance but equally because of the refusal of Charles II and then the inability of James II to learn from the circle of mistakes of the past. On the other hand, the poet laureate Dryden saw the return to Revolution, although "Glorious" because it was "Bloodless," as the collapse of his own hopes for the "new" Augustan age and as the death knell to the final remnants of enthusiasm with which he had welcomed and championed the Restoration. Ironically, the shape of Dryden's poetic career in several ways remarks Milton's emphasis on the essential need for human *change*; and unlike the cyclic decay or restless fluctuations of allegiance that Milton saw as endemic to his enemies, the shape of political, philosophical, and generic change in Dryden's career even reflects Milton's campaign for the re-creation of the paradise of man within, as Dryden moves from an enthusiastic championing of the Restoration monarchy (*Annus Mirabilis*, 1667) to a criticism of the weaknesses of the English political system of limited monarchy (*Absalom and Achitophel*, 1681) to a final movement to Roman Catholicism (*The Hind and the Panther*, 1687); he turns from the political to the personal, from propaganda to confessional poetry, from public panegyric to mock-heroic to medieval beast fable. The direction of Dryden's change, that

is, is consistently from the "modern" to the "ancient" – a line moving from public to private discourse and from panegyric to classical translation. ("Neander" – "the new man" – as Dryden termed himself in *Of Dramatick Poesie*, eventually "progressed" to what Milton certainly would have seen as *Neanderthal*.)

Dryden's "Neander" never concurred in Milton's definition of the "new" age, of course; his first published poem, as J. Douglas Canfield points out, "revealed Royalist sympathies in oblique references to rebellion and regicide" through its association of the deadly smallpox of Lord Hastings with a "Rebel-like . . . Insurrection," and even his early *Heroique Stanzas* on the death of Cromwell evince "perplexing ambiguities" that undercut the apparent panegyric: "Neander" was an Ancient from the start. In this sense, his movement from enthusiastic endorsement of the Stuart Restoration to "medieval" Catholicism might just as easily be seen as a "progress" in self-awareness and a movement directly to the "ancient" roots of the conservative, antirepublican, anti-Puritan position with which he began. In fact, the shape of his career might just as readily be viewed as a fulfillment of Donne's vision of "liberty" as a movement through *contemptus mundi* (*An Anatomy of the World*) to the "Paradise within" he called "The Progress of the Soul" (*The Second Anniversary*). (Although momentary in its dominance, it was Dryden's example, after all, even more than Milton's, that proved to be central to the mode of the next century of neoclassic nondramatic verse.)

Like Milton's, in fact, Dryden's eventual disillusionment may have derived from his initial faith in the ability of government to solve human problems; both strained to define their governments as the voice of Providence in "the race of Time"; and, despite his essential disagreement with Milton's political position, this poet of "Historical Poem[s]" came to share a vision of English political and social culture as a "circle" of decline from which only examples of the past might reclaim it. But this "new" poet of an age of public poetry initially characterized the Stuart Restoration as a sign of the nation's status as a new center of civilization. *Astraea Redux* concludes:

> O happy age! Oh times like those alone
> By fate reserved for great Augustus' throne!
> When the joint growth of arms and arts foreshow
> The world a monarch. . . .

This enthusiasm for the Stuart Restoration of a Golden Age is reiterated in his poetic restoration (or transformation) of the classical Ciceronian dialogue into a defense of English theater and dramatic language in *Of Dramatic Poesie* (composed in 1655), where "Neander," writing against the backdrop of "the late War," explains that the refinement of classical models into the "perfection" of English language and poetic meter has been central to the new culture. Like Sir Philip Sidney's defense of "Poesy" as the best "service" of the courtly maker to the English cause, Dryden's defense of rhyme and "our English writers from the censure of those who unjustly prefer the French before them" is posed in its dedication to Lord Buckhurst, as a "dispute betwixt some of our wits [about] some things of the ancient, and many of the modern ways of writing, comparing those with these, and the wits of our nation with those of others" – as a defense and essay of the triumph of *modern* England in the international cultural community. The "Genius of every age is different," he says, "and ours excel[s] in" rhymed verse – despite the misunderstanding of "the multitude" (for " 'tis no matter what they think; they are sometimes in the right, sometimes in the wrong: their judgement is a mere lottery"). Thus, just as *Astraea Redux* celebrates a new age in which the "lawless savage liberty" of Milton's Commonwealth has been "constrained" – even in the regularity of the meter of the public drama, by which "Wit's now arrived to a more high degree; / Our native language more refin'd and free" ("Epilogue" to *Conquest of Granada*, 1672) – so "Neander," following both classical and English examples in his reinvention of the new genre of the critical essay, presents the success of the "modern" English theater as complementary to "our Nation's victory" over the Dutch fleet. The modern English "heroic" play epitomizes the success (and the succession) of the "new" age of English culture as an international force and example to be reckoned with throughout the world. So it is not surprising that the opponents in his mock-debate (like those individuals with whom Dryden quarreled throughout his career) are figures who represent the weaknesses and failures of the "old" Stuart regime, such as "Lisideius" (Sedley) who came to defend the entire baggage of French art that Charles II unwisely wanted to import from the court of Louis XIV.

In the main, however, *Of Dramatic Poesie* and *Astraea Redux* are consistently enthusiastic about the Modern Age or Restoration – as is Dryden's next major poem, *Annus Mirabilis,* which was written during the time of the Great Fire, the Second Dutch War, and, as documented in Samuel Pepys's diary of these years, the first widespread stirring of discontent with "a king more concerned with his plea-

sures than his duties, more attentive to his mistresses than his ministers" (Paul Hammond, *John Dryden, A Literary Life,* 1991). Written in "the *proper* wit of an *heroic* or historical poem," says Dryden in the preface, *Annus Mirabilis* joins the account of the successes of the English navy in war and in trade to a fulsome encomium of the Royal Society's advances in "modern" learning in order to figure forth Charles II's England as a Providential force of international strength, through which, the hyperboles of the poem imply, even the Great Fire is "vanquished" (at least in part) by the authority and "royal bounty" of the monarch's word:

> The eternal heard. . . .
> Our king this more than natural change beholds,
>   With sober joy his heart and eyes abound;
> To the all-good his lifted hands he folds,
>   And thanks him low on his redeemed ground.

Framed through its epic comparisons and "heroic" portraits "to stifle domestic dissent by rallying the nation around the common causes of war abroad and disaster at home" (as Michael McKeon has shown, Canfield notes), this Virgilian poem of insistent Roman analogies challenges opposition to the Restoration by insisting on its divine *image*; even the imperial Royal Society, for instance, under Charles's tutelage and care managed to

> behold the law,
> And rule of beings in your Makers mind,
> And then, like Limbecks, rich Idea's draw,
> To fit the levell'd use of humane kind.

The poem is yet, of course, "troubled by time," in Hammond's words, and perhaps the hyperbole of its conceits and the fulsomeness of its praise evince a strain in Dryden's attempt to maintain the royal panegyric of his earlier poems; but, as Canfield points out, by and large the poem conveys Dryden's sustained faith in its "image of cooperation between government, venture capital, and guild labor in order to subdue the earth."

Not all shared Dryden's enthusiasm, of course, and when the fabrications of the Popish Plot of 1678 led to the Exclusion Crisis by which James, Duke of York, could have been denied succession, Dryden changed his mode from panegyric to satire: *Absalom and Achitophel.* Primarily an attack on the political theory of his parliamentarian enemies and what he characterizes as their "Hobbist" definition of *succession,* here he returns to the biblical David story on which the encomium of *Astraea Redux* relies and to the imagery of success/succession of *Annus*

Mirabilis in order to defend his "new" age from another corrupt legion of "liberal" political usurpers. Just as "Dryden's staunch belief in the Succession [underlay] the word-play" on British *successes* in *Annus Mirabilis* (Jose, *Ideas of the Restoration*), so his faith in the Providential authority of kingship sustains his (difficult) defense of Charles's rule in *Absalom and Achitophel*. Not even "the law of self-preservation empowers a Subject to rise in Arms against his Sovereign," he wrote in *His Majesties Declaration Defended* (1681); "we have the Examples of Primitive Christians, even under heathen Emperors, always suffering, yet never taking up Arms, during ten Persecutions. But we have no Text, no Primitive Example encouraging us to rebel against a Christian Prince" (cited in Michael J. Conlon, "Politics and Providence," Ph.D. dissertation, 1969). Like Vaughan, Dryden turns in *Absalom and Achitophel* to the typology of the Bible to base his criticism of the "new" political science of his enemies; somewhere in between mock-heroic and allegorical satire, his poem identifies Anthony Ashley Cooper, Earl of Shaftesbury, with Achitophel, James Scott, Duke of Monmouth, with Absalom, and King Charles II with David, as well as figuring other persons from the Popish Plot as biblical types. The authority of the biblical parallels is amplified by Dryden's association of the Whigs with current "liberal" political theory, by which Milton's Satan becomes Dryden's Achitophel. Achitophel's temptation of King David's son in the poem "attempts with studied arts" to convince Absalom that royal succession is but some "lucky revolution of [one's] fate, / Whose motions if we watch and guide with skill, . . . / Our fortune rolls as from a smooth descent"; "Nobler is a limited command . . . / Than a successive title, long and dark, / Drawn from the mouldly rolls of Noah's ark." Thus, in the name of self-preservation alone, Absalom/Monmouth should conspire with the rebels/Whigs, for "Already . . . the next heir [James, Duke of York] looks on you with jealous eyes [and] meditates revenge . . . : Resolve on death, or conquest by the sword, / . . . self-defense is nature's eldest law."

Achitophel's "diabolical" denial of the concept of "sacred" succession is underscored by the portrayal of the Israelites/English as embodying "ease" and "luxury." This "moody, murmuring race, . . . / God's pampered people, . . . debauched with ease," "These Adam-wits [are] too fortunately free"; and "The Plot" is but "The Good Old Cause revived." Yet the consistent imagery of the people and plotters as engaging in a political act of sexual transgression ("a pleasing rape upon the crown") serves in some ways to call into question the authority of the king in its admission of the prominent and public promiscuity of the monarch and his courtiers, as Conlon points out. But, Conlon explains, Dryden offsets these admissions to the limitations of the king and his subjects by urging that "men are subject to a set of prior obligations (beyond self-interest) imprinted on their souls and bound up with their status as sons of Adam [that] provide a ground for the government as a sacred institution binding God, king, parliament, and the people":

> If those who gave their sceptre could not tie
> By their own deed their own posterity,
> How then could Adam bind his future race?
> Or how could heavenly justice damn us all,
> Who ne'er consented to our father's fall?
> Then kings are slaves to those whom they command,
> And tenants to their people's pleasure stand.
> Add, that the power for property allowed
> Is mischievously seated in the crowd;
> For who can be secure of private right,
> If sovereign sway may be dissolved by might?
> . . . .
> All other errors but disturb a state,
> But innovation is the blow of fate.
> If ancient fabrics nod, and threat to fall,
> To patch the flaws, and buttress up the wall,
> Thus far 'tis duty. But here fix the mark
> For all beyond it is to touch the ark.
> To change foundations, cast the frame anew,
> Is work for rebels, who base ends pursue,
> At once divine and human laws control,
> And mend the parts by ruin of the whole.
> The tampering world is subject to this curse,
> To physic their disease into a worse.

And this concept of the universal *bond* (traced by Canfield in his *Word as Bond in Literature,* 1989) is supported in the poem by the example of Barzillai and his son who "All parts fulfilled of subject and of son": "Swift was the race, but short the time to run. / O narrow circle, but of power divine, / Scanted, but perfect in thy line!" Thus, even while admitting the sins of the king and court, Dryden finds authority in the concept of succession ("line") that the king embodies. As is *Annus Mirabilis,* that is, where another figurative oppressor (the Great Fire) threatens the peace of the Restoration – "As when some dire Usurper Heav'n provides, / To scourge his Country with a lawless sway" just as Cromwell had once before – and where Dryden countered the rapid spread of that would-be scourge by the constant reiteration of versions of the words *success* and *succession* (seventeen times, Jose points out), so in *Absalom and Achitophel* it is the authority of the king as *the successor* or agent of the divine word, the *heir* ultimately of a civilizing eloquence, and the *figure* of God as the king of both Justice and Mercy – figured as "the fusion of David's word with God's logos," Conlon points out – that finally brings the personal and civil threats to the nation under momentary control in the poem. Opposed to the "restlessness" and "innovation" of the Whig version of history/rebellion, Dryden's king wins the war of words against the new nominalists eventually through a speech of poetic *satire:*

> Beware the fury of a patient man.
> Law they require, let Law then show her face;
> They could not be content to look on grace,
> Her hinder parts, but with a daring eye
> To tempt the terror of her front and die.

Just as the Restoration project of civilization when threatened by writers such as Richard Flecknoe, Thomas Shadwell, and Rochester called Dryden to "wage Immortal War with Wit" (*Mac Flecknoe,* 1682) and to rely on the ancient vehicle of Roman satire to protect the succession of eloquent art and culture in the land, so the Exclusion Crisis called for the restoration of the voice of the Old Testament prophet and the ancient satirist to remind the public that it was the *line* of Stuart succession alone that figured forth the *circle* of Providential design in the history of English culture:

> *He said.* The mighty, nodding, gave consent;
> And peals of thunder shook the firmament.
> Henceforth a *series* of *new time* began,
> The mighty years in long *procession* ran:
> Once more the godlike David was *restored,*
> And willing nations knew their lawful lord.

England, as it turned out, did not remain (from Dryden's perspective anyway) a "willing nation" for long. And as it moved closer and closer to embody the dimensions of the mock-heroic as he had figured them in *Absalom and Achitophel* – even after James II came to the throne and tried to move the nation back to a "restoration" of its Catholic past – Dryden moved more deeply into the satiric mode. Indeed, he moved into the "ancient" forms of the mode as he went beyond the sort of Renaissance mock-heroic of his Exclusion Crisis satire back to the beast-fable genre in his "medieval" allegorical announcement of his Catholicism, *The Hind and the Panther,* and then back to ancient verse itself in his *Works of Virgil* (1697) and *Fables Ancient and Modern* (1700), completing the *linear* movement of his poetic career from a "modern" progressive to a satiric reactionary to a Restoration "ancient" – Tory, conservative, and Catholic. The line of Dryden's career,

then, is consistent in its ultimate concern with a concept of orderly succession that is political, religious, and poetic in its movement toward the *ancient* origins of the *modern* line of "proper wit."

From the beginning, Dryden's "new man" had had an ancient *Roman* name ("Neander"), after all; and the shape of Dryden's career evinces a sort of progress to or personal/professional search for the *authority* of his "name" or "word" and the "Roman" roots of his culture. His continuation of the assault on the leader of the liberal party in *The Medall* (1682) focuses again on Shaftesbury's own assault on the principle of succession:

> He preaches to the Crowds that Pow'r is lent,
> But not convey'd to Kingly Government;
> That *Claimes successive* bear no binding force;
> That *Coronation Oaths* are things of course;
> . . . .
> The reason's obvious: *Interest never lyes;*
> The most have still their Interest in their eyes;
> The power is always theirs, and power is ever wise.

Such was the "modern age," he wrote in the following year – overrun by "zealous sectarians [and] profane republicans: . . . fanatics [who] arrogate to themselves the right of disposing the temporal power according to their pleasure [and] nominal Christians who are otherwise *Hobbists* in their politics and morals" ("To His Grace the Duke of Ormond, Etc.," cited in Conlon). Counter to the "Hobbist" principle of self-interest for Dryden was the concept of succession, politically theocratic and poetically neoclassical. Even in that text in which he tries to affirm the rational foundations for Protestantism, *Religio Laici* (1682), his admissions about the individualistic tenor and latitudinarianism of the multiplying sects of the national religion so confound his efforts that the distinguishing characteristic of this most unstable of Dryden's texts is its failure to discover a principle of sufficient doctrinal and interpretative authority. Thus, his turn in his final works to Roman Catholicism, Roman satire, and the translation of pre-Reformation Catholic allegorists (Geoffrey Chaucer, Giovanni Boccaccio) and ancient Roman epic is largely an outgrowth and logical development of the "profound disquiet [and] consequent longing for some stronger principle of authority than the Anglican church was willing to claim" (Louis Bredvold, *The Literature of the Restoration,* 1962). His "doubts are done," he asserts in *The Hind and the Panther,* as he champions again the "weight of antient witness" over the claims of "private reason" in order to endorse Roman Catholicism's traditions and vision of "a better world." Assaulting the separation of church and state, the private and the public, the sacred and the profane he found endemic to the "modern" world, he urges that "As long as words a diff'rent sense will bear, / And each may be his own Interpreter, / Our airy faith will no foundation find." Just as his later *translations* are literally just that – attempts to reestablish the continuity of modern English culture with ancient literary civilization (*transferre* = "to carry across") – so his defense of his own *religious translation* in *The Hind and the Panther* is founded on his defense of the poetic traditions of his "mysterious writ." His own

> Muse has peopl'd *Caledon*
> With *Panthers, Bears,* and *Wolves,* and Beasts Unknown,
> As if we were not stock'd with monsters of our own.
> Let *Aesop* answer, who has set to view,
> Such kinds as *Greece* and *Phrygia* never knew;
> And mother *Hubbard* in her homely dress
> Has sharply blam'd a *British Lioness,*
> . . . .
> Let by those great examples, may not I
> The wanted organs of their words supply?

Literary tradition and convention underpin his own words, just as the tradition and authority of the Roman Church offer a solution to the legion of individual interpretations allowed in Protestant reading of the Word, in which each "innovating" conscience "grant[s] the words, and quarrel[s] for the sense." As Roman (Catholic) poet, then, Dryden maintains in *The Hind and the Panther* – and in the *Fables* and *Translations* (of Horace, Juvenal, Ovid, Persius, and Virgil) which occupy the last twelve years of his life – his pursuit of a "new" vision that might offset the tumult and instability – political, religious, and personal – which characterized seventeenth-century English culture. It is not despair, then, that dominates his valediction to the century in his final work, "The Secular Masque" (1700), when "Neander" is translated into "Janus," who then speaks as "Chronos" (Dryden the man) and "Momus" (Dryden the poet) in order to evaluate the age in neoclassical figures. (Janus is, of course, the wittily precise figure for this "new" poet of classicism and the "ancient" religion.) His allegory figures the age as having been dominated by "Diana" (the time before the civil wars, especially the age of the king in love with hunting, James I), then by "Mars" (the period of the civil wars and the Commonwealth), and then by "Venus" (the regime of the lascivious Charles II). But even in his insistence on the *absence* of a reigning, continuous, or successive principle in the age –

> *All, all of a piece throughout:*
> *Thy Chase had a Beast in view;*
> *Thy Wars brought nothing about;*
> *Thy Lovers were all untrue*

– he yet admits in his final poetical words some abiding faith or hope in his own version of "restoration." His final stanza is spoken by a *Chorus* – that most ancient of literary devices – which *joins* in a unified, single authoritative voice to announce his admission that " *'Tis well an Old Age is out*" even while it evokes again "Neander's" satiric-prophetic call that it is *"time to begin a new."*

* * * * * * * *

Dryden's final appraisal of his age has been cited frequently in twentieth-century attempts to evaluate the seventeenth century, and especially to remark the absence of a totally dominant author who figured best the various energies of the age. By the nineteenth century Milton would seem to have achieved such prominence, but during the seventeenth century he was less admired in some ways than even Cowley. Dryden certainly exerted a major influence on the next generation of English nondramatic and dramatic poets, when the Renaissance seems to have gasped its last breath of "medieval" air before the ascendancy of the "modern" Miltonic romantics. But this absence of a single "monarch of wit" among this generation of poets does express well the character of the age itself as *the century of revolution.*

Of course, looking from the perspective of our own *postmodern* age and its intent to "justify" all poetry and culture to be mere politics and ideology (what Donne called mere "opinion"), we might well take a lesson from the strong poets of this third generation of seventeenth-century British poets: those who spent their hopes and enthusiasm on the absolute *political* solution to national, poetic, and personal problems ended up disillusioned. Such a reminder cannot diminish, of course, the enduring brilliance and power of their achievement in their poetic essays of the "race of Time," and it is no dismissal of the pain and suffering they endured to suggest that (with one slight emendation) Adam's response to the record of human history at the end of the greatest single poem of the century evokes quite well an appropriate response to the poetry of this century:

> O . . . goodness immense!
> That all this good of [tumult] shall produce.

. . . .
Greatly instructed [we] hence depart,
. . . .
Greatly instructed [that] suffering for truth's sake
Is fortitude to highest victory.

– M. Thomas Hester

ACKNOWLEDGMENTS

This book was produced by Bruccoli Clark Layman, Inc. Karen L. Rood is senior editor for the *Dictionary of Literary Biography* series. Henry Cuningham was the in-house editor.

Photography editors are Edward Scott and Timothy C. Lundy. Layout and graphics supervisor is Penney L. Haughton. Copyediting supervisor is Bill Adams. Typesetting supervisor is Kathleen M. Flanagan. Samuel Bruce is editorial associate. Systems manager is George F. Dodge. The production staff includes Rowena Betts, Steve Borsanyi, Barbara Brannon, Patricia Coate, Rebecca Crawford, Margaret McGinty Cureton, Denise Edwards, Sarah A. Estes, Joyce Fowler, Robert Fowler, Jolyon M. Helterman, Tanya D. Locklair, Ellen McCracken, Kathy Lawler Merlette, John Morrison Myrick, Pamela D. Norton, Thomas J. Pickett, Patricia Salisbury, Maxine K. Smalls, Deborah P. Stokes, Jennifer Carroll Jenkins Turley, and Wilma Weant.

Walter W. Ross, Suzanne Burry, and Brenda Gross did library research. They were assisted by the following librarians at the Thomas Cooper Library of the University of South Carolina: Linda Holderfield and the interlibrary-loan staff; reference librarians Gwen Baxter, Daniel Boice, Faye Chadwell, Cathy Eckman, Gary Geer, Qun "Gerry" Jiao, Jean Rhyne, Carol Tobin, Carolyn Tyler, Virginia Weathers, Elizabeth Whisnant, and Connie Widney; circulation-department head Thomas Marcil; and acquisitions-searching supervisor David Haggard.

Seventeenth-Century British Nondramatic Poets
Third Series

Dictionary of Literary Biography

Jane Barker
(May 1652 – circa 1727)

John T. Shawcross
University of Kentucky

See also the Barker entry in *DLB 39: British Novelists, 1660–1800.*

BOOKS: *Poetical Recreations: Consisting of Original Poems, Songs, Odes &c. with several new translations. In two parts. Part I. Occasionally written by Mrs. Jane Barker. Part II. By Several Gentlemen of the Universities, and Others* (London: Printed for Benjamin Crayle, 1688);

Love Intrigues: Or, The History of the Amours of Bosvil and Galesia, As Related to Lucasia, in St. Germains Garden (London: Printed for E. Curll & C. Crownfield, 1713; facsimile, New York: Garland, 1973);

Exilius: or, The Banish'd Roman. A New Romance. In Two Parts: Written After the Manner of Telemachus (London: Printed for E. Curll, 1715; facsimile, New York & London: Garland, 1973);

The Entertaining Novels of Mrs. Jane Barker (2 volumes, London: Printed for A. Bettesworth & E. Curll, 1719; 1 volume, London: Printed for Bettesworth & Hitch, 1736);

A Patch-Work Screen for the Ladies; or, Love and Virtue Recommended: In a Collection of Instructive Novels (London: Printed for E. Curll, 1723; facsimile, New York & London: Garland, 1973);

The Lining of the Patch-Work Screen; Design'd for the Farther Entertainment of the Ladies (London: Printed for A. Bettesworth, 1726).

The daughter of Thomas and Anne Connock Barker, Jane Barker employed the pseudonyms Fidelia and Galesia in her novels, which have in recent times been discussed in critical studies of fiction and most of which have been republished in facsimile or new editions. But she was also a poet generally called "Mrs. Jane Barker," a title of respect ("Mistress"), for she was unmarried. In May 1652 Barker was born in Blatherwicke, Northamptonshire, to an Anglican and Royalist family, but she grew up in Wilsthorp, Lincolnshire. Her father provided some aristocratic associations, and her education was enhanced through her brother Edward, a student at St. John's College, Oxford, and Leyden. Both her father and brother dying in 1670, she and her mother moved to London, which proved a lonely place for her, if one can believe Galesia and her seemingly autobiographical novels. Galesia's thwarted love and acceptance of the single life are read as truthful to Barker's experience. Indeed much that is construed as biographical comes from the novels and poems.

Her mother died in 1685, and she continued to live on the inheritance from her father, who had been associated with Arthur Capel, Earl of Essex. *Poetical Recreations,* her collection of poems, appeared in 1688 with numerous verses by others, apparently men who were friends known through her brother. In the same year she went to France, following the exiled court of James II, deposed ostensibly for his Roman Catholicism, the religion which Barker now espoused. When she converted, or if her family had Catholic inclinations previously, is not known. She returned to England in 1713, and novels that she seems to have been working on in the 1680s and in France started to be published. *Exilius* was the earliest written, though not published until 1715. Aside from such publication, all that is known of her later life is that she developed cataracts and was functionally blind, that she had a serious illness in 1726, and that she may have gone back to France in 1727, after which nothing is recorded. Her current popu-

3

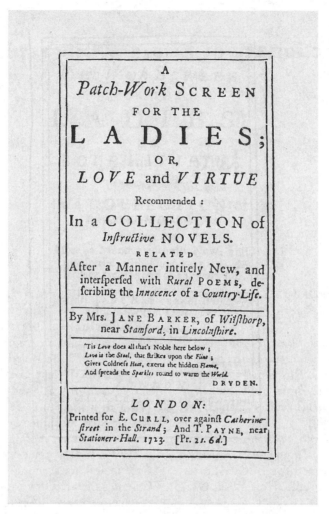

A

Patch-Work SCREEN

FOR THE

LADIES;

OR,

LOVE and *VIRTUE*

Recommended :

In a COLLECTION of

Instructive NOVELS.

RELATED

After a Manner intirely New, and
interspersed with *Rural* POEMS, describing the *Innocence* of a *Country-Life*.

By Mrs. JANE BARKER, of *Wilsthorp*,
near *Stamford*, in *Lincolnshire*.

'Tis *Love* does all that's Noble here below ;
Love is the *Steel*, that strikes upon the *Flint* ;
Gives Coldness *Heat*, exerts the hidden *Flame*,
And spreads the *Sparkles* round to warm the *World*.
DRYDEN.

LONDON:

Printed for E. CURLL, over against *Catherine-
street* in the *Strand*; And T. PAYNE, near
Stationers-Hall. 1723. [Pr. 2*s.* 6*d.*]

Title page for Barker's 1723 book, in which she describes her writing as
"Pieces of Romances, Poems, Love-Letters, and the like," put
together as patchwork

larity as a novelist derives primarily from her stance
for women faced with either marriage or independent achievement: she offers straightforward circumstances and characters that are not romanticized; and the fragments that are patched together
to make a "screen" and a "lining" often concern
women and women's psychology (though left unex-
plored). She is, at the same time, critical of some
women and satirizes those who are shallow or self-
serving. She champions those who are intellectual
and who should be able to assert themselves into
areas of life traditionally controlled by men. To
some feminist critics today she is antimasculinist, as
in "A Virgin Life" (published in *Poetical Recreations*
and *A Patch-Work Screen,* 1723):

Since, O good Heavens! you have bestow'd on me
So great a Kindness for *Virginity,*

Suffer me not to fall into the Powers
Of Man's almost Omnipotent Amours.
But let me in this happy State remain,
And in chaste Verse my chaster Thoughts explain;
. . . .
A *Virgin* bears the Impress of all Good,
Under that Name, all Vertue's understood.
. . . .
The Business of her Life to this extends,
To serve her God, her Neighbour and her Friends.

The poems consist of numerous kinds – odes,
sonnets, ballads, songs, those in heroic couplets,
and others. She writes of political issues, always siding with the Stuart monarchy and antagonistic toward James Scott, Duke of Monmouth, the Whigs,
and William III; of thwarted or lost love, female
friendship (which has led to a comparison with
Katherine Philips, the "Matchless Orinda"), fame,

religion, marriage, or the single life. Some of the poems of the collection reappear in the novels, which are often filled with verses that have an integral function with the plot. Of course, the earliest English prose narratives, such as George Gascoigne's *The Adventures of Master F. J.* (1573) or Sir Philip Sidney's *Arcadia* (1590), also worked out of poetic materials or employed poems to further the psychology of a character, and this was to continue in much eighteenth-century fiction. In *A Patch-Work Screen,* for instance, one finds "The Grove" in heroic couplets, "The Rivulet" in stanzas, "An Invocation of her Muse" in triplets, "Anatomy" in heroic couplets, two untitled odic stanzas, and twenty-three more poems on various subjects and in various meters or forms. The character Galesia says that "The Grove" (first published as "The Prospect of a Landskip, Beginning with a Grove" in *Poetical Recreations*) is the result of her fancy "to draw a Landskip in Verse" through her emulation of Katherine Philips's wit, although Philips's noble genius is inimitable "especially in Praise of a Country-Life, and Contempt of human Greatness":

> Well might the *Ancients* deem a *Grove* to be
> The sacred Mansion of Some DEITY;
> Its pleasing Shades, and gloomy Terrors, move
> Our *Souls* at once to *pious Fears* and *Love* [.]

A description of the trees, a catalogue of flowers, and an apostrophe to the birds follow, and the classic contrast between country life and the city (the *beata ille* theme) next appears:

> Methinks, I pity much the busy Town,
> To whom these Rural Pleasures are not known.
> But more I pity those whom Fate inthralls,
> Who can't retire when Inclination calls,
> By Business, Families, and Fortune ty'd;
> Beset, besieg'd, attack'd on ev'ry Side,
> By Friends & Foes; Wit, Beauty, Mirth & Wine,
> Piques, Parties, Policies, and Flatterers join
> To storm one's Quiet, Vertue undermine.

The last poem in the volume is separated from the text of the novel itself and is titled "An Ode in Commemoration of the Nativity of Christ," a set topic and a theme dear to Barker's heart:

> Well dost thou do, my Muse;
>   Ne'er envy Tuneful Bards, whoe'er they be,
> That Vain and Earthly Subjects chuse,
>   Yet vainly hope for Immortality.
> . . . .
> Yet, O thou Virgin! O thou Vestal-Muse!
>   That won't profane thy Voice, with Things below,
> One Theme, as Low as Earth can yield, I chuse,

> And yet as High as Heav'n can e'er bestow.
> . . . .
> Sing thou the Child, that seem'd like Mankind's Scorn.
> At Depth of Winter in a Stable born;
> Born among Beasts, and in a Manger laid:
> Yet if that Child will thee, inspiring, aid,
> The lovely Theme, exalting, shalt thou raise,
> Above the Kings and Heroes others praise.

She concludes the long poem with a wish for the conversion of the Jews, which would embark the prophesied millennium (the poem thus taking on the double vision of the birth and death of Christ):

> Tho' suff'ring still, they still thy Laws despise,
> Since Seventeen Cent'ries cannot make them wise:
> Since from their rooted Sin they cannot part;
> Melt (for Thou canst!) the hardest Heart,
>   And open Blindest Eyes:
> Make All on Earth, as All in Heav'n, join,
> Since All in Heav'n and Earth alike are Thine.

There is also in the last lines a play upon the text of 1 Corinthians 15:28: "And when all things shall be subdued unto him, then shall the Son also himself be subject unto him that put all things under him, that God may be all in all."

Love Intrigues (1713) has five poems, varying in triplets, tetrameter couplets, and heroic couplets. The other works such as *Exilius* likewise employ poems or poetic statements.

Poetical Recreations establishes links with earlier writers, such as Sir Philip Sidney, Ben Jonson, and Katherine Philips, in subject, treatment, and prosody. The verse epistle "An Invitation to my Friends at Cambridge" shows influence from John Milton's "At a Vacation Exercise" (1673) and *Paradise Lost* (1674). As might be understood from remarks above, Barker also engages the figure of Eve and Eden to criticize woman's continued exclusion from education at Cambridge, though it be likened to Eden: "For in our Maker's Laws [women]'ve made a breach, / And gather'd all that was within our reach." Wit, a major feature of late-seventeenth-century poetry, pervades her remarks about writing in "To Mr. Hill, on his Verses to the Dutchess of York, when she was at Cambridge":

> What fitter Subject could be for thy Wit?
> What Wit for Subject could there be more fit
> Than thine for this, by which thou'st nobly shew'd
> Thy Soul with Loyal Sentiments endew'd?
> . . . for now the World shall know
> That Woods and Hills of wit in Cambridge grow,
> Since here's a *Pisgah-Hill* whereon to stand

To take a project of Wit's holy Land,
Flowing with Milk of Christian innocence,
And Honey of Cic'ronian Eloquence.

A footnote identifies Woods as "Author of another Speech," and "Pisgah-Hill" (that is, Mount Pisgah, also called Mount Nebo, northeast of the Dead Sea) means that Hill's work provides a full panorama (guide) for other writers, in excellent style, to write well and with Christian worth. It becomes *A Pisgah-Sight of Palestine* (1650), as it were, such as commentators on biblical matters, like Thomas Fuller, called it.

That concern with writing is found as well in "Necessity of Fate," an ode in four numbered stanzas:

I.
In vain, in vain it is, I find,
To strive against our *Fate,*
We may as well command the *Wind,*
Or th' *Seas* rude Waves to gentle manners bind,
Or to *Eternity* prescribe a date,
As frustrate ought that *Fortune* has design'd.
For when we think we're *Politicians* grown,
And live by methods of our own;
We then *obsequiously* obey
Her Dictates, and a blindfull *Homage* pay.
II.
For were't not so, surely I cou'd not be
Still slave to Rhime, and lazy Poetry[.]

Accordingly, she forgoes "Soaring honours," "vain sweets of pleasure," "vainer fruits of *worldly treasure*" for her "*Muses* Melancholy *Tree.*" "In Commendation of the Female Sex. Out of Scipina" places a main concern of her writing, as noted above, within a religious context; the poem ends:

Nay more, we're taught *Religion* too by you:
For who can think that such Perfections grew
By chance? no, 'twas the divine Pow'rs which thus
Chose to exhibit their bright selves to us:
And for an Antepast of future bliss,
Sent you their Images from *Paradise.*

As a poet, Barker has had insufficient attention: she is in a mainstream of poetic writing as the centuries change, linking that of the past with that of the future, as in the work of Anne Finch, Countess of Winchilsea, or Elizabeth Rowe (Singer), and the meaningful use of poetry in novels continues throughout the eighteenth century.

References:
Jean B. Kern, "The Old Maid; or, 'To Grow Old, and Be Poor, and Laughed at,'" in *Fetter'd or Free? British Women Novelists, 1670–1815,* edited by Mary Anne Schofield and Cecilia Macheski (Athens: Ohio University Press, 1986), pp. 201–214;
Bridget G. MacCarthy, *Women Writers: Their Contribution to the English Novel 1621–1744* (Cork: Cork University Press / Oxford: Blackwell, 1944);
Myra Reynolds, *The Learned Lady in England 1650–1760* (Boston & New York: Houghton Mifflin, 1920), pp. 161–165, 434–439;
John Richetti, *Popular Fiction Before Richardson: Narrative Patterns 1700–1739* (Oxford: Clarendon Press, 1969), pp. 230–239;
Mary Anne Schofield, "Jane Barker," in her *Masking and Unmasking the Female Mind. Disguising Romances in Feminine Fiction, 1713–1799* (Newark: University of Delaware Press / London & Toronto: Associated University Presses, 1990), pp. 67–78;
Patricia M. Spacks, *Imagining a Self: Autobiography and Novel in Eighteenth-Century England* (Cambridge, Mass.: Harvard University Press, 1976), pp. 66–71, 176–177;
Jane Spencer, "Creating the Woman Writer: The Autobiographical Works of Jane Barker," *Tulsa Studies in Women's Literature,* 2 (Fall 1983): 165–181.

Papers:
Poems by Barker are included in two manuscripts. "Poems on Several Occasions in three parts" is found in the Bodleian Library, Oxford (Magdalen MS. 343). "A Collection of Poems referring to the times" is owned by the British Library (MS. Add. 21621).

Aphra Behn

(1640? – 16 April 1689)

Arlene Stiebel
California State University, Northridge

See also the Behn entries in *DLB 39: British Novelists, 1660–1800* and *DLB 80: Restoration and Eighteenth-Century Dramatists, First Series.*

BOOKS: *The Forc'd Marriage, Or The Jealous Bridegroom, A Tragi-Comedy, As it is Acted at His Highnesse The Duke of York's Theatre* (London: Printed by H. L. & R. B. for James Magnus, 1671);

The Amorous Prince, or, The Curious Husband. A Comedy, As it is Acted at his Royal Highness, the Duke of York's Theatre (London: Printed by J. M. for Thomas Dring, 1671);

The Dutch Lover: A Comedy, Acted At The Dukes Theatre (London: Printed for Thomas Dring, 1673);

Abdelazer, or The Moor's Revenge. A Tragedy. As it is Acted at his Royal Highness the Duke's Theatre (London: Printed for J. Magnes & R. Bentley, 1677);

The Town-Fopp: Or Sir Timothy Tawdrey. A Comedy. As it is Acted at his Royal Highness the Duke's Theatre (London: Printed by T. N. for James Magnes & Rich Bentley, 1677);

The Debauchee: Or, The Credulous Cuckold, A Comedy. Acted at His Highness the Duke of York's Theatre (London: Printed for John Amery, 1677);

The Rover. Or, The Banish't Cavaliers. As it is Acted At His Royal Highness the Duke's Theatre (London: Printed for John Amery, 1677); modern edition, edited by Frederick M. Link (Lincoln: University of Nebraska Press, 1967; London: Arnold, 1967);

The Counterfeit Bridegroom: Or The Defeated Widow. A Comedy, As it is Acted at His Royal Highness The Duke's Theatre (London: Printed for Langley Curtiss, 1677);

Sir Patient Fancy: A Comedy. As it is Acted at the Duke's Theatre (London: Printed by D. Flesher for Richard Tonson & Jacob Tonson, 1678);

The Feign'd Curtizans, Or, A Nights Intrigue. A Comedy. As it is Acted at the Dukes Theatre (London: Printed for Jacob Tonson, 1679);

The Revenge: Or, A Match In Newgate. A Comedy. As it was Acted at the Dukes Theatre (London: Printed for W. Cademan, 1680);

The Second Part Of The Rover. As it is Acted by the Servants of His Royal Highness (London: Printed for Jacob Tonson, 1681);

A Farce Call'd The False Count, Or, A New Way to play An Old Game. As it is Acted at the Duke's Theatre (London: Printed by M. Flesher for Jacob Tonson, 1682);

The Roundheads Or, The Good Old Cause, A Comedy As it is Acted at His Royal Highness the Dukes Theatre (London: Printed for D. Brown, T. Benskin & H. Rhodes, 1682);

The City-Heiress: Or, Sir Timothy Treat-all. A Comedy. As it is Acted at his Royal Highness his Theatre (London: Printed for D. Brown, T. Benskin & H. Rhodes, 1682);

Prologue to Romulus [single sheet with epilogue on verso] (London: Printed by Nath. Thompson, 1682); republished in *Romulus and Hersilia; or, The Sabine War. A Tragedy Acted at the Dukes Theatre* (London: Printed for D. Brown & T. Benskin, 1683);

The Young King: Or, The Mistake. As 'tis acted at his Royal Highness The Dukes Theatre (London: Printed for D. Brown, T. Benskin & H. Rhodes, 1683);

Poems upon Several Occasions: with A Voyage to the Island of Love (London: Printed for R. Tonson & J. Tonson, 1684);

Prologue [to John Fletcher's *Valentinian*, altered by John Wilmot, second Earl of Rochester] [single sheet] (London: Printed for Charles Tebroc, 1684);

Love-Letters Between a Noble-Man And his Sister, 2 volumes (London: Printed by Randal Taylor, 1684, 1687);

A Pindaric on the Death of Our Late Sovereign with an Ancient Prophecy on His Present Majesty (London: Printed by J. Playford for Henry Playford, 1685);

Aphra Behn (portrait attributed to Sir Peter Lely; from Montague Summers, ed., The Works of Aphra Behn, *volume 1, 1915)*

A Pindaric Poem on the Happy Coronation of His Most Sacred Majesty James II and His Illustrious Consort Queen Mary (London: Printed by J. Playford for Henry Playford, 1685);

La Montre; or, The Lover's Watch, Behn's translation of a work by Balthazar de Bonnecorse (London: Printed by R. H. for W. Canning, 1686);

The Luckey Chance, or An Alderman's Bargain. A Comedy. As it is Acted by their Majesty's Servants (London: Printed by R. H. for W. Canning, 1687);

The Emperor of the Moon: A Farce. As it is Acted by Their Majesties Servants, At the Queens Theatre (London: Printed by R. Holt for Joseph Knight & Francis Saunders, 1687);

A Congratulatory Poem to Her Most Sacred Majesty on the Universal Hopes of all Loyal Persons for a Prince of Wales (London: Printed for W. Canning, 1688);

The Fair Jilt: Or, The History of Prince Tarquin and Miranda (London: Printed by R. Holt for Will. Canning, 1688);

Oroonoko; Or, The Royal Slave. A True History (London: Printed for W. Canning, 1688);

The History of Oracles and the Cheats of the Pagan Priests, Behn's translation of Bernard Le Bovier Fontenelle's French adaptation of A. van Dale's *De oraculis ethnicorum* (London, 1688);

A Discovery of New Worlds. From the French. Made English by Mrs. A. Behn. To which is prefixed a preface, by way of essay on translated prose; wherein the arguments of Father Tacquet, and others, against the System of Copernicus . . . are likewise considered, and answered, Behn's translation of, and preface to, a work by Fontenelle (London: Printed for William Canning, 1688);

Agnes de Castro or, The Force of Generous Love. Written in French by a Lady of Quality. Made English by Mrs. Behn, Behn's translation of a novel by J. B. de Brilhac (London: Printed for William Canning, 1688);

Lycidus: Or The Lover in Fashion. Being an Account from Lycidus to Lysander, of his Voyage from the Island of Love. From the French. By the Same Author Of the

Voyage to the Isle of Love. Together with a Miscellany Of New Poems. By Several Hands, Behn's translation of a work by Paul Tallemant, with poems by Behn and others (London: Printed for Joseph Knight & F. Saunders, 1688) – includes the following poems by Behn: "Song. On Occasion"; "On the Honourable Sir Francis Fane, on his Play call'd the Sacrifice"; "To Damon. To inquire of him if he cou'd tell me by the Style, who writ me a Copy of Verses that came to me in an unknown Hand"; "To Alexis in Answer to his Poem against Fruition. Ode"; "To Alexis, On his saying, I lov'd a Man that talk'd much"; "A Pastoral Pindarick. On the Marriage of the Right Honourable the Earle of Dorset and Midlesex, to the Lady Mary Compton"; "On Desire A Pindarick"; "To Amintas, Upon reading the Lives of some of the Romans"; "On the first discovery of falseness in Amintas"; "To the fair Clarinda, who made Love to me, imagin'd more than woman";

The History of the Nun: Or, The Fair Vow-Breaker (London: Printed for A. Baskerville, 1689);

The Lucky Mistake: A New Novel (London: Printed by R. Bentley, 1689);

A Pindaric Poem to the Reverend Dr. Burnet (London: Printed for R. Bentley, 1689);

The Widdow Ranter or, The History of Bacon in Virginia. A Tragi-Comedy, Acted by their Majesties Servants (London: Printed for James Knapton, 1690);

The Younger Brother: Or, The Amorous Jilt. A Comedy, Acted at the Theatre Royal, By His Majesty's Servants (London: Printed for J. Harris & sold by R. Baldwin, 1696);

The Histories And Novels of the Late Ingenious Mrs. Behn: In One Volume. . . . Together with The Life and Memoirs of Mrs. Behn (London: Printed for S. Briscoe, 1696);

The Lady's Looking-Glass, to dress herself by; or, The Whole Art of Charming (London: W. Onley for S. Briscoe, 1697);

Histories, Novels, and Translations, written by the most ingenious Mrs. Behn; the second volume (London: Printed by W. O. for S. B. & sold by M. Brown, 1700).

Editions: *The Plays, Histories, and Novels of the Ingenious Mrs. Aphra Behn,* 6 volumes, edited by John Pearson (London: Pearson, 1871);

The Novels of Mrs. Aphra Behn, edited by Ernest A. Baker (London: Routledge, 1905: New York: Dutton, 1905);

The Works of Aphra Behn, 6 volumes, edited by Montague Summers (London: Heinemann, 1915);

Selected Writings of the Ingenious Mrs. Aphra Behn, edited by Robert Phelps (New York: Grove, 1950);

The Uncollected Verse of Aphra Behn, edited by Germaine Greer (Essex: Stump Cross, 1989).

OTHER: *Miscellany, Being A Collection Of Poems By Several Hands. Together with Reflections on Morality, Or Seneca Unmasqued,* includes ten poems by Behn (London: Printed for J. Hindmarsh, 1685);

Miscellany Poems Upon Several Occasions, edited by Charles Gildon, includes three poems by Behn (London: Printed for Peter Buck, 1692);

The Muses Mercury: Or The Monthly Miscellany, published twelve poems by Behn (March 1707 - January 1708).

Aphra Behn, one of the most influential dramatists of the late seventeenth century, was also a celebrated poet and novelist. Her contemporary reputation was founded primarily on her "scandalous" plays, which she claimed would not have been criticized for impropriety had a man written them. Behn's assertion of her unique role in English literary history is confirmed not only by the extraordinary circumstances of her writings, but by those of her life history as well.

No one really knows her birth name or when exactly she was born. Her parentage has been traced to Wye, and tradition has it that she was born in 1640. One version of her life postulates that her parents were a barber, John Amis, and Amy, his wife. Another speculation about Behn has her the child of a couple named Cooper. However, an essay by the unidentified "One of the Fair Sex" affixed to the collection of *The Histories And Novels of the Late Ingenious Mrs. Behn* (1696) maintains that Aphra was the daughter of Mr. and Mrs. John Johnson of nearby Canterbury. Johnson was a gentleman related to Francis, Lord Willoughby, who appointed him lieutenant general of Surinam, for which Willoughby was the royal patentee. Whether Aphra was Johnson's natural child or fostered by him is not known, but what has been established with reasonable certainty was that in 1663 Aphra accompanied Johnson, his wife, and a young boy, mentioned as Behn's brother, on a voyage to take up residence in the West Indies. Johnson died on the way, and the mother and two children lived for several months in Surinam. This episode was to

On the Death of Ed: Waller Esq:

How to thy Sacred Memory shall I bring
(Worthy thy Fame) a Gratfull offerings.
I, who by toyles of Sickness am becom
Almost as neere as thou art, to a Tombe.
While every soft and every tender straine
Is Ruffld and Ill Natur'd groune with Paine.
But at thy Name my Languisht Muse revives
And a New spark in the Dull Ashes strives;
I heave thy tunefull Voyce, thy Song divine!
And am inspir'd by every Charming line.!
But oh —————
What Inspiration at the second hand
Can an Immortall Eligie command?
Un less like Pious offerings mine shoud be
Made Sacred being Consecrate to thee.
Eternall as thy owne all mighty Verse
Shoud be those Trophies that adorn thy Herse
The thought Illustrious, & thy Fancy young
The Witt Sublime, the Judgment fine & strong
Soft as thy Notes to Sacarisa sung ———

Page from Behn's only extant literary manuscript, her elegy on Edmund Waller (Pierpont Morgan Library, MA 3585). She made this fair copy toward the end of her life for presentation to Waller's daughter-in-law.

have lasting effects on Behn's life. Her most famous novel, *Oroonoko* (1688), is based on her experiences there and her friendship with a prince of the indigenous peoples whom the colonials made a slave.

The facts about Behn's life after her return to England in 1664 are also unclear. She is known to have met and taken the name of a man considered to be her husband, who was perhaps a Dutch merchant whose name was either "Ben," "Beane," "Bene," or "Behn." Whatever the true circumstances, from that time on she was known publicly as "Mrs. Behn," the name she later used for her professional writing. Aphra Behn was propelled into writing for a living by the death of her husband in 1665, and her indebtedness as a result of her employment as a spy for King Charles II.

When her husband died, Behn was left without funds. Perhaps because of her association, through him, with the Dutch, she was appointed an intelligence gatherer for the king, who was, at least, to pay for her trip to Antwerp as his spy. But Charles did not respond to Behn's requests for money for her trip home, so in December 1666 she was forced to borrow for her passage back to England. Charles continued to refuse payment, and in 1668 Behn was thrown into debtor's prison. The circumstances of her release are unknown, but in 1670 her first play, *The Forc'd Marriage* (published, 1671), was produced in London, and Behn, having vowed never to depend on anyone else for money again, became one of the period's foremost playwrights. She earned her living in the theater and then as a novelist until her death on 16 April 1689.

Even before her arrest for indebtedness Aphra Behn had written poetry. These early poems are not as polished as the later incidental poems or those from her plays, but they indicate the versatility of her literary gifts and prefigure the skill and grace that characterize all of Behn's verse. Although it was impossible to make a living from writing poems exclusively, Behn, in the tradition of famous English playwrights whose poetry was also accorded distinction, pursued verse writing as an adjunct to her more lucrative work.

Behn's contemporary reputation as a poet was no less stunning than her notoriety as a dramatist. She was heralded as a successor to Sappho, inheriting the great gifts of the Greek poet in the best English tradition exemplified by Behn's immediate predecessor, Katherine Philips. Just as Philips was known by her pastoral nom de plume and praised as "The Matchless Orinda," so Behn was apostrophized as "The Incomparable Astrea," an appella-

tion based on the code name she had used when she was Charles's spy.

Some of Behn's lyrics originally appeared in her plays, and there were longer verses, such as the Pindaric odes, published for special occasions. But the majority of her poetry was published in two collections that included longer narrative works of prose and poetry as well as Behn's shorter verses. *Poems upon Several Occasions: with A Voyage to the Island of Love* (1684) and *Lycidus: Or The Lover in Fashion* (1688) reflect Behn's customary use of classical, pastoral, courtly, and traditionally English lyric modes. Forty-five poems appeared in *Poems upon Several Occasions;* ten poems were appended to *Lycidus.* Ten more works appeared in the 1685 *Miscellany.* Posthumous publications include poems in Charles Gildon's *Miscellany Poems Upon Several Occasions* (1692) and in *The Muses Mercury* (1707–1708).

Behn's distinctive poetic voice is characterized by her audacity in writing about contemporary events, frequently with topical references that, despite their allegorical maskings, were immediately recognizable to her sophisticated audience. Although she sometimes addressed her friends by their initials or their familiar names, she might just as easily employ some classical or pastoral disguise that was transparent to the initiated. Behn's poetry, therefore, was less public than her plays or her prose fiction, as it depended, in some cases, on the enlightened audience's recognition of her topics for full comprehension of both the expression and implications of her verse. Such poetic technique involved a skill and craft that earned her the compliments of her cohorts as one who, despite her female form, had a male intelligence and masculine powers of reason.

Behn's response to this admiration was to display even more fully those characteristics which had earned her praise. Frequently her poems are specifically addressed to members of her social community and might employ mild satire as commentary, present events of their lives, and detail or explore the emotional states of their frequently complex relationships, expecially those of love and sex. Less commonly Behn might use a translation or adaptation of another author's verse to discuss these issues in her own style. In these cases the poems are frequently redrawn to reveal Behn's own emphases and display more her artistic perspective than that of the original author.

Whatever the source of the texts, whether her plays, a political or personal occasion, an adaptation or translation, or an emotional or psychological exploration, Behn's verse style is particular and identifiable, with a very distinctive voice. The speaker is usually identified as a character or as "Astrea," Behn's poetic self, and there is usually a specific audience. There may be dialogue within a poem, but, unlike the dialogue in her plays, in the poetry the voices are joined in lyrical rather than dramatic expression. In fact, the musicality of Behn's verse is another identifying characteristic. Whereas many of Behn's predecessors and contemporaries, including Philips, to whom Behn was frequently compared, are known for the Metaphysical aspects of their verse, Behn's poems are more classical, in the tradition of Ben Jonson rather than John Donne. As such they rely more on the heritage of sixteenth-century ornate lyricism as practiced by Sir Philip Sidney, Edmund Spenser, and William Shakespeare, along with the epigrammatic tradition of light Juvenalian satire in Jonson and Robert Herrick, than the Marvellian wit and Miltonic grandeur of later seventeenth-century verse. Behn shares with John Dryden a preference for the couplet, but she also uses a modified ballad stanza and more varied verse forms if the content permits. The decorum of her verse is based in a very traditional relationship between structure and meaning, so that her discourse has a sense of immediacy and directness despite the conventionality of her literary forms. Perhaps it is because her use of vocabulary and form is so traditional that Behn, who was in her lifetime criticized as outrageous for the content of her works, was able, nevertheless, to thrive as a successful author.

The first of the *Poems upon Several Occasions,* "The Golden Age," presents Behn's customary combination of tradition and innovation. It is described in the text as "A Paraphrase on a Translation out of French," and although Behn criticism usually emphasizes that the poem is a translation, Behn herself presents rather more of the aspect of paraphrase. The poem restates well-known concepts in a typically idiosyncratic way. Behn conventionally places her paradise in a prelapsarian garden but then goes on to describe that sinless state as devoid also of "civilized" constraints. Lovers' vows are "Not kept in fear of Gods, no fond Religious cause, / Nor in obedience to duller Laws" but merely for joy alone. Honor, rather than being perceived as a desirable characteristic, is furiously attacked in two long verses as responsible for introducing the shame and formality that "first taught lovely Eyes the art, / To wound, and not to cure the heart." This, she maintains, is "a Cruel Law." She asserts that women have sexuality and can teach

men how to express their feelings if only this false value, honor, were not in the way.

Business and the rules of honor are also rejected in favor of a natural and easy "Love" in the poem "A Farewel to Celladon, On his Going into Ireland." These verses ask Celladon why he bothers with boring government business ("To Toyl, be Dull, and to be Great"), when he knows that success will not bring happiness. It is more important, the speaker advises him, to enjoy the company of his close good friend, Damon, to whom Celladon is "by Sacred Friendship ty'd," and from whom "Love nor Fate can nere divide" him. The tradition of close male friendships has both a literary and social history based in the classics. In this "Pindarique," Behn elevates such a relationship over politics and commerce. In her other poems as well, there is a precedence of close personal relationships over public enterprise. The portrayal of many of these relationships is in the classical pastoral tradition, and several of the poems also present the classical concept of the person with attributes of both sexes, the androgyne or hermaphrodite.

"Friendship" that is "Too Amorous for a Swain to a Swain" is the basis for one section in the long poem describing Behn's social circle, "Our Cabal." The verses on "Mr. Ed. Bed." describe the relationship between Philander and Lycidas as conventionally androgynous, with implicit overtones of sexuality. Philander, she writes, "nere paid / A Sigh or Tear to any Maid: / ... / But all the Love he ever knew, / On Lycidas he does bestow."

Homoeroticism is standard in Behn's verse, either in descriptions such as these of male to male relationships or in depictions of her own attractions to women. Behn was married and widowed early, and as a mature woman her primary publicly acknowledged relationship was with a gay male, John Hoyle, himself the subject of much scandal. Behn was known to have had male lovers throughout her lifetime, most notably the man allegorized as "Amintas" in her verses, but she also writes explicitly of the love of women for each other. Just as the emotional and physical closeness of males is justified by their androgynous qualities, so, for women, hermaphroditic characteristics transcend conventional boundaries by allowing the enjoyment of female and male qualities in lovers.

The breaking of boundaries in poetry, as in her life, caused Behn to be criticized as well as admired publicly. Her best-known poem, "The Disappointment," finely illustrates Behn's ability to portray scandalous material in an acceptable form. The poem was sent to Hoyle with a letter asking him to deny allegations of ill conduct circulating about his activities. Both the letter and the poem were reprinted in early miscellaneous collections. "The Disappointment" has been traditionally interpreted to be about impotence. But it is also about rape, another kind of potency test, and presents a woman's point of view cloaked in the customary language of male physical license and sexual access to females. The woman's perspective in this poem provides the double vision that plays the conventional against the experiential.

One evening Lysander comes across Cloris in the woods. They are in love, and he makes sexual advances. She resists and tells him to kill her if he must, but she will not give up her honor, even though she loves him. He persists. She swoons. He undresses her. She lies defenseless and fully exposed to him, but he cannot maintain an erection. He tries self-stimulation without success. She recovers consciousness, discovers his limp penis with her hand, recoils in confusion, and runs away with supernatural speed. He rages at the gods and circumstance but mostly directs his anger at Cloris, blaming her for his impotence.

The traditional interpretation of this poem is that Cloris, having been aroused by Lysander's advances, flees from him in shame and that the lovers are both disappointed by Lysander's inability to consummate their relationship sexually. But that is only one line of meaning in the poem. Embedded in the text is another interpretation of these fourteen stanzas. Cloris is definite: she says leave me alone or kill me. For her, defloration is a fate worse than death, and she will not endure dishonor even for one she loves. When Lysander continues to force her "without Respect," she lies "half dead" and shows "no signs of life" but breathing. Traditionally her passion and breathlessness have been read as sexual arousal, but they might just as easily be read as signs of her struggle to escape Lysander, which exhausts her. As soon as her struggle ends, he is "unable to perform." In the poem, even though Cloris is unconscious, Lysander unsuccessfully tries self-stimulation, ostensibly to continue the attack. Cloris awakens, however, and takes the first opportunity she has to run away from him as fast as she can. Her decision to flee may clearly be seen as an attempt to escape. When she sees the state of things, she shows no sympathy. Lysander's anger is greater than mere disappointment – he rants at the gods and the universe for his impotence and accuses Cloris of witchcraft. The extent of his rage is more that of a thwarted assailant than an embarrassed lover.

For the first thirteen stanzas of the poem, the story is told in the third person, with an omniscient speaker. But in the last verse, in a startling change of voice to the first person, the speaker identifies herself with Cloris and closes the narrative in sympathy with the "Nymph's Resentments," which the speaker, as a woman, can "well Imagine" and "Condole." The usual interpretation of "The Disappointment" will stand in a conventional reading, but this point of view ignores a particularly female perspective that Behn clearly asserts when, in the last stanza, she identifies with Cloris and not Lysander. The unconventionality of this poem is apparent when it is contrasted with the presentation of joyous amorous relations in some of Behn's other poems.

One of her best-known verses, happily juxtaposed to "The Disappointment," is "Song: The Willing Mistriss." This poem describes how the female speaker becomes so aroused by the excellent courtship of her lover that she is "willing to receive / That which I dare not name." After three verses describing their lovemaking, she concludes with the coy suggestion, "Ah who can guess the rest?" The poem is a good example of Behn's treatment of conventional courtly and pastoral modes, as is the "Song. Love Arm'd," which describes Cupid's power to enamour.

Convention and ingenuity are further united in the poem "Song: The Invitation," where, witnessing Damon's pursuit of Sylvia, the speaker interposes herself to meet "the Arrows" of love and save Sylvia "from their harms" because Sylvia already has a lover and Damon would more appropriately be paired with the speaker.

In her poems Behn uses the dramatic qualities of voice which gave her such great stage success. Her verses are always spoken by a specific, identifiable individual, whose self-characterization becomes clear in the text. The effect of this technique is to give the poems a sense of immediacy and energy that reveals Behn's personality through her works. She almost always speaks from the point of view of a female, and her attitudes convey a woman's confidence in dealing with men's amorous advances and betrayals. In the poem "A Ballad on M. JH to Amoret, asking why I was so sad," the speaker tells how she was betrayed by her lover, and she warns Amoret to be careful and be sure to get the better of the man. Here the relationship between women is primary, as they are allies on the same side of the war of love. Men are frequently shown as enemies in the battle of the sexes, as Behn's poem "The Return" illustrates. In it she warns a tyrannous shepherd not to stray, since "Some hard-hearted Nymph may return you your own."

"The Reflection" is a classic song of betrayal with a twist. It is written from the point of view of a woman who gave in to her lover. He used every means he could to get her; then, the more she wanted him, the less he wanted her. Although he made many vows, he betrayed her. Since her pain is too great for tears, traditional consolation is inadequate; therefore, she will die. This poem is a variation on the standard pastoral "lover's complaint" of the male: conventionally the courtly beloved refuses to give in to her suitor, and he proclaims he will die of lovesickness. This poem uses the conventional pastoral mode, including the appeal to nature, to witness and participate in the lover's grief. But although the woman's sorrow is conventional, the consequences of betrayal are far more profound for her than they would be for a male counterpart. She is, in the old-fashioned meaning of the word, "dis-maid," bereft of her maidenhood, and as one no longer virgin, banished from consideration by future suitors. In her society there is nothing for her to look forward to, so she may as well die.

In "To Alexis in Answer to his Poem against Fruition. Ode" Behn asserts that men are only interested in conquest and that once they get what they want from one woman, they go on to another. This point of view, as presented by a male speaker, is also a highlight of the poems interspersed throughout the prose text of *Lycidus: Or The Lover in Fashion*. The popular "A Thousand Martyrs I have made" presents the philanderer's scorn for "the Fools that whine for Love" in the context of the narrator's lighthearted appraisal of his unreformed self. The speaker of the poem takes delight in his ability to play the game of love in appearances only, exempting himself from serious hurt. Because of his emotional detachment, ironically, he scores more conquests than those for whom love is serious.

One of Behn's strongest statements on the failure of a double standard in heterosexual love is "To Lysander, on some Verses he writ, and asking more for his Heart then 'twas worth." This poem uses metaphors from banking and investment to illustrate Lysander's materialism, and the speaker promises to get even. She tells him to take back his heart, since he wants too much from her for it. He does not want an equal or fair return (her heart for his heart) but much more from her than he is willing to give. He does not allow her even to be friendly with others, but, at the same time, he is cheating on her.

She protests that he gives her rival easily what she only gets with pain, and his intimacy with another hurts her. She calls for fairness in love – if he takes such liberties, she should be allowed them as well. If Lysander does not maintain honesty with her, she warns, he will find that she can play a trick too. Her "P.S. A Song" declares: "Tis not your saying that you love, / Can ease me of my Smart; / Your Actions must your Words approve, / Or else you break my Heart."

Behn's poems express anticonventional attitudes about other topics as well. She makes a strong antiwar statement in "Song: When Jemmy first began to Love," concluding with the question of what is to become of the woman left behind. In "To Mr. Creech (under the Name of Daphnis on his Excellent Translation of Lucretius)," she praises the translator for making accessible to unlearned women a work originally in Latin. As a member of the female class, which is denied education in the classics, she would like, she says, to express her admiration to him in an acceptable, manly fashion. Because she is a woman, however, her response to his translation is not mere admiration, but a fiery adoration, since women are thereby advanced to knowledge from ignorance. She describes the state of women as her own: "Till now, I curst my Birth, my Education, / And more the scanted Customes of the Nation: / Permitting not the Female Sex to tread, / The mighty Paths of Learned Heroes dead."

Behn writes, then, as the representative of all women, allying herself openly with women against men in the war conventionally called love. She tells her friend Carola, "Lady Morland at Tunbridge," that even though she is a rival for Behn's lover, when she saw her, she grew to admire and love her. Because of that, she warns, beware of taking my lover as your own – he is experienced and can slip the chains of love. You deserve a virgin, she says, someone who has never loved before, who only has eyes for you and has a "soul as Great as you are Fair."

Women uniting to oppose a faithless male lover is the theme of Behn's entertainment, "Selinda and Cloris," in which the title characters befriend each other in order to deal with betrayal. First Selinda is warned by Cloris about Alexis, who was untrue to her. Selinda's response is to ally herself with the other woman and vow that Alexis will not conquer her as he did Cloris. The women praise each other's generosity and intelligence, agreeing to be good friends. The reciprocal relationship between the women includes both physical and intel-

Behn in her forties (engraving after a portrait by Riley)

lectual attraction, friendship, and sexuality. Cloris "will sing, in every Grove, / The Greatness of your Mind," to which Selinda responds, "And I your Love." They trade verses and sing together just as traditional pastoral speakers do. In this case, however, in addition to being poets, lovers, singers, and shepherds, the speakers are also, untraditionally, female. The celebration of their mutual joy is a variant on the conventional masque of Hymen, and it presents in song and dance a formal poetic drama that emphasizes the eroticism of the women's relationship.

The bonding of women in female friendship is most clearly stated by Behn in her explicitly lesbian love poem, "To the fair Clarinda, who made Love to me, imagin'd more than woman." This is the last of the poems appended to *Lycidus,* and in it Behn shows how important to her were those androgynous quali-

ties for which she herself was praised. Just as she was commended in the dedicatory verses of her *Poems upon Several Occasions* for having "A Female Sweetness and a Manly Grace," Behn asserts the unity of "masculine" and "feminine" characteristics in her "beloved youth." She cleverly argues that she "loves" only the "masculine" part of Clarinda and to the "feminine" gives merely friendship. Since Clarinda's perfection manifests the idealized Platonic form, loving her cannot and should not be resisted. Further, since that by which society defines sex is not found in the female form, that is, women do not have the necessary physical equipment to consummate what is culturally considered "the sex act," love between women is, by definition, "innocent," and therefore not subject to censure. Clarinda is a hermaphrodite, a "beauteous Wonder of a different kind, / Soft *Cloris* with the dear *Alexis* join'd."

The poem may be read as the speaker's justification of her own approach to a forbidden beloved, but Clarinda is not a passive fair maiden. She is the one who, the title states, "made Love" to the speaker, and, in the last quatrain, her "Manly part . . . wou'd plead" while her "Image of the Maid" tempts. Clarinda, therefore, may also be seen as the initiator of their sexual activity, with the speaker justifying her own response in reaction to the public sexual mores of her time. As the poem ends, Behn, in a witty pun on her first name, asserts the multigendered sexuality of both Clarinda and the speaker, and "the noblest Passions do extend / The Love to *Hermes, Aphrodite* the Friend."

The complexity of Behn's verse, its logical argument, pastoral and courtly conventions, biblical and classical allusions, and incisive social comment define a unique poetic vision. Through the centuries, interest in at least some of her poetry has been maintained.

Aphra Behn's later reputation as a playwright, novelist, and poet has benefited from her value as a model for women writers as noted first by those distinguished Victorian women of letters, Vita Sackville-West and Virginia Woolf. Sackville-West's early biography (1927) and Woolf's memorializing of Behn in *A Room of One's Own* (1929) as the first woman in England to earn her living by writing place Behn foremost in feminist literary history. Where she was previously criticized, today she is lauded, her poetry, along with her novels and plays, achieving the status it rightly deserves.

Bibliography:

Mary Ann O'Donnell, *Aphra Behn: Annotated Bibliography of Primary and Secondary Sources* (New York: Garland, 1986).

Biographies:

Vita Sackville-West, *Aphra Behn, The Incomparable Astrea* (London: Howe, 1927; N.Y.: Viking, 1928);

George Woodcock, *The Incomparable Aphra* (London: Boardman, 1948).

Frederick M. Link, *Aphra Behn* (New York: Twayne, 1968);

Maureen Duffy, *The Passionate Shepherdess* (London: Cape, 1977);

Angeline Goreau, *Reconstructing Aphra* (New York: Dial, 1980);

References:

W. J. Cameron, *New Light on Aphra Behn* (Auckland, New Zealand: University of Auckland, 1961);

Dorothy Mermin, "Women Becoming Poets: Katherine Philips, Aphra Behn, Anne Finch," *ELH,* 57 (Summer 1990): pp. 335–356;

Arlene Stiebel, "Not Since Sappho: The Erotic in Poems of Katherine Philips and Aphra Behn," in *Homosexuality in Renaissance and Enlightenment England,* edited by Claude J. Summers (Binghamton, N.Y.: Haworth, 1992), pp. 153–171;

Stiebel, "Subversive Sexuality: Masking the Erotic in Poems by Katherine Philips and Aphra Behn," in *Renaissance Discourses of Desire,* edited by Summers and Ted-Larry Pebworth (Columbia: University of Missouri Press, 1993), pp. 223–236.

Papers:

The Bodleian Library at Oxford has a manuscript copy of Behn's play, *The Younger Brother.* The Public Record Office in London has letters and documents regarding Behn's assignment as a spy for King Charles II in Antwerp. There are no other known papers or manuscripts surviving.

Sir Richard Blackmore

(22 January 1654 – 9 October 1729)

Deborah Wyrick
North Carolina State University

BOOKS: *Prince Arthur. An Heroick Poem* (London: Printed for Awnsham & John Churchil, 1695; facsimile, Menston: Scolar, 1971);

King Arthur (London: Printed for Awnsham, John Churchil & Jacob Tonson, 1697);

A Short History of the Last Parliament (London: Printed for Jacob Tonson, 1699);

A Satyr against Wit (London: Printed for Samuel Crouch, 1700);

A Paraphrase on the Book of Job (London: Printed for Awnsham & John Churchill, 1700);

The Report of the Physicians and Surgeons, Commanded to assist at the Dissecting the Body of His Late Majesty at Kensington, March the tenth MDCCI/II (London: Printed for John Nutt, 1702);

A Hymn to the Light of the World (London: Printed for Jacob Tonson, 1703);

Eliza: An Epick Poem (London: Printed for Awnsham & J. Churchill, 1705);

Advice to the Poets (London: Printed by H. M. for A. & J. Churchill, 1706);

The Kit-Kats (London: Printed for E. Sanger & E. Curll, 1708);

Instructions to Vander Bank, A Sequel to the Advice to the Poets (London: Printed for Egbert Sanger, 1709);

The Nature of Man (London: Printed for Sam Buckley, 1711);

Creation. A Philosophical Poem (London: Printed for S. Buckley & J. Tonson, 1712);

The Lay-Monastery, by Blackmore and John Hughes (London: Printed by Sam Keimer for Ferdinando Burleigh, 1714);

Essays upon Several Subjects, 2 volumes (volume 1, London: Printed for E. Curll & J. Pemberton, 1716; facsimile, New York: Garland, 1971; volume 2, London: Printed by W. Wilkins for A. Bettesworth & J. Pemberton, 1717);

A Collection of Poems on Various Subjects (London: Printed by W. Wilkins for Jonas Browne & J. Walthoe, 1718);

A Discourse Upon the Plague (London: Printed for J. Clark, 1721);

Just Prejudices Against the Arian Hypothesis (London: Printed by W. Wilkins for J. Peele, 1721);

A New Version of the Psalms of David, Fitted to the Tunes Used in Churches (London: Printed by John March and sold by the Company of Stationers, 1721);

Modern Arians Unmask'd (London: Printed for John Clark, 1721);

Redemption: A Divine Poem (London: Printed for A. Bettesworth & James MackEuen, 1722);

Alfred. An Epick Poem. In Twelve Books (London: Printed by W. Botham for James Knapton, 1723);

A Treatise upon the Small-Pox (London: Printed for John Clark, 1723);

A True and Impartial History of the Conspiracy against the Person and Government of King William III. Of Glorious Memory, in the Year 1695 (London: Printed for James Knapton, 1723);

A Treatise of Consumptions and other Distempers Belonging to the Breast and Lungs (London: Printed for John Pemberton, 1724);

A Treatise of the Spleen and Vapours: Or, Hypocondriacal and Hysterical Affections (London: Printed for J. Pemberton, 1725);

A Critical Dissertation upon the Spleen, So Far as concerns the Following Question: Whether the Spleen is necessary or useful to the Animal possess'd of it? (London: Printed for J. Pemberton, 1725);

Discourses on the Gout, A Rheumatism, and the King's Evil (London: Printed for J. Pemberton, 1726);

Dissertations on a Dropsy. A Tympany, the Jaundice, the Stone, and a Diabetes (London: Printed for James & John Knapton, 1727);

Natural Theology: Or, Moral Duties Consider'd apart from Positive (London: Printed for J. Pemberton, 1728);

The Accomplished Preacher (London: Printed for J. Downing, 1731).

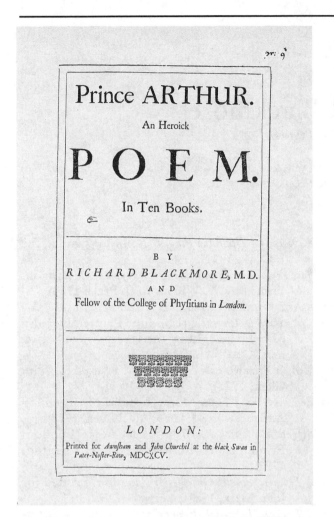

Prince ARTHUR.

An Heroick

POEM.

In Ten Books.

BY

RICHARD BLACKMORE, M.D.

AND

Fellow of the College of Phyſitians in *London*.

LONDON:

Printed for *Awnſham* and *John Churchil* at the *black Swan* in
Pater-Noſter-Row, MDCXCV.

*Title page for Blackmore's first epic, a political allegory drawing
on Arthurian legend to portray a "Pious British Prince," who
may be clearly identified as William of Orange*

Sir Richard Blackmore, physician and man of letters, was a cultural event. His ambitious epic poetry provoked pamphlet wars and coffeehouse cabals; it earned artistic scorn and royal gratitude. Although Blackmore was called the "British Elijah" by Nahum Tate and the equal of Lucretius by John Dennis, he was ridiculed by Sir Samuel Garth as a maladroit cit, by John Dryden as a fool who wrote "Dead-born Doggerel," and by Alexander Pope as the father of the bathos, "indeed as the Homer of it." As Theophilus Cibber wrote in 1753, it was "as if to be at enmity with Blackmore had been hereditary to our greatest poets." The reasons for this enmity extend beyond Blackmore's artistic lapses, into the political and cultural tensions that shaped Enlightenment England; yet his name has become a synonym for literary duncedom when it has not been forgotten altogether.

A small revival of interest did occur in the mid twentieth century. In 1949 Richard C. Boys pub-

lished a scholarly edition of the poems surrounding the dispensary controversy, a quarrel that largely revolved around Blackmore. In 1953 Albert Rosenberg wrote a biography concentrating more on Blackmore's professional life than on his art. Harry Solomon's fine critical biography (1980) remains the only sustained study of Blackmore's contributions to literature. Otherwise, modern scholarship is content to neglect Blackmore or to dismiss him; Maynard Mack's recent study of Pope, for instance, calls Blackmore a writer of "dreary exercise[s] in bombast," interesting only as a target for satire by his betters. Despite an undeniable ability to produce dreariness and bombast, however, Blackmore can be a rewarding subject for those concerned with the relationship of literature and culture, as well as with the symbiosis between limited talent and great art.

Richard Blackmore was born 22 January 1654, to Robert and Anne Blackmore, in the village of Corsham in Wiltshire. Robert Blackmore, an attorney, provided Richard, the third of his four surviving children, with a fine education: first a country school, then Westminster School, then Saint Edmund Hall at Oxford, where he entered as a commoner on 19 March 1669. A good student, he received his B.A. on 4 April 1674 and his M.A. on 3 June 1676; he remained at Oxford as a tutor until 1682. Perhaps prodded by the disruptions caused by Charles II's having moved Parliament to Oxford the year before, Blackmore left the university for a European tour, probably as a companion to a consumptive student named George Smith. They traveled through France and Switzerland, ending up at the University of Padua, where Blackmore studied for a doctorate in pure medicine, which he received in March 1684.

Considering the frightening state of medicine during the Restoration, Blackmore had an excellent, empirically based education. He set up a soon-to-be-prosperous practice in London and married a relation of a wealthy Whig family, Mary Adams, on 9 February 1685, three days after Charles II died. Although the succession of the Roman Catholic king James II doubtless troubled the devout Anglican doctor, the new ruler enlarged the Royal College of Physicians, and in April 1685 Richard Blackmore became a member. He spent the next ten years establishing himself in his profession; his only published poem was a commendatory Latin verse to a medical treatise by his friend William Cole, in 1693. This foray into the arts spurred Blackmore's interest in poetry. In 1695 he published his first epic, *Prince Arthur,* which he later explained had been "written in *Coffee-houses,* and in passing up and down the Streets; because I had little leisure elsewhere to apply to it" (preface to *King Arthur,* 1697).

In ten books of heroic couplets *Prince Arthur* presents the legendary monarch's exploits as he attempts to recover the Crown of Britain from the Saxon forces of King Octa. Based loosely on Geoffrey of Monmouth's *Historia regum Britanniae,* patterned on Virgil's *Aeneid,* and indebted to John Milton's *Paradise Lost* (1667), *Prince Arthur* enlists Lucifer and – for the first time in English poetry – Teutonic deities on the side of the archvillain Octa, while Uriel, Raphael, and Michael give aid and instruction to Arthur. Following the encyclopedic tendency of epic, Blackmore includes discourses on Creation, the life of Christ, the heavenly kingdom to come, the merits of contentment, and the future line of British rulers along with the requisite tempests, councils of war, royal unions, and battle pieces. What makes *Prince Arthur* unique, however, is its foregrounded political allegory. "The Pious British Prince" who saves the kingdom from paganism and chaos is clearly William of Orange, and the events in the poem parallel closely the events surrounding the Glorious Revolution. Blackmore's epic thus propagandizes for William's martial virtues and monarchal legitimacy; it reconstitutes cultural history in the service of a king whose authority is suspect, providing an epic countermyth of heavenly and historic approval to the exploded doctrine of the divine right of kings.

The ambitious scope, topical interest, and patriotic appeal of *Prince Arthur* intrigued the book-buying public, mandating two more editions in a little over one year. Not surprisingly, William III was also pleased. The king bestowed a medal and a gold chain on the poet and appointed him one of his physicians in ordinary, a post carrying an annual stipend of two hundred pounds. Two years later, Blackmore was knighted by his grateful monarch. Critical reception, on the other hand, was mixed. Some compared Blackmore favorably with Homer, Virgil, and Milton. Others were angered by the audacity of beginning one's poetic career with an epic, by – as John Oldmixon wrote – the "prodigious Muse" which "Huge Books of Verse can in a year produce / . . . / Rude and Dull / . . . / Created in despite of Sense" ("The Second Satire of Boileau, English'd," in *Poems on Several Occasions,* 1696). The finicky critic John Dennis turned René Le Bossu against Blackmore, who had invoked the French neoclassicist in his preface; Dennis charged Blackmore with violating the unities, with inappropriate

employment of Christianity, and with lack of stylistic decorum.

The aging Dryden also became an ardent opponent of Blackmore. In the preface to *Prince Arthur* Blackmore had not only discussed epic theory but had also excoriated the licentiousness of modern poetry, particularly that of playwrights who pander to irreligious and profligate tastes. Blackmore had then personalized his general criticism by placing an "old, revolted, unbelieving Bard" named Laurus (Dryden) in the middle of the epic; this passage depicts Dryden ingratiating himself with patrons and drowning "the Voice of modest Poets" with "endless Cries, and endless Songs." Dryden may have been even more infuriated by what he considered Blackmore's plagiarism. In the preface to his translation of Juvenal in 1692, Dryden disclosed that he had been planning to write an epic, one that would unite Christian doctrine with British history – such as "King Arthur, conquering the *Saxons*" – and that would display the author's "living Friends and Patrons"; this semiallegorical approach may have been rooted in his 1683 opera *King Arthur,* commissioned by Charles II to celebrate his new palace at Winchester, home of the Round Table. Unfortunately, Dryden explained, age and poverty had prevented him from accomplishing this epic work, "intended chiefly for the Honour of my Native Country." Dryden evidently believed that Blackmore had stolen his prescription for a modern epic and had added insult to injury by lampooning his unacknowledged benefactor.

Criticism by the poetic establishment neither silenced Blackmore's epic muse nor quieted his penchant for literary controversy. In March 1697 *King Arthur* was published. In its preface Blackmore claims that he wrote so "that the young Gentlemen and Ladys who are delighted with Poetry might have a useful, at least a harmless Entertainment, which in our Modern Plays and Poems cannot ordinarily be found." Accusing Dryden's circle of spearheading the attacks against *Prince Arthur,* he rather proudly suggests that his "*Provoking Preface* . . . must needs have engag'd a Considerable *Party,*" the "Committee that sits in *Covent Garden.*" Having "never kiss'd their Governour's hands, nor made the least court" to the reigning wits, Blackmore reasons that he was seen as a "pure, *downright Interloper.*" Using the language of Whig merchants to suggest that the poetic controversy involved ideological conflict between established privilege and entrepreneurial ambition, Blackmore claims that his detractors tried to "sink and ruin an unlicens'd Adventurer; notwithstanding I disturbed none of their

Factorys, nor imported any Goods they had ever dealt in."

The heroic poem itself continues the saga of Arthur/William up to the successful campaigns against Clotar/Louis XIV. Again Lucifer intercedes on the side of the evil empire; his machinations include an assassination attempt based on the 1695 Barclay plot against King William, a conspiracy about which Blackmore had been appointed to write the official history. As in his previous epic, Blackmore castigates poets who contribute to a nation's moral laxity:

> Poets the most Flagitious, and Profane,
> Neustria e'er fed, his bounty do's maintain,
> Who by their Wits procure to Vice applause,
> And loud Derision draw on Vertue's Cause.
> They easy Nature with fit Baits excite,
> And Youth to Crimes too prone before, invite.
> By artful Eloquence they strive to show
> Those Pleasures Lawful, which they wish were so.
> Against their Country they their Wit engage,
> Refine our language, but Corrupt the Age.
> Our Noble Youth enervated with Vice,
> Abhor the Field and Martial Fame despise.

Despite the literary contentiousness and political currency of the new epic, sales were slow, and no subsequent editions were called for.

In 1699 Blackmore published *A Short History of the Last Parliament,* a prose justification of Whig policy, and in the same year he was drawn into a political-poetical controversy that ended in a full-scale pamphlet war. The controversy was rooted in medical factionalism coalescing on the dispensary issue, which pitted "Society Physicians" in favor of free treatment for the deserving poor against "Apothecaries Physicians" who supported apothecaries' claims that such a scheme would ruin their business and effectively deny medical treatment to most indigent Londoners. The 1699 publication of Samuel Garth's *The Dispensary* brought the controversy to wide public attention. This mock-heroic poem named Blackmore as one of the "Apothecaries Physicians" and satirized him less for his failure of aristocratic philanthropy than for his literary malpractice. Garth has the goddess Disease lecture his fellow physician on "Th' offensive Discord of such hideous Verse" and advise him to study the ancients to learn polish and decorum. This advice, coupled with a defense of Charles Boyle against Richard Bentley, married the dispensary struggle to the literary war — most memorably enshrined in Jonathan Swift's *The Battle of the Books* (1704) — of the ancients and the moderns.

Just as Blackmore staunchly but unfruitfully opposed Lucan in Swift's fictional combat, he quickly responded to Garth with *A Satyr against Wit* (1700), a clever poem that engendered an outpouring of ridicule that ultimately helped ruin Blackmore's reputation. The satire pits men of reason, be they physicians or poets, against self-styled men of wit, whose sole business is to loaf, rail, mock, libel, and destroy hard work, progress, and common sense. It satirically suggests erecting a "Bank of Wit," where false wit can be recoined — a process that would purge the "leud Allay" from writers such as William Congreve, William Wycherley, and, especially, Dryden. Similarly, a Parnassian hospital to house those with diseased wit could be manned by the incompetent doctors so eager to establish their own dispensary. Behind the satire appears Blackmore's characteristic theme of the interrelationship of literary morality and public welfare. Predictably, the wits at Will's Coffeehouse were furious.

A Satyr against Wit engendered countersatires and counter-countersatires, including Daniel Defoe's mock-heroic battle of Covent Garden (site of Will's) and Cheapside (home of Blackmore) in *The Pacificator* (1700). Despite Defoe's sympathetic pronouncement that Blackmore's "Heroic Horse" had overthrown the "Troops of Wit" and "lies Encamped in the Field of Victory," the wits soon mounted a massive new attack. Under the leadership of Tom Brown and Christopher Codrington, the wits contributed scurrilous poems for an anti-Blackmore folio called *Commendatory Verses, on the Author of the Two Arthurs and the Satyr Against Wit* (1700). Its diatribes repeatedly combine Blackmore's medical and literary skills, "the most nauseous Mixture God can make." The submissions were anonymous, but scholarship has shown that writers such as Sir Charles Sedley, Richard Steele, and Elizabeth Montagu, Countess of Sandwich, conspired to compare Blackmore with turds, murderers, sadists, and dwarfs. As Boys maintains, the vitriolic tone of the volume indicates that Blackmore had wounded the wits' collective assumptions about society and culture; the diligent, morally vigilant upward mobility that Blackmore represented could not be laughed easily away with swipes at the doctor's by-then-quasi-legendary dullness.

Blackmore's friends quickly assembled *Discommendatory Verses* (1700), which responded to each of the *Commendatory Verses* through parody, transformative lampoon, and pure invective. Consequently, the verses do less to defend Blackmore than to lambaste the wits' talents and values. Partially because Blackmore's closest literary associates (Samuel Wesley, Isaac Watts, Thomas Rymer) tended not to be the types to write what Tom Brown called this "attempt to Poison . . . with Stink-Pots," the contributors to this volume have remained anonymous. Critics also are unsure about the extent of Blackmore's encouragement of or participation in the project.

Even if he had been so inclined, Blackmore may not have had time to join the poetic free-for-all. During this period he was shepherding his newest epic through the press and following, no doubt with some disappointment, its reception. *A Paraphrase on the Book of Job,* published on the last day of February 1700, emulates George Sandys's 1638 version in its use of heroic couplets and far exceeds its predecessor in metaphoric surprise, amplification, digressions, and the ability to induce reader fatigue. More interesting today than the poem, the preface presents a further variation on Blackmore's theory of the epic, this time calling for a genius to liberate the form from its classical shackles so that it can instruct and elevate members of a contemporary Christian commonwealth. Combining Lockean empiricism with religious rigor, he questions the validity of Aristotelian rules and the narrowness of those such as Nicolas Boileau-Despréaux who would exclude Christian themes from epic poetry. Further, Blackmore contends that epic heroes need not be active champions of their people and that epic narrative need not end with virtue being rewarded, even posthumously: Christian resignation and God's mysterious providence can serve just as well. Blackmore also slipped in yet another jab at Dryden by calling classical translations "a pardonable sort of Idleness." But despite the provocative and pious preface *A Paraphrase on the Book of Job* was burlesqued mercilessly and then quickly ignored by the public. Dryden, however, responded by denouncing Blackmore in the *Fables, Ancient and Modern* (1700) and in his final verses, the prologue to John Fletcher's *Pilgrim* (1700), which Dryden wrote in the last weeks before his death.

After Dryden's death Blackmore's war with the wits subsided to occasional skirmishes. The imminent death of William III commanded Blackmore's attention; medical duties outweighed poetic pleasures during the next two years. After William's death in 1702 Blackmore was asked to prepare the official autopsy report, a task demanding considerable political skill as well as scientific knowledge. Nonetheless, he found time to write a fifteen-page religious ode infused with his version of the Miltonic sublime. *A Hymn to the Light of the World*

(1703) was accompanied by couplets describing the Raphael cartoons, which Blackmore had seen often during his services at Hampton Court. This volume of poetry evoked little adverse attention and some praise, including a collection of religious poetry, *A Collection of Divine Hymns* (1704), that was dedicated to Blackmore. Yet the succession of Queen Anne gave occasion for Blackmore again to tempt fate. In 1705 the ten-book epic *Eliza* dropped, in Samuel Johnson's words, "dead-born from the press."

Eliza chronicles Elizabeth I's defense of Protestantism against Catholic opposition at home and abroad. As usual, the political allegory is transparent: Eliza is the prototype of Queen Anne, and Sir Francis Vere prefigures John Churchill, first Duke of Marlborough. Even this lackluster production was not without its attendant controversy, however. Blackmore's portrayal of Dr. John Radcliffe as Roderigo Lopez, the physician who tried to poison Queen Elizabeth, brought howls of protest from Radcliffe's supporters, inducing published attacks in the periodical the *Whipping Post*. Queen Anne nonetheless appointed Sir Richard one of her physicians in ordinary, cutting out Radcliffe because of his high-handedness in treating her fatally ill son, an event to which *Eliza* did not fail to refer.

After the successful battle of Ramillies in 1706, an anonymous poet urged Blackmore to add his pen to those celebrating Marlborough's victory. Sir Richard responded with *Advice to the Poets* (1706), part coterie compliment and part suggestion that England's finest writers produce a joint epic appropriate to the occasion. Blackmore's poem sold well and generated the expected flurry of replies ridiculing his prosody and defending John Philips, whom Blackmore had pilloried in his poem. Undeterred, Blackmore followed with *Instructions to Vander Bank* (1709), in which the narrator gives directions for a tapestry depicting English military successes.

Although published in 1708, *The Kit-Kats* was probably written four years earlier, when Blackmore was actively involved with the club. This comic poem seems to have tried to mediate a dispute between Jacob Tonson and other members of Joseph Addison's circle. The dissolution of the Kit-Kat club, Blackmore satirically predicts, will usher in a reign of "Dulness" in which lassitude and bad writing will overwhelm the nation. Stimulated by Dryden's in *Mac Flecknoe* (1682), Blackmore's vision of "Dulness" and her haunts appears to have inspired Pope in *The Rape of the Lock* (1714) and *The Dunciad* (1728).

Blackmore's flexibility once again manifested itself in 1711, when he published a long philosophical poem, *The Nature of Man,* exploring how climate shapes individuals and nations. Not surprisingly, the temperate climate of England is conducive to freedom, capitalism, right religion, and artistic accomplishment. This poem served as a warm-up exercise for Blackmore's next major work, *Creation* (1712). "If he had written nothing else," suggested Samuel Johnson, this poem "would have transmitted him to posterity among the first favourites of the English Muse."

The work that earned Johnson's respect, and that of Addison and of Blackmore's onetime opponent Dennis before him, is an elaborate discourse against impiety and a demonstration of "the existence of a Divine Eternal Mind." Written in seven books to recall the days of creation, the poem embeds interrogations of skeptical philosophers – atheists, Epicureans, and Aristotelians – in an "argument-by-design" framework, the first two books addressing Earth and the solar system, the last two books treating man and animals. Blackmore's penchant for late-Renaissance *copia* (abundance) serves him well in the central sections: every possible argument against divine creation is anticipated and met. Occasionally Blackmore salts his refutations with ridicule, as when the narrator asks Epicurus why farmers have not "found / A leg or arm unfinish'd in the ground," if humans were spontaneously generated from the soil. Most frequently, though, the poet adheres to meticulous and persuasive reasoning, irradiated by a sense of awe at the complexity and vastness of creation. Nowhere is this attitude more apparent than in discussions of scientific theory. By detailing the systems of Ptolemy, Nicolaus Copernicus, Tycho Brahe, Johannes Kepler, and Sir Isaac Newton, Blackmore suggests that scientific "truth" is always partial, relative to man's necessarily incomplete state of knowledge. Even the theory of gravitation describes rather than explains; it "solve[s] appearances with just applause" but does not penetrate to the source of "[t]his wondrous power." One suspects that Blackmore's years as a physician – categorizing symptoms, identifying diseases, yet often unable to discover their origins or prevent their ends – contributed to the humility that the poem presents as a concomitant to faith.

Blackmore's profession also influenced the last two books of the poem. His descriptions of human physiology travel into the anatomic baroque: the heart "[e]xpels and entertains the purple guest"; the glands "o'er the body spread / Fine complicated clues of nervous thread"; the lungs "this nitrous food impels / Through all the spungy parts and bladder'd cells"; the intestines' "little mouths in the large channel's side / Suck in the flood, and drink the cheering tide." Such flights are curious, even comic, but they are not silly. For a man who has watched illness ravage kings and commoners, who has cut into living tissue and dead flesh, to see beauty, poetry, and the mark of divine favor in the human body is itself an act of faith that supports the hypothesis of the poem.

Neither is *Creation* without political interest. Religion was inseparable from politics, and Blackmore rarely misses showing how fidelity to the church keeps the nation healthy. The physio-theological debate in which this poem partakes also had political implications: believing the world is shaped by grace, as Blackmore argued, rather than deformed by sin, as Thomas Burnet maintained, helps determine whether Britain is fulfilling God's plan for perfection. The late rise of "mechanic arts" brought England the "laurel honours" divinely intended as part of a progressive universe; the imperial destiny of Britain "through eight renown'd campaigns . . . Did through th'admiring realms around proclaim / Marlborough's swift conquest, and great Anna's name." Similarly, the power of the mind to form ideas from sense perceptions finds fruition in imperialist economics:

> The Mind a thousand skilful works can frame,
> Can form deep projects to procure her aim.
> Merchants, for eastern pearl and golden ore
> To cross the main, and reach the Indian shore,
> Prepare the floating ship, and spread the sail,
> To catch the impulse of the breathing gale.

Man's "projects" are "emulous of bright Seraphic Mind" and marks of the "Great Creator King's" existence and providential blessings.

Creation was the most widely praised and frequently reprinted of Blackmore's poems. Perhaps Blackmore felt that he had finally won the respect he sought; in any event, prose began to occupy more of his time than poetry. Extended commentary on his prose lies outside the scope of this volume, but students of literary theory will find much of interest in the *Lay-Monastery* (1714), an imitation of the *Spectator* that Blackmore began in 1713 (under the title of the *Lay Monk*) to fill the void left by Addison's retirement from periodical journalism, and in *Essays upon Several Subjects* of 1716, which folds discussions of epic and wit among discussions of science, civil law, and philosophy. He also began the series of medical treatises, notable because they are written in English rather than in Latin and because they espouse a modern empirical approach to diagnosis and treatment. He did publish a collection of poems ranging from the satiric to the religious in 1718; he also joined the growing stampede of metrical psalmists in 1721, with the publication of sacred versifications "Fitted to the Tunes Used in Churches." Blackmore even secured promises for use from a variety of bishops, but his psalmic hymns never seem to have become part of communal worship anywhere in the kingdom, despite the support of the Society for the Propogation of the Gospel.

At this time, Blackmore weighed in at the hoary Arian controversy with two books advocating the expulsion from the Church of England of those who rejected Christ's divinity. His *Redemption: A Divine Poem* of 1722 versifies the anti-Arian arguments he had delivered in prose. In the same year Blackmore announced his retirement from the Royal College of Physicians and moved from London to the village of Boxted in Essex. His epic muse gave one last, lengthy gasp the next year: *Alfred. An Epick Poem. In Twelve Books* (1723) flatters the house of Hanover with the same type of historical allegory previously lavished on William and on Anne. No more trenchant comment on the merits and reception of the poem exists than Johnson's. "Alfred took his place beside Eliza in silence and darkness," Johnson proclaimed; "Benevolence was ashamed to favor, and Malice was weary of insulting." Blackmore's final years were dedicated to his medical writing and to two devotional works in prose, one published posthumously. Pope's *Peri Bathous,* lampooning Sir Richard, appeared in 1727, effectively killing Blackmore's reputation once and for all. At the beginning of 1728 his wife died, and in 1729 the city knight himself followed her and his reputation to the grave.

Pope was the last and greatest of the literati who considered taking Blackmore to task a moral and artistic imperative. Pope had become the custodian of the Scriblerian project designed to invert Longinus, a project partially spearheaded by John Arbuthnot, who was Blackmore's professional rival; *Peri Bathous* flattens enemies as well as elevates taste through negative example. Of the approximately one hundred citations in the book, forty-four are attributed to Blackmore, far more than those drawn from any other poet's works. Less damaging than individual citations — after all, anyone can be made to look incompetent by out-of-context quotations — is their sheer number and the thumping epithets with which Martinus Scriblerus crowns Blackmore with barbed laurel. The "most celebrated Amplifier of our Age," a "universal Genius," "our excellent Modern," Blackmore "pours forth five or six Epick

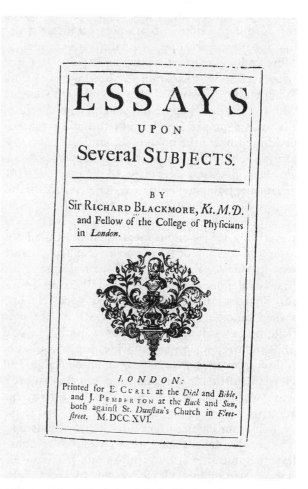

Title page for the book that includes Blackmore's essays on epic poetry, wit, science, civil law, and philosophy

Poems with greater Facility, than five or six Pages can be produc'd by an elaborate and servile Copyer after Nature or the Ancients." Further, Scriblerus's appendix includes a project for the advancement of the bathos, suggesting an incorporation of bad writers to make a rhetorical chest for universal use, thus parodying Blackmore's *Advice to the Poets* and his *Bank of Wit*; the appendix also includes the anti-Blackmore recipe for an epic – first printed in the *Guardian* in 1713. And Blackmore was more than a convenient scapegoat for the sinking sublime; he also pops up in *The Dunciad*, braying his own praise during the heroic games in book 2.

The causes of Pope's vehemence toward Blackmore are complex. Blackmore's unfortunate reference to Swift as "an impious buffoon" in *Essays upon Several Subjects* has been seen as the cause. But certainly Swift could take care of himself; he had involved Blackmore in *The Battle of the Books* and in a late poem consigned him to the literary hell of *The Le-*

gion Club (1736). And certainly Pope, an extremely careful craftsman and painstaking reviser, would be offended in principle by Blackmore's leaden ear and his apparent valuation of quantity over quality. More-compelling reasons may be Pope's outrage at what he saw as Blackmore's sheer presumption. Whereas Pope planned his career in consonance with the classically approved progression of genres, Blackmore jumped feet first into the epic, doggerel-paddling toward the noblest accomplishment in poetry without wading through proper apprenticeship. To Pope, Blackmore represented the worst of modern hustle, trampling on time-tested principles in his rush to literary notoriety, allying himself with mass taste rather than with elite judgment. Blackmore wore Whig values on his medical gown, while Pope aspired to the life of a Tory gentleman; Blackmore was a strident amateur, while Pope was among the first "professional" poets. Finally, Blackmore was, for Pope, a formidable precursor poet. He had staked out, perhaps even laid waste to, the epic field; he had written successful social satire; he had philosophized in verse to widespread applause. Milton's greatness may have been untouchable, and Dryden's difficult to undermine, but Blackmore's was vulnerable. Pope's campaign to destroy Sir Richard may indicate the need to clear space for himself in the eighteenth-century literary landscape. The serious debts Pope owes to his favorite dunce have been hinted at by Johnson and persuasively documented by John C. Hodges and by Harry Solomon; these debts add credence to the belief that Pope's vendetta was fueled by the anxiety of influence.

It is hard to read Blackmore without being swayed by Pope and his debunking forerunners. Thus a short look at *King Arthur,* an epic that escaped dissection in *Peri Bathous* and that has not been as roundly condemned as the later epics, allows contemplation with a relatively blank slate. Despite its prolixity, the narrative is easy to follow, even sprightly. One reason is the busily allusive texture that results from what Solomon aptly calls Blackmore's eclecticism. For instance, Lucifer uses Miltonic diction:

> With lab'ring Wings I beat the pondrous Air.
> Without a glimpse or ray of Light I past
> The Realms of Night, and all the *Stygian* wast

and soon his campaign against Arthur is described with a Homeric simile expanded with Christian reference:

> So when in ancient *Rome* a furious Beast
> With Hunger pinch'd was from his Den releast
> A constant Christian Martyr to devour
> Condemn'd by some Imperial Master's Power,
> He roar'd and ran with open Jaws to tear
> His Prey and pleas'd the bloody Theatre.
> Th'infernal Prince from Heav'n's Cerulean Top
> Shot thro' the liquid Gulph. . . .

Battle scenes recall Virgil; most of book 6, in which Arthur is tested by a monster and an enchantress, recalls Edmund Spenser.

Blackmore's notorious metaphors produce similarly lively effects. Often the language rises and plummets in metaphysical tropes that surprise even when they fail to delight. Storm clouds, for example, undergo a childbirth that slides into disembowelment:

> Their swagg'ring Wombs low in the Air depend
> Which struggling Flames, and imbred Thunder rend,
> O'ercharged with Stores and Heav'n's Artillery,
> They groan and pant and labour up the Sky.
> . . . .
> Rent Clouds a medley of Destruction Sport,
> And throw their dreadful Entrails round about.

Certainly Blackmore's taste for amplification can reach grotesque proportions, such as King Clotha's thirty-line dilation on the prophet Amos's two-line curse of his birthday. Nonetheless, the fecundity of expression exerts a fascination that balances its tedium.

Modern taste has even less patience with Blackmore's archaisms and periphrases. Swains too often cavort on the glebe; fish are "the Scaly people of the Main" or "Finny Murd'rers." But modern readers who can confront long poems in heroic couplets with equanimity may admire Blackmore's use of medial caesuras and run-on lines even as they condemn his awkward inversions and clumsy rhymes. The critics of today may also be intrigued by Blackmore's uninhibited endorsement of military adventurism and the social and ecological changes it entails:

> The Husbandman do's from his labour leap,
> To plough the Seas, and Gallic Laurels reap.
> He beats his Ploughshares into Helms and Shields,
> Deserts his Hamlet, and his flowing Fields,
> Neglects his Tillage, and his Rural Gains,
> To plant with *British* Spears Parisian Plains.
> . . . .
> Refulgent Arms *Augusta's* Merchants weild
> And to the busy *Change* prefer the Field.
> These brave Adventurers in the noble War,
> Will Honours fetch, as well as Wealth from far.
> . . . .
> To heal the Navy's with the Forest's Wounds,

For Masts, and Planks, they fell the fairest Trees,
The rest, for Supplemental Ribs and Knees.

In sum, Sir Richard Blackmore is not always a good poet, but he is often an interesting one.

More interesting may be his historical situation, astride two centuries. In a sense, he is the last Metaphysical poet, a terminal metastasis of baroque wit. He also culminates seventeenth-century epic experimentation which includes William Davenant's *Gondibert* (1651) and Abraham Cowley's *Davideis* (1656) as well as Milton's work; Blackmore, in fact, was among the first to praise Milton's stunning achievement and to recognize Adam as the hero of *Paradise Lost.* The highly political nature of Blackmore's work fits squarely within the practice of Restoration poetry, his eclecticism mirrors that of writers such as Thomas Burnet and Sir Thomas Browne as well as the spirit of the Royal Academy, and his layerings of history and allegory resemble not only Dryden's procedure in *Absalom and Achitophel* (1681) but also the political romances and scandalous chronicles that helped shape the early English novel. His cries about licentious theater anticipate Jeremy Collier's and, in general, show that the moral vigilance of the Cromwell years persisted beyond the Interregnum and was not restricted to Dissenters.

Yet Blackmore also belongs to the eighteenth century. He associated or squabbled with the major writers of Queen Anne's reign; he participated in the growth industry of periodical journalism; he sang the Whig virtues of industry and expansionism; with *Creation,* he was a founding father of the eighteenth-century long poem, such as James Thomson's *The Seasons* (1726–1730) and Pope's *Essay on Man* (1733), two works more indebted to Blackmore than is generally acknowledged. And one wonders whether, without Sir Richard to kick around, some of the age's masterpieces of satire and mock-heroism would ever have been written.

His long and not always illustrious career is marked by the highest level of integrity. From the early epics to the late devotional tracts, Blackmore's work is dedicated to improving morals, celebrating virtue, promoting religion, and cementing national pride. What some see as hubris may also be empirically based problem solving: England needs a patriotic epic, so Blackmore will write it; the Kit-Kats are divided, so Blackmore will reunite them; skepticism or Arianism threatens religious health, so Blackmore will diagnose the malady and try to cure it. His personal life was above reproach, and his professional skill seems to have been far above the average. He is known for friends such as John Locke and Addison as well as for enemies such as Dryden and Pope. That he aspired to literary greatness and hovered or sank more often than he soared makes him neither a madman nor a dullard, both of which he has been called. Yet if his work signified nothing, he would not have occupied the eyes of so many cultural and literary storms. To the extent that literary interest is produced by the reflection and generation of culture, Sir Richard Blackmore deserves renewed attention.

Biographies:
Samuel Johnson, "Blackmore," in his *Lives of the English Poets,* edited by George Birkbeck Hill, 3 volumes (Oxford: Clarendon Press, 1905);
Albert Rosenberg, *Sir Richard Blackmore: A Poet and Physician of the Augustan Age* (Lincoln: University of Nebraska Press, 1953);
Harry Solomon, *Sir Richard Blackmore* (Boston: Twayne, 1980).

References:
Richard C. Boys, *Sir Richard Blackmore and the Wits,* University of Michigan Contributions in Modern Philology, 13 (Ann Arbor: University of Michigan Press, 1949);
Roberta F. Brinkley, *Arthurian Legend in the Seventeenth Century,* Johns Hopkins Monographs in Literary History, 3 (Baltimore: Johns Hopkins University Press, 1932);
John Dryden, *The Essays of John Dryden,* 2 volumes, edited by W. P. Ker (Oxford: Oxford University Press, 1900);
F. H. Ellis, ed., *Poems on Affairs of State: Augustan Satirical Verse, 1660–1714,* volume 7 (New Haven: Yale University Press, 1975);
John C. Hodges, "Pope's Debt to One of His Dunces," *Modern Language Notes,* 51 (1936): 154–158;
Maynard Mack, *Alexander Pope: A Life* (New York: Norton, 1988);
Alexander Pope, *Peri Bathous,* edited by Edna Leake Steeves (New York: Octagon, 1968);
H. T. Swedenberg, *The Theory of the Epic in England: 1650–1800,* University of California Publications in English, 15 (Berkeley: University of California Press, 1953);
James Anderson Winn, *John Dryden and His World* (New Haven: Yale University Press, 1987);
Leah Rachel Clara Yoffie, "Creation, the Angels, and the Fall of Man in Milton's Paradise Lost and Paradise Regained and in the Work of Sir Richard Blackmore," Ph.D. dissertation, University of North Carolina at Chapel Hill, 1942.

Patrick Cary

(1623? – March 1657)

Louise Simons
Boston University

BOOK: *Poems from a Manuscript written in the time of Oliver Cromwell* (London: Printed for J. Murray, 1771).

Editions: *Trivial Poems and Triolets, written in obedience to Mrs Tomkin's Commands, by Patrick Carey, 20th Aug. 1651,* edited by Walter Scott (London: John Murray, 1819); revised in volume 2 of *Minor Poets of the Caroline Period,* edited by George Saintsbury (Oxford: Clarendon Press, 1906), pp. 445–482;

The Poems of Patrick Cary, edited by Veronica Delany (Oxford: Clarendon Press, 1978).

In most regards, Patrick Cary's life was a chaotic one, reflecting the damage done to private individuals by the political upheavals and religious controversies of the middle years of seventeenth-century England. Cary was born at the time of Charles I's ascension. He died during the Interregnum, the interlude of Puritan government, after Charles I had been beheaded by the English people in 1649 and before Charles II was recalled from France to restore the monarchy in 1660. Cary was the tenth of eleven children born to a Royalist family whose father, Henry Cary, a courtier, was named the first viscount Falkland. In general the Cary family had a flair for writing, as demonstrated by the accumulation of dramas, poems, biography, and voluminous and vivid correspondence left by Patrick Cary's parents, some of his siblings, and several of their descendants. These works attest to the range of the Falkland family's involvement in the political, economic, and religious changes that marked life in their time. Patrick Cary's slim collection of thirty-seven poems was undertaken as a private endeavor, and his status as a writer remains somewhat marginal; his poetry — which consists of a single manuscript volume of verse, penned in his own hand and illustrated emblematically — was evidently gathered for circulation among a small coterie of family and friends. The work remained unpublished during his lifetime.

As far as is known, the first publication of the poetry came in 1771, more than a century after Patrick Cary's death. Nine poems from the manuscript, then owned by the Reverend Pierrepont Cromp, were published as *Poems from a Manuscript written in the time of Oliver Cromwell.* Advertised as under the authorship of "one Carey," this quarto volume of four devotions and five ballads attracted no interest in the reading public, and the only known notice is negative: the *London Magazine* reviewer found it tedious. It was not until the nineteenth century that the poetry was rediscovered.

In Patrick Cary's background was a family that grew in propertied wealth from the time of Henry VIII, when the monasteries were dissolved and their land granted to aristocrats. His direct ancestor, John Cary (1491?–1552), a courtier during this period, acquired twenty thousand acres of former monastery land in Hertfordshire. In order to assure himself of descendants, at age forty he married Joyce Denny Walsingham. His wife's son by her first marriage, Francis Walsingham (1530–1590), became secretary of state to Queen Elizabeth. During the reigns of Elizabeth and of James I he was a helpful influence in favor of his half brother, Edward Cary (1539?–1618), who, like his father, John Cary, also married a wealthy widow, Katherine, Lady Paget.

The eldest son of this union, Henry Cary (1576–1633), was born in Berkhampstead. In 1599 he joined Robert Devereux, second Earl of Essex, in fighting in Ireland and was knighted by Essex at Dublin Castle. On Henry Cary's return to England he associated with Ben Jonson and other convivial London wits. An advantageous marriage was arranged for him with Elizabeth Tanfield (1586?–1639), the only child of the wealthy Baron Laurence Tanfield of Burford Priory, Oxfordshire, and his wife, Elizabeth Symonds Tanfield. Laurence Tanfield subsequently became chief baron of the Exchequer, a powerful post, and acquired the attractive manor of Great Tew, Oxfordshire; however, the Tanfield wealth and estates bypassed the daughter and her husband, despite their pressing needs. Both Henry and Elizabeth Cary were occasional writers, and Patrick inherited his literary talents from both parents. In the extant manuscript, Patrick Cary's poems fall under two general rubrics, secular and divine; "Triviall Ballades" comprise the types and topics usual for Caroline gentlemen – love poems, political satires, and celebrations of conviviality – while the divine poems are personal and comprise direct appeals for grace.

The marriage contract between Patrick Cary's parents was signed in 1602; intellectual and idiosyncratic as a young woman, Elizabeth became a religious controversialist as she grew older, whereas her husband was described by Thomas Fuller in his *Worthies of England* (1662) as the charming and adaptable "complete courtier." Because Henry Cary spent his time at court or abroad, the married couple did not live together for seven years, and some time elapsed before they discovered their incompatibility. In 1605 Henry Cary served as a volunteer against the Spanish troops in the Netherlands' war for independence. In the Battle of Mülheim he was captured during a gallant charge and was held for ransom. Cary was taken to Spain to await the payment, and he did not return to England until 1607. His valor and honor were praised at the time and are commemorated in Jonson's "To Sir Henrie Cary." The ransom payment reduced Henry Cary's patrimony so significantly that he never again recovered from financial difficulties, although for the rest of his life he tried in numerous ways to recoup. In 1620 he was created viscount Falkland of Fife in the peerage of Scotland. Although Cary received numerous preferments from the Crown, he was remarkably inept at increasing or even maintaining his wealth through court appointments. In *Rational Theology* (1872), John Tulloch wrote that Cary had "more address in gaining power than in maintaining it." This tendency was especially true of his appointment in 1622 as lord deputy of Ireland by James I during the final period of his reign: first, fitting Cary for his station as lord deputy necessitated heavy expenditures, and to pay for this need his wife mortgaged her jointure; second, his notions of Irish reform were so ill-timed that he had to be recalled in the early years of the rule of Charles I, although Charles received him warmly on his return to court.

Lord deputy of Ireland was the post Henry Cary held when his two youngest children, Patrick and Henry, were born. The parents took seven children with them to Ireland in September 1623. Catherine, the eldest child – who did not join the family because she had just been married to James, the Scottish earl of Home – was to die in childbirth at Burford just two years thereafter. Lucius and Lorenzo, the two eldest sons, were in Ireland; Edward, the third son, had died six years before the Irish appointment. The daughters descended in age from Anne, who was eight, through Elizabeth, Lucy, and Victoria, to Mary, who was not yet two.

It is known that Patrick Cary was born in Ireland, but records of his exact birth date and given name do not exist. It is thought that he was born in 1623 or 1624 and that approximately a year later, in 1625, he returned to England with some members of his family. Most often, he signed himself as John (or "J.") Patrick Carey. Patrick is not a family name, but since it is recognizably both Irish and Roman Catholic, it was perhaps intended to have political significance as a goodwill gesture and religious significance as a mark of Elizabeth Cary's growing preference for Catholicism.

Elizabeth Cary preceded her husband in the removal from Ireland to England, taking with her Anne, Mary, and the two youngest boys. On board the boat Patrick, approximately in his second year, was exposed to a stormy, dangerous crossing of the Irish Sea. During the voyage his baby brother Henry, while being nursed by his mother, was knocked unconscious and nearly washed overboard by a wave. On reaching England, Elizabeth Cary took her children to live in Oxfordshire with her mother in order to avoid the plague. The following year she moved her four children to London. In 1626 she avowed her conversion to Roman Catholicism, after which both her husband and her mother refused to contribute to her support. The children then lived in circumstances of extreme want, often being sent to the homes of their mother's friends for meals. Queen Henrietta Maria, who remained Patrick's benefactor for many years, and other ladies of the court contributed to the family's welfare until Parliament induced Henry Cary to make monetary arrangements.

Henry and Elizabeth Cary's quarrels over financial problems and religious differences grew from private bickering to public disputes that finally caused the throne and Parliament to intervene. Initially the Privy Council expressed displeasure over the conversion as emphatically as did Elizabeth Cary's husband and parents; later, when she was in dire financial difficulties, Charles I intervened on her behalf, and the quarrels between husband and

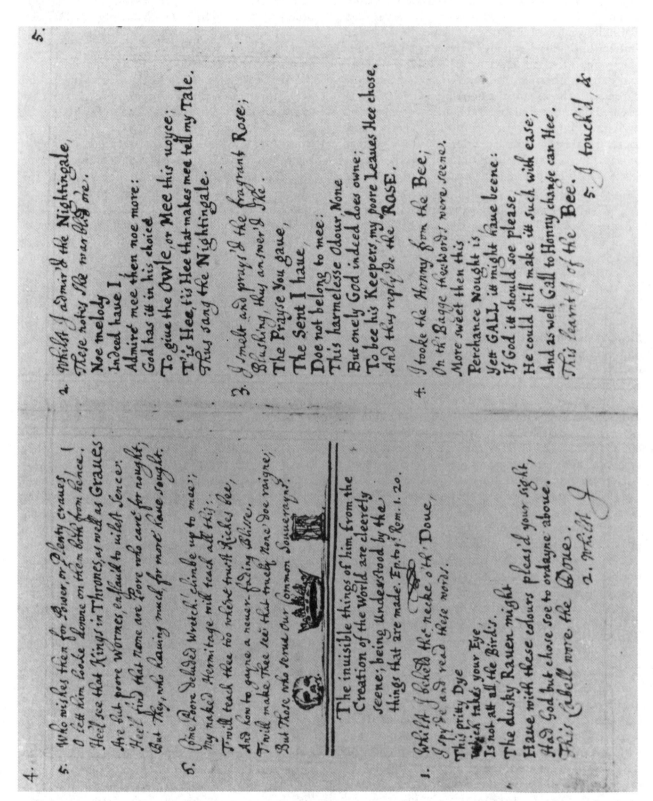

Pages from the only extant manuscript for Cary's poems, a fair copy made by Cary in the 1650s (Collection of Mrs. Maxwell-Scott, Abbotsford). The sketches are emblems related to the poems.

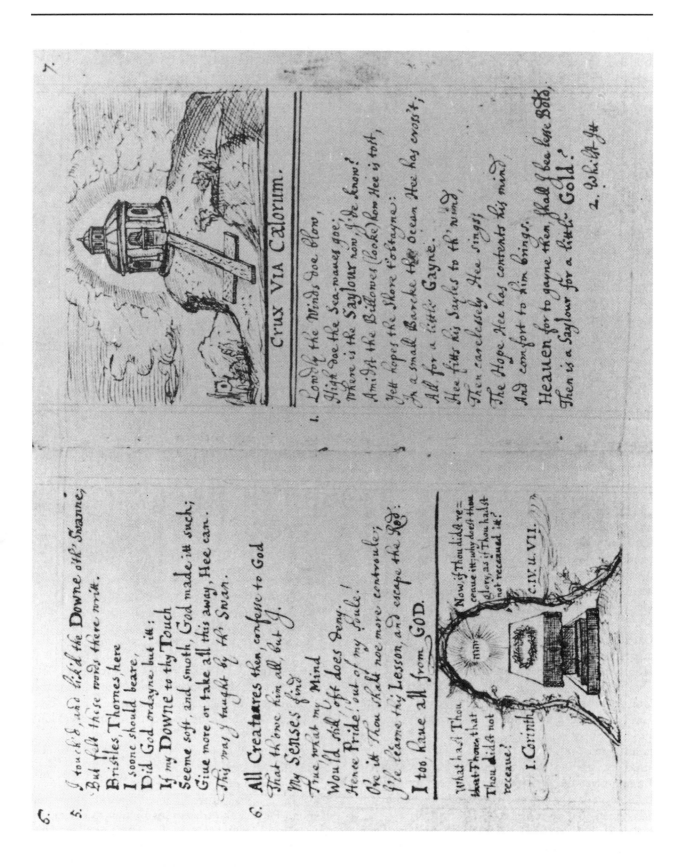

wife continued through correspondence with the Privy Council. Life for Patrick and the other children in residence in the insecure households of their parents was filled with financial, religious, and marital unrest. Patrick also endured extended periods of separation from his family, shuttling between England and Ireland in his early years and between England and the Continent later. It is understandable that pastoral poetry – which depicts independent, peaceful living, apart from favor-seeking situations – seems in Patrick Cary's hands to be given heartfelt expression. In "The Country Life," which is composed "To a French tune," Cary writes with feeling: "Here's noe Dinne, noe Hurry, / None seekes here to curry / Favour, by base meanes." His secular pieces comprise sixteen love poems that are either plaintive or lighthearted; five political satires; a country-house poem that is all-inclusive in its good wishes; and a lengthy pastoral, which extols virtue, congeniality, moderation amid abundance, and healthful employment and recreation.

The considerable Tanfield fortune that passed by Henry and Elizabeth Cary went to their eldest son, Lucius, who had been raised in the wealthy, stable home of his Tanfield grandparents. It is presumed that Laurence Tanfield disapproved of his daughter's improvident habit of spending beyond her means and especially of the use of her jointure to outfit her husband for his office in Ireland. In addition, the Tanfields heartily disapproved of their daughter's religious conversion and her estrangement from her husband. The instability of the Henry Cary household stemmed from both financial and religious causes: the inroads made by the ransom payment; his inability to profit (and his actual loss) from governing positions and economic ventures from which other men grew wealthy (Edward Hyde, first Earl of Clarendon, wrote that Cary, "instead of enriching himself by his great places, wasted a full fortune at court in those great offices and employments by which other men use to obtain a greater"); Elizabeth Cary's impetuosity and generosity; the expense of rearing the large family of eleven surviving children; and the passionately held religious convictions of the various family members. Although Patrick Cary was influenced by his mother and sisters to avow himself Roman Catholic, he did not have their conviction. Indeed, he later showed his flexibility when he reconverted to Anglicanism. It is worth noting that his devotional poems, which are thought to have been written in religious seclusion during his seminary life in France, give little evidence that they are informed by Roman Catholic liturgy or sensibility.

The writing shows intense desire for personal grace through communion with the Christian deity, but it seems to be the work of someone wishing to dedicate his song to general praise of his Lord without specific formal worship.

When Henry Cary rejoined his family in London, he and his wife were reconciled in obedience to the wishes of Queen Henrietta Maria. This reconciliation took place in 1633 only shortly before his death, which was probably caused by his deference to Charles I. Cary fell from his horse while hunting, fracturing his leg. When the concerned king came to his aid, Cary courteously and painfully rose to his feet, compounding his original fracture into a complicated medical problem. The negligent court surgeons sent by the king did not set the fractures, and when gangrene made amputation necessary, they did not seal the wound, causing hemorrhaging. An account of this calamity is given in "The Lady Faulkland her Life," a manuscript in the Imperial Archives at Lille. All the children were summoned to the hunting lodge where their father was undergoing surgery. One of the daughters wrote of her father that "as soone as ever it was done and he layd in his bed he sent for them in, smiling on them, spoke cheerfully seeking to comfort them, then giving them his last blessing, sent them home." This was Patrick's last occasion of seeing his father, who died within the week.

Like all his family, Patrick Cary was loyal to the Royalist cause, and during the time of Puritan rule he wrote political satire. In the ditty to be sung to the tune of *That we may row with my P. over the Ferry,* he mocks governmental zeal to eradicate sinful living. He summons the citizenry:

Good People of England! come heare mee relate
Some misteryes of our young *purse-sucking State,*
Whereby Ev'ry man may conceave out of 's pate
A reason for things here ordayned of late.

Cary continues, "What e're the State resolves, lett us bee merry," and proceeds wittily to lament the banishment of French claret by lampooning Oliver Cromwell's bulbous nose and ruddy complexion: "French Clarret was banish'd, (as most doe suppose) / Cause *Noll* would have nought here, soe red as his *Nose.*"

After the death of his father, Patrick's eldest brother, Lucius, now second viscount Falkland, brought Patrick and four of his siblings to live at the Oxfordshire estate, Great Tew. Lucius Cary was scholarly and philosophical, and his country house was the congenial meeting place for many noted Anglican writers, thinkers, statesmen, and divines.

There is no evidence that Patrick Cary, then approximately eleven, began to write his poems at this time; the country-house verse included in the manuscript clearly relates to a much later stay at his sister's home. William Chillingworth, who had once converted to Catholicism but then reconverted, was appointed as tutor to Patrick and Henry. Elizabeth Cary, who had previously entertained Chillingworth in her own home but had then broken off relations, was alarmed over her sons' religious education. Not only did Chillingworth attempt to influence the children, but Lucius Cary himself undertook disputation with Patrick, who, with his younger brother, was secretly observing the fasting days and was evidently inclined toward Catholicism. In an adventure that constituted a kind of kidnapping, the mother contrived in early May 1636 to have the boys escape from Great Tew under cover of darkness and be transported to London.

Anne Cary is probably the author of the manuscript that was written about her mother's life, which also gives a nine-page account of the escape. By the time "The Lady Faulkland her Life" was drafted, Anne had become Dame Clementia, a member of a Benedictine convent in Cambrai. Notably, there are interpolations and corrections to the text, some in Patrick Cary's handwriting. As Veronica Delany notes, the "account of the kidnapping . . . is surely one of the most complete records of a single incident in the youth of a seventeenth-century English poet." Anne and Mary asked to accompany their sister-in-law, Lettice Morison Cary, second Viscountess Falkland, on a trip to London. They further requested that the day be a holiday for their brothers, who were to rise by 3:00 A.M. and wake the sisters prior to the escape. Ushered off the premises by one of their sisters, the boys sped through the village in the early darkness, occasionally awakening homeowners and dogs with their flight, so that on occasion they had to hide behind bushes to avoid discovery. At an appointed spot they were met by two surly horsemen who furnished them with mounts, enforced silence on the ride, and guided them to Oxford and thence to Abingdon.

In Abingdon the men who were hired to row the boys by boat to London were so intoxicated that they could not leave, and the boys had to be hidden by the owner of the boat. He and the oarsmen quarreled so violently that Abingdon citizens summoned the constable, who turned out to be a friend of one of the horsemen. The constable allowed the boys to be taken to their mother. Anxiety about further delay prompted the boys to undertake the danger-

ous trip to London by water at 10:00 that evening under the dubious care of the still highly inebriated oarsmen, who were "not only not able to row, but ready every minute to over turne the boat with reeling and nodding."

In London after the "kidnapping," Elizabeth Cary withstood the bitter remonstrances of her eldest son and the infuriated questionings of the Privy Council. In order to evade authorities, for three weeks before the boys' passage to France she had Patrick and Henry moved from house to house. Eventually six siblings in all took the journey to the Continent. The four daughters who made the trip were settled in a Benedictine nunnery in Cambrai. A notation in the council book of Saint Edmund's Priory records the entry of Patrick and Henry into that Benedictine monastic school in Paris on 2 November 1636. Payment for the children's maintenance came from Queen Henrietta Maria, who was ever a staunch friend and supporter of their mother. Patrick Cary's poems show a fondness for the "wholsome, harmelesse Exercise" and food "spare, light, sweet to th'Pallett" that are found in "The Country Life." His praise for the rural life-style is coupled with a distaste for urban sophistications: "There y'have Ladyes gawdy; / Dames, that can talke bawdy." Included in the opprobrium is court life: "W'envy not your Cates att Court."

In lighthearted fashion, Cary's ballads, such as "To the tune *But that n'ere troubles mee Boyes* &c.," despise the national institutions of Parliament and the army:

> And now a Figge for th'lower House;
> The Army I doe sett att nought:
> I care not for them both, a louse
> For spent is my last Groat Boyes,
>   For spent is my last Groate.

As is the case, apparently, with all the secular verse, this song was written after Cary's return to England. Through their allusions to current topics, many of the "Triviall Ballades" can be dated to the period falling between September 1650 and February 1652. Prior to that, Cary was being educated, first in France and then in Italy, during the time that the English monarchy was collapsing. In the Civil-War years Lucius Cary became secretary of state to Charles I, and both Lucius (1610-1643) and the next oldest brother, Lorenzo (1613-1642), died fighting for the Cavalier cause in the Puritan revolution. Patrick Cary's unsettled youth in Ireland and England and his eventual removal to continental retreats are documented by his sister, Dame Clementia.

In 1638, nearly three years after his arrival in Paris, Cary was directed by his mother to move to Rome where her connections would be of use to him. On the trip to Rome an event of some significance took place. As Cary later wrote to Hyde in one of the letters preserved at the Bodleian Library, Oxford (M.S. C.S.P. 40, f. 169^v), "When I went into Italy (a very Boy) in the journey, being where many of the company made vowes, I then made mine allsoe; and itt was to enter a Religious life under S. Bennetts habitt." In Rome, Cary lived for twelve years with the English Benedictines under the guidance and protection of Father John Wilfrid. At the request of Henrietta Maria, Cardinal Francesco Barberini became a powerful friend and ally of her young protégé.

Through his family connections and his patrons, Cary was able to enjoy the company of other cultivated visitors from England, and perhaps his penchant for writing took shape from discourse with literary figures. The entry for 30 October 1638 in the Pilgrim Book of the English College in Rome reads, "The Hon. Mr Cary, brother of Lord Falkland, an English gentleman, dined." At the same dinner was the poet John Milton ("Mr. Milton, with his servant"), who was on a grand tour of the Continent following the death of his mother. In his *Diary* (1818), John Evelyn noted that on 5 November 1644, the morning after he arrived in Rome, losing no time, he "got acquainted with several persons that had long lived in Rome; being especially recommended to . . . Mr Patric Cary, an Abbot and brother to our Learned Lord Falkland, a pretty witty young priest; but one that afterwards came over to our Church." Again in the Pilgrim Book, on 27 December 1646, is to be found the notation that Cary dined in the English College vineyard with the visiting poet Richard Crashaw, another of Henrietta Maria's protégés. That Cary was aware of his good fortune during the time England was engulfed in war shows in his letter to Hyde (M.S. C.S.P. 39, 92^v-3) of about twelve years later: "Whilst the Queen had the wherewithall, I had a smale but sufficient pension under hand from her Majestye. Afterwards I was better provided by the last Pope [Urban VIII]; who uppon her Majestyes recommendation conferr'd uppon mee an Abbey and a priory *in commendum*; and besides, some pensions or other benefices: wherewith I subsisted well."

By 1650 Patrick Cary no longer had the competencies that had supported him. Urban VIII had died in 1644, his nephew Barberini was out of favor, and Cary wrote to Hyde that Innocent X sought to be "contrary" to his predecessor in all regards and had begun to show an aversion to foreigners. Innocent X dealt with Cary through fair words, but he gave no material assistance, and Cary began to feel the pinch of need. For this reason Cary and his cloistered sisters, especially Dame Clementia, began a letter-writing campaign in his behalf, contacting former English connections who might be able to help. Hyde, who considered himself bound by closest ties of friendship to Lucius Cary's family, was encouraging, but he was then experiencing difficulties and could do no more than reply with cordial warmth.

In acute financial distress during 1650, Cary considered renouncing Roman Catholicism if a position outside the church could be found. Despite his offers to return to Protestantism and Dame Clementia's letters reinforcing his intentions, little was forthcoming but hope of future preferment if he could wait. On 25 April, Hyde wrote to Dame Clementia, noting the death of her nephew (her brother Lucius's eldest son, also named Lucius, who had become the third viscount Falkland [1632–1649]) and asking her to join him in counseling Patrick to have patience. Hyde wrote that with only one young nephew remaining (Henry, fourth Viscount Falkland [1635–1663]) between Patrick and the Falkland title, Patrick should bear in mind his obligation to continue the family lineage. With no immediate prospects, however, and with a feeling close to desperation, Cary, who had resisted making a commitment up to that time, became a Benedictine novice at Douai.

It had seemed to him that the peace of Douai would calm his unquiet mind, and the monastery would provide a resting place after his years of bodily wandering. After three and a half months as a novice, however, Cary found he was constitutionally unable to endure the rigors of monastic life. He had begun the process of becoming a monk not through ardent desire to consecrate himself to his Lord, but through honorable fears that he had not lived up to his pledge to God. Though his attempt to enter the vocation was unsuccessful, Cary believed that the ordeal had released him from his vow. Many of the passionate, introspective devotional poems probably date from this period of soul searching. The verse dedicated to God indicates sincere repentance and spiritual release:

1. Open thy selfe, and then looke in;
   Consider what Thou mightst have bin,
   And what Thou art now made by Sin.
2. Asham'd o'th'State to which Th'art brought,
   Detest, and greeve for each past fault;
   Sigh, weepe, and blush for each foule thought.

Feare, but dispayre not, and still love;
Looke humbly up to God above,
And him Thou'lt soone to *Pitty* moove.

As George Saintsbury pointed out in *Minor Poets of the Caroline Period* (1906), the choice of triolet as a vehicle for devotion may appear inappropriate in English poetry, but Cary probably reflects French forms that he became familiar with in his Douai period.

      Unlike the four sisters who remained cloistered in France, Patrick left monastic life in young adulthood. In this defection from religious service he was followed by his youngest brother, who reverted to the name Henry, rather than Dom Placid as he had been called in France. Returning to England, Patrick Cary reconverted to Protestantism under the impression that through the possible death of his youngest nephew he might inherit the title of viscount Falkland. He wrote to Hyde that in case the title were to devolve on him, he would wish to marry in order to ensure heirs. Still without funds or means of support as of September 1650, he stayed for several months in Hampshire with his older sister Victoria (1620–1694). She had married Sir William Uvedale of Wickham, now treasurer of the chamber, formerly a soldier in the Low Countries with her father. Victoria had not felt any promptings of religious vocation; she alone had remained at the English court as a maid of honor to Henrietta Maria.

      The cordial, convivial Uvedales showered Cary with affectionate hospitality and included him into their bustling household. This was the first happy home life he had ever known. His songlike secular poems reflect the carefree enjoyment of this brief, golden period of his life. While he stayed with the Uvedales he wrote fluent, witty poetry that shows this was a time of energy and cheerfulness. The title page of the extant holograph manuscript of his poetry states that the secular poems are "writt here in obedience to M^es. *Tomkin*'s commands." The woman whose "commands" are referred to is Lucy, daughter of William Uvedale's first marriage; she was wedded to Thomas Tomkins at the time of Patrick Cary's congenial family visit.

      The first, abridged publication of Cary's work in 1771 received no continuing attention. The second publication came early in the nineteenth century when the manuscript was in the possession of Sir Walter Scott. In manifestation of the Romantic interest in the exotic, Scott, who was charmed by their antiquity and anonymity, published all thirty-seven of the poems in 1819 as *Trivial Poems and Trio-*

lets. Scott praised the work highly in his introduction, even while lamenting that further information was not known about the author. Later, after he learned the poet's identity, Scott included "Pat Carey" in his novel *Woodstock* (1826) as someone who was mentioned approvingly by a disguised Charles II. Scott has Charles encourage his desponding followers by singing "Patrick Carey's jovial farewell." When Scott borrows Cary's poem, he does not follow the manuscript exactly, but makes small improvements in the lines. Intending his poem to be sung to the tune of *The Healths,* Cary wrote:

Come (fayth) since I'me parting, & that God knowes
    when
The walls of sweet *Wickham* I shall see aghen;
Lett's e'ene have a frolicke, & drincke like tall men,
    Till Heads with healths goe round.

In chapter 31 of his novel, Scott has Charles sing the chorus of Cary's version of the country-house poem,

Come, now that we're parting, and 't is one to ten
If the towers of sweet Woodstock I e'er seen agen,
Let us e'en have a frolic, and drink like tall men,
    While the goblet goes merrily round.

The flowing effect of Scott's rendition comes closer to Jonson's abler management of joviality in verse than Cary himself was capable of achieving. In similar fashion, Jonson's dazzling country-house poetry, in which all nature joins in the celebration of the great house and its occupants, surpasses Cary's more modest efforts to commemorate his visit by praising the Uvedale household members and guests. Cary's verse, however, matches that of Charles Cotton, who similarly records the fleeting, happy moments in ordinary life.

      In the twentieth century there have been two notable editions of Cary's work: George Saintsbury included the poems in the second volume of *Minor Poets of the Caroline Period* (1906); and Veronica Delany gave both the poet and his original holograph manuscript full attention in *The Poems of Patrick Cary* (1978), including a biography, textual history, and scholarly apparatus, and, for the first time, presenting in their appropriate position facsimiles of the thirteen emblems that accompany and illustrate the religious meditations.

      The single known manuscript of Cary's poetry is in the Sir Walter Scott library in Abbotsford, Scotland. The volume, comprising sixty-two leaves that are handwritten and handsewn, is in two distinct halves. In the first half, dated "20 August 1651" and titled "Triviall Ballades," is a dedicatory octave and twenty-three works that include love poems, political satires, and occasional pieces. These secular poems are set to various tunes familiar to a contemporary audience. In the second half of the volume, dated "Warneford, 1651" and titled "I will sing unto the Lord," are thirteen devotional poems. In order to read these poems, the volume must be reversed and turned upside down. These pages are illustrated with thirteen devotional, emblematic ink drawings. The poems are penned by Cary himself, as can be ascertained by comparing them with his handwritten correspondence; almost certainly, the drawings are also in his hand. The volume is still in its leather binding, decorated with gold tooling. The cover is less ornate than it was formerly, having been, as Scott wrote in the 1819 introduction, "stripped of its silver clasps and ornaments." The two sections of the collection attest poignantly to the two distinct and incompatible sides – secular and religious – of Patrick Cary's rather brief life and form a tangible reminder of the two productive spells during which Cary had time for composition: his cloistered seminary life in Douai and his harmonious family life in Hampshire.

In the poems, Cary made use of a variety of celebratory modes. The secular poems are lyric pieces set to various known tunes, as indicated by the titles. Cary favors the lighthearted love lyric, as he shows in the lines, "I shall love you, whilst Y'are kind; / When Y'are not, forsake you" from "To the tune *Once I lov'd a Mayden Fayre* &c." ("Fayre-One! if thus kind You bee"). This type of playful poetry, including also such poems as "To the tune *I would give twenty pound* &c." ("There's noe Woeman, but I'me caught") and "To the tune of *Bobbing Joane*" ("I n'ere yett saw a lovely Creature") can be compared to the poetry of his contemporaries Sir John Suckling and Richard Lovelace for its interrogation of lovers and their vows of fidelity.

Cary illustrated his religious poems emblematically, with the charming effect of the amateur. Although it is possible that he intended his religious verse to form systematic steps to Ignatian meditation, this premise would be somewhat difficult to prove. Formally the poems are proficient though their subject matter is set by contemporary convention. Structurally, for the most part, they suffer from being overly regular both in meter and matter. The most accomplished of the divine works is the second poem. Cary's title, "O that I had wings like a Dove; for then I would fly away, and bee at rest," is somewhat cumbersome for so aerial a poem:

> I. By Ambition raysed high,
>   Oft did I
>   Seeke (though bruis'd with falls) to fly.
>   When I saw the pompe of Kings
>   Plac'd above,
>   I did love
>   To draw neare, and wish'd for wings.

In Cary's best religious poetry he is worthy of comparison with Henry Vaughan or even with George Herbert, whom, of all seventeenth-century religious poets, he most closely resembles in the personal sweetness of his devotion. "*Great God! I had been Nothing* but for Thee; / Thy all-creating Power first made mee *Bee,*" Cary begins one poem, which ends, "Thus, though to save mee God strove ev'ry way, / To Punishment I did my selfe betray / . . . . / Yett (God!) since Thou didst mee create, / Then ransome, then sanctificate; / Save what th'hast *bought* att such a Rate!" In such lines as these the piety and longing of the poem join together for Cary's most delicate and felicitous effects.

Subsequent to the visit to the Uvedale residence, Cary was admitted to Lincoln's Inn on 10 February 1652. Later he married Susan Uvedale, William Uvedale's niece. If Susan is mentioned in the poems, it would be in the line, "*Susan's* head is full of rattles" in "To the tune *But I fancy lovely Nancy* &c." Their first son, John, was born on 30 October 1654 at Great Tew, the scene of Patrick Cary's youthful nighttime escape, where he was now visiting with his nephew, Henry Cary, fourth Viscount Falkland. The following year in 1655, Patrick Cary voyaged to the West Indies as secretary to Admiral Sir William Penn on an unsuccessful expedition. The next year, his son Edward (1656–1692) was born in Dublin, where the family was now living. Patrick Cary had been appointed to commissionerships as early as 1653 for the precincts of Drogheda and Trim, and in 1654 his posts were extended to include county Louth. In 1655 he began to be assigned several court appointments in county Meath. Cary died of an unknown cause in early March 1657, at age thirty-four. An entry in the Irish Certificates Office (Records of Ulster Office) indicates he was buried on 15 March 1657. His daughter Susanna Patricia, evidently born after Cary's death, was baptized on 2 April 1657. Sadly, Cary's widow did not survive her husband by long; she died on 25 July 1658.

The Falkland title was continued by Anthony Cary (1657–1694), son of the fourth viscount, on whose death the descendance through Patrick's brother Lucius came to an end. It was by Patrick Cary's second son, Edward, that the line continued. Through Edward's son, Lucius Henry Cary (1687–1730), who succeeded to the title in 1694, the Falkland title has continued to the present time. Preservation of the Falkland name drove Hyde to suggest that Patrick Cary refrain from committing himself in the Benedictine order, even as it motivated the poet himself to revert from Catholicism to Protestantism. Through the continuity of the Falkland name and the recovery of his poetry, Cary has left two memorials that seem, with the passing of time, to compensate for the difficult and brief life that he lived.

References:

Veronica Delany, Introduction to *The Poems of Patrick Cary* (Oxford: Clarendon Press, 1978), pp. xiii–xcvi;

Fairfax Harrison, *The Devon Carys,* volume 2 (New York: De Vinne, 1920);

Edward Hyde, *The Life of Edward Earl of Clarendon, High Chancellor of England . . . in Which is Included a Continuation of his History of the Grand Rebellion. Written by Himself. A New Edition* (Oxford: Clarendon Press, 1827);

J. A. R. Marriot, *The Life and Times of Lucius Cary, Viscount Falkland* (New York: Putnam, 1907);

Richard Simpson, ed., *The Lady Falkland Her Life. From a MS. in the Imperial Archives at Lille. Also a Memoir of Father Francis Slingsby. From MSS. in the Royal Library, Brussels.* (London: Catholic, 1861);

Kurt Weber, "Patrick Cary," in *Lucius Cary: Second Viscount Falkland* (New York: Columbia University Press, 1940), pp. 301–326.

Papers:

The only surviving manuscript for Cary's poems is at Sir Walter Scott's library, Abbotsford, Scotland. Cary's letters are part of the Clarendon State Papers, a manuscript collection at the Bodleian Library, Oxford.

Margaret Lucas Cavendish, Duchess of Newcastle

(1623 – 15 December 1673)

Steven Max Miller
Millersville University of Pennsylvania

BOOKS: *Poems, and Fancies* (London: Printed by T. R. for J. Martin & J. Allestrye, 1653; second edition, revised, London: Printed by William Wilson, 1664); third edition, revised, published as *Poems, or, Several Fancies In Verse: With The Animal Parliament, In Prose* (London: Printed by A. Maxwell, 1668);

Philosophicall Fancies (London: Printed by Tho. Roycroft, for J. Martin & J. Allestrye, 1653);

The Worlds Olio (London: Printed for J. Martin & J. Allestrye, 1655);

The Philosophical and Physical Opinions (London: Printed for J. Martin & J. Allestrye, 1655; enlarged edition, London: Printed by William Wilson, 1663); revised as *Grounds of Natural Philosophy* (London: Printed by A. Maxwell, 1668);

Natures Pictures Drawn by Fancies Pencil to the Life (London: Printed for J. Martin & J. Allestrye, 1656);

Playes (London: Printed by A. Warren for John Martyn, James Allestry & Tho. Dicas, 1662);

Orations of Divers Sorts, Accommodated to Divers Places (London, 1662);

CCXI Sociable Letters (London: Printed by William Wilson, 1664);

Philosophical Letters: or, Modest Reflections upon some Opinions in Natural Philosophy, maintained by several Famous and Learned Authors of this Age, Expressed by way of Letters (London, 1664);

Observations upon Experimental Philosophy. To which is added, The Description of a New Blazing World (London: Printed by A. Maxwell, 1666);

The Description of a New World, called The Blazing World (London: Printed by A. Maxwell, 1666);

The Life of the Thrice Noble, High and Puissant Prince William Cavendishe, Duke, Marquess, and Earl of Newcastle (London: Printed by Anne Maxwell, 1667); translated as *De Vita et Rebus Gestis Nobilissimi Illustrissimique Principis, Guilielmi Ducis Novo-Castrensis, commentarii* (London: Excudebat T.M., 1668);

Plays, Never before Printed (London: Printed by Anne Maxwell, 1668).

Margaret Lucas Cavendish, first Duchess of Newcastle, remains one of the most remarkable authors of the mid seventeenth century. Praised by the influential philosophers and university faculty of her day, ridiculed by contemporary literati and later biographers, she published thirteen separate volumes of poetry and prose between 1653 and 1668, seeing most of her books through two or more revised editions during the same period. Although her works range from poetry, plays, and prose fiction to letters, orations, and natural philosophy, she has been noted most often as the writer of her husband's biography. Some three hundred years after her death, the range and complexity of Margaret Cavendish's writings are being reconsidered, especially in the context of social history, and she is being acknowledged as an important and underrated figure in the history of English literature.

The youngest child of Thomas Lucas and Elizabeth Leighton Lucas, Margaret was born at Saint John's Abbey, Colchester, Essex, in 1623. Along with three brothers and four sisters, she was raised by her widowed mother in the protected affluence of a close-knit, staunchly Royalist family. This early security was shattered by the civil wars of the 1640s, when the Lucas family was profoundly affected by the outbreak of hostilities. In 1642 Saint John's Abbey, the Lucases' principal residence, was plundered by an anti-Royalist mob. Margaret was to lose two brothers in the wars that followed. When Queen Henrietta Maria took up residence at Oxford in 1643, Margaret Lucas was permitted to join the court as a maid of honor to the queen, her married sisters having withdrawn to Oxford after the battle

Margaret Lucas (portrait by Sir Peter Lely; National Gallery of Victoria)

of Edgehill. Margaret accompanied Henrietta Maria into exile in 1644, and in Paris met William Cavendish, then Marquis of Newcastle, whom she married in December 1645. Newcastle was thirty years older than Margaret and a widower, an impressive horseman, and something of a military hero, although there were critics of his hasty flight to the Continent.

For the next fifteen years the Newcastles lived in exile, finally settling in Antwerp where they lived in Peter Paul Rubens's house, leased from Rubens's widow. Surviving almost entirely on credit, they maintained the trappings of nobility while the marquis maintained horses for manège and Margaret spent a good deal of time alone in reverie and writing. Her autobiography, "A True Relation of my Birth, Breeding, and Life" (in *Natures Pictures,* 1656), gives little detail of her private life, but Margaret characterizes herself as a very shy child and young woman, bashful to the point of awkwardness and homesick at court in Oxford. She consistently

praises her husband and says that he "did approve of those bashful fears which many condemned." Although their life in Antwerp was retired, the Newcastles visited and were visited by European notables and English exiles. Thomas Hobbes had a long association with the marquis's family, and the couple met at least once with René Descartes. Financial pressures grew steadily, with Royalist estates impounded and help from friends and relatives difficult to obtain.

In November 1651 Margaret and her brother-in-law Sir Charles Cavendish sailed to England in hope of securing funds. A traitor in the eyes of the Commonwealth, the marquis would have been imprisoned or executed in his homeland, and he remained in Antwerp to appease his creditors. Sir Charles managed to buy back his own estates and in addition retrieved a part of his brothers' lands at great personal sacrifice. Margaret sought an allowance that wives and widows of Cavaliers had been provided by the government, but her petition for a

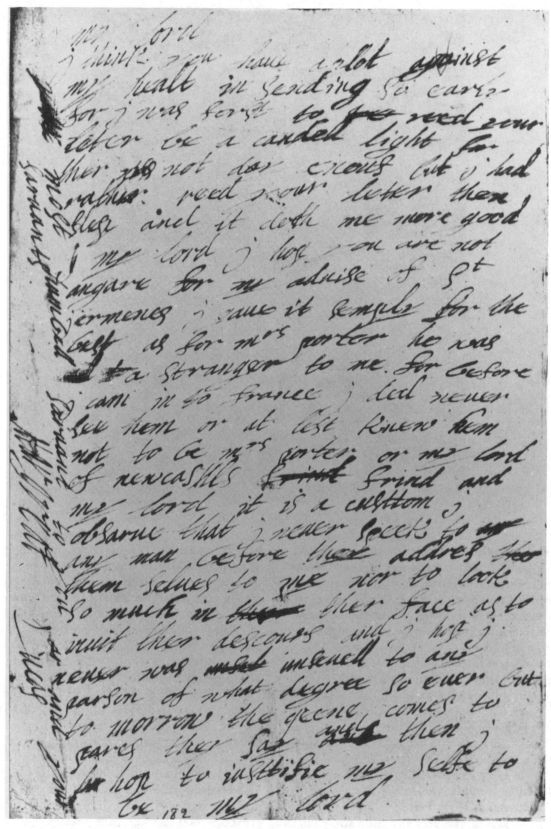

A 1645 letter from Margaret Lucas to William Cavendish, Marquis (later Duke) of Newcastle, whom she married in December of that year (Collection of the Duke of Portland, K.G.)

Title page for Cavendish's first published book, the principal collection of her poetry

share of William's estate was flatly denied on the grounds that she was married after the lands had been forfeited. She was also told her husband was "the greatest traitor to the state." This, she recorded bitterly, meant he was "the most loyall subject to his king and country." Virtually penniless in London, relying on the generosity of friends, she remained with Sir Charles over a year, going out little. By her account, she heard music at the house of Henry Lawes "three or four times" and sometimes rode in Hyde Park with her sisters. During this time she wrote a volume of scientific speculation, *Philosophicall Fancies,* and her first book of poetry, *Poems, and Fancies.* Both were published in London by John Martin and James Allestrye in 1653, *Poems, and Fancies* appearing in print first by about two months. Susan Hastings has recently called the prose philosophical work "an enchanting blend of fantasy and the popularization of current scientific inquiry," but it was received at the time more as a curiosity than a seri-

ous contribution to speculative science. Both volumes are marked by an adventurous imagination, the vigorous "fancy" named in both titles. In *Philosophicall Fancies* Margaret Cavendish explores atomist theories and offers her own speculations about the composition of matter and the characteristics of elemental particles. Both her first published books include verse in which she sets out her theories and contemplates natural phenomena.

Poems, and Fancies would be revised and reprinted in 1664 and 1668 and comprises the principal collection of her poetry. In 1653 she dedicated the volume to her brother-in-law in appreciation for his financial support and personal friendship; ironically, Sir Charles died just after Margaret returned alone to Antwerp in concern for her husband's faltering health. Her "Epistle Dedicatory" introduces imagery and implicit literary theory she returns to frequently in her works: "Spinning with the Fingers is more proper to our Sexe, then studying or writing

Poetry, which is the Spinning with the braine." Although she claims "no skill" at the distaff and admits that practical accomplishments might provide a "Garment to keep me from the cold," she refers to her writing as a "Garment of Memory, to lapp up my Name, that it might grow to after Ages." An acute sense of gender roles and an appeal to the memorial function of writing characterize all Margaret Cavendish's works of poetry, prose, and drama, including the supplementary bevy of prose and verse prefaces accompanying each of her printed works. Before her poems she includes prefaces addressed "To All Noble, and Worthy Ladies," "To Naturall Philosophers," and "To the Reader," with "An Epistle to Mistris Toppe," a serving lady, Elizabeth (Chaplain) Topp, who had known the Lucas family and would be employed by the Newcastles after the Restoration. These prefaces suggest the problematic self-fashioning that confronted Margaret Cavendish as a woman author in the mid seventeenth century. As Janet Todd, Elaine Hobby, and others have documented, the printing of works by women in this period often raised questions about the author's propriety, modesty, and morality. In her first venture into print, Cavendish contextualized and justified her work by combining conventional imagery, expressions of noble authorial ends, and prefaces designed for particular audiences. Later critics have often seen a defensive, insecure personality behind such prefatory material, but the preliminaries of Cavendish's volumes may also be read as a telling subtext and a record of social history.

During her eighteen-month stay in London, rumors spread about Cavendish's idiosyncratic manner of dress, an element of her personality that has continued to fascinate her biographers. Surviving portraits do not clearly account for what her contemporaries found eccentric in her clothing, but of her choice of fashion during the visit she wrote in her autobiography, "when I did dress myself, I did endeavor to do it to my best becoming." At her return to England in 1653, she had been out of the country for more than seven years, and she must have worn clothing from the Continent, garments possibly influenced by fashions of the French court. She traveled at a time when England was in the midst of parliamentary rule with Puritan ascendancy well established, and it was not in her character to conform. Cavendish describes her interest in clothing as an assertion of originality formed in her youth: "I took great delight in attiring ... and fashions, especially such fashions as I did invent myself. ... I always took delight in singularity, even in accoutrements of habits." Surely her "singularity"

would have been perceived with interest if not censure in the London of the 1650s. Her books met a similar response. *Poems, and Fancies* was received with a mixture of fascination and scorn, if surviving comments are representative. At the same time it must have been satisfying to the publishers and the debt-ridden author that copies of the volume were sought after by readers who were perhaps intrigued by the aristocratic writer who disappeared to the Continent almost as soon as the book appeared.

Poems, and Fancies may have caused a minor sensation in some circles. Dorothy Osborne wrote to her fiancé William Temple on 14 April 1653 inquiring if he had seen the volume and exclaiming, "for God sake if you meet with it send it me, they say 'tis ten times more extravagant than her dress." A short time later, Osborne had seen the book and wrote of its author, "I ... am satisfied that there are many soberer people in Bedlam; I'll swear her friends are much to blame to let her go abroad." Osborne may speak for many in her day as she continues, "Sure the poor woman is a little distracted" or "she would never be so ridiculous else as to venture at writing books and in verse too." Cavendish's public persona may have been another intentional device like her prefaces that sought to create and justify her authorship. Recent critics have shown that necessary self-justification faced women whose writing appeared in print during the period, and Cavendish may have used theatrical or extravagant gestures to reject social norms by standing outside them. The singular persona has been noted since her lifetime to explain and evaluate Cavendish's work, and the fame she says she sought has been only dimly parodied by the notoriety she found. Personality has all but obscured much of her writing, but judged as literature her poems are intriguing in themselves.

Poems, and Fancies comprises verse on a wide range of topics, with the poems of the final 1668 edition arranged into six sections. The first part begins with a "Council" called by Nature in which personified Destiny, Motion, and other forces describe the outline of Cavendish's scientific vision of the world. In this section are poems defining four sorts of atoms with their qualities and others exploring the components of Cavendish's natural philosophy. Here, poems examine physical properties of the echo, the circulation of the blood, the nature of human thought, and other scientific matters, including the question of multiple worlds. Admitting "It is hard to believe, that there may be other Worlds in this World" in a poem so titled, Cavendish creates several worlds in her verse, including "A World in

William Cavendish, Duke of Newcastle, soon after he was installed as Knight of the Garter in 1661 (portrait in the Collection of the Earl of Clarendon at the Palace of Westminster, a copy of a portrait by Sir Anthony Van Dyck at Welbeck Abbey) and Margaret Lucas Cavendish, Duchess of Newcastle (portrait attributed to Abraham van Diepenbeke; Collection of the Duke of Portland, K.G.)

an Ear-ring," a delightful speculation on microscopic lands and beasts that ends with imagined love and death in a micromicrocosm: "But when the *Ring* is broke, the *World* is done; / Then *Lovers* are into Elysium gone." Near the end of this and every section appear transitional poems, each titled "The Clasp," which comment on the poetic process and authorial purpose.

The second part of *Poems, and Fancies* addresses moral philosophy and includes "A Dialogue between an Oak, and a Man cutting it down" and "Moral Discourses" on human interaction with the natural world. The third part addresses poetry and poets, contrasting others' learned, allusive style with the imaginative creation Cavendish exercises in her own works of "Fancy," works she sees as "natural" and opposed to the mechanically artificial. The fourth part explores traditional roles of the fanciful in verse, and

includes poems that demystify the pastoral by focusing on the humble realities of country life, a set of three poems allegorizing Fame, and the frequently noted fairy poems with their wee creatures who dwell at the center of Earth. Cavendish's poems about Queen Mab are noted for descriptive, imaginative transformations of natural images: when "she goes to take the Air," the fairy queen rides

In coach, which is a Nut-shell fair:
The lining's Soft and Rich within,
Made of a glistering *Adder's* Skin.
And there six *Crickets* draw her fast,
When she a Journey takes in hast.

This section ends with imaginative natural philosophy, "The Clasp" titled "Of Fairies in the Brain," which concretizes an answer to its question, "Who knows, but that in every *Brain* may dwell / Those Creatures, we call Fairies? who can tell?" The fifth part addresses soldiers and uses military imagery for the allegorical explorations of "Doubt's Assault and Hope's Defence" and "A Battel Between Courage and Prudence." Here is included also "A Battel between King Oberon, and the Pigmies," continuing the fairyland motif. At the end are more serious poems subtitled "A Register of Mournful Verses," including an elegy "Upon the Funeral of my Dear Brother, Kill'd in these Unhappy Warrs." To her original collection of poetry Cavendish added in the 1668 edition a prose work, an internal debate titled "The Animal Parliament."

Among poems addressing the imagination and fancy as poetic faculties are many that proceed by "similizing," a term Cavendish uses to label her development of a comparison through energetic and sometimes alarming images. For example, Cavendish pursues the metaphor "Death is the Cook of Nature," and diseases become culinary processes that transform human bodies through the mortal art of "Nature's Cook": "Some Brains he dresseth with Apoplexy, / Or Sawce of Megrims, swimming plenteously." In the context of similar "fancies," Death as a male chef becomes part of a radically recreated world of metaphorical play that combines natural science, literary convention, and domestic imagery. The human brain in "Nature's Oven" is "Hot and Dry," and "like an Oven . . . / . . . bakes all sorts of Fancies low and high." "An Olio drest for Nature's Dinner" transforms a lover's heart into a savory dish by boiling it in tears and garnishing it with smiles so Life can serve it up "a Fair and Beauteous Mess."

Cavendish does not restrict herself to images from the realm of women's work, but builds comparisons on vivid observation, as the topography of "Man's Head similized to the Globe of the World" or the sounds of "Fancies similized to Gnats" demonstrates. The latter begins, "Some Fancies, like small Gnats, buz in the Brain." Insectlike fancies "do sting so sore, the Poet's Head, / His Mind is blister'd, and his Thoughts turn red." The "perfect Cure" is "Pen and Ink, to write on Paper plain," and the speaker prescribes "oyl of Fame" as the poem ends like a medicinal recipe. The effect created by Cavendish's strong images and direct language is difficult to describe, but poems of various lengths – often clustered in groups of related similes – follow one another in a stream of couplets almost always reminding the reader of the essential activity of making comparisons. Virtually all her poems are written in variations on the iambic pen-

tameter couplet; with the punctuation that appears in the 1668 edition, some lines are broken into a rhythm of halting reflection even when seemingly conventional personification and allusion are employed. "Nature's Officers" begins,

> *Eternity*, as Usher, goes before;
> And *Destiny*, as Porter, keeps the Door
> Of the Great World; who lets Life out and in.
> The *Fates*, her Maids, the Thread of Life do spin;
> Change Orders all, with Industry and Care.

At times Metaphysical conceit is concentrated into a couplet, as in the first lines of "Nature's Dessert": "Sweet *Marmalade* of *Kisses* newly gather'd: / Preserved Children, which were never Father'd." Cavendish's work shows the influence of John Donne, to whom she alludes, and of Ben Jonson, who had written masques for her husband and received his patronage. Her poetry includes nature imagery that has elicited comparison with Andrew Marvell and Robert Herrick; but in her emphasis on reflection, originality, and imagination, Cavendish anticipates eighteenth-century sentimentality and the Romantics.

"A Dialogue between Melancholy and Mirth" was praised in the eighteenth century and found its way into some nineteenth-century collections. In the musings of its speaker, personified Mirth is answered by Melancholy who lives "in a small House alone" and describes the solitary calm of contemplation as more satisfying than the burning sun, "blustering Storms," and sociable activity of Mirth "often smutch'd with Dust and Dirt." The long poem ends with Melancholy's advice, "Refuse me not, for I shall constant be; / Maintain your *Credit*, and your *Dignity*," an invitation the author seems to address to herself as well as to the reader. Many years later Cavendish's works appeared with an engraved frontispiece apparently selected by the author, a portrait of herself as a melancholy writer alone in her study with laurel-bearing putti (cupids) her only companions. Two narrative poems in her first published volume show another side of her contemplative character, the close observer and critic of aristocratic customs.

"The Hunting of the Hare" is a 106-line narrative poem that traces the flight of "poor Wat," a hare pursued by dogs and hunters. Told with complete sympathy for the small animal's fate, the poem describes the hare "press'd to th'Earth" with "His Head . . . always set against the Wind" anticipating the rush of his tormentors; "starting up with fear" he leaps, runs, and hides again. The reader shares his "relief," "thoughts," and "terror" until the hare is inevitably overtaken and killed. The hunters "spur-ring their Horses" and "hooping loud" are clearly condemned for destroying a life "that God did make; / Making their Stomacks Graves, which full they fill / With Murther'd Bodies, which in sport they kill." The poem moves from rapid action and minute attention to the hare's behavior to end with commentary on the arrogance of man who ironi-cally believes that his "God-like Nature" is license to tyrannize all other creatures. The depth of feeling and clear sympathy for the suffering of an animal "for Sport or Recreation's sake" is conveyed with confidence and strength one might not expect from an author of Cavendish's social class in the mid sev-enteenth century.

"The Hunting of a Stagg" is a second narrative with a similar theme. The 140 lines on the pursuit of a noble, antler-crowned male deer were perhaps more to the taste of her contemporary readers. Edmund Waller praised and ridiculed the piece, remarking that he would have given all his poems to have written this one by Cavendish. When he was chided for such pan-dering insincerity, he wittily answered that gallantry demanded nothing less than willingness to save Cavendish's reputation from the "disgrace of having written anything so ill." The anecdote, recorded by Katherine Philips, affirms that Waller could be witty and insincere, but his evaluation of the piece remains obscure. Published after the hunting scene in Sir John Denham's *Cooper's Hill* (1642) and before the similar passage in Alexander Pope's *Windsor Forest* (1713), "The Hunting of a Stagg" has a place in the history of the closed couplet and in the late-seventeenth-century subgenre of verse depictions of the hunt. Characteris-tically, Cavendish's poem focuses sharply on the deer and its perspective, opening with pithy description ("His *Leggs* were Nervous, and his *Joynts* were strong; / His Hair lay sleek and smooth . . .") and following the stag through shady forest, under-growth, and verdant pasture. She includes a cata-logue of trees that combines description ("The smooth-rind *Beech*, which groweth large and tall") with allusions to traditional associations ("The *Cypress* sad") and medicinal uses of these plants ("the *Poplar* green, / Whose Cooling-buds, in Salves, have healing been"). Developing the beast's anthropomorphic char-acter, Cavendish has the stag admire his reflection in a "Crystal Brook" and in pride forget "that *Doggs* might pull him down." Discovered by hunters on horseback, the stag runs for his life and is pursued by dogs, men, and horses through field and river. At bay, the deer is brave but outnumbered by "an Army" of pursuers, "a Multitude of Whelps" and "a Company of Men." Like Wat the hare, the stag is killed with

tears in his eyes, the victim of cruel human sport. Unlike "The Hunting of the Hare," Cavendish's de-piction of the stag's death does not end with com-mentary on the hunters' inhumanity. More subtly here the poem relies on the nobility of the quarry, the stag's imputed tragic flaw of pride, and refer-ences to the passions of dogs and men to suggest the author's criticism of such sport. At one point the hunters are "like to Boys" who risk their lives to see or do some "Mischief"; and near the end of the poem men and dogs are ambiguously identified, leaving questions about which animals are tossed aside by the stag's antlers. The hunted animal is the hero of the piece, and the hunters with their slaver-ing dogs are scarcely worthy adversaries. Subtle and elegant, the poem might well have been envied by contemporaries, and like much of Cavendish's poetry, it deserves reevaluation by students of Res-toration verse.

Her narrative and descriptive works show Cavendish was capable of creating poetic works well beyond the scope of the eccentric "lady philos-opher" her detractors have perpetuated. Current critics, who see her as "ahead of her time" and con-veying a "Blakean" quality in her verse, often refer to her feminist ideas and social criticism. Her poetry also abounds with a sense, uncharacteristic of her time, of wonder and delight in nature. Three short poems from her first volume – "Of the Knowledg of Beasts," "Of Fish," and "Of Birds" – begin with questions that ask whether animals might know more natural science than man is capa-ble of learning. "Who knows," Cavendish asks, but that birds understand the source of thunder and the composition of stars, that fish know why the sea is salt, and that beasts contemplate a message in the stars beyond "all Man's *Astrologie*." In simple lan-guage Cavendish explores the connections between the natural world and the realm of imagination, and she offers a poetic credo in "The Clasp" beginning, "Give me a Free and Noble Style, that goes / in an Uncurbed Strain, though Wild it shows." Striking a note that resounds throughout her work, Cavendish calls for a style that "shews more Courage, than it doth of Fear," a style "that Nature frames, not Art," a style that ultimately departs from the rules and conventions of her time and sets her among writers who are markedly out of step with their contempo-raries.

Mixed and negative reception of her poetry did not slow the rate at which Cavendish continued to write. After she returned to Antwerp, she com-pleted a third volume, *The Worlds Olio*, published in London in 1655 by Martin and Allestrye. Bearing a

Frontispiece, with a portrait of Cavendish, in her Worlds Olio *(1655; engraving by Peter van Schuppen after a portrait by Diepenbeke)*

dedication "to Fortune," the book is, as its title suggests, a miscellany or "stew" of diverse observations on literature, art, and life, prose meditations and pronouncements on the nature of matter, animal life, and historical figures ancient and modern. In prefaces and essays Cavendish returns to the idea of fame as her goal in writing, comparing the afterlife of literary reputation to the begetting of children as a means of escaping oblivion. Her marriage had proven childless, and although the marquis had at first hoped for children with his second wife, he seems to have become content with the heirs produced in his first marriage. It is difficult to determine Cavendish's own feeling on the subject of motherhood, and the association she makes between books and offspring may be as conventional a part of publishing as it is self-revealing. The prelim-

inary pages carry an interesting commendatory poem by her husband that continues the metaphor of the volume's title in offering up "Aromatick Spice of Phancy" and presenting "this Imaginary Feast" with the closing line, "Censure your worst, so you the Book will buy." Cavendish's works seem to have been attractive enough to her publishers, and in the same year appeared *The Philosophical and Physical Opinions* (1655), the work of natural philosophy that she would revise twice in later years, maintaining distrust of experimental science and embracing a "contemplative philosophy" rooted in her senses and powers of imagination. Her first folio volume devoted to scientific inquiry, the book modifies the atomism of *Philosophicall Fancies* and presents a skepticism radical for her day. As earlier reflection had left little room for conventional Christianity in her materialistic at-

Frontispiece for Cavendish's Natures Pictures *(1656) showing the author and her husband, crowned with laurel at the head of the table, surrounded by their family (engraving by Peter Clouwet after a portrait by Diepenbeke)*

omism, here too Cavendish's imagination is unbridled by a religious creed as she speculates freely in prose essays on the four elements, the nature of the brain, and the relationship between reason and fancy without reference to a deity.

Although her speculations were criticized, they were also read and praised by scientists of her time. The noted mathematician and experimental philosopher Robert Hooke owned a copy of Cavendish's second edition (1663) of *The Philosophical and Physical Opinions* and the 1668 edition of her later volume *Observations upon Experimental Philosophy* (1666). As Sophia B. Blaydes has pointed out in "Nature is a Woman" (1988), Cavendish wrote *The Philosophical and Physical Opinions* in isolation from the growing community of scientific thought. The author's prefaces mention that

the issues addressed in her philosophy were sometimes raised by conversations with her husband and brother-in-law, Sir William Cavendish having been adept at both amateur speculation and experiment. But she had not received the education, particularly in Latin, that would have given her access to the works of her male contemporaries. In later years she would abandon atomist theories in favor of what Lisa T. Sarasohn has termed "organic materialism," a theory maintaining the unity of all matter in which matter and motion are inseparable, dividing the universe into a descending hierarchy from rational to sensible and inanimate matter. After the Restoration and her return to England, Cavendish would read and reply to Descartes, Thomas Hobbes, Henry More, and Jan Baptista van Helmont in *Philo-*

sophical Letters (1664). She continued to correspond with the atomist Walter Charleton and with Constantijn Huygens, the father of mathematician Christian, into the last years of her life. Blaydes has demonstrated how the natural philosophy of Cavendish developed and was modified in ways similar to the thought of her scientific contemporaries, but in spite of Cavendish's aspirations to recognition in philosophical circles, she was barred from full participation in academic communities because she was a woman.

Before the Restoration, Cavendish completed one more volume of literary works, *Natures Pictures Drawn by Fancies Pencil to the Life* (1656), a collection of prose and verse narratives and characters. Perhaps inspired by traditional storytelling or the literary works of Geoffrey Chaucer and Marguerite of Navarre, Cavendish created a series of verse tales told by alternating male and female narrators who offer gender stereotypes only to subvert them. *Natures Pictures* includes prose and verse character sketches, sometimes set in dialogue, and allegorical fables in which Cavendish explores human traits or, in the prose of "Heavens Library," comments on the received literary canon. Her prefaces further explore the importance of imagination or fancy in her work as Cavendish seems to apologize for not meeting contemporary criteria for lively imitative description, although she simultaneously asserts her "natural genius" for fanciful creation. Perhaps not as intriguing as the "similizing" of *Poems, and Fancies*, her verse shows variety and a critical eye for the society around her. In the first edition of *Natures Pictures* Cavendish included her short autobiography, "A True Relation of my Birth, Breeding, and Life," a modest chronicle offered, she says, "not to please the fancy, but to tell the truth." Written ostensibly to record the major events of her life "lest after-ages should mistake" and confuse her with her husband's first wife or some future spouse, the "True Relation" was to serve as a model and inspiration to later women who also sought to leave written traces.

With the Restoration and their return to England, Margaret and William Cavendish withdrew to the restored but reduced estates that had survived the civil wars and Interregnum. No longer part of the life at court now surging up around Charles II, the couple retired to life in the country, principally at Welbeck Abbey in Nottinghamshire. Margaret continued to write, publishing her first folio volume of plays in 1662. In the same year also appeared *Orations of Divers Sorts*, as she began to settle into a new life after exile. This volume shows Margaret continuing to explore social questions and philosophical ideas, addressing social issues, especially those related to gender. Possibly her plays were never meant to be performed, but it is easy to imagine their being read at Welbeck and, with the opening of the theaters and the marquis's longstanding interest in drama, performance was not out of the question. Much more dialogue than action, the plays explore relationships among women and between women and men, compare characters of different social classes, and criticize the superficiality of life à la mode, the stylish world in which life could be seen as itself a foppish art.

The years after 1660 were busy as dwellings were repaired and refurnished, trees were planted to restore lands from virtual deforestation, and revenues began to be managed after long years of debt. William Cavendish was never repaid the huge sums he had contributed to the Royalist cause, and rebuilding his estates proved costly. During this period Cavendish was exploring new genres and revising her earlier works. In 1663 she revised *The Philosophical and Physical Opinions* for a new printer, William Wilson. Revising the misprint-ridden first edition of *Poems, and Fancies* in 1664, she published two volumes of prose epistles, *Philosophical Letters* and *CCXI Sociable Letters* , in the same year. Often noted as perhaps her most successful prose genre, the first work continues Cavendish's exploration of speculative philosophy and shows that she began studying contemporary theories in the period following the Restoration. *CCXI Sociable Letters* is a collection of opinion and observation addressed to a real or convincingly imagined friend; touching on philosophical ideas, the letters discuss social issues and share the author's reflections and criticism with a clarity of tone some have found lacking in her other works. More and more absorbed in scientific speculation, in her last works Cavendish primarily employed prose except for songs in plays, but her dedication to the imagination and its vast possibilities continued to flourish.

In 1665 Margaret and William went to London for ceremonies creating him duke of Newcastle, the title by which he is commonly known. The duchess completed her *Observations upon Experimental Philosophy* and had it handsomely printed by Anne Maxwell, widow of a London stationer, in 1666. At the end of this philosophical work appears *The Description of a New World, called The Blazing World*, which Maxwell also issued separately (1666). This remarkable imaginary voyage recapitulates many tenets of Cavendish's scientific theory and her criticism of experimentation in a combination of fantasy and autobiography. Touching also on political theory, the prose tale reasserts the author's exuberance and probably contributed to her reputation for eccentricity. The next year was marked by two events which assured Cavendish's place in history. The year after the Great Fire of London, 1667, the duchess attended a meeting of the Royal Society and observed experiments performed for her amusement by members of the learned group at Arundel House. Her visit was recorded by Samuel Pepys and other contemporaries with varying degrees of curiosity and disdain, but her persistence in philosophical thought and publication had been recognized – whatever pressures may have been exerted by her rank – by the society's invitation. Cavendish was the first woman to be so acknowledged. Also in 1667 she published her most widely read work, *The Life of the Thrice Noble, High and Puissant Prince William Cavendishe, Duke, Marquess, and Earl of Newcastle*. Meticulously chronicling his financial losses, the biography was written in a plain style approved by the duke. Cavendish conveys admiration for her husband without ornamentation or absurdity, recording with acknowledged bias the career of a notable Cavalier, patron, and spouse. Ironically her own fame as an author has rested most heavily on her tribute to him.

In the final years of Cavendish's life she was engaged in revisions and final editions of her literary and philosophical works. In 1668 three new editions were published and a final version of her scientific work appeared as *Grounds of Natural Philosophy*, beautifully printed by Anne Maxwell and accompanied by engraved frontispiece portraits. One additional volume, *Plays, Never before Printed*, also appeared in 1668, adding another folio collection to her dramatic works. In 1671 new editions of *The Worlds Olio* and *Natures Pictures* proved to be her last ventures in print. Margaret Lucas Cavendish, first Duchess of Newcastle, died on 15 December 1673. In tribute to his second wife William Cavendish provided a funeral with all the ceremony appropriate to her station, and her body was interred in Westminster Abbey. In 1676 the duke published a 182-page volume of *Letters and Poems* addressed to the duchess during her lifetime in praise of her work, demonstrating that universities, philosophers, and gentleman poets had showered her with ornate and flattering panegyric, even as peers had ridiculed her in private letters and diaries.

The reputation of Margaret Lucas Cavendish has continued to be mixed, but the complex author of a remarkable range of works may still be seen through the contradictory clouds of praise and blame. Her works were read and admired by Charles Lamb and Samuel Taylor Coleridge, but her poetry was never widely reprinted. Virginia Woolf considered Cavendish with both interest and uneasiness. Biographers have tended to exploit her

Effigy of Cavendish from the monument to the duke and duchess of Newcastle in Westminster Abbey

eccentricities and carefully qualify praise of her work. Over three hundred years after her death, Cavendish is being studied by social historians and feminist critics with increased sensitivity to the complexity of her work and the problematic context in which she lived and wrote. Hampered by her sex, her lack of formal education, the society in which she lived, and perhaps even by her social rank, Cavendish nonetheless wrote voluminously to record her views, and she wrote very specifically for print publication. Her poetry is not now widely available or currently recognized as a significant part of English literary history, but in the history of literature still to be written she deserves careful and thorough consideration. She has already come to be acknowledged in women's studies, and her works are beginning to be republished for a wider scholarly audience. Not easily assigned a position in traditional periodization, Cavendish wrote with and about the power of imagination as she created worlds of her own and attempted to share her vision with a receptive audience. When her originality is recognized, she may be seen as an important woman, a significant pre-Romantic poet, and a powerful visionary.

Letters:

Letters of Margaret Lucas to her Future Husband, edited by Richard William Goulding (London: J. Murray, 1909);

The Phanseys of William Cavendish Marquis of Newcastle Addressed to Margaret Lucas and her Letters in Reply, edited by Douglas Grant (London: Nonesuch, 1956).

Bibliography:

Elizabeth R. Hageman, "Studies in Women Writers of the English Seventeenth Century (1604–1674)," *English Literary Renaissance,* 18 (Winter 1988): 138–167.

Biographies:

Henry Ten Eyck Perry, *The First Duchess of Newcastle and Her Husband as Figures in Literary History* (Boston & London: Ginn, 1918);

Douglas Grant, *Margaret the First* (London: Rupert Hart-Davis, 1957);

Kathleen Jones, *A Glorious Fame: The Life of Margaret Cavendish, Duchess of Newcastle, 1623–1673* (London: Bloomsburg, 1988).

References:

Sophia B. Blaydes, "Nature is a Woman," in *Man, God, and Nature in the Enlightenment*, edited by Donald C. Mell, Theodore E. D. Braun, and Lucia M. Palmer (East Lansing, Mich.: Colleagues, 1988), pp. 51–64;

Blaydes, "The Poetry of the Duchess of Newcastle: A Pyramid of Praise," *Bulletin of the West Virginia Association of College English Teachers,* 6 (Spring 1981): 26–34;

Sylvia Bowerbank, "The Spider's Delight: Margaret Cavendish and the 'Female' Imagination," *English Literary Renaissance,* 14 (Autumn 1984): 392–408;

Moira Ferguson, "A 'Wise Wittie and Learned Lady': Margaret Lucas Cavendish," in *Woman Writers of the Seventeenth Century*, edited by Katharina M. Wilson and Frank J. Warnke (Athens: University of Georgia Press, 1989), pp. 305–340;

James Fitzmaurice, "Fancy and the Family: Self-Characterizations of Margaret Cavendish," *Huntington Library Quarterly,* 53 (Summer 1990): 199–209;

Jean Gagen, "Honor and Fame in the Works of the Duchess of Newcastle," *Studies in Philology,* 56 (1959): 519–538;

Elizabeth Hampsten, "Petticoat Authors: 1660–1720," *Women's Studies,* 7 (1980): 21–38;

Susan Hastings, "Margaret Cavendish, Duchess of Newcastle," in *An Encyclopedia of British Women Writers*, edited by Paul and June Schlueter (New York & London: Garland, 1988), pp. 91–93;

Elaine Hobby, *Virtue of Necessity: English Women's Writing 1649–88* (Ann Arbor: University of Michigan Press, 1989);

Sara Heller Mendelson, *The Mental World of Stuart Woman: Three Studies* (Amherst: University of Massachusetts Press, 1987);

Samuel I. Mintz, "The Duchess of Newcastle's Visit to the Royal Society," *Journal of English and Germanic Philology,* 51 (April 1952): 168–176;

Dolores Paloma, "Margaret Cavendish: Defining the Female Self," *Women's Studies,* 7, nos. 1–2 (1980): 55–66;

Mary Beth Rose, "Gender, Genre, and History: Seventeenth-Century English Women and the Art of Autobiography," in *Women in the Middle Ages and the Renaissance*, edited by Mary Beth Rose (Syracuse: Syracuse University Press, 1986), pp. 245–278;

Leona Rostenberg, *The Library of Robert Hooke* (Santa Monica: Modoc, 1989);

Lisa T. Sarasohn, "A Science Turned Upside Down: Feminism and the Natural Philosophy of Margaret Cavendish," *Huntington Library Quarterly,* 47 (Autumn 1984): 289–307;

Hilda L. Smith, *Reason's Disciples: Seventeenth-Century English Feminists* (Urbana: University of Illinois Press, 1982).

Janet Todd, *The Sign of Angellica: Women, Writing, and Fiction, 1660–1800* (New York: Columbia University Press, 1989).

Papers:

The Portland Papers, housed at the British National Library with other Cavendish manuscripts, and the Portland Collection, University of Nottingham, contain the most frequently cited manuscripts, especially letters.

An Collins

(floruit circa 1653)

Eugene R. Cunnar
New Mexico State University

BOOK: *Divine Songs and Meditacions* (London: Printed by R. Bishop, 1653); abridged facsimile published as *An. Collins Divine Songs and Meditacions (1653),* edited by Stanley N. Stewart (Los Angeles: William Andrews Clark Memorial Library, University of California, 1961).

An Collins's *Divine Songs and Meditacions* (1653) represents one of the first significant religious publications by a woman. Her volume, composed of numerous religious songs and poetic meditations, reveals the difficulties that women had to overcome in order to publish and how they could employ religious writing to begin creating their own voice. In "The Preface" she tells the reader that some have objected to her effort: "Yet this cannot prevail to hinder me / From publishing those truths I do intend." Her work captures the beginnings of a feminine sensitivity expressed as a positive statement of the empowerment that her religious experiences and writing gave her.

The only biographical information available about Collins comes from her "To the Reader," "The Preface," "The Discourse," and other poems in *Divine Songs and Meditacions,* and any discussion of her life is necessarily speculative. In "To the Reader" she says that she has "been restrained from bodily employments" because of chronic ill health that apparently began in childhood. To ease her mind she turned first to "prophane Histories" but found no relief. In writing religious verse, however, she experienced a "peacefull temper, and spirituall calmness." She explains, "To be brief, I became affected to Poetry, insomuch that I proceeded to practise the same; and though the helps I had therein were small, yet the thing it self appeared unto me so amiable, as that it enflamed my faculties, to put forth themselves, in a practise so pleasing." In both "The Preface" and "The Discourse" she expands on these statements and develops a Protestant theology influenced by Calvinism. She explains in "The Pref-

ace" that the volume is the result of her "morning exercise," her devotions and meditations on how God deals with his creatures. In an apologetic and humble tone she says of her verse,

Now touching that I hasten to expresse
Concerning these, the ofspring of my mind,
Who though they here appeare in homly dresse
And as they are my works, I do not find
But ranked with others, they may go behind,
Yet for theyr matter, I suppose they bee
Not worthlesse quite, while they with Truth agree.

Nevertheless, she expresses hope because God reveals himself "To his elect in divers Dispensacions." Working from the Protestant tradition of individual biblical interpretation, she states her intention to publish religious truth as she perceives it. She also tells her reader that her own sorrows have produced these poems: "So sorrow serv'd but as springing raine / To ripen fruits, indowments of the minde."

"The Discourse" is a poem of 102 stanzas in which the author provides more autobiographical information as well as a long poetic account of her Protestant theology – a daring feat for a woman at the time. Although her poems were initially intended for private use, she hopes that they will be as spiritually beneficial and morally edifying to others as they have been for her. On another level the poems are meant to be praises to God for sustaining her through a lifelong chronic illness by giving her a Job-like patience: "Even in my Cradle did my Crosses breed, / And so grew up with me, unto this day." She further justifies her publication by arguing that "by the mouths of sucking babes doth he [God], / Reveal his power, and immortall fame." Thus, if her verses will cause others to read the biblical passages she invokes as well as help them to be pious and bear their own crosses, then the difficulties have been worthwhile.

The following long section of "The Discourse" further develops her Protestant theology. She be-

Title page for Collins's only book, a collection of religious verse that grew out of her daily devotions and meditations

gins by professing her belief in the Trinity, stating that God is "A mistrey past all imagination." She acknowledges that "Touching my selfe and others, I conceive, / That all men are by nature dead in sin." Although not an explicit statement of Calvinistic total depravity, this is a concept that Collins frequently repeats. For her, Christ's sacrifice becomes the major means by which salvation is achieved. She also emphasizes, however, the roles of the Word and grace: "His word doth take when grace shall have possession, / For by the word no good effect is wrought / But where the heart is by Gods spirit taught." She defines faith as "a Grace which doth the soul refine, / Wrought by the Holy-Ghost in contrite hearts, / And grounded on Gods promise divine." Collins analyzes the process of faith as when

First God doth take the hammer of the Law,
And breaks the heart which he for Grace will fitt
Then the seduced soul is brought in aw,
And doth immediately it selfe submitt,
When sight of sinne, and sorrowing for it,
Hath wrought humility, a vertu rare
Which truly doth the soul for Grace prepare.

In the next ten stanzas she paraphrases and comments on the Ten Commandments, suggesting that each person must examine his life against these moral laws.

The last thirty-four stanzas of this poem outline and discuss the Protestant paradigm for salvation. She discusses the need to examine conscience in order to institute "Saving faith" and experience "th'assurance of his Love." In order to have assurance, the sinner must practice "Repentance with

Sincerity" as well as prayer and praise of God. This is necessary because of "sinne Original, / Corruption of our nature we it call." Given the burden of original sin, she addresses those "dispairing of salvation." Then she argues that "By Faith in Christ much profit we do gain, / For thereby only are we justified, / And thereby only are we sanctifide." According to Collins, justification and sanctification are dependent on God's grace: "To be accepted as for just indeed, / With God, whose grace it is that justifies." Sinners cannot achieve this state through good works or their own efforts: "Then far from doing any work whereby / They might deserve Salvation on their part." Nevertheless, she writes that "Though by good works we do not gain Salvacion / Yet these good Duties that our God requires." For Collins, sanctification involves a "quickening to holinesse" that produces a spiritual "renovacion." This process, however, is never completed in earthly life because "continuall combates will arise, / Between Gods image, on the soul renewede, / And Sathans image." She concludes by stating that sinners must constantly fight temptation and, although undeserving, will receive God's grace.

Collins's poems and meditations must be read against her own exposition of theology. Her work resembles a spiritual autobiography in which she has examined her own conscience, suffering, and pain. From this perspective her work is within the larger tradition of Protestant meditational verse written by George Herbert, Henry Vaughan, Thomas Traherne, and others. According to Louis Martz in *The Meditative Poem* (1963), the "central meditative action consists of an interior drama, in which a man projects a self upon a mental stage, and there comes to understand that self in the light of a divine presence." While Collins's meditative poetry clearly functions within this concept, it also is distinctively Protestant as Barbara Kiefer Lewalski has defined Protestant meditations (*Protestant Poetics and the Seventeenth-Century Religious Lyric,* 1979). While Collins seems familiar with Ignatian and Salesian forms of meditation, she clearly modifies those forms according to the Protestant prescriptions of focusing on the Word of God and by applying that Word to oneself. One of her major themes revolves around the necessary resignation of the will to God in order to overcome physical and mental suffering and achieve a sense of peace. Another major theme that emerges in her verse is the sudden happiness or bliss that comes about through grace.

Although her autobiographical work resembles the poetical and spiritual diaries of Puritans, it

nevertheless displays a variety of metrical practices and structural approaches to religious verse that give it a distinct sense of craft. For example, the long metrical "Preface" is written in rhyme royal while other poems employ different types of stanzaic and metrical approaches that were traditional to songs, ballads, and imitations of the Psalms. Although her poems are not structured as formal meditations, she develops major themes of retirement from this world, union with Christ, and corollary themes of moderation and patience. In seeking solace and peace from personal and public conflict, she tells her reader that she experiences spiritual regeneration through the act of writing. Frequently these themes are presented in biblical images of dark and light, drought and fruition, winter and spring, derived from both the Old and New Testaments.

In "A Song expressing their happinesse who have Communion with Christ," Collins develops the metaphor of the wintertime of the soul caused by her sorrows. Only a call from God will bring spring:

> He too, thats Lord of all
>   Will thee beloved call,
> Though all else prove unkind;
>   Then chearfull may I sing
> Sith I enjoy the Spring,
>   Though Sesterns dry I find.

The union with God fills the soul with bliss and allows one to "beare their Crosse." The distressed soul, following Canticles, must say to God, "Open to me my Love, / My Sister, and my Dove."

In "A Song shewing the Mercies of God to his people, by interlacing cordiall Comforts with fatherly Chastisments," Collins again uses the metaphor of spiritual winter:

> So though that in the Winter
> Of sharp Afflictions, fruits seem to dy,
> And for that space, the life of Grace
> Remayneth in the Root only.

Christ, however,

> Shall make Summer with us, our spirits to chear,
> Warming our hearts with the sense of his favour,
> Then must our flowers of piety savour,
> And then the fruits of righteousnesse
> We to the glory of God must expresse.

Those fruits are Collins's poems.

In "This Song showeth that God is the strength of his People, whence they have support and comfort," Collins develops the metaphor of "God is the Rock of his Elect / In whom his grace is incoate." As the rock of strength and love, God provides spiritual succor and nourishment:

> Therfore my soule do thou depend,
> Upon that Rock which will not move,
> When all created help shall end
> My Rock impregnable will prove,
> Whom still embrace with ardent Love.

The metaphor allows her effectively to contrast her own instability with God's stability.

In a variation on the theme of spiritual winter, Collins in "Another Song" manipulates the metaphor in a witty and moving way. She begins with "The Winter of my infancy being over-past" as she waits for spring and spiritual renewal. However, when spring arrives and nature blooms, she says, "But in my Spring it was not so" because "a comfortlesse Eclips, / Disconsolation and sore vexacion, / My blossom nips." Subsequently she discovers consolation in her meditations:

> Yet as a garden is my mind enclosed fast
> Being to safety so confind from storm and blast
> Apt to produce a fruit most rare,
> That is not common with every woman
> That fruitfull are.

Because Collins was most likely unmarried and childless, she found succor in producing her verse. In doing so she, like other women writers such as Margaret Cavendish, recovers for women's verse the traditional male appropriation of the creativity/childbirth trope.

In her five poetic meditations Collins reveals that she clearly understands the structure of formal meditations when in "The first meditacion" she writes that "The Understanding, Will, Affections cleare, / Each part of Soule and Body instantly / Losing their purity, corrupted were." It is also clear, however, that she modifies the formal structure to fit her own experiences as filtered through her Protestantism. In that meditation she contemplates the Fall and its manifestations in current sinfulness, a state in which "The Conscience sleeps, the Soule is dead in sin." The wakening of conscience leads her to consider God's mercies to the sinner and the subsequent need to purify oneself:

> Each member of thy body thou dost guide,
> Then exercise them in Gods service most
> Let every part be thoroughly sanctifide
> As a meet Temple for the Holy Ghost;

> Sin must not in our mortall bodies raign
> It must expelled be although with pain.

In "The Preamble" to "The second Meditacion," the reader is told that the work was written in a state of misery and depression. As Collins contemplates God's mercies in the meditation itself, she receives consolations for her sufferings so that "Gods Favour toward me is hereby proved, / For that he hath not quite dejected me." She concludes by stating that

> Who can his servants from all troubles free
> And would I know my Crosses all prevent,
> But that he knowes them to be good for me
> Therefore I am resolv'd to be content,
> For though I meet with many Contradictions
> Yet Grace doth alwayes sweeten my Afflictions.

Overall, Collins perceives her sufferings and tribulations as trials sent by God. In "The third Meditacion" she explains,

> So it is no small mercy, though we see
> Gods Countenance not alwaies shining bright
> That by the same our minds enlightened be,
> And our affections guided by that Light,
> And whilst the winter-fruits as it were we find
> In Pacience, Sufferings, and Peace of mind.

Her resignation to God's will and her contemplation of his mercy leads her to understand and accept her situation better: "But wait till God do manifest his grace, / For thy deliverance, prefix no day, / But patiently the Lords due leisure stay."

In "The fourth Meditacion" she explores the extremes that those who suffer often take. On the one hand are those who are "too light takeing thy Distresse," while on the other are those who express "hopelesse Greife or Pensivenesse." The first group will never learn to see their tribulations in the proper perspective and will not have a means of achieving spiritual health. The second group will wallow in self-pity and despair. According to Collins the proper way to approach one's sufferings is to see them as part of God's plan or punishments meant to try the soul. One should "Endeavour in the right way to be led, / With tru Repentance, hope of pardon join." In this endeavor Collins realizes that "Whereas if God his blessing doth restrain / We by the creature can no help attain"; that is, one is dependent on God's grace and not one's self. All the sinner can do is "to lowest thoughts thy self retire, / To seek the cause that moved God to ire." Next, the sinner can "look to Christ, who doth thy weaknesse view / And of compassion will thy strength renew."

Collins reiterates similar themes in "The fifth Meditacion," which focuses on the mysterious workings of God's grace and love:

The fruits of this his Love or Favour deare,
Are likewise called Graces everywhere,
Election and redemption, graces are,
And these his Favour cheifly do declare.

Life without God's grace is compared to life at the North Pole:

Who should inhabit neare the Northern-Pole,
Though Moon & Stars may there apear most bright
Yet while the Sun is absent, still tis night,
And therefore barren, cold, and comfortlesse,
Vnfit for humane creatures to possesse.

No earthly comfort or wealth can compare to God's graces, according to Collins. She concludes by advocating that the sinner purge out sin, have faith in Christ, love God, and practice patience.

The one explicit political poem in the collection, "A Song composed in time of Civill Warr, when the wicked did much insult over the godly," laments what the "Foes of Truth" have done to religion and society. The poem is allusive in terms of identifying the historical foes and Collins's specific politics. Inspired by Satan, these foes "The Soule to circumvent / In that they seeds of Error sow / And to false Worships tempt, / And Scripture falsly they apply / Their Errors to maintain." Her attack on those "who no Religion prise, / But carnall Liberty" may be implicit criticism of the Cavaliers and their notorious life-style. Whatever Collins's specific political position, it is clear that the foes of religion aflict the "Saints," who are "most severely try'd." Insofar as the poem addresses the political conflicts of the period, it is a daring authorization of the female voice to speak to such issues.

Nothing was known of Collins's reputation until short selections from her volume were included in an anthology, *Restituta* (1814–1816), edited by Sir Samuel Egerton Brydges. Samuel Austin Allibone included a brief reference to her in *A Critical Dictionary of English Literature* (1859–1871). The only known copy of her poems is that in the Henry E. Huntington Memorial Library, a selection of which has been edited by Stanley N. Stewart. Only in the late twentieth century have scholars once again recognized her poems, which are now seen as serious examples of the obstacles encountered and overcome by women writers in the seventeenth century as well as serious expressions of women's religious experiences.

References:

Elspeth Graham, Hilary Hinds, Elaine Hobby, and Helen Wilcox, eds., *Her Own Life: Autobiographical Writings by Seventeenth-Century Englishwomen* (London: Routledge, 1989), pp. 54–57;

Germaine Greer, Susan Hastings, Jeslyn Medoff, and Melinda Sansone, eds., *Kissing the Rod: An Anthology of Seventeenth-Century Women's Verse* (London: Virago Press, 1988; New York: Farrar, Straus & Giroux, 1989), pp. 148–154;

Elaine Hobby, *Virtue of Necessity: English Women's Writing 1649–88* (Ann Arbor: University of Michigan Press, 1989), pp. 59–62;

Stanley N. Stewart, Introduction to *An. Collins Divine Songs and Meditacions (1653),* edited by Stewart (Los Angeles: William Andrews Clark Memorial Library, University of California, 1961), pp. i–iii.

Charles Cotton
(28 April 1630 – February 1687)

Jean Gagen
University of Kansas

BOOKS: *A Panegyrick to the King's Most Excellent Majesty* (London: Printed by Tho. Newcomb, 1660);

The Valiant Knight (London: Printed for J. Johnson, 1663);

The Morall Philosophy of the Stoicks, Guillaume Du Vair's *Philosophie morale des Stoïques*, translated by Cotton (London: Printed for Henry Mortlock, 1664);

Scarronides; or, Virgile Travestie. A Mock-Poem. Being the First Book of Virgils Æneis in English, Burlesque (London: Printed by E. Cotes for Henry Brome, 1664);

Scarronnides; or, Virgile Travestie. A Mock-Poem in Imitation of the First and Fourth Books of Virgil's Æneis in English; Burlésque (London: Printed by J. C. for Henry Brome, 1670);

The History of the Life of the Duke of Espernon, the Great Favourite of France. Englished by Charles Cotton, Esq. (London: Printed by E. Cotes & A. Clark for Henry Brome, 1670);

Horace, A French Tragedy of Monsieur Corneille. Englished by Charles Cotton, Esq. (London: Printed for Henry Brome, 1671);

The Commentaries of Messire Blaize de Montluc, Mareschal of France, translated by Cotton (London: Printed by Andrew Clark for Henry Brome, 1674);

The Fair One of Tunis; Or, The Generous Mistress; A New Piece of Gallantry. Out of French, translated by Cotton (London: Printed for Henry Brome, 1674);

The Compleat Gamester (London: Printed by A. M. for R. Cutler, sold by Henry Brome, 1674);

Burlesque Upon Burlesque; or, The Scoffer Scoft. Being Some of Lucian's Dialogues, Newly Put Into English Fustian (London: Printed for Henry Brome, 1675);

The Planter's Manual: Being Instructions for the Raising, Planting and Cultivating All Sorts of Fruit-Trees (London: Printed for Henry Brome, 1675);

The Universal Angler, Made So, By Three Books of Fishing: The First Written by Mr. Izaak Walton, The

Charles Cotton, circa 1667 (portrait by Peter Lely; from John Beresford, ed., Poems of Charles Cotton, *1923)*

Second by Charles Cotton, Esq, The Third by Col. Robert Venables, all which may be bound together, or sold each of them severally (London: Printed for Richard Marriott, 1676);

The Wonders of the Peake (London: Printed for Joanna Brome, 1681);

Essays of Michael, Seigneur de Montaigne, 3 volumes, translated by Cotton (London: Printed for T. Basset, M. Gilliflower & W. Hensman, 1685–1686).

Editions: *Poems on Several Occasions* (London: Printed for Tho. Basset, Will. Hensman & Tho. Fox, 1689);

Beresford Hall, Cotton's ancestral home (engraving by John Linnell for an 1815 edition of The Compleat Angler*)*

Memoirs of the Sieur de Pontis, translated by Cotton (London: Printed by F. Leach for James Knapton, 1694).

The Genuine Works of Charles Cotton, Esq. (London: Printed for R. Bonwicke & others, 1715);

Poems of Charles Cotton, 1630–1687, edited by John Beresford (London: R. Cobden-Sanderson, 1923; New York: Boni & Liveright, 1923);

Poems of Charles Cotton, edited by John Buxton (London: Routledge & Kegan Paul, 1958; Cambridge, Mass.: Harvard University Press, 1958).

Charles Cotton entered the world under unusually propitious circumstances. His father, Charles Cotton the Elder, was considered to be the model of a gentleman and was on friendly terms with many poets of distinction, including Ben Jonson, Sir Henry Wotton, John Donne, Robert Herrick, Sir William Davenant, and Richard Lovelace. Young Charles was also descended from aristocratic stock on his mother's side. Olive Stanhope Cotton was the only daughter and heiress of Sir John Stanhope and his wife Alivia Beresford Stan-

hope. It was through his mother that Charles eventually inherited Beresford Hall, located on the borders of Staffordshire and Derbyshire. At his ancestral home on the banks of the river Dover, surrounded by mountains, valleys, and moorlands, the poet would live for most of his life. Cotton's physical environment fostered a love of nature just as his social and cultural background fostered an appreciation for literature, especially poetry.

He was born on 28 April 1630 at Beresford Hall. Little is known about Cotton's childhood and youth, though his father apparently took great interest in his only son's education. Whether he attended Cambridge or Oxford is unknown, but his prose and poetry reveal thorough training in Greek, Latin, French, and Italian. Cotton wrote his best poetry during the Restoration; yet his verse is not stamped by any particular poetic movement or period. The clarity, freshness, and honesty of Cotton's poetry are the traits most frequently praised, as well as his penchant for graphic description.

Whether or not he intended to become known as a poet, financial difficulties forced him to devote

Why was not th'etyre dust in prodigious formes
To grone in thunder, and to weepe in stormes?
 Had (as at some mens fall) why did his
In Nature worke a Metamorphosis?
Noe, hee was gentle; and his fayre soule went
A sylent vigtime t'heaven, whence t'was sent.
Ledyes weepe, lament greate Hastings fall
Perfections buried at his Funerall:
Bath him in teares till there appeare no trace
Of these sad blushes in his lovely face.
That there be int of guilt no seeming sence
Nor other Colour then of innocence:
For, hee was wise, and good, though hee was young
Well suited to the stock from whence hee sprung;
And what in Youth is ignorance, and vice
In him proved piety of an excellent price.

Farewell (deare Lord) and since thy body must
In time returne to its first matter; dust:
Rest in thy melancholy Tomb in peace, for who
would longer live that could but now dye so?

Charles Cotton.

Second page of the manuscript for Cotton's first published poem, "An Elegie upon the Lord Hastings," one of two poems surviving in Cotton's hand (Yale University Library, MS. Vault. Shelves. Cotton; CnC 18) much of his time to more lucrative prose. He published many translations, compilations, and commentaries that reveal the breadth and depth of his knowledge. He managed to write a large amount of poetry in spite of these other pursuits, although most of it remained unpublished during his lifetime. Many of his early poems were commendatory verses of no real distinction. His first published poem was an elegy appearing in Richard Brome's *Lachrymae Musarum* (1649), a volume occasioned by the death of Henry, Lord Hastings. There were several distinguished contributors to this volume, including Herrick and John Dryden. Among his early verses Cotton's strongest poem is undoubtedly "An Invitation to Phillis," written in imitation of Christopher Marlowe's "Come live with me and be my love" (1599).

Cotton married his cousin Isabella Hutchinson in 1656 despite family opposition because of the close blood relationship. The marriage was apparently a happy one. While Cotton was on a trip to the Continent before his marriage, he may have written "The Retreat" for Isabella. In this love poem of three neatly turned quintets, the poet pays tribute to the beauty of his beloved in a fresh and humorous way:

> I am return'd, my Fair, but see
> Perfection in none but thee,
>   Yet many Beauties have I seen,
>   And in that search a Truant been,
> Through fruitless curiositie.

As a result of his search, the speaker concludes "That all, but I, in love are blinde, / And none but thee, divinely fair." He further claims that

>   now grown wise
> All objects, but thy face, despise;
>   Taught by my folly now I swear,
>   If you forgive mee nere to erre
> Nor seek impossibilities.

Another poem, "The Separation," undoubtedly refers to the family opposition Cotton and Isabella encountered during their courtship. The speaker of the poem rails against "superstitious Laws! / That us from our mutuall embraces tear, / And separate our blouds, becaus too near."

Unfortunately Isabella died young in April 1669, leaving five of the children she had borne, including a son. Cotton's father had died the previous year, leaving the poet an estate encumbered by debt. Conveniently, Cotton's second wife was a wealthy widow, Dame Mary, Countess Dowager of Ardglass, whom he married shortly before 1675. Even with the considerable means she brought to him, the poet still suffered from the financial carelessness of his father.

Fortunately Cotton's first marriage had been free of financial problems, and during these years he probably wrote some of his most cheerful verse, including the four poems on a summer day: "Morning Quatrains," "Noon Quatrains," "Evening Quatrains," and "Night Quatrains." In the first poem he describes homely rural scenes with mythological allusions:

> Now through the morning doors behold
> *Phœbus* array'd in burning Gold,
> Lashing his fiery Steeds, displays
> His warm and all enlight'ning Rays.

When the sun reaches its zenith in the "Noon Quatrains," however, the heat becomes almost unendurable. The speaker predicts that if there is no respite,

>   our fertile Lands,
> Will soon be turn'd to parched Sands,
> And not an Onion that will grow
> Without a *Nile* to overflow.

The poet compares the sun to kings "Who mildly do begin to reign, / But to the *Zenith* got of pow'r, / Those whom they should protect devour." The people who seek refuge from the heat in underground cellars and grottoes are compared to persecuted Christians, who, "When Pagan Tyranny grew hot," sought shelter in "the dark but friendly womb / Of unknown Subterranean *Rome*." After a few scorching hours, the power of the sun wanes, and "In a more mild and temp'rate Ray / We may again enjoy the day."

In the "Evening Quatrains" the steeds of the sun have become so tired and thirsty that they can "Scarce lug the Chariot down the Hill." The setting sun casts long shadows, so "That Brambles like tall Cedars show, / Mole-hills seem Mountains, and the Ant / Appears a monstrous Elephant." A small flock of sheep now "Shades thrice the ground that it would stock," while the small shepherd "Appears a mighty *Polypheme*." The remainder of the poem shows the completion of a day's work. The sheep are brought into the fold; clothing that was left to dry on the hedges is brought in; the bees are hived; the cock stands on his roost; and "The Sow's fast pegg'd within the Sty." After everyone "has had his Supping Mess," the dishes are washed and left "Rear'd up against the Milk-house Wall" to dry.

Charles Cotton, circa 1674 (portrait by Edmund Ashfield; Collection of Samuel W. Lambert, Jr., New York)

And now on Benches all are sat
In the cool Air to sit and chat,
Till *Phœbus,* dipping in the West,
Shall lead the World the way to Rest.

"Night Quatrains" also features vivid imagery, such as "Nights sable Steeds," which "mount the Sky" and "Ravish all Colour from the Eye." The first eleven stanzas emphasize the intensity of the darkness, followed by a series of typical night sounds: "lustful Cats make ill-tun'd Love"; a "watchful Nurse sings Lullabies"; "*Haggs* meet to mumble o'er their Charms"; and "The Drunkard now supinely snores, / His load of Ale sweats through his Pores."

While these verses depict the calm beauty of nature, some of Cotton's best-known poems deal with its violence. In the fifty-three stanzas of "Winter Quatrains," the season is memorably rendered as an invader from the sea intending "To ravish from our fruitful Fields / All that the teeming Season yields." The visual imagery is remarkably graphic. The first thirty-eight stanzas describe "Winter and all his blust'ring train" aboard a ship, which on reaching land "Vomits her burthen" of ice and snow, binding "The Earth in Shining chains." From the thirty-ninth stanza to the conclusion of the poem, the mood shifts from terror to tranquillity, for the people threatened by Winter have retreated to an underground fortress where they have "a Magazine / of Sovereign juice" sufficient to sustain them even if "*Phœbus* ne're return again." Protected from the storm,

we together jovial sit
Careless, and Crown'd with Mirth and Wit;
Where though bleak Winds confine us home,
Our Fancy round the World shall roam.

Through "the plump Grapes Immortal Juice" and the power of imagination,

The Brave shall triumph in Success,
The Lover shall have Mistresses,
Poor unregarded Virtue Praise,
And the Neglected Poet Baies.

For these revelers the fury of "Old Winter" is merely their sport as long as "Sack and Claret Man the Fort."

In the final stanza there is a lighthearted political reference in the suggestion that Winter turn his attention to Scotland and there "Confine the plotting Presbyter; / His Zeal may Freeze, whilst we kept warm / With Love and Wine, can know no harm." Although Cotton was a Royalist, he was apparently never embroiled in the Civil War, and this is one of the rare political allusions in his poetry. It has been suggested that Winter's ravishment of the land may represent the Presbyter destruction of much that Cotton and the Royalists considered beautiful in England.

Another nature poem, "The Storm," is distinguished by Cotton's use of rhyming pentameter couplets. Reminiscing about a sea voyage, the speaker describes a beautiful May day and a calm sea, a setting with no portent of disaster. "All nature seemed to court us to our woe," the speaker muses, for as soon as his ship had passed out of the still harbor, "the false wind (that seem'd so chaste before) / The Ship's lac'd smock began to stretch and tear." The violence of the storm increased until even

Men born and bred at sea, did ne're behold
Neptune in such prodigious furrows roll'd;
Those winds which with the loudest terror roar
Never so stretched their lungs and cheeks before[.]

The narrator and other passengers are so fearful "T'was strange our little Pink" was "not sunk with weight of our despair." After ten hours the "rude Tempest" abates, and the ship is able to return safely to its point of departure. The speaker knows, however, that "The dangers we escap'd must tempt agen."

Some of Cotton's best poems are addressed to Izaak Walton, author of *The Compleat Angler* (1653). So close was the relationship of the two men that Cotton called Walton "father" and Walton called Cotton "son." A poem dated 17 January 1673, "To my Old and most Worthy Friend, Mr. Izaak Walton, on his Life of Dr. Donne, etc.," is a tribute both to Walton and to four of his *Lives:* Donne (1640), Wotton (1651), Richard Hooker (1665), and George Herbert (1670). Although Cotton recognizes that "their great works . . . can never dye,"

only Walton's biographies of these men can show "how th' Almighties grace, / . . . / Brought them to be the Organs of his praise." Cotton's poem, written in triplets, also praises Walton for his impartiality:

Your pen, disdaining to be brib'd or prest,
Flows without vanity or interest:
A Vertue with which few good Pens are blest.

In the penultimate stanza, Cotton declares, "I ask no more of Fame" than to be known as Walton's "*true Friend.*"

A poem written in quatrains, "To my dear and most worthy Friend, Mr. Izaak Walton," is one of many in which Cotton complains of the "cold and blust'ring Clime" that prevailed in the winter where his ancestral home was located. This particular season is the "roughest" in many a year, but Cotton is comforted at the thought "That in a better Clime than this / You our dear Friend have more repose." He is also comforted by knowing that nature will soon smile again. "We'll recompense an Age of these / Foul days in one fine fishing day," Cotton predicts. Perhaps they may even have a week to try their skill "With the most deadly killing Flie." On some day with "A warm, but not a scorching Sun," they will wait "behind some bush," their aim, "The Scaly People to betray." Cotton concludes on a mournful note:

This (my best Friend) at my poor Home
Shall be our Pastime and our Theme,
But then should you not deign to come
You make all this a flatt'ring Dream.

"Contentation. Directed to my Dear Father, and most Worthy Friend, Mr. Izaak Walton" is a comparatively long poem in quatrains that, despite its title, directs no personal remarks to Walton. Cotton is concerned here with what brings contentment and begins by citing false ways of seeking peace. For example, those who vie for wealth and power often miss "the sweets of Life." Likewise, men who engage in public business are often betrayed "Through Labyrinths of policy, / To crooked and forbidden ways." Since the "beaten Roads" are "yet so slippery, withal, / . . . / Untrodden paths are then the best." The happiest person is one

Who from the busie World retires,
To be more useful to it still,
And to no greater good aspires,
But only the eschewing ill.

Nothing is closer to Cotton's personal ideal of contentment than the person "Who, with his Angle, and his Books, / Can think the longest day well spent."

Cotton's poem "The Retirement. Stanzes Irreguliers To Mr. Izaak Walton" was published at Walton's request in *The Universal Angler* (1676). This volume, the fifth edition of Walton's *Compleat Angler*, was the first to include Cotton's prose "instructions" on "how to angle for trout or grayling in a clear stream," also known as part 2 of Walton's original treatise. "The Retirement" is a tribute to the beauty of the natural surroundings of Cotton's ancestral estate. The piece also reveals much about the poet's temperament, especially his love of solitude and the quiet life:

> How calm and quiet a delight
>   It is, alone
> To read, and meditate, and write,
> By none offended, nor offending none[.]

Despite the severe cold of the winter and the excessive heat of the summer, Cotton writes he is so happy at Beresford that he could live contented there for "sixty full years" and then "contented die."

Cotton was apparently living at Beresford as late as 1686, but he was in London when he died in February the following year and is listed in the burial register of Saint James Church, Piccadilly. At the time of his death, Cotton was known, if at all, for his translations and burlesques, most of his poetry having been circulated only among close friends. The first collection of his verse, *Poems on Several Occasions* (1689), was not published until two years after his death.

In the nineteenth century Cotton's poems drew some distinguished admirers, including William Wordsworth, Charles Lamb, and James Russell Lowell. Perhaps the poet's most notable advocate was Samuel Taylor Coleridge, who in his *Biographia Literaria* (1817) described the best of Cotton's verse as "replete with every excellence of thought, image and passion" and "so worded, that the reader sees no reason either in the selection or the order of the words, why he might not have said the very same in an appropriate conversation, and cannot conceive how indeed he could have expressed such thoughts otherwise, without loss or injury to his meaning."

Biographies:

Alexander Chalmers, "The Life of Charles Cotton," in volume 6 of *The Works of the English Poets from Chaucer to Cowper*, edited by Chalmers (London: Printed for J. Johnson & others, 1810; facsimile, Hildesheim & New York: Georg Olms, 1970), pp. 699–701;

Thomas Campbell, "Charles Cotton," in volume 4 of *Specimens of the British Poets*, edited by Campbell (London: J. Murray, 1819), pp. 293–316;

Charles Jacob Sembower, *The Life and the Poetry of Charles Cotton* (Philadelphia: University of Pennsylvania / New York: Appleton, 1911).

Abraham Cowley

(1618 – 28 July 1667)

Thomas O. Calhoun
University of Delaware

BOOKS: *Poetical Blossomes* (London: Printed by Bernard Alsop & Thomas Fawcett for Henry Seile, 1633); second edition, enlarged to include *Sylva,* published as *Poeticall Blossomes* (London: Printed by Elizabeth Purslowe for Henry Seile, 1636; third edition, London: Printed by Elizabeth Purslowe for Henry Seile, 1637);

Loves Riddle. A Pastorall Comædie (London: Printed by John Dawson for Henry Seile, 1638): adapted by Daniel Bellamy as *The Rival Nymphs, or, The Merry Swain* (London: Printed by E. Say for the Author, 1723);

Naufragium Joculare, Comædia (London: Printed for Henry Seile, 1638); translated by Charles Johnson as *Fortune In Her Wits* (London: Printed for Bernard Lintott, 1705); adapted by Daniel Bellamy, Jr., and Daniel Bellamy as *The Perjur'd Devotee: or, The Force of Love. A Comedy* (London, 1741);

The Prologue and Epilogue to a Comedie [*The Guardian*] (London: Printed by Francis Cole for James Calvin, 1642);

A Satyre Against Seperatists [*The Puritans Lecture*], as A. C. Generosus (London: Printed for A. C., 1642); republished with *Ad Populum* in 1660, 1675, and with full attribution to Cowley in 1678; second edition published as *A Satyre Against Separatists* (London: Printed for A. C., 1642); republished in *The Foure Ages of England* (London, 1648);

A Satyre. The Puritan and the Papist. By A Scholler in Oxford (Oxford: Henry Hall, 1643); excerpted in *The Character of a Moderate Intelligencer* (London, 1647) and reprinted under Cowley's name in *Wit and Loyalty Reviv'd* (London: Printed for W. Davies, 1682); a second edition, under the same title but without title page, appeared in 1643; third edition published as *Sampsons Foxes Agreed to Fire a Kingdom: or, the Jesuit, and the Puritan, met in a Round, to Put a Kingdom Out of Square* (circa 1644);

The Mistresse (London: Printed by William Wilson for Humphrey Moseley, 1647; second edition, 1647); revised and expanded as *The Mistress,* in *Poems* (1656);

The Guardian. A Comedie (London: Printed by Thomas Newcomb for John Holden, 1650);

Poems (London: Printed by Thomas Newcomb for Humphrey Moseley, 1656; facsimile, Scolar, 1971) — includes *Miscellanies, Anacreontiques, The Mistress, Pindarique Odes, Davideis,* and "Davideidos liber primus"; posthumously reprinted, with changes made by Cowley's literary executor Thomas Sprat, in *The Works of Mr. Abraham Cowley;* "Davideidos liber primus" republished as *Davideidos Sacri Poematis operis imperfecti, liber unus,* in *Poemata Latina* (1668);

Ode, Upon the Blessed Restoration and Returne of His Sacred Majestie, Charls the Second (London: Printed for Henry Herringman, 1660); republished as "Ode. Upon his Majesty's Restoration and Return," in *Verses, Written Upon Several Occasions* (1663);

The Visions and Prophecies Concerning England, Scotland, and Ireland, as Ezekiel Grebner (London: Printed for Henry Herringman, 1661); republished as *A Vision, Concerning His Late Pretended Highnesse Cromwell, the Wicked* (London: Printed for Henry Herringman, 1661); republished as "A Discourse By Way of Vision Concerning the Government of Oliver Cromwell," in *The Works of Mr. Abraham Cowley;* excerpted in "The Definition of a Tyrant," in *A Fifth Collection of Papers Relating to the Present Juncture of Affairs in England* (London, 1688); and *The Learned and Loyal Abraham Cowley's Definition of a Tyrant* (London, 1688); verse extracts republished as "A True and Faithful Narrative of Oliver Cromwell's Compact with the Devil," in *Eachard's History of England,* second edition (London, 1720); republished in *Enthusiasm Display'd* (London, 1743);

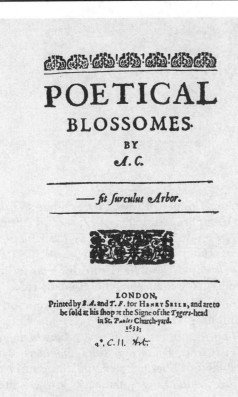

Frontispiece and title page for Cowley's first collection of verse, prepared for publication when he was thirteen and published two years later

A Proposition for the Advancement of Learning (London: Printed by J. M. for Henry Herringman, 1661); republished, with new dedicatory material, as *A Proposition for the Advancement of Experimental Philosophy* (1661);

A. Covleii Plantarum Libri Duo (Londini: Typis J. Flesher & Prostant apud Nath. Brooks, 1662); expanded to six books as *Plantarum,* in *Poemata Latina* (London, 1668); sixth book of *Plantarum* translated as *Plantarum. Being A Poem upon the late Rebellion, the Happy Restoration of His Sacred Majesty, and the Dutch War Ensuing* (London: Printed for Samuel Walsall, 1680); republished as *An Heroick Poem. Upon the Late Horrid Rebellion* (London: Printed for T. D., 1683); another translation "by several hands" published as *Six Books of Plants,* in *The Second Part of the Works of Mr. Abraham Cowley*; republished as *Cowley's History of Plants* (London: Printed and sold by J. Smeeton, 1795);

Cutter of Coleman-Street. A Comedy (London: Printed for Henry Herringman, 1663);

Verses, Written Upon Several Occasions (London: Printed for Henry Herringman, 1663); republished as *Verses, Lately Written Upon Several Occasions* (London: Printed for Henry Herringman,

1663); enlarged as *Verses, Lately Written Upon Several Occasions . . . To Which is Added A Proposition for the Advancement of Experimental Philosophy* (London: Printed for Henry Herringman, 1663);

Abraham Couleij Angli, Poemata Latina (Londini: Typis T. Roycroft, Impensis Jo. Martyn, 1668); second edition (Londini: Typis M. Clark, Impensis Jo. Martyn, 1678);

A Poem of the Late Civil War (London: Printed for Langly Curtis, 1679).

Editions: *The Works of Mr. Abraham Cowley* (London: Printed by John Macocke for Henry Herringman, 1668 – includes *Several Discourses by Way of Essays in Verse and Prose*; reprinted, 1668, 1669, 1672, 1674, 1678, 1680, 1681, 1681, 1684, 1688, 1700, 1708, 1710, 1721);

The Second Part of the Works of Mr. Abraham Cowley (London: Printed by Mary Clark for Charles Harper & Jacob Tonson, 1681; reprinted, 1681, 1684) – enlarged to include *The Third Part of the Works of Mr. Abraham Cowley* (1689; reprinted, 1700, 1708, 1711, 1721);

Select Works of Mr. A. Cowley, 2 volumes, edited by Richard Hurd (London: Printed by W. Boyer & J. Nichols for T. Cadell, 1772);

The Poetical Works of Abraham Cowley, 4 volumes, edited by John Bell, Poets of Great Britain Complete from Chaucer to Churchill, 36–39 (Edinburgh: Printed at the Apollo Press by the Martins, 1777);

Prose Works of Abraham Cowley, Esq. Including His Essays in Verse and Prose (London: Pickering, 1826);

The Complete Works in Verse and Prose of Abraham Cowley, 2 volumes, edited by Alexander B. Grosart (Edinburgh: Constable, 1881);

Cowley's Prose Works, edited by J. Rawson Lumby (Cambridge: University Press, 1887); revised by Arthur Tilley as *Cowley's Essays* (Cambridge: University Press, 1923);

The English Writings of Abraham Cowley, 2 volumes, edited by A. R. Waller (Cambridge: University Press, 1905, 1906);

Essays and Selected Verse of Abraham Cowley, edited by John Max Attenborough (London & New York: Walter Scott, 1915);

The Essays and Other Prose Writings, edited by Alfred B. Gough (Oxford: Clarendon Press, 1915);

The Mistress with Other Select Poems, edited by John Sparrow (London: Nonesuch, 1926);

Poetry & Prose, edited by L. C. Martin (Oxford: Clarendon Press, 1949);

The Civil War, edited by Allan Pritchard (Toronto: University of Toronto Press, 1973);

The Collected Works of Abraham Cowley, edited by Thomas O. Calhoun, Laurence Heyworth, Allan Pritchard, et al (Newark: University of Delaware Press / London: Associated University Press, 1989–   ).

PLAY PRODUCTIONS: *Naufragium Joculare,* Cambridge, Trinity College, 2 February 1638;

The Guardian, Cambridge, Trinity College, 12 March 1642;

Cutter of Coleman Street, Lincoln's Inn Fields, Duke's Theater, 16 December 1661.

"Abraham Cowley was beloved by every muse he courted," states Henry Felton in his *Dissertation on Reading the Classics* (1713); Cowley excelled in every literary genre he undertook. In his early years, he was best known as a dramatist and satirist; in mid life he was most widely read for the love lyrics of *The Mistresse* (1647, 1656) and for the Pindaric odes; later readers have alternately preferred Cowley's Anacreontic verse and his essays. It is not for lack of talent that Cowley is accorded secondary status as a poet next to his contemporary John Milton, but because his epics – *The Civil War* (1679)

and *Davideis* – were not or could not be completed. Cowley's four books on the troubles of the first biblical kings, however, broke new ground for the epic, preparing the way for Milton's *Paradise Lost* (1667), and John Dryden considered Cowley the master and reformer of English poetry, according him the title "mentor."

Much of what is known about Cowley's life comes from the author's essay "Of My Self" and the "Life" by Thomas Sprat, prefixed to the *Works* of 1668 and subsequent editions. One matter that seems to bedevil modern readers, though, the pronunciation of "Cowley," may be resolved by spellings in other documents. Not to satisfy the matter, it is certain that the name was pronounced "Cooley" during the seventeenth century but nowadays, even in places where the poet lived such as Oxford and Chertsey, people refer to him in the bovine as "Cowley." The poet was born in London in 1618, the youngest of seven children. His father, Thomas, a London stationer of sufficient estate, died before Abraham's birth, making provision in a will dated 24 July 1618 for "the Childe or Children wch Thomasyn my wife now goeth withall." In the poem "To his very much honoured Godfather, Master A. B.," first published in the collection *Sylva* (1636), Cowley explains that the name Abraham was given him from his godfather, of whom nothing more is known. An exact date of birth is uncertain, since the parish records of Saint Michael le Quern (Or Corn), Cheapside, where the poet was born, were destroyed in the Great Fire of London in 1666, the year before Cowley died. He must, however, have been born during the latter five months of 1618, after his father's death.

Cowley himself reports that the most significant event of his childhood was the discovery, among his mother's religious books, of a copy of Edmund Spenser's *Faerie Queene* (1590, 1596). Though he was delighted by the stories of knights and giants and monsters, it was "the tinkling of the rhyme and the dance of the numbers" that made a deeper impression. When he was ten years old, Cowley began drafting his earliest published poem, "The Tragicall Historie of Pyramus and Thisbe," with a copy of Arthur Golding's Ovid (1565, 1567) near at hand but with the rhythms of Spenser's lines and stanzas in his mind. Rhythms and phrases from Spenser recur in many of his later writings.

For all his reported precocity, and the clear evidence of it in *Poetical Blossomes* (1633), which was prepared for publication when he was thirteen years old, Cowley was a stubbornly independent student. His schoolmates at Westminster (where records

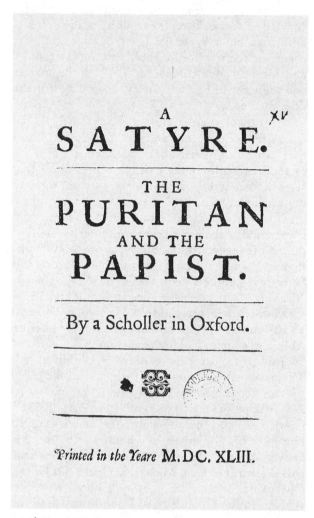

A

SATYRE. XV

THE
PURITAN
AND THE
PAPIST.

By a Scholler in Oxford.

Printed in the Yeare M.DC. XLIII.

Title page for Cowley's second political verse satire, which attacks the two extreme religious parties of his time

show Cowley as a king's scholar at Saint Peter's College as of July 1630) compared him to the similarly independent, constant, and stable Cato Utican. He learned grammar by reading, listening, and imitating, rather than by-the-book — that is, William Lily's Latin grammar *Brevissima Institutio* (1549), which Cowley mocks, along with schoolmasters who themselves do not understand it, in the poem "A Vote" (published in *Sylva*). Cowley was the product of the most successful educational system for the humanities in England; he was celebrated in 1631, when a portrait showing him a laureate at age 13 was engraved by Robert Vaughan. Cowley was the model of what a king's scholar could be, yet from the start he was a child apart from the other "Anthony's pigs" at Westminster. He remarks in the autobiographical essay that as a boy at school he preferred to be alone with his books, or with some one companion of similar tem-

per, rather than playing with his fellows. Among public events or attractions, only the theater appears to have held his genuine interest. The Cockpit and the Red Bull were near Westminster School, and Cowley's early satires imply that he was not an infrequent visitor to these places. *Loves Riddle,* a perfect vehicle for school-age actors, was written at Westminster and probably performed there before its publication in 1638. Cowley's interest in Anacreontic verse began during his Westminster years. "The merry waves dance up and downe" and "It is a punishment to love," songs appearing in acts 1 and 4 of *Loves Riddle,* are loose adaptations from the Anacreontea. These poems reappear in the 1656 *Anacreontiques* newly translated as "Drinking" and "Gold."

It is remarkable that this unusual boy should have been so welcomed and admired by schoolmates such as Ben Masters and Robert Meade, whose testaments preface *Poetical Blossomes.* Throughout his life Cowley was able to maintain his reserve, his distance, while winning the admiration and affection of virtually everyone he encountered.

Cowley's first try for Cambridge, probably in 1636, was unsuccessful, but later in the same year he was admitted (perhaps provisionally and perhaps with the aid of Sir Kenelm Digby) to Trinity College as a "dry chorister" — a student who, though he did not sing, received a chorister's stipend. He was chosen as a scholar a year later, in June of 1637. At Cambridge, according to Sprat, "before the twentieth year of his Age, he laid the design of divers of his most Masculine Works that he finished long after." Such works include the *Davideis*; some poems ("To the Lord Falkland. For His Safe Return from the Northern Expedition Against the Scots," "On the Death of Sir Henry Wootton," "On His Majesties Return Out of Scotland," "On the Death of Sir Anthony Vandike") that later appeared in the 1656 *Miscellanies;* some of the poems later published in *The Mistresse;* and even some verses (the "Ode. Acme and Septimius out of Catullus," for example) that were not published until after the poet's death. Not everything he wrote, however, was sequestered. The Latin comedy *Naufragium Joculare* was performed at Trinity College in 1638 and published in the same year with a dedication to the master of Trinity, Dr. Thomas Comber. Cowley contributed poems to university anthologies in 1637, 1640, and 1641, and in 1642 he was chosen to prepare the major entertainment for the royal visitor Prince Charles, who saw *The Guardian* performed at Trinity on 12 March. The prologue and epilogue to this

Warwick ye publick Tyrat, ~~for brings them ayde~~
And dares, like an high Tyde, ye Land invade,
How seekes his prey both uppon earth & Sea,
Soe livs ye doubtfull Crocodile, & he.
what dares not he who can like Jonas sleepe,
In midst of his Rebellion and ye Deepe.
who can a Mind constant in Sinne ytaine
Amidst those dreadfull wonders of ye Mayne
who feares not Shipwrack, wth ye stormy forth
when mutinous waves rise up, and winds rebell //
And yet on Exes streames hee learnt to grone
There rose a new and deadlier Tempest then,
The Canons murthring blasts from either shore
Their canvas pride, and thin-built safety tore,
Here a tall Ship sunck by degrees to low,
The decks yt firm now meets, and nothing now.
~~How~~ , and then ye men aboat.
In rush ye waves, and crowd their wt foule out.
Some forth hot wounds that through ye dashing flood,
They drinke in water, and supplyt wth Blood.
Some not yt staine, are caught by Fish beneath,
And forth their painfull Buriall in their Death.
Here on ye streame two ships for waters call,
The streame lookes on, and brings noe helpe at all.
A naturall hate though to ye Flame hee borne,
Hee will not quencht: but hates ye Rebells more.
Soe Cold and Heat on Ætnas top conspire,
Here Frosts ly bound, and by them breaks out Fire.
A strange peace ye faithfull neighbours keene.
Th' emboldned Snow next to ye Flame doy sleepe.
Some to avoyde ye firy embrace a wave,
Some burning planks from waves their life to save.
What help, alas could in this change appeare,
Onely yt death yt s next them, yt they feare.
Warwick beholds dead corps around him swimme,
And their last breath, heard, when it curssed him.
Hee dares not longer his iust fortune try;
In hast, but slow, ye batterd Vessels fly.
How was ye towring Towne yt night dismayde,
When ye next Tide cast up to them their aide.

Page from the second book of Cowley's manuscript for The Civil War, *one of two incomplete epic poems in which Cowley attempted to trace the workings of Providence in history (Hertfordshire Record Office, D/EP F48, "The Second Booke," fol. 6ʳ)*

Letter from Cowley to Sir Robert Long, another member of Queen Henrietta Maria's court in exile (Maggs Bros. catalogue, no. 480, 1926) political comedy circulated widely in manuscript during the years of the first civil war. So too did Cowley's two political verse-satires. The first, in the style of Juvenal and John Donne, survives in manuscript copies under the title "The Puritans Lecture." This satire was written at Cambridge, and it was printed in London as *A Satyre Against Seperatists* in 1642 under the pseudonym A. C. Generosus. After later reprintings, Cowley had to take considerable pains to disown this unequivocally Royalist poem, along with his other political writings, in the preface to his Commonwealth-era folio *Poems* (1656). The second verse-satire, *A Satyre. The Puritan and the Papist* (1643), is based on a Horatian model and shows direct influence of John Marston. It was started at Cambridge but probably finished at Oxford, where it was published "By a Scholler in Oxford." Ten manuscript versions of this satire are extant.

Cowley's deepest friendships at Cambridge were with men from outside his college – William Hervey, cousin to Henry Jermyn, Cowley's future employer, and Richard Crashaw, both of Pembroke, whose deaths occasioned two of Cowley's finest poems. His circle of friends extended to include George Villiers, second Duke of Buckingham, and Lucius Cary, Lord Falkland, later one of the principal secretaries of state, whom Cowley may have met by way of his Trinity chamber fellow Robert Creswell. Cowley took his M.A. in March 1643 and was ejected from his college and from the university immediately thereafter. Sprat records that his "affection to the King's Cause" occasioned the ejection and drew Cowley to Oxford, where he became the poet of the Falkland group of Cavaliers and the king's party.

In his essay "Of My Self," Cowley writes of his departure from the university and the quiet life of learning and letters he had known there, stating that he was "torn from thence by that violent Publick storm which would suffer nothing to stand where it did, but rooted up every Plant, even from the Princely Cedars to Me, the Hyssop." In March 1643, however, Cowley was of a mind more eager for public themes. His published or performed work during the early 1640s, like that of most poets at this time, was exclusively political, and at the beginning of the Civil War his reputation stood higher than that of other Royalist poets. The task to which he felt both obliged and suited kept him in the ranks of learning and the arts. As he states in *The Civil War*, Cowley found himself in the forefront of those "unapt themselves to fight, / [Who] promised noble pens the Acts to write." In the summer or early autumn of 1643 Cowley began his war epic, tracing

the military action through the battle of Newbury within a cosmic, providential frame designed to affirm the Royalist cause.

The Civil War was not Cowley's first attempt to trace, in epic form, the workings of Providence in history. The *Davideis*, written in draft at Cambridge, treats the same theme, and it appears that at Oxford Cowley had manuscript copy of the earlier poem from which he could adapt passages to the ongoing endeavor of *The Civil War*.

Sprat reports that Cowley served the king on several journeys and expeditions during the time of the Oxford court. The poet is also connected with the well-known anecdote of King Charles I's *Sors Virgiliana* – the sport of telling the future by picking a random passage from the *Aeneid*. As the story goes, during the time that Parliament sat at Oxford (22 January 1644–10 March 1645), Charles determined to try his fate. He opened the *Aeneid* to book 4 and picked lines 615–620, Dido's curse on Aeneas. The lines were sent to Cowley, who translated them:

> By a bold people's stubborn arms oppressed,
> Forced to forsake the land which he possessed,
> Torn from his dearest son, let him in vain
> Seek help, and see his friends unjustly slain;
> Let him to base, unequal terms submit,
> In hope to save his crown, yet lose both it
> And life at once; untimely let him die,
> And on an open stage unburied lie.

Queen Henrietta Maria left England for France on 14 July 1644. It is probable that Henry Jermyn, her secretary, traveled with her. Cowley, by now in Jermyn's employ, may have been part of the entourage, but the date of his arrival at Paris is not known. A letter in his hand, sent from Paris, is dated 1 February 1645 (this could mean 1646 new calendar style). A cipher letter from Paris that Cowley wrote for the queen, sent to King Charles at Oxford, is dated 1 September 1645.

For almost a decade Cowley remained secretary to Lord Jermyn and thus, in effect, a secretary of Henrietta Maria's. Documents dated 1647, 1649, and 1651 also establish that the poet had some responsibility for Jermyn and Henrietta Maria's financial affairs. Sprat adds that Cowley accompanied Jermyn on "several dangerous journeys." These would include Jermyn's trip to Jersey in June 1646 to bring Prince Charles to his mother in Paris; a trip to Holland in December 1650 to advise Mary, Princess Royal of Orange; a journey to Scotland in February 1651 to confer with Charles II; and other trips to Jersey to negotiate the sale of Crown lands.

Frontispiece for Poemata Latina, *a collection of Cowley's Latin poems published in the year after his death (engraving by W. Faithorne)*

The honors that Cowley anticipated for his service – mastership of the Savoy; the post of secretary for the colony of Virginia – were promises only and, in Caroline manner, they were not fulfilled.

If Cowley's secretarial services produced no personal reward, the poet was at least in a position to assist others in the literary community. Anthony Wood in his *Athenæ Oxonienses* (1691, 1692) wrote that Cowley was an intermediary for his old friend Richard Crashaw during arrangements for the latter poet's clerical appointment in Italy. Cowley transcribed a warrant for reimbursement of money to William Davenant, prior to Davenant's America venture, and he kept track of John Denham's various travels in the interest of the exiled court. Among Cowley's other literary associates during the period of exile were Edmund Waller, Thomas Hobbes, and John Evelyn.

Cowley's literary endeavors during the Paris exile are marked by the publication of *The Mistresse, The Guardian* (1650), and *Poems. The Guardian,* written and performed in 1642, brings down the curtain on prewar theater. It was printed in 1650 by Thomas Newcomb, with whom Cowley later worked on *Poems,* for John Holden, whose shop at the Anchor in the New Exchange was later run by Henry Herringman, publisher of Cowley's collected works. Cowley remarks in the preface to *Poems* that *The Guardian* was published, "mangled and imperfect," without his knowledge or consent, but given his later collaboration with both printer and publisher, this remark ought to be considered in context of the poet's political situation in 1656.

Cowley returned to England in 1654. According to Sprat, he traveled under the pretense of "retirement" but was actually employed to report on conditions in England. He had other business as well, for which he arranged a meeting between the duke of Buckingham and one of Oliver Cromwell's representatives. The specific subject of this meeting is not known, but it was regarded by some staunch Royalists as more than compromising, and Cowley's participation was maliciously reported to Charles II, damaging his status with the king. The Protectorate authorities in England grew suspicious of him also. On the night of 12 April 1655 Cowley was arrested; on the following day he was taken to Whitehall and interrogated by Cromwell and John Thurloe. He was then imprisoned, for most of the remainder of the year. Prior to his arrest, Cowley had been working with Humphrey Moseley, preparing copy for the publication of *Poems*. He wrote the preface to *Poems,* which includes disclaimers of any earlier political poems and *The Guardian,* alongside declarations of his present "peaceable intentions" and desire to retire to America, while he was in prison. He was released after Dr. Charles Scarborough, a Cambridge friend who later became one of Charles II's physicians, posted bail.

Poems was published early in 1656, before 8 April, when Scarborough wrote to Aubrey de Vere, Earl of Oxford, presenting him with a copy of Cowley's book. It comprises both old and new work, including a third, expanded edition of *The Mistresse.* This collection of love poems, which Moseley had first published in 1647, proved to be enormously popular: at least forty of its eighty-four poems were set to music in the later seventeenth century. The section of *Poems* titled *Miscellanies* includes prewar poems, delightful paraphrastic translations from the Anacreontea, and the prologue and epilogue to *The Guardian* (sounding just as political as they did in 1642), as well as new Pindaric odes perhaps written at Jersey and Cowley's elegy on the death of Richard Crashaw. The *Davideis,* four books of a biblical epic based on the story of Saul and David, was drafted before Cowley left Cambridge and revised for publication. The 1656 printed text is given a scholarly cast by way of detailed endnotes that the poet prepared either in France or before his arrest in England. The same kind of apparatus accompanies the *Pindarique Odes.* "The occasion of his falling on the Pindaric way of Writing," Sprat claims, "was his accidental meeting with Pindar's works in a place where he had no other books to direct him." Such an apology would have appeared hardly necessary to younger university poets of the 1660s who seized on the Pindarics as their measure of poetic liberty. The form was widely imitated. Cowley was idolized

as its inventor and consequently as the reformer of English verse.

On 26 June 1656 Cowley presented a large-paper copy of *Poems,* inscribed with a dedicatory Pindaric ode, to the Bodleian Library. Sprat tells that Cowley studied medicine during 1656 and 1657, retiring to Kent for that purpose, and was then inspired to write his *Plantarum,* two books of which were published in 1662 as *A. Couleii Plantarum Libri Duo.* The remaining books were published in the posthumous collection of his Latin poems, *Poemata Latina* (1668). This volume also includes a Latin version of Sprat's "Life" that differs in significant ways from the English edition. While a medical student, Cowley wrote a Pindaric ode to William Harvey. As a result of his studies, he was created doctor of medicine by Oxford University on 2 December 1657. This does not mean, however, that Cowley had given up his involvement with the Royalist cause. It may be, as Sprat suggests, that the medical studies served to disguise his main activities. Sprat may have had firsthand knowledge, since he made Cowley's acquaintance at Oxford in 1657.

Cowley's activities in England were connected with the affairs of the duke of Buckingham, who, in an effort to regain some of his estates, married in September 1657 Mary Fairfax, daughter of Thomas Fairfax, the Parliamentarian general. By one account, Cowley was best man. The protector disapproved of the marriage and had Buckingham imprisoned. Cowley wrote an ode on the occasion of the wedding and appears to have served Buckingham's interests during his confinement and after his release, following Cromwell's death.

The Visions and Prophecies Concerning England, Scotland, and Ireland, published in 1661 and republished as *A Vision, Concerning His Late Pretended Highnesse Cromwell, the Wicked,* is a political satire written according to the advertisement in the second edition, during the reign of Richard Cromwell. The "vision" came to him, the writer claims, as he stood spectator to Oliver Cromwell's funeral. Cowley's *Cutter of Coleman-Street* is set at about this time, "in the year 1658," though there is no record of it being performed before 1661 and much of the text as printed in 1663 had to have been set after the Restoration.

Cowley returned to France in 1659 to renew his services to Lord Jermyn and the court, but not without much troubled negotiation. The preface to *Poems* and the Pindaric ode "Brutus" gave evidence supporting suspicions held by the king and others (including Edward Hyde, first Earl of Clarendon)

Abraham Cowley, circa 1667 (portrait by Sir Peter Lely; National Portrait Gallery, London)

about the poet's loyalty. Correspondence from 1659 and 1660 reveals Cowley's efforts to reinstate himself, his excitement at the impending Stuart recall, and his future prospects, including a dramatic enterprise with Buckingham. He was in England for Charles II's entrance into London on 29 May 1660. George Thomason dates his copy of Cowley's lengthy *Ode, upon the blessed Restoration* as 31 May. After yet another journey across the Channel, accompanying Jermyn, in whose estimation the poet had never fallen short, Cowley settled successively in London, Barnes, and Chertsey.

Cowley's former association with William Davenant grew into some form of collaboration at the Duke's Theater, where *Cutter of Coleman Street* was first performed in 1661 – attended by most of the London literati, including John Dryden. The play was also performed at court before its publica-

tion in 1663. According to Davenant's son, Cowley held part interest in the Duke's Theater and assisted Sir William as a literary adviser, soliciting and editing plays and other entertainments for the stage.

Cowley's association with the Royal Society is documented in his *A Proposition for the Advancement of Learning* (1661) and his ode "To the Royal Society" that prefaces Sprat's 1667 *A History of the Royal Society.* The treatise is a detailed plan for a new educational institution, like that imagined as Solomon's House in Francis Bacon's "New Atlantis." Cowley's approach in *A Proposition for the Advancement of Learning,* however, is entirely practical, and according to Sprat the proposal much hastened the establishment of the society. Cowley's ode satisfies a grand theme contrasting old and new science that was outlined by John Evelyn, with whom Cowley developed a close relationship during the later years of his life. Evelyn notes that in 1664 Cowley participated in meetings at Gray's Inn sponsored by the society for the improvement of the English language.

A. Couleii Plantarum Libri Duo is dedicated to Trinity, Cambridge, and Cowley was incorporated doctor of medicine at Cambridge on 11 June 1664. No evidence suggests that he took up residence again at Trinity, though he was reinstated in his fellowship there and absolved from the statutory obligation to take holy orders. To the stipend of his fellowship and dividends from his interest in the Duke's Theatre, Cowley was able to add income from leases granted him by Jermyn, now titled Saint Albans, and perhaps a pension granted by Buckingham. In his essay "Of Greatness," Cowley suggests that his income, in retirement, was around five hundred pounds a year.

Cowley continued to write occasional verses, some of which appear in a 1663 Dublin miscellany, *Poems, by Several Persons,* which also includes poems by Katherine Philips, Clement Paman, Peter Pett, and Roger Boyle, Baron Broghill. Cowley's poems were reprinted in London, along with the Restoration ode and an ode to Dr. Harvey, as *Verses, Written Upon Several Occasions* in the later part of 1663. Many of his verse translations from Claudian, Horace, and others appear among the *Essays* in the posthumous *Works* of 1668.

Cowley was ultimately disappointed in his hopes for greater preferment at the Restoration, but if one can trust in a connection between the Horatian themes of the *Several Discourses by Way of Essays in Verse and Prose* (1668) and actual living or trust the rhetoric of Katherine Philips's ode "Upon Mr. Abraham Cowley's Retirement," he found genuine satisfaction in retirement at Barnes and later at Porch House, in Chertsey. Books 3 and 4 of the *Plantarum* may have been written at Barnes, where the poet suffered a severe illness in 1663–1664. The last two books of the Latin epic were written after the illness, at Chertsey. Sprat makes the point that books 5 and 6 of the *Plantarum* show no diminution of Cowley's poetic powers, praising particularly the allegory of book 6 that traces recent English history from the Interregnum to the beginning of the Dutch Wars – in a sense completing the design Cowley had set forth in *The Civil War.*

Of the essays, Sprat says "these he intended as a real Character of his own thoughts, upon the point of his Retirement" and that he had intended to write many more of them and dedicate them to his patron Saint Albans. Cowley's health, however, was in decline. He suffered an attack of diabetes shortly after his move to Chertsey and then, in July 1667, contracted an illness that developed into pneumonia. He died on 28 July 1667. His age, 49, is supplied by the monument on his tomb at Westminster Abbey, where he was laid next to Geoffrey Chaucer and Spenser. Of the many eulogistic reports of the time, one in the 4 August *London Gazette* is typical: mourners included the London wits, members of the clergy, and the court; more than a hundred coaches of "noble men and persons of quality" followed the funeral procession from Wallingford House to Westminster Abbey, "to perform this last office to one who had been the great ornament of our nation, as well by the candour of his life as the excellency of his writings." The boy beloved of the muses died a man whose poems, songs, and plays, whose years of dedicated service to the nation, and whose open and honest character made him at last a poet loved by the masses.

Bibliographies:
Dennis G. Donovan, "Recent Studies in Cowley," *English Literary Renaissance,* 6 (Autumn 1976): 446–475;

M. R. Perkin, *Abraham Cowley: A Bibliography,* Pall Mall Bibliographies, no. 5 (Folkestone: Dawson, 1977);

Thomas O. Calhoun, Laurence Heyworth, and Allan Pritchard, eds., *The Collected Works of Abraham Cowley* (Newark: University of Delaware Press / London: Associated University Press, 1989–).

Biographies:
Thomas Sprat, "An Account of the Life and Writings of Mr. Abraham Cowley," in *The Works of Mr. Abraham Cowley* (London: Printed by John Macocke for Henry Herringman, 1668);

Alexander B. Grosart, "Memorial Introduction," in *The Complete Works in Verse and Prose of Abraham Cowley,* 2 volumes, edited by Grosart (Edinburgh: Constable, 1881);

Samuel Johnson, "Cowley," *Lives of the English Poets,* 3 volumes, edited by George B. Hill (Oxford: Clarendon Press, 1905), I: 1–69;

Jean Loiseau, *Abraham Cowley, Sa vie, son oeuvre* (Paris: Henri Didier, 1931);

Arthur H. Nethercot, *Abraham Cowley: The Muse's Hannibal,* second edition (New York: Russell & Russell, 1967).

References:
Raymond A. Anselment, "Abraham Cowley and the 'Soule Compos'd of th'Eagle and the Dove,' " in his *Loyalist Resolve* (Newark: University of Delaware Press / London & To-

ronto: Associated University Presses, 1988), pp. 155–184;

Thomas O. Calhoun, "Cowley's Verse Satire, 1642–43, and the Beginnings of Party Politics," *Yearbook of English Studies,* 21 (1991): 197–206;

Nicholas Jose, "Ideal Restoration and the Case of Cowley," in *Ideas of the Restoration in English Literature 1660–71* (Cambridge, Mass.: Harvard University Press, 1984), pp. 67–96;

Peter Malekin, *Liberty and Love: English Literature and Society: 1640–88* (London: Hutchinson, 1981);

Graham Parry, *The Seventeenth Century: Intellectual and Cultural Context of English Literature* (London & New York: Longman, 1990);

Ted-Larry Pebworth, "Cowley's *Davideis* and the Exaltation of Friendship," *The David Myth in Western Literature,* edited by R. Frontain and J. Wojick (West Lafayette, Ind.: Purdue University Press, 1979), pp. 96–104;

Louise Schleiner, "Cowley and Restoration Song," in *The Living Lyre in English Verse* (Columbia: University of Missouri Press, 1984), pp. 158–183;

W. David Trotter, *The Poetry of Abraham Cowley* (Totowa, N.J.: Rowman & Littlefield, 1979);

Geoffrey Walton, "Abraham Cowley," in volume 3 of *The New Pelican Guide to English Literature* (Harmondsworth, U.K.: Penguin, 1982), pp. 356–363.

Papers:

Peter Beal's *Index of English Literary Manuscripts* (1987) lists Abraham Cowley's autograph manuscripts and manuscript copies, with their locations in various libraries, public archives, and private collections. Manuscript descriptions and analyses may be found in present and forthcoming volumes of *The Collected Works of Abraham Cowley* (1989–). Cowley's correspondence, including some of the letters he wrote for Henrietta Maria and Henry Jermyn, is planned for publication in volume six. M. R. Perkin's *Abraham Cowley: A Bibliography* (1977) includes a list of published letters in approximate chronological order of composition. Beal expands this inventory with a chronological list of letters that Cowley wrote on his own behalf and that survive in his own hand.

Charles Sackville, Lord Buckhurst, Earl of Dorset and Middlesex

(24 January 1643 – 29 January 1706)

James E. Gill
University of Tennessee

SELECTED WORKS: Twelve poems included in *Poetical Miscellanies: The Fifth Part. Containing a Collection of Original Poems, With Several New Translations. By the Most Eminent Hands* (London: Printed for Jacob Tonson, 1704).

Edition: *The Poems of Charles Sackville, Sixth Earl of Dorset,* edited by Brice Harris (New York: Garland, 1979).

Charles Sackville, Lord Buckhurst (1652), fourth Earl of Middlesex (1675), and sixth Earl of Dorset (1678), was the son of Richard Sackville, fifth Earl of Dorset (died 1677). Charles was a Restoration courtier-patron-poet. He became an influential participant in King Charles II's "ministry of pleasure" and ended his career as a high-ranking but uninfluential member of King William III's cabinet; he was an important companion and patron of many Restoration poets and playwrights from Sir Charles Sedley, Sir George Etherege, John Wilmot, Earl of Rochester, John Dryden, and Samuel Butler at the beginning of the period to Thomas Shadwell, Nahum Tate, Thomas Durfey, Robert Gould, and Matthew Prior at the end; and he was a poet of some significance in his own right – just important enough in Samuel Johnson's view to be included in *The Lives of the Poets* (1779–1781). Although Johnson valued him very little, he quoted Dryden's *Discourse Concerning the Original and Progress of Satire* (1693), which ranked Dorset as a rival of the ancients in satire. In the crucial period from about 1675 to 1680, when long-standing bonds among aristocrats in Charles II's court were loosening, Dorset maintained his friendships with George Villiers, second Duke of Buckingham, the earl of Rochester, and the king, among others. After Rochester's death in 1680, Dorset was sometimes compared favorably to his dead comrade and fellow rake, but nothing of Dorset's is as forceful or original as Rochester's best

work, and Dryden's satire is far above Dorset's in every respect.

The poet lived a long, rich, and varied life. Descended from the earls of Dorset on his father's side and from the earls of Middlesex on his mother's, Charles Sackville was born 24 January 1643 probably at Copt Hall in Essex and was the second son of Richard Sackville, Lord Buckhurst, and Lady Frances Cranfield. Unlike his father, who became impoverished in the Royalist cause, or his mother, who had been a governess of the royal princes Charles and James, or his older brother, who died in the king's service, Richard Sackville was prudent and pedestrian, and thus little is known of the childhood of his witty and charming son, Charles, who entered Westminster School on 28 October 1657, where he lasted only a year under the strenuous regimen of the famous teacher and disciplinarian Richard Busby. He then was placed under an apparently easygoing tutor and completed the grand tour just in time to enjoy the fruits of his father's conniving during the return of Charles II in 1660. At court the father became an important figure, and the son devoted himself to wit and pleasure. He managed to secure pardons for manslaughter in 1662 and for his part in the Cock Tavern affair the following year with Sir Charles Sedley and Sir Thomas Ogle. The first charge stemmed from the killing of a highwayman on 18 February 1662. The second charge had resulted when Sackville, Sedley, and Ogle nearly incited a riot when, from the balcony of the Cock Tavern, they taunted a mob of about one thousand people on 16 June 1663. Sedley, the chief culprit, went so far as to strip naked and shout blasphemy. In 1664 Etherege dedicated *The Comical Revenge* to Sackville, and the translation of Pierre Corneille's *La Mort de Pompée* by Edmund Waller, Sir Edward Filmer, Sir Charles Sedley, and Sidney Godolphin was published; Sackville is responsible for act 4 according to Dryden. In the same year he sailed with

Charles Sackville, Earl of Dorset (portrait from the studio of Godfrey Kneller; National Portrait Gallery, London)

James, Duke of York, against the Dutch, composed before battle his gallant Cavalier ballad "To all you ladies now at land," and thereafter presumably sat for the picture of Eugenius, the enlightened and progressive patron of the moderns, in Dryden's great *Essay of Dramatic Poesie* (1668), which was also dedicated to Sackville. By 1667 he was keeping as his mistress the comic actress Nell Gwyn, who eventually graduated to serve the king, her Charles III, as she wittily observed (her first Charles had been the actor Hart, and her second was Sackville). By 1670 he had undertaken several diplomatic missions to France for the king and in 1670 became gentleman of His Majesty's bedchamber for life. In 1671, the same year that he fought a duel, his poems began to appear in miscellanies and drolleries. Between 1671 and 1678 he fathered three illegitimate daughters by one Phillipa Waldegrave. In the meantime by 1673 he began wooing the dazzling, disreputable widow Mary, Countess of Falmouth, and when on the death of his uncle he became fourth earl of Middlesex in 1675, he announced his secret marriage to the countess. He became earl of Dorset on his father's death in 1677. His first wife died in childbirth in 1679, and in 1685 he married Mary Compton, a beautiful and intelligent daughter of James Compton, third Earl of Northampton; she bore Dorset several children but died in 1691. His activities in the closing years of Charles II's reign were limited by illness and travel, and after participating in James II's 1685 coronation, he tried to absent himself from public affairs. When he refused, as lord lieutenant of Sussex, to assist in James's efforts to relieve Catholics by repealing the Penal Laws and Test Act in 1687, he was discharged from his post; he was among twenty peers who offered to stand bail for the seven Anglican bishops whom James accused of sedition and libel; and during the Glorious Revolution of 1688, in which William III and Mary II ascended the throne, Dorset was a member of the protective escort of Mary's sister, Princess Anne. After assuming the throne, William III promptly appointed him lord chamberlain, an important and demanding position (but in this case an uninfluential one) that he held until 1697. Brice Harris, his twentieth-century biographer and editor, describes Dorset during this period as a loyal Whig, a member of the Kit Cat Club, and patron of many writers. He drifted into retirement, his mind and health declining. In October 1704 he married Anne Roche, his housekeeper. He died on 29 January 1706 at Bath. He was, according to Harris, "endlessly lauded by his own and the next generation." Over the years he had patronized many poets and dramatists – Dryden, Shadwell, Gould, and Prior, to name a few.

Dorset's verse, though nearly always fluent, is varied and uneven in quality, and his slender production is strewn over a period of forty years. Known today chiefly for a few polished songs, his real strength is satire. Despite Johnson's descriptions of them as "little personal invectives," Dorset's satires sometimes rise to become powerful indictments of their subjects. Among his best lyrics is the "Advice," written about 1670, in which the speaker counsels his beloved to seize courageously the time for love despite intimidation by the foppish discretion and wisdom of the world. The poem is built on clarity of statement, fluency, and solid contrasts between courageous pride and slavish shame, inner desire and external compulsion, the life-giving moment and barren prudence.

> Phyllis, for shame let us improve
> 　A thousand several ways
> These few short minutes stol'n by love
> 　From many tedious days.
>
> Whilst you want courage to despise
> 　The censure of the grave,
> For all the tyrants in your eyes
> 　Your heart is but a slave.
>
> My love is full of noble pride
> 　And never will submit
> To let that fop, discretion, ride
> 　In triumph over it.
>
> False friends I have, as well as you,
> 　Who daily counsel me
> Fame and ambition to pursue,
> 　And leave off loving thee.
>
> When I the least belief bestow
> 　On what such fools advise,
> May I be dull enough to grow
> 　Most miserably wise.

There are several other "advices" to lovers that are less philosophical and general than this one. In "The Answer to Phyllis" (written in 1665; confusingly titled in Harris's edition because the poem's speaker responds to a song titled "To Phyllis"), a lady responds to her lover's complaint that the power of her eyes has "forc'd me from my Celia's arms." Her lover warns that age sets a limit on her power over him. To maintain her influence, she must either pretend to love him or, better yet, to "forever fix your throne: / Be kind, but kind to me

alone." In the accompanying reply, the lady roundly asserts her contempt for "all your courtly fallacies / Which your dissembling justifies." Rather she knows how to maintain her independence of all men "and better on you fix our throne, / By being kind t'ourselves alone." (It is probably not far-fetched to see in this defiant declaration of proud self-sufficiency a hint of the autoerotic). Another lyric, "Knotting," is described by Harris as "precise, proportioned (every fourth line rhymes, for example), elegant, and unimpassioned." Knitting while sitting in the shade of a tree, the lady of this poem invites her favorite swain to lay his head in her lap and take a nap, but he arouses her anger when he takes her at her word and does in fact fall asleep. The woman's knitting or knotting is in the first instance an erotic binding, as the second stanza makes clear:

> Each slender finger play'd its part
> With such activity and art
> As would enflame a youthful heart
> And warm the most decay'd.

But her angry frustration and disappointment when she finds "him fast asleep all o'er" constitute a greater and more painful knotting (with the obligatory puns on naught-ing) or angry entanglement.

While the poems so far discussed embody the coy eroticism of much seventeenth-century pastoral lyric poetry, many of Dorset's poems are even more mundane. Judging from his verse as well as his life, Dorset liked women who were beautiful, adventurous, and witty (but not learned). He also liked women of low degree as well as the nobly born. "On Dolly Chamberlain, A Sempstress in the New Exchange," for example, shows his lordship raking and punning among the lower classes:

> Dolly's beauty and art
> 　Have so hemm'd in my heart
> That I cannot resist the charm:
> 　　In revenge I will stitch
> 　　Up the hole next her breech
> With a needle as long as my arm.

"A Song on Black Bess" prefers "the truth" of a woman of low degree to the beauty and cruelty of court ladies:

> Methinks this poor town has been troubled too long
> With Phyllis and Chloris in every song,
> 　By fools who at once can both love and despair,
> And will never leave calling them cruel and fair:
> 　Which justly provokes me in rhyme to express
> The truth that I know of bonny Black Bess.

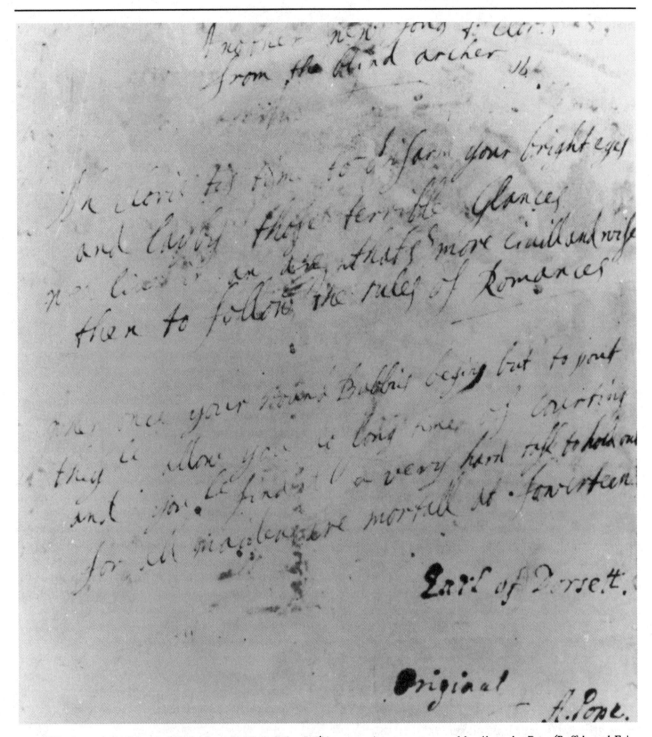

Draft for Dorset's "A Song to Chloris, from the blind Archer." This manuscript was once owned by Alexander Pope (Buffalo and Erie County Public Library, Gluck Collection).

Having conquered "the plowman and squire, the arranter clown" in the country, Bess now "adorns the boxes and pit" of the theater, where "all hearts fall a leaping whenever she comes, / And beat day and night." Her open sexuality cannot be allowed at Whitehall, however, because "she'd outshine the ladies, paint, jewels, and all," make fools of all the lecherous lords there, and be sent away by the queen. Dorset had the contempt of his age for prudes and coquettes.

One woman who provoked his special scorn was Katherine Sedley, Countess of Dorchester, daughter of his old drinking companion Sir Charles Sedley. The countess irritated Dorset, one suspects, for several reasons. First, she was by all accounts a rather plain woman; second, she was not only extremely witty but intelligent and better read than many women of her day; and last, she was for a time a mistress of James II, for whom Dorset had little respect.

> Sylvia, methinks you are unfit
>   For your great Lord's embrace:
> For tho' we all allow you wit,
>   We Can't a handsome face.
> Then where's the pleasure, where's the good
>   Of spending time and cost?
> For if your wit ben't understood,
>   Your keeper's bliss is lost.

A second poem complains of her too brilliant wit, and a third scorns her pride and learning and mocks her choice of husband, Sir David Colyear, a naval hero lamed and blinded in one eye in battle. A fourth poem mocks her superannuated attempts to appear young and fashionable:

> So have I seen in larder dark
> Of veal a lucid loin,
>   Replete with many a heatless spark,
> As wise philosophers remark,
>   At once both stink and shine.

The sad truth is that some of Dorset's lyrics are by modern standards downright rapacious, crude, or even sometimes criminal. One poem, "Phyllis, the fairest of love's foes," is Surley Strephon's crude poetic revenge on a woman of low degree who has rejected his advances until she is "compell'd by want" to "sad complaints begin." Strephon's response is that "it was both a shame and sin / To pity such a lazy jade / That wou'd neither kiss nor spin." The poem makes clear that a pretty woman who will neither work nor submit to gentlemanly lusts is beneath pity. Yet another lyric, "An Advice to Lovers," answers a critical but poetically lame attack by a minor court figure on "Damon's" beloved, who "must be as nature has made her, / A prey to false hearts, a plague to the true." Dorset's smooth but repellent reply urges Damon to an expedient which may have been all too common at the time – in effect, he urges him to force himself on his reluctant beloved on the grounds that

> Love gives out a large commission,
>   Still indulgent to the brave;
> But one sin of base omission
>   Never woman yet forgave.
> But true vigor in performing,
>   Turns the tragic scene to farce;

> And she'll rise appeas'd next morning,
>   With Dry eyes and a wet a_____.

Similarly, Dorset's poem on "A Young Heiress of Lincoln's Inn Fields" (written circa 1690) seems common and callous. Such poems lack any real feeling for the qualms, confusions, desires, and misfortunes of others.

Scatology, frank sexuality, and even sexual contempt and hatred have honored places in Restoration poetry because they vigorously and forcefully express dislike of unthinking conformity, hypocrisy, and pretense and because, for better or worse, they frankly represent the sexual vigor and strong feelings of robust young men and women; and so one must distinguish some of the deficient performances just described from other, less cruel works of Dorset, as well as those of other Restoration poets, about which a strong case can be made for the satirical expressiveness or representative truth of the scatological. To this last category belong some of Dorset's earliest poems – for example, his two contributions to the "Four Letters in Verse between Dorset and Etherege" (written 1664). Dorset initiates the exchange by announcing his forthcoming visit to the town, but he does so indirectly:

> Dreaming last night on Mrs. Farley [an actress],
>   My p_____ was up this morning early;
> And I was fain without my gown
>   To rise in th' cold to get him down.

This scarcely conventional beginning, with its immediate sequel – a digression about how Cleopatra made those men who serviced her maintain their erections – is perhaps a witty, "poetic" way of informing Etherege that he has finished collaborating on the translation of Corneille's *La Mort de Pompée* and is coming to town to celebrate. His first request is for information about sound ladies of pleasure, and the letter is a frank declaration that man is governed by his lusts: "I must entreat you by this letter, / To inquire for whores, the more the better." His second request is significant: he wishes Etherege to collect for him all the high-blown love poetry he can find or "any paltry poetry" of the kind that ordinarily would find its way to the fireplace or the privy. The poem is thus not merely an exercise in adolescent prurience but an invitation to discuss poetry and particularly to criticize old-fashioned and, especially, "platonic" and academic verse. It is, in a very real and immodest sense, a declaration of poetic independence from the past. The muses of the new kind of poetry Dorset and Etherege write are not imaginary goddesses but reeking, flesh-and-blood harlots, as Etherege's reply makes clear. Along with his graphic accounts of his sexual adventures, Etherege sends Dorset

> some paltry rhymes,
> The greatest grievance of our times,
> When such as Nature never made
> For poets daily do invade
> Wit's empire, both the stage and press –
> And what is worse, with good success.

Dorset's response elaborates the theme, railing against Etherege's fit against the wit emanating from the pudenda.

> What horrid fury could provoke thee
> To use thy railing, scurrilous wit
> 'Gainst p_____ and c____ the source of it
> For what but p_____ and c____ do's raise
> Our thoughts to songs and roundelays[?]

He concludes that his muse stumbles because he lacks the proper inspiration – encouragement which he hopes again to find in London. Etherege's second response further embellishes the connections between desire and art.

To deny the force of such verse, which successfully aims to shock, is as mistaken as to ignore its self-mockery. The wits of Charles's court could mock others because they could mock themselves and their king, and their libertine sentiments are very close to the sources of their poetry – not only of their amatory verse but also of their political satire. As Dorset declares in an early poem on the Commonweath and Restoration,

> Both p_____ and prelate then went down
> . . . .
> In every street
> We daily meet
> Instead of whore an armed train.
> But now honest c____
> Shall flourish as 'twas wont,
> For the King enjoys his own again.

Because the wits of Charles's court were not blind to their king's faults and weaknesses, this version of the Restoration is not without its serious ironies, but the scurrilous victory of "love" over "war" suggests the recovery of a certain minimal honesty, safety, and freedom. The fact that the king (as opposed to everyone else) "enjoys his own again" suggests both the hopes of others that they too may be "restored" and the cynical possibility that without vigorous self-assertion they as underlings may not so easily recoup their losses.

Extravagantly praised by Dryden in his "Discourse on Satire" (1692), Dorset's satiric poems are of uneven quality – the worst are lame, and the best are vigorous and cutting. Several early poems attack the poet Edward Howard, whose work, according to Harris, "quickly gained a reputation for ineptness and stupidity that has seldom been equalled." The first satire, "To Mr. Edward Howard, on his Incomparable, Incomprehensible Poem Called 'The British Princes,'" anticipates some of the themes that Dryden exploited in *Mac Flecknoe* (1682) a decade later. Poetic techniques reflexively become the stuff of the poem, and the theme of "nonsense absolute" is stunningly sounded:

> Come on, ye critics! Find one fault who dare,
> For, read it backward like a witch's prayer,
> 'Twill do as well; throw not away your jests
> On solid nonsense that abides all test.
> Wit, like tierce claret, when't begins to pall,
> Neglected lies and's of no use at all;
> But in its full perfection of decay,
> Turns vinegar and comes again in play.
> This simile shall stand in thy defence
> 'Gainst such dull rogues as now and then write sense.

The poem then develops several analogous figures of speech – the maggot that survives the stuff it feeds on, the "stumbling, founder'd jade"; the diver skilled in the art of sinking; and "the dull eel [which] moves nimbler in the mud / Than all the swift-finn'd racers in the flood." In the last analysis, however, Howard's greatest reproach is his own work and name: "Thou sett'st thy name to what thyself dost write; / Did ever libel yet so sharply bite?" A series of sharp jabs, the thirty-four-line poem has only a hint of the deep structure or continuity that the great satirists of the period – Dryden, Rochester, and Oldham – were developing. Using similar techniques and themes (along with quip and retort) with about the same success, Dorset also attacked Howard's 1671 play *The Six Days' Adventure, or The New Utopia.*

Another early satire of interest is "The Duel of the Crabs" (written 1668), a ribald burlesque of Sir Robert Howard's "Duel of the Stags" (1668), a poem dealing with the public turmoil surrounding the attempt to impeach Edward Hyde, Earl of Clarendon. Dorset's travesty reduces Howard's epic treatment of the imperialistic rivalry of two mighty stags to the struggles of two heroic lice inhabiting the ample, pilose pubes of a prostitute. When both champions die in the fray (their military struggle vaguely recollects military metaphors describing coition), their waiting armies (hitherto unmentioned) are so "in doubt," that "they both agree / A commonwealth their government shall be." A witty reduction of politics and its poetry to verminous, prostituted activity, the poem is one of Dorset's more successful satires.

His most powerful satires, however, are his most extended efforts and attack the rank corruption at the court of the aging Charles II and the court of James II. In the first of these, the title "Colon" (written 1679) derives from the frame story. The aged shepherd of that name is driving his sheep (or hogs) by Whitehall palace on the day that Charles's reigning mistress Louise Renée de Kéroualle, Duchess of Portsmouth, is auctioning her office to the highest bidder because stories of her depravity and involvement in the Popish Plot have aroused the hostility of the populace and the court. The public sale attracts various aspirants to the position. Accompanied by stories of their sordid and complicated relationships with different lovers (some succeeding others within minutes), various court ladies are pilloried as they assert their claims to the king's friendship and slink off to various degenerate alternatives, but some like Carey Fraser cannot "swear, drink, and talk bawdy – / Virtues more requisite for that place / Than wit, or youth, or a good face." But although old Rowley (the king) owns his passion for the last woman to bid ("young Lady Jones"), he suspends the proceedings because he is engaged to hear debate on some trivial matters in council. The disgruntled shepherd returns to his herding "Swearing there were at every fair / Blither girls than any there." The more apt comparison, however, is between the congregation of would-be royal whores (and their associates) and the common beasts of the shepherd's flock. "Colon" has a primitive vigor and biting humor appropriate to its speaker, but it lacks the skillful development and subtlety of Rochester's best satires of the same period. There is some evidence that this poem, like some others, was never revised for polish or consistency.

"A Faithful Catalogue of our most Eminent Ninnies" (written 1687) does for the court of James II what "Colon" did for the court of the late King Charles. Instead of a dismayed herdsman, however, an outraged and disgusted poet speaks here in a Juvenalian diatribe in couplets which are more polished than the doggerel verse of "Colon":

> Go on, my muse, and with bold voice proclaim
> The vicious lives and long detested fame
> Of scoundrel lords and their lewd wives' amours,
> Pimp statesmen, bug'ring priests, court bawds, and
> whores;

> Exalted vice its own vile name does sound,
> To climes remote, and distant shores renown'd.

James's court has become the vile, moribund, and brazen repository of all the sins of Charles's reign, including his mistresses and royal bastards, as well as the nursery of its own sins – without one iota of Charles's saving charm, sense, and wit. The stifling and corrupt incense of James's Catholic establishment, including the lascivious and diseased priest Father Dover, is often in evidence; and the rebellion and execution of James Scott, Duke of Monmouth, and the self-serving behavior of various aristocrats concerning these bloody events darken the atmosphere of the poem. Monmouth's widow, for example, called a "trimming beast," has had not one, but two lovers. The proliferation of sexual excess, crime, and personal and family betrayal in this poem symbolizes gross political disorder and religious apostasy. Speaking of the minor courtier, Sir Edward Hales, who turned Catholic on the ascent of James II and reaped numerous rewards, Dorset rails,

> But Hales has sure, to his eternal curse,
> Left his own strumpet and espous'd a worse [Popery].
> That Blazing star still rises with the sun,
> And will, I hope, whene'er it sets, go down.
> St. Peter ne'er deny'd his Lord but thrice,
> But good St. Edward scorns to be so nice;
> He, ev'ry mass, abjures what he before
> On tests and sacraments so often swore.
> His mother church will have a special son,
> Of him, by whom his father was undone.

Dorset is conscious of the classical and English past here as he is in no other poem, and, after excoriating Monmouth's weakness and lamenting some of the lost leaders of his rebellion, the poem abruptly returns to the depraved courtiers of James's court. It ends suddenly and tragically: "Caetera desunt" (As for the rest, they are absent). Though it, like "Colon," does not really qualify as a formal verse satire in the manner of Rochester's greatest satires – indeed, William C. Dowling states that it derives from the lampoon tradition – "A Faithful Catalogue" is Dorset's most complex and effective depiction of the depravities of his time.

Extravagantly praised and admired in his own time as a great patron and model of polite learning, Dorset today is virtually unknown except by historians and literary specialists. Now he is liable to strike the common reader as one born in the lap of privilege who entered more fully than many of his class into the literary and political worlds of his time. He sinned exuberantly in his youth, aided numerous writers throughout his life, enjoyed his existence at all times without regrets, and in bad times acted with some courage. He entered political life a firm supporter of the Stuarts, and he died an honored Whig. In the meanwhile he wrote poems sometimes above the ordinary. He was a man of his times.

Biography:

Brice Harris, *Charles Sackville, Sixth Earl of Dorset: Patron and Poet of the Restoration* (Urbana: University of Illinois Press, 1940).

References:

Helen A. Bagley, "Checklist of the Poems of Charles Sackville, Sixth Earl of Dorset and Middlesex," *Modern Language Notes,* 47 (November 1932): 454–461;

Bror Danielsson and David M. Vieth, eds. *The Gyldenstolpe Manuscript Miscellany of Poems by John Wilmot, Earl of Rochester, and other Restoration Authors. A Collection of English Poetry Principally Political &tc Satyrs from the Last Years of Charles II* (Stockholm: Almqvist & Wiksell, 1967);

William C. Dowling, *The Epistolary Moment: The Poetics of the Eighteenth-Century Verse Epistle* (Princeton, N.J.: Princeton University Press, 1991), p. 67;

Dustin Griffin, "Rochester and the Holiday Writers," in *Rochester and Court Poetry* (Los Angeles:

William Andrews Clark Memorial Library, 1988), pp. 47–53;

R. G. Howarth, "Some Additions to the Poems of Lord Dorset," *Modern Language Notes,* 50 (June 1935): 457–459;

Vivian de Sola Pinto, *Enthusiast in Wit: A Portrait of John Wilmot Earl of Rochester, 1647–1680* (Lincoln: University of Nebraska Press, 1962);

Pinto, *Restoration Carnival. Five Courtier Poets: Rochester, Dorset, Sedley, Etherege, and Sheffield* (London: Folio, 1954), pp. 109–148;

Pinto, *Sir Charles Sedley 1639–1701: A Study in the Life and Literature of the Restoration* (London: Constable, 1927);

K. E. Robinson, "The Disenchanted Lyric in the Restoration Period," *Durham University Journal,* 73 (1980): 67–73;

David M. Vieth, *Attribution in Restoration Poetry: A Study of Rochester's Poems of 1680* (New Haven & London: Yale University Press, 1963);

Howard D. Weinbrot, *Eighteenth-Century Satire: Essays on Text and Context from Dryden to Peter Pindar* (Cambridge: Cambridge University Press, 1988), pp. 28–29;

John Harold Wilson, *Court Satires of the Restoration* (Columbus: Ohio State University Press, 1976);

Wilson, *The Court Wits of the Restoration: An Introduction* (Princeton, N.J.: Princeton University Press, 1948).

John Dryden

(9 August 1631 – 1 May 1700)

J. Douglas Canfield
University of Arizona

See also the Dryden entries in *DLB 80: Restoration and Eighteenth-Century Dramatists: First Series* and *DLB 101: British Prose Writers, 1660–1800: First Series.*

SELECTED BOOKS: *Astraea Redux. A Poem On the Happy Restoration and Return Of His Sacred Majesty Charles the Second* (London: Printed by J. M. for Henry Herringman, 1660);

To His Sacred Majesty, A Panegyrick On His Coronation (London: Printed for Henry Herringman, 1661);

To My Lord Chancellor, Presented on New-years-day (London: Printed for Henry Herringman, 1662);

The Rival Ladies (London: Printed by W. W. for Henry Herringman, 1664);

The Indian Emperour, or The Conquest of Mexico by the Spaniards (London: Printed by J. M. for H. Herringman, 1667); second edition republished with "A Defence of An Essay of Dramatique Poesie" in some copies (London: Printed for H. Herringman, 1668);

Annus Mirabilis: The Year of Wonders, 1666 (London: Printed for Henry Herringman, 1667);

Of Dramatick Poesie: An Essay (London: Printed for Henry Herringman, 1668 [i.e., 1667]);

Secret-Love, or The Maiden-Queen (London: Printed for Henry Herringman, 1668);

Sr Martin Mar-All, or The Feigned Innocence (London: Printed for H. Herringman, 1668);

The Wild Gallant (London: Printed by Tho. Newcomb for H. Herringman, 1669);

The Tempest, or The Enchanted Island, by Dryden and William Davenant (London: Printed for Henry Herringman, 1670);

Tyrannick Love, or The Royal Martyr (London: Printed for H. Herringman, 1670);

An Evening's Love, or The Mock Astrologer (London: Printed by T. N. for Henry Herringman, 1671);

The Conquest of Granada by the Spaniards: In Two Parts (London: Printed by T. N. for Henry Herringman, 1672);

Marriage A-la-Mode (London: Printed by T. N. for Henry Herringman & sold by Joseph Knight & Francis Saunders, 1673);

The Assignation: or, Love in a Nunnery (London: Printed by T. N. for Henry Herringman, 1673);

Amboyna (London: Printed by T. N. for Henry Herringman, 1673);

Notes and Observations on the Empress of Morocco, by Dryden, John Crowne, and Thomas Shadwell (London, 1674);

Aureng-Zebe (London: Printed by T. N. for Henry Herringman, 1676);

The State of Innocence and Fall of Man (London: Printed by T. N. for Henry Herringman, 1677);

All for Love: or, The World Well Lost (London: Printed by Tho. Newcomb for Henry Herringman, 1678);

Oedipus, by Dryden and Nathaniel Lee (London: Printed for R. Bentley and M. Magnes, 1679);

Troilus and Cressida, or, Truth Found too Late (London: Printed for Jacob Tonson & Abel Swall, 1679);

The Kind Keeper; or, Mr. Limberham (London: Printed for R. Bentley & M. Magnes, 1680);

His Majesties Declaration Defended (London: Printed for T. Davies, 1681);

Absalom and Achitophel (London: Printed for J. T. & sold by W. Davis, 1681);

The Spanish Fryar, or The Double Discovery (London: Printed for Richard Tonson & Jacob Tonson, 1681);

The Medall. A Satyre against Sedition (London: Printed for Jacob Tonson, 1682);

Mac Flecknoe, or a Satyr Upon the True-Blew Protestant Poet, T.S. [unauthorized edition] (London: Printed for D. Green, 1682);

Religio Laici or a Laymans Faith (London: Printed for Jacob Tonson, 1682);

John Dryden, circa 1662 (portrait by an unknown artist; Bodleian Library, Oxford)

The Duke of Guise, by Dryden and Lee (London: Printed by T. H. for R. Bentley & J. Tonson, 1683);

The Vindication [of the Duke of Guise]: or The Parallel of the French Holy-League, and The English League and Covenant (London: Printed for Jacob Tonson, 1683);

Threnodia Augustalis: A Funeral-Pindarique Poem Sacred to the Happy Memory of King Charles II (London: Printed for Jacob Tonson, 1685);

Albion and Albanius, by Dryden, with music by Lewis Grabu (London: Printed for Jacob Tonson, 1685);

A Defence of the Papers Written by the Late King of Blessed Memory and Duchess of York (London: Printed for H. Hills, 1686);

The Hind and the Panther (London: Printed for Jacob Tonson, 1687);

A Song for St Cecilia's Day, 1687, with music by Giovanni Baptista Draghi (London: Printed for T. Dring, 1687);

Britannia Rediviva: A Poem on the Birth of the Prince (London: Printed for J. Tonson, 1688);

Don Sebastian, King of Portugal (London: Printed for Jo. Hindmarsh, 1690);

Amphitryon; or The Two Socia's, with music by Henry Purcell (London: Printed for J. Tonson & M. Tonson, 1690);

King Arthur: or The British Worthy, with music by Purcell (London: Printed for Jacob Tonson, 1691);

Eleonora: A Panegyrical Poem Dedicated to the Memory of the Late Countess of Abingdon (London: Printed for Jacob Tonson, 1692);

Cleomenes, The Spartan Heroe (London: Printed for Jacob Tonson, 1692);

Love Triumphant; or, Nature Will Prevail (London: Printed for Jacob Tonson, 1694);

An Ode, on the Death of Mr. Henry Purcell; Late Servant of his Majesty, and Organist of the Chapel Royal, and of St. Peter's Westminster (London: Printed by J. Heptinstall for Henry Playford, 1696);

Alexander's Feast; Or The Power of Musique. An Ode, In Honour of St. Cecilia's Day (London: Printed for Jacob Tonson, 1697).

Editions: *The Works of John Dryden,* 18 volumes, edited by Walter Scott (London: William Miller, 1808); revised by George Saintsbury (Edinburgh: William Paterson, 1882–1893);

The Dramatic Works of John Dryden, 6 volumes, edited by Montague Summers (London: Nonesuch Press, 1931);

The Works of John Dryden [The California Dryden], 20 volumes, edited by Edward Niles Hooker, H. T. Swedenberg, and others (Berkeley: University of California Press, 1955–);

The Poems of John Dryden, 4 volumes, edited by James Kinsley (Oxford: Clarendon Press, 1958);

John Dryden: Of Dramatic Poesy and Other Critical Essays, 2 volumes, edited by George Watson (London: J. M. Dent / New York: E. P. Dutton, 1962).

PLAY PRODUCTIONS: *The Wild Gallant,* revised from an older play, possibly by Richard Brome, London, Vere Street Theatre, 5 February 1663;

The Rival Ladies, London, Theatre Royal, Bridges Street, possibly autumn of 1663;

The Indian-Queen, by Dryden and Sir Robert Howard, London, Theatre Royal, Bridges Street, January 1664;

The Indian Emperour, London, Theatre Royal, Bridges Street, early months of 1665;

Secret Love, London, Theatre Royal, Bridges Street, final days of January 1667;

Sir Martin Mar-All, by Dryden and William Cavendish, Duke of Newcastle, London, Lincoln's Inn Fields, 15 August 1667;

The Tempest, revised from William Shakespeare's play by Dryden and William Davenant, London, Lincoln's Inn Fields, 7 November 1667;

An Evening's Love; or, The Mock Astrologer, London, Theatre Royal, Bridges Street, 12 June 1668;

Tyrannic Love, London, Theatre Royal, Bridges Street, 24 June 1669;

The Conquest of Granada, part 1, London, Theatre Royal, Bridges Street, December 1670; part 2, January 1671;

Marriage A-la-Mode, London, Theatre Royal, Bridges Street, probably late November or early December 1671;

The Assignation; or, Love in a Nunnery, London, Lincoln's Inn Fields, not later than early autumn of 1672;

Amboyna, London, Lincoln's Inn Fields, possibly February 1673;

Aureng-Zebe, London, Theatre Royal, Drury Lane, 17 November 1675;

All for Love, London, Theatre Royal, Drury Lane, probably 12 December 1677;

The Kind Keeper; or, Mr. Limberham, London, Dorset Garden Theatre, 11 March 1678;

Oedipus, by Dryden and Nathaniel Lee, London, Dorset Garden Theatre, autumn 1678;

Troilus and Cressida, revised from Shakespeare's play, London, Dorset Garden Theatre, not later than April 1679;

The Spanish Fryar, London, Dorset Garden Theatre, 1 November 1680;

The Duke of Guise, by Dryden and Lee, London, Theatre Royal, Drury Lane, 30 November 1682;

Albion and Albanius, opera with text by Dryden and music by Louis Grabu, London, Dorset Garden Theatre, 3 June 1685;

Don Sebastian, London, Theatre Royal, Drury Lane, 4 December 1689;

Amphitryon, London, Theatre Royal, Drury Lane, probably early October 1690;

King Arthur, opera with text by Dryden and music by Henry Purcell, London, Dorset Garden Theatre, early June 1691;

Cleomenes, by Dryden and Thomas Southerne, London, Theatre Royal, Drury Lane, on or before 16 April 1692;

Love Triumphant, London, Theatre Royal, Drury Lane, probably late January 1694; "The Secular Masque," inserted into *The Pilgrim,* revised from John Fletcher's play by John Vanbrugh, London, Theatre Royal, Drury Lane, late April or early May 1700.

OTHER: "Upon the Death of the Lord Hastings," in *Lachrymae Musarum: The Tears of the Muses: Exprest in Elegies; Written By divers persons of Nobility and Worth, Upon the death of the most hopefull, Henry Lord Hastings* (London: Printed by Thomas Newcomb, 1649);

"To his friend the Authour on his divine Epigrams," in *Sion and Parnassus,* by John Hoddesdon (London: Printed by R. Daniel for G. Eversden, 1650);

"Heroique Stanzas, Consecrated to the Glorious Memory of his most Serene and renowned Highnesse Oliver Late Lord Protector of this Common-Wealth, &c.," in *Three poems Upon the Death of his late Highnesse Oliver Lord Protector of England, Scotland & Ireland* (London: Printed by William Wilson, 1659);

"To My Honored Friend, Sr Robert Howard, On his Excellent Poems," in *Poems,* by Sir Robert Howard (London: Printed for Henry Herringman, 1660);

"To My Honour'd Friend, Dr Charleton," in *Chorea Gigantum, or The most Famous Antiquity of Great-Britain, Vulgarly called Stone-Heng, Standing on Salisbury Plain, Restored to the Danes,* by Walter Charleton (London: Printed for Henry Herringman, 1663 [i.e., 1662]);

The Indian-Queen, by Dryden and Howard, in *Four New Plays,* by Howard (London: Printed for H. Herringman, 1665);

Ovid's Epistles, Translated by Several Hands, includes a preface, and translations of three epistles, by Dryden (London: Printed for Jacob Tonson, 1680);

Nahum Tate, *The Second Part of Absalom and Achitophel,* includes contributions by Dryden (London: Printed for Jacob Tonson, 1682);

"The Life of Plutarch," in volume 1 of *Plutarchs Lives, Translated from the Greek by Several Hands,* 5 volumes (London: Printed for Jacob Tonson, 1683–1686);

Miscellany Poems, includes the authorized version of *Mac Flecknoe* and twenty-five other contributions by Dryden (London: Printed for Jacob Tonson, 1684);

Louis Maimbourg, *The History of the League,* translated by Dryden (London: Printed by M. Flesher for Jacob Tonson, 1684);

"To the Memory of Mr. Oldham," in *The Remains of Mr. John Oldham in Verse and Prose* (London: Printed for Jo. Hindmarsh, 1684);

Sylvae; or, the Second Part of Poetical Miscellanies, includes a preface and seventeen contributions by Dryden (London: Printed for Jacob Tonson, 1685);

"To the Pious Memory Of the Accomplisht Young Lady Mrs Anne Killigrew, Excellent in the two Sister-Arts of Poësie, and Painting. An Ode," in *Poems By Mrs. Anne Killigrew* (London: Printed for Samuel Lowndes, 1686 [i.e., 1685]);

Dominique Bouhours, *The Life of St. Francis Xavier, of the Society of Jesus,* translated by Dryden (London: Printed for Jacob Tonson, 1688);

The Satires of Decimus Junius Juvenalis Translated into English Verse. By Mr. Dryden, and Several other Eminent Hands. Together with the Satires of Aulus Persius Flaccus Made English by Mr. Dryden . . . To which is Prefix'd a Discourse concerning the Original and Progress of Satire (London: Printed for Jacob Tonson, 1693 [i.e., 1692]);

Examen Poeticum: Being the Third Part of Miscellany Poems, includes fifteen contributions by Dryden (London: Printed by R. E. for Jacob Tonson, 1693);

"A Character of Polybius and His Writings," in *The History of Polybius the Megalopolitan,* translated by Sir Henry Sheeres (London: Printed for S. Briscoe, 1693);

"To my Dear Friend Mr. Congreve, On His Comedy, call'd, The Double-Dealer," in *The Double-Dealer,* by William Congreve (London: Printed for J. Tonson, 1694);

"To Sir Godfrey Kneller," in *The Annual Miscellany: for the Year 1694. Being the Fourth Part of Miscellany Poems* (London: Printed by R. E. for Jacob Tonson, 1694);

Charles Alphonse du Fresnoy, *De Arte Graphica,* Latin text, with prose translation and "A Parallel of Poetry and Painting" by Dryden (London: Printed by J. Heptinstall for W. Rogers, 1695);

The Works of Virgil: Containing His Pastorals, Georgics, and Æneis, translated by Dryden (London: Printed for Jacob Tonson, 1697);

Fables Ancient and Modern; Translated into Verse, from Homer, Ovid, Boccace, & Chaucer; with Original Poems, translated by Dryden (London: Printed for Jacob Tonson, 1700);

"A Dialogue and Secular Masque," in *The Pilgrim,* by John Fletcher, revised by John Vanbrugh (London: Printed for Benjamin Tooke, 1700);

"The Life of Lucian," in volume 1 of *The Works of Lucian, Translated from the Greek by Several Eminent Hands,* 4 volumes (London: Printed for S. Briscoe, 1711);

[Heads of an Answer to Rymer], in volume 1 of *The Works of Mr Francis Beaumont and Mr John Fletcher,* 7 volumes (London: Printed for J. Tonson, 1711).

After John Donne and John Milton, John Dryden was the greatest English poet of the seventeenth century. After William Shakespeare and Ben Jonson, he was the greatest playwright. And he has no peer as a writer of prose, especially literary criticism, and as a translator. Other figures, such as George Herbert or Andrew Marvell or William

Wycherley or William Congreve, may figure more prominently in anthologies and literary histories, but Dryden's sustained output in both poetry and drama ranks him higher. After Shakespeare, he wrote the greatest heroic play of the century, *The Conquest of Granada* (1670, 1671), and the greatest tragicomedy, *Marriage A-la-Mode* (1671). He wrote the greatest tragedy of the Restoration, *All for Love* (1677), the greatest comitragedy, *Don Sebastian* (1689), and one of the greatest comedies, *Amphitryon* (1690). As a writer of prose he developed a lucid professional style, relying essentially on patterns and rhythms of everyday speech. As a critic he developed a combination of methods – historical, analytical, evaluative, dialogic – that proved enabling to neoclassical theory. As a translator he developed an easy manner of what he called paraphrase that produced brilliant versions of Homer, Lucretius, Horace, Ovid, Juvenal, Persius, Giovanni Boccaccio, Geoffrey Chaucer, and above all Virgil. His translation of *The Aeneid* remains the best ever produced in English. As a poet he perfected the heroic couplet, sprinkling it with judicious enjambments, triplets, and metric variations and bequeathing it to Alexander Pope to work upon it his own magic.

Dryden the poet is best known today as a satirist, although he wrote only two great original satires, *Mac Flecknoe* (1682) and *The Medall* (1682). His most famous poem, *Absalom and Achitophel* (1681), while it contains several brilliant satiric portraits, unlike satire comes to a final resolution, albeit tragic for both David and his son. Dryden's other great poems – *Annus Mirabilis* (1667), *Religio Laici* (1682), *The Hind and the Panther* (1687), "To the Pious Memory Of the Accomplisht Young Lady Mrs Anne Killigrew" (1686), *Alexander's Feast* (1697), and "To My Honour'd Kinsman" (1700) – are not satires either. And he contributed a wonderful body of occasional poems: panegyrics, odes, elegies, prologues, and epilogues.

Dryden was born 9 August 1631 into an extended family of rising Puritan gentry in Northamptonshire. But as a teenager he was sent to the King's School at Westminster to be trained as a King's Scholar by the brilliant Royalist headmaster Richard Busby. Dryden's family sided with the Commonwealth; however, in his first published poem, the elegy "Upon the Death of the Lord Hastings" – included in a commendatory volume (1649) of verses upon this young aristocrat's untimely death from smallpox – Dryden revealed Royalist sympathies in oblique references to rebellion and regicide. In a bold opening for a young (Puritan) poet – and such bold openings were to be-

come characteristic – Dryden hurls a series of theodicean questions about why the good die young. In the middle of the poem he proffers the only answer the poem yields: "The Nations sin." He seems indirectly to identify this sin when subsequently describing the pustules of Hastings's smallpox: "Who, Rebel-like, with their own Lord at strife, / Thus made an Insurrection 'gainst his Life." What would perhaps have been worse to Dryden's family is his patent refusal to add religious consolation at the end of the elegy. Instead, he suffocates his continuing theodicean challenge – could Heaven choose "no milder way" than the smallpox to recall Hastings? – by the tears of grief instead of the prayers of faith and outrageously suggests that Hastings's disappointed fiancée mate with his soul and engender ideal representations of him. The brash youngster may have been suggesting that she patronize such poets as himself and such ideal "Irradiations" as the current poem.

Aside from two other minor juvenilia (one in a private letter) – and perhaps because of family pressure – Dryden did not go public again until he had left Cambridge, where he was an undergraduate at Trinity College, and had been in the employ of Oliver Cromwell's government, probably in the Office of Latin Secretary along with Milton and Marvell. This is perhaps the first evidence of Dryden's trimming his sails to the political winds, as centuries of critics have accused him. His cousin, the prominent Puritan Sir Gilbert Pickering, lord chamberlain to Cromwell, probably procured employment for Dryden, and when the Protector died, Dryden, perhaps out of a sense of duty either internally or externally imposed, published his "Heroique Stanzas, Consecrated to the Glorious Memory . . ." of Cromwell in a commendatory volume (1659). People – especially young people – change their opinions all the time, so we should feel no compulsion to make Dryden consistent. But this poem is filled with so many perplexing ambiguities, as especially Steven N. Zwicker has noted, that no coherent republican ideology emerges from it. Dryden skates on perilous ice by outrageously employing in the opening stanzas the metaphor of "treason" to refer to his "best notes": he seems to mean that however good his praise, it cannot properly measure Cromwell's "fame," yet "duty" and "interest" both dictate that he offer such praise as he "can."

Not only does he stumble awkwardly through these early stanzas, Dryden goes on to talk of Cromwell's "*Grandeur*" as if it seemed greater than it really was; to call attention to Cromwell's ambivalence toward being crowned (especially the ambiguity of Cromwell's "Vertue" not being "poyson'd" with "*too early* thoughts of being King" – emphasis added); to a potentially embarrassing implicit reminder of Charles I as one of those "rash *Monarch's* who their youth betray / By Acts their Age too late would wish undone" – surely no cause for beheading. Even when his praise for Cromwell seems unambiguous as he relates Cromwell's series of victories, Dryden raises the general problem of infidelity when he accuses "Treacherous *Scotland*" of being "to no int'rest true." In the light of these and other inappropriate tropes, readers might well have sensed that Dryden's seeming praise of Cromwell's putting an end to the bloodshed "by breathing of the vein" was a grotesque reference to the regicide. But if so, perhaps what Dryden has done is subtly to undercut his apparent praise and therefore to dissociate himself from the mourners. Perhaps his final references to Tarpeia, the traitorous virgin, and to the beached Leviathan leave us with the image of a prodigious monster, who performed great feats, some of them for the good of the empire, but who nonetheless was something of a scourge of God. (Dryden would implicitly portray Cromwell as such in *Annus Mirabilis*). That might make sense of Dryden's strange last stanza:

> His Ashes in a peacefull Urne shall rest,
> His Name a great example stands to show
> How strangely high endeavours may be blest,
> Where *Piety* and *valour* joyntly goe.

The praise sounds unexceptionable, were it not for the troubling adverb "strangely." Maybe at this point we are to reflect back over the poem and wonder at the strangeness of a valor that commits treason and regicide in the name of piety. Are we to remember another "great example" in Western story, another conqueror who pretended to refuse the crown he lusted after, only to be taken off on the verge of it in strangely poetical justice?

If in "Heroique Stanzas" Dryden's ambivalence is expressed in the halting use of the quatrain made fashionable in Sir William Davenant's *Gondibert* (1651), the assuredness of his heroic couplets in *Astraea Redux* (1660), his poem celebrating Charles Stuart's restoration, may perhaps indicate Dryden's comfort with a feudal monarchist rather than a bourgeois republican ideological myth. Moreover, the first twenty-eight lines of *Astraea Redux* can be read as seven quatrains made up of couplets rather than alternating rhymes – as if to show Dryden could write sophisticated quatrains his own way:

> We sigh'd to hear the fair *Iberian* Bride
> Must grow a Lilie to the Lilies side,
> While Our cross Stars deny'd us *Charles* his Bed
> Whom Our first Flames and Virgin Love did wed.
> For his long absence Church and State did groan;
> Madness the Pulpit, Faction seiz'd the Throne:
> Experienc'd Age in deep despair was lost
> To see the Rebel thrive, the Loyal crost.

The special effects here are manifold: the delightful internal rhyme ("sigh'd ... Bride"); the image of lily yielding to lily (a play on the Spanish infanta's whiteness and purity being allied to the French fleur-de-lis as metonymy for Louis XIV) subtly underwritten by the collapse of the intervening iamb; the spondees of the last two lines of the first quatrain (the second reinforced by alliteration) underscoring the portrayal of England and Charles as star-crossed lovers; the substitution of initial trochee for iamb to emphasize the irrationality of the "Madness" that has taken over the Puritan "Pulpit"; the assonance that unites and thus equates both "Madness" in the "Church" and "Faction" in the "State"; the enjambment of the last couplet coming to rest in the final caesura, underlining by the rush toward the "Rebel" and the isolation of the "Loyal" the theodicean problem of evil's thriving while the good are star-"crost." Moreover, these images of the monarch as lover and his land as either loyal or disloyal spouse are integral to Dryden's ideological myth throughout the rest of his career. Central to this myth is the ultimate theodicean problem/solution: if power is the essence of government, then God himself can be stormed and "violated"; that is, there is no metaphysical guarantee to enforce the bonds of fidelity between leaders and people. For Dryden, normally absent Astraea (Justice) does return. In this poem "Providence" rules not by sheer power but by law and thus ensures that Charles's "right" is ultimately upheld, that he cannot be "Gods Anointed" in vain.

In many ways *Astraea Redux* anticipates foundational tropes in Dryden's later, greater political poems: the iron law of oligarchy that belies rebellion's rhetoric; the analogy between King Charles and King David; the analogy between the Puritans' Solemn League and Covenant in Charles's England and the Catholics' Holy League in Henri IV's France; the hypocrisy of glozing the "sin" of rebellion with the name of "Religion"; the counseling of mercy over justice; and, finally, exhortation of the king to concentrate on England's navy and its trade. What little positive Dryden saw in Cromwell – his contribution to British imperialism – can now be extended exponentially:

Dryden's brother-in-law and collaborator on The Indian-Queen *(engraving by R. White after a portrait by Sir Godfrey Kneller; first published as the frontispiece to Howard's* Five New Plays, *1692)*

> Our Nation with united Int'rest blest
> Not now content to poize, shall sway the rest.
> Abroad your Empire shall no Limits know,
> But like the Sea in boundless Circles flow.

Dryden identifies civilization itself, as opposed to a primitive "lawless salvage Libertie," with the "Arts" of "Empire" from Rome to contemporary England, an empire that is at once patriarchal, hierarchal, monarchal, and commercial.

In between the poems celebrating Cromwell and Charles, Dryden appears to have moved toward his career as a professional writer, his deceased father not having left him a sufficient income to survive where Dryden wanted to live – in the hub of political and cultural activity, London. In the late 1650s he seems to have lived with and written prefaces for the bookseller Henry Herringman, and by the early 1660s he had moved into lodgings with Sir Robert Howard, a younger son of Thomas Howard, first Earl of Berkshire, with impeccable Royalist credentials and a budding literary career. In a system of symbiosis between patrons and poets, Dryden had found himself a patron, and Howard had found himself an editor and collaborator. Dryden helped prepare Howard's first volume of poems for the press in 1660, for which he wrote the first of many panegyrics to prominent individuals, "To My Honored Friend, Sir Robert Howard," and in 1664 they collaborated on *The Indian-Queen,* a drama that contributed significantly to the Restoration fashion of rhymed heroic play (influenced, among other things, by those the exiled court witnessed in France) and that introduced what was to be the staple of Dryden's later contributions, the *noble savage,* whose powerful energy is eventually socialized.

Dryden's relationship with Howard is important in other ways: Dryden married his sister Lady Elizabeth Howard in 1663. Why a member of so prestigious a family would have stooped to a member of the lesser gentry remains a subject for speculation. But the match was certainly advantageous for Dryden, who was now a member of the powerful Howard family, several members of which aside from Sir Robert were playwrights. Along with his brothers-in-law Dryden tried his hand at his own plays. His first, a comedy entitled *The Wild Gallant* (1663), despite being a failure, won the support of another influential aristocrat, Barbara Villiers Palmer, Countess of Castlemaine, to whom Dryden addressed another verse epistle. Indeed, with such encouragement, abetted by his collaboration with Sir Robert (who had become a shareholder in the new Theatre Royal in Bridges Street), Dryden became a stable writer for the King's Company under Sir Thomas Killigrew and began to succeed on his own with his first tragicomedy, *The Rival Ladies* (late 1663?), and with a sequel to *The Indian-Queen, The Indian Emperour* (early 1665).

Dryden wrote three other panegyrics during the early 1660s: *To His Sacred Majesty, A Panegyrick On His Coronation* (1661), *To My Lord Chancellor* (1662), and "To My Honour'd Friend, Dr Charleton" (1663). In them he perfected the witty compliment begun with the poem to Sir Robert. But he also perfected the device of giving advice under cover of compliment, for example reminding the rakish Charles in the Coronation poem that political stability depends on his choosing a bride with all deliberate speed in order to ensure the succession. And the Charleton poem reflects Dryden's interest in the new science, an interest rewarded by invitation in the early 1660s to become a member of the Royal Academy of Science, although he appears not to have participated and was subsequently dropped.

In 1665 the plague was so bad in London that Dryden had to rusticate himself and his wife at her family estate in Charlton, Wiltshire. There he wrote three excellent works: *Of Dramatick Poesie: An Essay* (1667), the first great sustained work in English dramatic theory; *Secret-Love* (1667), the tragicomedy that perfected the gay couple motif, complete with proviso scene; and *Annus Mirabilis: The Year of Wonders, 1666* (1667). This "Historical Poem" celebrating English victories at sea during the Second Dutch War and Charles II's conduct during the Great Fire of London won Dryden the poet laureateship in 1668.

Because it was published in 1667, Dryden's heroic poem invites comparison with Milton's great epic *Paradise Lost,* first published in its ten-book format that same year. Ironically, Milton's epic – written by this radical Puritan secretary to Cromwell – despite its bourgeois elements of antimonarchism, emphasis on the individual and the domestic, and celebration of the *paradise within* of the private religious sphere, looks back through its aristocratic mode to classical and medieval times. Dryden's poem, despite its aristocratic elements of monarchism and heroic valor, its classical allusions and epic similes, looks forward through its bourgeois celebration of mercantile expansion, maritime dominance, and homely imagery of laboring citizens to the rule of a capitalist Britannia under a constitutional monarch.

Michael McKeon has brilliantly demonstrated that the poem is essentially political propaganda designed to stifle domestic dissent by rallying the nation around the common causes of war abroad and disaster at home. Dryden mythologizes Charles II, his brother James, Duke of York, and the triumphant admirals and generals as classical and Christian heroes and even gods. The care of the king is portrayed as being analogous to divine providence. The Great Fire of London (1666) is portrayed as a scourge for no particular sins (such as Charles's promiscuity, as his enemies would have it) but for the general sins of the nation and indeed humankind. And the fire's final extinction, having burned temples but not palaces, is portrayed as the result of Jove's melting with ruth upon hearing Charles's humble, pious prayer. This mythologizing seems deployed especially to defuse opposition to Charles and thereby to avert the potential unraveling of the Restoration compromise. Thus Charles is portrayed as the bride of his loyal country, or, even more explicitly, of the loyal City of London, and Dryden – from his Dedication to the City through his portrayal of the restored ship *Loyal London* to the restoration of the city itself as a "Maiden Queen" of commerce – exhorts almost desperately a fidelity on the part of the emergent bourgeoisie.

Underneath the mythologizing, Dryden is attempting to placate the growing power of the city as the center of trade and finance by getting it to view the *real* challenge for England as the battle over who controls world trade. Only one nation, one navy can and should control it ("What peace can be where both to one pretend?"). Therefore, the logic of the poem goes, Britain should defeat Holland, eclipse the trade of the rest of Europe, and make the world's waters a "British Ocean." Thus British "Commerce" will make "one City of the Universe." But this universal city will not mark the end of competition in some sort of utopian distribution of the cornucopia. Dryden's model is one of acquisitive crypto-capitalism: "some may gain, and all may be suppli'd." Then as now such a trickle-down theory results in the "some" gaining a disproportionate amount of the world's wealth at the expense and exploitation of the many. Behind Dryden's cornucopia lies an imperialist theory of dominance.

Nevertheless, at his very best Dryden the mythologizer of late feudalism and incipient capitalism descends occasionally from his highly allusive and allegorical mode to portray real people in material situations. Witness the momentary descent in these stanzas:

> Night came, but without darkness or repose,
>   A dismal picture of the gen'ral doom:
> Where Souls distracted when the Trumpet blows,
>   And half unready with their bodies come.
>
> Those who have homes, when home they do repair
>   To a last lodging call their wand'ring friends.
> Their short uneasie sleeps are broke with care,
>   To look how near their own destruction tends.
>
> Those who have none sit round where once it was,
>   And with full eyes each wonted room require:
> Haunting the yet warm ashes of the place,
>   As murder'd men walk where they did expire.

The opening allegorical yet human image is worthy of Donne. For anyone who has lived through fire, hurricane, tornado, or (in our century) saturation or nuclear bombing, the stanzas painting the near or already homeless are quite poignant. And Dryden's maturity as a poet is evidenced here by his masterful handling of not only image but sound: the reversed iambs and spondees, the frequent alliteration and occasional assonance ("Souls . . . blows"), and especially the freeze-frame quality of successive emphasized syllables imitating the eyes' movement from room to room around the absent house.

Dryden also insightfully imagines the contrasting dreams of the English and Dutch sailors during an evening's respite from the battle. But he dares most by his inclusion, in these new heroic stanzas, of indecorously technical and vulgar terms for material work by the laboring force of shipbuilders called upon to repair the British fleet, from picking "bullets" out of planks, to caulking seams with "Okum" and "boiling Pitch," to binding "gall'd ropes" with "dawby Marling," to re-covering masts

"with strong Tarpawling coats." Dryden is no democrat; he has no love here as elsewhere in his poetry for "th'ignoble crowd," and he hints at the anarchy unleashed by republican rebels. However, in his image of these industrious laborers demonstrating their loyalty and contributing to the cause, he raises them to the stature of the heroic. However he mythologizes the duke of York and Prince Rupert and George Monck, Duke of Albemarle, and King Charles himself, the reader experiences the following realistic snapshots within the same poem: Albemarle, his breeches ignominiously blown off, as Dryden's audience would know, "All bare, like some old Oak which tempests beat, / He stands, and sees below his scatter'd leaves"; and while the King harmlessly amuses himself playing with the "newcast Canons," among the shipworkers "To try new shrouds one mounts into the wind, / And one, below, their ease or stifness notes." By diminishing heroes and exalting workers Dryden has at least leveled them into a common humanity, united in a bourgeois image of cooperation between government, venture capital, and guild labor in order to subdue the earth.

Dryden's return to London in the winter of 1666–1667 was triumphant. Several of his plays were staged, old (*The Wild Gallant* and *The Indian Emperour*) and new (not just *Secret Love* but *Sir Martin Mar-All* and an adaptation of Shakespeare's *The Tempest*, plays he collaborated on with William Cavendish, Duke of Newcastle, and Sir William Davenant, respectively, and which were performed by the rival Duke's Company); the *Essay* was published; the King's Company signed Dryden to a contract in which he became a shareholder and agreed to give them three new plays per year; and he received the laureateship – all before the end of 1668. By the end of 1671 he had produced four more plays, including two masterpieces, *The Conquest of Granada,* a rhymed heroic play in ten acts, and *Marriage A-la-Mode,* a split-plot tragicomedy. Dryden had established himself as the greatest dramatist of his time. And if one can separate out his development as a poet per se – a difficult task when his plays have so much verse, so many songs, and prologues and epilogues in couplets – one would have to conclude that, despite the absence during these years of isolated poems, Dryden achieved a virtuosity of verse and wit unequaled during the Restoration. Palmyra's description of her falling in love with Leonidas in *Marriage A-la-Mode* is lovelily lyrical. The prologue to *An Evening's Love* (1668) concerning poets as worn-out gallants and the songs concerning wet dreams and worn-out marriage vows from *The Conquest of Granada* and *Marriage A-la-Mode* respectively are wickedly witty and wonderfully versified. But Dryden's masterpiece is probably his puckish epilogue to *Tyrannic Love* (1669), spoken by Nell Gwyn, outrageously rakish actress and mistress to Charles II (among others). Having played Valeria, daughter of the Roman emperor Maximin who martyrs Saint Catharine, and having herself been a martyr to love, Nell is about to be carried off at the end of the play, when she leaps up — most certainly to the audience's delight in such comic relief — and speaks the epilogue in couplets that rival Alexander Pope's for their colloquial and dramatically conversational style:

> To the Bearer. *Hold, are you mad? you damn'd*
> *confounded Dog,*
> *I am to rise, and speak the Epilogue.*
> To the Audience. *I come, kind Gentlemen, strange news to*
> *tell ye,*
> *I am the Ghost of poor departed* Nelly....
> *O Poet, damn'd dull Poet, who could prove*
> *So sensless! to make* Nelly *die for Love;*
> *Nay, what's yet worse, to kill me in the prime*
> *Of Easter-Term, in Tart and Cheese-cake time!*
> *I'le fit the Fopp; for I'le not one word say*
> *T'excuse his godly out-of-fashion Play:*
> *A Play which if you dare but twice sit out,*
> *You'l all be slander'd, and be thought devout.*
> *But farewel, Gentlemen, make haste to me,*
> *I'm sure e're long to have your company.*
> *As for my Epitaph when I am gone,*
> *I'le trust no Poet, but will write my own.*
>
> Here *Nelly* lies, who, though she liv'd a
> Slater'n,
> Yet dy'd a Princess, acting in S. *Cathar'n.*

The laughter must have brought down the house. Yet twentieth-century critics do not seem to understand that such wit does not *undercut* (their favorite metaphor) the seriousness of such plays as *Tyrannic Love, The Conquest of Granada,* and *Marriage A-la-Mode.* Urbanity does not mean a supercilious, ironic rejection of all values but rather a witty reflexivity and studied insouciance about them.

By 1672, then, Dryden was at the height of his powers and reputation. He had added to the title poet laureate that of historiographer royal. He hobnobbed with the powerful and, despite his increasing family (by then, three sons), appears to have aped the manners of his betters by fashionably taking a mistress, the actress Ann Reeves. But the first hints of the tarnishing of his triumph had also appeared: his feud with his brother-in-law Sir Robert over the aesthetic merit of rhyme in drama escalated through Dryden's *Essay* to Howard's preface

to *The Great Favourite; or, The Duke of Lerma* (1668) to Dryden's extremely intemperate "Defence" of the *Essay,* prefixed to the second edition of *The Indian Emperour* in the same year. Because this preface was removed from most copies of this edition, one can speculate that Dryden realized his error in judgment, but his relationship with his brother-in-law may have been permanently damaged. A few years later, perhaps out of pique at Dryden's pride in his success, George Villiers, second Duke of Buckingham, attacked Dryden as a poetaster in *The Rehearsal* (1671). The era of Dryden's public brawls with his critics had begun.

Things got worse when fire destroyed Dryden's company's theater at the inopportune time of the rival company's moving into an extravagant new theater in Dorset Garden. Furthermore, the Duke's Company was beginning to have the best actors as Thomas Betterton gathered great young talent around him, and it was beginning to attract new and successful playwrights: Thomas Shadwell, Edward Ravenscroft, and Elkanah Settle. Dryden's own new comedy, *The Assignation* (1672), failed, and even his jingoistic propaganda attack against the Dutch during the outbreak of the Third Dutch War, *Amboyna* (1673), did not salvage the fortunes of the King's Company. When their new theater in Drury Lane opened in 1674, Dryden, in an attempt to rival the extravaganzas of the Duke's Company, tried to turn his great admiration for Milton's *Paradise Lost* to account by creating an operatic version, *The State of Innocence.* He appears even to have gone so far as to visit the aged and blind poet, with whom he had once worked, in order to ask his permission. From all his references to Milton's great poems throughout his works, beginning perhaps as early as 1669, one can infer in what respect Dryden held Milton, but unfortunately nothing is known of this meeting. Even more unfortunately, for Dryden and the King's Company at least, the company could not afford to produce the opera, and it was never performed. At this nadir of his career, Dryden sought an appointment at Oxford where he could retire from the stage and write his own epic poem. Neither desideratum was ever to be realized.

Whether caused by Milton's great aesthetic achievements and his attack on rhymed plays, or by Settle's embarrassingly bathetic popular successes in Dryden's erstwhile favorite genre of rhymed heroic play, or just by Dryden's own study (perhaps of plays by the great French dramatist Jean Racine), Dryden began his comeback by moving toward a more neoclassical form of drama. In *Notes and Observations on the Empress of Morocco* (1674), he joined in an attack on Settle's extravagance. In 1675, although he gave the King's Company another excellent rhymed heroic play, *Aureng-Zebe,* in the prologue he bade farewell to his "long-lov'd Mistris, Rhyme" (and probably his other mistress, Ann Reeves, as well) as he began to imitate Racine. His next three serious plays were blank-verse, neoclassical tragedies, and one – *All for Love* (1677) – was the greatest tragedy of the Restoration; indeed, it remains the greatest tragedy in English after Shakespeare, and it is still performed in England. His theory of the late 1670s ("Heads of an Answer to Rymer," "The Grounds of Criticism in Tragedy"), influenced by Thomas Rymer and the French critics, as well as by Racine, became more neoclassical. And he turned his attention to the translation of classics. In his dramatic compositions he was also influenced by the initial successes of two new playwrights, Thomas Otway and Nathaniel Lee. Dryden entered into a temporary rivalry with Otway, who wrote for the Duke's Company. Dryden entered into a friendship with Lee, who wrote for the King's Company, that produced mutual praise (commendatory poems addressed to each other prefixed to Dryden's *The State of Innocence and Fall of Man* and Lee's *The Rival Queens,* both published in 1677) and mutual work (by 1678 they had both abandoned the King's Company and moved to the Duke's Company, for whom they wrote *Oedipus* in 1678 and *The Duke of Guise* in 1682). Dryden's severing of ties with the King's Company had begun as early as 1677, when he insisted on the third night's profits from *All for Love.* It continued with the Duke's Company's production of *The Kind Keeper* in 1678 (apparently because the King's Company did not want it).

In the meantime, however, before Dryden made the transition from King's to Duke's, from romance to neoclassical tragedy, from depression to renewed vigor as dramatist, he had some scores to settle. When his fortunes were sinking, he had appealed to John Wilmot, Earl of Rochester, to patronize him, but, after some initial flirtation, Rochester proved inconstant, supported Dryden's rival Shadwell instead, and lampooned Dryden in "An Allusion to Horace." Dryden had been feuding with Shadwell over the theory of comedy for years in various prefaces and dedications, but the two had remained relatively conciliatory and had collaborated with John Crowne in the attack on Settle. In early 1676, however, the same year Rochester's satire was circulating in manuscript, Shadwell broke the facade of civility and degenerated into lampoon. He pilloried Dryden throughout his comedy *The*

Virtuoso, especially in the dedication to the published text.

Dryden responded with a vengeance probably doubled by displaced anger at Rochester and compounded by his own poor fortunes, both literal and figurative, in the first half of the decade. Beginning most likely in the summer of 1676, Dryden wrote one of the two greatest satires in English against rival poets, *Mac Flecknoe* (the other is Pope's *Dunciad,* 1728-1743). He certainly had finished it by 1678, though it circulated in manuscript until unauthorized publication in 1682. The controlling fiction of the poem is succession, a daring motif in a country where the restored monarch had produced no legitimate male heir. Witness the brashness of the opening lines:

> All humane things are subject to decay,
> And, when Fate summons, Monarchs must obey[.]

The phenomenology of the first reading dictates that the reader's expectations for a heavy, topical political poem have been aroused. The next couplet provides a crashing diminuendo:

> This *Fleckno* found, who, like *Augustus,* young
> Was call'd to Empire, and had govern'd long.

The poem is a mock panegyric, a paradoxical encomium, complete with parodic procession and coronation. Dryden the poet laureate destroys his rival by crowning him anti–poet laureate, king of "the Realms of *Non-sense*": "from *Ireland* let him reign / To farr *Barbadoes* on the Western main" – that is, he reigns over the unpopulated Atlantic Ocean! By making Richard Flecknoe his poetic forebear, Dryden denies Shadwell the lineage he has claimed, to be a new Son of Ben (Jonson) because of his dedication to a comedy of humors. Instead, Flecknoe was a poetaster who paid to have his plays published, who sometimes changed a title and added a little window dressing to get one produced (*Erminia* [1661] to *Emilia* [1672]), whose plays, whether produced or not were uniformly bad. Yet Flecknoe may also have earned Dryden's professional envy by having the courage to appeal to Cromwell to reopen the stage in the dedication to *Love's Dominion* (1654) and by trying his own hand at a history of the English stage in the preface to that play's revision as *Love's Kingdom* (1664). To make Shadwell Flecknoe's heir was to put down another upstart, especially by portraying him as impotent, capable of producing urine and feces and freaks but no legitimate, manly poetic progeny.

John Dryden, circa 1683 (portrait by John Riley; from David Piper, The Development of the British Literary Portrait up to Samuel Johnson, *1968)*

Throughout the poem Dryden combines references to dirt with references to myth. The latter does not "transcend" the former (another favorite metaphor of critics) but coexists with it, cocreates the joke, which is intended to amuse Dryden's friends, antagonize his enemies, and hurt Shadwell himself – as if Dryden were saying, "Don't touch me!" Dryden's technique perhaps can be best illustrated by the following lines:

The hoary Prince in Majesty appear'd,
High on a Throne of his own Labours rear'd.

The second line echoes Satan's ascent to his parodic throne in the opening of book 2 of Milton's *Paradise Lost,* and its metaphor of "Labours" alludes to the leitmotiv of labor in Virgil's *Aeneid,* upon which

alone can a lasting empire be built. But "Labours" of course refers primarily to a pile of Flecknoe's worthless books. Yet by extension of the repeated references to "Sh____" in the poem – ostensibly *Shadwell* but implicitly *shit* every time, as in "loads of *Sh____* almost chokt the way" – "Labours" refers metaphorically to piles of material more than just books. Dryden may be portraying Shadwell as an Antichrist of Wit (in anticipation of Pope), but he is also and at the same time debasing him through folk humor as being full of shit. Neither level of meaning supersedes the other.

Another instance of the technique occurs at the end. Playing off the controlling fiction of succession, Dryden's elaborate use of classical and Christian allusions throughout allows him to compare Shadwell to Ascanius, Iulus, Christ himself, or, in the closing lines, Elisha to Flecknoe's Elijah. Flecknoe's last lines of encomium are lost as he disappears through a trapdoor mischievously engineered by a couple of Shadwell's comic characters:

> Sinking he left his Drugget robe behind,
> Born upwards by a subterranean wind.
> The Mantle fell to the young Prophet's part,
> With double portion of his Father's Art.

The *f, P, p* pattern of the penultimate line begs to be repeated in a *p, F,* [*f*] pattern in the last, so that the "subterranean wind" (perhaps an allusion to Milton's wind off the backside of the world that blows hypocrites awry in book 3 of *Paradise Lost*) gets positively identified in the reader's mind sotto voce: this mock-Elisha inherits his mantle upward not downward from his *Father's fart.* Curiously, the Dryden who seems so preoccupied in his prologues and epilogues with establishing a bourgeois community of taste that contemns "low" artistic techniques and types such as slapstick and farce reveals himself to be the master of Rabelaisian humor. In the cruelest cut of all, he has Flecknoe say to Sh____, "With whate'er gall thou sett'st thy self to write, / Thy inoffensive Satyrs never bite." Dryden's satire has bitten so well that he has effectively decapitated Shadwell for three centuries, precisely because he has so masterfully combined high and low. Playing a mock–John the Baptist to Shadwell's mock-Messiah, Flecknoe prepares the way for a mock–Triumphal Entry into Jerusalem-London, where not palm leaves

> But scatter'd Limbs of mangled Poets lay:
> From dusty shops neglected Authors come,
> Martyrs of Pies, and Reliques of the Bum.

This mixing of sacred and scatological is positively medieval in its folk humor. Dryden can pretend that Shadwell has debased Jonson into selling "Bargains, Whip-stitch, kiss my Arse," but this last phrase is exactly what Dryden has commanded Sh____ to do.

After the success of *All for Love* and the growing chances for his security with the Duke's Company, Dryden must have felt emboldened enough to settle his other score by attacking Rochester himself in his preface to the published version of the new play in early 1678. While suggesting that Rochester specifically had bitten off more than he could chew in imitating Horace, that he ought to leave writing to professionals, that his own literary heritage descends from the poetaster translator of the Psalms, Thomas Sternhold, Dryden indicts not just Roches-

ter but his "witty" comrades, such as Buckingham, Rymer, and Sir Charles Sedley, but also his *zanies,* such as Shadwell and Otway. Squire Dryden asserts his talents as a literary professional to be superior to those of the court wits, who properly ought to confine their literary dabbling to being good patrons. Perhaps Dryden was feeling protected by his new patron, the dedicatee of *All for Love,* Lord Treasurer Thomas Osborne, Earl of Danby. Indeed, shortly after Danby's fall from power in 1679, Dryden was attacked by thugs in Rose Alley and beaten soundly. Did Rochester and his friends finally take their revenge? Or by that time had Dryden offended someone else (suggestions have included the King's mistress, Louise de Kéroualle, Duchess of Portsmouth, and the Whig Opposition)? The point of the beating is that Dryden was considered uppity enough for some group to want to teach him a lesson. But if they thought they would intimidate him, they were mistaken.

In 1678 occurred the infamous Popish Plot. Several witnesses, most notorious among them Titus Oates, offered perjured testimony to the effect that the Jesuits were planning the overthrow of the government and a return of England to the yoke of Catholicism – a threat that Englishmen, in the light of characters in their history since the time of Henry VIII, from Bloody Mary to Guy Fawkes, found credible. (Indeed, they were right to be suspicious, for the Stuarts had made an unholy alliance with France eventually to deliver their nation back into the Catholic fold.) Several Catholic heads rolled; Catholic peers were removed from the House of Lords; the duke of York and his new Catholic duchess, Maria Beatrice, had to go into exile; and a new Parliament was elected, one that was ready to pass legislation to exclude James from the throne because of his religion: thus the name given to this political turmoil, the Exclusion Crisis. Some of the principals tried to get Charles to declare his bastard son, James Scott, Duke of Monmouth, his legitimate heir. Several playwrights jumped on the anti-Catholic bandwagon as if to say, "we might disagree with the exclusionists, but we are not therefore in favor of a foreign-based Catholic takeover, ultimately by Rome through France." Dryden himself grabbed onto the wagon in his next play, *The Spanish Fryar* (1680), in which he satirizes a priest; nevertheless, in the high plot he strenuously upholds the principle of hereditary, patrilineal monarchal succession. He apparently (his authorship is disputed) even more stridently defended Charles's dissolution of Parliament in a pamphlet entitled *His Majesties Declaration Defended* (1681). And finally he wrote the greatest political poem in the English language, *Absalom and Achitophel* (1681).

Dryden's controlling fiction in this poem is the familiar trope of superimposing scriptural story over current events. He had already availed himself of the David story in *Astraea Redux*. The consequences for propaganda are obvious. Dryden endows his vision of events with sacred authority: the social and the sacred Logos are the same. Thus a theoretical dispute over the mode of political succession gets mythologized and mystified. Parliament's struggle to control succession becomes a blasphemous, ultimately Satanic revolt against "heavens Anointing Oyle." Absalom's sacrilegious revolt against David gets reenacted in contemporary history. The evil counselor Achitophel becomes Anthony Ashley Cooper, third Earl of Shaftesbury, one of the leaders of the Parliamentary party, who was caricatured repeatedly in ways reminiscent of Shakespeare's treatment of Richard III. Dryden adds the further fillip of overlaying Miltonian pattern: Achitophel/Shaftesbury becomes Satan tempting an anti-Messiah to be the people's "*Saviour.*"

One of the problems with the biblical parallel is that its arc is tragic. It is as if Dryden wrote Monmouth into a text from which he could not escape. David threatens at the end, "If my Young *Samson* will pretend a Call / To shake the Column, let him share the Fall." David's urge, on the other hand, is to be lenient. But Monmouth never did heed the poet's advice; he led a revolt upon his father's death in 1685 and was executed. Moreover, as with the biblical David, Dryden's David/Charles is trammeled up in the consequences of his adultery. Dryden opens again brilliantly:

In pious times, e'er Priest-craft did begin,
Before *Polygamy* was made a sin;
When man, on many, multiply'd his kind,
E'r one to one was, cursedly, confind:
When Nature prompted, and no law deny'd
Promiscuous use of Concubine and Bride;
Then, *Israel*'s Monarch, after Heaven's
   own heart,
His vigorous warmth did, variously, impart
To Wives and Slaves: And, wide as his Command,
Scatter'd his Maker's Image through the Land.

However wittily Dryden opens the poem, the ultimate point of its portrayal of David's promiscuity is that "No True Succession" can "attend" the "seed" of David's concubines. Another of Dryden's bold openings has cut to the heart of the matter. When Absalom and David both later complain that Absalom was born too high but not high enough,

they may blame "Fate" or "God," but the fault is clearly David's own, as it was in 2 Samuel when God punished David with Absalom's rebellion for David's adultery with Bathsheba and the murder of her husband, and as Dryden's pointed reference to Bathsheba would remind his audience.

However, the main point of Dryden's poem is neither to recuperate Monmouth nor admonish Charles. It is to discredit thoroughly Charles's enemies and their putative political theory, praise his steadfast friends, and vindicate Charles himself. The first objective Dryden accomplishes with perhaps the most devastating rogues' gallery of satiric portraits ever assembled. The portraits are not devastating solely because of vitriolic lampooning, though there is plenty of that. They are devastating because they at first appear evenhanded, a studied moderation designed to appeal to the common sense of Dryden's contemporary audience. After praising Achitophel/Shaftesbury for being an excellent judge, Dryden breaks out in calculated lamentation:

Oh, had he been content to serve the Crown,
With vertues only proper to the Gown; . . .
David, for him his tunefull Harp had strung,
And Heaven had wanted one Immortal song.

That is, David would not have had to write Psalm 109 attacking Achitophel. "But," Dryden continues with studied sadness:

   wilde Ambition loves to slide, not stand;
And Fortunes Ice prefers to Vertues Land:
Achitophel, grown weary to possess
A lawfull Fame, and lazy Happiness;
Disdain'd the Golden fruit to gather free,
And lent the Croud his Arm to shake the Tree.
Now, manifest of Crimes, contriv'd long since,
He stood at bold Defiance with his Prince:
Held up the Buckler of the Peoples Cause,
Against the Crown; and sculk'd behind the Laws.

What could be more temperate, more measured than this cool judgment? After all, Shaftesbury's prince had been lenient with him, forgiven him for supporting Cromwell. Nevertheless, "Restless, unfixt in Principles and Place," Shaftesbury was not content to await the descending benefits of a merciful king but, because of ambition, preferred "Fortunes Ice." Thus Dryden avails himself not only of the posture of fair judgment but also the leitmotiv of inconstancy versus steadfastness. By his very nature or character, Shaftesbury cannot remain fixed; driven by desire, he "loves to slide, not stand." The implication, of course, is that "Fortunes Ice" is perilously thin, that Shaftesbury's use of Parliament and the law is a flimsy ruse.

Dryden's portrait of Absalom also appears balanced. He is like one of Dryden's noble savages. But the difference is that he does not turn out to be the legitimate heir, and he knows it, acknowledging David's "Right" to rule and that of his "Lawfull Issue," if he should have any, or of his "*Collateral Line*," that is, his brother. When through ambition fostered by his noble nature Monmouth succumbs to Achitophel's Satanic temptation, Dryden again assumes the strategy of lamentation:

> Unblam'd of Life (Ambition set aside,)
> Not stain'd with Cruelty, nor puft with Pride;
> How happy had he been, if Destiny
> Had higher plac'd his Birth, or not so high!
> His Kingly Vertues might have claim'd a Throne,
> And blest all other Countries but his own:
> But charming Greatness, since so few refuse;
> 'Tis Juster to Lament him, than Accuse.

The master stroke here is Dryden's sympathy toward Monmouth's ambiguous position in the hierarchy resulting from the circumstances of his birth (not his but Charles's fault) coupled with his insistence (as well as Charles's own) that nevertheless he remains illegitimate. Even if he were legitimate, Dryden implies, he would never be the heir (because he has shown by his character that he could never merit it?); he might have blessed other countries with his noble virtues (through royal intermarriage), but not — and never — his own.

Dryden also portrays the "Best" of the "Malecontents" assembled by Achitophel — that is, primarily, the Country party among the Lords — as being essentially well-meaning but "Seduc'd by Impious Arts" into believing the "power of Monarchy" a threat to "Property." Thus identifying with and appealing to the moderates in the House of Lords, Dryden does not want to seem to be maligning his betters. He saves his nastiness generally for the middle and lower classes, whom he portrays as motivated by "Interest," parsimonious "Husbandry," desire for "Preferment," or, under the hypocritical guise of (dissenting) religion, the sheer desire "all things to Destroy," especially monarchy itself. Dryden portrays the common "herd" as mindless, those "Who think too little, and who talk too much."

Dryden's next justly famous portraits are representatives of the three classes. From the truly rebellious aristocrats (implicitly a mere fringe group) he selects his old enemy Buckingham, whom he portrays as similar to Shaftesbury, too inconstant in his moods, postures, and political positions to remain constant to any one – or, by implication, to the king:

> Some of their Chiefs were Princes of the Land:
> In the first Rank of these did *Zimri* stand:
> A man so various, that he seem'd to be
> Not one, but all Mankinds Epitome.
> Stiff in Opinions, always in the wrong;
> Was every thing by starts, and nothing long:
> But, in the course of one revolving Moon,
> Was Chymist, Fidler, States-Man, and Buffoon:
> Then all for Women, Painting, Rhiming, Drinking;
> Besides ten thousand freaks that dy'd in thinking.

In the whole passage, but especially in the last two couplets, Dryden is at his absolute best at wielding the rhetoric of satire. The zeugma of the antepenultimate line is worthy of Pope's more famous lists, especially when one considers that "States-Man," potentially a pejorative term anyway, gets completely leveled to the status of the concluding "Buffoon." Then the jingle of the participles dances through the feminine ending of the penultimate line, pausing for a moment on the spondee in the middle of "Besides ten thousand freaks" before tripping into the final feminine ending, creating a contemporary mindless marionette.

Dryden's representative of the middle class is the hypocritical Puritan Shimei (Slingsby Bethel, sheriff of London), whose animosity against the office of king itself is so strong he fears not to curse "Heavens Annointed," and whose very religion is simply a means for his personal "Gain." As do modern satirists with televangelists, Dryden turns Shimei's canting rhetoric against him:

> For *Shimei*, though not prodigal of pelf,
> Yet lov'd his wicked Neighbour as himself:
> When two or three were gather'd to declaim
> Against the Monarch of *Jerusalem*,
> *Shimei* was always in the midst of them:
> And, if they Curst the King when he was by,
> Would rather Curse, than break good Company.

In a wonderful marriage of sound, sight, and sense, the middle triplet here inserts a third line into the usual couplet form as if in imitation of the insinuation of Antichrist Shimei into the midst of his disciples.

Dryden's representative of the lower class is Corah, who stands for Titus Oates, the weaver's son who was the archwitness of the Popish Plot. Dryden portrays him with dripping sarcasm:

> His Memory, miraculously great,
> Could Plots, exceeding mans belief, repeat;
> Which, therefore cannot be accounted Lies,
> For humane Wit could never such devise.

If Shimei perverts the words of Scripture for his interest, Corah perverts words in the very citadel of justice, where oaths are supposed to guarantee the truth. Indeed, all of Dryden's villains assault the social logos through disloyalty, hypocrisy, and perjury, thus challenging the underwriting divine Logos.

In addition to discrediting his opponents thus, Dryden discredits their political theory. Achitophel's articulation of Lockean theory – "the People have a Right Supreme / To make their Kings; for Kings are made for them. / All Empire is no more than Pow'r in Trust" – is belied by his own ambition for power. But Dryden appears to take his theory seriously and to approach the question moderately. Rejecting the position of absolute monarchy, Dryden equally rejects the position of social-contract theorists who argue that the people can take their bond back, a secession resulting, for Dryden, in Hobbist political instability:

> If they may Give and Take when e'r they please,
> Not Kings alone, (the Godheads Images,)
> But Government it self at length must fall
> To Natures state; where all have Right to all.

Purloining Locke's own concept of prudence, Dryden then asks in his most conciliatory mode, "Yet, grant our Lords the People Kings can make, / What Prudent men a setled Throne woud shake?" While Dryden appears to be adopting a Burkean conservatism based on the weight of tradition – as is obvious from all the references to God's involvement in anointing and supporting kings throughout the poem – the grammatical uncertainty of the first line images forth the political anarchy that would ensue if anyone but God – lords, commoners, kings themselves, by tampering with succession – were to make a king.

Dryden then proceeds to portray the king's friends as a loyal group of peers, bishops, judges, and even the former speaker of the (now rebellious) House of Commons. Unlike the conspirators, these men kept their words of loyalty and, like Dryden the poet, used their words to defend the king and to rebut his attackers – most notably, perhaps, Jotham, who represents George Savile, Marquis of Halifax, whose golden tongue in debate turned the tide against the Exclusion Bill in the House of Lords.

The greatest wielder of words in the poem is David himself, who comes forward finally to vindicate his power and position. Weary of abuse despite his wonted clemency and long-suffering, David insists that even if he has only a part of government, the part belongs to him, cannot be attenuated by any other part, and is "to Rule." Dryden endows his speech with magisterial authority:

> Without my Leave a future King to choose,
> Infers a Right the Present to Depose:
> True, they Petition me t'approve their Choise,
> But *Esau*'s Hands suite ill with *Jacob*'s Voice.

David becomes more aggressive as he progresses:

> What then is left but with a Jealous Eye
> To guard the Small remains of Royalty?
> The Law shall still direct my peacefull Sway,
> And the same Law teach Rebels to Obey.

Thus Dryden stakes out for David/Charles a middle ground between extremes of arbitrary or anarchic rule. He insists on the king's lawful prerogative granted by the unwritten constitution and forming part of a balanced system of government. The other parts of that balance have threatened the very Ark of the Covenant, and so David himself now threatens, "Law they require, let Law then shew her Face," for "Lawfull Pow'r is still Superiour found." So David will punish the transgressors, who will actually devour themselves by turning against each other. Dryden closes the poem by underwriting David's words with the Word of God: "He said. Th'Almighty, nodding, gave Consent: / And Peals of Thunder shook the Firmament." Dryden's final touch, then, is a kind of apotheosis: David and God become one: "And willing Nations knew their Lawfull Lord."

Absalom and Achitophel was a celebration of Charles's triumph over his foes in the Exclusion Crisis. As it was published in November of 1681, Shaftesbury was on trial for treason. But that triumph seemed short-lived, for Shaftesbury, to Dryden the archconspirator, got off scot-free, and his supporters cast a medal in his honor. Early in 1682 Dryden published another attack on Shaftesbury and his followers, *The Medall. A Satyre against Sedition*. He relinquished the moderate stance of the earlier poem and wrote a scathing Juvenalian satire, prefaced by an equally scathing "Epistle to the Whigs." The controlling fiction of the poem is the two sides of the medal, one with a portrait of Shaftesbury, the other with a portrait of the City of London. Again portraying Shaftesbury's political inconstancy as a function of inconstancy of character, Dryden says sardonically of the medal, "Cou'd it have form'd his ever-changing Will, / The various Piece had tir'd the Graver's Skill." Dryden traces him through his

John Dryden, 1693 (portrait by Kneller; National Portrait Gallery, London)

tortuous twists of allegiance until his final revelation of the "fiend" within.

On the other hand, Dryden addresses "*London,
thou great Emporium* of our Isle" again in a lamen-
tory mode, and one cannot help remembering his
praise of the city in *Annus Mirabilis* as the emporium
of England's imperialist trade. As in *Absalom and
Achitophel,* Dryden spares the virtuous Londoners
from blame, but he stridently attacks the "Fool and
Knave" who corruptly misdirect the city's great energies. Here one sees as plainly as anywhere Dryden's
fear of and contempt for the rising middle class
that couched its political ambitions in religious
rhetoric:

In Gospel phrase their Chapmen they betray:
Their Shops are Dens, the Buyer is their Prey.
The Knack of Trades is living on the Spoyl;
They boast, ev'n when each other they beguile.

Customes to steal is such a trivial thing,
That 'tis their Charter, to defraud their King.

Dryden has perceived the inherent danger of bourgeois individualism and incipient capitalism: the
selfish, predatory accumulation of wealth by means
of fraud and tax evasion. These are descendants of
the Commonwealth's men who murdered a previous king and who are still bent on the destruction
not only of "Kings" but of "Kingly Pow'r" per se.

In both sections of the poem, Dryden satirizes
(this time he does not pretend to rational debate)
the political theory of the Whigs. In both he reduces
republican theory to a version of might makes right,
here applied to the concept of majority rule, "The
Most have right, the wrong is in the Few":

Almighty Crowd, thou shorten'st all dispute;
Pow'r is thy Essence; Wit thy Attribute!

Nor Faith nor Reason make thee at a stay,
Thou leapst o'r all eternal truths, in thy *Pindarique* way!

The wit in these lines resides not only in the brilliant imitative spillover of the concluding alexandrine but also in the mock theology: as in the disputes over whether God's will or his reason be his primary essence, Dryden follows his sarcastic reference to the crowd as "Almighty" with a pseudovoluntarist position, reducing reason or "Wit" to a mere "Attribute." But, as he had suggested early in his writing,

If Sovereign Right by Sovereign Pow'r they scan,
The same bold Maxime holds in God and Man:
God were not safe, his Thunder cou'd they shun
He shou'd be forc'd to crown another Son.

The marvelous irony of the last line works especially well when one reads from the caesura of the penultimate line through the enjambment to fall hard upon the reversed iamb of the last line: the implication is that even *He* would be forced, like Charles, to declare another son his legitimate heir. The pun on *crown,* referring to Christ's crown of thorns, is savage.

The best – because, perhaps, the most prophetic – parts of the poem are the early series of analogies to political majority rule and the later series of images of clipping of the royal power until the monarch is purely ceremonial – as indeed he/she became after the revolution Dryden so desperately feared. Dryden mocks the notion that majority rule is stable, citing historical examples of mistakes resulting in the deaths of heroes, among them Socrates. As he comes closer to his own time, he wickedly asserts, "Crowds err not, though to both extremes they run; / To kill the Father, and recall the Son." His most scathing indictment of this creeping relativism occurs in the following lines:

Some think the Fools were most, as times went then;
But now the World's o'r stock'd with prudent men.
The common Cry is ev'n Religion's Test;
The *Turk*'s is, at *Constantinople,* best;
Idols in *India,* Popery at *Rome;*
And our own Worship onely true at home:
And true, but for the time; 'tis hard to know
How long we please it shall continue so.
This side to day, and that to morrow burns;
So all are God-a'mighties in their turns.

Instead of mythologizing the political theory he defends, Dryden attempts to justify it on pragmatic grounds, that their British forefathers attempted to avoid factional civil war by securing peaceful succession of both power and property through primogeniture. God has already tried us, Dryden argues, by giving the republicans what they wanted during the Commonwealth, and look what happened. And he predicts a similar cannibalistic civil war if Shaftesbury and his cronies succeed, for all will want a piece of the power, and none will be constrained by law. His concluding prophecy seems a bitter wish-fulfillment:

Thus inborn Broyles the Factions wou'd ingage,
Or Wars of Exil'd Heirs, or Foreign Rage,
Till halting Vengeance overtook our Age:
And our wild Labours, wearied into Rest,
Reclin'd us on a rightfull Monarch's Breast.

If as at the end of *Absalom and Achitophel* Dryden is again collapsing both earthly and heavenly monarch together, his vision has progressed from apotheosis to apocalypse, the ultimate curse of the satirist.

In the immediate aftermath of the Exclusion Crisis, Dryden continued to attack the Stuarts' enemies. He contributed satiric portraits of old nemeses now openly Whiggish, Settle and Shadwell, to a sequel to *Absalom and Achitophel,* written mostly by another young protégé, Nahum Tate. He contributed politically satirical prologues and epilogues to several plays. He wrote another play with Nathaniel Lee, *The Duke of Guise* (1682), which exploited the analogy between current events and those in France a century before; he wrote a *Vindication* of that play (1683); and in 1684 he translated Louis Maimbourg's *History of the League,* the source of most of his knowledge of that French analogue. The stridency of Dryden's tone increases proportionally to the growing strength of the Stuart position, especially after the discovery in the summer of 1683 of the Rye House Plot, an alleged plan to assassinate Charles and James and foment a radical revolution based in London.

In the midst of this political activity Dryden published another major poem on an apparently radically different topic, *Religio Laici or a Laymans Faith* (1682). The poem is a response to another French work, recently translated by a friend of his into English as *A Critical History of the Old Testament* (1682). The original was by a French priest, Richard Simon, and employed emerging modern methods of scholarship to examine the biblical text, its errors and contradictions. Dryden's response is essentially a declaration of faith in the few fundamental truths of Christianity that are "uncorrupt, sufficient, clear, intire, / In *all* things which our needfull *Faith* require," among them such doctrines as Original Sin and its consequences, especially death and the loss of heaven; the Incarnation of Christ; His Redemption and the consequent justification for the sin of Adam by means of the imputed righteousness of Christ extended to mankind. Astonishingly, the divinity of Christ is *not* among these essential doctrines, and Dryden is convinced that many, not only heathens but Christians, have been saved without "this Question" even "brought in play." On the other hand, Dryden attacks Deists by insisting that revelation is necessary for those essential truths to be known, that reason cannot discover them by itself, for, as he insists in another bold opening:

> Dim, as the borrow'd beams of Moon and Stars
> To *lonely, weary, wandring* Travellers,
> Is *Reason* to the *Soul:* And as on high,
> Those rowling Fires *discover* but the Sky
> Not light us *here;* So *Reason*'s glimmering Ray
> Was lent, not to *assure* our *doubtfull* way,
> But *guide* us upward to a *better Day.*
> And as those nightly Tapers disappear
> When Day's bright Lord ascends our Hemisphere;
> So pale grows *Reason* at *Religions* sight;
> So *dyes,* and so *dissolves* in *Supernatural Light.*

Here Dryden perfects a casual epistolary mode of heroic couplets to be later employed by Pope in *An Essay on Man* (1733), among other philosophical poems of the age. The strong medial caesuras, the enjambments, the triplet, and the metric variety lend an air of almost casual conversation. The imagery is worthy of Dante or Donne or Henry Vaughan. At the end Dryden maintains that he has chosen "this unpolish'd, rugged Verse . . . As fittest for Discourse, and nearest Prose." Not even Matthew Arnold could take this quite polished verse for prose. But Dryden had become a master of the philosophical epistle in verse, whose apparent casualness disguises its richly tropic nature.

Dryden had not really made a radical departure from his concurrent political poems, however. His attempt to steer a middle way between what he calls "Extreme[s]" concerning the issue of tradition in biblical interpretation is really a political stance, a proto-Burkean conservatism, indeed, a proto-Swiftian Erastianism:

> 'Tis some Relief, that points not clearly known,
> Without much hazard may be let alone:
> And, after hearing what our Church can say,
> If still our Reason runs another way,
> That private Reason 'tis more Just to curb,
> Than by Disputes the publick Peace disturb.
> For points obscure are of small use to learn:
> But *Common quiet* is *Mankind*'s *concern.*

The extremes he attacks in the religious sphere are the same he has been attacking in the political: Catholics and Dissenters, the Catholics especially for their gnostic priesthood, the Dissenters for their pernicious doctrine of individual interpretation, which leads ultimately to the kind of political instability, disturbance of the "Peace," and loss of "Common quiet" detailed above. Dryden would have sided with Edmund Burke against the French Revolution, and he would have been appalled by Thomas Jefferson and Thomas Paine.

By 1685, with the publication of *Sylvae,* a poetical miscellany, Dryden had become a major translator, having turned his hand to Ovid and Virgil as early as 1680 (*Ovid's Epistles*) and adding more Ovid and Theocritus in 1684 (*Miscellany Poems*) and then especially Lucretius and Horace in 1685 (*Sylvae*). Dryden also apparently polished William Soames's translation of Nicolas Boileau-Despréaux's *Art of Poetry* (1684) and contributed a dedication and life of Plutarch to a new edition of *Plutarchs Lives* (1683). While he would return to and memorably refine his versifying of Virgil in the next decade, among these early translations most notable are his deft handling of libertine psychology in Ovid's epistles, especially the incestuous "Canace to Macareus"; his inspired if somber rendition of Lucretius's atheistical arguments against fear of death; and his dextrous attempt at Pindarics in Horace's Ode 3.29. In these poems Dryden engages in some of his most experimental prosody. That Dryden was occupied with issues of translation is evidenced not only by his preface to *Sylvae* but also by his panegyric "To the Earl of Roscomon, on his Excellent Essay on Translated Verse," prefaced to the edition of that essay in 1684. Dryden's poem celebrates translation as an imperialist act whereby Greece, Rome, Italy, France, and now England appropriate the best from the countries they have (ostensibly) superseded.

In 1684 Dryden also published what many consider his best elegiac poem, "To the Memory of Mr. Oldham." Dryden's praise is doubly generous: first, he honors this kindred spirit in satire as having arrived at the goal and won the prize, that is, honor in the field of satire per se, before himself (Oldham's *Satyrs upon the Jesuits* was published in 1681, before *Mac Flecknoe,* *The Medall,* and, for that matter, *Absalom and Achitophel* were officially published, although it is ironic that Oldham's manuscript copy of *Mac Flecknoe* is dated August 1678 – if Oldham was inspired by it, that fact would increase the generosity of Dryden's gesture); second, Dryden laments Oldham's early death but insists that longer time would have added nothing to Oldham's wit and verse but metrical regularity and "the dull sweets of Rime" – like those of Dryden himself in his satires and indeed in this poem. The poem, like the early elegy to Hastings, closes with no metaphysical consolation, but with these grim, haunting lines:

> Once more, hail and farewel; farewel thou young,
> But ah too short, *Marcellus* of our Tongue;
> Thy Brows with Ivy, and with Laurels bound;
> But Fate and gloomy Night encompass thee around.

Despite the honors garnered by this bright, young star (analogous to Augustus's young poet, about whom Virgil sang), he sinks into a "gloomy" land of shades. Dryden achieves a poignant world-weariness in his *ave atque vale* motif.

Dryden's next major poetic task was another unpleasant one, another elegy, this time for Charles II, who died in February 1685. As poet laureate and historiographer royal, Dryden had to produce an official, public elegy, one that lamented the deceased king, praised his accomplishments, and underwrote the transition to a new king, around whom swirled such tempests of controversy. For some time Dryden had been preparing an opera to celebrate Charles II, one that was finally produced in late 1685 as *Albion and Albanius*. In it he continued the metrical experimentations of his translations. Relying on this metrical virtuosity, Dryden produced *Threnodia Augustalis: A Funeral-Pindarique Poem Sacred to the Happy Memory of King Charles II* (1685).

As in *Annus Mirabilis*, Dryden attempts to portray real people in the most material of situations – death – while at the same time mythologizing his subject in the light of the theory of the king's two bodies, public and private. For example, Dryden portrays James's rushing to Charles's bedchamber upon first hearing of his illness in terms that mingle allegorical with realistic details:

> Half unarray'd he ran to his Relief,
> So hasty and so artless was his Grief:
> Approaching Greatness met him with her Charms
>   Of Pow'r and future State;
> But look'd so ghastly in a Brother's Fate,
>   He shook her from his Armes.

The rolling alliterative *r*'s in this passage lend force to the tempting "Charms" of Greatness's arms entwining with those of James, who asserts himself by thrusting her and the ambition to which he is susceptible aside.

Dryden draws a scene of pathos designed to extract pity and loyalty from even the most recalcitrant of his audience, especially in the light of his re-

hearsal of Charles's mild temper, forgiveness, and contributions to an English renascence of both arts and trade after the havoc wreaked by "Rebellion" and "Faction." Dryden portrays Charles's greatest contribution as his intrepid support of the principle of legitimate succession. In imitative rhythms Dryden delineates the progress of this principle down through British history:

> Succession, of a long Descent,
>   Which Chastly in the Channells ran,
>   And from our Demi-gods began,
> Equal almost to Time in its extent,
>   Through Hazzards numberless and great,
> Thou hast deriv'd this mighty Blessing down,
> And fixt the fairest Gemm that decks th'Imperial Crown.

That succession, Dryden insists, falls upon Charles's brother, whether the Opposition likes it or not, and he deserves it because of his – as opposed to their – unswerving devotion to the "plighted vows" of loyalty. In *Annus Mirabilis*, Dryden praised London for its loyalty; in *Absalom and Achitophel* and *The Medall* he blamed Shaftesbury for attempting to effect a divorce, to break "the Bonds she plighted to her Lord"; here Dryden appeals to his countrymen to honor their vows of fealty sworn to their earthly lord in the sight of their heavenly: "Faith is a Christian's, and a Subject's Test." In a desperate wish fulfillment, Dryden pretends to prophesy, "with a distant view, I see / Th'amended Vows of *English* Loyalty" – a vision that he once again transforms into the prosperity of British imperialism in the wake of its "Conquering Navy," which, under James, will reduce the oceans of the world to acknowledging their rightful "Lord." In the finale of *Albion and Albanius*, Dryden would try again to rally the nation behind this theme. Amid the final chorus, "Fame *rises out of the middle of the Stage, standing on a Globe; on which is the Arms of* England." The epilogue concludes a crescendo of appeals to trust with the following version of the myth of human word-as-bond underwritten by the Divine Word:

> *He Plights his Faith; and we believe him just;*
> *His Honour is to Promise, ours to Trust.*
> *Thus Britain's Basis on a Word is laid,*
> *As by a Word the World it self was made.*

Unlike earlier elegies that omitted theodicean resolutions by means of metaphysical consolations, here (as briefly in the portrait of Young Barzillai in *Absalom and Achitophel*) Dryden in the name of excessive "Grief" stifles the "Impious thought" of his theodicean complaint and acknowledges that

Heaven did not take Charles too soon but instead gave him double the dozen years he spent in exile to bring England close to the "Promis'd Land" of political stability.

His next major poem, "To the Pious Memory Of the Accomplisht Young Lady Mrs Anne Killigrew" (1686), also an elegy, is devoid of theodicean complaint and provides the consolation of apotheosis throughout. Even when Dryden, in one of the best images in the poem ("*Destiny* . . . like a hardn'd Fellon," that is, a rapist, refused to finish the "Murder at a Blow, . . . But . . . took a pride / To work more Mischievously slow, / And plunder'd first, and then destroy'd"), laments Killigrew's premature death from smallpox, he concludes immediately that she, like Katherine Philips, the matchless "*Orinda,*" died only to be "translate[d]" to heaven. Moreover, the person praised is a poet — and a woman to boot. Dryden uses the occasion to apotheosize art itself. Anne is a Beatrice, a descendant of "*Sappho,*" whose transmigrating soul now leaves its peregrinations to sing eternally in a heavenly choir and to whom Dryden and other poets can now pray for poetic inspiration:

> Hear then a Mortal Muse thy Praise rehearse,
>   In no ignoble Verse;
> But such as thy own voice did practise here,
> When thy first Fruits of Poesie were giv'n;
> To make thy self a welcome Inmate there:
>   While yet a young Probationer,
>   And Candidate of Heav'n.

Dryden portrays this "Poetess" as having "Wit . . . more than Man," as being indeed quasi-divine, a second Christ who "attone[s]" for the "Second Fall" of mankind through bad poetry, bad art, and bad drama; a second Noah in her ability to people creation itself through her portraits; and a cocreator who has the power to paint not only James II's "Outward Part" but to "call out" with her very "hand" the "Image of his Heart." Dryden thus portrays Anne's agency on earth as a second Incarnation, one that, like Christ's, raises mankind up to higher status — especially the "Sacred Poets," who, at the sound of the "Golden Trump" on Judgment Day, will, because "they are cover'd with the lightest Ground," spring first from the earth "And streight, with in-born Vigour, on the Wing, / Like mounting Larkes, to the New Morning sing," led by Anne "As Harbinger of Heav'n, the Way to show." Dryden has granted this "Virgin-daughter of the Skies" the status of the Blessed Virgin or Sophia, by implication a coequal member of the Trinity (from which the figure of woman has been conspicuously absent). And one of the main fictions of the poem is that his Pindaric poetry itself participates in the divine emanation. Without music itself, this poem is as wonderfully lyrical as anything the age produced. Witness the last stanza in its entirety:

> When in mid-Aire, the Golden Trump shall sound,
>   To raise the Nations under ground;
>   When in the valley of *Jehosaphat,*
> The Judging God shall close the Book of Fate;
>   And there the last Assizes keep
>   For those who Wake, and those who Sleep;
>   When ratling Bones together fly,
> From the four Corners of the Skie,
> When Sinews o're the Skeletons are spread,
> Those cloath'd with Flesh, and Life inspires the Dead;
> The Sacred Poets first shall hear the Sound,
>   And formost from the Tomb shall bound:
> For they are cover'd with the lightest Ground
> And streight, with in-born Vigour, on the Wing,
> Like mounting Larkes, to the New Morning sing.
> There Thou, Sweet Saint, before the Quire shalt go,
> As Harbinger of Heav'n, the Way to show,
> The Way which thou so well hast learn'd below.

The play off the inverted iamb every time the line begins with "When" and then leads, in the first instance — or slams, in the third — into a spondee provides wonderful metrical variation, even as the foot-lengths vary, producing, along with the alliterative *f*'s and the collapsed iambs of the second line, these great sound effects: "When ratling Bones together fly, / From the four Corners of the Skie." The use of medial caesuras is masterful especially in the last five lines, including double caesuras that allow the succeeding lines to explode forth in imitation of the mounting larks/resurrected bodies. Even the flirtation with the grotesque in the image of the re-creation of those resurrected bodies seems a bold anticipation of the cinematic, cartoonlike process later perfected in Modest Mussorgsky's *Night on Bald Mountain* (1867) in *Fantasia* (1940). Finally, the passage seems reminiscent of Donne, Milton, and Shakespeare — their images respectively of the Last Judgment ("At the round earth's imagin'd corners, blow"), the lady's song "creat[ing] a soul / Under the ribs of Death" (Milton's *Comus,* 1637), and the lover's soul "Like to the lark at break of day arising / From sullen earth, sing[ing] hymns at heaven's gate" (Shakespeare's Sonnet 29).

On his deathbed, Charles II declared his conversion to Catholicism, and his Catholic brother James succeeded to the throne, issuing some "Royal Papers" detailing not only Charles's but James's first wife's Catholic faith. Meanwhile, Dryden himself converted, and he was ordered to defend those

John Dryden, circa 1698 (portrait by Kneller; Trinity College, Cambridge)

Royal Papers, which he did in a pamphlet exchange with prominent Anglican bishop Edward Stillingfleet. Apparently Dryden felt obliged to publish another philosophical poem, documenting his own confession of faith and answering his earlier *Religio Laici*. The result was *The Hind and the Panther* (1687), Dryden's longest original poem. Ever since, he has been attacked for insincerity and opportunism. James Anderson Winn, Dryden's modern biographer, argues that from the time of his relationship with the Howards, Dryden was intimately connected with Catholic recusants, one of whom was a prominent cardinal, and one of whom may have been his own wife. His sons were Catholic, and the youngest was studying to be a priest. So his conversion may have taken place over a long period of time. And he himself argues persuasively in the third part of *The Hind and the Panther* that he really

stood little to gain and far more to lose by becoming Catholic, mostly because up until that time the aging James had no son, and his new duchess, Maria Beatrice, had lost several babies: the throne would revert to a Protestant upon his death.

Biographers will never ascertain just why Dryden converted, and critics will probably always accuse him of being a trimmer. But there is a logic to his conversion if one studies his works. They are preoccupied with the need for political stability and the concomitant necessity of loyalty to de jure monarchs, whose titles are inherited through primogenitive patrilinearity. As Dryden shifted from his early optimism concerning Britain's future as an expansionist imperial power to his defensive posture with regard to the principle of succession amid threats of civil war, his own loyalty to James and to unbroken succession grew stronger. It appears that the more he examined his *Religio Laici* position, the more he came to doubt the Church of England's claim to authority. By the time he wrote *The Hind and the Panther* the analogy between church and state was ironclad. Only Catholicism can trace its origins in unbroken succession back to the primitive church; Anglicanism dates from Henry VIII's break with Rome (a break that occurred for dubious reasons at that, Dryden argues throughout). And without a final arbiter in doctrinal matters, no church can claim authority: "Because no disobedience can ensue, / Where no submission to a Judge is due." Dryden's fears of political anarchy are reflected in his fears of doctrinal anarchy, especially where the Protestant theory of individual interpretation of the Bible obtains. Thus it should come as no surprise that he would finally swear allegiance to Rome. Moreover, Dryden's religious theory of infallibility as residing in both pope *and* General Council can be seen as homologous to his political theory of a government balanced between king and Parliament. And his religious theory of authority based upon historical priority can be seen as homologous to not just a political but an economic theory of succession: "An old possession stands, till Elder quitts the claim" is as true for power and property as it is for the True Church. The problematics of the transmission of the Savior's "Testament" are developed in terms of homology to a contested will, precisely because an unerring guide is needed in both religious and sociopolitical realms. Dryden has the Catholic Hind assert to the Anglican Panther, "For that which must direct the whole, must be / Bound in one bond of faith and unity": both church and state need one leader, to whom his subjects are bound by word-as-bond. In language that expresses Dryden's merged religious and political theory, the Hind concludes triumphantly that "the mother church . . . with unrivall'd claim ascends the throne."

Not only Dryden's theory but also his very fable mingles political with religious. All along the poem seems to have a dual raison d'être: to explain Dryden's conversion but also to achieve an alliance between Catholics and Anglicans against the Dissenters. Dryden's antipathy to the latter is essentially political: their theory of individual interpretation leads to not only religious but political anarchy. The heritage of the Presbyterian Wolf may go all the way back to the Old Testament "When the proud *Sanhedrim* [the ancient homologue to Parliament] oppress'd the Prince" or better still, "When *Corah* with his brethren did conspire, / From *Moyses* hand the sov'reign sway to wrest." Even earlier, both the Wolf and the Deistic (read *atheistic*) Fox descend ultimately from "some [postdiluvian] wild currs, who from their masters ran / Abhorring the supremacy of man," and who "In woods and caves the rebelrace began." Passing through "*Wickliff,*" with his "innate antipathy to kings," in their modern manifestation in mid-seventeenth-century England, these radical Protestants (now Roundheads) "fastn'd on the miter'd crown, / And freed from God and monarchy your town" – the City of London. They would draw the nation "to the dreggs of a Democracy," which for Dryden is anarchy. They are the fomenters of "Rebellion" against both "heav'n" and "Prince."

Rebellion is a leitmotiv in the poem, from this early satirical description of the Dissenters through the description of Henry VIII's rebellion, which but teaches others to rebel in part 2, to the final ungrateful rebellion of the Anglican pigeons against their rightful sovereign at the end of part 3. In this last part of the poem Dryden reveals himself as the controversialist he always was, arguing with the bishops Stillingfleet and Gilbert Burnet over not doctrinal but political disputes: why would the Anglicans keep the Test Act, a device introduced in the fright of the Popish Plot to exclude Catholics from power, when the plot has been shown to be a fraud and when James has shown himself to be tolerant? Of course, Dryden's problem was that he was defending an inept king who kept making matters worse by privileging Catholics. The Panther's fable of the swallows and the martins is a displaced attack on James's policy, which attack, of course, holds his Catholic advisers, especially one Father Edward Petre, primarily responsible. As usual, Dryden is offering advice against potential disaster.

Finally the ending – and perhaps the real import – of Dryden's poem is secular. The Hind finally despairs of an accommodation with the Panther. In vatic style Dryden offers an optimistic, wish-fulfillment prophecy of Catholic hegemony over an Anglican establishment ungrateful ultimately to James's new policy of religious tolerance. But it is as if he could not sustain the optimism. Instead he tacked on a dire prophecy of the advent, at the death of James, of the "Usurper," William of Orange. There is no final apotheosis, no final apocalypse, no final justice. The "Glorious" Revolution that did occur almost immediately forever destroyed Dryden's faith in a fulfillment of his religious/political vision in his own lifetime. Instead, he moved to the margins of the new order to carry on his critique.

In the meantime, the one event Catholics desired most occurred: James and his queen had a son in June of 1688. Of course, it was the one event most feared by the Protestants. Almost as Dryden had prophesied, the Protestants invited William and Mary to become cosovereigns, and James fled the country. In *Britannia Rediviva* (1688) Dryden's celebration of the prince seems strained, almost hysterical. He desperately prays that England be spared another civil war: "Here stop the Current of the sanguine flood, / Require not, Gracious God, thy Martyrs Blood." Yet he cautions the Catholic (potential) martyrs, "Nor yet conclude all fiery *Trials* past, / For Heav'n will exercise us to the last." And all he can praise at the end is no new order but James's "Justice" – darling attribute of God himself – and James's stoic endurance of whatever "Fortune" and "Fate" will bring. James Garrison seems right when he argues that Dryden has run out of enabling myth to sustain the Stuarts.

In a famous passage in *The Hind and the Panther,* Dryden assumes the posture of one who has humbled his ambitious desire for fame. Almost self-pityingly he writes of his (eventual) loss of his offices of poet laureate and historiographer royal, as well as the income that was supposed to go with them:

> ' Tis nothing thou hast giv'n, then add thy tears
> For a long race of unrepenting years:
> ' Tis nothing yet; yet all thou hast to give,
> Then add those *may-be* years thou hast to live.
> Yet nothing still: then poor, and naked come,
> Thy father will receive his unthrift home,
> And thy blest Saviour's bloud discharge the mighty sum.

At some level Dryden may have believed that, but immediately after the revolution he began to write again for the stage, partly to make money but also partly to assert himself: his talent, even as his nemesis Shadwell was made the new poet laureate; his spirit amid the storm of political conflict; his worth and thus his justifiable fame. Moreover, though the Hind claims to "discipline" her son, Dryden, "Whose uncheck'd fury to revenge wou'd run," Dryden could not control his Jacobitical rage, which broke out in his later works in various satiric fashions.

Don Sebastian (1689) has as its central theme loyalty to one's king, whatever the circumstances. And when the tragicomic pattern is ruptured by the tragic ending – itself the result of a breach of society's patrilineal codes – Dryden closes with a Christian/Stoic acceptance of the inscrutability of God's ways. But in his next play, *Amphitryon* (1690), Dryden retells the story of Jupiter's seduction of Amphitryon's wife in a witty but ultimately sar-

donic way, imaging for his audience a world run by a god who is sheer power, without justice as his darling attribute – as if Dryden were Jobishly complaining about the absence of his God's justice in the postrevolutionary world. In *Cleomenes* (1692), Dryden (and Thomas Southerne, who helped him finish the play because he was in poor health) portrays a king in exile, betrayed and abandoned, who fails to rally a revolution that might result in his restitution in his native land. Several details seem calculated to arouse Jacobite sympathies, especially that of Cleomenes' wife and infant child starving to death, and God finally seems absent, as the play emphasizes Stoic resignation and self-reliance.

In subtler ways Dryden inculcated his Jacobitism into *King Arthur* (1691), an opera that celebrates Britain's resistance to foreign invaders, and *Love Triumphant* (1694), his final play, a tragicomedy featuring a prince who rebels against his father and against the incest taboo, and concluding with a nonresolution to the issues because the prince turns out to be unrelated to either father or sister (by implication, Mary Stuart is still her father's daughter and a usurper). Dryden also inculcated Jacobitism into a series of prologues and epilogues, prose works, and especially brilliant new translations, most notably selected satires of Juvenal and Persius (1693), his Virgil (1697), and *Fables Ancient and Modern* (1700).

Most of the work of his last years was in translation, apparently as a way of achieving a modicum of independence, both political and economic. He returned to favorites, such as Ovid, Virgil, and Homer, and added Boccaccio and Chaucer. Especially noteworthy is the malleability of Dryden's heroic couplets. In the *Aeneis,* for example, he occasionally opens up the couplet rather than, like Pope, closing it virtually all the time. He spices couplets with triplets, masculine with feminine endings. He is a past master at the enjambment and particularly of metric variation in the first hemistich. He is also a master weaver of motif, as in the leitmotiv of *labor* in the *Aeneis,* a Virgilian key word and concept he variously translates as *Labour* and *Toyl* – sometimes adding to the Virgilian original and always emphasizing the need to build a kingdom on hard work, as opposed to the easy gains in Carthage. He also embellishes the original with lines such as the following, which emphasize the emerging theme of self-reliance in his final works: Dryden's Sybil praises Aeneas as being "secure of Soul, unbent with Woes" and advises him, "The more thy Fortune frowns, the more oppose." Dryden's Aeneas answers, in lines that expand on the original:

no Terror to my view,
No frightful Face of Danger can be new.
Inur'd to suffer, and resolv'd to dare,
The Fates, without my Pow'r, shall be without my Care.

Dryden's Aeneas, then, must learn – like Cleomenes before him and Dryden's "Honour'd Kinsman," John Driden of Chesterton, after him in Dryden's canon – to stand fixed on his own firm center. Aeneas's boast seems Dryden's own.

Meanwhile, Dryden continued to write excellent occasional verse, from prologues and epilogues to elegies to verse epistles. *Eleonora* (1692), a commissioned elegy, was originally to be entitled "The Pattern," and Dryden indeed makes the countess a pattern of Christian piety and charity, as well as of aristocratic wife and motherhood. On the topic of friendship, Dryden achieves one of his best extended similes, one employing his later motif of conveying the fixed self no matter where one goes:

The Souls of Friends, like Kings in Progress are;
Still in their own, though from the Pallace far:
Thus her Friend's Heart her Country Dwelling was,
A sweet Retirement to a courser place:
Where Pomp and Ceremonies enter'd not;
Where Greatness was shut out, and Buis'ness well
   forgot.

In the midst of this pattern panegyric, however, Dryden's satiric muse once again asserts herself, first in rather misogynistically suggesting that good wives should show "Love and Obedience to [their] Lord": Dryden jibes at his contemporaries, "So Subjects love just Kings, or so they shou'd." At the end Dryden bitterly comments on his own situation:

Let this suffice: Nor thou, great Saint, refuse
This humble Tribute of no vulgar Muse:
Who, not by Cares, or Wants, or Age deprest,
Stems a wild Deluge with a dauntless brest:
And dares to sing thy Praises, in a Clime
Where Vice triumphs, and Vertue is a Crime:
Where ev'n to draw the Picture of thy Mind,
Is Satyr on the most of Humane Kind:
Take it, while yet 'tis Praise; before my rage
Unsafely just, break loose on this bad Age.

In the genre of the verse epistle, sometime around 1686, Dryden wrote a wonderfully witty and wicked letter in Hudibrastics to George Etherege, who had become envoy to Ratisbon, in Bavaria. Again Dryden plays off the Virgilian theme of *labor,* as he addresses the aging libertine as if he were scattering his maker's image through the frozen north of Europe:

Like mighty Missioner you come
Ad partes Infidelium.
A work of wondrous merit sure
So farr to go so much endure,
. . . .
you have made your zeal appear
Within the Circle of the Bear.
What region of the Earth so dull
That is not of your labours full?
Trioptolemus (so sing the nine)
Strew'd plenty from his Cart divine
But spight of all those fable makers
He never sow'd on Almain Acres.

In "To my Dear Friend Mr. Congreve" (1694), as in his elegy on Oldham, Dryden assumes a magnanimous pose, answering, as it were, his mock-panegyric *Mac Flecknoe* with a genuine panegyric, featuring this time a legitimate succession. Dryden's laurels should descend to Congreve, representative of a new generation of dramatic poets, but they have been intercepted, "For *Tom* the Second reigns like *Tom* the first," that is, Tom Rymer has succeeded Tom Shadwell as historiographer royal (not poet laureate). Nevertheless, Dryden prophesies,

Thou shalt be seen,
(Tho' with some short Parenthesis between:)
High on the Throne of Wit; and seated there,
Not mine (that's little) but thy Lawrel wear.

Though never actually poet laureate, Congreve certainly rose "high on a throne of his own labors rear'd," for he became for centuries considered the premier Restoration comedic playwright.

Dryden also praises the painter Sir Godfrey Kneller in a miscellany poem of 1694:

The fair themselves go mended from thy hand:
Likeness appears in every Lineament;
But Likeness in thy Work is Eloquent:
Though Nature, there, her true resemblance bears,
A nobler Beauty in thy Piece appears.
So warm thy Work, so glows the gen'rous frame,
Flesh looks less living in the Lovely Dame.

The strong emphasis on the word "Flesh" leads so musically into the lilting alliteration of *l*'s in the last line. But Dryden cannot forbear his satire – and at the expense of women:

Our Arts are Sisters; though not Twins in Birth:
For Hymns were sung in *Edens* happy Earth,
By the first Pair; while *Eve* was yet a Saint;
Before she fell with Pride, and learn'd to paint.
Forgive th'allusion; 'twas not meant to bite;
But Satire will have room, where e're I write.

And at the center of the poem Dryden again has recourse to his emergent theme:

> Thou hadst thy *Charles* a while, and so had I;
> But pass we that unpleasing Image by.
> Rich in thy self; and of thy self Divine,
> All Pilgrims come and offer at thy Shrine.

Self-reliance will compensate for the loss of patrons – and even, perhaps, for the loss of God.

In 1697 Dryden took time out from his other chores to pen one of the greatest odes in the English language, *Alexander's Feast; Or The Power of Musique*. He had written a less remarkable poem on the subject a decade earlier. The original setting by the composer Jeremiah Clarke has been lost, but George Frideric Handel's magnificent setting of 1736 exists, and anyone who has ever heard it must marvel at the incredible virtuosity on the parts of both poet and musician. As has been often noted, the poem is a celebration of the power of art. The musician Timotheus modulates Alexander the Great through several moods, manipulating him with sure hand. Not only is Timotheus the real hero, but Alexander is shown, as in Dryden's friend Nathaniel Lee's portrait of him in his *The Rival Queens* (1677), to be the victim of his own reckless passions, from his pride in his quasi-divinity to his proverbial drunkenness, to his martial vanity followed immediately by pity for the vanquished foe, to his destructive amorousness, and finally to pointless, destructive vengeance. Some critics have seen an implied critique of William III in the poem, and the pitiable portrait of the vanquished Darius, "Deserted at his utmost Need, / By those his former Bounty fed," would certainly have reminded Dryden's audience of the deserted James II. But the poem is a paean to the triumph of art over all military power, over all rulers with delusions of divinity. The seventh stanza, expounding the supposed transcendence of Saint Cecilia and her organ, calls upon "old *Timotheus*" to "yield the Prize," for "He rais'd a Mortal to the Skies," while "She drew an Angel down" to listen to her. But Dryden qualifies the victory of Saint Cecilia by offering an alternative, "Or both divide the Crown": Dryden seems to identify with "old *Timotheus*" himself, and his humility would be false. Proud? He must have been proud to see men not afraid of God for breaking their oaths of loyalty, afraid enough of him and the few others of his courage to restrict further satire on the stage and to enact further punitive laws against Catholics.

In 1698 Dryden published two verse epistles, "To Mr. Granville, on his Excellent Tragedy Call'd *Heroic Love*" and "To My Friend Mr. Motteux." The latter bears some comment, for it includes a response to Jeremy Collier's attack on the supposed immorality and profanity of the English stage:

> 'Tis hard, my Friend, to write in such an Age,
> As damns not only Poets, but the Stage.
> That sacred Art, by Heav'n it self infus'd,
> Which *Moses, David, Salomon* have us'd,
> Is now to be no more: The Muses Foes
> Wou'd sink their Maker's Praises into Prose.
> Were they content to prune the lavish Vine
> Of straggling Branches, and improve the Wine,
> Who but a mad Man wou'd his Faults defend?
> All wou'd submit; for all but Fools will mend.
> But, when to common sense they give the Lie,
> And turn distorted words to Blasphemy,
> *They* give the Scandal.

Dryden is willing to admit when he has been excessive in his works, provided clerics such as Collier (whom he has made appear a Puritan but who was in fact a nonjuring Anglican, that is, one who refused to take the oaths of loyalty to William and Mary) acknowledge their own faults and grant that "Their Faults and not their Function I arraign" when Dryden attacks corrupt clergy in such plays as *The Spanish Fryar*.

In the last year of his life, though suffering from continual illness, Dryden published his last group of translations, *Fables Ancient and Modern,* along with two last original verse epistles of praise. The first, "To Her Grace the Dutchess of Ormond," contains some of his most graceful compliments. On her recent journey to Ireland, the Ormonds' family seat, Dryden writes, "The Land, if not restrain'd, had met Your Way, / Projected out a Neck, and jutted to the Sea." Perhaps influenced by Dante, Edmund Spenser, and the Neoplatonists, Dryden repeatedly praises great beauty in his poems (for example, Maria Beatrice of Modena, James II's second duchess and eventually his queen, whose name is not insignificant). In this poem he maintains that the duchess's beauty is so great that it is capable of obliterating the recent suffering in Ireland, suffering Dryden must have particularly sympathized with, since a great deal of it was in the cause of James and at the hands of William up to the climactic Battle of the Boyne in 1690, which ended the first Jacobite war:

> The Waste of Civil Wars, their Towns destroy'd,
> *Pales* unhonour'd, *Ceres* unemploy'd,
> Were all forgot; and one Triumphant Day
> Wip'd all the Tears of three Campaigns away.
> Blood, Rapines, Massacres, were cheaply bought,
> So mighty Recompence Your Beauty brought.

The latter end of last week, I had the honour of a visite from my cousine your Mother, & my Cousine Dorothy, with which I was very much comforted: within this Month, there will be played for my profit, an old play of Fletcher's, calld the pilgrim, corrected by my good friend Mr Vanbrook; to which I have added A New Masque, & am to write a New prologue & Epilogue. Your Lyons tragedy, calld the Revolt of Capoua, will be playd at Betterton's House within this fortnight. I am out with that Company, & therefore, if I can help it, will not read before tis Acted; though the Author much desires I should. I do not think I will refuse a present from fair hands, but I am resolvd to save my Bacon. I beg your pardon for this slovenly Letter, but I have not health to transcribe it. My service to my Cousin your Brother, whom I hear is happy in your Company, which he is not, who most desires it, & who is, Madam,

　　　　　　　Your most oblig'd, Obedient
　　　　　　　　　　servant
　　　　　　　　　　　John Dryden.

Thursday, April the 11
1700.

Second page of Dryden's last surviving letter. Writing to a young cousin, Mrs. Elizabeth Steward, Dryden mentions "The Secular Masque" that he has written for John Vanbrugh's revision of John Fletcher's The Pilgrim. *This letter also refers to Dryden's falling-out with Thomas Betterton's acting company at Lincoln's Inn Fields, perhaps because – as Dryden had written to Mrs. Steward earlier – he felt that the company could have given a better performance of* The Way of the World, *a new play by his friend William Congreve (MA 130, Pierpont Morgan Library).*

In "To my Honour'd Kinsman, John Driden," Dryden praises a relative of different political and religious persuasion – perhaps because Driden had sent money and goods to his cousin in an act of familial friendship and Christian charity that transcended partisan politics and religion, but also because Driden provides the poet with an opportunity to portray the emergent hero. One of the dominant images in the poem is the circle, as in this famous passage about the hare:

> The Hare, in Pastures or in Plains is found,
> Emblem of Humane Life, who runs the Round;
> And, after all his wand'ring Ways are done,
> His Circle fills, and ends where he begun,
> Just as the Setting meets the Rising Sun.

The circle is traditionally an emblem of perfection, of the human soul, which ends where it began, as Dryden's poem does, referring to the blessedness Driden will finally attain in "Heav'n." Moreover, the circle is an emblem for the "Integrity" Dryden praises in his cousin, for the man with such integrity stands fixed on his own firm center, no matter what the strife. Dryden portrays Driden as "void of Strife" in his country retirement and as "composing Strife" in his role of justice of the peace. He is "Lord" of him "self" and, Dryden adds in one of his increasingly misogynistic portraits of women, "uncumber'd with a Wife," who, by her nature, farther removed from God (Dryden exaggerates even Milton's misogynistic hierarchy), would only drag him down. Perhaps Dryden intended this as a witty compliment to an aging bachelor in a family with an increasing number of childless patriarchs. And he certainly wanted the iconography of the One Just Man standing alone. But the misogyny is an unwelcome alloy.

Dryden also avails himself of another emerging motif, the Younger Brother. Driden is not the heir to his father's fortunes but to his mother's. Yet unlike his older brother, whom Dryden did not like, Driden made the best of his more limited means by being charitable to the poor and by being a generous host.

Driden thus becomes the figure for the new "Patriot," a word usually appropriated by the Whiggish Country party. It is a figure appropriated by the rebels in the American Revolution: not the eldest, but nevertheless an equal citizen. Furthermore, Dryden portrays his cousin as unselfishly willing to serve his turn in Parliament if elected, where he, fixed on his own center, will help to balance contending elements:

> Betwixt the Prince and Parliament we stand;
> The Barriers of the State on either Hand:
> May neither overflow, for then they drown the Land.

Note that Dryden has employed the first-person plural pronoun "we." By doing so he identifies himself with his cousin as a patriot, one who helps the politician teach England to avoid disastrous foreign wars (the poem is full of criticisms of William III and his military policies, from war to a standing army). When Dryden reminds his cousin of his ancestor, Erasmus Dryden, who bravely refused in an earlier Parliament "to lend the King against his Laws," he of course implies their common heritage. And by his praise of Erasmus, who "in a lothsom Dungeon doom'd to lie, / In Bonds retain'd his Birthright Liberty, / And sham'd Oppression, till it set him free," Dryden obviously intends his own portrait as one who, though in exile, retained his liberty. Dryden closes by asking Driden to accept this portrait, for poets also serve: "Praise-worthy Actions are by thee embrac'd; / And 'tis my Praise, to make thy Praises last." Dryden has drawn the portrait of his cousin round and, as the portrait maker, shares the praise.

Dryden ended his life in squabbles with his publisher and in bitterness over his own fate and that of not only his king but the principle of succession he had fought so hard to defend. He concluded his career with a contribution to a revision of John Fletcher's *Pilgrim* by his new friend, Sir John Vanbrugh. His prologue continues his attack, begun in "To my Honour'd Kinsman, John Driden" on the latest of his detractors, Sir Richard Blackmore and Luke Milbourne, poetaster and quack doctor, and the epilogue continues his ongoing attack against self-righteous Puritans who attack the stage and the age in general. But his best contribution is a fitting epitaph, both for himself and his century. In "The Secular Masque" (1700) Dryden portrays Momus, the god of mockery, showing up at a celebration of the century. Momus's comments are devastating, as he attacks the god or goddess associated with each third of the century. To Diana, patroness of the early Stuarts, Momus comments, "Thy Chase had a Beast in View"; to Mars, patron of the Interregnum, "Thy Wars brought nothing about"; to Venus, patroness of the later Stuarts, "Thy Lovers were all untrue." This last is perhaps his most devastating statement, for it refers not only to the licentious loves of Charles's time but to James's subjects' infidelity. No wonder the expiring poet would with his last breath sing, " 'Tis well an Old Age is out, / And time to begin a New." Dryden meant not only the century itself but his own old age. As a frustrated but nevertheless believing Catholic, he could only hope that he was on his way to a new life, one free from the strife and disappointment of this life, one appreciative of the celestial strains of his great poetry.

Letters:

The Letters of John Dryden: With Letters Addressed to Him, edited by Charles E. Ward (Durham, N.C.: Duke University Press, 1942).

Bibliographies:

Hugh McDonald, *John Dryden: A Bibliography of Early Editions and Drydeniana* (Oxford: Oxford University Press, 1939);

John A. Zamonski, *An Annotated Bibliography of John Dryden: Texts and Studies, 1949–1973* (New York: Garland, 1975);

David J. Latt and Samuel Holt Monk, *John Dryden: A Survey and Bibliography of Critical Studies, 1895–1974* (Minneapolis: University of Minnesota Press, 1976);

James M. Hall, *John Dryden: A Reference Guide* (Boston: G. K. Hall, 1984).

Biographies:

Samuel Johnson, "John Dryden," in *The Works of the English Poets, With Prefaces, Biographical and Critical,* 68 volumes (London: Printed by H. Hughes for C. Bathurst and others, 1779–1781); in volume 1 of the standard edition, *Lives of the English Poets,* 3 volumes, edited by George Birkbeck Hill (Oxford: Clarendon Press, 1905);

Edmond Malone, volume 1 of *The Critical and Miscellaneous Works of John Dryden,* 4 volumes, edited by Malone (London: Cadell & Davis, 1800);

Walter Scott, *The Life of John Dryden,* volume 1 of Scott's edition of *The Works of John Dryden* (London: William Miller, 1808); published separately in 1826;

Charles E. Ward, *The Life of John Dryden* (Chapel Hill: University of North Carolina Press, 1961);

James M. Osborn, *John Dryden; Some Biographical Facts and Problems,* revised edition (Gainesville, Fla.: University of Florida, 1965);

George McFadden, *Dryden: The Public Writer, 1660–1685* (Princeton: Princeton University Press, 1978);

James Anderson Winn, *John Dryden and His World* (New Haven & London: Yale University Press, 1987);

Paul Hammond, *John Dryden: A Literary Life* (New York: St. Martin's Press, 1991).

References:

Donald R. Benson, "Dryden's *The Hind and the Panther:* Transubstantiation and Figurative Language," *Journal of the History of Ideas,* 43 (April–June 1982): 195–208;

Benson, "Space, Time, and the Language of Transcendence in Dryden's Later Poetry," *Restoration,* 8 (Spring 1984): 10–16;

Benson, "Theology and Politics in Dryden's Conversion," *Studies in English Literature, 1500–1900,* 4 (Summer 1964): 393–412;

Louis I. Bredvold, *The Intellectual Milieu of John Dryden* (Ann Arbor: University of Michigan Press, 1934);

Sanford Budick, *Dryden and the Abyss of Light: A Study of "Religio Laici" and "The Hind and the Panther"* (New Haven: Yale University Press, 1970);

David Bywaters, *Dryden in Revolutionary England* (Berkeley: University of California Press, 1991);

J. Douglas Canfield, "Anarchy and Style: What Dryden 'Grants' in *Absalom and Achitophel,*" *Papers on Language and Literature,* 14 (Winter 1978): 83–87;

Canfield, "The Authorship of *Emilia:* Richard Flecknoe's Revision of *Erminia,*" *Restoration,* 3 (1979): 3–7;

Canfield, "Flecknoe's Early Defence of the Stage: An Appeal to Cromwell," *Restoration and 18th-Century Theatre Research,* second series 2 (Winter 1987): 1–7;

Canfield, "The Image of the Circle in Dryden's *To My Honour'd Kinsman,*" *PLL,* 11 (Spring 1975): 168–176;

Canfield, "Poetical Injustice in Some Neglected Masterpieces of Restoration Drama," in *Rhetorics of Order / Ordering Rhetorics in English Neoclassical Literature,* edited by Canfield and J. Paul Hunter (Newark: University of Delaware Press, 1989), pp. 23–45;

Canfield, "*Regulus* and *Cleomenes* and 1688: From Royalism to Self-Reliance," *Eighteenth-Century Life,* 12 (November 1988): 67–75;

Canfield, "Royalism's Last Dramatic Stand: English Political Tragedy, 1679–89," *Studies in Philology,* 82 (Spring 1985): 234–263;

Canfield, *Word as Bond in English Literature from the Middle Ages to the Restoration* (Philadelphia: University of Pennsylvania Press, 1989);

Michael J. Conlon, "The Passage on Government in Dryden's *Absalom and Achitophel,*" *Journal of En-*

glish and Germanic Philology, 78 (January 1979): 17–32;

Conlon, "The Rhetoric of *Kairos* in Dryden's *Absalom and Achitophel,*" in *Rhetorics of Order / Ordering Rhetorics in English Neoclassical Literature,* pp. 85–97;

Elizabeth Duthie, " 'A Memorial of My Own Principles': Dryden's *To My Honour'd Kinsman,*" *Journal of English Literary History,* 47 (Winter 1980): 682–704;

Mother Mary Eleanor, "*Anne Killigrew* and *Mac Flecknoe,*" *Philological Quarterly,* 43 (January 1964): 47–54;

T. S. Eliot, *John Dryden: The Poet, the Dramatist, the Critic* (New York: Holliday, 1932);

William Empson, "A Deist Tract by Dryden," *Essays in Criticism,* 25 (January 1975): 74–100;

Empson, "Dryden's Apparent Scepticism," *EIC,* 20 (April 1970): 172–181;

William Frost, *Dryden and the Art of Translation* (New Haven: Yale University Press, 1955);

Paul H. Fry, *The Poet's Calling in the English Ode* (New Haven: Yale University Press, 1980);

Thomas H. Fujimura, "Dryden's Changing Political Views," *Restoration,* 10 (Fall 1986): 93–104;

Fujimura, "The Personal Drama of Dryden's *The Hind and the Panther,*" *PMLA,* 87 (May 1972): 406–416;

James D. Garrison, *Dryden and the Tradition of Panegyric* (Berkeley: University of California Press, 1975);

Dustin Griffin, "Dryden's Charles: The Ending of *Absalom and Achitophel,*" *Philological Quarterly,* 57 (Summer 1978): 359–382;

Griffin, "Dryden's *Oldham* and the Perils of Writing," *Modern Language Quarterly,* 37 (June 1976): 133–150;

Phillip Harth, *Contexts of Dryden's Thought* (Chicago: University of Chicago Press, 1968);

Harth, Alan Fisher, and Ralph Cohen, *New Homage to John Dryden* (Los Angeles: William Andrews Clark Memorial Library, 1983);

Arthur W. Hoffman, *John Dryden's Imagery* (Gainesville: University of Florida Press, 1962);

D. W. Jefferson, "The Poetry of *The Hind and the Panther,*" *Modern Language Review,* 79 (January 1984): 32–44;

Oscar Kenshur, "Scriptural Deism and the Politics of Dryden's *Religio Laici,*" *ELH,* 54 (Winter 1987): 869–892;

Bruce King, ed., *Dryden's Mind and Art* (Edinburgh: Oliver & Boyd, 1969);

James and Helen Kinsley, eds., *Dryden: The Critical Heritage* (New York: Barnes & Noble, 1971);

Jay Arnold Levine, "John Dryden's Epistle to John Driden," *JEGP,* 63 (July 1964): 450–474;

Thomas E. Maresca, "The Context of Dryden's *Absalom and Achitophel,*" *ELH,* 41 (Fall 1974): 340–358;

Michael McKeon, "Historicizing *Absalom and Achitophel,*" in *The New 18th Century: Theory, Politics, Literature,* edited by Felicity Nussbaum and Laura Brown (New York: Methuen, 1987), pp. 23–40;

McKeon, *Politics and Poetry in Restoration England: The Case of Dryden's 'Annus Mirabilis'* (Cambridge, Mass.: Harvard University Press, 1975);

Earl Miner, *Dryden's Poetry* (Bloomington: Indiana University Press, 1967);

Miner, ed., *John Dryden* (Athens: Ohio University Press, 1972);

Douglas Murray, "The Musical Structure of Dryden's *Song for St. Cecilia's Day,*" *Eighteenth-Century Studies,* 10 (Spring 1977): 326–334;

Murray, "The Royal Harmony: Music and Politics in Dryden's Poetry," *Restoration,* 11 (Spring 1987): 39–47;

William Myers, "Politics in *The Hind and the Panther,*" *Essays in Criticism,* 19 (January 1969): 19–34;

Maximillian E. Novak, "Shaping the Augustan Myth: John Dryden and the Politics of Restoration Augustanism," in *Greene Centennial Studies,* edited by Paul J. Korshin and Robert R. Allen (Charlottesville: University Press of Virginia, 1984), pp. 1–20;

Richard L. Oden, ed., *Dryden and Shadwell: The Literary Controversy and Mac Flecknoe (1668–1679): Facsimile Reproductions* (Delmar, N.Y.: Scholars' Facsimiles & Reprints, 1977);

H. J. Oliver, *Sir Robert Howard, 1626–1698: A Critical Biography* (Durham, N.C.: Duke University Press, 1963);

Cedric D. Reverand, *Dryden's Final Poetic Mode: The "Fables"* (Philadelphia: University of Pennsylvania Press, 1988);

Reverand, "Patterns of Imagery and Metaphor in Dryden's *The Medall,*" *Yearbook of English Studies,* 2 (1972): 103–114;

Alan Roper, *Dryden's Poetic Kingdoms* (London: Routledge & Kegan Paul, 1965);

Roper, "Dryden's *Secular Masque,*" *Modern Language Quarterly,* 23 (March 1962): 29–40;

Bernard N. Schilling, *Dryden and the Conservative Myth: A Reading of "Absalom and Achitophel"* (New Haven: Yale University Press, 1961);

Judith Sloman, *Dryden: The Poetics of Translation* (Toronto: University of Toronto Press, 1985);

Ruth Smith, "The Argument and Contexts of Dryden's *Alexander's Feast*," *Studies in English Literature, 1500–1900,* 18 (Summer 1978): 465–490;

Peter Stallybrass and Allon White, *The Politics and Poetics of Transgression* (London: Methuen, 1986);

Donna Elliot Swaim, "Milton's Immediate Influence on Dryden," Ph.d. dissertation, University of Arizona, 1978;

H. T. Swedenberg, ed., *Essential Articles for the Study of John Dryden* (Hamden, Conn.: Archon, 1966);

W. K. Thomas, *The Crafting of "Absalom and Achitophel"* (Waterloo, Ont.: Wilfred Laurier, 1978);

Mark Van Doren, *John Dryden: A Study of His Poetry* (New York: Harcourt, Brace & Howe, 1920);

David M. Vieth, "The Discovery of the Date of *Mac Flecknoe*," in *Evidence in Literary Scholarship: Essays in Memory of James Marshall Osborn,* edited by René Wellek and Alvaro Ribeiro (Oxford: Clarendon Press, 1979), pp. 63–87;

David Wykes, *A Preface to Dryden* (London & New York: Longman, 1977);

Steven N. Zwicker, *Dryden's Political Poetry: The Typology of King and Nation* (Providence: Brown University Press, 1972);

Zwicker, *Politics and Language in Dryden's Poetry: The Arts of Disguise* (Princeton: Princeton University Press, 1984).

Papers:

Few Dryden manuscripts remain. The only poetic manuscript extant, the fair copy of the elegy for Cromwell, is on display at the British Library. The primary collection of Dryden materials is at the William Andrews Clark Memorial Library, University of California at Los Angeles; letters can be found in several collections, including those at the British Library, the Bodleian Library, and the libraries at Harvard and Yale Universities.

Anne Killigrew

(1660 – 16 June 1685)

Ann Hurley
Skidmore College

BOOK: *Poems By Mrs Anne Killigrew* (London: Printed for Samuel Lowndes, 1686 [i.e., 1685]); facsimile published as *Poems (1686) by Mrs. Anne Killigrew, a Facsimile Reproduction with an Introduction,* edited by Richard Morton (Gainesville, Fla.: Scholars' Facsimiles & Reprints, 1967).

Anne Killigrew, "A *Grace* for Beauty, and a *Muse* for Wit," according to the publisher of her verse, was one of the maids of honor to Mary of Modena, Duchess of York (and later queen of James II), in the court of Charles II and was noted as both poet and painter. She was celebrated by John Dryden in the ode "To the Pious Memory Of the Accomplished Young Lady, Mrs Anne Killigrew, Excellent in the two Sister-Arts of Poësie, and Painting," which introduced the volume of her poems.

Killigrew's fame rests on this single volume of poetry, a collection of verse probably composed over relatively few years, as she died young. Although one scholar, Margaret J. M. Ezell, describes Killigrew as "the female poet most celebrated by her contemporaries," such an assertion is probably more the product of the hyperbole of Dryden's ode than of other seventeenth-century evidence, as relatively little contemporary mention of her poetry has been found. Nevertheless, her volume of poems offers an engaging instance of a lively mind commenting on court settings and the conventions, both social and literary, that a young member of the court, male or female, might have encountered in the early years of the Restoration. Killigrew tries her hand at a variety of poetic genres – heroic, pastoral, epigrammatic, occasional, panegyrical – from a variety of stances, old and young, male and female, engaged by or disenchanted with the court. While occasional passages from the poems praise "Reason" or warn court "nymphs" of the dangers of Love, the overall effect of Killigrew's poetry is less "Pious" than Dryden's ode implies. Instead, an examination of the poetry suggests a young poet's striking out on

her own, essaying and frequently mastering the intricacies of her chosen craft.

The daughter of Dr. Henry Killigrew, master of the Savoy and one of the prebendaries of Westminster, Anne Killigrew was born in 1660 shortly before the Restoration, at Saint Martin's Lane, London. She was christened in a private chamber because the offices in the common prayer were not yet being publicly allowed. Her education, in keeping with her social level, stressed poetry and painting, and her contemporaries praised her for excelling in these two sister arts. At a relatively young age she was appointed one of the maids of honor to the duchess of York, but she was stricken with smallpox and died, at the age of twenty-four or twenty-five, in her father's lodgings in the cloisters of Westminster Abbey. She was buried in the chancel of Saint John the Baptist's Chapel in the Savoy, where a marble monument (since destroyed by fire) was erected to her memory and graced with a Latin epitaph.

In 1685 her family permitted the publication of a thin quarto of poems (of about one hundred pages) titled *Poems By Mrs Anne Killigrew*. They are prefaced by an epitaph by one "E. E." titled "On the Death of the Truly Virtuous Mrs. Anne Killigrew who was Related to my (Deceased) Wife" and by a conventional "Publisher to the Reader" poem by Samuel Lowndes, which is then followed by Dryden's ode and the long Latin epitaph from her tomb and its translation, both by her father; the collection concludes with some fragments from her own poetry and that of others.

The circumstances of this publication can be conjectured with some accuracy. While it was still not the rule for poets to publish during their own lifetimes, posthumous publication did frequently occur, particularly for women poets whose families sought to commemorate them. That this was the case for Killigrew is implied by a reference made to her *Poems* by a female contemporary, Damaris, Lady Masham, who, on being urged to publish her own verse, refused. In a 14 December 1685 letter to John

This self-portrait published in Anne Killigrew's Poems *is one of her many paintings.*

Locke, Masham wrote, "How ever perhaps you may see me in Print in a little While, and then need not be Beholden to me, it being growne much the Fasion of late for our sex, Though I confess it has not much of my Approbation because (Principally) the Mode is for one to Dye First; and at this time if I might Have my owne Choice I Have no Great Inclination That Way."

Most probably Dryden, as family friend and recently appointed poet laureate, was invited to contribute the ode as an appropriate gesture toward someone who had been associated with the court of Charles II. That her family played a central role in the publication can be inferred not only from her father's epitaph but also from Anthony Wood's comment in *Athenæ Oxonienses* (1691, 1692) that "if there had not been more true history in her praises,

than compliment, her father would never have suffered them to pass the press." Publication occurred quickly; the volume was licensed to be printed on 30 September 1685, three months after her death, and was listed in the Stationers' Register on 2 October. Thus the 1686 date on the title page was predated by actual publication.

The poems themselves were not given extended or thoughtful analysis by her contemporaries, nor has Killigrew been the subject of a monograph or similarly focused treatment by modern criticism. Among the early reactions to her poetry is Horace Walpole's, who comments in *Anecdotes of Painting in England* (1726–1780) that her verses show a "versatility of subject," adding, by way of example, that they include "Pastoral Dialogues, Four Epigrams, and the Complaint of a Lover, and lastly, 'upon the saying that my verses were made by another.' " Dryden's ode, of course, praises them fulsomely, if faintly condescendingly:

Her *Arethusian* Stream remains unsoil'd,
Unmix't with Forreign Filth, and undefil'd,
Her Wit was more than Man, her Innocence a Child!

Others responded more to Dryden's prefatory ode than to the poems themselves, most notably Samuel Johnson, who considered that ode to be the "noblest in our language." Theophilus Cibber, in his *Lives of the Poets* (1753), summarizes Killigrew's initial reputation when he observes that "Mr. Dryden is quite lavish in her praise; and we are assured by other contemporary writers of good probity, that he has done no violence to truth in the most heightened strains of his panegyric." Although Killigrew's own poems also include some lines addressed to Katherine Philips, nothing similar has been discovered to record a more extended reaction of her contemporaries to her own verse.

Greater praise, it would appear, was given to her skill as an artist. Her volume of poetry includes a print of her, taken, Walpole tells us, from a "portrait drawn by herself." Dryden praises her portraits of James II and his queen and makes reference to some landscapes which Killigrew also produced. She mentions three of her paintings in her poems, and six more were sold from the collection of her brother Adm. Henry Killigrew in 1727. The paintings that she mentions in her poetry are concerned with biblical or mythological subject matter, including a Saint John in the Wilderness, Herodias with the head of that saint, and two of Diana's nymphs. Of the paintings sold from her brother's collection, little is known except that they represented a Venus and Adonis, a satyr playing on a pipe, Judith and Holofernes, a woman's head, the Graces dressing Venus, and one of the poet's self-portraits. In general, the subject matter of her paintings, mythological and biblical, seems consistent with the subject matter of her poetry. Walpole comments that, as a portrait artist, Killigrew worked "in the manner of Sir Peter Lely." She was herself painted by that artist, and an engraving made from his portrait of her is included in *Anecdotes of Painting in England.* Walpole himself does not appear to have seen any of Killigrew's paintings; his discussion of them relies on notes from the engraver George Vertue, who did see at least the ones from Admiral Killigrew's collection. Of these, Vertue comments, "These pictures I saw, but can say little." In *The Obstacle Race* (1979) Germaine Greer reports that the Venus and Adonis

painting was recorded as being in a private collection in Folkestone in 1915. The portrait of King James II is in the possession of Her Majesty the Queen, and an engraving by Blooteling from Killigrew's self-portrait and a mezzotint by B. Lens from the Venus and Adonis are in the Paul Mellon Collection.

Anne Killigrew's character, or personality, can be faintly seen behind the traditional praises that her rank and accomplishments called forth. Both Dryden's ode and Anthony Wood's notes on her (appended to his discussion of her father's life) imply qualities of both charm in person and tenacity of purpose. Walpole, evidently relying on Wood and Vertue, comments that she "gave very early testimonies of singular powers." He goes on to acknowledge the difficulty of assessing individual merit in an age of courtly compliment, asserting that "To have received such elevated praise, in the prose of the ascetic A. Wood; and in the enthusiastic strains of Dryden, argues transcendent merit; or was owing to a fortunate combination of circumstances." The "fortunate circumstances" may well have included family talent as well as connections, as both Killigrew's uncles, William and Thomas, were celebrated for dramatic poetry, and her father published sermons and a tragedy, written when he was seventeen.

The volume of poems that Killigrew's family published serves well to extend the family's reputation for literary activity. Thirty of the thirty-three poems in the collection, including two fragments and one longer but unfinished attempt, are by Killigrew. The remaining three are described as "found among Mrs. Killigrews Papers." The titles give some suggestion of their variety. Along with conventional epigrams – "On Billinda," "On an Aetheist," "On Galla" – are mixed some instances of pastoral and some occasional verse – "On the Birthday of Queen Katherine" and "To My Lady Berkley, Afflicted upon her Son my Lord Berkley's early Engaging in the Sea-Service." Some poems sound like conventional takes on poetical or philosophical topics: "On Death," "An Invective against Gold," "The Miseries of Man," and "Farewel to Worldly Joys" all have the ring of exercise rather than of experience. A more personal note is sounded in the three poems describing Killigrew's own paintings and in the poem most frequently cited by modern critics interested in gender studies or manuscript circulation, "Upon the saying that my Verses were made by another." More startling yet are the nineteen lines titled "On my Aunt Mrs A. K. Drown'd under London-bridge, in the

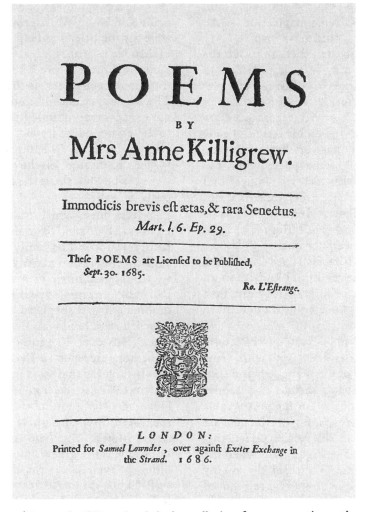

POEMS

BY

Mrs Anne Killigrew.

Immodicis brevis eſt ætas,& rara Senectus.
Mart. l. 6. Ep. 29.

Theſe POEMS are Licenſed to be Publiſhed,
Sept. 30. 1685.

Ro. L'Eſtrange.

LONDON:
Printed for *Samuel Lowndes* , over againſt *Exeter Exchange* in
the *Strand.* 1 6 8 6.

Title page for Killigrew's only book, a collection of verse commenting on the Restoration court

Queen's Bardge, Anno 1641," not only for the curious incident they commemorate, but even more so for their scathing reference to the recent Civil War where Killigrew's Royalist sympathies are strongly apparent:

> When angry Heav'n extinguisht her fair Light,
> It seem'd to say, *Nought's Precious in my ſight;*
> As I in Waves this Paragon have drown'd;
> *The Nation next, and King I will confound.*

The poems may have been arranged chronologically in order of composition as the volume begins with two poems that identify themselves as early and because Killigrew's mastery of her craft seems to grow as the volume progresses. Additionally, some effort also seems to have been given to grouping the poems by genre or by subject matter. The epigrams, for example, appear together, and the pastoral dialogues are for the most part similarly grouped. Killigrew's three poems on her own paintings are printed in sequence, while several of the philosophical pieces appear linked together as well. The occasional poems, some of the most interesting of the collection, are scattered throughout.

The first two poems, evidently the earliest composed of those Killigrew chose to save or her family elected to publish, are intriguing both for their choice of subject and for the deft way in which the failure of the first is appropriated for the success of the second. The first, "Alexandreis," although unfinished ("*first Essay of this young Lady in Poetry,*" her editor – probably a Killigrew – remarks, laid "*by till Practice and more time should make her equal to so great a Work*"), has a confident, exuberant tone, not particularly tempered by Killigrew's acknowledgment that by age, experience, and sex she is perhaps not ready for such an effort. It begins in true epic fashion – "I sing the Man that never Equal knew, /

Whose Mighty Arms all *Asia* did subdue" – and conventionally requests divine inspiration – "Ah that some pitying *Muse* would now inspire / My frozen style with a Poetic fire." Yet, although the poet admits that her sex may be an impediment to celebrating a male conqueror – "Great my presumption is, I must confess, / But if I thrive, my Glory's ne're the less; / Nor will it from his Conquests derogate / A Female Pen his Acts did celebrate" – she rather neatly answers her own objection in the second part of the poem when the troops described there, with "Scarlet Plumes" and "haughty Crests," turn out to be Amazons, not Alexander's, and are clearly identified as his rivals in both splendor and reputation. Thus the Amazons by their very presence qualify the opening line of the poem, shifting its stress from Alexander, "the Man that never Equal knew," to an implied "among *men,*" but Killigrew may not have intended that small irony as the poem does not in any way call attention to it.

In contrast the second poem in the collection, "To the Queen," refers overtly and with some amusement to the failure of the first poem and then converts that amusement to a serious point about the limitations of heroic poetry for the present age. "So thought my *Muse* at her first flight," the poet announces with reference to the earlier poem, that "she had chose the greatest height"; but when the queen's "Eye wholly divine / Vouchsaf'd upon my Verse to Shine," then the poet found herself moved to "Pitty" for "him the World called *Great*" and instead smiled at his "Unequal (though Gigantick) State." In this poem Alexander becomes not a hero but a clumsy giant, flailing with "Frantick Might" against "Wind-Mills," an absurd Don Quixote when contrasted with the queen's quiet "Grace" and "Charms." The poem then proceeds to work skillfully through a series of oppositions between hyperactive, absurdly dimensioned brutal and often ludicrous force and nondimensioned "Goodnesse," which, itself inactive, activates others by ruling "mens Wills, but with their Hearts." At the same time, the tone shifts from the banter of the opening lines to a serious indictment of a second "Giant," "bold Vice unmasked," who blatantly shows his "Ulcerous Face," lacking even the hypocrisy to hide the effects of the moral equivalent of venereal disease. Against such corruption, the poem points out, an Alexander's force has no relevance, and even a queen's virtue can offer no more than a "Shelter," not full conquest. The poem concludes that in such an age the heroic has no operative force, and a poet can only "Mourn," not "sing."

The poem does not make clear which queen is being addressed. Most probably the editor, responsible for the title, assumed the "queen" to be Mary of Modena, who had assumed the throne with James II shortly before Killigrew's death and would thus have been queen as the volume went to press. The less-experienced handling of verse form and meter, however, coupled with the direct reference to the earlier poem implies composition before the reign of James II. As Killigrew was later to address "Queen Katherine" on the occasion of her birthday, it is possible that she is the queen of the title for this poem as well.

The poem which follows these first two, "A Pastoral Dialogue," completes the introduction to Killigrew's world by implying the same rather pessimistic conclusion about the nonheroic nature of the times, although in a different context, love. Dorinda, the female speaker, offers Alexis, the traditional pastoral shepherd-lover, her gifts of song if he will accept her love. Already plighted to Lycoris (Lust), however, he gently refuses Dorinda and refutes her reference to Lycoris's less-than-virginal past by arguing that what occurred between Lycoris and an earlier lover, because it took place before he knew her, was "not to be my Care." To Dorinda's reiterated offer of a purer "Virgin love ... that's newly blown / ... / not once mis-plac't," he acknowledges the greater purity but refutes its possibility, or even its desirability, for mortals like himself: "Thus do our Priests of Heavenly Pastures tell, / Eternal Groves, all Earthly, that excell: / And think to wean us from our Love below, / By dazzling Objects which we cannot know."

The three opening poems can thus be seen as introducing the variety that follows, for while different groupings are clearly distinguished from each other, there is constantly the implication that the world in which Killigrew lives is no longer heroic. Her epigrams, for example, while skillfully delivering a typically witty turn at their respective closings, often do so with a cynicism that sounds more local than conventional. The fourth epigram, "On Galla," for instance, opens with an indictment of a winter cold spell so severe that even "*Corinna's* youthful cheeks ... / Look pale and bleak, and shew a purple hew, / And Violets stain, where Roses lately grew." The poem concludes, however, with a bitter tribute to "*Galla* alone," who "with wonder we behold, / Maintain her Spring, and still out-braves the Cold." "Sure Divine beauty in this Dame does shine?" the naive voice admiringly questions. "Not Humane" comes the response, "yet not Divine." As cosmetic art is given its dubious due, the imagery of the natural world in the earlier lines is called into question, converted to, and indicted as the artifice of the world of the court. Corinna, it is implied, in this world is always Galla, her virtue, like her violets, more stained than pure.

The Restoration world that Anne Killigrew inhabited admittedly supplied an abundance of material for indictment, of a magnitude on a significantly greater scale than that of the use of cosmetics. Nonetheless, Mary of Modena's immediate household, both before she became queen and after, seems to have endeavored to remain self-consciously exempt from the more general corruption. The duchess of York and her ladies lived in an atmosphere where the liberal arts were honored and practiced and where the discussion of serious topics was encouraged. A list of the maids of honor, drawn up in 1683 by Gregario Leti, historiographer to Charles II, includes Anne Kingsmill, later to become Anne Finch, Countess of Winchilsea, another poet; Penelope O'Brien, Countess of Petersborough, accomplished in French, who had been with the duchess since her marriage; Susanna Armine, Lady Belasyse, who as a young widow in 1670 had so attracted James with her remarkable powers of mind that he had once "wooed her for his wife"; and Catherine Sedley, who drew the highest salary, a brilliant woman and celebrated wit.

Killigrew's pastoral poems, traditionally opening the way to commentary on court matters, would certainly bear investigation in this light. The first pastoral dialogue, already mentioned, in its concluding lines invites contemporary reference, and some scholars have suggested that the "Dorinda" of this poem might be equated with either Katherine Philips or Catherine Sedley. More generally, the second "Pastoral Dialogue" strikes a note consistent with the moral ambitions of the duchess of York's court, as a tough-minded and witty Alinda rejects the shepherd-suitor Amintor's complaint that her avoidance of him should be curtailed by this strenuous effort of pursuit. Turning his own argument back on him, Alinda replies:

> What wonder, Swain, if the Pursu'd by Flight,
> Seeks to avoid the close Pursuers Sight?
> And if no Cause I have to fly from thee,
> Then thou hast none, why dost thou follow me.

Prompted to woo by less insulting means than sophistry, Amintor then succeeds in shifting from conventional flattery to sincere admiration. Rightly praising Alinda's virtue over beauty, he remarks, in lines that seem strikingly suitable to Killigrew herself, that he loves her because

> Thou still Earliest at the Temple art,
> And still the last that does from thence depart;
> *Pans* Altar is by thee the oftnest prest,
> Thine's still the fairest Offering and the Best;
> . . . .
> Strict in thy self, to others Just and Mild;
> Careful, nor to Deceive, nor be Beguil'd;
> . . . .
> Even on thy Beauty thou dost Fetters lay,
> Least, unawares, it any should betray.
> . . . .
> Beholding with a Gen'rous Disdain,
> The lighter Courtships of each amorous Swain;
> Knowing, true Fame, Vertue alone can give;
> Nor dost thou greedily even that receive.

Although Alinda remains cautious, she nonetheless concedes that if she ever surrenders to any it will be to one who "does, like to *Amintor* love," and the poem becomes less seductive than instructive in the proper ways of wooing the serious court lady. In this context the poem might even be read as a tribute, for it is tempting to see it as occasioned by the exemplary courtship and marriage in 1684 of Killigrew's friend Anne Kingsmill to Heneage Finch, captain of the halberdiers of the duke of York and the future Lord Winchilsea.

The longest and most ambitious of Killigrew's pastorals, "A Pastoral Dialogue: Melibæus, Alcippe, Asteria, Licida, Alcimedon, and Amira," invites a similar reading out of the context of Mary of Modena's court, and, although generalized in its images and morality, might also reward the effort to align its speakers with specific historical figures from Killigrew's circle.

The three poems dealing with her own paintings, however, strike an individual note that separates Killigrew's collection of verse from similar efforts by her contemporaries. The poems are brief — two on biblical subjects, one on a scene drawn from mythology. Interestingly, they do not directly address the topic one might have expected from a poet/painter, the relative merits of word and image, nor do they explicitly acknowledge the sister arts tradition to which the title of Dryden's ode refers. Nevertheless, Killigrew's handling of her material, if not direct in acknowledging the sibling rivalry between the arts, nonetheless implies a decided bias in favor of poetry. Each poem, for example, is spoken by a subject from its respective painting, certainly implying Killigrew's assent to the traditional Renaissance view of painting as "mute" poetry in need of a viewer to give it voice. That the viewer here is also the artist, and thus the "voice" an act of ventriloquism, is something that Killigrew regrettably does not make much of, although that point is underscored by each title (most likely not of Killigrew's choosing): "St. John Baptist Painted by her self," "Herodias Daughter . . . also Painted by her self," and "On a Picture Painted by her self." The concluding lines of the third poem – "If you ask where such Wights do dwell, / In what Bless't Clime, that so excel? / The Poets onely that can tell" – indeed claim special knowledge for the poet without whom the painter's art is, from this stance at least, tellingly incomplete and thus morally inefficacious.

The effort to derive Killigrew's biography from her poetry is probably best served by a final grouping of her poems, the occasional pieces. Their topics range from the conventional, in poems addressed to royalty or "On a Young Lady Whose Lord was Travelling," to the curious lines on the death of her aunt by drowning. Some of the most interesting include specific reference to Killigrew's own poetry.

The two poems in which Killigrew refers directly to her own verse are placed closely together in the collection. The first, "Upon the saying that my Verses were made by another," though its topic is commonplace among women's poetry of the time, does seem to have been occasioned by a specific incident. In response to her accuser, Killigrew recounts her initial commitment to poetry in terms that invoke the purity and idealism of her first enthusiasm for her craft – "Next heaven my Vows to thee (O Sacred *Muse!*) / I offer'd up" – and makes it clear that neither money nor reputation motivated her original devotion:

> O Queen of Verse, said I, if thou'lt inspire,
> And warm my Soul with thy Poetic Fire,
> No Love of Gold shall share with thee my Heart,
> Or yet Ambition in my Brest have Part[.]

Her sincerity is rewarded: her verse flows easily and is praised by her peers, most probably the circle surrounding Mary of Modena and her ladies. Killigrew's indignation, when her lines, though praised, are attributed to another, makes an interesting departure from convention, however. Rather than defending her own integrity, she turns self-accuser and chastises herself, not without some amused self-deprecation, for having violated what she knew to be a sacred contract. Seduced by "False Hope" for her dedication to earthly, not heavenly, "Fame," she is punished less by "shame" than by loss of that balanced insight with which she was graced before. To "False Hope" she says, rather ruefully, "By thee deceiv'd, methought each Verdant Tree, / *Apollos* transform'd *Daphne* seem'd to be," and wittily recounts how every leaf of her own

poetry became for her a "garland"; hence her shock when her verse is attributed to another, better-known collector of such "Sacred Wreaths." She concludes that her punishment is deserved and agrees to accept it with good grace should her gifts be restored: "so *Phebus* I by thee / Divinity Inspired and possest may be; / I willingly accept *Cassandras Fate,* / To speak the Truth, although believ'd too late." One slightly digressive passage in the poem deserves further mention because it implies that Killigrew's effort to correct her own vanity might not have been entirely successful. Katherine Philips, she suggests, escaped the common female fate of being denied the rewards of her own talent, in part because she was not a great beauty. "What she did write, not only all allow'd / But ev'ry Laurel, to her Laurel, bow'd!" Her sex did not "obstruct her Fame," for she "Ow'd not her Glory to a Beauteous Face." Envy, Killigrew seems to be saying, is an inevitable companion of physical beauty, and one she herself cannot escape.

The other poem which strikes a personal note is addressed "To My Lord Colrane, In answer to his Complemental Verses sent me under the Name of Cleanor." The poem is intriguing, not only because it offers a clue to the circulation of verse within a system of fanciful names and courtly compliment, but also for its delicate adjustment of status, which implies Killigrew's sophisticated awareness of the dangers of condescension and triviality that a female poet might risk in appealing to an older, male, mentor. Henry Hales, second Baron Coleraine (1636–1708), was an antiquary of Tottenham, Middlesex. (A copy of Killigrew's *Poems* bearing his bookplate, dated 1702, is in the University of Michigan Library.) Killigrew's poem to him opens with a narrative account of the verse, evidently highly complimentary, which Coleraine had sent in response to a poem of hers and thus raises the question of a suitable reaction. Should the younger poet be pleased, flattered, reinspired? Before answering, however, she ostensibly digresses to commend Coleraine in respectful lines, which honor him for the fact that among the "Great," whose status is usually given to "dang'rous Politicks, and formal Pride," he should stand out as "One, who on Ancestors does not rely / For Fame, in Merit, as in Title, high!" The passage, while digressive, in its exchange of compliment for compliment thus serves the more important function of clarifying the relationship between the two poets as one between equals. Hence Killigrew can conclude that the proper use for her of his verse should be that "This Use of these Applauding Numbers make / Them for Example, not Encomium, take."

Taken together, then, these two poems yield some insight into Killigrew's reflections on her own verse and into the kind of circulation she sought for it. She seems to have been sensitive to the dangers of excessive praise and aware that the beauty or status of a female poet could impede an accurate assessment of her verse. Yet she also appears willing to permit the circulation of her poems within a select circle, warily testing them by using the good taste of others and her own good sense as guides.

Recent scholarship has yet to address Killigrew's accomplishments at length. The most extensive discussion to date is the introduction by Richard Morton in the facsimile edition of her poems. Morton generalizes about Killigrew's verse, describing it as bearing a "conventionality which inevitably borders on the derivative." Although he allows that "at her best" she does move beyond the conventional to achieve some surprisingly Metaphysical intensity, Morton nonetheless locates the individuality of her work in its "evangelical moral tone" and agrees with Dryden's characterization of her verse as "cold," citing the line " 'Twas *Cupid* bathing in *Diana's* Stream."

More appreciative readings, although usually of relatively few poems, are offered by Kristina Straub, Ann Messenger, and Maureen E. Mulvihill. In most other instances Killigrew's verse is assessed in the context of discussions of Dryden's ode or rapidly summarized in surveys of seventeenth-century women poets and artists.

The original volume of her poetry is relatively rare. An account of it is given in George Ballard's *Memoirs of Several Ladies* (1752), and a bibliographical analysis of it is given by Hugh Macdonald in *John Dryden, a Bibliography* (1939). The facsimile reprint was made from the copy in the Alexander Turnbull Library, Wellington, which was originally in the collection of Dr. Philip Bliss.

Because the poetry is all one has at present from which to tease out the details of the life and personality of this young poet, it is enticing. As a text reflective of life at court in the first decades of the Restoration, it certainly engages interest. Finally, as a verbal artifact of words, wit, taste, craft, and intelligence, Killigrew's collection of poems rewards reading. As such it continues to pose an engaging challenge to scholarship and should certainly be of interest in future studies of seventeenth-century literature and life.

References:

Ellen Creathorne Clayton, *English Female Artists,* volume 1 (London, 1876), pp. 59–70;

Margaret Doody, *Daring Muse* (Cambridge, Mass.: Harvard University Press, 1985);

Margaret J. M. Ezell, *The Patriarch's Wife: Literary Evidence and the History of the Family* (Chapel Hill & London: University of North Carolina Press, 1987);

Germaine Greer, Susan Hastings, Jeslyn Medoff, and Melinda Sansone, eds., *Kissing the Rod: An Anthology of Seventeenth-Century Women's Verse* (London: Virago, 1988; New York: Farrar, Straus & Giroux, 1989);

Elaine Hobby, *Virtue of Necessity: English Women's Writing 1649–88* (Ann Arbor: University of Michigan Press, 1990);

Ann Messenger, *His and Hers: Essays in Restoration & 18th-Century Literature* (Lexington: University Press of Kentucky, 1986);

Maureen E. Mulvihill, "Essential Studies of Restoration Women Writers: Reclaiming a Heritage, 1913–1986," *Restoration: Studies in English Literary Culture, 1660–1700,* 11 (Fall 1987): 122–131;

Carol Virginia Pohli, "Formal and Informal Space in Dryden's Ode, 'To the Pious Memory of Anne Killigrew,' " *Restoration: Studies in English Literary Culture, 1660–1700,* 15 (Spring 1991): 27–40;

Myra Reynolds, ed., *The Poems of Anne Countess of Winchilsea* (Chicago: University of Chicago Press, 1903), pp. xxiii–xxiv;

C. Anderson Silber, "Nymphs and Satyrs: Poet, Readers and Irony in Dryden's 'Ode to Anne Killigrew,' " *Studies in Eighteenth-Century Culture,* 14 (1985): 193–212;

Kristina Straub, "Indecent Liberties with a Poet: Audience and the Metaphor of Rape in Killigrew's 'Upon the Saying that My Verses' and Pope's Arbuthnot," *Tulsa Studies in Women's Literature,* 6 (Spring 1987): 27–45;

Horace Walpole, *Anecdotes of Painting in England,* volume 3 (London: Shakespeare, 1828), pp. 52–55.

Jane Ward Lead

(March 1623 – 19 August 1704)

John T. Shawcross
University of Kentucky

BOOKS: *The Heavenly Cloud Now Breaking. The Lord Christ's Ascension-Ladder Sent down; To shew the way to reach the Ascension, and Glorification, through the Death and Resurrection* (London: Printed for the author, 1681); revised as *The Heavenly Cloud Now Breaking . . . A New Edition. With a Postscript now added, which was in the last edition of it in the High Dutch* (London: Printed by J. Bradford, 1701);

The Revelation of Revelations Particularly as an Essay Towards the Unsealing, Opening and Discovering the Seven Seals, the Seven Thunders, and the New-Jerusalem State (London: Printed & sold by A. Sowle, also by J. Lead, 1683; second edition, London: Printed by J. Bradford, 1701);

The Enochian Walks with God, found out by a Spiritual-Traveller, Whose face towards Mount-Sion above was set . . . with an experimental account of what was known, seen, and met withal there (London: Printed & sold by D. Edwards, 1694; second edition, London: Printed by J. Bradford, 1702);

The Laws of Paradise (London: Printed & sold by T. Sowle, 1695);

The Wonders of God's Creation Manifested in the Variety of Eight Worlds as they were made known experimentally to the author (London: Printed & sold by T. Sowle, 1695?);

The Tree of Faith; or, The Tree of Life Springing up in the Paradise of God (London: Printed & sold by J. Bradford, 1696);

A Message to the Philadelphian Society, withersoever dispersed over the whole earth. Together with a call to the several gathered churches among Protestants in this nation of England (London: Printed & sold by J. Bradford, 1696);

A Fountain of Gardens: Watered by the rivers of divine pleasure, and springing up in all the variety of spiri-

tual plants; blown up by the pure breath into a paradise. To which is prefixed a poem, introductory to the Philadelphian age, called Solomons porch, or the beautiful gate to Wisdoms Temple, 3 volumes (London: Printed & sold by J. Bradford, 1696–1701);

The Ark of Faith: or a Supplement to the Tree of Faith, &c., For the Further Confirmation of the Same. Together with a Discovery of the New World (London: Printed by J. Bradford, 1696);

A Revelation of the Everlasting Gospel-Message, which shall never cease to be preach'd till the hour of Christ's eternal Judgment shall come (London: Sold by the Booksellers of London & Westminster, 1697);

The Messenger of an Universal Peace: or, A Third Message to the Philadelphian Society (London: Printed for the Booksellers of London & Westminster, 1698);

The Ascent to the Mount of Vision; Where Many Things were shown, concerning I. The First Resurrection; II. The State of Separated Souls; III. The Patriarchal Life; IV. The Kingdom of Christ (London, 1699);

The Signs of the Times; Forerunning the Kingdom of Christ, and Evidencing where it is come (London, 1699);

The Wars of David, and the Peaceable Reign of Solomon, Symbolizing the Times of Warfare and Refreshment of the Saints (London: Printed by J. Bradford, 1700);

A Living Funeral Testimony: or, Death Overcome, and Drown'd in the Life of Christ (London: Printed by J. Bradford, 1702).

A prolific author, Jane Ward Lead (Leade) was an important religious personage and founder of the Philadelphian Society, whose prose is frequently punctuated with verse. It has been only recently, with the growth of interest in women authors and thinkers, that she has become known to a current audience. A few excerpts of her prose writings will be found in recent anthologies. Her married name appears in both spellings.

She was the daughter of Schildknap Ward of Norfolk, receiving at home only the inadequate customary education given to middle-class women. The mysticism which was to dominate her later life and writing first emerged when she was fifteen, at which time during Christmas celebrations, she records, she heard a whispering voice. Her subsequent melancholy ended at eighteen when another vision pardoned a lie told earlier in her life. In 1644, at twenty-one, she married William Lead (Leade), six years her senior and a relative. He died in February 1670, leaving their daughter, Barbara, who lived into adulthood. During the 1640s Lead was influenced by the growing belief in an oncoming millennium (to occur for some in 1657); the belief remained to emerge in all her later works. In 1663 she had met Dr. John Pordage, Rector of Bradfield, Berks, a follower of Jakob Boehme, who propounded the doctrine of the Light of Nature (mystic revelation of all true knowledge of divine and human concerns). The Boehmenists achieved "visible and sensible communion with angels" in their ceremonies, believing in an indwelling of Christ in their souls and a mixing of his fiery deity in their flesh. From April 1670 onward, as "a widow of God," she experienced nightly visions, as recorded in *A Fountain of Gardens* (1696–1701), her spiritual biography, the major source of her mystic experiences. Sophia, Goddess of Wisdom, was significant in Boehme's philosophy, and Lead's visions often revolve around her. Lead's first published works were well received in Holland and Germany by members of the sect, and brought her to the attention of Dr. Francis Lee of Oxford. These works and later ones were published in Dutch and German translations. Lee met her on his return to England, and was later adopted by her as her son. His marriage to Barbara (at that time the widow of Izaac Walton) came through a "divine order."

Lead and Lee formed the Philadelphian Society in 1694, its monthly (but short-lived) journal *Theosophical Transactions by the Philadelphian Society* being published by Lee and Richard Roach of Oxford. While not being Dissenters, those varying sects that commanded attention as the century drew to a close, the Philadelphians were aligned with the numerous groups that developed from midcentury onward and stressed spiritual life and the inner light. Lead became blind (around 1699), and Lee functioned as her conduit for recording her frequent visions; publication of them occurred, she wrote, through the command of God. Most noteworthy, perhaps, in the prose and poetry that appear are the strong images in arresting metaphor, with complex rhetorical expression, labeled ungrammatical by some. Attention in her mystic works is paid to genderization: she emphasized the female aspects of God (a God of eternal Love), understood Adam as androgynous until the Fall when sexual discrimination took place, and looked forward to a Third Coming of Christ when such discrimination would disappear. With this Coming life would return to its original divine existence.

Impoverished and the object of professional jealousy in her last years, Lead received a pension from Baron Knyphausen, lived in an almshouse in Stepney, and died, after periods of intermittent consciousness, "in the 81st year of her age, and 65th of her vocation to the inward life." She was buried in Bunhill Fields; Roach delivered the funeral sermon. Lee communicated the circumstances of her death to various friends on the Continent and wrote "The Last Hours of Jane Lead, by an Eye and Ear Witness." (The original was translated into German before the manuscript was lost. A manuscript of an English retranslation from the German is in the Walton Library of Dr. Williams's Library, London.)

As remarked above, Lead's prose is interspersed with poetry, generally in stanzaic form (usually quatrains) or in iambic pentameter couplets. The poetry versifies the ideas of the ecstatic prose: the greatness of love and the greatness of sacrifice for others (such as Christ's). It employs scriptural allusions and language, and its metaphors are Metaphysical in their ethereal nature and in their being unexpected and complex. The long poem "Solomons Porch: or The Beautiful Gate of Wisdoms Temple," in heroic verse, is signed "Onesimus" (a Roman surname but perhaps implying here the superlative of "one") and exhibits the themes noted above: millennialism, wisdom, the triumph of wisdom over materiality, the necessity of thought and its wisdom to be able to pass into the temple of God, and the significance of the female and female qualities in passing through the Gate. A major influence on the poem, and indeed on some of the ideas of the prose, is John Milton's *Paradise Lost* (1667). There are echoes of language and images as well as content. A contrastive thought is Adam's that Death becomes the Gate of Life: here it is Wisdom as seen in Boehmenist terms that becomes the Gate to the Edenic world.

References:

Myra Reynolds, *The Learned Lady in England, 1650–1760* (Boston & New York: Houghton Mifflin, 1920);

Catherine F. Smith, "Jane Lead: Mysticism and the Woman Cloathed with the Sun," in *Shakespeare's Sisters: Feminist Essays on Women Poets*, edited by Sandra M. Gilbert and Susan Gubar (Bloomington: Indiana University Press, 1979), pp. 3–18;

Smith, "Jane Lead's Wisdom: Women and Prophecy in Seventeenth-Century England," *Poetic Prophecy in Western Literature*, edited by Jan Wojick and Raymond-Jean Frontain (Rutherford, N.J.: Fairleigh Dickinson University Press, 1984), pp. 55–63;

Smith, "A Note on Jane Lead, with Selections from her Writings," *Studia Mystica,* 3, no. 4 (1980): 79–82;

Smith, "Three Guineas: Virginia Woolf 's Prophecy," in *Virginia Woolf and Bloomsbury: A Centenary Celebration,* edited by Jane Marcus (Bloomington: Indiana University Press, 1987), pp. 225–241;

Joanne Magnani Sperle, "God's Healing Angel: A Biography of Jane Ward Lead," Ph.D. dissertation, Kent State University, 1985;

Nils Thune, *The Behemenists and the Philadelphians. A Contribution to the Study of English Mysticism in the Seventeenth and Eighteenth Centuries* (Uppsala, Sweden: Almqvist & Wiksells, 1948).

Richard Lovelace

(1618 – 1657)

Sharon Cadman Seelig
Smith College

BOOKS: *Lucasta: Epodes, Odes, Sonnets, Songs, &c. To Which Is Added Aramantha, A Pastorall* (London: Printed by Thomas Harper, sold by Tho. Evvster, 1649; facsimile, Menston: Scholar, 1972);

Lucasta: Posthume Poems (London: Printed by William Godbid for Clement Darby, 1659 [i.e., 1660]).

Edition: *The Poems of Richard Lovelace,* edited by C. H. Wilkinson (Oxford: Clarendon Press, 1930).

Richard Lovelace, Royalist, soldier, and poet, perhaps more than any of his contemporaries embodies the spirit of the Cavalier. Like his fellow poets Sir John Suckling and Thomas Carew, Lovelace was an accomplished amateur following in the tradition of Baldassare Castiglione's *Courtier* (1528; translated, 1561), in which writing poetry, like proficiency in arms, love, and music, was one of the accomplishments expected of the gentleman. Lovelace's work, consisting of two volumes of poetry published in 1649 and 1660, is certainly uneven, but it includes singularly beautiful and graceful lyrics that stand as exemplary for the casual grace and elegance of this group of poets.

Richard Lovelace was born in 1618, probably in Woolwich, Kent. He was the eldest son of Sir William Lovelace and his wife Anne Barne Lovelace. Sir William, a member of an old and distinguished military and legal family and owner of a considerable amount of landed property in Kent, died in battle when Lovelace was only nine, leaving "his Lady ritch only in great store of children" (there were five sons and three daughters). At the age of eleven Richard was sent to the Charterhouse School in London, where, during the next five years, he would have known a future poet of quite different talents and inclinations, Richard Crashaw. Thereafter Lovelace enrolled as a student at the University of Oxford (in Gloucester Hall, now Worcester College). He was then, according to the seventeenth-century historian Anthony Wood, "accounted the most amiable and beautiful person that ever eye beheld; a person also of innate modesty, virtue and courtly deportment, which made him then, but especially after, when he retired to the great city, much admired and adored by the female sex."

Lovelace was early associated with the brilliant and extravagant court of Charles I, which was a center not only of political interaction but also of artistic and literary patronage, a place that attracted and supported the painters Anthony Van Dyck, Peter Paul Rubens, and Peter Lely, the musician Henry Lawes, and the poets Ben Jonson, Thomas Carew, Sir John Suckling, Abraham Cowley, and Edmund Waller. At the age of fifteen Lovelace became a "Gentleman Wayter Extraordinary" to the king; in 1636, at the age of eighteen, during a three-week celebration at Oxford, he was granted the degree of master of arts. Wood describes Lovelace as coming in 1638 in "great splendour" to the court; a year later, when the Princess Katherine died on her birthday, Lovelace contributed verse to a volume of commemorative elegies. Although Lovelace's poetry shows a good many signs of his acquaintance with classical as well as contemporary poets, as a gentleman he took care to appear a connoisseur rather than a scholar, one who engaged in graceful allusion or response to the work of others, in a mode of social interaction rather than studious effort. Lovelace wrote to commemorate an occasion, to praise a friend or fellow poet, to give advice in grief or love, to define a relationship or the nature of honor, to articulate the precise amount of attention a man owes a woman, to celebrate beauty, and to persuade to love. That a good many of the poems of *Lucasta* (1649) were set to music by Lawes and others further indicates the social function of these lyrics, which elegantly and wittily articulate common themes.

Lovelace also tried his hand at drama: while a student at Oxford he wrote a comedy, titled "The Scholars," which was acted first in his own college and later in London but was never printed; later in

Richard Lovelace (portrait in the Dulwich Gallery)

1640, after some military experience of his own, Lovelace wrote a tragedy titled "The Soldier," which was never performed. Neither of these plays survives, but their titles suggest a combination of conventional genre and personal experience. After leaving Oxford, Lovelace spent several months at Cambridge University, where he met another prominent poet of his generation, Andrew Marvell, with whom he remained on friendly terms.

Having met George, Lord Goring (later Earl of Norwich), at court, Lovelace became a member of the regiment of Goring's son and served in the Bishops' Wars of 1639 and 1640. This ill-advised attempt to impose the forms of worship of the Anglican church on Scotland not only failed but in fact marked the beginning of the decline of the power of Charles I. In this demoralizing campaign, in which Suckling also took part, Lovelace served first as se-

nior ensign (1639) and then as captain (1640). Only one poem clearly grew out of this experience: the "Sonnet. To Generall Goring" is a poem of bacchanalian celebration rather than a glorification of military action.

When Lovelace returned home to Kent in 1640, having come of age, he took possession of his lands and assumed the usual duties of the country gentleman, including service as justice of the peace. But the civil turmoil that was to dominate England for the next generation and affect Lovelace until his death at the age of thirty-nine soon intervened. In the struggle over religious doctrine and ritual, over church government, and over the amount of authority inherent in or ceded to the monarchy that led to the Civil War, Lovelace's sympathies, by class and by temperament, were with the supporters not so much of Charles's policies as of the monarchy itself.

But Lovelace, although standing in the popular imagination as the ideal Cavalier, as soldier as well as poet and lover, actually spent comparatively little time in arms, a fact that derived from his early and decisive devotion to the Royalist cause rather than from any lack of enthusiasm: for Lovelace was prohibited first by imprisonment and later by parliamentary decree from participating in military action.

The kind of idealism expressed in perhaps his most famous poem, "To Lucasta. Going to the Warres," is also revealed in Lovelace's first recorded political action. In December 1640 a petition for the abolition of episcopal rule, signed with fifteen thousand names, was presented to the House of Commons. This movement, which was opposed by moderates such as Edward Hyde, later first Earl of Clarendon, and Lucius Cary, second Viscount Falkland, led to a counterpetition, framed by Sir Edward Dering, in support of the rights of the king, governance of the church by bishops, and the reinstatement of the Anglican liturgy. There followed a chain of reactions – anger in Parliament and counterpetitions. When in Lovelace's home county of Kent such an anti-Royalist, antiepiscopal petition was being drafted, Lovelace in 1641 led a group of men who seized the petition and tore it up. That dramatic action led to his being chosen in 1642 for a far more dangerous task – to present Dering's pro-Royalist petition, which had been ordered burned, to the House of Commons on behalf of the county of Kent. In response to questioning by the Commons, Lovelace answered forthrightly, acknowledging the shredding of the anti-Royalist petition in Kent and asserting that he spoke for all the Kentish justices of the peace who had joined in rejecting it.

For his actions in Kent and for his candor in London, Lovelace was imprisoned in the Gatehouse in Westminster. After seven weeks Lovelace submitted a petition to the House of Commons, expressing submission and asking for clemency, but without any statement of regret for his past actions. In his petition Lovelace notes that in "beeinge confined here in the Springe-tide of Action, when open Rebellion treads on the late peacefull bosome of his Maiesties Kingdome of Ireland, [he] is to his farther Greefe disabled from discharging parte of that duetie, which he owes unto his Kinge and Countrie by his service there."

Lovelace's desire to serve the king in Ireland or elsewhere was hardly an inducement to the Commons to free him, but on 21 June he was released on bail, with the stipulation that he not go beyond the lines of communication without a pass from the speaker of the House of Commons. Thus Lovelace,

a forthright young man of twenty-four who had already done his best to serve King Charles in the Bishops' Wars, was effectively denied participation in the first phase of the Civil War.

But this first experience of imprisonment, so frustrating to Lovelace's hopes and intentions, seems also to have given rise to one of his finest lyrics, "To Althea, From Prison," in which he asserts an inner freedom of spirit in contrast to his physical confinement. In this poem Lovelace presents himself as a lover, visited by "divine Althea," who comes "to whisper at the Grates," as a member of a good fellowship whom he depicts in a grief-assuaging festivity, and most of all as the courtier whose confinement only makes him the more devoted to the cause for which he is punished:

> When (like committed Linnets) I
>   With shriller throat shall sing
> The sweetnes, Mercy, Majesty,
>   And glories of my KING[.]

In each of these instances there is a contradiction between the poet's apparent situation – physical imprisonment – and what he declares to be the actual one – moral and spiritual freedom. Although imprisoned, either by love ("tangled in her haire / And fettered to her eye") or by the walls of a prison, Lovelace asserts, at the end of each stanza, his essential freedom, concluding with his famous declaration of supremacy:

> Stone Walls do not a Prison make,
>   Nor I'ron bars a Cage;
> Mindes innocent and quiet take
>   That for an Hermitage[.]

This four-stanza lyric embodies much that is characteristic of Lovelace's best poetry. It represents the voice of a single speaker who defines himself and his situation in a way that is both noble and paradoxical, that shows his independence of thought and action, his refusal to be overwhelmed or controlled by his circumstances. The general level of diction is simple, tending even to the colloquial and casual ("Fishes that tipple in the Deepe") but spiced with a good deal of the sensuous and the concrete ("When I lye tangled in her haire / And fettered to her eye") and with surprising word choices – "committed Linnets," "shriller throat," "no allaying *Thames*" – that keep Lovelace's verse lively and interesting and raise it above the level of the mere gentleman amateur. In "To Althea, From Prison" Lovelace places clause against clause, line against line, yet interrupts that balanced structure with the surprising word so that the result is a sense of grace, elegance, and control that never ceases to seem spontaneous. The poem moves from its depiction of the three instances in which the poet, though imprisoned, is yet by his assertion free, to a ringing and climactic articulation of the general principle:

> If I have freedome in my Love,
> 　And in my soule am free;
> Angels alone that sore above,
> 　Injoy such Liberty.

Lovelace was free in body and in mind by late June 1642, but he was not allowed to join the king's army in Ireland. Nevertheless he did what he could, selling most of his land in 1643 and using the proceeds, according to Wood, "to keep up the credit and reputation of the king's cause by furnishing men with horse and arms." Lovelace supplied his two brothers, Col. Francis Lovelace and Capt. William Lovelace, who did fight for the king, with men and money, and he supported his youngest brother, Dudley Posthumus Lovelace, during his study of tactics and fortifications in Holland.

Lovelace appears to have spent a good deal of time abroad in 1643–1646, in Holland and France. He may well have accompanied his former chief officer General Goring to Holland, where he met Princesss Louisa of Bohemia and wrote a complimentary poem to her on her drawing. Unable to join the struggle in Great Britain, Lovelace was among those who fought against the Spanish in Holland and was wounded at Dunkirk in October 1646.

It is to this period that "To Lucasta, Going beyond the Seas," a song set by Lawes, has generally been assigned. This graceful lyric is the opening poem of Lovelace's first published volume, where it appears in close proximity to several of his best-known and most successful poems. The identity of Lucasta is unknown: poets writing in the tradition of courtly love commonly addressed a (sometimes fictitious) lady whose name reflected the qualities ascribed to her: Lucasta, from *lux casta,* means "chaste light." Although Wood confidently identified Lucasta with Lucy Sacheverel, "a gentlewoman of great beauty and fortune," that claim has been doubted and was disputed by Lovelace's modern editor C. H. Wilkinson, who associates "that bright Northern star" with the Lucas family. Whoever her original may have been, Lucasta, represented in Peter Lely's engraving as a rather healthy-looking young woman with bared breast, is addressed in twenty-seven of Lovelace's poems.

"To Lucasta, Going beyond the Seas" is one of the poems by Lovelace with obvious similarities to work by John Donne, in this case "A Valediction, Forbidding Mourning" (1633), in which a lover urges his beloved not to mourn his absence, arguing that "They who one another keep alive, / Ne'er parted be." But whereas Donne offers a series of extravagant yet precise analogies to the lovers' situation, Lovelace's poem, characteristically, is much less detailed, exact, and elaborate in working out a conceit. The conditional opening stanza looks as if it might set up a Donnean paradox:

> If to be absent were to be
> 　Away from thee;
> 　Or that when I am gone,
> 　You or I were alone;
> Then my *Lucasta* might I crave
> Pity from blustring winde, or swallowing wave.

But instead of proceeding to a dramatically executed triumph over fate and fact, Lovelace in stanza 2 simply declares his indifference to these forces and, in a milder, dilute evocation of Donne, asserts that the lovers inhabit a realm beyond the dictates of space and time:

> Though Seas and Land betwixt us both,
> 　Our Faith and Troth,
> 　Like separated soules,
> 　All time and space controules:
> Above the highest sphere wee meet
> Unseene, unknowne, and greet as Angels greet.

Lovelace's poem takes for granted the reader's acquaintance with Donne and, rather than an ingenious working-out of a conceit, offers a kind of graceful insouciance, a blithe assertion of independence in the face of unkind fate that has been seen by Cyril H. Hartmann as characteristic of the Cavaliers in general, an affirmation of the independence of mind from body, a refusal to identify freedom of the spirit with bodily freedom.

The mid 1640s – which drove Lovelace to Holland and led to such poems as "To Lucasta, Going to the Warres" and "To Althea, From Prison" – reveal him as soldier, poet, and courtier, as an attractive and magnetic personality, but also suggest his wider intellectual and aesthetic interests. Lovelace was a friend of the Dutch painter Lely, who succeeded Anthony Van Dyck at court and who designed the plates for Lovelace's two volumes of poems, as well as of Endymion Porter, patron of poets and painters and artistic purchasing agent for Charles I. Both Lovelace and Lely were admitted to the Freedom of the Painters' Company on 26 October 1647, and one of Lovelace's poems offers discriminating praise of Lely's portrait of Charles I and James, Duke of York, painted during the king's imprisonment at Hampton Court. Lovelace was also on friendly terms with Thomas Stanley and George Sandys, poets and translators; with both the elder and younger Charles Cottons; and with Andrew Marvell and John Hall, both of whom, though closely connected with the parliamentary cause, wrote prefatory poems for the 1650 edition of *Lucasta.*

In the spring and summer of 1648, with Charles I forcibly detained on the Isle of Wight and the parliamentary forces dominant, sympathy for the king's cause was manifested in a series of uprisings in Wales, Essex, Surrey, and Kent. Once again Lovelace appears to have taken a significant part, since once again his punishment was more severe than that of his companions. The rebellion in Kent was quelled by the army under Gen. Thomas Fairfax, and Lovelace was imprisoned in early June and held, despite a petition for his release, until April 1649.

When Lovelace emerged from prison, the cause he had fought for seemed irretrievably lost: the king had been executed in January 1649, the army under Oliver Cromwell was in the ascendancy, and Lovelace's own economic circumstances were increasingly insecure. But the time of his imprisonment led, as in the case of the earlier "To Althea, From Prison," to an assertion of spiritual freedom. Having used the enforced leisure to revise his verse, Lovelace published his first volume of poetry, *Lucasta,* in May 1649. Although, as Manfred Weidhorn points out, the act of publication itself may be a sign of Lovelace's straitened circumstances, in a time when writing poetry was a gentlemanly thing to do but publishing it was not, and although Lovelace's imprisonment may have delayed publication (the book had already been licensed for the press in February 1648), the appearance of his poems increased his contemporary reputation beyond the court circle and ensured the preservation of his work to the present day. Although 1649 was hardly the ideal year for a poet of Lovelace's views to break into print (nor do sales appear to have been brisk), his poetry was welcomed by men who, like him, held the rank of colonel in the Royalist forces, and praised in a commendatory poem by Marvell as an example of an earlier, higher standard in the arts, likely to be censured by the present

> . . . *swarms*
> *Of Insects which against you rise in arms.*
> *Word-peckers, Paper-rats, Book-scorpions[.]*

Of the final decade of Lovelace's short life we know relatively little. His financial circumstances were certainly difficult, for he sold the remainder of the property he had inherited, including the family manor house at Bethersden, Kent, and the family portraits. But whether he lived the life of acute poverty described by Wood ("in ragged clothes, mostly lodged in obscure and dirty places, more befitting the worst of beggars and poorest of servants") has been much doubted. Though no longer the man who "when he was in his glory . . . wore cloth of gold and silver," Lovelace was not altogether friendless; he was supported to a significant degree by Edmund Wyld and by his old friend Charles Cotton, who is reported to have sent him twenty shillings every Monday morning. Like many others who had supported the king's cause, Lovelace surely found it advisable to maintain a low profile. He died in London, most probably in 1657, and was buried near his kinsman Sir William Lovelace in the Church of Saint Bride's in Fleet Street, which was destroyed in the Fire of London in 1666.

Lovelace appears to have contemplated a second volume of poems, which appeared only after his death. *Lucasta: Posthume Poems,* listed in the Stationers' Register for 1659 but published in 1660, was seen through the press by his youngest brother Dudley Posthumus and by Elwood Revett, who appears to have acted as a literary agent for Lovelace. Although this second volume of poetry includes fewer brilliant lyrics than the first, it does expand our sense of Lovelace's range. Besides occasional poems and love lyrics, many with a world-weary or sardonic twist, there are several quasi-emblematic poems about small creatures, translations, and some satires. There is plenty of evidence of the poet's disillusionment with the topsy-turvy world in which he and fellow Royalists found themselves after the execution of Charles I and before the Restoration of Charles II, which Lovelace did not live to see.

As one of what Alexander Pope would later describe as the "mob of gentlemen who wrote with ease," Lovelace had the ability to write graceful lyrics that look as if they had been tossed off without effort. But as Castiglione pointed out, such grace and apparent ease (*sprezzatura*) are the results of a good deal of practice. Often in Lovelace's best lyrics only the effortless effect appears; but in a good many other deservedly less well known poems, the effort is obvious and the result sometimes contorted and confusing. As an accomplished amateur poet whose self-conception and self-presentation differ sharply from those of the professional writer of later days, Lovelace's versatility is shown in the number

Engraving of Lucasta in Lovelace's first collection of verse

of styles he employed. If his work often fails to achieve the level of what he imitates, he often achieves a particular grace or elegance, a flash of perspective not present in his models.

The two volumes of *Lucasta* comprise just over a hundred original poems and several translations. The largest group consists of amatory poems, the majority addressed to Lucasta but also to Althea, Gratiana, Amarantha, and Ellinda, all of them courtly or Petrarchan idealizations of the power of the beloved. There are many occasional poems of compliment, elegies and poems of consolation (on the death of Princess Katherine, to his brother Francis on the death of their brother William, on the death of the sister of Charles Cotton the elder). Like Donne, Lovelace composed poems that ideal-

ize and elevate love as well as those that are cynical about it, that reject notions of constancy as irrelevant or fraudulent, that are dismissive or manipulative of women. There are satiric poems, such as "Against the Love of Great Ones," that have been associated with the Roman satirist Juvenal but are more immediately related to the social attitudes of Jonson. There is a poem in the country-house tradition ("Being treated To Ellinda") that recalls Robert Herrick, and a group of poems on small creatures ("The Grasse-hopper," "The Ant," "The Snayl") with roots in the classical moral fable.

The Cavalier ideal for which Lovelace has often been taken as an exemplar is most clearly set out in "To Lucasta, Going to the Warres," a poem that defines the two central activities of that ideal, love and war, and articulates wittily and forcefully the relationship between them. The tension is heightened by making war not simply a rival activity but "a new Mistresse," whom the poet chases, thus making his decision to fly "the Nunnerie" of Lucasta's "chaste breast, and quiet minde" look like what it is called in stanza 3 – "Inconstancy" – with clear implications of both sexual and religious infidelity. Seemingly apostate, the poet "with a stronger Faith imbrace[s] / A Sword, a Horse, a Shield," until, in the ringing final stanza, the deserted lady herself is made a devotee of the speaker's new faith.

This brief lyric, which serves both as self-defense and self-definition, is a kind of litmus test for the Cavalier attitudes idealized by earlier generations of critics, such as Mark Van Doren, who found in the two lovers a commonality of interests rather than a tension. While the poem compliments Lucasta, that chaste light, so pure as to be designated a kind of sanctuary, the poet's position is both active and definitive, while hers is static and passive. He not only leaves her but places her, with the parenthetical designations "(Sweet)" and "(Deare)," defining first her new religion and then defining, not the terms on which she would find him worthy of love (as, for example, a courtly lover who failed to do his duty would not be highly regarded by a lady) but the terms on which *he* will love *her*:

Yet this Inconstancy is such,
    As you too shall adore;
I could not love thee (Deare) so much,
    Lov'd I not Honour more.

Both the stance – the Cavalier who leaves a woman not through infidelity but as an instance of faith to, as it has long been known, "a higher cause" – and the rhetorical means by which it is accomplished are characteristic of Lovelace. His poem is supremely graceful, deft, and masterful; but its persuasion depends not only on the kinds of manipulation of logical categories that we would find in Donne but on the finessing of oppositions, so that what has appeared to be inconstancy is redefined as the highest form of faith. The lady is both sweet and dear, but Lovelace asserts that he must yield, not with regret but with adoration, to the new mistress, which turns out not to be merely "Warre and Armes" but "Honour," a realm in which war and love are inseparably linked.

Lovelace plays the equally conventional role of the courtly lover in "Lucasta's World," in which the power of the lady creates a world that is frozen or incinerated by her glance. Such exaggerated effects are the sort of Petrarchism mocked by Donne

in the opening of "The Canonization," but Lovelace, though he does not transform the convention, nevertheless creates some striking lines in his description of a world that is both natural and yet supremely artificial, whose artifice is its chief attraction:

Cold as the breath of winds that blow
To silver shot descending snow

    LUCASTA sight [sighed]; when she did close
    The World in frosty chaines!
    And then a frowne to Rubies frose
        The blood boyl'd in our veines[.]

Lovelace attributes similarly cosmic powers to his poetic mistresses in two even more successful poems, "Gratiana dauncing and singing" and "To Amarantha, That she would dishevell her haire," both of which go beyond the conventions of Petrarchism to a quite fascinating baroque instability of images. There is in Gratiana's "constant Motion / Even, and glorious, as the Sunne" a trace of what would be a Metaphysical conceit if it were more fully or precisely elaborated. Gratiana, rather like Lucasta, shapes a larger order imagined by the poet, but whereas Lucasta expresses her power by burning and freezing, Gratiana simply dances. Yet that action becomes the cosmic dance itself and transforms her surroundings to the very heavens:

She beat the happy Pavement
By such a Starre made Firmament,
    Which now no more the Roofe envies;
But swells up high with *Atlas* ev'n,
Bearing the brighter, nobler Heav'n,
    And in her, all the Dieties.

Rather than extending and elaborating this conceit, as he does in "Lucasta's World" or as Donne does in "The Sun Rising," Lovelace quickly shifts perspective, bringing his reader back to the realm of the love poem, in which the dance is not only the cosmic pattern but also a kind of morris of "a Lovers thought." Like the Petrarchan mistress, Gratiana is a paradox of beauty and power, sweetness and refusal: it is not until the breathtaking climax of the poem that we see how much destruction she has wrought: "As when she ceas'd, we sighing saw / The floore lay pav'd with broken hearts." The poem concludes with a compliment that makes explicit the meaning of Gratiana's name as it reestablishes her within the realm of the classical pantheon and the music of the spheres:

So did she move; so did she sing
Like the Harmonious spheres that bring

Unto their Rounds their musick's ayd;
Which she performed such a way,
As all th' inamour'd world will say
The *Graces* daunced, and *Apollo* play'd.

The beloved at the center of the universe, as the arbiter, the mistress as a paradoxical being, combining "sweet command and gentle awe" — these ideas and tropes, central to Petrarchism, are hardly new with Lovelace. But the rendering of them is supremely graceful (except for the false step of "*Gratiana* steeres that Noble Frame" of line 3, in which the idea of a woman dancing collides rather awkwardly with the notion of cosmic movement). Lovelace's treatment yields moments of illumination, such as "The floore lay pav'd with broken hearts," which suddenly casts the metaphor in a new light, conveying the human dimension of pain as well as the image of a starry sky and an inlaid Renaissance pavement. The poem moves from graceful articulation of a conventional compliment to a quite remarkable sense of unstable perspective that is properly termed baroque.

Lovelace also makes striking use of paradoxical images in the "Song" set by Lawes, "To Amarantha, That she would dishevell her haire," which goes beyond precise or even admiring observation to a kind of baroque splendor, even to decadence. The argument that there is a special "Delight in Disorder," a particular beauty in the absence of rigid perfection, is seen in both Herrick and Jonson, but Lovelace goes further than either poet, beyond Herrick's sensuous enjoyment of "a wilde civility" to a sensual delight in which the lady's liberty becomes the poet's license:

Amarantha sweet and faire,
Ah brade no more that shining haire!
As my curious hand or eye,
Hovering round thee let it flye.

Lovelace's complicated syntax, which sometimes leads to confusion, here seems purposeful, for, in the act of urging Amarantha to allow her hair to fly freely, he also gives an image of his controlling gaze, which "As my curious hand or eye" is also "Hovering round" her. In each case what appears a simile for the woman's freedom in fact becomes an image of enclosure by a male observer or actor: "As my curious hand or eye"; "As it's calme Ravisher, the winde." The oxymoronic images of sexual violence and possession coupled with references to peace seen here are continued in the description of Amarantha's hair, "neatly tangled," "excellently ravelled." The association of the woman with the sun, and the assumption that her hair must be blond, both conventional, are then combined in the brilliantly imaginative conclusion:

Doe not then winde up that light
In Ribands, and o're-cloud in Night;
Like the Sun in's early ray,
But shake your head and scatter day.

As in "Lucasta's World," the sensuous realm created by Amarantha's hair becomes a kind of imaginary refuge for lovers, a place of sexual fulfillment:

Within this Grove,
The Bower, and the walkes of Love,
Weary lye we downe and rest,
And fanne each others panting breast.

There are even more explicit sexual suggestions in the stanza that follows:

Heere wee'l strippe and coole our fire
In Creame below, in milke-baths higher:
And when all Well's are drawne dry,
I'le drink a teare out of thine eye.

But the stanza is remarkable, not so much for the decadence of its imagery as for its resemblance to the kind of sensuous excess found in Crashaw's poem on Mary Magdalene called "The Weeper." "To Amarantha" lacks the tight structure of "To Althea, From Prison" or "To Lucasta, Going to the Warres"; it is instead a series of brilliant and rather unstable images, images that associate Lovelace not only with the Cavalier poetry of compliment but also with the powerfully shifting perspectives of the baroque.

That kind of taste for the sensuously excessive is evident in several other poems. In "A loose Saraband" (1649), Lovelace recounts how Cupid, "The little Tyrant Theefe," stole his heart, subjecting it to all kinds of torments, treating it as a ball, a top, a pin cushion, until it is washed with Lucasta's tears and healed with the balm of her kisses. In the rather decadent "La Bella Bona Roba" Lovelace extends a cool gaze toward the body of, as the title tells us, a harlot, whom he considers as if she were nothing but flesh, and whose chief interest consists in the varying substance and texture of skin and flesh:

Such whose white-sattin upper coat of skin,
Cut upon Velvet rich Incarnadin,
Ha's yet a Body (and of Flesh) within.

There are certainly poems in Lovelace's repertory that seem the result of a too-curious consideration: in "A Black patch on Lucasta's Face" Lovelace wittily, almost Metaphysically, reinterprets the patch which appears first as a blemish, resulting from the presumption of "a Court Fly," as the "large Monument" of "th'industrious Bee," which "Mistook her glorious Face for Paradise." This poem, like "Ellinda's Glove," is closer to the Metaphysical mode in creating a more unified approach to the subject, which it explores in great detail, finding significance in every aspect of it. In "A Black patch," the bee, which may be presumed to have stung Lucasta, enacts an elaborate fantasy: though a mere spark, he tries to emulate the sun (indeed the double suns of her eyes) and "Acts the *Romantick Phoenix* fate": "chaft" and "set on fire" by the beauty of her eyes, he "in these holy flames doth glad expire."

The plot is less complicated but the examination similarly thorough in "Ellinda's Glove," in which, in the absence of his mistress, the poet pays tribute instead to the glove, which he calls "Thou snowy Farme with thy five Tenements." His action looks like an image of self-abasement, but the poem concludes with the suggestion of a much more direct and possessive sexual relationship. The lover who would scarcely be allowed to kiss the lady, or even her hand, at last proceeds to imply something more substantial, as he addresses the glove:

Then give me leave to leave my Rent with thee;
　Five kisses, one unto a place:
　For though the *Lute's* too high for me;
Yet Servants knowing Minikin nor Base,
Are still allow'd to fiddle with the Case.

That shifting to the physical implications, to the ground bass of what has been until this point in the poem a Petrarchan compliment, wrought to the highest pitch, is evident also in "Her Muffe," in which after strained conceits exploring the significance of the lady's hands being incased in fur, Lovelace moves from the highly wrought and passionate yet clearly limited adulation of Petrarchism to the more explicitly sexual desires of the would-be lover:

But I, in my Invention tough,
　Rate not this outward bliss enough,
But still contemplate must the hidden Muffe.

Lovelace, then, is sometimes the Cavalier in the most idealized sense – the courtly lover, the embodiment of honor, in love and in war – but there are also poems in which he approximates the more dangerous character Samuel Richardson named after him in *Clarissa* (1747–1748), a man of superb and gallant manners, but importunate and finally

menacing. And there are poems in which the witty formulas of the "Cavalier spirit" are engaged in the service of sexual domination, as for example in "The faire Begger," which elaborates a popular baroque paradox, that of the beautiful and desirable woman who must beg ("Commanding Asker"). The speaker, after turning striking phrases on the subject of her inadequately clothed beauty, offers to satisfy her hunger if she satisfies his, moving from an initial emphasis on feeding his "Fancy" to a more usual suggestion:

Thou shalt be cloath'd above all prise,
　If thou wilt promise me imbrac't;
Wee'l ransack neither Chest or Shelfe,
I'll cover thee with mine owne selfe.

Lovelace also wrote poems in which he analyzes in detail the life or activities of small creatures – "The Ant," "The Grasse-hopper," "The Snayl," "The Falcon," "The Toad and Spyder" – but as one would expect of a poet of his era, these poems are neither "nature study" nor romantic celebrations of the natural world but are rather a moralizing, nearly an allegorizing of the subject and have their root in a rich tradition of such beast fables, from Aesop and the Greek Anthology to Jean La Fontaine and emblem literature, in which such creatures are seen as exemplifying the qualities of human life and experience.

In the best known of these poems, "The Grasse-hopper," Lovelace addresses his friend Charles Cotton the elder. Based on a lyric by the Greek poet Anacreon in which the grasshopper sings with delight in the summer, a virtual owner of all that it sees, Lovelace's poem depicts the grasshopper as the type of carefree pleasure, a creature lacking foresight and, unlike the provident and industrious ant, making no preparation for the winter, a point that leads to Lovelace's striking apostrophe:

Poore verdant foole! and now green Ice! thy Joys
　Large and as lasting as thy Peirch of Grasse,
Bid us lay in 'gainst Winter, Raine, and poize
　Their flouds, with an o'reflowing glasse.

The opening five stanzas emphasize first the fullness of the grasshopper's joys, "Drunke ev'ry night with a Delicious teare," and then their fragility and transiency, seen in relation to the cycle of the seasons:

But ah the Sickle! Golden Eares are Cropt;
　Ceres and *Bacchus* bid good night;
Sharpe frosty fingers all your Flowr's have topt,
　And what sithes spar'd, Winds shave off quite.

After the apostrophizing of Cotton in the sixth stanza – "Thou best of *Men* and *Friends*" – the poem goes on to create an image of a warmth and fellowship which is both indoors and internal, as well as more lasting than the external summer which is past:

> we will create
> A Genuine Summer in each others breast;
> And spite of this cold Time and frosen Fate
> Thaw us a warme seate to our rest.

As in "To Althea, From Prison," Lovelace movingly depicts the notion that internal peace and warmth, like internal freedom, are truer and more lasting than anything dependent on external forces. The poem concludes with a similar emphasis on the independence of spirit that constitutes true liberty:

> Thus richer than untempted Kings are we,
>   That asking nothing, nothing need:
> Though Lord of all what Seas imbrace; yet he
>   That wants himselfe, is poore indeed.

Like its Anacreontic source, this poem emphasizes the consolation to be found in wine and good fellowship. But it also treats the situation of Cavaliers left out in the cold by the ascendancy of the parliamentary forces and the execution of King Charles I. The image of the grasshopper, Don Cameron Allen has argued, far from being a type of folly or imprudence, is associated in classical sources with nobility, with warmth, abundance, and light, with music and the Muses. If, as he suggests, it is also a representation of the poet, of a king in exile, of men in political disfavor, the reader may see in the concluding stanzas images of the king who though deposed is about to be reinstated, an amalgam of King Charles and the King of Christmas, both banished by the parliamentary powers, set in the context of the Roman Saturnalia and preserved in an inner kingdom of hope and good fellowship:

> Dropping *December* shall come weeping in,
>   Bewayle th'usurping of his Raigne;
> But when in show'rs of old Greeke we beginne,
>   Shall crie, he hath his Crowne againe!

There are complementary political messages in several other small animal poems, poems that give poignant indications of the situation of a Cavalier in the Interregnum. "The Ant," in contrast to the grasshopper a type of prudence and foresight, has clear similarities to Puritans who work even on festival days: he "drive[s] on sacred Festivals, [his] Plow." Although the poet seems to praise the ant's virtues ("thou great good Husband"), he presents him as out of tune with the rhythm and harmony of the seasons, as in effect committing an act of sacrilege in persisting in labor on a holiday (a day made holy by Lucasta), like the Puritans who forbade indulgence in holiday sports. The ant in its incessant labor becomes an image of meaningless activity, of a miserable life, finally subject only to predators: "Thus we unthrifty thrive within Earths Tomb / For some more rav'nous and ambitious Jaw." In contrast to the short-lived but saturnalian grasshopper, the ant, though always working, never lives.

In two poems on the snail ("The Snayl" and "Another") Lovelace depicts the qualities of prudence and self-containment, of discretion and diplomacy needed in the Interregnum: "Sage Snayl, within thine own self curl'd; / Instruct me softly to make hast." Like the Royalist, or even like the future King Charles II in exile, the snail is a mysterious creature – cautious, self-protective, associated with gold, silver, and the rising sun. Lovelace concludes "Another" with words that make explicit the theme of human and political exile:

> But banisht, I admire his fate
> Since neither Ostracisme of State,
> Nor a perpetual exile,
> Can force this Virtue change his Soyl;
> For wheresoever he doth go,
> He wanders with his Country too.

In *Lucasta: Posthume Poems* Lovelace goes beyond the assertions of spiritual or psychic independence of the first volume to a rather darker mood, such as that expressed in "A Mock-Song," which ironically represents the topsy-turvy world of postmonarchical England:

> Now *Whitehalls* in the grave,
>   And our *Head* is our slave.
> The bright pearl in his close shell of Oyster;
> . . . .
> And the *Body* is all but a Belly:
>   Let the *Commons* go on,
>   The Town is our own,
>   We'l rule alone;
> . . . .
> For our Dragon hath vanquish'd the St. *George*.

Not only has the king been executed at his palace at Whitehall, but order, as Lovelace conceives it, is overthrown, and any virtues (such as "the bright pearl") must be concealed. In these later poems, Lovelace's earlier assertions of freedom within confinement are replaced by visions of confinement with more serious consequences, such as "A Fly caught in a Cobweb";

images of fatal attraction, as in "A Fly about a Glass of Burnt Claret"; or images of mortal conflict, as in "The Toad and Spyder" or "The Falcon," which dies impaled on the beak of a heron. That these poems have political implications is clear, but their message is necessarily muted. While this second volume includes fewer of the brilliant and graceful poems most often associated with Lovelace, it does include a group of by no means negligible meditations that reflects the somber conditions of his life and enlarges his poetic range. The greater predominance in this volume of rhymed couplets over more-varied stanza forms also links it with the general tendencies of later-seventeenth-century verse.

In his own time Lovelace, who was best known as the poet of "To Althea, From Prison," clearly had some reputation as writer of lyrics, as soldier and courtier, but he was less well known for his poetry than were his contemporaries Suckling and Carew. His work was largely forgotten from the later seventeenth century to the later eighteenth century, when several accounts of his life and selected poems were republished in anthologies. In 1817 and 1818 S. W. Singer published an edition of both volumes of *Lucasta,* but with all passages considered obscene or improper excised and with the addition of other poems no longer thought to be Lovelace's. The first full edition of Lovelace's poems since his death was published in 1864 by William Carew Hazlitt. Although Lovelace has benefited from the renewed interest in seventeenth-century poetry that arose early in the twentieth century, he has more often been treated as an example of a type than as a writer of great individual interest, and, other than Weidhorn's book published in 1970, there are no recent full-length studies.

Lovelace wrote a few nearly perfect lyrics which are the deservedly famous staple of anthologies. But both the range of his work and the number of fine poems are greater than might be judged by those few examples. Sometimes his verse is heavily indebted, most obviously to Donne but also to Jonson and others. Lovelace's verse is also often remarkably complex, not always, as in the case of Donne or Jonson, owing to its density and complexity of style but because he simply has not bothered to untangle his syntax and make his meaning clear. But, despite his unevenness, Lovelace also wrote remarkably well in a variety of genres: as courtly lover; cynical amorist; poet of occasion, compliment, and consolation; animal fabulist; and satirist. Some of his most interesting work tends rather to the baroque than the Metaphysical, to the cynical and skeptical rather than the romantic. Because nei-

ther the voice nor the stance of the Cavalier is much akin to our own time, Lovelace has received relatively little attention in recent years. Yet his place is assured, not as one of the greatest voices in a century so rich in epic, dramatic, and lyric poetry, but as a poet finely representative of the virtues and limitations of Cavalier and Caroline verse, one who wrote lines that, to borrow the words of his great contemporary John Milton, later generations would "not willingly let . . . die."

Bibliography:

David C. Judkins, "Recent Studies in the Cavalier Poets: Thomas Carew, Richard Lovelace, John Suckling, and Edmund Waller," *English Literary Renaissance,* 7 (Spring 1977): 243–258.

References:

Don Cameron Allen, "An Explication of Lovelace's 'The Grasse-hopper,' " *Modern Language Quarterly,* 18 (1957): 35–43; republished as "Richard Lovelace: 'The Grasse-hopper,' " in *Seventeenth-Century English Poetry,* edited by William R. Keast (New York: Oxford University Press, 1962), pp. 280–289;

Raymond A. Anselment, " 'Griefe Triumphant' and 'Victorious Sorrow': A Reading of Richard Lovelace's 'The Falcon,' " *Journal of English and Germanic Philology,* 70 (July 1971): 404–417;

Cyril H. Hartmann, *The Cavalier Spirit and Its Influence on the Life and Work of Richard Lovelace* (London: Routledge, 1925);

Bruce King, "Green Ice and a Breast of Proof," *College English,* 26 (March 1965): 511–515;

Leah S. Marcus, "Pastimes without a Court: Richard Lovelace and Andrew Marvell," in her *The Politics of Mirth* (Chicago: University of Chicago Press, 1986), pp. 213–263;

Earl Miner, *The Cavalier Mode from Jonson to Cotton* (Princeton: Princeton University Press, 1971);

Randolph L. Wadsworth, Jr., "On 'The Snayle' by Richard Lovelace," *Modern Language Review,* 65 (October 1970): 750–760;

Geoffrey Walton, "The Cavalier Poets," in *From Donne to Marvell,* volume 3 of *The New Pelican Guide to English Literature,* edited by Boris Ford (Harmondsworth, U.K.: Penguin, 1982), pp. 205–218;

C. V. Wedgwood, "Cavalier Poetry and Cavalier Politics," in her *Velvet Studies* (London: Cape, 1946), pp. 15–31;

Manfred Weidhorn, *Richard Lovelace* (New York: Twayne, 1970).

Andrew Marvell

(31 March 1621 – 16 August 1678)

R. V. Young

Franciscan University of Steubenville

BOOKS: *The First Anniversary of the Government Under His Highness the Lord Protector* (London: Printed by Thomas Newcomb & sold by Samuel Gellibrand, 1655);

The Rehearsal Transpros'd: Or, Animadversions Upon a late Book, Intituled, A Preface Shewing What Grounds there are of Fears and Jealousies of Popery (London: Printed by A. B. for the assigns of John Calvin & Theodore Beza, 1672);

The Rehearsal Transpros'd: The Second Part (London: Printed for Nathaniel Ponder, 1673);

Mr. Smirke; or The Divine in Mode (N.p., 1676);

An Account of the Growth of Popery, and Arbitrary Government in England (Amsterdam, 1677);

Remarks Upon a Late Disingenuous Discourse, Writ by one T. D. Under the pretense De Causa Dei (London: Printed & sold by Christopher Hussey, 1678);

Miscellaneous Poems. By Andrew Marvell, Esq. (London: Printed for Robert Boulter, 1681).

Editions: *The Complete Works in Prose and Verse of Andrew Marvell,* 4 volumes, edited by Alexander B. Grosart (London: Robson, 1872–1875);

The Poems and Letters of Andrew Marvell, 2 volumes, edited by H. M. Margoliouth (Oxford: Clarendon Press, 1927); third edition, revised by Pierre Legouis with E. E. Duncan-Jones (Oxford: Clarendon Press, 1971);

Andrew Marvell: The Complete Poetry, edited by George deF. Lord (London: Dent, 1968; New York: Random House, 1968);

The Rehearsal Transpros'd and The Rehearsal Transpros'd: The Second Part, edited by D. I. B. Smith (Oxford: Clarendon Press, 1971);

Andrew Marvell: The Complete Poems, edited by Elizabeth Story Donno (Harmondsworth, U.K.: Penguin, 1972);

Andrew Marvell, edited by Frank Kermode and Keith Walker, Oxford Authors Series (Oxford & New York: Oxford University Press, 1990).

Andrew Marvell, circa 1655–1660 (artist unknown; National Portrait Gallery, London)

OTHER: "Ad Regem Carolum Parodia" and Πρὸς Κάρυλον τὸν βασιλέα, in Συνωδια *Musarum Cantabrigiensium Concentus et Congratulatio ad Serenissimum Britanniarum Regem Carolum* (Cambridge, 1637);

"To his Noble Friend Mr. Richard Lovelace, upon his Poems," in Richard Lovelace, *Lucasta* (London: Printed by Tho. Harper & sold by Tho. Ewster, 1649);

"Upon the death of Lord Hastings," in *Lachrymæ Musarum; The Tears of the Muses. . . . Collected and set forth by R. B.* (London: Printed by Tho. Newcomb, 1649);

"Dignissimo suo Amico Doctori Wittie. De Translatione Vulgi Errorum D. Primrosii" and "To his worthy Friend Doctor Witty upon his Translation of the Popular Errors," in James Primrose, *Popular Errours. Or the Errours of the People in Physick,* translated by Robert Wittie (London: Printed by W. Nelson for Nicholas Bourne, 1651);

"A Dialogue between Thyrsis and Dorinda," in John Gamble, *Ayres and Dialogues, . . . The Second Book* (London: Printed by W. Godbid for Nathaniel Ekin, 1659);

"The Character of Holland," lines 1–100, in *Harleian Miscellany,* volume 613 (London: Printed by T. Mabb for Robert Horn, 1665);

"Clarindon's House-Warming," in *Directions To A Painter. For Describing our Naval Business: In Imitation of Mr. Waller. Being The Last Works of Sir John Denham. Whereunto is annexed Clarindons House-Warming. By an Unknown Author* (London, 1667);

"On the Victory Obtained by Blake over the Spaniards in the Bay of Santacruze, in the Island of Teneriff. 1657," in *A New Collection of Poems and Songs. Written by several Persons* (London: Printed by J. C. for William Crook, 1674);

"On Mr. Milton's *Paradise lost,*" in John Milton, *Paradise Lost,* second edition (London: Printed by S. Simmons, 1674).

In an era that makes a better claim than most upon the familiar term *transitional,* Andrew Marvell is surely the single most compelling embodiment of the change that came over English society and letters in the course of the seventeenth century. Author of a varied array of exquisite lyrics that blend Cavalier grace with Metaphysical wit and complexity, Marvell turned, first, into a panegyrist for the Lord Protector and his regime and then into an increasingly bitter satirist and polemicist, attacking the royal court and the established church in both prose and verse. It is as if the most delicate and elusive of butterflies somehow metamorphosed into a caterpillar.

To be sure, the judgment of Marvell's contemporaries and the next few generations would not have been such. The style of the lyrics that have been so prized in the twentieth century was already out of fashion by the time of his death, but he was a pioneer in the kind of political verse satire that

would be perfected by his younger contemporary John Dryden and in the next generation by Alexander Pope (both writing for the other side) – even as his satirical prose anticipated the achievement of Jonathan Swift in that vein. Marvell's satires won him a reputation in his own day and preserved his memory beyond the eighteenth century as a patriotic political writer – a clever and courageous enemy of court corruption and a defender of religious and political liberty and the rights of Parliament. It was only in the nineteenth century that his lyrical poems began to attract serious attention, and it was not until T. S. Eliot's classic essay (first published in the *Times Literary Supplement,* 31 March 1921), marking the tercentenary of Marvell's birth, that Marvell attained recognition as one of the major lyric poets of his age.

In recent years postmodernist theory has once again focused on Marvell as a political writer, but with as much attention to the politics of the lyric poems as to the overtly partisan satires. Doubtless what sustains critical interest in Marvell and accommodates the enormous quantity of interpretive commentary attracted by his work is the extraordinary range and ambiguity of theme and tone among a comparatively small number of poems. Equally uncertain are the nature and timing of his personal involvement and his commitments in the great national events that occurred during his lifetime. Nevertheless, despite the equivocal status of many of the details of Marvell's life and career, the overall direction is clear enough: he is a fitting symbol for England's transformation in the seventeenth century from what was still largely a medieval, Christian culture into a modern, secular society. In his subtle, ironic, and sometimes mysterious lyrics, apparently written just at the middle of the century, we have one of our finest records of an acute, sensitive mind confronting the myriad implications of that transformation.

The son of the Reverend Andrew Marvell and Anne Pease Marvell, Andrew Marvell spent his boyhood in the Yorkshire town of Hull, where his father, a clergyman of Calvinist inclination, was appointed lecturer at Holy Trinity Church and master of the Charterhouse when the poet was three years old. His father was, Marvell wrote years later in *The Rehearsal Transpros'd: The Second Part* (1673), "a Conformist to the established Rites of the Church of *England,* though I confess none of the most overrunning or eager in them." Not surprisingly then, at the age of twelve in 1633, Marvell was sent up to Trinity College, Cambridge. This was the very year that William Laud became archbishop of Canter-

Miniature of Marvell, possibly by Samuel Cooper (Harry Ransom Humanities Research Center, University of Texas at Austin)

Marvell's earliest surviving verses lead to no conclusions about his religion and politics as a student. In 1637 two pieces of his, one in Latin and one in Greek, were published in a collection of verses by Cambridge poets in honor of the birth of a fifth child to Charles I. Other contributors were as diverse as Richard Crashaw, who would later be a Catholic priest, and Edward King, whose death by drowning that same year was the occasion for John Milton's *Lycidas* (1638). Marvell's Latin poem, "Ad Regem Carolum Parodia," is a "parody" in the sense that it is a close imitation – in meter, structure, and language – of Horace, *Odes* I.2. While the Roman poet hails Caesar Augustus as a savior of the state in the wake of violent weather and the flooding of the Tiber, Marvell celebrates the fertility of the reigning sovereign and his queen on the heels of the plague that struck Cambridge at the end of 1636. Marvell's contribution in Greek asserts that the birth of the king's fifth child had redeemed the number five, of ill omen since attempts had been made on the life of James I on 5 August 1600 and 5 November 1605. It would be easy enough to condemn the poem's frigid ingenuity but for a reluctance to be harsh with the work of a sixteen-year-old capable of writing Latin and Greek verse.

If little can be made of these student exercises, the poems written in the 1640s that imply a close association between Marvell and certain Royalists furnish intriguing (if meager) grounds for speculation. The mystery is further complicated by a lack of evidence regarding Marvell's whereabouts and activities during most of the decade. In 1639 he took his B.A. degree and stayed on at the university, evidently to pursue the M.A. In 1641, however, his father drowned in "the Tide of *Humber*" – the estuary at Hull made famous by "To his Coy Mistress." Shortly afterward Marvell left Cambridge, and there is plausible speculation that he might have worked for a time in the shipping business of his well-to-do brother-in-law, Edmund Popple. It is known that sometime during the 1640s Marvell undertook an extended tour of the Continent. In a letter of 21 February 1653 recommending Marvell for a place in his own department in Oliver Cromwell's government, Milton credits Marvell with four years' travel in Holland, France, Italy, and Spain, where he acquired the languages of all four countries. Regrettably Milton casts no light upon the motives and circumstances of this journey. Modern scholarship has generally assumed that Marvell served as the companion/tutor of a wealthy and perhaps noble youth, but all the candidates brought forward for this role have been eliminated by one

bury. If not such a stronghold of Puritanism as Emmanuel College (alma mater of Marvell's father), Trinity was characterized by a moderation that contrasted sharply with a college such as Peterhouse (Richard Crashaw's college), which ardently embraced the Arminianism and ritualism of the Laudian program. Indeed, the liberal, rationalistic tenor of Marvell's religious utterances in later life may owe something to the influence of Benjamin Whichcote, who in 1636 as lecturer at Trinity Church began to lay the foundation for the latitudinarian strain that was so important in the Church of England after the Restoration. Such tenuous evidence as exists, however, does not suggest Puritan enthusiasm on the part of the youthful poet. The story that Marvell, converted by Jesuits, ran away from Cambridge and was persuaded to return by his father, who found him in a London bookshop, has never been properly verified (although embarrassment over such a youthful indiscretion might go far to explain the virulent anti-Catholicism of his later years). More provocative is the lack of any evidence that he participated in the English Civil War, which broke out a few months after his twenty-first birthday, and the Royalist tone of his poems before 1650.

consideration or another. Some have suggested that Marvell was merely avoiding the war, others that he was some kind of government agent. Although the explanation that he was a tutor seems most plausible, there is no certainty about what he was doing.

Whatever the purpose of his travel, its lasting effects turn up at various points in Marvell's writings. The burlesque "Character of Holland" (1665), for example, draws on reminiscences of the dikes of the Netherlands: "How did they rivet, with Gigantick Piles, / Thorough the Center their new-catched Miles." "Upon Appleton House" describes a drained meadow by evoking a Spanish arena "Ere the Bulls enter at Madril," and a letter "To a Friend in Persia" recalls fencing lessons in Spain (9 August 1671). The circumstantial detail of "Fleckno, an English Priest at Rome," a satire very much in the manner of John Donne's efforts in that genre, suggests that Marvell actually met the victim of his poem in Rome when Richard Flecknoe was there in 1645–1647. Flecknoe is, of course, the man immortalized as Thomas Shadwell's predecessor as king of dullness in John Dryden's *Mac Flecknoe* (1682). Marvell mercilessly ridicules both the poverty of Flecknoe's wit and his literal poverty and consequent leanness. The jokes at the expense of Catholic doctrine seem almost incidental to the abuse of Flecknoe's undernourished penury:

> Nothing now Dinner stay'd
> But till he had himself a Body made.
> I mean till he were drest: for else so thin
> He stands, as if he only fed had been
> With consecrated Wafers: and the *Host*
> Hath sure more flesh and blood than he can boast.

Doubtless these lines play irreverently with the Thomist teaching that the Body and Blood of Christ are both totally contained under each of the eucharistic species, as well as with accounts of the life of Saint Catherine of Siena, who is said to have subsisted for several years with no other nourishment than daily Communion. But the real object of this quasi-Scholastic wit (again, much in the style of Donne) is the absurdity of Flecknoe, and it lacks the virulent loathing that characterizes Marvell's attack on the doctrine of Transubstantiation years later in *An Account of the Growth of Popery* (1677). His mockery of the narrowness of Flecknoe's room makes a similar joke with the doctrine of the Trinity, which was accepted by virtually all Protestants at the time:

> there can no Body pass
> Except by penetration hither, where

> Two make a crowd, nor can three Person here
> Consist but in one substance.

While the jocular anti-Catholicism of "Fleckno" hardly implies militant Puritanism, by placing Marvell in Rome between 1645 and 1647, it raises the possibility that he met Lord Francis Villiers, who was also in Rome in 1645 and 1646. This would strengthen the case for Marvell's authorship of "An Elegy upon the Death of my Lord Francis Villiers" and bring to three the number of Royalist poems that he wrote. Two poems published in 1649, "To his Noble Friend Mr. Richard Lovelace, upon his Poems" and "Upon the death of Lord Hastings," are both indisputably by Marvell and indisputably Royalist in sentiment. It is not simply that both poems celebrate known adherents of the king's failed cause, but that they do so with pungent references to the triumphant side in the Civil War. The death of Henry, Lord Hastings, in 1649 at the age of nineteen may have resulted immediately from smallpox, but the ultimate source of his fate is that "the *Democratick* Stars did rise, / And all that Worth from hence did *Ostracize*." The poem to Lovelace is one of the commendatory pieces in the first edition of *Lucasta* (1649). Marvell observes how "Our Civill Wars have lost the Civicke crowne" and refers with explicit scorn to the difficulty encountered in acquiring a printing license for the volume:

> The barbed Censurers begin to looke
> Like the grim consistory on thy Booke;
> And on each line cast a reforming eye,
> Severer then the yong Presbytery.

In subsequent lines Marvell refers to Lovelace's legal difficulties with Parliament, especially his imprisonment for presenting the Kentish petition requesting control of the militia and the use of the Book of Common Prayer.

"An Elegy upon the Death of my Lord Francis Villiers" was first published in the H. M. Margoliouth edition (1927) from an apparently unique pamphlet left to the Worcester College Library by George Clarke (1660–1736) with an ascription of the poem to Marvell in Clarke's hand. Villiers (1629–1648), posthumous son of the assassinated royal favorite George Villiers, first Duke of Buckingham, died in a skirmish against Parliamentary forces. Here the poet celebrates not just a Royalist, but a Royalist killed in military action against the revolutionary government. "Fame" had "Much rather" told "How heavy *Cromwell* gnasht the earth and fell. / Or how slow Death farre from the sight of day / The long-deceived *Fairfax* bore away." Villiers is credited with erecting "A whole Pyramid / Of Vulgar bodies," and the poet recommends that those who lament him turn to military rather than literary "Obsequies":

> And we hereafter to his honour will
> Not write so many, but so many kill.
> Till the whole Army by just vengeance come
> To be at once his Trophee and his Tombe.

All the evidence suggests that Clarke was a reliable witness; there is nothing in the style of the poem that rules out Marvell as the author; and, though more extreme politically, it is certainly compatible in sentiment and tone with the Hastings elegy and the commendatory poem for *Lucasta,* which Marvell is known to have written about the same time. If the Villiers elegy is in fact Marvell's, then it casts a rather eerie light on the man who would the following year write "An Horatian Ode upon Cromwel's Return from Ireland" and in 1651 become tutor to the daughter of Thomas, third Baron Fairfax.

The "Horatian Ode" is undoubtedly one of the most provocatively equivocal poems in English literature. It has been read both as a straightforward encomium of Cromwell and as an ironic deprecation. There is plentiful evidence for both extremes as well as for intermediate positions. Interpretations are only more confused by the fact that the poem can be narrowly dated. Its occasion is the return of Oliver Cromwell from one of the more brutally successful of the many British efforts to "pacify" the Irish, at the end of May 1650. It anticipates his invasion of Scotland, which occurred on 22 July 1650. These dates furnish a reasonable terminus a quo and terminus ad quem. During the interval Thomas, Lord Fairfax, already unhappy about the execution of King Charles, resigned his position as commander in chief of the Parliamentary army because he disapproved of striking the first blow against the Scots. His lieutenant general, Cromwell, was appointed in his place and proceeded with the attack. Little is known about Marvell's footing with the Royalists whom he honored with poems in 1649 or with his Puritan employers, Fairfax beginning in 1651 and later Cromwell himself; hence it is futile to infer the attitude of the 1650 ode from the sketchy biographical facts.

Whatever was in Marvell's mind at the time, the "Horatian Ode" succeeds in expressing with surpassing finesse and subtlety a studied ambivalence of feeling sharply bridled by the decisive grasping of a particular point of view. Written near the exact midpoint of the century and very nearly in the middle of the poet's fifty-seven years, the ode on Cromwell establishes its portentous subject as a paradigmatic figure of the great transformation of English culture then unfolding – as both a cause and effect of the final dissolution of the feudal order of medieval Christendom. The *argument* of the ode, which shares something of the driving energy of the "forward Youth" and of "restless *Cromwel*" himself, is almost completely devoted to the exaltation of the victorious general as a man in whom a relentless individual will to power and an inevitable historical necessity have converged to refashion the world. Cromwell is described both as conscious, deliberating agent and as an ineluctable force of nature:

> So restless *Cromwel* could not cease
> In the inglorious Arts of Peace,
> > But through adventrous War
> > Urged his active Star.
> And, like the three-fork'd Lightning, first
> Breaking the Clouds where it was nurst,
> > Did through his own Side
> > His fiery way divide.

He is exonerated for the violence and destruction of his campaigns because he is the instrument of divine wrath, but he is also given credit for character, courage, and craftiness:

> 'Tis Madness to resist or blame
> The force of angry Heavens flame:
> > And, if we would speak true,
> > Much to the Man is due.

Marvell accepts the contemporary rumor that Cromwell deliberately engineered Charles's flight from Hampton Court, by "twining subtile fears with hope," so that after the king's recapture his loss of crown and head was more likely; but the device is adduced not to exemplify Cromwell's malice, but his "wiser Art." Cromwell is thus the rehabilitation of Niccolò Machiavelli. Even the closing stanzas, while asserting the continued necessity of military force to maintain the regime, in no way condemn it. Writing in the year before Thomas Hobbes published *Leviathan* (1651), Marvell has come independently to the same conclusion, that power is essentially its own justification:

> But thou the Wars and Fortunes Son
> March indefatigably on;
> > And for the last effect
> > Still keep thy Sword erect:
> Besides the force it has to fright
> The Spirits of the shady Night,
> > The same *Arts* that did *gain*
> > A *Pow'r* must it *maintain*.

Undoubtedly Marvell means that Cromwell is to keep his "Sword erect" by keeping the blade up, ready to strike; but the assertion that it would thus "fright / The Spirits of the shady Night," notwithstanding precedents in Homer's *Odyssey* and Virgil's *Aeneid,* still calls to mind the opposite procedure: holding up the hilt as a representation of the cross. By implicitly rejecting the cross as an instrument of political power, Marvell obliquely indicates that one effect of the vast cultural revolution set in motion by the Civil War was the banishing of religion from political life, just one aspect of the general secularization of Western civilization already under way at the time.

Of course what distinguishes the "Horatian Ode" is the emotional shudder that pervades it, acknowledging the wrenching destructiveness of massive social change. Marvell concedes that Charles I, in some sense, has *right* on his side, but he will not concede that the right, or justice, is an inviolable absolute to which a man must remain unshakably committed. A terrible exhilaration marks the stanza in which the "ruine" of "the great Work of Time" is regretted but unblinkingly accepted:

> Though Justice against Fate complain,
> And plead the antient Rights in vain:
> But those do hold or break
> As Men are strong or weak.

There is a finely calculated irony in the way "the *Royal Actor*" on the "*Tragick Scaffold*" occupies the very center of an ode dedicated to Cromwell's victories and furnishes the poem's most memorable lines:

> *He* nothing common did or mean
> Upon that memorable Scene:
> But with his keener Eye
> The Axes edge did try:
> Nor call'd the *Gods* with vulgar spight
> To vindicate his helpless Right,
> But bow'd his comely Head,
> Down as upon a Bed.

These lines are moving, and they seem to reflect Marvell's genuine admiration for the king as well as a vivid realization that some ineffable cultural value was lost irrecoverably with Charles's head, but nostalgia for what was passing away is subsumed in the excited awareness of the advent of what was new: "This was that memorable Hour / Which first assur'd the forced Pow'r." The word *forced* is not pejorative here; force is, finally, the hero of the poem even more than the individual Cromwell.

The brilliant ambivalence of feeling is enhanced by Marvell's deft deployment of classical precedents. The obvious Horatian model is *Odes* I.37, a celebration of Augustus's naval victory at Actium that closes with a tribute to Cleopatra's courage in committing suicide rather than facing the humiliation of a Roman triumph. In addition, Marvell has drawn upon the language and imagery of Lucan's *Pharsalia,* both in the original and in Thomas May's English translation. That Marvell's language describing Cromwell is mainly borrowed from Lucan's descriptions of Caesar (whom Lucan detested) is not an encoded condemnation of the English general; it is an aspect of Marvell's strategy for praising Cromwell not merely in spite of, but because of, qualities that are conventionally condemned. The point of the "Horatian Ode" is that Cromwell has ushered in a new era that renders "the antient Rights" obsolete.

Given the radical character of the "Horatian Ode," it is actually easier to account for the apparent anomaly of Marvell's poem "Tom May's Death." May, who died on 13 November 1650 and whose translation of Lucan seems to have influenced some passages of the "Horatian Ode," had made his reputation as a poet at the court of Charles I and apparently hoped to succeed Ben Jonson as poet laureate upon Jonson's death in 1637. According to his enemies – including the author of "Tom May's Death" – it was chagrin at having been passed over in favor of William Davenant that led May to switch sides and became a propagandist for Parliament. In the major action of the poem the shade of Ben Jonson, in "supream command" of the Elysian Fields of poets, expels May from their number for "Apostatizing from our Arts and us, / To turn the Chronicler of *Spartacus*." Critics have wondered how the same man who celebrated Cromwell in the "Horatian Ode" could only a few months later scornfully equate the Parliamentary rebellion against the king with the revolt of Roman slaves under Spartacus, or depict the two best-known regicides of the classical world thus: "But how a double headed Vulture Eats, / *Brutus* and *Cassius* the Peoples cheats." What Marvell may well be doing in this poem is simply distancing himself from May, who seems to have been a loutish individual (according to contemporary accounts he died in a drunken stupor) and whose political choices seemed to have been determined by sheer expediency as well as personal pique. His death perhaps afforded Marvell an opportunity to deal with residual Royalist sentiment in conflict with his judgment and even to assure himself that his own changing allegiances were not motivated by venality. Given the ambiguity of Marvell's politics in 1650, it is not reasonable to exclude a poem from the canon because it seems politically incompatible with another poem. It is also difficult to deny Marvell lines such as these:

When the Sword glitters ore the Judges head,
And fear has Coward Churchmen silenced,
Then is the Poets time, 'tis then he drawes,
And single fights forsaken Vertues cause.
He, when the wheel of Empire, whirleth back,
And though the World's disjointed Axel crack,
Sings still of ancient Rights and better Times,
Seeks wretched good, arraigns successful Crimes.

It is by no means displeasing to think that Marvell had second thoughts about his dismissal of the "antient Rights" in the "Horatian Ode."

Perhaps before the end of 1650, but certainly by 1651, Marvell was employed as tutor in languages to the twelve-year-old daughter of Thomas, Lord Fairfax, who had returned to his Yorkshire estates after resigning his military command. It is not known who recommended Marvell for the post, but doubtless his own Yorkshire background was a factor. Marvell remained with Fairfax until early 1653 when he sought employment in the Cromwell government with John Milton's recommendation. Instead Cromwell procured Marvell a position as tutor to William Dutton, who was being considered as a husband for Cromwell's youngest daughter, Frances. Marvell served as Dutton's tutor until 1657, living in the house of John Oxenbridge, a Puritan divine who had spent time in Bermuda to escape Laud's reign over the Church of England. In 1657 Marvell did receive a government post with Milton as his supervisor. The period of the poet's employment as a tutor is generally thought to be the time when his greatest lyrics and topographical poems — the works on which his twentieth-century reputation is founded — were written.

Undoubtedly having their source in Marvell's sojourn with Fairfax are three poems on the general's properties at Bilbrough and Nun Appleton: "Epigramma in Duos montes Amosclivum Et Bilboreum. Farfacio," "Upon the Hill and Grove at Bill-borow To the Lord Fairfax," and "Upon Appleton House, to my Lord Fairfax." The first two of these poems, the Latin epigram and its English companion piece, allegorize topographical features in and around the Fairfax manor at Bilbrough to praise the character of Marvell's patron. The Latin poem attributes to Fairfax both the forbidding ruggedness of Almscliff and the gentleness of the hill at Bilbrough: "Asper in adversos, facilis cedentibus idem" (the same man is harsh to enemies, easy on those who yield); while the English poem elaborates upon the agreeable qualities of Bilbrough as an emblem of the man who modestly withdrew from "his own Brightness" as a military leader to a life of rural retirement. "Upon Appleton House" takes up the theme and develops it through nearly eight hundred lines into a subtle and complex meditation on the moral implications of choosing a life of private introspection over action, of withdrawal from the world rather than involvement in its affairs. Beginning as a country-house poem in the mode of Jonson's "To Penshurst," Marvell's poem expands into a leisurely survey of the entire landscape that moves with an ease that is the antithesis of the urgency of the "Horation Ode."

"Upon Appleton House" covers an array of topics with an extraordinary range of wit and tone, but its central preoccupation is the identical theme of the ode on Cromwell, only in reverse: while that poem gives an exhilarating account of the career of Cromwell's "active Star," moderated by a keen sense of the violence of "the three-fork'd Lightning," the poem on Fairfax expresses a deep affection as well as respect for its hero, tempered by just a hint that Fairfax's scruples and modesty may have been excessive and detrimental to his country. Marvell comments on the incongruity between the floral ordinance of Nun Appleton's fort-shaped flower beds and the actual warfare that had laid England waste; then he suggests that, had Fairfax's conscience been less tender, it might have been within his power to set England right:

And yet their walks one on the Sod
Who, had it pleased him and *God*,
Might once have made our Gardens spring
Fresh as his own and flourishing.
But he preferr'd to the *Cinque Ports*
These five imaginary Forts:
And, in those half-dry Trenches, spann'd
Pow'r which the Ocean might command.

The fine discrimination of these lines defies comment: Is there an intimation, however slight, that preference for "imaginary Forts" is not worthy of a man of Fairfax's gifts during a national crisis? But even to suggest this much is to suggest too much: it is never put in doubt that Fairfax is listening to his conscience; that is, to God. While there is regret that the best man is impeded by his very goodness from assuming the position for which he is fitted, there is no recrimination; the sorrow is, finally, a result of the inherent condition of fallen mankind:

Oh Thou, that dear and happy Isle
The Garden of the World ere while,
Thou *Paradise* of four Seas,
Which *Heaven* planted us to please,
But, to exclude the World, did guard
With watry if not flaming Sword;
What luckless Apple did we tast,
To make us Mortal, and The Wast?

If Fairfax himself has succeeded in withdrawing from the world – now become "a rude heap together hurled" – into the "lesser *World*" of Nun Appleton, "*Heaven's Center, Nature's Lap. / And Paradice's only Map,*" his daughter must go out into that world in marriage to carry on "beyond her *Sex* the *line*." Always the individual hope of happy retirement is threatened by the historical necessity of society:

Whence, for some universal good,
The *Priest* shall cut the sacred Bud;
While her *glad Parents* most rejoice,
And make their *Destiny* their *Choice.*

We can only wonder how Marvell responded to the marriage of his former pupil when it came in 1657, and Maria Fairfax was joined with George Villiers, second Duke of Buckingham, elder brother of Lord Francis Villiers, and one of the most notorious rakes of the notorious Restoration era. Such a "destiny" may have shaken even the poet's cool detachment.

Many of Marvell's best-known lyrics are associated with his tenure as Maria Fairfax's tutor because they deploy language and themes that appear in "Upon Appleton House." The Mower poems, for example, provide a particular focus on the undifferentiated figures of the mowing section of "Upon Appleton House" (lines 385–440). Four in number, the Mower poems are a variant of the pastoral mode, substituting a mower for the familiar figure of the shepherd (as Jacopo Sannazaro's *Piscatorial Eclogues* [1526] substitutes fishermen). "The Mower against Gardens" is the complaint of a mower against the very idea of the formal enclosed garden planted with exotic hybrids – an increasingly fashionable feature of English country estates in the seventeenth century, condemned by the mower as a perverted and "luxurious" tampering with nature at her "most plain and pure." The theme is unusual, if not unprecedented, with the most familiar treatment coming in Perdita's argument with Polixenes in William Shakespeare's *The Winter's Tale* (IV.4). As is so often the case in Marvell's poems, the point is stated in its most extreme form by his censorious mower: it is not just excess that offends him, the "Onion root

[tulip bulb] they then so high did hold, / That one was for a Meadow sold"; but the very notion of the luxuriant, ornamental garden as an improvement over nature: "'Tis all enforc'd; the Fountain and the Grot; / While the sweet Fields do lye forgot." The poem is thus pervaded by hints of timely references to the revolutionary situation of England at mid-century: the mower's strictures against formal gardens recall the Puritan's suspicion of religious images and courtly extravagance, the laboring man's bitter disdain for the self-indulgent idleness of his social "betters," and the whole vexed issue of land enclosures. Yet these are overtones not arguments, and the single-minded moralizing of the mower is certainly not in the poet's own style, although a part of his nature would doubtless sympathize with the mower's "root-and-branch" viewpoint.

The other three Mower poems, "Damon the Mower," "The Mower to the Glo-Worms," and "The Mower's Song," all express Damon's frustration at his rejection by a certain "fair Shepheardess," Juliana. It cannot be determined whether Damon is to be identified with the speaker of "The Mower against Gardens," but the voice in all the Mower poems displays the belligerent intensity of wounded self-righteousness. "Damon the Mower" is in a line of pastoral figures beginning with the Polyphemus of Theocritus (*Idylls* 11) and Ovid (*Metamorphoses* 13) and the Corydon of Virgil (*Eclogues* 2), all of whom enumerate their clownishly rustic wealth and personal attributes with incredulous frustration at the beloved's refusal to respond favorably to their advances. In keeping with the classical precedents, Marvell tempers the lugubriousness of his unhappy mower by endowing him with a certain threatening aura. In "Damon the Mower" the frantic activity of the lovesick laborer results in "Depopulating all the Ground" as he "does cut / Each stroke between the Earth and Root." When he inadvertently cuts his own ankle, he is solemnly mocked with the line "By his own Sythe, the Mower mown"; but Damon dismisses this wound as inconsequential compared to that given by "*Julianas* Eyes," and the poem closes with a sinister reminder of the symbolism of the Mower: "'Tis death alone that this must do: / For Death thou art a Mower too." Similarly, in "The Mower's Song" his obsessive fixation on desire disdained is expressed in a grim refrain, the only one in Marvell's verse, closing out all five stanzas: "For *Juliana* comes, and She / What I do to the Grass, does to my Thoughts and Me." Even "The Mower to the Glo-Worms" leaves its disconsolate speaker benighted despite the friendly efforts of the

66.

May it please your Excellence,

It might perhaps seem fit for me to seek out words to giue your Excellence thanks for my selfe. But indeed the onely Ciuility which it is proper for me to practise with so eminent a Person is to obey you, and to performe honestly the worke that you haue set me about. Therefore I shall use the time that your Lordship is pleas'd to allow me for writing, onely to that purpose for which you haue giuen me it. That is to render you some account of Mr Dutton. I haue taken care to examine him seuerall times in the presence of Mr Oxenbridge, as those who weigh and tell ouer mony before some wytnesse ere they take charge of it. For I thought that there might possibly be some lightnesse in the Coyn, or errour in the telling, which hereafter I should be bound to make good. Therefore Mr Oxenbridge is the best to make your Excellence an impartiall relation thereof. I shall onely say that I shall striue according to my best understanding (that is according to those Rules your Lordship hath giuen me) to increase whatsoeuer Talent he may haue already. Truly, he is of a gentle and waxen disposition; and, God be praisd, I can not say that he hath brought with him any euill Impression; and I shall hope to set nothing upon his Spirit but what may be of a good Sculpture. He hath in him two things which make Yowth most easy to be managed, Modesty which is the bridle to Vice, and Emulation which is the Spurr to Virtue. And the Care which your Excellence is pleas'd to take of him is no small incouragement and shall be so represented to him. But aboue all I shall labour to make him sensible of his Duty to God. For then we begin to serue faithfully, when we consider that he is our Master. And in this both he and I ow infinitely to your Lordship, for hauing placed us in so godly a family as that of Mr Oxenbridge whose Doctrine and Example are like a Book and a Mapp, not onely instructing the Eare but demonstrating to the Ey which way we ought to trauell. And Mrs Oxenbridge.

Letter to Oliver Cromwell written soon after Marvell began tutoring William Dutton (Society of Antiquaries) hath a great tendernesse over him also in all other things. She has looked so well to him that he hath already much mended his complexion: And how she is busy in ordring his Chamber, that he may delight to be in it as often as his Studyes require. For the rest, most of this time hitherto hath been spent in acquainting our selves with him: and truly he is very chearfull and I hope thinks us to be good company. I shall upon occasion henceforward informe your Excellence of any particularityes in our litle affairs. For so I esteem it to bee my Duty. I have no more at present but to give thanks to God for your Lordship, and to beg grace of him, that I may approve my selfe

Windsor July 28
1653

Mr Dutton presents his most humble service to your Excellence.

Your Excellencyes most humble and faithfull Servant

Andrew Marvell

fireflies, "For She my Mind hath so displac'd / That I shall never find my home." There are undoubtedly political resonances in the vociferous mower – sprung out of the soil, brandishing his scythe, and denouncing wealthy gardeners and shepherds and scornful shepherdesses – but his menacing air is blended with a larger measure of absurd pathos. The Mower poems are thus characteristic of Marvell's aloof irony.

"The Garden" shares in this equivocal detachment, as the endless debates about its sources (in classical antiquity, the church fathers, the Middle Ages, hermeticism, and so on), its relation to contemporary poetry, and its own ultimate significance show. The poem has been regarded as an account of mystical ecstasy by some commentators, of Horatian Epicureanism by others; some find in it an antilibertine version of the poetry of rural retirement, while others interpret it in terms of "the politics of landscape." What seems indisputable is its congruence with the vision of reality proposed by the "Horatian Ode" and "Upon Appleton House": a virtually unbridgeable chasm is seen between contented withdrawal into contemplation and the actual life of man in the world. Ostensibly a celebration of the contemplative garden, hinting equally at the Garden of Eden and the enclosed garden of the Song of Songs, and the garden of the mind of classical philosophy, "The Garden" subverts the solemnity of the meditative theme by engulfing it in irony. The dismissal of the active life, of ambition or love, in the first four stanzas is stated in terms of absurd hyperbole: the strenuous efforts of politicians, soldiers, and even poets are disparaged because they result, at best, in only the "short and narrow verged Shade" of a single wreath, "While all Flow'rs and all Trees do close / To weave the Garlands of repose." Similarly, the "lovely green" of "am'rous" plants is preferred to the conventional red and white of the Petrarchan mistress's complexion; and Apollo and Pan are supposed to have pursued Daphne and Syrinx not for the sake of their feminine charms, but for the laurel and reed into which the nymphs were transformed. The wit of these first four stanzas is highlighted by the labored elaboration of the same conceits in the Latin version of the poem, "Hortus," which lacks any lines corresponding to stanzas 5–8 of "The Garden." Sharply contrasted to, but never wholly free of, this foolery is the stunning depiction of "The Mind" and its transcendent activity, "Annihilating all that's made / To a green Thought in a green Shade." But this introspective solitude can be known only as a longed-for impossibility by the self-conscious intelligence that defines itself in relation to the Other:

> Such was that happy Garden-state,
> While Man there walk'd without a Mate:
> After a Place so pure, and sweet,
> What other Help could yet be meet!
> But 'twas beyond a Mortal's share
> To wander solitary there:
> Two Paradises 'twere in one
> To live in Paradise alone.

The speaker's petulant misogyny expresses at a deeper level a loathing for the social nature of the human condition, which creates the longing for total withdrawal into contemplative solitude and also renders it impossible.

"The Nymph complaining for the death of her Faun" posits the dichotomy in even starker terms: retirement into the innocence of nature, epitomized by a sublimely exquisite beast, is disrupted by warfare, that most violent manifestation of social conflict. Whether the "wanton Troopers riding by," who have slain the fawn belong to Prince Rupert's Royalist forces, to the Scotch covenanting army of 1640, or to Cromwell's New Model Army is finally irrelevant to their significance in the poem. They personify the turbulent strife of the world outside the garden of contemplative withdrawal that, on this occasion, they have invaded. The casual indifference with which they kill the fawn aligns them with the Cromwell of the "Horatian Ode" who, as "The force of angry Heavens flame," wreaks indiscriminate havoc. Similarly, the Nymph and the fawn are attractive but ineffectual figures, much like the King Charles of the "Ode." The Nymph, in contrast to Isabel Thwaites and Maria Fairfax of "Upon Appleton House," attempts to maintain a life of perpetual virginity and solitude, already disillusioned by "Unconstant *Sylvio*" before the advent of the "Ungentle men" who kill the fawn. At the center of the poem is the dying fawn itself. Swathed in a web of allusions to the Song of Songs and Virgil, as well as to other scriptural and classical passages, the fawn has been regarded as a symbol for Christ or the Church of England, or a *surrogatus amoris* for the deceived Nymph. The ambiguity of the fawn's significance does not, however, obscure the meaning of the poem; it *is* the meaning of the poem. In the seventy years since, it has not been better expressed than in T. S. Eliot's tercentenary essay: "Marvell takes a slight affair, the feeling of a girl for her pet, and gives it a connection with that inexhaustible and terrible nebula of emotion which surrounds all our exact and practical passions and mingles with them." Of course, in surrounding the "slight affair" of personal emotion with a panoply of traditional references with mystical overtones, Marvell anticipated the enhanced role of subjective experience in the modern world and manifested a poignant awareness of the alienation of the private individual from the public objective realm.

Alienation is likewise the keynote of Marvell's love poems, which frequently elaborate the treatment of love in "Upon Appleton House," where William Fairfax wins Isabel Thwaites by force, wresting her away from the nuns, and Maria Fairfax's marriage is anticipated as a ritual sacrifice. "Young Love" and "The Picture of little T.C. in a Prospect of Flowers" both take up a theme which originates in the Greek Anthology and proceeds through Horace to several seventeenth-century poets, including Thomas Randolph and Thomas Carew, before Marvell: that is, love for an unripe girl before or just at the threshold of nubility. What is striking in Marvell's poems is a certain ominousness: both girls are reminded that they may perish before their mature charms become threatening to men, and it is the threat of their growing beauty that leads the poet to seek peace before he is stricken. The application to a little girl of the full Petrarchan topos of the woman who murders by a combination of beauty and disdain, as in these lines from "The Picture of little T.C.," borders on grotesquery:

> O then let me in time compound,
> And parly with those conquering Eyes;
> Ere they have try'd their force to wound,
> Ere, with their glancing wheels, they drive
> In Triumph over Hearts that strive,
> And them that yield but more despise.

The war of the sexes is similarly depicted in "The Fair Singer"; here the object of the poet's desire adds to the advantage of her captivating eyes the charms of an exquisite singing voice, which combine to defeat all his resistance conceived in martial terms: "And all my Forces needs must be undone, / She having gained both the Wind and Sun." "The Match" portrays the beauties of one Celia as the storehouse of Nature's vitality, the poet as the conflagration of Love's powder magazine in her presence; and in "The Gallery" the poet's soul is a portrait gallery containing pictures only of Clora in an endless variety of guises and poses. She is both "Enchantress" and "Murtheress," both Aurora and Venus. The poet confesses that he prefers the painting "at the Entrance" where she appears as

Marvell in 1662 (artist unknown; Wilberforce House Museum, Hull)

a shepherdess, "with which I first was took"; but of course the point is that this "Posture," like all the rest, is just a pose, a disguise – the real "Clora" cannot be finally identified, and certainly not relied upon.

The negative view of love suggested by these heightened Petrarchan conceits is intensified by two poems which blend tragic despair with an ingenious baroque extravagance. "The unfortunate Lover" deploys a series of emblematic images of the lover as a gallantly embattled knight of despair, born by "a *Cesarian Section*" to a woman shipwrecked on rocky shoals. The state of the lover is likened to the torment of Tityrus in hell (in Lucretius's *De rerum natura*). Cormorants "fed him up with Hopes and Air, / Which soon digested to Despair." Hence the birds both nurture and consume him: "And as one Corm'rant fed him, still / Another on his Heart did bill." The lover thus exists in a condition of endlessly frustrated hope. The heraldic image at the poem's close suggests that the lover's tormented dissatisfaction makes him the hero *only* of romantic stories, but that such hopeless love is valuable not in reality, but *only* in romance:

Yet dying leaves a Perfume here,
And Musick within every Ear:
And he in Story only rules,
In a Field *Sable* a Lover *Gules*.

These lines are reminiscent of the Charles I of the "Horatian Ode," who is a "*Royal Actor*" upon the "*Tragick Scaffold*" but not really fit to rule.

"The Definition of Love" depicts the hopelessness of love in geometric terms. The lovers are like opposite poles of the globe, enviously separated by Fate's "Decrees of Steel"; to consummate this love would require the destruction of the world: "And, us to joyn, the World should all / Be cramp'd into a *Planisphere*." It is the very perfection of such love that renders impossible its temporal and physical realization:

As Lines so Loves *oblique* may well
Themselves in every Angle greet:
But ours so truly *Paralel,*
Though infinite can never meet.

The alternative to fateful, despairing passion would seem to be cynicism. In "Daphnis and Chloe" the latter, whom nature "long had taught . . . to be coy," offers to yield when Daphnis announces that he has given over his suit and will depart forever. Daphnis refuses this desperate offer for several high-sounding reasons, but the penultimate stanza reveals that his real motive is casual cruelty: "Last night he with *Phlogis* slept; / This night for *Dorinda* kept; / And but rid to take the Air."

The masculine assault upon the reluctance of the "coy" woman lies at the heart of Marvell's best-known love poem – perhaps the most famous "persuasion to love" or carpe diem poem in English – "To his Coy Mistress." Everything we know about Marvell's poetry should warn us to beware of taking its exhortation to carnality at face value. Critics from T. S. Eliot on took note of the poem's "logical" structure, but then it began to be noticed that the conditional syllogism in that structure is invalid – a textbook case of affirming the consequent or the fallacy of the converse. Has Marvell made an error? Or does he attribute an error to the speaking persona of the poem? Or is the fallacy part of the sophistry that a seducer uses on an ingenuous young woman? Or is it a supersubtle compliment to a woman expected to recognize and laugh at the fallacy? These alternatives must be judged in the light of the abrupt shifts in tone among the three verse paragraphs. In the opening lines the seducer assumes a pose of disdainful insouciance with his extravagant parody of the Petrarchan blason:

An hundred years should go to praise
Thine Eyes, and on thy Forehead Gaze.
Two hundred to adore each Breast:
But thirty thousand to the rest.
An Age at least to every part,
And the last Age should show your Heart.

Although the Lady is said to "deserve this State," the compliment is more than a little diminished when the speaker adds that he simply lacks the time for such elaborate wooing. It is also likely that most women would be put off rather than tempted by the charnel-house imagery of the poem's middle section where the seducer, sounding like a fire-and-brimstone preacher, warns that "Worms shall try / That long preserv'd Virginity." Finally, the depiction of sexual intimacy at the poem's close, with its vision of the lovers as "am'rous birds of prey" who will "tear our Pleasures with rough strife," is again a disconcerting image in an ostensible seduction poem. The persona's desire for the reluctant Lady is mingled with revulsion at the prospect of mortality and fleshly decay, and he manifests an ambivalence toward sexual love that is pervasive in Marvell's poetry.

Marvell's poems of religious inclination are few in number and so equivocal in status that one critic, J. B. Leishman, puts "religious" in quotation marks. The first problem is to decide which pieces in the Marvell canon count as religious poems. "Clorinda and Damon" and "A Dialogue between Thyrsis and Dorinda" are both pastorals with quasi-religious overtones. In the first of these Damon has met "Pan" (pastoral jargon for Jesus, as Good Shepherd) and loftily informs Clorinda that he will no longer wanton with her in "that unfrequented Cave," which she calls "Loves Shrine" but which to him is now "Virtue's Grave." Clorinda is easily (too easily?) convinced to join Damon in praising "Pan" in place of wanton frolic. In "A Dialogue between Thyrsis and Dorinda," Dorinda is so enraptured by her religious vision (of "Elizium") that she persuades Thyrsis to enter into a suicide pact with her so they can reach "Elizium" as quickly as possible. Insofar as these dialogues touch on religious themes, they might be taken as sardonic parodies of Richard Crashaw's pastoral Nativity hymn, which also includes a shepherd named Thyrsis and concludes with the shepherds offering to burn as a sacrifice in the fiery eyes of the Christ Child. "Eyes and Tears" could similarly be taken as a not altogether pious imitation of Crashaw's "The Weeper." Only the eighth stanza of Marvell's poem, a translation of his own Latin epigram on Mary Magdalene, makes an explicitly Christian reference. "Eyes and

*Letter to the "Commissioners of the Militia for the town & Country of Kingston upon Hull," written on 29 May 1660,
the day on which Charles II arrived in London to assume the British throne (Pierpont Morgan Library)*

Tears" employs the baroque extravagance of "The Weeper" without Crashaw's devotional intensity.

"A Dialogue, Between The Resolved Soul, and Created Pleasure" and "A Dialogue between the Soul and Body" are essentially philosophical in tone and substance although the former does make glancing allusion to the Pauline "whole armor of God" (Eph. 6:13–17) and the delight of "Heaven" in the soul's triumphant resistance to the temptation of worldly pleasure. The soul/body dialogue makes no expressly Christian references and, contrary to the usual fashion of such poems, shows the body getting the better of the argument and undercutting the aloof smugness of the "Resolved Soul":

What but a Soul could have the wit
To build me up for Sin so fit?
So Architects do square and hew,
Green Trees that in the Forest grew.

By the same token "On a Drop of Dew," for all its perfect meditative form, is more Neoplatonic than Christian in mood, and this is equally true of its Latin companion piece, "Ros." Both poems deploy the similitude of an evaporating drop of dew for the soul "dissolving" back into its natural home, "the Glories of th'Almighty Sun," and only a further comparison to evaporating manna provides a scriptural reference.

"Bermudas" and "The Coronet" of all Marvell's poems most resolutely develop Christian themes. The former doubtless dates from the time Marvell spent as a tutor to William Dutton in the Eton home of John Oxenbridge, who had sought refuge in Bermuda during Laud's persecution of Puritans. In part the poem is polemical: in Bermuda the psalm-singing English boatmen are "Safe from the Storms, and Prelat's rage"; but mainly it develops a vision of an earthly paradise as symbol for that withdrawal from the workaday world that is Marvell's constant preoccupation. The remote island is a garden spot of contemplative retirement, and its imagery is reminiscent of "The Garden": "He hangs in shades the Orange bright, / Like golden Lamps in a green Night." "The Coronet" is perhaps the most witheringly self-conscious poem of a poet of studied self-consciousness. Written in the tradition of John Donne's "La Corona" and George Herbert's "A Wreath," Marvell's effort at repentance by weaving "So rich a Chaplet . . . / As never yet the king of Glory wore" can be said almost to "deconstruct" the devotional tradition that it invokes. "Dismantling all the fragrant Towers / That once adorn'd my Shepherdesses head" in order to weave a garland for Christ is clearly a fig-

ure for sacred parody – application of the tropes and themes of profane love poetry to devotional poetry. Marvell finds the whole procedure, central to the religious verse of the seventeenth century, flawed by an inevitable lack of purity of intention or of sincerity. The result is implicitly idolatry, the worship of our own devices and desires:

Alas I find the Serpent old
That, twining in his speckled breast,
About the flow'rs disguis'd does fold,
With wreaths of Fame and Interest.

Hence in a sophisticated manner, Marvell shares the Puritan suspicion of any ritual worship as not only inadequate but unworthy to express true devotion to God. Religious gesture and image (and perhaps the religious poem) must be destroyed to destroy the devil lurking within: "Or shatter too with him my curious frame: / And let these wither, so that he may die, / Though set with Skill and chosen out with Care." Thus is Puritanism a recipe for secularization: since there can be no fitting or innocent expression of religious feeling, religion must remain silent; and art and culture are left to what is profane.

During the years that Marvell served as tutor to Dutton, Cromwell's virtual ward, the poet evidently came to be on intimate footing with the Lord Protector. Toward the end of 1654 Marvell commemorated *The First Anniversary of the Government under O.C.* in more than two hundred heroic couplets. The poem was published in quarto early in the following year by Thomas Newcomb, the government printer. The praise here is considerably less equivocal than in the "Horatian Ode," but even so scholars have debated the ultimate intention of *The First Anniversary*. Is it a simple panegyric, a deliberative poem urging Cromwell to legitimate and solidify his power by having himself crowned king (the thesis of John M. Wallace), or an apocalyptic poem that celebrates Cromwell as the herald and architect of a new order of things? The last seems by far most probable, since Marvell pointedly contrasts Cromwell with "Unhappy Princes, ignorantly bred, / By Malice some, by Errour more misled," who fail to recognize "Angelique *Cromwell*" as the "Captain" under whom they might pursue "The Great Designes kept for the latter Dayes!" The greatest design in which the subordinate monarchs should join the Protector is, evidently, the destruction of the Catholic church, "Which shrinking to her *Roman* Den impure, / Gnashes her Goary teeth; nor there secure." Indeed, this poem, with its apocalyptic overtones, is the first sample of the virulent

The cottage in Highgate where Marvell lived from 1673 until his death in 1678. This photograph was taken by John Haynes before the house was demolished in 1868 (Heal Collection, Camden Borough Libraries).

anti-Catholicism which will become central to Marvell's post-Restoration politics. He approaches the prophecy that Cromwell is the harbinger of the Millennium, but draws back into a cautious uncertainty: "That 'tis the most which we determine can, / If these the Times, then this must be the Man." What *The First Anniversary* leaves us with, finally, is a sense of the fragility of the regime that depended so much on one man, whose mortality was so pointedly signaled by his potentially fatal Hyde Park coach accident in September 1654, a central incident in the poem.

In 1657 Marvell was appointed Latin secretary, the post for which Milton had recommended him four years earlier, and wrote two different though equally public poems: "On the Victory Obtained by Blake over the Spaniards in the Bay of Santacruze, in the Island of Teneriff. 1657" and "Two Songs at the Marriage of the Lord Fauconberg and the Lady Mary Cromwell." The following year Cromwell died, and Marvell celebrated the late Lord Protector in *A Poem upon the Death of O.C.* Although the closing lines of this poem seem to proffer allegiance to Oliver's son, Richard Cromwell, who succeeded to his father's place, when Richard's government failed and he fled the

country, the poet was a member of the Parliament that restored Charles II to the throne his father had lost. Elected member of Parliament for Hull in 1659, a position he held until the end of his life, Marvell was safe himself in the wake of the Restoration and well placed to help other members of the Interregnum government, including Milton, whose life he may well have saved.

Apart from two diplomatic journeys in the service of Charles Howard, Earl of Carlisle, in Holland (1662–1663) and in Russia, Sweden, and Denmark (1663–1665), Marvell remained generally in London, faithfully and energetically representing his Hull constituency of middle-class merchants. Naturally he became increasingly disenchanted with and alienated from the court of Charles II, who resorted to secret subsidies from Louis XIV and high-handed taxation measures to circumvent Parliament's reluctance to support his pro-French foreign policy and toleration of Catholicism. The most charming of Marvell's poems of this period is "On Mr. Milton's *Paradise lost*," first published in the second edition of Milton's great epic (1674). Better than anyone else, Marvell expresses the wonder that most readers have felt upon perusing Milton's work: "Where couldst thou Words of such a compass find? / Whence furnish such a vast expense of Mind?" Otherwise, Marvell's Restoration poetry is almost exclusively confined to political satire of an extremely topical bent. With these poems questions of text and authenticity of attribution are extremely vexed. During an age of severe censorship, such fierce attacks upon the government could be published or circulated only anonymously; while still alive Marvell could not safely claim authorship, and after his death a poem gained immediate currency if attributed to the renowned patriot, whether he actually wrote it or not. Among the satires that Marvell certainly wrote, the most important are "Clarindon's House-Warming," "The last Instructions to a Painter," and "The Loyall Scot." Reasonable arguments can also be made for "The Kings Vowes," "The Statue in the Stocks-Market," "The Statue at Charing Cross," "A Dialogue between the Two Horses," and one or two other minor satires. George deF. Lord argues vigorously for the inclusion in the Marvell canon of the second and third "Advice to a Painter" poems, but his contention has not been widely accepted.

"Clarindon's House-Warming" reverses the architectural symbolism of "Upon Appleton House" by attacking the character of Henry Hyde, Earl of Clarendon, the king's chief minister, through ridicule of the ostentatious and very expensive house he built between 1664 and 1667, a time when London was suffering from the combined effects of fire, plague, and unsuccessful war with the Dutch. "The last Instructions to a Painter" is one of several satirical burlesques of Edmund Waller's panegyric on a naval victory commanded by the king's brother, James, Duke of York, titled *Instructions to a Painter, For the Drawing of the Posture and Progress of His Majesties Forces at Sea* (1666). Running to almost one thousand lines, "The last Instructions to a Painter" is the longest poem Marvell wrote. Although not infrequently enlivened by flashes of wit and intensity that anticipate the satires of Dryden and Pope, on the whole it lacks the clarity and universal appeal of Dryden's *Absalom and Achitophel* (1681) or Pope's *Dunciad* (1728, 1742). Perhaps the most effective of Marvell's satires is *The Loyall Scot*, which purports to be a recantation by the ghost of John Cleveland of his Royalist anti-Presbyterian satire, *The Rebel Scot* (1644). Marvell's satire on the ineptitude of the Royal Navy in an encounter with the Dutch under Michiel Adriaanszoon de Ruyter (1667) is highlighted by contrast with the heroic death of the Scottish captain Archibald Douglas. In lines that also appear in "The last Instructions to a Painter," Marvell captures the young Scot's fiery

death with the baroque intensity of his earlier manner:

> Like a glad lover the fierce Flames he meets
> And tries his first Imbraces in their sheets.
> His shape Exact which the bright flames enfold
> Like the sun's Statue stands of burnisht Gold:
> Round the Transparent fire about him Glowes
> As the Clear Amber on the bee doth Close;
> And as on Angells head their Glories shine
> His burning Locks Adorn his face divine.

Marvell also wrote satires in prose, which are generally more successful in themselves while providing a model, in this case, for the prose of Jonathan Swift. Of these the best are surely the two parts of *The Rehearsal Transpros'd* (1672, 1673), in which Marvell takes on the Reverend Samuel Parker, an erstwhile Puritan turned intolerant Tory Anglican, who recommended severe persecution of Protestant dissenters from the established church. The title of Marvell's work comes from George Villiers, second Duke of Buckingham's farcical mockery of Dryden's poetry, *The Rehearsal* (1672), and it engages in the same sort of high-spirited, if scurrilous, mockery in religious controversy that Buckingham had introduced into a literary quarrel. For once Marvell found himself, superficially at least, in agreement with the king, who had just issued the short-lived Declaration of Indulgence, which removed criminal penalties against Protestant dissenters and Catholic recusants alike. Charles, however, was mainly interested in protecting the recusants, and Marvell had sympathy only for the dissenters, so the marriage of convenience did not last long. Marvell continued his attack on Anglican intolerance in *Mr. Smirke; or The Divine in Mode*, which was published with his *Historical Essay on General Councils* (1676), and he is probably the author of *Remarks Upon a Late Disingenuous Discourse* (1678), which defends the independent nonconformist John Howe from the strictures of a severe Calvinist dissenter, Thomas Danson. Finally, just before his death, Marvell produced *An Account of the Growth of Popery, and Arbitrary Government in England* (1677), which blends shrewd insights into the devious machinations of the government of Charles II in circumventing Parliament with Marvell's own brand of furiously anti-Catholic intolerance.

By the time of Marvell's death, generally attributed to a fever, on 16 August 1678, there was a reward offered by the government for the identity of the author of *An Account of the Growth of Popery*, though there was little doubt who the author was. Popular rumor attributed Marvell's death to poisoning by the Jesuits. Whatever the event, the ensuing decades would see Marvell remembered essentially as a patriot, and a great many political satires, most of which he could not have written, were attributed to him. In 1681 the folio edition of *Miscellaneous Poems. By Andrew Marvell, Esq.*, including the lyrics that made the poet's twentieth-century reputation, was published under mysterious circumstances. Although there is no record that Marvell ever married, the volume is prefaced by a short note by a woman claiming to be the poet's widow and calling herself "Mary Marvell." She was in fact his housekeeper, Mary Palmer, and no one except William Empson believes that the marriage ever took place. Instead it is generally regarded as a ruse to protect Marvell's small estate from the depredations of his business partners' creditors. Whatever their motivations, the editors of the *Miscellaneous Poems* have earned the gratitude of modern readers, and it seems fitting that a certain ambiguity should surround the posthumous publication of such ambiguous poetry.

Letters:

Volume 2 of *The Complete Works in Prose and Verse of Andrew Marvell*, 4 volumes, edited by Alexander B. Grosart (London: Robson, 1872–1875);

Volume 2 of *The Poems and Letters of Andrew Marvell*, third edition, 2 volumes, edited by H. M. Margoliouth, revised by Pierre Legouis with E. E. Duncan-Jones (Oxford: Clarendon Press, 1971).

Bibliographies:

Gillian R. Szanto, "Recent Studies in Marvell," *English Literary Renaissance*, 5 (Spring 1975): 273–286;

Dan S. Collins, *Andrew Marvell: A Reference Guide* (Boston: G. K. Hall, 1981).

Biography:

Pierre Legouis, *Andrew Marvell: Poet, Puritan, Patriot*, second edition (Oxford: Clarendon Press, 1968).

References:

Don Cameron Allen, "Andrew Marvell: 'The Nymph Complaining for the Death of her Faun'" and "Andrew Marvell: 'Upon Appleton House,'" in his *Image and Meaning: Metaphoric Traditions in the Renaissance*, revised edition (Baltimore: Johns Hopkins Press, 1968), pp. 165–186, 187–225;

Anne E. Berthoff, *The Resolved Soul: A Study of Marvell's Major Poems* (Princeton, N.J.: Princeton University Press, 1970);

Harold Bloom, ed., *Andrew Marvell: Modern Critical Views* (New York: Chelsea House, 1989);

M. C. Bradbrook and M. G. Lloyd-Thomas, *Andrew Marvell* (Cambridge: Cambridge University Press, 1940);

R. L. Brett, ed., *Andrew Marvell: Essays on the Tercentenary of his Death* (Oxford & New York: Published for the University of Hull by Oxford University Press, 1979);

John Carey, ed., *Andrew Marvell: A Critical Anthology* (Baltimore: Penguin, 1969);

Warren L. Chernaik, *The Poet's Time: Politics and Religion in the Work of Andrew Marvell* (Cambridge: Cambridge University Press, 1983);

Rosalie L. Colie, *"My Ecchoing Song": Andrew Marvell's Poetry of Criticism* (Princeton, N.J.: Princeton University Press, 1970);

Michael Craze, *The Life and Lyrics of Andrew Marvell* (London: Macmillan, 1979);

Patrick Cullen, *Spenser, Marvell, and Renaissance Pastoral* (Cambridge, Mass.: Harvard University Press, 1970);

T. S. Eliot, "Andrew Marvell," in his *Homage to John Dryden: Three Essays on Poetry of the Seventeenth Century* (London: Hogarth Press, 1924);

William Empson, "Marvell's Garden," in his *Some Versions of Pastoral* (London: Chatto & Windus, 1935), pp. 117–145;

Empson, "Natural Magic and Populism in Marvell's Poetry," in *Andrew Marvell: Essays on the Tercentenary of his Death*, edited by Brett, pp. 36–61;

Kenneth Friedenreich, ed., *Tercentenary Essays in Honor of Andrew Marvell* (Hamden, Conn.: Shoestring Press, 1977);

Donald F. Friedman, *Marvell's Pastoral Art* (Berkeley: University of California Press, 1970);

George R. Guffey, *A Concordance to the English Poems of Andrew Marvell* (Chapel Hill: University of North Carolina Press, 1974);

John Dixon Hunt, *Andrew Marvell: His Life and Writings* (Ithaca, N.Y.: Cornell University Press, 1978);

Lawrence Hyman, *Andrew Marvell* (New York: Twayne, 1964);

J. B. Leishman, *The Art of Marvell's Poetry* (London: Hutchinson, 1966);

George deF. Lord, ed., *Andrew Marvell: A Collection of Critical Essays* (Englewood Cliffs, N.J.: Prentice-Hall, 1968);

Louis L. Martz, "Andrew Marvell: The Mind's Happiness," in his *The Wit of Love* (Notre

Dame, Ind.: Notre Dame University Press, 1969), pp. 151–190;

C. A. Patrides, ed., *Approaches to Andrew Marvell: the York Tercentenary Essays* (London: Routledge & Kegan Paul, 1978);

Annabel M. Patterson, *Marvell and the Civic Crown* (Princeton, N.J.: Princeton University Press, 1978);

Maren-Sofie Røstvig, *The Happy Man: Studies in the Metamorphosis of a Classical Idea*, 2 volumes (Oslo: Akademisk forlag, 1954, 1958);

Kitty W. Scoular, *Natural Magic: Studies in the Presentation of Nature from Spenser to Marvell* (Oxford: Clarendon Press, 1965);

Phoebe S. Spinrad, "Death, Loss, and Marvell's Nymph," *PMLA*, 97 (January 1982): 50–59;

Spinrad, "Marvell and Mystic Laughter," *Papers on Language and Literature*, 20 (1984): 259–272;

Harold E. Toliver, *Marvell's Ironic Vision* (New Haven: Yale University Press, 1965);

James Turner, *The Politics of Landscape: Rural Scenery and Society in English Poetry 1630–1660* (Cambridge, Mass.: Harvard University Press, 1979);

John M. Wallace, *Destiny His Choice: The Loyalism of Andrew Marvell* (Cambridge: Cambridge University Press, 1968);

Ruth Wallerstein, "Marvell and the Various Light," in her *Studies in Seventeenth-Century Poetic* (Madison: University of Wisconsin Press, 1950), pp. 149–342;

Michael Wilding, ed., *Marvell: Modern Judgments* (London: Macmillan, 1969);

R. V. Young, "Andrew Marvell and the Devotional Tradition," *Renascence*, 38 (Summer 1986): 204–227.

Papers:
There are Marvell manuscripts in the collections of the British Library; the Bodleian Library, Oxford; the Public Record Office, London; and the Codrington Library, All Souls College, Oxford.

John Milton

(9 December 1608 – 8? November 1674)

Albert C. Labriola
Duquesne University

SELECTED BOOKS: *A Maske Presented at Ludlow Castle, 1634* [*Comus*] (London: Printed for Humphrey Robinson, 1637);

Epitaphivm Damonis. Argvmentvm (London: Printed by Augustine Mathewes?, 1640?);

Of Reformation Touching Chvrch-Discipline in England: And the Cavses that hitherto have hindered it (London: Printed for Thomas Underhill, 1641);

Of Prelatical Episcopacy, and Whether it may be deduc'd from the Apostolical times by vertue of those Testimonies which are alledg'd to that purpose in some late Treatises: One whereof goes under the Name of Iames' Archbishop of Armagh (London: Printed by R. O. & G. D. for Thomas Underhill, 1641);

Animadversions upon the Remonstrants Defence, against Smectymnvvs (London: Printed for Thomas Underhill, 1641);

The Reason of Church-governement Urg'd against Prelaty (London: Printed by E. G. for Iohn Rothwell, 1641 [i.e., 1642]);

An Apology Against a Pamphlet Call'd A Modest Confutation of the Animadversions upon the Remonstrant against Smectymnuus (London: Printed by E. G. for Iohn Rothwell, 1642);

The Doctrine and Discipline of Divorce: Restor'd to the Good of Both Sexes, From the bondage of Canon Law, and other mistakes, to Christian freedom, guided by the Rule of Charity (London: Printed by Thomas Payne & Matthew Simmons, 1643; second edition, "revis'd and much augmented," London, 1644);

Of Education: To Master Samuel Hartlib (London: Printed for Thomas Johnson, 1644);

The Ivdgment of Martin Bucer, Concerning Divorce. Writt'n to Edward the sixt, in his second Book of the Kingdom of Christ. And now Englisht (London: Printed by Matthew Simmons, 1644);

Areopagitica: A Speech of Mr. John Milton For the Liberty of Vnlicenc'd Printing, To the Parlament of England (London, 1644);

John Milton, circa 1670 (pastel by William Faithorne; Princeton University Library)

Colasterion: A Reply to A Nameless Answer Against the Doctrine and Discipline of Divorce (London: Printed by Matthew Simmons, 1645);

Tetrachordon: Expositions Upon The foure chief places in Scripture, which treat of Mariage, or nullities in Mariage (London: Printed by Thomas Payne & Matthew Simmons, 1645);

Poems of Mr. John Milton, Both English and Latin, Compos'd at Several Times. Printed by His True Copies. The Songs were Set in Musick by Mr. Henry Lawes (London: Printed by Ruth Raworth for Humphrey Moseley, 1645);

The Tenure of Kings and Magistrates (London: Printed by Matthew Simmons, 1649; second edition, enlarged, 1650);

ΕΙΚΟΝΟΚΛΑ'ΣΤΗΣ. *in Answer to a Book Intitl'd* ΕΙΚΩ'Ν ΒΑΣΙΛΙΚΗ, *The Portraiture of his Sacred Majesty in His Solitudes and Sufferings* (London: Printed by Matthew Simmons, 1649; second edition, enlarged, London: Printed by T. N. & sold by Tho. Brewster & G. Moule, 1650);

Joannis Miltoni Angli Pro Populo Anglicano Defensio Contra Claudii Anonymi, alias Salmasii, Defensionem Regiam (Londini: Typis DuGardianis, 1651);

Joannis Miltoni Angli Pro Populo Anglicano Defensio Secunda. Contra infamen libellum anonymum cui titulus, Regii sanguinis clamor ad cælum adversus parricidas Anglicanos (Londini: Typis Neucomianis, 1654);

Joannis Miltoni Angli pro se Defensio contra Alexandrum Morum Ecclesiasten, Libelli famosi, cui titulus, Regii sanguinis clamor ad cælum adversuç Parricidas Anglicanos, authoren recteç dictum (Londini: Typis Neucomianis, 1655);

Considerations Touching The likeliest means to remove Hirelings out of the church. Wherein is also discourc'd of Tithes, Church-fees, Church-revenues; and whether any maintenance of ministers can be settl'd by law (London: Printed by T. N. for L. Chapman, 1659);

A Treatise of Civil Power in Ecclesiastical Causes: Shewing That it is not lawfull for any power on earth to compell in matters of Religion (London: Printed by Tho. Newcomb, 1659);

The Readie & Easie Way to Establish a Free Commonwealth, and the Excellence thereof Compar'd with The inconveniences and dangers of readmitting kingship in this nation (London: Printed by T. N. & sold by Livewell Chapman, 1660; second edition, "revis'd and augmented," London: Printed for the author, 1660);

Brief Notes Upon a late Sermon, titl'd, The Fear of God and the King; Preachd, and since Publishd, By Matthew Griffith, D. D. And Chaplain to the late King (London, 1660);

Paradise lost. A Poem Written in Ten Books by John Milton (London: Printed & sold by Peter Parker, Robert Boulter, and Matthias Walker, 1667);

Accedence Commenc't Grammar, Supply'd with Sufficient Rules, For the use of such as, Younger or Elder, are desirous, without more trouble then needs, to attain the Latin Tongue; the elder sort especially, with little teaching, and their own industry (London: Printed by S. Simmons, 1669);

The History of Britain, That part especially now call'd England. From the first Traditional Beginning, continu'd to the Norman Conquest (London: Printed by J. M. for James Allestry, 1670);

Paradise Regain'd. A Poem In IV Books. To Which Is Added Samson Agonistes. The Author John Milton (London: Printed by J. M. for John Starkey, 1671);

Joannis Miltoni Angli, Artis Logicæ Plenior Institutio, Ad Petri Rami Methodum concinnata (Londini: Impensis Spencer Hickman, 1672);

Of True Religion, Hæresie, Schism, Toleration, and what best means may be us'd against the growth of Popery (London, 1673);

Poems, &c. upon Several Occasions. By Mr. John Milton: Both English and Latin, &c. Composed at several times. With a small Tractate of Education To Mr. Hartlib (London: Printed for Tho. Dring, 1673);

Joannis Miltoni Angli, Epistolarum Familiarum Liber Unus: Quibus Accesserunt, Ejusdem, jam olim in Collegio Adolescentis, Prolusiones Quædam Oratoriae (Londini: Impensis Brabazoni Aylmeri, 1674);

A Declaration, or Letters Patents of the Election of this present King of Poland John the Third, Elected on the 22d of May last past, Anno Dom. 1674, translated by Milton (London: Printed for Brabazon Aylmer, 1674);

Paradise Lost. A Poem in Twelve Books. The Author John Milton. The Second Edition Revised and Augmented by the Same Author (London: Printed by S. Simmons, 1674);

Literæ Pseudo-Senatûs Anglicani, Cromwellii, Reliquorumque Perduellium nomine ac jussu conscriptæ (Amsterdam: Printed by Peter & John Blaeu, 1676);

A Brief History of Moscovia: and of Other Less-Known Countries Lying Eastward of Russia as far as Cathay. Gather'd from the Writings of Several Eyewitnesses (London: Printed by M. Flesher for Brabazon Aylmer, 1682);

Letters of State, Written by Mr. John Milton, to most of the Sovereign Princes and Republicks of Europe. From the Year 1649. Till the Year 1659. To Which Is Added, an Account of His Life. Together with Several of His Poems (London, 1694);

Joannis Miltoni Angli De Doctrina Christiana libri duo posthumi, quos ex schedis mauscripts deprompsit et typis mandari primus curavit C. R. Sumner (Cantabrigiae: Typis Academicis excudit Joannes Smith, 1825);

A Common-place Book of John Milton, and a Latin Essay and Latin Verses Presumed To Be by Milton, edited by A. J. Horwood, Camden Society Publications, new series 16 (Westminster: Printed for the Camden Society, 1876; revised, 1877);

A Common-Place Book of John Milton. Reproduced by the Autotype Process from the Original Manuscript in the Possession of Sir Frederick J. U. Graham. . . . With an Introduction by A. J. Horwood (London: Privately printed at the Chiswick Press, 1876).

Editions: *The Poetical Works of Mr. John Milton. Containing Paradise Lost, Paradise Regain'd, Sampson Agonistes, and His Poems on Several Occasions. Together with Explanatory Notes on Each Book of the Paradise Lost and a Table Never before Printed,* with notes to *Paradise Lost* by David Hume (London: Printed for Jacob Tonson, 1695);

The Works of Mr. John Milton (London, 1697);

A Complete Collection of the Historical, Political, and Miscellaneous Works of John Milton, both English and Latin; with som Papers Never Before Publish'd, 3 volumes (Amsterdam [i.e. London], 1698);

The Poetical Works of Mr. John Milton, 2 volumes (London: Printed for Jacob Tonson, 1705);

Paradise Regain'd. A Poem in Four Books. To Which is Added Samson Agonistes: and Poems on Several Occasions. . . . From the text of Thomas Newton, D.D. (Birmingham: Printed by John Baskerville for J. & R. Tonson, London, 1758);

Paradise Lost. A Poem, in Twelve Books. . . . From the Text of Thomas Newton D.D. (Birmingham: Printed by John Baskerville for J. & R. Tonson, London, 1758);

Poems upon Several Occasions, English, Italian and Latin, With Translations by John Milton. . . . With Notes Critical and Explanatory and Other Illustrations, edited by Thomas Warton (London: Printed for J. Dodsley, 1785);

The Poetical Works of John Milton. With a Life of the Author, by William Hayley, 3 volumes (London: Printed by W. Bulmer for John & Josiah Boydell & George Nicol, 1794–1797);

Latin and Italian Poems of Milton Translated into English Verse, and a Fragment of a Commentary on Paradise Lost, translated by William Cowper, edited by William Hayley (London: Printed by J. Seagrave for J. Johnson & R. H. Evans, 1808);

The Poetical Works of John Milton, with Notes of Various Authors. To Which are added Illustrations, and Some Account of the Life and Writings of Milton. . . . Second edition, with considerable additions and with a Verbal Index to the whole of Milton's poetry, 7 volumes, edited by H. J. Todd (London: Printed for J. Johnson by Law & Gilbert, 1809);

Milton's Life and Poetical Works with Notes by William Cowper. . . . With Adam, a Sacred Drama, 4 vol-

umes, edited by Hayley (Chichester: Printed by W. Mason for J. Johnson, London, 1810);

The Poetical Works of John Milton. . . . with Imaginative Illustrations by J. M. W. Turner, 6 volumes, edited by Sir Egerton Brydges (London: J. Macrone, 1835);

The Prose Works of John Milton, 5 volumes, edited by J. A. St. John, Bohn's Standard Library (London: Bell, 1848–1881);

The Works of John Milton in Verse and Prose, Printed from the Original Editions with a Life of the Author, 8 volumes, edited by John Mitford (London: Pickering, 1851);

The Poems of John Milton, 2 volumes, edited by Thomas Keightley (London: Chapman & Hall, 1859);

English Poems by John Milton, 2 volumes, edited by R. C. Browne (Oxford: Clarendon Press, 1870; revised, 1873);

The Poetical Works of John Milton, 3 volumes, edited by David Masson (London: Macmillan, 1874; revised, 1890);

The Cambridge Milton for Schools, 10 volumes, edited by A. Wilson Verity, Pitt Press series (Cambridge: Cambridge University Press, 1891–1896; revised edition of *Comus,* 1909; revised edition of *Paradise Lost,* 1910);

The Poetical Works of John Milton, Edited after the Original Texts, edited by H. C. Beeching (Oxford: Clarendon Press, 1900);

The Poetical Works of John Milton, edited by William Aldis Wright (Cambridge: Cambridge University Press, 1903);

The Poems of John Milton, 2 volumes, edited by H. J. C. Grierson (London: Chatto & Windus, 1925);

Milton's Prose, edited by Malcolm W. Wallace (London: Oxford University Press, 1925);

Areopagitica and Other Prose Works (London: Dent, 1927; New York: Dutton, 1927);

The Student's Milton, Being the Complete Poems of John Milton, with the Greater Part of His Prose Works, Now Printed in One Volume, Together with New Translations into English of His Italian, Latin and Greek Poems, edited by Frank Allen Patterson (New York: Crofts, 1930; revised, 1933);

The Works of John Milton, 18 volumes in 21, edited by Patterson (New York: Columbia University Press, 1931–1938);

Paradise Regained, the Minor Poems and Samson Agonistes, Complete and Arranged Chronologically, edited by Merritt Y. Hughes (New York: Odyssey Press, 1937);

The English Poems of John Milton, from the Edition of H. C. Beeching Together with an Introduction by Charles Williams, and a Reader's Guide to Milton Compiled by Walter Skeat (London: Oxford University Press, 1940);

The Complete Poetical Works of John Milton, edited by Harris Francis Fletcher (Boston: Houghton Mifflin, 1941);

John Milton's Complete Poetical Works, Reproduced in Photographic Facsimile, 4 volumes, edited by Fletcher (Urbana: University of Illinois Press, 1943–1948);

John Milton: Prose Selections, edited by Hughes (New York: Odyssey Press, 1947);

The Poetical Works of John Milton, 2 volumes, edited by Helen Darbishire (Oxford: Clarendon Press, 1952–1955); republished with Latin poems edited by H. W. Garrod and Italian poems edited by John Purves (London & New York: Oxford University Press, 1958);

Complete Prose Works of John Milton, 8 volumes in 10, edited by Don M. Wolfe and others (New Haven: Yale University Press, 1953–1982);

Poems, edited by B. A. Wright (London: Dent / New York: Dutton, 1956);

Complete Poems and Major Prose, edited by Hughes (New York: Odyssey Press, 1957);

The Complete Poetical Works of John Milton, edited by Douglas Bush (Boston: Houghton Mifflin, 1965; London: Oxford University Press, 1966);

The Prose of John Milton, edited by J. Max Patrick (Garden City, N.Y.: Doubleday, 1967);

The Poems of John Milton, edited by John Carey and Alastair Fowler (London: Longmans, Green, 1968);

The Complete Poetry of John Milton, revised edition, edited by John T. Shawcross (Garden City, N.Y.: Doubleday, 1971);

Selected Prose of John Milton, edited by C. A. Patrides (Harmondsworth, U.K.: Penguin, 1974);

John Milton: The Complete Poems, edited by Wright, with an introduction by Gordon Campbell (London: Dent / New York, Dutton, 1980);

John Milton, edited by Stephen Orgel and Jonathan Goldberg (Oxford & New York: Oxford University Press, 1991).

OTHER: "An Epitaph on the admirable Dramaticke Poet, W. SHAKESPEARE," in *Mr. William Shakespeares Comedies, Histories, and Tragedies,* Second Folio (London: Printed by Tho. Cotes for Robert Allot, 1632);

"Lycidas," in *Justa Edovardo King, naufrago, ab Amicis moerentibus, amoris & μνείας χάριν* (Cantabrigiæ: Apud Thomam Buck & Rogerum Daniel, 1638); part 2: *Obsequies to the Memorie of Mr. Edward King, Anno Dom. 1638* (Cambridge: Printed by Th. Buck & R. Daniel, 1638), pp. 20–25;

Sonnet to Henry Lawes, in *Choice Psalmes, Put into Musick for Three Voices,* by Henry and William Lawes (London: Printed by James Young for Humphrey Moseley, 1648);

"Observations on the Articles of Peace," in *Articles of Peace, made and concluded with the Irish Rebels, and Papists, by James Earle of Ormond, for and in behalfe of the late King, and by vertue of his Autoritie* (London: Printed by Matthew Simmons, 1649);

The Cabinet-Council: Containing the Chief Arts of Empire, and Mysteries of State . . . By . . . Sir Walter Raleigh, published by Milton from a manuscript (London: Printed by Thomas Newcomb for Thomas Johnson, 1658).

John Milton's career as a writer of prose and poetry spans three distinct eras: Stuart England; the Civil War (1642–1648) and Interregnum, including the Commonwealth (1649–1653) and Protectorate (1654–1660); and the Restoration. When Elizabeth I, the so-called Virgin Queen and the last of the Tudors, died, James VI, King of Scots, was enthroned as Britain's king. Titled James I, he inaugurated the House of Stuart. His son and successor, Charles I, continued as monarch until he lost the Civil War to the Parliamentarians, was tried on charges of high treason, and was beheaded on 30 January 1649. For eleven years thereafter England was governed by the military commander and later Lord Protector Oliver Cromwell, who was succeeded by his son, Richard. By 1660 the people, no longer supportive of the Protectorate, welcomed the Restoration, the return of the House of Stuart in the person of Charles II, son of the late king.

Milton's chief polemical prose was written in the decades of the 1640s and 1650s, during the strife between the Church of England and various reformist groups such as the Puritans and between the monarch and Parliament. Designated the antiepiscopal or antiprelatical tracts and the antimonarchical or political tracts, these works advocate a freedom of conscience and a high degree of civil liberty for humankind against the various forms of tyranny and oppression, both ecclesiastical and governmental. In line with his libertarian outlook, Milton wrote *Areopagitica* (1644), often cited as one of the most compelling arguments on the freedom of the press. In March 1649 Milton was appointed secretary for foreign tongues to the Council of State. In that capacity his service to the government, chiefly in the field of foreign policy, is documented by official correspondence, the *Letters of State,* first published in 1694. In that capacity, moreover, he was a vigorous defender of Cromwell's government. One of his assignments was to counteract the erosion of public support of the Commonwealth, a situation caused by the publication of the *Eikon Basilike* (1649) or King's Book, which had widespread distribution after Charles I's execution. Believed to have been written by the king himself — though composed chiefly by an episcopal divine, Dr. John Gauden, who later became a bishop — the work sought to win public sympathy by creating the image of the monarch as a martyred saint. *Eikonoklastes* (1649), or Imagebreaker, is Milton's refutation, a personal attack on Charles I which likened him to William Shakespeare's duke of Gloucester (afterward Richard III), a consummate hypocrite. As a result Milton entered into controversy with Claude de Saumaise, a French scholar residing in Holland and the polemicist who wrote on behalf of Charles I's son in exile in France.

The symptoms of failing eyesight did not deter Milton, who from an early age read by candlelight until midnight or later, even while experiencing severe headaches. By 1652 he was totally blind. The exact cause is unknown. Up to the Restoration he continued to write in defense of the Protectorate. After Charles II was crowned Milton was dismissed from governmental service, apprehended, and imprisoned. Payment of fines and the intercession of friends and family, including Andrew Marvell, Sir William Davenant, and perhaps Christopher Milton, his younger brother and a Royalist lawyer, brought about Milton's release. In the troubled period at and after the Restoration he was forced to depart his home which he had occupied for eight years in Petty-France, Westminster. He took up residence elsewhere, including the house of a friend in Bartholomew Close; eventually, he settled in a home at Artillery Walk toward Bunhill Fields. On or about 8 November 1674, when he was almost sixty-six years old, Milton died of complications from gout.

While Milton's impact as a prose writer was profound, of equal or greater importance is his poetry. He referred to his prose works as the achievements of his "left hand." In 1645 he published his first volume of poetry, *Poems of Mr. John Milton, Both English and Latin,* much of which was written before

Milton at age ten (portrait attributed to Cornelis Janssen; Pierpont Morgan Library)

he was twenty years old. The volume manifests a rising poet, one who has planned his emergence and projected his development in numerous ways: mastery of ancient and modern languages — Greek, Latin, Hebrew, Italian; awareness of various traditions in literature; and avowed inclination toward the vocation of poet. The poems in the 1645 edition run the gamut of various genres: psalm paraphrase, sonnet, canzone, masque, pastoral elegy, verse letter, English ode, epigram, obituary poem, companion poem, and occasional verse. Ranging from religious to political in subject matter, serious to mock-serious in tone, and traditional to innovative in the use of verse forms, the poems in this volume disclose a self-conscious author whose maturation is undertaken with certain models in mind, notably Virgil from classical antiquity and Edmund Spenser in the English Renaissance.

Like the illustrious literary forebears with whom he invites comparison, Milton used his poetry to address issues of religion and politics, the central concerns also of his prose. Placing himself in a line of poets whose art was an outlet for their public voice and using, like them, the pastoral poem to present an outlook on politics, Milton aimed to promote an enlightened commonwealth, not unlike the *polis* of Greek antiquity or the cultured city-states in Renaissance Italy. When one considers that the 1645 volume was published when Milton was approximately thirty-seven years old, though some of the poems were written as early as his fifteenth year, it is evident that he sought to draw attention to his unfolding poetic career despite its interruption by governmental service. Perhaps he also sought to highlight the relationship of his poetry to his prose and to call attention to his aspiration, evident in several works in the 1645 volume, to become an epic poet. Thus, the poems in the volume were composed in Stuart England but published after the onset of the English Civil War. Furthermore, Milton may have begun to compose one or more of his mature works – *Paradise Lost, Paradise Regained,* and *Samson Agonistes* – in the 1640s, but they were completed and revised much later and not published until after the Restoration.

This literary genius whose fame and influence are second to none, and on whose life and works more commentary is written than on any author except Shakespeare, was born at 6:30 in the morning on 9 December 1608. His parents were John Milton, Sr., and Sara Jeffrey Milton, and the place of birth was the family home, marked with the sign of the spread eagle, on Bread Street, London. Three days later, at the parish church of All Hallows, also on Bread Street, he was baptized into the Protestant faith of the Church of England. Other children of John and Sara who survived infancy included Anne, their oldest child, and Christopher, seven years younger than John. At least three others died shortly after birth, in infancy or in early childhood. Edward Phillips, Anne's son by her first husband, was tutored by Milton and later wrote a biography of his renowned uncle, which was published in Milton's *Letters of State* (1694). Christopher, in contrast to his older brother on all counts, became a Roman Catholic, a Royalist, and a lawyer.

Milton's father was born in 1562 in Oxfordshire; his father, Richard, was a Catholic who decried the Reformation. When John Milton, Sr., expressed sympathy for what his father viewed as Protestant heresy, their disagreements resulted in the son's disinheritance. He left home and traveled to London, where he became a scrivener and a professional composer responsible for more than twenty musical pieces. As a scrivener he performed services comparable to a present-day attorney's assistant, law stationer, and notary. Among the documents that a scrivener executed were wills, leases, deeds, and marriage agreements. Through such endeavors and by his practice of money lending, the elder Milton accumulated a handsome estate, which enabled him to provide a splendid formal education for his son John and to maintain him during several years of private study. In "Ad Patrem" (To His Father), a Latin poem composed probably in 1637–1638, Milton celebrated his "revered father." He compares his father's talent at musical composition, harmonizing sounds to numbers and modulating the voices of singers, to his own dedication to the muses and to his developing artistry as a poet. The father's "generosities" and "kindnesses" enabled the young man to study Greek, Latin, Hebrew, French, and Italian.

Little is known of Sara Jeffrey, but in *Pro Propulo Anglicano Defensio Secunda* (The Second Defense of the People of England, 1654) Milton refers to the "esteem" in which his mother was held and to her reputation for almsgiving in their neighborhood. John Aubrey, in biographical notes made in 1681–1682, recorded that she had weak eyesight, which may have contributed to her son's similar problems. She died on 3 April 1637, not long before her son John departed for his European journey. Her husband died on 14 March 1647.

In the years 1618–1620 Milton was tutored in the family home. One of his tutors was Thomas Young, who became chaplain to the English merchants in Hamburg during the 1620s. Though he departed England when Milton was approximately eleven years old, Young's impression on the young pupil was long standing. Two of Milton's familiar letters, as well as "Elegia quarta" (Elegy IV), are addressed to Young. (The term *elegy* in the titles of seven of Milton's Latin poems designates the classical prosody in which they were written, couplets consisting of a verse of dactylic hexameter followed by a verse of pentameter; *elegy,* when used to describe poems of sorrow or lamentation, refers to Milton's meditations on the deaths of particular persons.) Also dedicated to Young is *Of Reformation* (1641), a prose tract; and the "TY" of the acronym SMECTYMNUUS in the title of Milton's antiprelatical tract of 1641 identifies Young as one of the five ministers whose stand against church government by bishops was admired by Milton.

From 1620 until 1625 Milton attended St. Paul's School, within close walking distance of his home and within view of the cathedral, where almost certainly he heard the sermons of Dr. John Donne, who served as dean from 1621 until 1631. The school had been founded in the preceding century by John Colet, and the chief master when Milton attended was Alexander Gill the Elder. His son, also named Alexander and an instructor at the school, did not teach Milton. Some of Milton's familiar letters are addressed to the elder and the younger Gills, with whom he maintained contact, chiefly to express gratitude for their commitment to learning and to communicate to them his unfolding plans and aspirations. During his years at St. Paul's, Milton befriended Charles Diodati, who became his closest companion in boyhood and to whom he wrote "Elegia prima" (Elegy I) and "Elegia sexta" (Elegy VI). They maintained their friendship even though Diodati attended Oxford while Milton was at Cambridge.

On 9 April 1625 Milton, then sixteen years of age, matriculated at Christ's College, Cambridge, evidently in preparation for the ministry. For seven years he studied assiduously to receive the bachelor of arts degree (1629) and the master of arts degree (1632). With his first tutor at Cambridge, the logician William Chappell, Milton had some sort of disagreement, after which he may have been whipped. Thereafter, in the Lent term of 1626, Milton was rusticated or suspended, a circumstance to which he refers in "Elegia prima." After his return to Cambridge later that year and for the remainder of his years there he was tutored by Nathaniel Tovey. At Cambridge Milton was known as "The Lady of Christ's," to which he refers in his sixth prolusion, an oratorical performance and academic exercise that he presented in 1628. While the reasons for the sobriquet are uncertain, one suspects that Milton's appearance seemed feminine to some onlookers. In fact, this theory is supported by a portrait of Milton commissioned by his father when the future poet was ten years old. The delicate features, pink-and-white complexion, and auburn hair, not to mention the black doublet with gold braid and the collar with lace frills, project a somewhat feminine image. Another portrait, painted while he was a student at Cambridge, shows a handsome youth, appearing somewhat younger than his twenty-one years. His long hair falls to the white ruff collar that he wears over a black doublet. His dark brown hair has a reddish cast to it, and his complexion is fair. Apart from his appearance, Milton may have been called "The Lady of Christ's" because his commitment to study caused him to withdraw from the more typical male activities of athletics and socializing.

By 1632 Milton had completed a sizable body of poetry. At St. Paul's he had translated and paraphrased Psalms 114 and 136 from Greek into English. Throughout his Cambridge years he composed many of the poems in the 1645 volume: the seven Latin elegies (three verse letters, two funeral

Milton, circa 1629 (artist unknown; National Portrait Gallery, London)

tributes, a celebration of spring, and an acknowledgment of the power of Cupid), other Latin verse, seven prolusions, six or seven sonnets (some in Italian), and numerous poems in English. The works in English include "On the Morning of Christ's Nativity," "The Passion," "On Shakespeare," the Hobson poems, "L'Allegro," and "Il Penseroso."

The circumstances of composition of Milton's Nativity poem, classified as an ode, are recounted in "Elegia sexta," a verse letter written to Diodati in early 1630. To his close friend Milton confided that the poem was composed at dawn on Christmas day in December 1629. In "Elegia sexta" Milton summarizes the poem, which, he says, sings of the "heaven-descended King, the bringer of peace, and the blessed times promised in the sacred books." Likewise, the Christ child "and his stabling under a mean roof " are contrasted with the "gods that were suddenly destroyed in their own shrines" (translation by Merritt Y. Hughes). "On the Morning of Christ's Nativity" is divided into two sections, the induction and the hymn. The induction is composed of four stanzas in rime royal, a seven-line stanza of iambic pentameter; the hymn consists of twenty-seven stanzas, each eight lines long, combining features of rime royal and the Spenserian stanza.

POEMS

OF

Mr. *John Milton*,

BOTH

ENGLISH and LATIN,

Compos'd at several times.

Printed by his true Copies.

The S O N G S were set in Musick by
Mr. H E N R Y L A W E S Gentleman of
the K I N G S Chappel, and one
of His M A I E S T I E S
Private Musick.

——— *Baccare frontem*
Cingite, ne vati noceat mala lingua futuro;
Virgil, Eclog. 7.

Printed and publish'd according to
ORDER.

LONDON,
Printed by *Ruth Raworth* for *Humphrey Moseley,*
and are to be sold at the signe of the Princes
Arms in *Pauls* Church-yard. 1645.

Title page for the volume in which Milton collected his early poems,
many written before he was twenty

The poem develops thematic opposition between the pagan gods – associated with darkness, dissonance, and bestiality – and Christ – associated with light, harmony, and the union of divine and human natures.

In addition to the contrasting themes, the poem addresses two of the major paradoxes or mysteries of Christianity: the Virgin Birth and the two natures of Christ. By using oxymoron or succinct paradox – "wedded Maid, and Virgin Mother" – to describe Mary, the poet suggests the mystery of the Virgin Birth, whereby Mary retains her purity and chastity despite impregnation by the godhead. To describe the combination of two natures in Christ, the poet resorts to biblical allusion, particularly Paul's letter to the Philippians (2:6–11), which recounts how the Son emptied himself of his godhead in order to take on humanity. Paul states that the

Son having assumed the form of a servant or slave was obedient unto death on the cross. In the Nativity poem Milton indicates that the Son, while customarily enthroned "in Trinal Unity," has "laid aside" his majesty to undergo suffering. By such biblical allusion Milton interrelates the Incarnation and Redemption. Paradoxically, Milton affirms that the heroism of the Son is attributable to his voluntary humiliation, so that, in effect, his triumph over the pagan gods is anticlimactic. Significantly, in a poem about the birth of the Savior, Milton foreshadows the death of Jesus, the consummate gesture of voluntary humiliation. The manger is described as a place of self-sacrifice, where the light from the star overhead and the metaphoric reference to the fires of immolation converge: "secret altar touched with hallowed fire."

Not to be overlooked is Milton's use of mythological allusions to dramatize the effect of Christ's coming. Thus, the Christ child is characterized as triumphant over his pagan adversaries, one of whom, Typhon, is "huge ending in snaky twine." Typhon, the hundred-headed serpent and a leader of the Titans, rebelled against Zeus, who cast a thunderbolt against him. After his downfall he was incarcerated under Mount Aetna and tormented by the active volcano. Such myths were typically related to the Hebraic-Christian tradition in numerous ways: in illustrated Renaissance dictionaries and encyclopedias, editions of Ovid's *Metamorphoses,* and other lexicons known to Milton. Indeed, early biographers report that Milton himself was planning a similar compilation and interpretation of myths, though this work was never completed. Traditionally, Typhon, his revolt against Zeus, and his subsequent punishment are analogues of Satan's rivalry of the godhead, of his downfall thereafter, and of his everlasting torment in the fires of Hell. Thus, the triumph in the Nativity poem looks backward to the War in Heaven while anticipating the final conquest over Satan foretold in the Apocalypse. The appearance of Typhon as a multiheaded serpent is further correlated by Renaissance commentators with the biblical figure of Leviathan, the dragonlike monster associated with Satan in interpretations of the Hebraic and Christian scriptures. At the same time, the Christ child is likened to the infant Hercules, who overcame the serpent that attacked him in his cradle. The foregoing examples typify how Milton's erudition and literary imagination enabled him to pursue and synthesize a wide range of mythological and biblical allusions.

Illustrated Renaissance lexicons, along with manuals of painting, which guided artists and authors in the use and significance of visual details, may be employed to interpret other allegorical figures in the Nativity poem. Thus, at the birth of the Savior, the poem recounts how "meek-eyed Peace" descends, "crowned with Olive green," moved by "Turtle wing," and "waving wide her myrtle wand." Such visual details suggest the peace and harmony between the godhead and humankind when the dove returned with the olive branch after the Deluge and when the Holy Spirit, figured as a dove, descended at the baptism of the Lord.

A dominant feature of the Nativity poem is the frequent reference to pagan gods, many of whom are included in the epic catalogue in book 1 of *Paradise Lost* (1667). One such figure is Osiris, whose shrine in the Nativity poem is described: "with Timbrel'd Anthems dark / the sable-stoled Sorcerers bear his worship Ark." This description suggests a funeral procession, thereby dramatizing the causal relationship between the birth of Christ and the death of the pagan gods. Additionally, the phrase "worshipt Ark" calls attention to the ark of the Covenant, associated with the tablets of law from the Old Dispensation. Christ, however, rewrites the law in the hearts of humankind, a process to which Milton's poem alludes. The Chosen People of the Old Dispensation thus anticipate the faithful Christian community centered on Jesus. The poem presents the first such community when the holy family, shepherds, angels, and narrator unite in their adoration of the Christ child. The narrator endeavors to join his voice to the chorus of angels so that his sacred song and devotional lyrics are harmonized with theirs. He also informs us of the imminent arrival of the Magi, who will enlarge the community of worshipers and chorus of praise. Characteristically, the poem highlights unity and harmony between humankind and the godhead, earth and Heaven, the Old and New Dispensations.

What also emerges from the Nativity poem is an overriding awareness of Christian history, which is both linear and cyclical. As time unfolded, Old Testament events were fulfilled in Christ's temporal ministry. Thereafter, the faithful community looks toward the Second Coming. Along this linear disposition of time there are recurrent foreshadowings and cyclical enactments of triumphs over God's adversaries. Like the Apocalypse, the Nativity poem foresees that the ultimate defeat of Satan, having been prefigured in numerous ways, will be one of the climactic events of Christian or providential history.

Despite its early date of composition, the Nativity poem foreshadows many features of Milton's major works: the allusions to mythology and their assimilation to the Hebraic-Christian tradition, the conflict between the godhead and numerous adversaries, the emphasis on voluntary humiliation as a form of Christian heroism, the paramount importance of the redemptive ministry of the Son, and the Christian view of history.

Probably intended as a companion piece to the Nativity poem, "The Passion" was written at Easter in 1630. Only eight stanzas in rime royal were composed, presumably as the induction. Appended to the unfinished work is a note indicating that the author found the subject "to be above the years he had, when he wrote it, and nothing satisfied with what was begun, left it unfinished." The eight stanzas clarify Milton's unfulfilled intent: to dramatize more fully the humiliation of the Son, "sovereign Priest" who "Poor fleshly Tabernacle entered."

"On Shakespeare," Milton's first published poem, was composed in 1630 and printed in the Second Folio (1632) of Shakespeare's plays, where it was included with other eulogies and commendatory verses. Milton's poem, a sixteen-line epigram in heroic couplets, was included perhaps because of the intercession of his friend and eventual collaborator Henry Lawes, a musician and composer, who wrote the music for Milton's *Comus* (1637) and probably for the songs of "Arcades" in Milton's 1645 *Poems*. Milton celebrates his friend's musical talent in Sonnet XIII. Milton's poem echoes a prevalent opinion evident in other commendatory verses — that Shakespeare, the untutored genius with only a grammar-school education, was a natural poet whose "easy numbers flow" in contrast to "slow-endeavoring art." Perhaps the implied contrast is between the spontaneity of Shakespeare and the more deliberate and learned composition of Ben Jonson. The foregoing contrast is explicit in "L'Allegro," where Shakespeare's plays, the products of "fancy's child" who composes his "native Wood-notes wild," are contrasted with Jonson's "learned Sock." The reference to Jonson calls attention to the sock or low shoe worn by actors during comedy, as well as to the learned imitation of classical dramaturgy practiced by Jonson, who had a university education. Ironically, Jonson's commendatory poem on Shakespeare, included in the First Folio (1623) and republished in the folios thereafter, is the most renowned of the lot. It cites the excellence and popularity of Shakespeare as a dramatist despite his "small Latin, and less Greek," an allusion, no doubt, to his lack of education beyond grammar school. More to the point, Jonson used the metonymy of the sock to appraise Shakespearean comedy as nonpareil: "when thy socks were on / Leave thee alone." Therefore, Milton may have appropriated but adapted the allusion in order to contrast the learned and spontaneous playwrights, respectively Jonson and Shakespeare.

Central to the poem is Milton's recognition that an erected monument, possibly even the Stratford burial site with its bust of Shakespeare, is unsuitable to memorialize the playwright's unique genius. Ultimately, Milton argues that Shakespeare alone can and does create a "livelong Monument": his readers transfixed by wonder and awe. So long as his works are read, his readers will be immobilized when confronting his transcendent genius. To be sure, the inadequacy of stone or marble monuments to perpetuate one's memory is one major theme in Shakespeare's sonnets; a complementary theme is the permanence of literary art despite the mutability and upheaval in the human condition. Milton integrates both themes from Shakespeare's sonnets into his poem, perhaps to emphasize that the unique achievement of Shakespeare must be memorialized by the words and ideas of none other than the master poet and dramatist himself. Despite his admiration for Shakespeare, Milton in his prose and poetry explicitly referred to the playwright only three times: in "On Shakespeare," "L'Allegro," and *Eikonoklastes*. Despite the paucity of explicit reference, commentators have, nonetheless, sought to identify verbal parallels between the works of Shakespeare and Milton. Though such parallels or apparent echoes abound, they are inadequate to establish source or influence. Virtually identical similarities may be adduced between the works of Milton and the writings of other Elizabethans. It seems unlikely that Milton, having prepared himself to be an author of religious and biblical poetry, relied heavily on Shakespeare, whose dramatic works are vastly different in conception and subject matter.

Two of the most amusing poems of the Cambridge years were written about Thomas Hobson, the coachman who drove the circuit between London and Cambridge from 1564 until shortly before his death on 1 January 1631. Several of Milton's fellow students also wrote witty verses. In Milton's first poem, "On the University Carrier," Death is personified; his attempts to claim Hobson have been thwarted in various ways. Hobson, for instance, is described as a "shifter," one who has dodged Death. In effect, his perpetual motion made him an evasive adversary until he was forced to discontinue his trips because of the plague; then Death "got him down." The allusion is to a wrestling

match, Hobson having been overthrown. Death is personified, in turn, as a chamberlain, who perceives Hobson as having completed a day's journey. He escorts the coachman to a sleeping room, then takes away the light. The second poem, "Another on the Same," is more witty as it elaborates a series of paradoxes. Thus, "an engine moved with wheel and weight" refers at once to Hobson's coach – the means of his livelihood – and to a timepiece. The circuit of the coachman is likened to movement around the face of a timepiece, motion being equated with time. The assertion that "too much breathing put him out of breath" refers to the interruption of his travel caused by the plague. While idle, in other words, he himself took ill and died. Furthermore, the poem likens his former travel to the waxing and waning of the moon, a reciprocal course of coming and going. These playful poems that treat the topic of death may be contrasted with Milton's lamentations, such as his funeral tributes, "Elegia secunda" (Elegy II) and "Elegia tertia" (Elegy III), and the later renowned pastoral elegies: "Lycidas," which memorializes Edward King, and "Epitaphium Damonis" (Damon's Epitaph), which mourns the loss of Charles Diodati.

Probably in 1631, toward the end of his stay at Cambridge, Milton composed "L'Allegro" and "Il Penseroso," companion poems. They may have been intended as poetic versions or parodies of the prolusions, the academic exercises at Cambridge that sometimes involved oppositional thinking. Clearcut examples include Milton's Prolusion I ("Whether Day or Night Is the More Excellent") and Prolusion VII ("Learning Makes Men Happier than Does Ignorance"). The correspondences and contrasts between "L'Allegro" and "Il Penseroso" – in themes, images, structures, and even sounds – are innumerable. Essentially, Milton compares and contrasts two impulses in human nature: the active and contemplative, the social and solitary, the mirthful and melancholic, the cheerful and meditative, the erotic and Platonic. Some commentators have identified Milton with the personality type of "Il Penseroso" and Diodati with that of "L'Allegro." Though the poems anatomize each personality type and corresponding life-style apart from the other, the overall effect may be to foster the outlook that a binary unit, which achieves a wholesome interaction of opposites, is to be preferred. While it is difficult to assess the autobiographical significance of the companion poems or to develop a serious outlook when Milton himself may have composed them playfully, "L'Allegro" and "Il Penseroso" graphically demonstrate the dialectic that dis-

Manuscript for Sonnet VII, probably written in 1631 or 1632 (Trinity College Library, Cambridge, MS. R. 3. 4)

tinguishes much of Milton's poetry, particularly the dialogues and debates between different characters in various works, including the Lady and Comus in *Comus,* the younger and elder brothers in the same work, Satan and Abdiel in *Paradise Lost,* Adam and Eve, Samson and his visitors, and the Christ and the tempter in the wilderness of *Paradise Regained* (1671).

Having spent seven years at Cambridge, Milton entered into studious leisure at his parents' home in Hammersmith (1632–1635) and then at Horton (1635–1638). Perhaps he was caring for his parents in their old age because his sister and brother were unable to do so. Anne had become a widow in 1631 and had two young children. Probably in 1632 she married Thomas Agar, a widower who had one young child. Milton's younger brother, Christopher, was a student at Christ's College. The situation with his parents may explain why Milton, after Cambridge, did not accept or seek a preferment in the church. Although he may still have intended to become a minister, it seems likely that the prevailing influence of William Laud, Archbishop of Canterbury, who established and enforced ecclesiastical and religious regulations, deeply affected Milton's outlook. The most concise but cryptic explanation for his eventual rejection of the ministry as a career is provided by Milton himself, who in one of his prose treatises, *The Reason of Church-governement* (1642), comments that he was "church-outed." An undated letter to an unidentified friend, a document surviving in manuscript in the Trinity College Library at Cambridge, sheds further light on Milton's view of the ministry as a career. Some commentators speculate that Thomas Young is the addressee. Another influential factor in Milton's decision may have been his long-standing inclination to become a poet, evident in poems written in his Cambridge years and published in the 1645 edition. One of the most self-conscious, though ambiguous, statements concerning Milton's sense of vocation is Sonnet VII ("How soon hath time"). Unfortunately, it cannot be accurately dated, though 1631–1632 seems likely. In the poem he refers to the rapid passing of time toward his "three and twentieth year." His "hastening days fly on with full career," though the direction of movement, toward the ministry or poetry, goes unidentified. In any case, he contends that his process of development toward "inward ripeness" continues under the all-seeing eye of Providence.

Milton's course of study in his leisure is outlined in Prolusion VII, which was influenced by Francis Bacon's *Advancement of Learning* (1605). History, poetry, and philosophy (which included natural science) are celebrated as important to individual growth and to civic service. Milton's *Of Education* (1644), an eight-page pamphlet written in the early 1640s, elaborates on many of the ideas in Prolusion VII and cites specific authors to be read. Autobiographical statements in various forms emerge from Milton's period of private study, which enabled him to supplement extensively his education at Cambridge and to read numerous authors of different eras and various cultures. In a 23 November 1637 letter to Charles Diodati, Milton indicated the progress of his study, particularly in the field of classical and medieval history, involving the Greeks, Italians, Franks, and Germans. At this time, moreover, Milton kept two important records of his reading and writing. The "Trinity Manuscript" or "Cambridge Manuscript," so called because it is kept in the Library of Trinity College, Cambridge, includes works such as "Arcades," *Comus*, the English odes, "Lycidas," "At a Solemn Music," and other later, but short, poems. Also in the manuscript are sketchy plans and brief outlines of dramas, some of which were eventually transformed and assimilated to *Paradise Lost*. For some of the poems, the "Trinity Manuscript" includes various drafts and states of revision. The second record kept during this period is the commonplace book (now in the British Library), which lists topics under the threefold Aristotelian framework of ethics, economics, and political life, topics that aroused Milton's interest and that were later incorporated into his prose works. The entries include direct quotations or summaries, with sources cited, so that one learns not simply what books Milton read but also what editions he used.

Two important works that Milton wrote during the years of studious leisure include *A Maske Presented at Ludlow Castle* and "Lycidas." The masque was first performed on 29 September 1634, as a formal entertainment to celebrate the installation of John Egerton, Earl of Bridgewater, as lord president of Wales. The performance was held in the Great Hall of Ludlow Castle in Shropshire, close to the border of Wales. The composer of the music was Lawes, also the music tutor of the Egerton children. The three children – Alice (fifteen), John (eleven), and Thomas (nine) – enacted the parts of the Lady, the elder brother, and the younger brother. Lawes himself was the Attendant Spirit, named Thyrsis. Other characters include Comus, a tempter, by whose name the masque has been more commonly known, at least since the eighteenth century, and Sabrina, a nymph of the Severn River. Because the earl of Bridgewater had taken up his viceregal position without his family having accompanied him, a reunion was planned. To honor the earl of Bridgewater and to use the occasion of family reunion so that his children could act, sing, and dance under his approving eye are other purposes of the masque.

While *Comus* may be examined in relation to masques of the same era, most notably the collaborations of Jonson and Inigo Jones, the remoteness of Ludlow prevented Milton and Lawes from mounting the sort of spectacle with elaborate scenery, complicated machinery, and astounding special effects that Jones and Jonson produced. Nor were trained dancers and singers transported from London. Nevertheless, *Comus* does have scenery, chiefly for its allegorical significance; singing, especially by individuals, such as the Lady, Sabrina, and Thyrsis; and dancing, both the riotous antimasque of Comus and his revelers and the concluding song and dance of triumph featuring the three children and others referred to as "Country-Dancers," all under the direction of Lawes in his role as the Attendant Spirit. The three major settings of the masque are the "wild Wood" at the outset, actually a location indoors decorated with some foliage (more imaginatively depicted by vivid language); the palace of Comus, in which the tables are "spread with all dainties"; and the outdoors, near the lord president's castle and within view of the town of Ludlow. These elements of spectacle are incorporated into a plot severely limited by the circumstances of the celebration and by the fact that only six notable players, three of them children of the earl of Bridgewater, participated.

Within these limitations Milton wrote a masque – actually, it is more a dramatic entertainment – that develops the theme of temperance and its manifestation in chastity. The theme evolves against the three major settings and by reference to the character of the Lady. From the outset of the masque, the Lady is separated from her two brothers in the "wild Wood," which suggests the mazes and snares that confuse and entrap unwary humankind. Allegorically, the topography signifies the vulnerability of humankind to misdirection, the result of having pursued intemperate appetites rather than the dictates of right reason, or the consequence of having been deceived by an evil character who professes "friendly ends," the phrase used by Comus in his plans to entrap the Lady. Misled by Comus, who appears to be a "gentle Shepherd" and innocent villager, the Lady travels to his "stately Palace set out with all manner of deliciousness," where she, while "set in an enchanted chair," resists the offer to drink from the tempter's cup. Thereafter, she sits "in stony fetters fixed and motionless" though continuing to denounce the tempter and his blandishments. Despite her immobility, she affirms the "freedom of my mind." Her brothers "rush in with Swords drawn," so that Comus is put to flight; and Sabrina, "a Virgin pure" and "Goddess" of the Severn River, sprinkles drops of water on the breast of the Lady to undo the spell of the enchanter. When liberated, the Lady and her brothers "triumph in victorious dance / Over sensual folly and Intemperance."

The suspense, adventure, and dramatic rescue enhance the conflict between the tempter and his prospective victim. Typically, Milton uses classical analogues to cast light on the situation. The Lady is likened to the goddess of chastity, Diana, who frowned at suggestions of lasciviousness and whose role as huntress made her a formidable adversary, one whose virtue was militant, not passive. The Lady is also likened to Minerva, the goddess of wisdom, on whose shield is pictured one of the Gorgons, whose look would turn one to stone. By analogy, the Lady's disapproving glance casts dread into lustful men. The classical analogues of the enchanter are best explained by his parentage, Bacchus and Circe. His father is the god of wine and revelry; his mother is the sorceress who turned Ulysses' mariners into swine when they imbibed the drink that she proffered. In fact, the journey of Ulysses and the temptations encountered by him and his men provide a context in which to understand the travel of the Lady through adversity, her endeavor to withstand temptation, and the reunion that she anticipates.

These classical analogues and others like them call attention to a moral philosophy that contrasts the lower and higher natures of humankind. Degradation or sublimation, respective inclinations toward vice or virtue, are the opposite impulses adumbrated in the masque. Accordingly, Comus's followers, having yielded to the vice of intemperance, are degraded so that they appear "headed like sundry sorts of wild Beasts." They were imbruted when, "through fond intemperate thirst," they drank from Comus's cup. Their "foul disfigurement" is a defacement of the "express resemblance of the gods" in the human countenance. With his charming rod in the one hand and the glass containing the drink in the other, Comus is indeed akin to his mother, Circe. Like her, he has attracted a rout of followers, whose antimasque revelry, both in song and dance, suggests a Bacchanal, the sensualis-

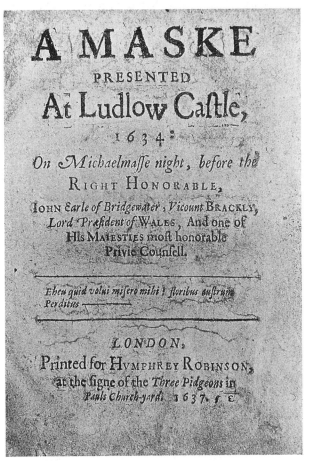

Title page for the first edition of Comus, written for performance by the three children of John Egerton, Earl of Bridgewater, and their music tutor, Henry Lawes

tic frenzy associated with his father. Before, during, and after her encounter with Comus, the Lady has a "virtuous mind," and she is accompanied by "a strong siding champion Conscience," enabling her to see "pure-eyed Faith," "white-handed Hope," and the "unblemished form of Chastity." In this series of three virtues chastity is substituted for charity, which typically appears along with faith and hope. Milton therefore suggests that chastity and charity are interrelated. Chastity is a form of self-love, not vanity but a wholesome sense of self-worth that enables one to value the spirit over the flesh and to affirm the primacy of one's higher nature. When viewed from this perspective, chastity is the necessary prerequisite to one's love of God, not to mention one's neighbor.

The moral philosophy of Comus reflects the imprint of Neoplatonism. In the Renaissance, particularly between 1450 and 1600, the works of Plato were reinterpreted and the central ideas emphasized. Beginning in Italy at the Platonic Academy of

Florence, Renaissance Neoplatonism eventually spread throughout the Continent and entered the intellectual climate of England. The Renaissance version of Platonism synthesized the ideas of Plato and Plotinus with elements of ancient mysticism, all of which were assimilated, in turn, to Christianity. The fundamental tenet of Renaissance Neoplatonism asserted by Marsilio Ficino (1433–1499), one of the foremost intellectuals of the Florentine Academy, is that "the soul is always miserable in its mortal body." The soul, having descended from the realm of light, strives to return homeward. While on earth, the soul is immersed in the darkness of the human condition and imprisoned in the human body. In effect, the soul and the body are in a state of tension, the one thriving at the other's expense. When the appetites are denied virtue prevails, and the soul is enriched. When, on the other hand, the appetites of the flesh are indulged, vice predominates, and the soul suffers. The term *psychomachia,* which means "soul struggle," designates the inner conflict that one experiences as virtue and vice contend for dominance. The foregoing paradigm is typical of certain Renaissance paintings of the fifteenth and sixteenth centuries. Several works of Perugino and Andrea Mantegna, having been influenced by Neoplatonic philosophy, depict the contention between *ratio* and *libido,* or reason and desire. These paintings show classical gods and goddesses whose allegorical significance was established. Venus and Cupid embody desire and its attendant vices; Diana and Minerva, to whom the Lady of *Comus* is likened, signify reason and its accompanying virtues.

Another tradition that may have contributed to *Comus* is the morality drama of the late Middle Ages, which uses allegorical characters to present the conflict between the virtues and vices. Furthermore, Edmund Spenser's allegorical treatment of temperance and chastity in *The Faerie Queene* (1590, 1596) is pertinent to an understanding of Milton's work. After all, Milton in *Areopagitica* refers to the "sage and serious poet Spenser," whom he calls "a better teacher than Scotus and Aquinas, describing true temperance under the person of Guyon." Much as Sir Guyon's temperance in book 2 of Spenser's epic anticipates the Lady's virtue in *Comus,* so too Britomart, the female knight in book 3, by her chastity foreshadows the Lady's heroism. While the depiction of the natural setting in *Comus,* such as the maze of woods in which the Lady is lost, resembles at times the topography in *The Faerie Queene,* both English and Continental pastoral dramas of the Renaissance also provide ana-

logues, including John Fletcher's *Faithful Shepherdess* (1610) and Torquato Tasso's *Aminta* (1573).

Within the dynamic conflict between virtues and vices, the role of reason, particularly in maintaining one's inner liberty, is crucial. If right reason, or *recta ratio,* enables one to see the light of virtue, then the Lady has a rational and imaginative vision of the Platonic ideals of faith, hope, and chastity, for which she is the earthly embodiment. But when reason is misled by the appetites, it is no longer effective. Upstart appetites gain control of a person in whom the legitimate predominance of reason has been subverted. Such a person in whom right reason no longer functions is enslaved by vice. Inward servitude having been permitted, enslavement by an external captor becomes a sign of one's loss of self-government. The congruence of inner and outer thralldom is emphasized by Milton in various works, ranging from *The Tenure of Kings and Magistrates* (1649), an antimonarchical tract in which he argues that "bad men" are "all naturally servile," to *Paradise Lost,* where in book 12 the archangel Michael explains to Adam that Nimrod has tyrannized others under the sufferance of God, who permits "outward freedom" to be enthralled as a sign and consequence that one is enslaved by "inordinate desires" and "upstart Passions," which create a condition of effeminacy. Thus, Neoplatonism may be combined with moral philosophy and Christian theology in order to contrast the rational or virtuous freedom of the Lady in *Comus* with the enslaved state of the enchanter's followers. Renaissance faculty psychology is also involved because it highlights the interaction of sensory perception, the appetites or passions, reason, and the will.

Milton himself may be used as a commentator on the contest between virtue and vice in *Comus.* His private exposition of Christian theology, *De Doctrina Christiana* (The Christian Doctrine), which was discovered in the nineteenth century and published in 1825, includes a section in which he defines and classifies virtues and vices, then cites scriptural passages, called proof-texts, to substantiate his views. Temperance is "the virtue which prescribes bounds to the desire of bodily gratification." Under it are "comprehended sobriety and chastity, modesty and decency." Chastity "consists in temperance as regards the unlawful lusts of the flesh." Opposed to chastity is effeminacy, which licenses the appetites and promotes sensual indulgence. *De Doctrina Christiana* may also be used to distinguish the two kinds of temptation at work in *Comus:* evil and good. In De Doctrina Christiana Milton explains that a temptation is evil "in respect of him who is

Tyrannus. vide. 248.

Sigerbertus West-saxonum tyrannus leges patrias conculcans, meritas luit poenas Malmesbur. l.1. 5to.

Richard the 2d. in his 21 yeare holding a violent parlament shorten'd his days. see in Sto. the violences of that parl. see other tyrannicall acts, an. 22. and of this parl. Holinsh. 490.

his definition see. de Rege out of Sr. Tho. Smith. 7. et 8. C. and Basil. distinguishes a tyrant from a K. breifly thus Τύραννός ἐστιν ὁ ἀφρόνως τυραννῶ βασιλεύς, ὅτι οὐ μετὰ τὸ ταῦτα πάντα χάριν ὀκονει, ἀλλὰ τὸ τοῖς ἀρχομένοις ὠφέλιμον ἐκποιεῖ τι. tom. 1. 456.

Tyrannicall practizes of Rich. 2. and his accomplices. see Holinsh. p. 456. an. reg. 11. 457. 458. 462. 487. see also the parl. Holinsh. 490. 493: black charters. 496. and other tyrannical actions. ibid. see also the articles against him in parliament. Holin. 502. also 508.

Aiding tyrants. the Black Prince, by aiding the cruel tyrant Peeter of Arragon Castile brought him selfe to all the mischeifs that fell on his latter days and his fathers for besides the suspicion of poyson in the voiage he brought him self into. so deep debt, beeing defrauded of his soldiers pay by yt ingratefull tyrant, that he was fain to raise that sharp taxation of fuage in Aquitain wherby he lost the country. see our writers. and spe. p. 597.

Whether it be lawfull to rise against a tyrant. Sr Thomas Smith prudently answers that the common people judge of that act according to the event, and successe, and the learned according to the purpose of the doers ez. com. wealth of Engl. C. 5.

Ludovicus pius beeing made iudge of a certain German tyrant, approves the people who had depos'd him, & sets his younger brother up in his stead. Girard. Hist. France. 14. c. 218.

Scoti proceres missis ad Elizabetha legatis post Mariam regno pulsam jure id factum multis exemplis contendunt Thuan. hist. l.58. Rich the 2d was not only depos'd by parliament, but suite made by the commons that he might have judgement decreed against him to avoid furder mischeif in the realm. Holinsh. 512.

Petrus Martyr in 3 c. Iud. eos qui potestatem superiorem eligunt certis legibus reipub. proficiunt, ut hodie electores imperii &c. licere, si princeps pactis, et promissis non steterit eum in ordinem cogere ac coadigere, ut conditiones, et pacta quae fuerat pollicitus, compleat, idque bellarmio cum aliter fieri non possit. citatque authorem Polydoru nostros homines aliquando suos reges compulisse ad rationem reddendam pecuniae administratae.

Ad un principe scelerato non é altro rimedio che'l ferro. Amori la mali via del principe basciano le pacie, nò ma a quella del principe bisogna il ferro Macchiavel discorsi c. 58.

nec imperatorem opprobriis flagitiis urgere metuunt principes Germaniae quo quidem rex quivis Europaeus regq major, imo sanctior potest esse, ut quis facinus esse putet regem justas ob causas accusationibus appetere. vide Sleidan. l. 18. 299.

Vitam principum aerumnosam, et perpetuo sollicitam, etiam eorum, qui rem prospere in superbiis, felices habent & videnti describit cominaeus testis & saepe oculatus. comines l. 8. c. 13. p. 684.

De monarchia Gallica ad tyrannidem Turcicam redigenda consilium Blesis fuisse initum a rege Car., regina matre, alijs tradit Thuanus. et ratio res ejus rei efficienda p sane commodas a Pomcero quodam explicatur narrata. Hist: l. 56. 7. p. 970.

Reges a subditis potestate exuti, aut minuti, nulla reconciliatione ne quidem juramento postea placantur. exempla recentis memoriae extant l. 71. 423.

Page from the commonplace book that Milton began circa 1635 and kept for about thirty years (British Library, Add. MS. 36354). These notes probably date from 1639 to 1641.

tempted." Having yielded to temptation, one suffers the evil effects, enslavement to upstart passions and at times external thralldom, precisely what befall the enchanter's victims in *Comus*. A good temptation, on the other hand, is directed at the righteous "for the purpose of exercising or manifesting their faith or patience," a definition that aptly pertains to the Lady in *Comus*. Biblical examples, particularly Abraham and Job, are cited in *De Doctrina Christiana*. The results of good temptation are described as "happy issue," an assertion supported by a biblical proof-text, James 1:12: "Blessed is the man that endureth temptation; for when he is tried, he shall receive the crown of life." In *Comus*, phrases such as "happy trial" and "crown of deathless praise" are succinct references to the good temptation undergone by the Lady and the heavenly reward for her Christian heroism.

When the rich and diverse contexts surrounding *Comus* are thus recognized, Milton's composition becomes more meaningful. Seemingly minor details, including references to birds, fit into the overall design. Snares are mentioned, such as "lime-twigs," which result from the application of a glutinous substance that prevents a bird from flying away. A bird thus trapped signifies a foolish person enslaved to his or her passions. The virtuous Lady, on the other hand, is described by her elder brother in another way: "She plumes her feathers, and lets grow her wings." Her freedom to elude Comus's temptations is signified by her readiness to fly. Flight also connotes her sublimated and rarefied ascent from the human condition. Other verbal images are auditory but at times may involve actual music. Comus and his followers when performing the antimasque revelry create "barbarous dissonance," whereas verbal imagery suggests that the Lady's "Saintly chastity" causes "Angels" to communicate with her: "in clear dream and solemn vision" she learns "of things that no gross ear can hear."

The characterization of the Lady as an exemplar of temperance and chastity and the definition of her Christian heroism acquire focus in two debates, one between the two brothers, the other between the Lady and Comus. The younger brother stresses the pathos of his sister's situation: she is helplessly and hopelessly lost in the woods and vulnerable to threats from beasts and mankind alike. The elder brother counters his younger brother's anxieties, arguing that their "sister is not defenceless left" but armed with "a hidden strength," chastity. In his unfolding exposition of the strength afforded by chastity, the elder brother alludes to Neoplatonism, moral philosophy, Christian theol-

ogy, faculty psychology, and the other contexts in which the Lady's defense against the wiles of Comus is more clearly understood.

In the Lady's debate with the enchanter the theoretical exposition of the elder brother is translated into action. The debate, reminiscent of Milton's prolusions at Cambridge, pits the sophistry of Comus against the Lady's enlightened reasoning, which is informed by her commitment to virtue, specifically temperance and chastity. Comus's palace, with "all manner of deliciousness" and "Tables spread with all dainties," is intended to arouse the Lady's appetites. The intricacies of the debate are manifold, but the essence of Comus's argument is simply stated: that appetites are naturally licit and innocent when gratified. Having exhibited "all the pleasures" in his palace, Comus alleges that such plenitude or bounty was provided by Nature for the use and consumption of humankind – in particular, to "sate the curious taste." The Lady, on the other hand, perceives that overindulgence or even exquisite indulgence is unnatural. To pursue one's appetites without rational self-control is to degrade human nature. Such rebuttal is accompanied by the Lady's external rejection of the "treasonous offer" of the cup, which signifies licensed passions that would overthrow the predominance of reason. As the debate intensifies, Comus resorts to a form of sophistry in which he reasons by analogy, likening the Lady's beauty to a coin or comparing her to a "neglected rose." Much as coins are to be used, so also the Lady's beauty should be put into circulation. A rose is to be admired, and the Lady likewise is to be appreciated. A corollary of Comus's argument is that the Lady's beauty, comparable to a rose, is ephemeral, an allusion to a prevalent theme – "carpe diem," or seize the day – in seventeenth-century poetry. Comus strives to engender a sense of urgency in the Lady so that she will respond affirmatively and immediately to his overture.

While Comus's sophistical arguments and the Lady's compelling counterarguments are more subtle than the foregoing account suggests, the upshot is that the Lady's virtue, right reason, and wariness enable her to affirm her "well-governed and wise appetite" while she refutes and debunks the "false rules pranked in reason's garb" and "dear Wit and gay Rhetoric" of her would-be seducer. The Lady's "freedom" of mind is manifested while she is physically restrained in the enchanted seat, where she remains immobilized even after her brothers enter with drawn swords to disperse Comus and his followers. When Sabrina, the nymph who is invoked by the Attendant Spirit, emerges from the Severn River and sprinkles drops on the breast of the Lady, the Attendant Spirit's comment – "Heaven lends us grace" – interprets Sabrina's presence and gesture as divine assistance, which may be explained theologically. In *De Doctrina Christiana* Milton comments that natural virtue is elevated to supernatural status only with an infusion of grace from above. Such, indeed, may be the case with the Lady, whose heroism is rewarded by divine approval and whose joyous reunion with her father at the end of the masque anticipates the relationship of the sanctified soul and the Lord in the heavenly hereafter.

In *Areopagitica* Milton comments that he "cannot praise a fugitive and cloistered virtue, unexercised and unbreathed, that never sallies out and sees her adversary." Rather, he extols virtue that has undergone "trial . . . by what is contrary," then triumphed. In line with this view, *Comus,* a theatrical presentation in the Marches or border region between England and Wales, may advance the Lady as an exemplar of the virtue and moral rectitude, not to mention civility, that the lord president seeks to establish in his jurisdiction. As the seat of both the council and the court of the Marches, Ludlow Castle was the central location from which administrative and judicial policy and decisions were issued. Accordingly, the corruptions among the people in the border region – drunkenness, gambling, sexual immorality, witchcraft, and occultism – may suggest the sociopolitical context in which Milton's masque was composed and the relation of the work to the local populace.

Despite the early date of composition, *Comus* is a sophisticated foreshadowing of Milton's later poetry. The contention between virtue and vice is reenacted in "Lycidas," *Paradise Lost, Samson Agonistes,* and *Paradise Regained.* Though each poem presents the archetypal conflict somewhat differently, long expositions and debates, or certainly meditations, are crucial in all the works, especially the later ones.

The second important work written during Milton's studious leisure is "Lycidas," a pastoral elegy commemorating Edward King, a fellow student of Milton's at Christ's College, Cambridge, who died on 10 August 1637 when a vessel on which he was traveling capsized in the Irish Sea. King, like Milton, was a poet who intended to enter the ministry. Milton's poem was included in a collection of thirty-five obsequies, *Justa Edouardo King* (1638), mostly in Latin but some in Greek and English. *Justa* refers to justments or the due ceremonies and rites for the dead. By writing a pastoral elegy that is heavily allegorical, Milton taps into an inveterate tradition of lament, one that dates back at least to the third century B.C., when poets in Greek Sicily, like Theocritus, Bion, and Moschus, presumably initiated the genre. From the pre-Christian era through the Renaissance in Italy, France, and England, pastoral elegies were written by notable authors, including Virgil, Petrarch, Mantuan, Baldassare Castiglione, Pierre de Ronsard, and Spenser. Of the works by these poets, the fifth and tenth eclogues of Virgil's *Bucolics* and Spenser's *Shepheardes Calender* (1579) were exceptionally influential. As the literary tradition of the pastoral elegy unfolded, certain conventions were established, creating a sense of artificiality that amuses or antagonizes, rather than edifies, some readers, including Samuel Johnson in the eighteenth century. Some of the major conventions include the lament by a shepherd for the death of a fellow shepherd, the invocation of the muse, a procession of mourners, flower symbolism, satire against certain abuses or corruptions in society and its institutions, a statement of belief in immortality, and the attribution of human emotions to Nature, which, in effect, also mourns the loss of the shepherd.

Through the use of such conventions Milton recounts his association with Edward King at Cambridge, likening himself and his friend to fellow shepherds together from early morning, through the afternoon, and into nightfall. Because of their friendship Milton, through the narrator, expresses an urgency, if not compulsion, to memorialize his friend. As a simple shepherd, he will fashion a garland of foliage and flowers to be placed at the site of burial. Allegorically, the garland signifies the flowers of rhetoric woven together into a pastoral elegy. The narrator also expresses modesty and humility concerning his talent to memorialize his friend: "with forced fingers rude" he may "shatter" the leaves of the foliage that he strives to fashion into a garland. The allegorical significance relates to the daunting challenge of crafting a pastoral elegy. The three kinds of foliage cited by the narrator – laurels, myrtles, and ivy – are evergreens, which symbolically affirm life after death. At the same time they are associated with different mythological divinities. The laurel crown of poetry was awarded by Apollo; the love of Venus was reflected in the myrtle; and Bacchus wore a garland of ivy. Signified thereby is the poetry written at Cambridge by King and Milton in imitation of classical Greek and Latin literature. Later in "Lycidas," when the narrator mentions the "oaten flute" and its "glad sound," to which "rough satyrs danced" while accompanied by "fauns with cloven heel," he is alluding to the erotic

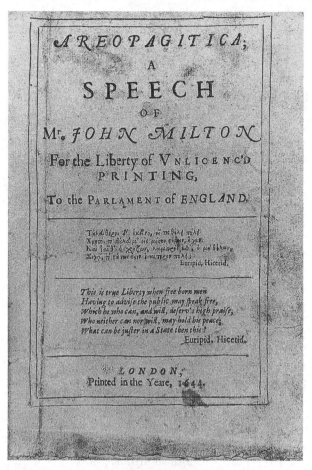

Title page for the work that Milton wrote "in order to deliver the press from the restraints with which it was encumbered"

and festive poetry, perhaps Ovidian, that King and Milton composed as students under the supervision of a tutor at Cambridge.

Despite the conventions that Milton assimilates to his poem and the artificiality of his pose as a naive shepherd, "Lycidas" is still an outlet for earnest sentiment. The poem is Milton's endeavor to write a pastoral elegy in order to test his talent, to manifest his proficiency in a genre associated with the most reputable poets, and to signal his readiness to progress to other challenges. But King, who died before he fulfilled his potential as a poet and priest, no doubt reminds Milton of his own mortality. By implication in "Lycidas" and explicitly in other poems, Milton registered concern that his unfolding career as a poet might be interrupted not only by early death but by the failure to progress in his development as a poet or because of failed inspiration. Milton, in short, may be alluding to himself when he complains that Lycidas, who equipped himself "to scorn delights, and live laborious days," died without having achieved the fame as a poet to

which he aspired. While the allusions recount King's abstemiousness and strict regimen of study, they glance, as well, at Milton's similar habits. But lament turns to bitterness, so that the narrator in the allegorical framework of the poem impugns God's justice: "the blind Fury with th'aborred shears" cuts "the thin spun life." Some critics suggest that Milton erred in his reference to the Furies, whose keen sight — they are by no means "blind" — enables them to serve as agents of divine vengeance. From this vantage point, Milton should have alluded to the Fates — Clotho, Lachesis, and Atropos — who spin the thread of life. In particular, Atropos, whose name means "inflexible," is equipped with shears to cut the thread. The more likely explanation is that Milton conflates the Furies and Fates into one allusion in order to heighten the narrator's bitterness, which emerges from his misperception that vengeance was misdirected and, therefore, that justice is blind. The narrator's bitterness is also aroused because he associates the death of Lycidas with that of Orpheus, who was dismembered by the Thracian women. The mythological figure's remains scattered on the Hebrus River and in the Aegean Sea suggest the route of King's travel from the River Deva to the Irish Sea.

Appropriately, Apollo, the classical patron of poetry who intervenes to rectify the shortsightedness of the narrator, distinguishes "broad rumor" from "fame." Although Lycidas did not achieve earthly renown through "broad rumor," he was elevated much earlier into the hereafter, where an eternal reward, "fame," will be conferred on him under the eyes of the godhead. Apollo's speech, which some critics perceive as a digression, is integral to the poem because it affirms that the godhead is both clear-sighted and just.

Balancing Apollo's commentary on the role and reward of the poet is Saint Peter's perspective on the priesthood. For Milton, King was the ideal clergyman, whose pastoral ministry would have been exemplary. King's premature death at first appears to be another example of injustice, for the corrupt clergymen and bishops of the Church of England continue to prosper. Against the clergy and most notably the bishops, Milton issues a virtual diatribe, a poetic counterpart of his enraged denunciation of them in the antiprelatical or antiepiscopal tracts. The speaker of the diatribe is "the pilot of the Galilean lake," Saint Peter. As the principal Apostle, Saint Peter is perceived, in effect, as the first bishop. As the one who wields the keys — "The golden opes, the iron shuts amain," images that signify, respectively, access to Heaven and incarceration in

Hell – Saint Peter functions as the sharp-sighted judge. Inveighing against the bishops as "Blind Mouths!," Saint Peter thus likens them to tapeworms that infest the sheep. Later they are equated with infectious diseases tainting the flock. Saint Peter's stern tone anticipates his eventual use of the "two-handed engine at the door," an instrument of divine justice that he wields in judgment against reprobates. His message, in sum, is that corrupt clergy and bishops may thrive in the present life, but justice will be exacted in the hereafter. In his prose treatises Milton uses the odious term "hireling," derived from the Gospel of John, to describe a venal clergyman. In John's Gospel the "hireling" is contrasted with the Good Shepherd, whose faithful service would have been reembodied in King.

Across the panorama of the poem, the narrator undergoes a change in outlook. At first sorrowful and depressed, he projects his mood onto the landscape. The flowers that he enumerates in a virtual catalogue manifest the human emotion of grief, as well as the ritualistic appearance and gestures of mourning – "Cowslips . . . hang the pensive head"; "every flower . . . sad embroidery wears"; and "Daffadillies fill their cups with tears." Later in the poem, when the narrator comes to recognize that Lycidas has been elevated into the heavenly hereafter, his outlook and tone change noticeably. Whereas Lycidas's "drooping head" has sunk into the waves, the narrator likens this downfall to the sunset, followed by sunrise. Lycidas, like the sun, "tricks his beams" and "flames in the forehead of the morning sky," enhanced by the sheen of the water. Both fire and water bring about baptismal cleansing so that Lycidas enters Heaven, where he "hears the unexpressive nuptial song," the intimate union of the sanctified soul and the Lord celebrated in the Book of Revelation. Like the resurrected Christ, Lycidas is finally triumphant and glorified. At the end of the poem most of the biblical allusions that celebrate joy after sorrow are from Revelation.

Despite its brevity (only 193 lines), "Lycidas" anticipates a recurrent theme in Milton's major poems: the justification of God's ways to humankind. In *Paradise Lost,* for example, the downfall of Adam and Eve and the introduction of sin and death into the human condition are interpreted from a providential perspective. From this vantage point, the deity is not vengeful but merciful, not misguided or blind but instrumental in humankind's ultimate triumph. In *Samson Agonistes* (1671), the downfall of the protagonist results in bitterness toward God. Samson, having been chosen by God to liberate the Israelites from the tyranny of

Engraving by William Marshall that was published as the frontispiece to Milton's 1645 Poems. *Milton wrote the Greek caption, which says: "That an unskillful hand had carved this print / You would say at once, seeing that living face; / But, finding here no jot of me, my friends, / Laugh at the botching artist's misattempt."*

the Philistines, is himself enslaved. By the end of the dramatic poem Samson and others who have impugned God's justice come to recognize that the "unsearchable dispose" or providential intent is very different from what they had alleged.

As a capstone to his education at Cambridge and to the years of private study, the twenty-nine-year-old Milton, with an attendant, traveled abroad for fifteen months in 1638–1639, to France but chiefly through Italy. The principal source of information about the grand tour is Milton's *Defensio Secunda.* Despite his vocal opposition to Roman Catholicism, while he was abroad Milton fraternized with numerous Catholics, including Lucas Holstenius, the Vatican librarian; presumably Cardinal Francesco Barberini; and Giovanni Battista Manso, the patron of both Giambattista Marini and Tasso. In his poem "Mansus," Milton, who recognizes the importance of patrons such as Manso, yearns for such friendship and support in order to write a poem about King Arthur. Milton did not compose an Arthuriad, probably because his concept of heroism was very different by the time that he wrote *Paradise Lost.* In Italy, moreover, Milton viewed numerous works of art that depicted biblical episodes central to his later works – *Paradise Lost, Samson Agonistes,* and *Paradise Regained.* The relationship of the works of art to the visual imagery in the major poems is the subject of much critical commentary. During his stay in Florence, Milton visited the aged and blind Galileo. Having suffered through the Inquisition, Galileo was under virtual house arrest in his later years. In *Paradise Lost* Milton refers to Galileo's telescope and to the view of the heavens that it provided. As a victim of persecution, Galileo became for Milton a symbol of the adversity that a spokesperson of the truth underwent. Also in Florence, Milton read his Italian poetry at the academies, where he elicited the plaudits of the humanists for his command of their language. Milton corresponded with his Florentine friends, such as Carlo Dati, after his return to England. Years later, Milton continued to remember his friends at the Florentine academies with intense affection. Before his departure from Italy he shipped home numerous books, including musical compositions by Claudio Monteverdi. From Venice, Milton headed to Geneva. In Italy or in Switzerland, he learned of the deaths of his sister, Anne, and of Charles Diodati. To memorialize Diodati, Milton wrote a pastoral elegy, "Epitaphium Damonis," in Latin.

After his return to England, Milton assisted in the education and upbringing of Anne's children, John and Edward Phillips. He also became embroiled in the controversies against the Church of England and the growing absolutism of Charles I. The freedom of conscience and civil liberty that he advocated in his prose tracts were pursued at a personal level in the divorce tracts. Milton married three times; none of the relationships ended in divorce. His first wife, Mary Powell, left Milton shortly after their marriage in summer 1642 in order to return to her parents. This separation evidently motivated the composition of *The Doctrine and Discipline of Divorce* (1643). By 1645 they were reunited. Mary died in 1652. His second wife, Katherine Woodcock, whom he married on 12 November 1656, died in 1658. Milton's third wife, Elizabeth Minshull, whom he married on 24 February 1663, survived him. In addition to his marital woes Milton faced the deaths of his infant son, John, in 1651 and of an infant daughter in 1658. In the same period Milton's relationship with his three daughters by Mary Powell – Anne, Mary, and Deborah, all of whom survived their father – was troublesome, especially because they did not inherit their father's interest in and aptitude for learning. Further adversity resulted from his failing eyesight and total blindness by 1652. These adversities, along with Milton's involvement in politics, may have delayed the composition of the major poetry, and *Paradise Lost, Samson Agonistes,* and *Paradise Regained* surely bear the imprint of Milton's personal experience and public service.

Milton's major work, *Paradise Lost,* was first published in ten books in 1667, then slightly revised and restructured as twelve books for the second edition in 1674, which also includes prose arguments or summaries at the outset of each book. *Paradise Lost,* almost eleven thousand lines long, was initially conceived as a drama to have been titled "Adam Unparadised," but after further deliberation Milton wrote a biblical epic that strives to "assert Eternal Providence, / And justify the ways of God to men." To vindicate Providence, Milton attempts to make its workings understandable to humankind. In accordance with epic conventions, he begins his work in medias res. An overview of major characters and their involvement in the action are the prerequisites to further critical analysis. In the first two books the aftermath of the War in Heaven is viewed, with Satan and his defeated legions of angels having been cast down into Hell, a place of incarceration where they are tormented by a tumultuous lake of liquid fire. By the end of the first book they have been revived by Satan, under whose leadership they regroup in order to pursue their war against God either by force or guile. Most of the second book depicts the convocation of the fallen angels in Hell. Rather than continue their warfare directly against God and his loyal angels, they choose to reconnoiter on the earth, the dwelling place of God's newly created human beings, whose lesser nature would make them more vulnerable to onslaught or subversion. Satan, who volunteers to scout the earth and its inhabitants, departs through the gates of Hell, which are guarded by two figures, Sin and Death. He travels through Chaos, alights on the convex exterior of the universe, then descends through an opening therein to travel to earth. While Satan is traveling, God the Father and the Son, enthroned in Heaven at the outset of book 3, oversee the progress of their adversary. Foreknowing that Adam and Eve will suffer downfall, the Father and the Son

John Milton was born the 9th of December
1608 die Veneris half an howr after 6 in the
morning
Christofer Milton was born on Friday about
a month before Christmass at 5 in the morning
1615
Edward Phillips was 15 year old August 1645
John Phillips is a year younger about Octob.

My daughter Anne was born July the 29th
on the fast at eebning about half an houre
after six 1646.
My daughter Mary was born on Wedensday
Octob. 25th on the fast day in the morning about
6 a clock 1648.
My son John was born on Sunday March the
16th about half an hower past nine at night 1650
My daughter Deborah was Born the 2d of May
Being Sunday ffomwhat before 3 of this clock in the
morning. 1652.
his my wife hir mother dyed about 3. days after. And my
son about ~6. weeks after his mother
Katherin my daughter by Katherin my second wife, was
borne y.e 19.th of October, between 5 and 6 in y.e morning
and dyed y.e 17.th of March following, 6 weeks after hir
mother, who dyed y.e 3.rd of Feb. 1657

Flyleaf in Milton's Bible, with entries in the handwriting of Milton and his amanuensis Jeremy Picard (British Library, Add. MS. 32310) discuss the conflicting claims of Justice and Mercy. The Son volunteers to become incarnate, then to undergo the further humiliation of death in order to satisfy divine justice. At the same time his self-sacrifice on behalf of humankind is a consummate act of mercy, one by which his merits through imputation will make salvation possible.

In a soliloquy at the beginning of book 4, a vestige of the dramatic origin of the epic, Satan, having arrived in the Garden of Eden, laments his downfall from Heaven and his hypocritical role in instilling false hope in his followers, whom he misleads into believing that they will ultimately triumph against God. Satan's first view of Eden and of Adam and Eve arouses his admiration, which is rapidly replaced by his malice and hate for the creator and his creatures. Overhearing the conversation of Adam and Eve, Satan learns that God has forbidden them to partake of the fruit of a certain tree in the Garden of Eden. By the end of book 4 Satan has entered the innermost bower of Adam and Eve while they are asleep. In the shape of a toad at Eve's ear, he influences her dream. When detected by the good angels entrusted with the security of Eden, Satan reacquires his angelic form, confronts Gabriel, but departs Eden. At the outset of book 5 Eve recounts her dream to Adam. In the dream Satan, who appears as a good angel, leads Eve to the interdicted tree, partakes of the fruit, and invites her to do likewise. Adam counsels Eve that her conduct in the dream is blameless because she was not alert or rational. He concludes his admonition by urging Eve to avoid such conduct when she is awake. Also in book 5 God sends the angel Raphael to visit Adam and Eve, chiefly to forewarn them that Satan is plotting their downfall. Midway through book 5, in response to a question from Adam, Raphael gives an account of the events that led to the War in Heaven.

Book 6 describes the war in detail as the rival armies of good and evil angels clash. Personal combat between Satan and certain good angels, such as Michael, is colorfully rendered, but a virtual stalemate between the armies is the occasion for intervention by the godhead. God the Father empowers the Son to drive the evil angels from Heaven. Mounting his chariot, the Son, armed with thunderbolts, accelerates toward the evil angels and discharges his weaponry. To avoid the onrushing chariot and the wrathful Son, the evil angels, in effect, leap from the precipice of Heaven and plummet into Hell. Also in response to a question from Adam, Raphael provides an account of the seven days of Creation, highlighting the role of the Son, who is em-

powered by the Father to perform the acts by which the cosmos comes into being, including the earth and its various creatures, most notably humankind. This account takes up all of book 7. In book 8 Adam recalls his first moments of consciousness after creation, his meeting with Eve, and their marriage under God's direction. Using that account as a frame of reference, Raphael admonishes Adam to maintain a relationship with Eve in which reason, not passion, prevails.

Book 9 dramatizes the downfall of Eve, then Adam. Working apart from Adam, Eve is approached by Satan, who had inhabited the form of a serpent. Led by him to the interdicted tree, Eve yields to the blandishments of the serpent and partakes of the fruit, and the serpent rapidly departs. Eve, having rejoined Adam, gives him some fruit. His emotional state affects his power of reasoning, so that he eats the fruit. Book 10 begins with the Son having descended from Heaven to judge Adam and Eve. Though they are expelled from Eden, his merciful judgment, their contrition, and the onset of grace will eventually convert sinfulness to regeneration. Satan, who retraces his earthward journey to return to Hell, encounters Sin and Death, who had followed him. He urges them to travel to the earth and to prey on humankind. For the last two books of the epic, Adam, having been escorted to a mountaintop by the angel Michael, has a vision of the future. Narrated by Michael, the vision presents biblical history of the Old and New Testaments, with emphasis on the redemptive ministry of Jesus and the availability of salvation to humankind. The vision concludes with a glimpse of the general conflagration at Doomsday, the Final Judgment, and the separation of the saved from the damned in the hereafter.

Milton's work differs significantly from the epic traditon of Greco-Roman antiquity, the Middle Ages, and the Renaissance. Earlier epics developed ideas of heroism that celebrate martial valor, intense passions such as wrath or revenge, and cunning resourcefulness. If indeed such traits of epic heroism are retained by Milton, they tend to be embodied in Satan. In other words, Milton uses the epic form simultaneously as a critique of an earlier tradition of heroism and as a means of advancing a new idea of Christian heroism for which the crucial virtues are faith, patience, and fortitude. Undoubtedly, this idea of heroism was influenced by Milton's personal experience with adversity and by his public service as a polemicist and an opponent of Stuart absolutism and the episcopacy of the Church of England. Under attack from his adver-

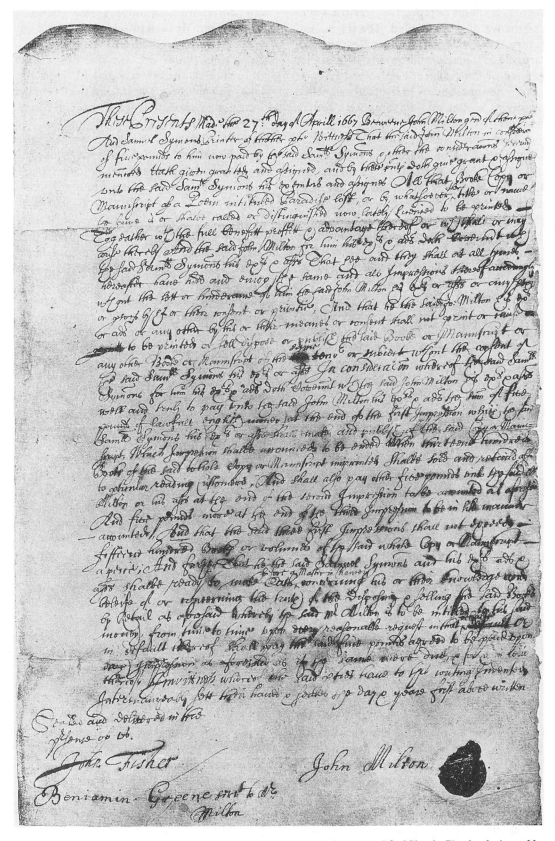

Contract between Milton and Samuel Simmons for the printing of Paradise Lost, *signed for Milton by Picard and witnessed by one John Fisher and Milton's servant Benjamin Greene (British Library, Add. MS. 5016)*

saries, Milton, from his perspective, was the advocate of a righteous cause that failed. The triumph of his adversaries, his solitude after the Restoration, and his struggle to understand how and why, under the sufferance of Providence, evil seemingly prevailed – and other questions – presumably impelled him to modify an earlier plan to compose a British epic on Arthur. At the same time, however, one may acknowledge that some traditional traits of epic heroism are embodied in characters such as the Son. Surely wrath and martial effectiveness are manifested in the War in Heaven, but Milton more emphatically affirms that the greater triumph of the Son is his voluntary humiliation on behalf of humankind. Accordingly, faith, patience, and fortitude are the crucial virtues to be exercised by the Son in his redemptive ministry, which he has agreed to undertake because of meekness, filial obedience, and boundless love for humankind.

Heroism is simply one of a series of epic conventions used but adapted by Milton. Another is the invocation of the muse, who is not precisely identified – whether the Holy Spirit or, more generally, the spirit of the godhead. At times, Milton alludes to the classical muse of epic poetry, Urania. The intent, however, is to identify her not as the source of inspiration but as a symbol or imperfect type of the Hebraic-Christian muse through which the divine word was communicated to prophets or embodied in Jesus for dissemination to humankind. A third convention is intrusion by supernatural beings, action that takes place throughout the epic – when, for example, the godhead sends Raphael to forewarn Adam and Eve of the dangers of Satan or when the Son descends to Eden as the judge of humankind after the fall. In Adam's vision of the future, the Son's role as the Incarnate Christ and the unfolding of his redemptive ministry are highlights. The descent into the underworld, a fourth epic convention, occurs in *Paradise Lost* as early as book 1, which shows the punishment of the fallen angels in Hell. A fifth convention is the interrelation of love and war. The love of Adam and Eve before and after their expulsion from Eden is central to the epic, but the self-sacrifice of the Son on behalf of fallen humankind is the most magnanimous example of love. Warfare in *Paradise Lost* is sensational when the good and evil angels clash and as the Son expels Satan and his followers from Heaven; but the epic develops another form of struggle, humankind's experience of temptation after Satan conceals his malice behind external friendliness and solicitude. Finally, the style of *Paradise Lost,* including the extended similes and catalogues, is a sixth epic convention. In book 1 Satan, who had plummeted from Heaven into Hell, is prone on the fiery lake. Across several lines, the narrator compares Satan's enormous size with that of the Titans. Later in book 1, as the fallen angels file from the burning lake, an epic catalogue is used to cite their names as false gods whose idols were worshiped in infidel cultures, particularly in Asia Minor. Both the similes and catalogues, when examined closely, provide insight into other, but related, aspects of style, such as the Latinate diction and periodic sentence structure, which when accommodated to blank verse create a majestic rhythm, a sense of grandeur, and at times sublimity.

While contributing to Milton's grand design, each book in the epic has distinctive features. The first book begins with an invocation, and three other books – three, seven, and nine – have similar openings. In all four instances the narrator invokes divine assistance or inspiration to begin or continue his epic poem. Furthermore, the invocations enable the narrator periodically to characterize himself, to announce his aspirations, and to assess his progress in composing the epic. Thus, in the invocation of book 1, the narrator pleads for inspiration comparable to what Moses experienced in his relationship with the Lord. Topography is mentioned, including Horeb and Sinai, the mountains, respectively, where God announced his presence to Moses and gave him the Commandments, and Siloa's brook, where Christ healed the blind man. By implication the narrator interrelates Hebraic-Christian landscapes with the haunts of the classical muses. With his vision thus illuminated, he hopes to describe events of biblical history. At the same time, he invites comparison with epic writers of classical antiquity; but his work, which treats the higher truth of biblical history and interpretation, will supersede theirs.

After the invocation to book 1, the narrator's description of Hell incorporates accounts of the volcanic fury of Mt. Aetna, where the leaders of the Titans, Typhon and Briareos, were incarcerated when cast down by Jove's thunderbolts. Coupled with this analogue and others, including classical descriptions of Hades, is Milton's adaptation of details from Dante's *Inferno*. When, for example, the narrator describes how the fires of Hell inflict pain but do not provide light, the allusion is to Dante. And the lines "Hope never comes / That comes to all," which describe the plight of the fallen angels, paraphrase the inscription on the gate to Hell in the *Inferno:* "Abandon all hope, ye who enter here." In reviving the fallen angels, Satan, upright and with wings outstretched over the fiery lake, resembles the dove brooding on the abyss (book 1) or the Son (book 7) standing above Chaos to utter the words that result in Creation. Satan also parodically resembles Moses, who led his followers away from the threat of destruction. His speeches instill false hope in the angels, who are gulled by his public posturing, but the narrator alerts the reader to Satan's duplicity. Privately the archfiend is in a state of despair. By the end of book 1 the fallen angels assemble in a palace called Pandemonium to deliberate on a course of action: to pursue the war against God by force or guile. As this convocation begins, Satan is not only the ruler in the underworld but its virtual deity.

Book 2 opens with Satan enthroned above the other angels. The first of the speakers to address the topic of ongoing warfare with God is Moloch, the warrior angel who urges his cohorts to ascend heavenward and to use black fire and thunder as weaponry. Despite his call to action, he recognizes that force will not prevail against God. To disrupt Heaven and to threaten its security, though not military triumphs, are nevertheless vengeful. The second speaker, Belial, debunks the argument of Moloch. Not to endure one's lot in defeat is a sign of cowardice rather than courage, Belial argues. Moreover, he says, the fiery deluge is not as tumultuous as it was immediately after the expulsion of the fallen angels from Heaven, thus suggesting that God's ire is remitting. Under these circumstances the fallen angels may become more acclimated to the underworld. By diverting attention from the stated premise of ongoing war against God and by urging the fallen angels to orient themselves toward their present habitat, Belial lays the groundwork for the third speaker, Mammon, who advocates the creation of a kingdom in Hell. To redirect the debate to its fundamental premise of ongoing war, Beelzebub, Satan's chief lieutenant, intervenes. He mocks the fallen angels, particularly Belial and Mammon, by calling them "Princes of Hell" to indicate where their attention and energies are presently focused. At the same time he knows implicitly that if Moloch, the warrior angel, despairs of military success, then no one will be eager to pursue open war against God. Accordingly, he revives Satan's earlier suggestion – that the earth and its newly created inhabitants should be assessed and then overcome by force or seduced by guile. After the hazards of travel to the newly created world are described, the fallen angels become silent until Satan agrees to undertake the mission. Seemingly voluntary, the decision is virtually constrained. Recogniz-

ing that an antagonistic relationship with God is essential to the pretense that the fallen angels are hopeful rivals, not vanquished foes, Satan revives the possibility of victory on the middle ground of earth. Having agreed to scout the earth, he emphasizes that he will travel alone. By preventing others emboldened by his lead from accompanying him, he reserves the glory for himself.

At the gates of Hell, Satan accosts Death, a wraithlike figure who challenges him. Nearby is Sin, a beautiful woman above the waist but a serpent below, tipped with a deadly sting. Her transmogrification prefigures Satan's own degradation. As an allegorical figure, she synthesizes Homer's Circe and Spenser's Error. In her appearance and interactions with Satan and Death, she dramatizes the scriptural account that uses an image of monstrous birth to describe how Sin and Death emerge from lustful urges, which include both pride and concupiscence (James 1:15). Having recalled that she emerged from Satan's forehead, an allusion to the birth of Athena from the head of Zeus, Sin incestuously consorts with the archfiend, a relationship that begets Death. What results is an infernal trinity, in which the offspring, Death, even copulates with his mother, Sin. The remainder of the book follows Satan's journey through Chaos.

The invocation of book 2, like that of book 1, is a petition by the narrator for light or illumination, so that he may report events that occur in Heaven. Having ascended from Hell, through Chaos, to the convex exterior of the universe, the blind narrator likens himself to a bird, particularly the nightingale, which sings in the midst of darkness. He mentions many of the same topographic features – the mountains and waters associated with classical and Hebraic-Christian inspiration – cited in the invocation of book 1. Building on the earlier invocation, in which he courts comparison with earlier epic authors, he acknowledges a desire for fame comparable to that of Homer and Thamyris, a blind Thracian poet. Like the blind prophets of classical antiquity, Tiresias and Phineus, the narrator affirms that his physical affliction is offset by the gift of inward illumination. As he reports the dialogue in Heaven, the narrator develops structural and thematic contrasts between books 2 and 3, not to mention differences between Satan and the Son. The infernal consult, which aimed to bring about the downfall of humankind, is balanced against the celestial dialogue, which outlines the plan of redemption. If Satan is impelled by capital sins, such as hate, envy, revenge, and vainglory, then the opposite virtues are the Son's meekness, obedience, love, and humility.

13

First Book

Hung on his shoulders like the moon whose orb
Through optick glasse the Tuscan Artist views
At evening from the top of Fesole,
290 Or in Valdarno, to descry new lands,
Rivers or Mountaines in her spotty globe.
His Speare, to equall which the tallest pine
Hewn on Norwegian hills, to be the mast
Of some great Ammirall, were but a wand,
He walkt with, to support uneasy steps
Over the burning Marle, not like those steps
On Heavens azure; and the torrid clime
Smote on him sore besides, vaulted with fire;
Nathlesse hee so endur'd, till on the beach
300 Of that inflamed sea, hee stood and calld
His legions, Angell forms, ~~that~~ who lay intranc't
Thick as Autumnall leaves that strow the brooks
In Vallombrosa, where th' Etrurian shades
High overarcht imbowre: or scatterd sedge
Afloat when with fierce winds Orion arm'd
Hath vext the red-sea coast, whose waves o'rthrew
Busiris and his Memphian chivalry
While with perfidious hatred they persu'd
The sojourners of Goshen, who beheld
310 From the safe shore their floating carcases

Page from the setting copy for the 1667 edition of Paradise Lost *(Pierpont Morgan Library), dictated by Milton to an amanuensis circa 1665*

The interaction of Justice and Mercy is also a central topic of the dialogue, which is interrupted by the Father's question: Who among the angels "will be mortal" to redeem humankind? The question and the silence that ensues are contrasted structurally and thematically with book 2, when Satan, amid the hushed fallen angels, agrees to risk the threats of Chaos to travel to earth. As the Son volunteers to die on behalf of humankind the dialogue resumes, with emphasis on the imputation of his merits and the theology of atonement. In the meantime Satan, having traveled to the opening in the cosmos, alongside the point at which the world is connected to Heaven by a golden chain, descends. He flies first to the sun, where, by posing as a lesser angel, he acquires directions from Uriel to earth, where he arrives at the top of Mount Niphates in Eden.

Book 4 begins with a soliloquy by Satan, the speech that was to have opened the drama "Adam Unparadised." At this point the so-called heroic nature of Satan as the archetypal rebel is offset by his candid awareness that downfall was caused by his own ambition; that his repentance is prevented by vainglory, which impelled him to boast to the fallen angels that they would overcome God; and that reconciliation with God, if possible, would lead inevitably to another downfall because of ambition. Satan thus becomes the prototype of the obdurate sinner. As he takes on the shapes of various animals – a cormorant, other predators, a toad, and finally a serpent – Satan's degradation contrasts markedly with his earlier vainglorious posturing. Satan observes the resemblance of Adam and Eve to their maker, assesses the complementary relationship of male and female, learns of the divine prohibition concerning the Tree of Knowledge, and overhears Eve's account of her creation, especially her attraction to her self-image reflected from the surface of a pool of water. Led from her reflected image by the voice of God, Eve encountered Adam, to whom she is wed. From the first, she acknowledges her hierarchical relationship with Adam, wherein "beauty is excelled by manly grace." Appellations that she applies to him, such as "Author" and "Disposer," reaffirm the relationship, along with her other assessments: "God is thy law, thou mine." Satan, who becomes a toad at Eve's ear, influences her dream while she and Adam are asleep in their bower of roses. He regains his shape as an angel when accosted by Gabriel and the other attendants in Eden.

When Eve at the outset of book 5 recounts her dream, it is evident that Satan has appealed to her potential for vainglory, the narcissistic inclinations toward self-love, which when magnified disproportionately would elevate her above Adam. Thus, the appellations that the tempter applies to Eve during her dream – "Angelic Eve" and "Goddess" – may engender in her the psychology of self-love and pride, precisely what brought about Satan's downfall. Much as Satan challenged his hierarchical relationship with God, so too Eve is tempted to question her subordination to Adam. Dividing Book 5 in half is the visit by Raphael, who descends to earth at the behest of God to forewarn Adam and Eve of the wiles of the tempter. In his account of hierarchy, which is a discourse on the great chain of being, Raphael emphasizes how "by gradual scale sublimed" humankind, through continuing obedience, will ascend heavenward. His discourse, an apt commentary on Eve's dream, particularly the temptation to disobedience, prepares for the account of Satan's rebelliousness, the occasion for the emergence of Sin from the archfiend. The context for Satan's rebellion is the so-called begetting of the Son, which does not refer to his origin as such but to his newly designated status as "Head" of the angels or to his first appearance in the form and nature of an angel. The latter possibility is the more likely because Satan's hate and envy would emerge from his subordination to a being like himself, at least in external appearance. Having summoned numerous angels to a location in the northern region of Heaven, ostensibly to celebrate the begetting of the Son, Satan argues that God's action is an affront to the dignity of the angels. One of the angels, Abdiel, refutes Satan's argument. He contends that the manifestation of the Son as an angel is not a humiliation of the godhead but an exaltation of the angelic nature. Such an argument anticipates the eventual Incarnation of the Son, who unites his deific nature with the human nature. In both instances, with the Son having manifested himself in lesser natures, the solicitude of the deity for angels and humankind alike is paramount.

Approximately one-third of the angels rally behind Satan, who leads them in the three-day War in Heaven, the subject of book 6. Typical epic encounters include the personal combat of Satan and Abdiel, then Satan and Michael, not to mention the large-scale clashes of angels. On the dawn of the third day, a situation that prefigures the glorification of Christ at the Resurrection, the Son as the agent of the Father's wrath speeds in his chariot toward the evil angels. His onrush, accompanied by lightning and a whirlwind, suggests the chariot of Ezekiel. Having described the wrathful godhead in the War in Heaven, Raphael balances this terrifying example by presenting a picture of the benevolent and bountiful deity in book 7. First, however, the narrator in the invocation alludes to his work's half-finished state, expressing anxiety that his inspiration may be interrupted or that his personal safety is threatened. Through the narrator, Milton perhaps alludes to his own situation at the Restoration, his intercessors presumably having negotiated an agreement that spared his life, so long as he observed certain conditions. After the invocation, book 7 includes an account of Creation, which elaborates on the catalogues of Genesis to highlight how the plenitude, continuity, and gradation are manifestations of God's benevolence. Most significant is the interactive relationship of male and female principles in Nature – for example, the sun's rays against the earth – a model for the union of Adam and Eve.

Across books 5–7, the begetting of the Son, Satan's sinfulness, the War in Heaven, and Creation are episodes that build toward a pointed commentary by Raphael on the relationship of Adam and Eve. Adam, however, first gives an account of his creation, the first moments of his consciousness, and his marriage to Eve. Whereas Eve was led shortly after her creation by the voice, not by the visible presence, of the Lord, Adam at his creation first experiences the warmth of sunlight, falls asleep, and in a dream is led by a "shape Divine" toward the summit of the Garden of Eden. When he awakens, he views among the trees his "Guide" or "Presence Divine," who speaks to Adam: "Whom thou sought'st, I am." This disclosure is comparable to what the Lord from the bush on Horeb uttered to Moses. Adam's recognition of "single imperfection" moves him to request a helpmate, who is created from his side. At once in his relationship with Eve, Adam experiences "passion" and "commotion strange," which cause Raphael to warn him not to abandon rational control. Discoursing on the hierarchy of reason and passion, the distinction between love and lust, and the scale or ladder along which humankind is to ascend heavenward, Raphael, by conflating Neoplatonic philosophy and traditional Christian theology, amplifies the context in which to understand obedience and disobedience.

The invocation of book 9 recapitulates Milton's earlier plans to write an epic on "hitherto the only argument / Heroic deemed": the exploits of "fabled knights," like Arthur. As an index of his departure from epic tradition, Milton, through his narrator, argues that "the better fortitude / Of patience and heroic martyrdom," previously "Unsung," will distinguish his work. After the invocation the narra-

tor describes how Satan, who enters as a serpent, utters a soliloquy ("O foul descent!") that laments his degradation, an outlook that contrasts with the Son's willingness to inhabit the nature and form of humankind. Because he is implementing a strategy of deception, Satan conceals his true nature behind a disguise; whereas the Son by becoming human intends to reveal and implement the divine plan of salvation.

In her first speech to Adam in book 9 Eve proposes that she and Adam "divide" their "labors" because their mutual affection has diverted them from their duties of gardening. Adam counters her proposal by affirming that he and Eve when together are "More wise, more watchful, stronger." Despite the cogency of his argument, Adam twice urges Eve to "Go," thereby forfeiting his responsibility to issue a lawful command for Eve to remain with him, a command that she would be free to obey or disobey. The topic of a lawful command recurs at the end of book 9, when during their mutual recrimination Eve faults Adam: "why didst not thou, the head, / Command me absolutely not to go . . . ?" Agreeing to reunite with Adam by noon, Eve works alone among the roses, propping up the flowers with myrtle bands. Ironically, the very duty of gardening that she performs should bring to mind her relationship with Adam, from whom she is separated. Satan is pleased to have found her alone. Eve's beauty momentarily awes Satan, who is rendered "stupidly good," a phrase suggesting that he is disarmed of his enmity. In his approach to Eve the serpent/tempter seeks to re-create in her the psychology of transcendence, which he had engendered during her dream. Feigning submissiveness and awe because of her beauty, Satan deceives Eve into believing that his power of reasoning derives from the forbidden fruit. Characterizing God as a "Threatener" and "Forbidder" who denies the fruit to others to prevent them from becoming his equals, the serpent/tempter capitalizes on Eve's unwariness, influences her perception, and thus affects her will. Having engorged the forbidden fruit, Eve for a time contemplates possible superiority over Adam; but fearful that death may overtake her and that Adam would be "wedded to another Eve," she resolves to share the fruit with him. As he was awaiting the return of Eve, Adam had fashioned a garland of roses. Astonished to learn at their reunion that Eve violated the divine prohibition, he drops the wreath, which withers. This dramatic event foreshadows the process of dying that will be introduced into the human condition as a consequence of the downfall of Adam and Eve. Whereas Eve was deceived by the tempter, Adam is "overcome with Female charm," a reaction whereby judgment gives way to passion, precisely the concern that Raphael had expressed at the end of book 8. Not unlike the phantasmic experience of Eve's dream, Adam and Eve undergo illusory ascent, then sudden decline. With the onset of concupiscence, moreover, their lustful relationship contrasts with the previous expression of love in their innermost bower. Besieged by turbulent passions, Adam and Eve become involved in mutual recrimination, each faulting the other for their downfall, both denying culpability.

At the outset of book 10 the Father sends the Son to earth as "the mild Judge and Intercessor both," as one who will temper justice with mercy. Despite the retribution meted out to Adam and Eve, the greater emphasis of the Son's ministry is to encourage an awareness of sinfulness and the onset of sorrow and contrition as steps in the process of regeneration. Satan, who has begun to return to Hell, where with the fallen angels he plans to revel in his triumph over humankind, meets Sin and Death, who traveled earthward in the wake of his earlier journey. He urges them to prey on Adam and Eve and all their progeny. Though Adam and Eve have continued their mutual recrimination, each eventually acknowledges responsibility for sinfulness. Despite their evident frailties and imperfections, Adam and Eve are neither victims nor victors. Having been created "Sufficient to have stood, though free to fall," they are endowed with the capability to withstand temptation; but when they suffer downfall, they cannot undergo regeneration without divine assistance. Their predicament, which typifies the human condition, provides the context for the Christian heroism of Milton's epic. When measured in relation to humankind, heroism is manifested as one resists temptation in the manner of the Lady of *Comus* or when one, having yielded to temptation, experiences regeneration.

Books 11 and 12 include Adam's dream vision of the future, which is narrated by the angel Michael, who presents a panoramic overview of the implementation of the divine will in human history. As Adam views Hebraic and Christian biblical history, the prophets and patriarchs of the Old Testament, such as Noah, Abraham, Isaac, Jacob, Moses, and Joshua, are presented as "shadowy Types," prefiguring the Son's incarnate ministry of redemption. Interspersed with descriptions of the Old Testament types are accounts of evildoers, such as the tyrant Nimrod. The cyclical interaction of goodness and evil, which continues under the sufferance of Providence, is the context wherein obedience and hero-

ism are manifested, for which Christ is the perfect exemplar. Indeed, the Pauline view that Jesus was obedient even unto death on the cross is the Christian heroism at the center of Adam's dream vision. In addition to its typological emphasis, the vision of human history in books 11 and 12 is also apocalyptic, with focus on the Second Coming, when the final victory over Satan will occur and the union of sanctified souls with the godhead will take place in the heavenly hereafter. More immediate for Adam and Eve, however, is their expulsion from Eden and the change in their perception of Paradise – from an external garden to "A paradise within," which results from the indwelling of the godhead in one's heart.

Because of its length, complexity, and consummate artistry, *Paradise Lost* is deemed Milton's magnum opus, the great work for which he had prepared himself since youth and toward which, in his view, the godhead guided him. As a biblical epic, *Paradise Lost* is an interpretation of Scripture: a selection of biblical events, their design and integration according to dominant spiritual themes – downfall and regeneration, the presentation of a Christ-centered view of human history, a virtual dramatization of the phenomenon of temptation to create psychological verisimilitude, and final affirmation about personal triumph over adversity and ultimate victory over evil. Imprinted in the epic are Milton's personal and political circumstances: his blindness, on the one hand, and the dissolution of the Protectorate, on the other. Thus, Milton may have identified himself with intrepid spokespersons who advocated a righteous cause despite the adversity confronting them. Such figures include Abdiel, whose "testimony of Truth" is the single refutation of Satan and the fallen angels in book 5, and Noah, the "one just man" who, while surrounded by reprobates, continues to advocate the cause of goodness. Though evil may be ascendant for a time, including the Stuart monarchy at the Restoration, goodness in the cyclical panorama of history will have its spokesperson and, ultimately, will prevail.

After *Paradise Lost* Milton's two major works are *Paradise Regained* and *Samson Agonistes,* published in the same volume in 1671. As such, the works may be perceived as complementary, if not companion, pieces on the topic of temptation. The Christ of *Paradise Regained* successfully withstands the temptations of Satan in the desert, whereas Samson, who yields to temptation earlier in his career, undergoes the cycle of spiritual regeneration. Like the Lady in *Comus,* the Christ of *Paradise Regained* heroically refutes his tempter. Like Adam in *Paradise Lost,* Sam-

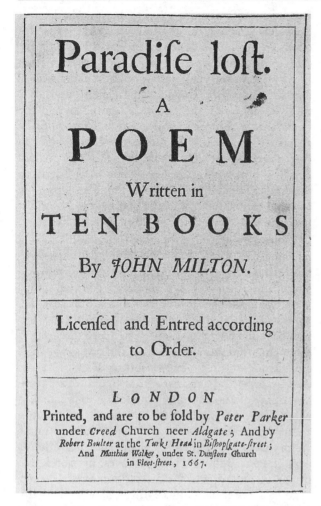

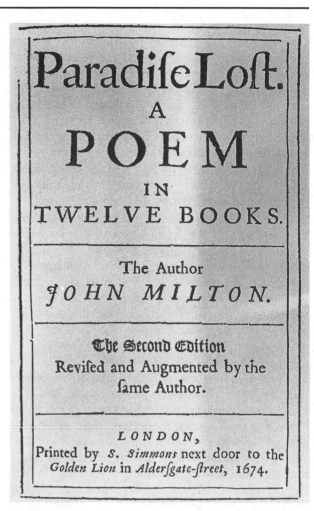

Title pages for the first and revised editions of the Christian epic in which Milton hoped to "assert Eternal Providence, / And justify the ways of God to men"

son manifests his heroism in recovery after downfall.

If *Paradise Lost* treats "man's disobedience," then *Paradise Regained* presents Christ, whose human nature is emphasized, as the example of consummate obedience. The work, approximately one-fifth the length of *Paradise Lost,* is divided into four books. In the first book, after the Holy Spirit is invoked, Satan overhears the announcement by the Father, "the great proclaimer," that Christ is his "beloved Son." At Satan's command a convocation of the fallen angels is held in "mid air," after which the tempter travels earthward to use his wiles in order to learn the identity of Christ. His fear is that Christ fulfills the prophecy that "Woman's seed" will inflict the "fatal wound" on him. Christ enters the desert, where he cogitates on the Old Testament prophecies of his coming, the earlier events of his life, and his role in the divine plan of redemption. After Christ has been in the wilderness for forty

days, the tempter, disguised as an old man, accosts him. Urging him to convert stones into bread so that the two of them can alleviate their hunger, Satan is refuted by Christ, who acknowledges that he is being tempted to "distrust" God. In book 2 the absence of Christ troubles especially his mother. Satan in the meantime has convoked the fallen spirits in order to plan a more subtle seduction, which will begin with a temptation of food, then proceed to an appeal to one's desire for "honor, glory, and popular praise." Christ, who experiences hunger, dreams of food; when he awakens, he beholds "A table richly spread." Rejecting the "guiles" of the tempter, Jesus also dismisses materialism and worldly power, symbolized by the scepter: "who reigns within himself, and rules / Passions, Desires, and Fears, is more a King."

By the third book Satan is focusing on fame and glory, but Christ rejects earthly fame as false, decrying military heroes and extolling spiritual heroism. From a high mountain Christ views ancient kingdoms, over which he could become the ruler by commanding the numberless troops that he also sees. Christ remains unmoved by "ostentation." Continuing the temptation in book 4, Satan shows Christ the Roman Empire, of which he could become the benevolent sovereign. Jesus, however, notes that "grandeur and majestic show" are transitory, whereas "there shall be no end" to his kingdom. Thereafter Satan presents him with a view of the whole world, a temptation that Jesus rejects outright. Still endeavoring to tempt Jesus with glory, Satan offers him the total learning of Greek antiquity – art, philosophy, and eloquence. By such gifts he would be equipped to rule the world. Christ dismisses Greek learning because his own direct knowledge of the Lord is the higher truth. While Jesus sleeps, Satan strives unsuccessfully to trouble him with dreams and a storm. The climax of the work occurs when Satan, having brought Christ to the pinnacle of the temple of Jerusalem, tells him to stand or to cast himself down so that angels will rescue him. Christ's rebuke causes the tempter to flee. Angels then minister to Jesus, who by resisting temptation has begun the liberation of humankind from the wiles of the devil to which Adam had succumbed.

Milton follows the order of the temptations outlined in the Gospel of Luke, rather than in Matthew. Despite the focus on the trial in the desert, Milton interrelates this experience of the Son to earlier and later biblical history. Thus, Christ meditates on the events of his childhood and youth but also remembers Old Testament biblical prophecy that anticipates the coming of the Messiah. Furthermore, God the Father announces his intention to "exercise" Christ in the desert, where "he shall first lay down the rudiments / Of his great warfare" in preparation for his conquest over "Sin and Death" at the Crucifixion and Resurrection. At the same time the patience, faith, and fortitude that Christ manifests in the desert perfect the previous exercise of similar virtues by Old Testament precursors, notably Job, who is cited by Christ in one of his refutations of Satan. From this perspective the Book of Job is another biblical source of Milton's so-called brief epic. Perhaps Milton was also modeling the trials and triumphs of Jesus after Spenser's account of Sir Guyon in book 2 of *The Faerie Queene,* where a demonic figure tests the knight with temptations of materialism, worldly power, and glory. *Christs Victorie and Triumph in Heaven and Earth* (1610) by Giles Fletcher the Younger is another model possibly adapted by Milton.

When one considers the grand scale across which the action of *Paradise Lost* takes place – in Hell, Chaos, Heaven, the Cosmos, and Earth – *Paradise Regained* seems both limited and limiting in its outlook. When one recalls the grand events of *Paradise Lost* – from the War in Heaven to the Creation – what occurs in *Paradise Regained* appears to be static. Furthermore, the dramatic elements of *Paradise Lost,* such as motives for action, suspense, and conflict, excite the reader and encourage both intellectual and psychological responses. In *Paradise Regained,* on the other hand, the tempter is doomed to failure from the start because Christ does not heed the temptations at all but rejects them outright, with little or no internal conflict. Probably Milton is depending on the contrast between Christ's wholesale dismissal of the temptations and the more engaged response by the reader, who is perhaps allured by the attractiveness of earthly glory. In his exercise of perfect obedience and of virtues such as faith, patience, and fortitude, Christ is the exemplar after whom we model our own conduct.

Though *Paradise Regained* lacks the grand and spectacular events of Milton's longer epic, its purpose is vastly different. Milton's plan is to provide a context for philosophical meditation and debate by Christ, who, at the outset of his public ministry, is being equipped for his role as the Savior. As such, Christ meditates on the significance of the two natures, divine and human, united in him. The drama of the brief epic derives in part from the tension in Christ between these two natures and the questions that emerge therefrom – how divine omniscience is balanced against human reasoning, why suffering is the prelude to triumph, and when Providence should rectify the misperceptions of the people, who expect the Messiah to be an earthly conqueror. While it is a foregone conclusion that Satan will not succeed with his wiles, the meditations of Christ and the debates with his adversary enable him to reconcile his two natures, to develop his message to the people, and to prepare for public service as a preacher and exemplar. Related to these perspectives is the tension between the ongoing relationship of Christ with the other divine persons and his disengagement from them after he becomes incarnate. Though the Father and the Spirit manifest themselves at the baptism of the Son in order to affirm his divinity in spite of his humanity, afterward the Son enters the human condition as fully as possible to enact his role as the suffering servant. This role, which becomes evident to him in the wilderness, culminates with his death on the cross.

PARADISE
REGAIN'D.
A
POEM.
In IV BOOKS.
To which is added
SAMSON AGONISTES.

The Author,
JOHN MILTON.

LONDON,
Printed by J. M. for John Starkey at the
Mitre in Fleetstreet, near Temple-Bar.
MDCLXXI.

Title page for the book that includes Milton's epic of "Recover'd Paradise to all mankind" and his attempt to write a tragedy "after the ancient manner" that incorporates the Christian concept of redemption

If suffering, temptation, and heightened self-perception are characteristic of *Paradise Regained,* they are equally significant in *Samson Agonistes,* a dramatic poem not intended for stage performance. Using the Book of Judges as his chief source, Milton refocuses the saga of Samson in order to emphasize regeneration after downfall, rather than sensational feats of physical strength. Beginning the work with Samson's degradation as a prisoner in a common workhouse in Gaza, Milton portrays a psychologically tormented character, confused about his downfall and at times antagonistic toward the godhead. Throughout the work a chorus of Danites from Samson's tribe both observe his plight and speak with him. Three successive visitors also converse with Samson: Manoa, his father; Dalila, his wife; and Harapha, a Philistine giant. In the course of these three visits Samson acquires gradual, not complete, understanding of himself and of his relationship with the godhead. With the departure of Harapha, the change in Samson is noticeable to the chorus, which praises his psychological resurgence

from a state of acute depression and his faith in the higher, though obscure, workings of Providence. The poem concludes with Samson in the theater of Dagon, collapsing its pillars of support so that the falling structure kills more of his adversaries than he has slain cumulatively in the past. He himself is killed in the process.

One of the chief ironies of Milton's rendition is that Samson, though physically strong, is spiritually weak. After he becomes a captive of the Philistines, a consequence and manifestation of his having yielded to temptation, he gradually undergoes spiritual regeneration, which culminates in his renewed role as God's faithful champion against the Philistines. Within the framework of temptation and regeneration Milton recasts the concept of heroism, debunking or at least subordinating feats of strength to the heroism of spiritual readiness, the state in which one awaits God's call to service. In line with this outlook the structure of the work and the developing characterization of Samson are discernible. At the outset Samson is tormented by the irony of his captivity. The would-be liberator is himself enslaved. He questions the prophecy to his parents that they would beget an extraordinary son "Designed for great exploits." At first Samson laments the contrast between his former, seemingly heroic, status and his present state of captivity and degradation. He and others recall his past feats: slaying a lion, dislodging and transporting the gates of Gaza, and slaughtering vast numbers of Philistines with only the jawbone of an ass.

As the poem progresses Samson's self-knowledge increases, and he comes to realize that "like a petty God" he "walked about admired of all," until "swollen with pride into the snare" he fell. This realization, as it gradually develops in Samson, is crucial to his self-knowledge and to the understanding of his relationship with God. Samson and others, such as the chorus and Manoa, have questioned, indeed impugned, Providence, likening God's justice to the wheel of fortune, which is turned blindly. They allege that God, after having chosen Samson to be his champion, inexplicably rejected him. Samson believes that he is alienated from God. As the poem unfolds it first becomes evident to the reader, rather than to the characters, that God had guided Samson into an encounter with the woman of Timna in order to warn his champion of the dangers of pride. In particular, Samson married the woman of Timna, a Philistine, who cajoled him until he disclosed the secret of a riddle that he had posed to the thirty groomsmen at his wedding. When he yields the secret of the riddle to her, she divulges it to the groomsmen. Despite God's plan to use this episode as a warning, Samson continues to be blinded by pride so that he falls into the snare of Dalila. Thus, his external blinding by the Philistines aptly signifies Samson's benighted spiritual state. In Milton's poem, moreover, Dalila is not simply a concubine, her role in Scripture, but Samson's wife. This point emphasizes the parallel between the woman of Timna and Dalila, though the essential difference is that Samson violates divine prohibition when he reveals the secret of his strength to Dalila. The marital relationship of Samson and Dalila also enables Milton to suggest contrasts with the conjugal union of Adam and Eve. Whereas Samson rejects Dalila, Adam and Eve pursue their regeneration cooperatively.

After his downfall, therefore, Samson must clarify his perception in order to begin the process of regeneration. By recognizing that pride was the cause of his downfall, Samson becomes contrite. In the course of his trials, which involve both physical affliction and psychological torment, Samson exercises patience, faith, and fortitude until he regains the state of spiritual readiness that will enable him to serve as an instrument of God. Ironically, no one, not even Samson, believes that he will again be called to service by God.

The three visitors Manoa, Dalila, and Harapha function unwittingly – another source of irony – to assist Samson in the process of regeneration. Paternal solicitude impels Manoa to negotiate with the Philistines for his son's liberation. If their desire for revenge against Samson is satisfied, Manoa believes, the Philistines may release his son. He does not recognize that enslavement by the Philistines is simply a sign of Samson's inward thralldom to sinful passions. Nor does he recognize that God's justice, rather than Philistine revenge, is to be satisfied and that Samson's suffering is both a means of divine retribution and a source of wisdom. Dalila, who seeks by various arguments to elicit Samson's forgiveness and to persuade him to be reunited with her, is rejected wholesale. In short, a measure of his progress is that Samson, who previously yielded to Dalila, resists her wiles.

Of all three visitors, Dalila is perhaps the most important because of past and present relationships with Samson. In his earlier relationship with Dalila, Samson recalls, he was "unwary" so that her "gins and toils" ensnared him. He likens her to a "bosom snake," suggesting that she had gained access to, and influence over, his innermost being. Though it has been anticipated by the woman of Timna, Samson calls Dalila's betrayal of him both "Matrimonial treason" and "wedlock-treachery." To describe his present rejection of Dalila, Samson resorts to classical allusions. He shuns her "fair enchanted cup" and remains impervious to her "warbling charms," thereby likening her to Circe and the Sirens, respectively. In his encounter with Dalila, Samson for the first time is gratified, rather than displeased, by the contrast between his past status and his present self. Another way of perceiving Samson's relationships with Dalila is by reference to Milton's *De Doctrina Christiana*. When Samson yielded to Dalila, he experienced evil temptation; as he resists her, he exercises virtue in the course of good temptation. Additionally, the rage that Dalila elicits in Samson carries over to his encounter with Harapha, who expects to see a crestfallen captive. Instead, Samson challenges the Philistine giant, who retreats.

The climax of the poem occurs when Samson, at first unwilling to attend the activities at the theater of Dagon, the Philistine idol, is impelled by "rousing motions" to go there. Initially, Samson feared that he would be publicly humiliated when performing feats of strength to entertain the Philistines; but his faith in the higher, though obscure, plan of Providence is rewarded not simply by the impulsion to attend the Dagonalia but by the inner light. "With inward eyes illuminated," Samson, who becomes aware of the divine will, exercises his volition in concert with it by collapsing the pillars that support the theater of Dagon. Significantly, Samson's death is described more as a resurrection, whereby he is likened to the phoenix that emerges from the conflagration at its funeral pyre. Finally, the fame that Samson achieves by his renewed spiritual readiness and service as God's agent transcends his previous glory from feats of strength and slaughter of the Philistines. After all, he is included among the heroes of faith celebrated in the Epistle to the Hebrews.

Not to be overlooked are the political dimensions of the poem, at times counteracting the more traditional outlook on Samson. The saga of Samson may allegorize the heroic ambitions and failings of the Puritan revolution, and his demise, rather than a sign of heroism, may be the product of self-delusion. *Samson Agonistes* may also emerge from Milton's personal and political circumstances – his blindness and his role during the rise and fall of a political movement in Britain toward which providential intent was obscure.

If Milton conceived of his dramatic poem after the manner of Greek tragedy, the resemblance is clearcut. The unities of time, place, and action are observed. The poem begins at dawn and ends at noon on the same day. The single place for the action is the workhouse, where, after the destruction of the Philistines, a messenger gives an account of the catastrophe. The action centers on Samson's spiritual regeneration, culminating in his heroism. Because of Samson's death and victory, the poem combines features of classical tragedy and Christian drama of regeneration, for which the saga of Samson is a Hebraic prefiguration. When *Paradise Lost, Paradise Regained,* and *Samson Agonistes* are juxtaposed in their probable order of composition, the threefold arrangement, a virtual triptych, depicts Old Testament types – Adam and Samson – yielding to temptation, then undergoing regeneration; Christ's triumph over the tempter is the New Testament antitype at the center.

Milton's influence in later eras derives from his prose and his poetry. His treatises against various forms of oppression and tyranny have elicited admiration in many quarters and in different eras. In fact, his influence as a political writer was felt in the American, French, and Russian revolutions,

when he was cited to justify the opposition to monarchs and absolutists. Among the English Romantics, Milton was extolled as a libertarian and political revolutionary. His refusal to compromise on matters of principle, his blindness, and his punishment after the Restoration have caused many admirers to cite Milton as a model of the spokesperson of truth and of someone who pursues idealism despite adversity.

Milton's reputation as one of the finest English poets was widespread soon after his death in 1674. While most of the critical attention was directed at *Paradise Lost,* it is essential to realize that his other works drew extensive commentary. In 1712 Joseph Addison devoted eighteen *Spectator* papers to *Paradise Lost* – six general essays and twelve others, one on each book of the epic. At times the outlook on Milton as a poet reflected the biases of the commentators. In the eighteenth century, for example, Tories and Anglicans had little admiration for him, but the Whigs were laudatory. Interestingly, *Paradise Lost* was cited for its contributions to the teaching of traditional Christianity because most interpreters were inattentive to possible implications in the epic that the Son might be subordinate to the Father. Also at the center of attention in the eighteenth century were the grandeur and sublimity of the poem. By the nineteenth century the critical outlook shifted to technical and stylistic features of the verse; but the Romantic admirers of the figure of Satan in *Paradise Lost,* including William Blake and Percy Bysshe Shelley, implicitly attacked the traditional theological and philosophical ideas in the work. Through the nineteenth and twentieth centuries Milton's reputation as a poet becomes quite complex. For a time, in fact, Milton fell into disrepute because of T. S. Eliot's adverse comments decrying the artificiality of his verse.

More recently, *Paradise Lost,* in particular, has been at the center of rich and diverse critical commentary. The theology of the epic, its indebtedness to works of classical antiquity, its adaptation of Scripture and the Genesis tradition, its Christian humanism, its political overtones, and its varied perspectives on gender relations – these and other topics are explored and debated. Even Milton's reputation as a misogynist has been challenged by feminists, who perceive tension in the Genesis tradition and in *Paradise Lost* between the orthodox hierarchical relationship of Adam and Eve and their reciprocal or complementary interaction, especially after their downfall and through their regeneration. Such commentary and the controversies that it ignites demonstrate that Milton's poetry, like his prose, has durability and applicability beyond the era in which it was composed. It is not simply of an age but for all time.

Bibliographies:

David H. Stevens, *A Reference Guide to Milton from 1800 to the Present Day* (Chicago: University of Chicago Press, 1930);

Harris F. Fletcher, *Contributions to a Milton Bibliography, 1800–1930* (Urbana: University of Illinois Press, 1931);

Calvin Huckabay, *John Milton: An Annotated Bibliography, 1929–1968,* revised edition (Pittsburgh: Duquesne University Press, 1969);

James Holly Hanford and William A. McQueen, *Milton,* second edition, Goldentree Bibliographies (Arlington Heights, Ill.: AHM, 1979);

John T. Shawcross, *Milton: A Bibliography for the Years 1624–1700* (Binghamton, N.Y.: Medieval & Renaissance Texts & Studies, 1984).

Biographies:

David Masson, *The Life of John Milton: Narrated in Connexion with the Political, Ecclesiastical, and Literary History of His Time,* 7 volumes (Cambridge & London: Macmillan, 1859–1894; volume 1 revised, 1881; index, 1894);

Helen Darbishire, ed., *The Early Lives of Milton* (London: Constable, 1932);

James Holly Hanford, *John Milton, Englishman* (New York: Crown, 1949);

Joseph Milton French, ed., *The Life Records of John Milton,* 5 volumes (New Brunswick, N.J.: Rutgers University Press, 1949–1958);

William Riley Parker, *Milton: A Biography,* 2 volumes (Oxford: Clarendon Press, 1968);

A. N. Wilson, *The Life of John Milton* (New York: Oxford University Press, 1983).

References:

Robert M. Adams, *Ikon: John Milton and the Modern Critics* (Ithaca, N.Y.: Cornell University Press, 1966);

Arthur Barker, ed., *Milton: Modern Essays in Criticism* (New York: Oxford University Press, 1965);

Joan S. Bennett, *Reviving Liberty: Radical Christian Humanism in Milton's Great Poems* (Cambridge, Mass.: Harvard University Press, 1989);

Boyd M. Berry, *Process of Speech: Puritan Religious Writing and Paradise Lost* (Baltimore: Johns Hopkins University Press, 1976);

Harry Blamires, *Milton's Creation: A Guide Through Paradise Lost* (London: Methuen, 1971);

Francis C. Blessington, *Paradise Lost and the Classical Epic* (London: Routledge, 1979);

C. M. Bowra, *From Virgil to Milton* (London: Macmillan, 1945);

John B. Broadbent, *Some Graver Subject: An Essay on Paradise Lost* (London: Schocken, 1967);

Archie Burnett, *Milton's Style* (London: Longman, 1981);

Douglas Bush, *Paradise Lost in Our Time: Some Comments* (New York: P. Smith, 1957);

Jackson I. Cope, *The Metaphoric Structure of Paradise Lost* (Baltimore: Johns Hopkins University Press, 1962);

Roy Daniells, *Milton, Mannerism, and Baroque* (Toronto: University of Toronto Press, 1963);

Dennis Danielson, ed., *The Cambridge Companion to Milton* (Cambridge: Cambridge University Press, 1989);

Helen Darbishire, *Milton's Paradise Lost* (Oxford: Clarendon Press, 1951);

Stevie Davies, *Images of Kingship in Paradise Lost* (Columbia: University of Missouri Press, 1983);

John G. Demaray, *Milton and the Masque Tradition* (Cambridge, Mass.: Harvard University Press, 1968);

Demaray, *Milton's Theatrical Epic: The Invention and Design of Paradise Lost* (Cambridge, Mass.: Harvard University Press, 1980);

John S. Diekhoff, *Milton's Paradise Lost: A Commentary on the Argument* (New York: Humanities Press, 1958);

T. S. Eliot, "Milton I," in his *On Poetry and Poets* (London: Faber & Faber, 1957);

William Empson, *Milton's God,* revised edition (London: Chatto & Windus, 1965);

J. M. Evans, *Paradise Lost and the Genesis Tradition* (London: Oxford University Press, 1968);

Anne Davidson Ferry, *Milton's Epic Voice: The Narrator in Paradise Lost* (Cambridge, Mass.: Harvard University Press, 1963);

Stanley Fish, *Surprised by Sin: The Reader in Paradise Lost* (New York: Macmillan, 1967);

Michael Fixler, *Milton and the Kingdoms of God* (Evanston, Ill.: Northwestern University Press, 1964);

Harris F. Fletcher, *The Intellectual Development of John Milton,* 2 volumes (Urbana: University of Illinois Press, 1956, 1962);

Northrop Frye, *The Return of Eden: Five Essays on Milton's Epics* (Toronto: University of Toronto Press, 1965);

Roland Mushat Frye, *Milton's Imagery and the Visual Arts: Iconographic Tradition in the Epic Poems*

(Princeton, N. J.: Princeton University Press, 1978);

Helen Gardner, *A Reading of Paradise Lost* (Oxford: Oxford University Press, 1965);

Christopher Grose, *Milton's Epic Process: Paradise Lost and Its Miltonic Background* (New Haven: Yale University Press, 1973);

Christopher Hill, *Milton and the English Revolution* (New York: Viking, 1977);

John Spencer Hill, *John Milton, Poet, Prophet, Priest* (London: Macmillan, 1979);

E. A. J. Honigmann, *Milton's Sonnets* (New York: St. Martin's, 1966);

Merritt Y. Hughes, *Ten Perspectives on Milton* (New Haven: Yale University Press, 1965);

G. K. Hunter, *Paradise Lost* (London: Allen & Unwin, 1980);

William B. Hunter, Jr., C. A. Patrides, and J. H. Adamson, *Bright Essence: Studies in Milton's Theology* (Salt Lake City: University of Utah Press, 1971);

Hunter, gen. ed., *A Milton Encyclopedia,* 9 volumes (Lewisburg, Pa.: Bucknell University Press, 1978–1983);

John R. Knott, Jr., *Milton's Pastoral Vision: An Approach to Paradise Lost* (Chicago: University of Chicago Press, 1971);

Burton O. Kurth, *Milton and Christian Heroism: Biblical Epic Themes and Forms in Seventeenth-Century England* (Hamden, Conn.: Shoe String Press, 1966);

Jon S. Lawry, *The Shadow of Heaven: Matter and Stance in Milton's Poetry* (Ithaca, N.Y.: Cornell University Press, 1968);

Edward S. Le Comte, *Milton and Sex* (New York: Columbia University Press, 1978);

J. B. Leishman, *Milton's Minor Poems* (London: Hutchinson, 1969);

Barbara Kiefer Lewalski, *Milton's Brief Epic: The Genre, Meaning, and Art of Paradise Regained* (Providence: Brown University Press, 1966);

C. S. Lewis, *A Preface to Paradise Lost,* revised edition (London & New York: Oxford University Press, 1960);

Michael Lieb, *Poetics of the Holy: A Reading of Paradise Lost* (Chapel Hill: University of North Carolina Press, 1981);

Lieb, *The Sinews of Ulysses: Form and Convention in Milton's Works* (Pittsburgh: Duquesne University Press, 1989);

Anthony Low, *The Blaze of Noon: A Reading of Samson Agonistes* (New York: Columbia University Press, 1974);

Isabel G. MacCaffrey, *Paradise Lost as Myth* (Cambridge, Mass.: Harvard University Press, 1959);

William G. Madsen, *From Shadowy Types to Truth: Studies in Milton's Symbolism* (New Haven: Yale University Press, 1968);

Louis L. Martz, *Poet of Exile: A Study of Milton's Poetry* (New Haven: Yale University Press, 1980);

Diane McColley, *Milton's Eve* (Urbana: University of Illinois Press, 1983);

Anna K. Nardo, *Milton's Sonnets and the Ideal Community* (Lincoln: University of Nebraska Press, 1979);

C. A. Patrides, *Milton and the Christian Tradition* (Oxford: Clarendon Press, 1966);

Patrides, ed., *Milton's Lycidas: The Tradition & the Poem,* second edition (Columbia: University of Missouri Press, 1983);

Elizabeth M. Pope, *Paradise Regained: The Tradition and the Poem* (Baltimore: Johns Hopkins University Press, 1947);

Mary Ann Radzinowicz, *Toward Samson Agonistes: The Growth of Milton's Mind* (Princeton, N. J.: Princeton University Press, 1978);

Balachandra Rajan, *The Lofty Rhyme: A Study of Milton's Major Poetry* (London: Routledge, 1970);

Rajan, *Paradise Lost and the Seventeenth-Century Reader* (London: Chatto & Windus, 1947);

Stella P. Revard, *The War in Heaven: Paradise Lost and the Tradition of Satan's Rebellion* (Ithaca, N.Y.: Cornell University Press, 1980);

Christopher Ricks, *Milton's Grand Style* (Oxford: Clarendon Press, 1963);

William G. Riggs, *The Christian Poet in Paradise Lost* (Berkeley: University of California Press, 1972);

Murray Roston, *Milton and the Baroque* (Pittsburgh: University of Pittsburgh Press, 1980);

John T. Shawcross, *Paradise Regain'd: Worthy T'Have Not Remain'd So Long Unsung* (Pittsburgh: Duquesne University Press, 1988);

Shawcross, *With Mortal Voice: The Creation of Paradise Lost* (Lexington: University of Kentucky Press, 1982);

Shawcross, ed., *Milton 1732–1801: The Critical Heritage* (London: Routledge, 1972);

John M. Steadman, *Epic and Tragic Structure in Paradise Lost* (Chicago: University of Chicago Press, 1976);

Steadman, *Milton and the Renaissance Hero* (Oxford: Clarendon Press, 1967);

Arnold Stein, *Answerable Style: Essays on Paradise Lost* (Seattle: University of Washington Press, 1953);

Stein, *The Art of Presence: The Poet and Paradise Lost* (Berkeley: University of California Press, 1977);

Joseph H. Summers, *The Muse's Method: An Introduction to Paradise Lost* (Cambridge, Mass.: Harvard University Press, 1962);

Edward Tayler, *Milton's Poetry: Its Development in Time* (Pittsburgh: Duquesne University Press, 1980);

James Thorpe, *John Milton: The Inner Life* (San Marino, Cal.: Huntington Library, 1983);

E. M. W. Tillyard, *Milton,* revised edition (London: Chatto & Windus, 1966);

James Grantham Turner, *One Flesh: Paradisal Marriage and Sexual Relations in the Age of Milton* (Oxford: Clarendon Press, 1987);

Rosemond Tuve, *Images and Themes in Five Poems by Milton* (Cambridge, Mass.: Harvard University Press, 1957);

A. J. A. Waldock, *Paradise Lost and Its Critics* (Cambridge: Cambridge University Press, 1947);

Joan M. Webber, *Milton and the Epic Tradition* (Seattle: University of Washington Press, 1979);

Joseph A. Wittreich, Jr., *Feminist Milton* (Ithaca, N.Y.: Cornell University Press, 1987);

Wittreich, *Visionary Poetics: Milton's Tradition and His Legacy* (San Marino, Cal.: Huntington Library, 1979);

Don M. Wolfe, *Milton in the Puritan Revolution* (New York: Humanities Press, 1963).

Papers:

Milton materials are scattered around the world, but most of the important collections of manuscripts and early printed editions are in Britain and the United States. In Britain, the important depositories are the British Library in London, the Bodleian Library in Oxford, and the Trinity College Library in Cambridge. In the United States the important depositories are the New York Public Library, the Folger Shakespeare Library, the Henry E. Huntington Library, the Yale University Libraries, the University of Kentucky Libraries, the Columbia University Library, the Union Theological Seminary Library, the University of Illinois Library, and the Princeton University Library.

John Oldham

(9 August 1653 – 5 December 1683)

Anne Barbeau Gardiner
John Jay College of Criminal Justice

BOOKS: *Upon the Marriage of the Prince of Orange with the Lady Mary* (London: Printed by T. N. for Henry Herringman, 1677);

Garnets Ghost, Addressing to the Jesuits, met in a private Caball, just after The Murther of Sir Edmund-Bury Godfrey. Written by the author of the Satyr against Virtue, (not yet Printed.) (London, 1679);

A Satyr against Vertue (London, 1679);

A Pindarick ode describing the excellency of true virtue, with reflexions on the satyr against virtue (London, 1679);

The Clarret Drinker's Song: Or, The Good Fellows Design (London, 1680);

Satyrs Upon The Jesuits: Written in the Year 1679. Upon occasion of the Plot, Together with the Satyr against Vertue, And Some other Pieces by the same Hand (London: Printed for Joseph Hindmarsh, 1681 [i.e., 1680]; second edition, revised, 1682);

Some New Pieces Never before publisht. By the author of the Satyrs upon the Jesuits (London: Printed by M. C. for Joseph Hindmarsh, 1681);

Poems, and Translations. By the Author of The Satyrs upon the Jesuits (London: Printed for Joseph Hindmarsh, 1683);

Remains of Mr. John Oldham In Verse and Prose (London: Printed for Joseph Hindmarsh, 1684);

The Works of Mr. John Oldham, Together with his Remains (London: Printed for Joseph Hindmarsh, 1684);

A Second Musical Entertainment Perform'd on St. Cecilia's day. November XXII. 1684. The Words By the late ingenious Mr. John Oldham, Author of the Satyrs against the Jesuits, & c. Set to Music in two, three, four, and five Parts, by Dr. John Blow (London: Printed by John Playford for John Carr, 1685).

Editions: *The Works of Mr. John Oldham, Together with his Remains. In Two Volumes To this Edition are added, Memoirs of his Life, and Explanatory Notes upon some obscure Passages of his Writings,* 2 volumes (London: Printed by J. Bettenham for D. Brown, B. & S. Tooke, G. Strahan, S. Ballard, W. Mears & F. Clay, 1722);

The Compositions in Prose and Verse of Mr. John Oldham. To which are added Memoirs of his Life, and Explanatory Notes upon some obscure passages of his writings, 3 volumes, edited by Edward Thompson (London: Printed for W. Flexney, 1770);

"Satyrs upon the Jesuits," in volume 2 of *Poems on Affairs of State,* edited by Elias F. Mengel, Jr. (New Haven & London: Yale University Press, 1965), pp. 17–82;

Selected Poems, edited by Ken Robinson (Newcastle upon Tyne: Bloodaxe, 1980);

The Poems of John Oldham, edited by Harold F. Brooks (Oxford: Clarendon Press, 1987).

John Oldham's poetry developed in eight years from pious panegyrics, to mock-heroic satires on libertinism and violence, to self-conscious meditations on art, to moral satires about his era. In most of these works his theme is liberty from the middle way, whether in pursuit of virtue, lust, revenge, or artistic creation. Oldham, who died at age thirty, seems forever caught like Catullus in the brashness of youth. He celebrates, whether in panegyrical or mock-heroic mode, the escape from popularity and mediocrity, from the conventional constraints on personal and artistic self-will. His fame first rested on four mock-heroic *Satyrs Upon The Jesuits* (1681) started in December 1678 at the height of the public hysteria over the pretended Popish Plot. In his lifetime they remained his claim to fame. Oldham, however, was also a scholar-poet in the line of two other scholar-poets of the seventeenth century, Ben Jonson and Abraham Cowley. Before the close of his brief life he turned Roman and French satires into well-tempered weapons against contemporary evils. Literary critics now argue that he ought to be remembered chiefly for these adaptations which inspired Augustan poets down to Alexander Pope.

John Oldham (from E. and S. Harding, The Biographical Mirror, *volume 1, 1795)*

John Oldham was born 9 August 1653 at Shipton-Moyne in Gloucestershire, where his grandfather was a clergyman. In the biographical introduction to his 1987 edition of Oldham's poems, Harold F. Brooks relates how Oldham's father, John Oldham, also a clergyman, lost his living in 1662 in nearby Newnton, Wiltshire, along with other Presbyterians ejected at the resettling of the Church of England. Educated in his father's own school and then in Tetbury for two years, Oldham proceeded to Saint Edmund Hall, Oxford, in 1670 and returned home to serve as schoolmaster in 1674 after receiving his bachelor's degree. He lived only nine more years.

Although Oldham's poems were not published in the order he wrote them, he often included a date of composition with his titles, making it possible to trace his artistic and political development. His first poems are valuable for showing him as he was before meeting the libertine circle of John Wilmot, Lord Rochester. Even making some allowance for the style of panegyric, Oldham shows early on a deep love of contemplative piety. In 1675 he wrote two elegies where he distanced himself from Puritan notions of grace by insisting that one may be miraculously preserved in large part from Original Sin. Oldham hinted at the Virgin Mary's sinless conception in "On the Death of Mrs. Katherine Kingscote," when he described his subject as a "Saint" who had "scarcely ever sully'd been / By the least Foot-steps of Original Sin." He wittily justified medieval monks for pondering about angels on a pin, for this child had crowded "so much Divinity" in her small compass that "By her we credit what the Learned tell, / That many Angels in one point can dwell." In "To the Memory of Mr. Charles Morwent," a 784-line ode about a college friend who died in August 1674, Oldham reflected on sainthood and true religion as transcending national boundaries: his friend Morwent's "Heart no Island was, disjoyn'd / (Like thy own Nation) from all human kind," but embraced "every member of the world's great Family." Although monastic life in England had ended around 1530, Oldham praised Morwent for being like "holy *Hermits*" who spend their days "twixt Extasie and Prayer." This ideal of solitary contemplation seems close to the center of Oldham throughout life. His friend's "God-like" virtues had turned Oldham into one of the "new Idolaters," that is, one who worshiped Morwent as Catholics were accused of worshiping saints.

By the summer of 1676 Oldham was assistant master at Whitgift School, Croydon. In his later "A Satyr Address'd to a Friend, that is about to leave the University, and come abroad in the World," he said teaching was slavery to him, a "Grammar-Bridewel," and wished he had a "small Estate" he could retreat to in obscure solitude. That year Oldham wrote another poem about sainthood as liberty to pursue contemplative piety. In "Presenting a book to Cosmelia," he calls his lady a living saint without any trace of Adam's Fall. Like the love that ties "Saints above" to the beatific vision, her virtue is "all free Choice" without necessity. Having escaped "uncurs'd" from the Fall, and having kept herself free of the least "stain of native Sin," she spends her days like "holy Hermits" between "Extasie, and Prayer." In these works Oldham seems like a medieval Catholic poet in love with a lady's purity. In another poem to Cosmelia, "Complaining of Absence," he is a "poor Lover militant below" enslaved by Fate, while she is triumphant, ruling destiny with God.

Oldham offered a mock-tribute to libertine freedom in July 1676, when he composed *A Satyr against Vertue* (1679), a dramatic monologue about debauchery as a form of escape from mediocrity, featuring Rochester posing as a stage atheist. A subtitle for Oldham's manuscript version of the poem alludes to an exploit of the earl of Rochester's, his "Breaking of ye Sun-Diall in ye Privy-Garden." Written in the same style and format as the *Satyrs Upon The Jesuits* and published with them late in 1680 (though it was printed separately without the author's approval in 1679), *A Satyr against Vertue* is very likely a clue to the way the speaker operates in those four satires as well. Oldham's Rochester promotes sexual freedom through a denial of immortality, contending that debauchery restores him to his first "Charter" of liberty. He curses the inventor of religion for robbing men of self-will and leaving them with guilt over their brutish lust. He also scoffs at "vile Canters," modern clergymen who trick the rabble with fear of divine punishment. How foolish were early Christians, he says, to suffer martyrdom just for the glory of being thought

saints in the church calendar. They could have enjoyed "Gospel-Freedom" (a cant phrase for alleged Puritan antinomianism) or sexual promiscuity. With this libertine mouthpiece Oldham breaks out of the middle way as in his early poems, only now he creates a saint in reverse, one who flies from ordinary, middling vice to unbounded carnality. But Oldham also evokes contemporary heroic plays, since such larger-than-life displays of limitless self-will had appeared in characters such as John Dryden's Maximin, in *Tyrannic Love* (1670). Oldham aesthetically distances his reader by this theatrical heightening.

Late in 1676 Oldham turned Psalm 137 into a Pindaric poem, revealing a fascination with unlimited self-will in revenge. The speaker of the psalm conceives of and prays for total eradication of the national enemy, including terrifying deaths of infants, virgins, and aged people, till Babylon is a heap of corpses. Oldham will direct this curse against England and place it in the mouth of *Garnets Ghost* in 1679 in the first of the Jesuit satires.

In 1677 Oldham returned to the theme of sainthood as extreme liberty from the via media in an elegy on Harman Atwood, a benefactor for the school at Croydon who died that year. Here was a lawyer nearly untainted by Original Sin who helped the poor with such "holy Prodigality" that he was present to them all as God is in the Eucharist: he could "only by diffusing greater grow" as it was "his chiefest Glory to communicate." Praising Atwood for having come to his faith not by dull inheritance but by a private journey of the soul, Oldham writes that this lawyer had "no false Religion which from Custom came, / Which to its Font and Country only ow'd its Name," but knew what and why he believed and was prepared to "out-suffer ancient Martyrology." In the same poem Oldham attacked Puritans of the Interregnum for making sullenness and anger "marks of Grace" – perhaps hinting at the source of his discomfort with that type of nonconformity.

At the other extreme from this tribute to Atwood is the Rabelaisian prose "Character of a Certain Ugly Old P[arson]," probably written around this time but printed, only after his death, in the 1684 *Remains*. This scatological piece shows Oldham's profound hostility to the Low Church party, as represented by a very old Puritan clergyman who remains within the Church of England. This parson, who torments his parish with deafening sermons given from a perch "high against a Pillar," has physical deformities of mythical proportions which are signs of his spiritual monstrosity. For example, his ears, party emblems, are big enough for "a whole Regiment of Round-Heads." His religion is so sour that his face during a sermon resembles Lodowicke Muggleton's being pilloried. Oldham even warns he should be approached with an "Exorcism," the "Parsonage House" having been "haunted since he moved there."

Late in 1677 Oldham wrote a topical poem for publication in early November, *Upon the Marriage of the Prince of Orange with the Lady Mary*. At this time James, Duke of York, and Charles II had shifted their support to the Dutch in the six-year war of Holland with France. Oldham wrote that the marriage brings to Dutch William (later William III) "far greater Conquests" than the "Pow'rs of France" have so far taken by war and slaughter. Yet Oldham gives tribute as well to the deceased queen Henrietta Maria, who bore "mighty York," Mary's "great Father." David M. Vieth contends that Oldham and his *Satyr against Vertue*, featuring Rochester, were yet unknown to the court wits, since this poem fell completely flat.

According to Vieth, Oldham would have met Lord Rochester between November 1677 and the end of 1678. There is an unverified tradition that Rochester and other wits went to the school at Croydon to see the schoolmaster-prodigy who had produced *A Satyr against Vertue*. Oldham was supposedly introduced then to the Rochester circle, known as the Guinea (Guinny) Club. Yet Oldham may well have been present on 5 August 1677, when Lord Rochester gave the speech at the club which Oldham mock-celebrated in "A Dithyrambique on Drinking." John H. O'Neill calls this poem a "mock-encomium on the rake's life," parallel to *A Satyr against Vertue*. Here Rochester, onstage and tipsy, argues that wine is the first substance, the "World's great Soul." Wine frees men from inherited religion, for it antedates the gods, having first inspired the poets to create the gods. The speaker exits "reeling," a gambit which detaches the author from blasphemy. Oldham obviously enjoys the freedom to scoff that using masks and dramatic monologues gives him. He writes scoffery in coarser language after meeting the court wits: "Upon the Author of a Play called 'Sodom,' " "Sardanapalus," and "A Satyr Upon a Woman, who by her Falshood and Scorn was the Death of my Friend." The obscene poem "Sardanapalus," O'Neill shows, is another mock-praise of libertinism, while the "Satyr upon a Woman," composed at Croydon in 1678, goes from the hieratic courtliness of his poems to Cosmelia three years before to the opposite extreme: it curses a woman with ugliness, disease, unsatisfied lust,

and damnation by "mere Necessity," and it brands womankind as the "viler Sex" that first damned men and plagues "us" still.

While still teaching at Croydon in 1678, Oldham wrote about art as his divinity in a poem on the artist's vocation. In the panegyric "Upon the Works of Ben Johnson," it is art, not sainthood or libertinism, which leads to liberty from mediocrity. Jonson gave the poets who came after him freedom to outdo the ancients because he made a "full Discovery" of art's compass; now poets may venture out on a "trackless Ocean" beyond the coasting of antiquity. "Fanaticks and Enthusiasts in Poetry" who think art is "all Revelation, Trance and Dream" are wrong, since the wise Jonson created his works consciously, with "all-seeing judgment." Here Oldham downplays inspiration, but elsewhere he admits he sometimes writes as in a trance. He is again impatient with national limits, as in his earlier ode on Morwent: he insists that Jonson's work must reach not just an English but a universal stage. He makes art divine by calling Jonson's poetry a sun not only lighting and warming God's own "Poem" – the globe – but also, after doomsday, still treading "the endless circle of Eternity." Thus, while remaining wary of "Enthusiasm" in art, a private inspiration associated with Puritans, Oldham sees the poet's calling as being intrinsically a venture into limitless freedom, beyond nature and beyond tradition or ancients.

As usual with him, he goes to the other extreme soon after, showing the absurd underside of what he has just praised to the limit. Looking at his worldly condition, Oldham reveals in July 1678 that a poetic vocation is ruining him. In "A Letter from The Country to a Friend in Town," he makes a pretended sacramental confession: his "shrifted Muse" tells his "secret sins" to this "gentle Confessor" in the hopes of getting "ghostly counsel" and an easy pardon. Oldham warns the confessor that he must give that easy pardon, since he is one who "help'd debauch" Oldham by praising his poetry. Now rhyming has become not freedom from mediocrity but personal slavery: it is a "Disease," a secret "lust," a "darling sin" obtruding even in prayer, a "barren Trade." Oldham asks why he is cursed to be a poet: has he robbed an altar, killed a priest, or raped virgins receiving the sacrament? Instead of his divinity, his muse seems now a demon out of hell. Alluding perhaps to the libertine circle of Lord Rochester, he records that "bad Company and Wine" seem to bring on a demonic possession that drives him to compose: "The Spirit, which I thought cast out before," enters with "stronger force" and "tyrannizes more." But the "Prayers of the Church can dispossess" him. Yet even here, in a passage on poetic invention, Oldham speaks lovingly of the creative process, which he represents as starting with passive contemplation. Initially he gazes at bits of light that slowly break from chaos. This process is unlike the Creation ex nihilo in Genesis, on which poets usually modeled their inventive act. Oldham waits as lights form by themselves in the void and dawn into sense; then he begins to select and form. He admits, though, that at times he is less a craftsman and more an ecstatic writing in a trance. Later, perhaps as late as 1682, Oldham again complains wryly about his vocation dooming him to poverty, this time in a monologue given by Edmund Spenser's ghost, "A Satyr . . . Dissuading the Author from the Study of Poetry, and shewing how little it is esteem'd and encourag'd in this present Age." Here Spenser seems to emerge from purgatory, looking like "some poor sinner, who by Priest had been / Under a long Lent's Penance, starv'd and whip'd." Spenser warns Oldham that no gifted poet thrives in England, for even Abraham Cowley and Samuel Butler were treated ungratefully, the rich having long since learned to admire poets instead of paying them. Better to "Preach, Plead, Cure, Fight, Game, Pimp, Beg, Cheat, or Thieve," he advises, than starve writing verse.

When the pretended Popish Plot ignited panic in the fall of 1678 — a plot Titus Oates invented about a papal army poised to take over England with the help of Jesuits and other Catholics — Oldham embarked on four satires about the Jesuits. Jesuits were the first Catholics tried, hanged, and quartered on those trumped-up charges in 1679. *Garnets Ghost* was printed in a pirated edition early in 1679, after which Oldham wrote the three other satires comprising *Satyrs Upon The Jesuits*. Politically and artistically Oldham had now traveled, like Dryden, from a Presbyterian family to a Royalist milieu. According to Brooks, Oldham wrote the last three satires in 1679 while living under the roof of the seventy-three-year-old Sir Edward Thurland, solicitor-general to the duke of York. According to the entry in the *Dictionary of National Biography,* Thurland was also known as the friend of Anglican clergymen John Evelyn and Jeremy Taylor. Oldham was supposedly tutoring Thurland's two grandsons while composing the satires. From this time all of Oldham's works were published by Joseph Hindmarsh, the duke of York's bookseller, whom Oldham, in an adaptation of an epigram by Martial, called "the noted'st TORY in the Town" and whom the Whigs refused to patronize. Hindmarsh special-

ized in those writers attacking Anthony Ashley Cooper, Lord Shaftesbury, and his Whig-Presbyterian clique in 1679–1688 — writers such as Thomas Durfey, Nahum Tate, and Thomas Otway. In 1682 Hindmarsh went so far as to publish two panegyrics celebrating the return of the duke of York from exile. In James II's reign Hindmarsh published among other things two works by Jesuit Louis Maimbourg and after 1688 promoted the nonjuring cause. Since Oldham's satires came out under his aegis, it is safe to conclude that they served the duke of York.

Published by Hindmarsh in November 1680 and in a second edition in 1682, the *Satyrs Upon The Jesuits* were framed with a prologue hinting that Oldham had donned the mask of a true-blue Whig poet. The mock-heroic monologues, which are delivered by ghostly Jesuits of the past, in one case to an audience of Jesuits executed in 1679, seem intended to deflect public hate from other Catholics — from the duke of York, the lords in the Tower, and the secular priests. Dead Jesuits make good scapegoats. Dryden spoke of Oldham in 1684 as having been a kindred soul, a Euryalus to his Nisus: "For sure our Souls were near ally'd; and thine / Cast in the same Poetick mould with mind." They two had come a long way from a Puritan background to serve the duke of York with their pens during the attempt to keep him from the throne: "One common Note on either Lyre did strike."

Read straight, as most critics have read them, the *Satyrs Upon The Jesuits* are a stream of imaginary revelations about the diabolic depths of depravity of which Jesuits are supposedly capable. But first Oldham seems to distance himself from the preposterousness of these dramatic monologues by making a frame. A Mac Flecknoe–like speaker introduces all four satires and delivers the second one in his own voice. Presumably the monstrous Jesuits come out of his admittedly poisonous pen. Oldham also distances his subject from the English by repeatedly calling Jesuits the scourge of the Huguenots, the vowed enemies of Lutherans, and the opponents of Sorbonne doctors. The Jesuit speakers of the monologues are distanced also as long-since dead. Nothing in the war on Jesuits waged by Blaise Pascal and Jansenists in France resembles Oldham's phantasmagoric work, a kind of Restoration horror movie. The one thing Oldham will not mock here is the Bible, which, in the tradition of William Chillingworth and Edward Stillingfleet, seems to be (far more than a church) the basis of what religion he has.

In the verse introduction to the four satires, the anonymous speaker vows, like Mac Flecknoe, to

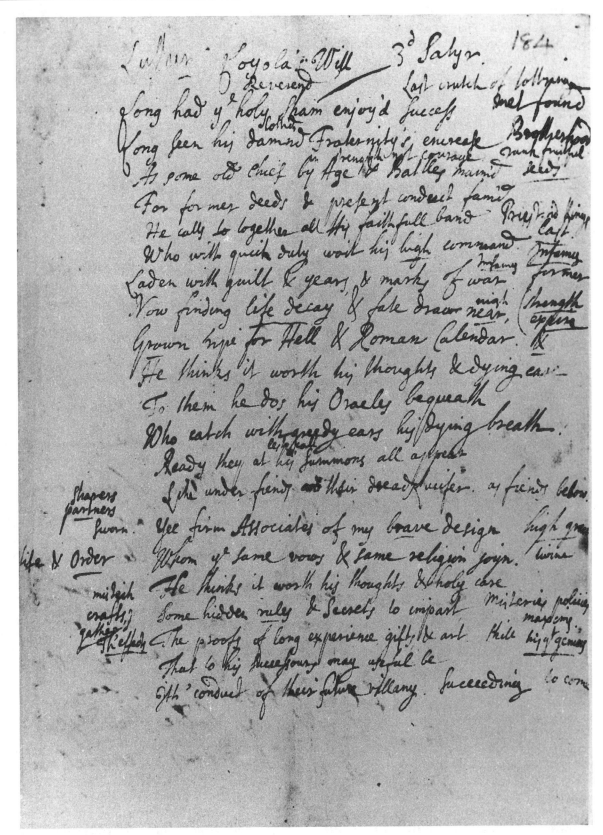

Early draft for the third of Oldham's Satyrs Upon The Jesuits, *"Loyola's Will"; from the notebook in which Oldham wrote drafts and fair copies of his poems (Bodleian Library, Oxford, MS. Rawlinson poet. 123)*

remain Hannibal-like in "endless War" against Jesuits and Rome and to use a pen envenomed with malice. Brooks relates that Oldham transcribed Dryden's *Mac Flecknoe* (1682) from a manuscript at the start of 1678. The allusions here to that mock-heroic monologue would have been recognized by the in-group of court wits who had read *Mac Flecknoe*. But Oldham reverses Dryden's order of box within box: his overall speaker is a true-blue Mac Flecknoe through whom one hears the long-gone Jesuits speaking, only Flecknoe is now divided into Garnet and Loyola. This gambit allows Oldham to be as outrageous as he had been when using Rochester as a mouthpiece. In effect he makes his poem — at least in the eye of his own circle — a self-destructing artifact. In "Satyr I, Garnet's Ghost," the wraith of Jesuit Henry Garnet, executed for supposed guilt in the Gunpowder Plot, delivers a sermon full of monstrous visions of revenge to an audience made up of the English Jesuits blamed in the Popish Plot. Garnet, just risen from hell, lauds the Jesuits for murdering Sir Edmund Berry Godfrey and tells them to go on now and kill the king. He urges them to burn London to the ground, kill members of Parliament, rip out wombs, rape virgins, and make England a pile of corpses. Here Oldham reaches for unlimited self-will in violence as he had earlier in libertinism. He has more than one target too: he slyly sends Irish Presbyterians to hell by having Garnet's ghost say he welcomed "Vast shoals" of heretics "thronging down" when Connor Lord Maguire allegedly killed Ulster Protestants in 1641.

"Satyr II" is a monologue in the voice of the Mac Flecknoe–like Whig poet of the frame. The speaker debunks the Jesuits' declarations of innocence in 1679, scaffold speeches made by those hanged and quartered. Such dying oaths cannot be trusted, he insists, because Jesuits live only for the glory of being called saints by their church, a goal which Rochester attributes to early Christians in the *Satyr against Vertue*. In this second satire the Jesuit founder, Saint Ignatius of Loyola, is misrepresented as having an unlimited appetite for cruelty: he is shown as abandoning a military career for a greater liberty to be cruel in the name of religion, preferring to undo whole realms, murder kings, and baptize myriads of pagans in their blood. The sight of Jesuits dying with false oaths in their mouths makes atheists "Firm in their Creed," the speaker wishing for an English law like the alleged Swedish one allowing the hunting and castrating of Jesuits like beavers or the bringing of their bodies in like wolves to be quartered for bounty. Here the speaker contends that unlimited savagery against Jesuits is warranted because they can be presumed guilty.

"Satyr III, or Loyola's Will" seems heavily influenced by *Mac Flecknoe*. The speaker is a Loyola decaying from wounds received in war and debauchery, like the Jesuit Flecknoe in Dryden's poem. Before sinking to hell, he gives a long speech about the unwritten rules of his order, as if Jesuits were a secret lodge of freethinkers. This satire of almost seven hundred lines is twice as long as the others but follows the same style of mock-heroic invective. For instance, the first rule of the lodge is to obey the pope blindly, even if he be an "Atheist, Heathen, *Turk,* or Jew," a "Pander, Bawd, Pimp, Pathick, Buggerer," a "Tyrant, Traitor, Pois'ner, Parricide, / Magician, Monster." The second rule is to imitate ancient Rome or Mecca and admit everyone whom gambling, drink, and lust have reduced to "Need and Popery." The third is to let young Jesuits enjoy wine and brothels to develop "well-bred Shamelessness." The fourth is to deceive audiences with tales of miracles such as apparitions of the Virgin Mary. The fifth is to instruct young Jesuits in the art of seducing women during confession by obscene questions on sexual matters. The sixth is the keep the Bible away from laymen, the seventh to prepare young Jesuits to commit regicide and start a rebellion. Finally, all Jesuits must, Hannibal-like, swear "Eternal Enmity," oddly enough, to Lutherans. Since the speaker, himself Hannibal-like, vowed eternal war with Rome in the frame of these satires, he makes the Jesuits a distorted mirror image of himself, which is precisely the Tory position in 1681 — that fanaticism is to be found in the extremes of both Catholic and Presbyterian camps.

In "Satyr IV" is a self-destructing artifact — a poem ridiculing icons uttered by a garrulous icon created by a venomous iconoclast. Oldham's speaker envisions a statue of Saint Ignatius that has watched for a century and has total recall of all the gross sins committed in front of it in the church. It is this statue, then, which mocks statues, holy water, candles, and crosses. At the climax of the poem, it mocks the Eucharist itself, at least in the Greek Orthodox, Catholic, and Lutheran sense of it, where Christ is present with the bread and wine at the altar. The conscious statue jeers, "Tis Bread you see; / *Presto be gone!* Tis now a Deity." This scoffing at the Eucharist even sinks to the scatological, as the statue-mouthpiece tracks the Communion bread from "Altar to Close Stool," and the hands of the "mighty God-maker" from the altar to a prostitute. Oldham's true-blue speaker and the garrulous sculpture are together a distorted yet revealing mirror held up to the insular iconoclasm and polemical coarseness prevalent in Restoration England. This was a time when religious statues and paintings were not allowed in the Church of England.

In the "Counterpart to the Satyr against Virtue, In Person of the Author," published with *Satyrs Upon The Jesuits* and later included in Oldham's *Remains*, is a trace of the poet's early remorse for mock-encomiums of vice. Oldham asks forgiveness of the "blest Souls" above and of souls who strive below if he disparaged virtue. Virtue makes people the "Heirs and Image of the Deity," while Vice tricks them, so that they give away jewels for glass beads, like the American Indians. In this poem Oldham ridicules the sacramental Test Act, which excluded Catholics from public office and from Parliament, saying there is finally only one true test: "That grand inevitable Test which all must bear, / Which best distinguishes the blest and wretched here."

In February 1680 Oldham wrote a paraphrase on the Hymn of Saint Ambrose, known as the *Te Deum*. Before the climax Oldham puts great stress on the fixed verticality of the spiritual order: the people of God are "vassals"; angels are of "lesser Honour" than seraphs; the sun's rays are "coarse"; the stars are garbage next to God's luster; Heaven is full of "menial Saints"; and Christ is "debas'd" to rescue man. Oldham sounds the note of groveling meniality for our human state until the liberating élan of the Incarnation:

Th'Almighty thought it no disdain
To dwell in the pure Virgin's spotless Womb,
There did the boundless Godhead and whole Heav'n
     find room,
And a small Point the Circle of Infinity contain.

With sudden ardor Oldham sees the "pure" and "spotless" Virgin's womb as fleshly but not lowly, an echo of his earlier poems on sainthood.

Eight months before the publication of the four *Satyrs Upon The Jesuits*, Oldham composed on 9 March 1680 "The Careless Good Fellow," published that year as *The Clarret Drinker's Song*. Here he reveals how cynical some Tories have become about the Popish Plot. The wine bibber is supposed to be a Tory, for court supporters in 1680 (like Cavaliers in the 1640s) were associated with wine toasts. Our "Good-Fellow" finds the "Rabble" has "run mad with Suspicions and Fears" over the plot. Even so, the Catholics hanged and quartered in the plot are not to be pitied: they were fools to be martyred for their faith in a wafer, that is, for believing in a real presence of Christ's body under the bread at mass:

What Coxcombs were those, who would barter their
     ease
And their Necks for a Toy, a thin Wafer and Mass?
At old *Tyburn* they never had needed to swing,
Had they been but true Subjects to Drink, and their
     King[.]

This tipsy Tory faults the martyrs for caring so much about religious doctrine. He himself would certainly not die for any religious profession: "No, I swear, Mr. *Fox,* pray excuse me for that." His only "Profession" is his bottle. Far from being "Careless," he is careful of his neck. Over the Catholic succession and Catholic victories abroad he thinks it not worth troubling himself. Louis XIV, the "Bully of *France,*" may go on dully cutting throats and venturing his own neck for fame, while the "Good Fellow" drinks unconcerned. Oldham hints here that the Tories knew very well that the Whigs were exploiting mass fear of the French king (from whom, Lord John Dalrymple showed in *Memoirs of Great Britain and Ireland* [1771], Whigs such as William Lord Russell and Algernon Sidney were taking bribes at this time) to weaken the monarchy. The Tories could see that the plot stories were improbable but were indifferent about the scapegoated Catholics. A year later in an adaptation of ode 14 of Horace's second book, Oldham echoes this unperturbed view of Louis XIV, stating that "the busie, restless *Monarch* of the times" keeps "a pother" merely to "fill Gazettes," and, in an adaptation of satire 9 of Horace's first book, saying that the "*French* king," who was thought to represent Catholicism, actually has no religion at all.

When Rochester died on 26 July 1680, Oldham adapted a classical elegy for him entitled "Bion." Here he uses the mask of an ancient poet so as to avoid having to flatter Rochester or his family with Christian hope. This elegy more than any other work shows Oldham's awkwardness at courtly praise. He presents Rochester as a poet from whom he had learned much of his skill, yet he ignores the satires and limits Rochester's range to love lyrics: "Love ever was the subject of his lays, / And his soft lays did *Venus* ever please." Alluding to Rochester's sexual license, he declares, "No Sheperdess" ever could "withstand" his voice, and he was dearer "to *Venus* than her *Loves.*" Oldham does not suggest this libertinism derogated from Rochester's superiority to other, mediocre human beings: "Better ten thousand meaner Swains had dy'd, / Than this best work of Nature been destroy'd." Five years earlier Oldham's elegies were contemplations of sainthood, of persons superior by their piety and almsgiving, but now in this ode superiority is based on artistic gifts. He gives no hint of salvation but uses the mask of an ancient poet to deny Rochester hope of resurrection, declaring no human being shall ever have life again except by the power of poetry. At the end of the ode Rochester is left forever to abide in the undergloom, Oldham mourning that his elegy cannot "move the rigid King of Hell." Although the "vilest Weeds" shall spring again and grow more vigorous after dying, "The great'st, the brav'st, the witti'st of mankind" will "in vain / Ever expect the dawn of Life again." This is an odd conclusion, but Dryden's elegy on Oldham in 1684 likewise ends in a descent to a classical undergloom with no hint of resurrection.

At the end of 1680, when *Satyrs Upon The Jesuits* and *Satyr against Vertue* were published together, the text of the latter was set from the pirated version of 1679. Disappointed that the satire had reappeared in mangled form, Oldham wrote a curse on his bookseller Hindmarsh, though Hindmarsh had passed the blame on to printer Mary Clark. Speaking comically as a bully who is "Fond of a quarrel," Oldham boasts his pen can still run a man through and through, for he is no "Drone" drained of his venom by the five satires just published. He curses Hindmarsh to print memoirs of criminals executed at Tyburn or to be "Compell'd by want" to "print Popery" and to end up at the pillory, there to be mauled worse than the Catholic midwife Elizabeth Cellier had been in the fall of 1680 with "Turnips," "rotten Eggs," and "filth" for publishing that year her work against Lord Shaftesbury and his party, *Malice Defeated*.

In 1681 Oldham may have tried to live briefly on his own in London, but he soon returned to private teaching for sustenance. *Some New Pieces Never before publisht. By the author of the Satyrs upon the Jesuits* appeared in the fall of 1681. In the prefatory remarks he said he had adapted Horace after a "libertine way," keeping "religiously strict" to the sense of the original but putting it in modern dress, as if Horace were living and writing now. Oldham defended his *Satyrs Upon The Jesuits* from the charge of "roughness" in the verse – a charge Dryden would echo in his elegy on Oldham. He said those shocked at his satires were "too nice and censorious" at his Juvenalian "lashing of Vice and Villany." His defen-

siveness may have been prompted in part by Sir William Soames's reproaches in the manuscript "To the Author of Sardanapalus, upon that, and his other Writings." Soames told Oldham to study the rules of his art, and so, perhaps in response, Oldham cheerfully announced that Horace's *Art of Poetry* had been imposed on him as a sort of penance. In his adaptation of Horace's work, he showed himself a modern, saying Dryden was free to introduce new words, as William Shakespeare and Ben Jonson had, for vogue was the "sole Judg and Law" of speech. He praised Charles II for bringing "back the Arts with him from Banishment" in 1660. Connecting reliance on private inspiration in poetry with Puritanism, he jeered at "wild Enthusiasts" who would turn invention to "rapture," as if "Lunacy" were a "mark of the Elect in Poetry," and commended such eloquence as that of "*Sprat,* or *Tillotson,*" rationalist Anglican preachers. Exorcising the Puritan from himself, Oldham declared he would rather compose poems that are "Fit for the learned *Bodley* to admit / Among its Sacred Monuments of Wit" than be one of those "crack-brain'd" poets damn'd to Rhime" and fit for asylum at "*Bedlam,* or *Hogsdon.*"

In this same collection of verses appeared "An imitation of Horace Book I Satire IX," written June 1681, in which Oldham hints he was under suspicion of being Catholic and had to lean over backward to deny it. Here the "bore," who is chattering about the pretended Popish Plot, insinuates that Oldham might have been "known to *Oats.*" Immediately the poet protests too much: "*I no Priest have been: / Have never* Doway *nor* St Omers *seen.*" As in the song of the drunken "Good Fellow," Oldham dismisses as utterly boring the panic fears of fire and inquisition, adding slyly that a man as poor as he is does not fear the restitution to the Catholic church of monastery lands distributed to the English gentry in the 1530s: "why should I? / I've no Estate in Abby-Lands to lose."

In this fall 1681 collection also appeared "The Praise of Homer," spoken by an idolater of Homer who rejects revealed religion. Homer is at once the Bible and Roman Catholic church, the "sole Text and holy Writ" a bard ever needs and also his "Judg infallible." Evoking Oldham's earlier mock-heroics on violence in his paraphrase of Psalm 137 and *Satyrs Upon The Jesuits,* the speaker praises Homer for inspiring the military conquest of the world: for after Alexander was through with "dull Pedants" and was filled with "lust of Honor," he turned to the writings of Homer and learned there the "Art of Reigning" and the "Art of War." Here Oldham echoes his earlier mockery of Louis XIV and of his pursuit of glory through war. Carrying aestheticism even beyond blasphemy to a new religion, Oldham's speaker adds that God never formed Homer: rather, "by chance" Nature formed a "God" in Homer, who was not blind since by him "all others see." Those ancients who raised temples to Homer were therefore justified, and even doomsday will not destroy anything in the world worth more than Homer. The poem concludes with the speaker's bewailing the insularity of the English language, wishing that English, like Greek, were a universal tongue that traveled to "every Coast of Wit." After this mock-panegyric, however, Oldham soon runs to the other extreme in "A Satyr . . . Dissuading from Poetry," probably written the next year. Now, using Spenser's ghost as a mask, he warns against idolizing Pindar, who glorifies jockeys, and Homer, who glorifies Greek bullies fighting for a whore.

In April 1682 Oldham wrote "The Thirteenth Satyr of Juvenal Imitated," a moral satire conveying his profound disgust with the perjuries abounding during the Popish Plot years. He finds only two precedents for the plot era, the age destroyed in Noah's Flood and the one ended by brimstone at Sodom. In the 1680s atheism is rampant despite the pretended religious furor: are not God and hell now mere names "Devis'd by Priests, and by none else believ'd / E're since great *Hobbes* the world has undeceiv'd?" Yet the rabble with loud cries on Queen Bess's day (an anti-Catholic holiday) demand a Pope or "*Antichrist* burnt in Effigie." Oldham cuts through the argument about whether Norman kings had encroached on Saxon liberties by saying that England went downhill ever since the Saxon invasion, when "mingling with corrupted forein Seed, / We learnt their Vice, and spoil'd our native Breed." The poet here identifies with ancient Britons who were part of the larger Roman world. In this clever application of Juvenal's satire, he seems to target mainly Whigs for the perjuries of the plot era. Like Dryden he scores the Shaftesbury camp for Epicurean views, which allow them to take false oaths with imagined impunity. Some disavow "all Providence" and calmly take false oaths, while others still own a God but fear poverty much more than his vengeance. The perjurers – evidently in the Whig camp – pass for innocent "with the Rabble," while the truly innocent lose their faith and blaspheme, asking why anyone should believe priests "if this be Providence." But Oldham tries to spread the blame a bit, too, and hints that perjuries must have occurred on the Catholic side since there

were oaths to make the plot "nothing," and he still thinks there was some grain of truth in Oates's accusations. He takes the Tory line that both extreme Presbyterians and Catholics are capable of regicide, but he names John Bradshaw, chief of the Protestant judges who condemned Charles I to death, and François Ravailliac, the lone Catholic assassin of Henry IV of France: not all "that *Fox* his Bloody Records tell, / Can match what *Bradshaw* and *Ravilliac* feel." The English should not seek revenge but imitate "mild good *Socrates*" and "good *Martyr'd King*" Charles I. "Sound Divinity and Sense" teach that wicked rebels and murderers carry a hell within their breast and that God is just and all-seeing.

This serene conclusion does not lead one to expect the next piece, "A Satyr, In Imitation of the Third of Juvenal," written a month later in May 1682. Here Oldham adapts Juvenal's satire on Greek immigrants into a hundred-line satire on Huguenot immigrants. Following the new oppression of the Huguenots starting in 1681, a flood of Huguenot immigrants sharing the politics of English Puritans (and swelling that anti-Stuart camp) arrived in England. By refusing to consider the religion of the French arrivals, Oldham's speaker Timon chooses to see them merely as outlaws and/or economic refugees. Timon laments that London is the sewer where France pours out her "Filthe and Ordure." Their very mode of arrival is against the law: they disembark with shiploads of "prohibited Goods" and sexual aids from France. Having been "Slaves at home," these immigrants quickly rise by sycophancy to "Lord it" over the native English. They come straight out of French jails to the English court or to houses where they "wriggle into Great Mens Service" and worm out secrets for blackmail. These "true-born Slaves" start by "wiping Shoes" and become "Masters of the House," reducing the English under them to be the slaves of slaves. When Timon ends his tirade, he explains he is not of the "Silk-Weavers Mutiny," alluding to English workers hostile to the Huguenot migrant weavers. This poem also echoes previous laments by Oldham on his poverty: Timon complains how badly a poor man is treated in London churches, where he is not even allowed to enter a pew reserved for his supposed betters "*Gripe* and *Cheatwel*," obviously Whig merchants of Puritan background attending the services of the national church merely to fulfill the law. Oldham also alludes here to a storm that accompanied Oliver Cromwell's death as a wind that "blew old Noll to Hell," giving still another jab at Puritans, native as well as foreign.

In October 1682 Oldham adapted Nicolas Boileau's eighth satire but added lines that would have offended French Catholics, lines mocking the worship of the real presence of Christ's body under the symbol of the sacrament: "And now each day in every street abroad / Sees prostrate Fools adore a breaden God." Like the latitudinarian divine he calls "great *Stillingfleet*" here, Oldham compares Catholic worship of Christ in the Eucharist with ancient Egyptian worship of a baboon and a crocodile. This attack refers not to the sacrament during mass but during procession, carried in a monstrance, a favorite target of iconoclasts. Yet when examples of learned doctors are adduced in this satire, two Jesuits – Saint Robert Bellarmine and Richard Simon, the biblical critic – come to Oldham's mind.

Constitutionally unable to praise living men so as to win a patron and survive by his pen in London, Oldham returned in 1682 to teaching the eldest son of Sir William Hickes of Rookwood, in Low Leyton, Essex. At this time he studied medicine with Richard Lower. Declining to go with Hickes on a grand tour, Oldham found a patron or pupil around June 1682 in William Pierrepont, Baron of Kingston-upon-Hull. Pierrepont was only twenty-one years old when Oldham died at age thirty of smallpox at his home on 5 December 1683. One of Oldham's undated works that might possibly come from his last period is "Sunday Thought in Sickness," where he laments having made his talents the "Patrons of Debauchery."

In the weeks before his death in 1683, Oldham composed "An Ode For an Anniversary of Musick on S. Cecilia's Day," performed a year later in 1684. This libretto was published in *A Second Musical Entertainment* in 1685. Since the annual gala honoring music began on 22 November 1683, two weeks before Oldham's death, it seems he was invited the first year to contribute something to the feast of the virgin-martyr. The feast of music was probably meant to displace the November parade for Queen Bess usually put on by the Whigs, who were now disgraced by the Rye House Plot disclosures of June 1683 (this plot was a conspiracy to assassinate Charles II and the duke of York). Oldham's tribute to Saint Cecilia shows art in harmony with revealed religion, a far cry from the "Praise of Homer" of 1681. Music, under which rubric Oldham would include poetry, brings "Exstasy" to mortals so that they "antedate" their "future Bliss on high." Without "Melody" to "tune our Vital Breath," life would be empty. Wine is not the world's soul, as in the "Dithyrambique on Drinking" of 1677, but rather music "gives Relish to our Wine" and "Rapture to our Love." Music heals, refines, and lifts the soul to contemplative heights, "wings Devotion to a pitch Divine." The last poem Oldham composed in his life seems closest in spirit to his early panegyrics on sainthood, as if he had come full circle in eight years to relish anew the contemplative piety he had loved in his youth.

Some elegies prefixed to his *Remains* provide a final glimpse of Oldham as he was known to his friends. He seems to have won the affection as much as the esteem of these Tory writers. They saw him as a quiet, scholarly, and "modest" person roused to satire by the excesses of the age in which he lived. Such a character may explain his being drawn to contemplative piety and his using masks of antiquity to satirize modern vice. Thomas D'Urfey recalls Oldham as skilled in all "that did with Learning dwell," a scholar-poet who remained "calm" and "Modest" till the wickedness of the times roused the "drowsie Satyr from his Den" – to attack general vices, not private persons. Thomas Andrews claims he was puzzled by Oldham's having "So sharp a Pen, and so serene a Mind," by his being a *Juvenal* in Rage" and yet of such "Modesty." He adds that "learned" Oldham had the honesty to "flatter none for Greatness, Love or Hire." Still another friend, in "Damon, an Eclogue," recalls Oldham's unusual "Modesty" and his piety so remarkable that, had he lived, he would have taught "Priests to pray." One wonders if this anonymous friend knew Oldham to the end of his life. A university associate lauds Oldham as the glory of Oxford, but admits that he went pretty far in mock-praising vice and disgracing virtue: "The first *Excess* of Wit that e'er did please." He calls Oldham's soul a "pure Etherial Flame" gone up to replace the fallen seraphs. Thomas Flatman, in his elegy, hints that Oldham was disliked by London's lower class and by rich Whigs: he triumphs now "O'er the unthinking Rabble's Spite, / And the dull wealthy Fool's disdain." The populace and merchants, who would have sided then with the Whigs, were apparently not fooled by the *Satyrs Upon The Jesuits* into thinking Oldham was one of them. Finally, in his masterpiece "To the Memory of Mr. Oldham," John Dryden mourns Oldham with genuine emotion, depicting him as a boyish Euryalus full of risky enthusiasm for the royal cause and as the Marcellus of the English tongue, crowned already with laurel but cut off from life too soon to reign as poet laureate in his turn. The feeling behind these poems is that of older poets mourning a fiery young genius who burned himself out young.

Bibliography:

Harold F. Brooks, *A Bibliography of John Oldham, the Restoration Satirist,* Oxford Bibliographical Society Proceedings and Papers, 5, part 1 (Oxford, 1936);

Brooks, "The Chief Substantive Editions of Oldham's Poems, 1679-1684," *Studies in Bibliography,* 27 (1974): 188-226.

References:

Harold F. Brooks, "The 'Imitation' in English Poetry, especially in formal Satire, before the Age of Pope," *Review of English Studies,* 25 (April 1949): 124-140;

Brooks, "John Oldham: some problems of biography and annotation," *Philological Quarterly,* 54 (Summer 1975): 569-578;

Brooks, "John Shepheard, Master of Whitgift School when John Oldham the Poet was Under Master," *Notes and Queries for Somerset and Dorset,* 30 (1979): 435-444;

Brooks, "The Poems of John Oldham," *Restoration Literature: Critical Approaches,* edited by Harold Love (London: Methuen, 1972), pp. 177-203;

Chester H. Cable, "Oldham's Borrowing from Buchanan," *Modern Language Notes,* 66 (December 1951): 523-527;

Paul Hammond, *John Oldham and the Renewal of Classical Culture* (Cambridge: Cambridge University Press, 1983);

Cooper R. Mackin, "The Satiric Technique of John Oldham's *Satyrs upon the Jesuits,*" *Studies in Philology,* 62 (January 1965): 78-90;

John H. O'Neill, "Oldham's 'Sardanapalus': A Restoration Mock-Encomium and its Topical Implications," *Clio,* 5 (Winter 1976): 193-210;

Raman Selden, "Oldham's Version of the Classics," *Poetry and Drama 1570-1700: Essays in Honour of Harold F. Brooks,* edited by Antony Coleman and Antony Hammond (London: Methuen, 1981), pp. 110-135;

Selden, "The Young Marcellus of Our Tongue," *Restoration,* 9 (Spring 1985): 26-30;

Roger Sharrock, "Modes of Satire," in *Restoration Theatre,* Stratford-upon-Avon Studies, 6 (London: Arnold, 1965), pp. 120-132;

David M. Vieth, *Attribution in Restoration Poetry: A Study of Rochester's Poems of 1680* (New Haven: Yale University Press, 1963);

Vieth, "John Oldham, the Wits and *A Satyr against Vertue,*" *Philological Quarterly,* 32 (January 1953): 90-93;

Weldon M. Williams, "The Genesis of John Oldham's *Satyrs upon the Jesuits,*" *PMLA,* 58 (December 1943): 958-970;

Williams, "The Influence of Ben Jonson's *Catiline* upon John Oldham's *Satyrs upon the Jesuits,*" *ELH,* 11 (March 1944): 38-62;

James Zigerell, *John Oldham* (Boston: Twayne, 1983).

Katherine Philips

(circa 1 January 1632 – 22 June 1664)

Elizabeth H. Hageman
University of New Hampshire

BOOKS: *Pompey. A Tragedy,* Pierre Corneille's *Mort de Pompée,* translated by Philips (Dublin: Printed by John Crooke for Samuel Dancer, 1663); republished as *Pompey. A Tragedy. Acted with Great Applause* (London: Printed for John Crooke, 1663);

Poems. By the Incomparable Mrs. K.P. (London: Printed by J. G. for Richard Marriott, 1664);

Poems. By the most deservedly Admired M^{rs}*. Katherine Philips, the matchless Orinda. To which is added, Monsieur Corneille's Pompey & Horace, Tragedies. With several other Translations out of French* (London: Printed by J. M. for Henry Herringman, 1667);

Letters from Orinda to Poliarchus (London: Printed by W. B. for Bernard Lintott, 1705; second edition, enlarged, London: Printed for Bernard Lintott, 1729).

Edition: *The Collected Works of Katherine Philips: The Matchless Orinda,* volume 1: *The Poems,* edited by Patrick Thomas (Stump Cross, Essex: Stump Cross, 1990).

OTHER: "To the Memory of the most Ingenious and Vertuous Gentleman Mr: Will Cartwright, my much valued Friend," in William Cartwright, *Comedies, Tragi-Comedies, with Other Poems . . . The Ayres and Songs set by M*^r *Henry Lawes* (London: Printed for Humphrey Moseley, 1651);

"To the much honoured Mr Henry Lawes, on his Excellent Compositions in Musick" and "Mutuall Affection between Orinda and Lucasia," in Henry Lawes, *Second Book of Ayres, and Dialogues* (London: Printed by T. Harper for John Playford, 1655);

Poems, by Several Persons, includes three poems by Philips (Dublin: Printed by John Crooke for Samuel Dancer, 1663);

Familiar Letters. Written by the Right Honourable John, late Earl of Rochester, and several other Persons of Honour and Quality. With Letters Written by Thomas Otway and Mrs. K. Philips. Published from their Original Copies. With other Modern Letters by Tho. Cheek, Esq; Mr. Dennis; and Mr. Brown (London: Printed by W. Onley for Samuel Briscoe, 1697).

Best known today for her poems on female friendship, Katherine Philips wrote some 125 poems on a variety of subjects; she translated plays by Pierre Corneille and five shorter Italian and French pieces; and she wrote a series of letters to Sir Charles Cotterell that were published after her death as *Letters from Orinda to Poliarchus* (1705). Philips (whose non de plume was Orinda) was one of a relatively small number of British women writers whose poems were widely circulated in the 1650s and early 1660s, and she seemed to her contemporaries to be, as the title pages of the first two editions of her *Poems* declared, "the Incomparable" (1664) or "the Matchless Orinda" (1667).

The only daughter of Katherine and John Fowler, she was born in early January 1632 in the parish of Saint Mary Woolchurch Haw in London. There is no exact record of her birth, but the poem "On the 1. of January 1657," in which she says her "time / . . . / is swell'd to six and twenty years," may indicate that her birthday coincided exactly with the first day of the new year. In any case, that she was born early in January 1632 was confirmed by John Aubrey, who cited in his *Brief Lives* (1813) the parish record to indicate that she was baptized on 11 January. She had an elder half brother, Joshua Fowler, and, as a result of her mother's later marriages, a younger half brother, Daniel Henley, and a half sister, Elizabeth Phillipps (*sic*). Although none of these siblings is mentioned in any of Philips's extant works, other relatives are important figures in her poetry and letters.

Of Katherine Philips's father, not a great deal is known. John Fowler was a relatively prosperous cloth merchant. When he died in December 1642, he left a legacy of some thirty-three hundred

Katherine Philips (portrait by an unknown artist; Collection of Lord Sackville of Knole)

pounds, most of which was divided between his wife, his son, Joshua, and his daughter. The Fowler household also included a "cosen Blacket" who, after the poet's death, told Aubrey that young Katherine "was mighty apt to learne . . . she had read the Bible thorough before she was full foure years old."

Philips's mother, born Katherine Oxenbridge, was the granddaughter of an early Separatist, John Oxenbridge, and one of seven children of the physician Daniel Oxenbridge and his wife Katherine Harby Oxenbridge. One of Katherine Oxenbridge's brothers, John Oxenbridge (1608–1674), is known to literary scholars for his friendship with John Milton and Andrew Marvell. A Puritan and Parliamentarian, John Oxenbridge went, two years after the Restoration of the English monarchy in 1660, to Su-

rinam, then to Barbados, and finally to Massachusetts, where he became the pastor of the First Church of Boston. Philips's other two uncles, Daniel and Clement Oxenbridge, were also Parliamentarians, and Philips herself was sent, when she was eight, to a boarding school run by a Mrs. Salmon, whom Aubrey identifies as "a famous schoolmistris, Presbyterian." At Mrs. Salmon's school in Hackney, Aubrey's notes go on to indicate, Philips was trained in the Puritan John Ball's catechism: "She was very religiously devoted when she was young; prayed by herself an hower together, and tooke sermons *verbatim* when she was but ten years old." With clear High Church sympathy, Aubrey adds that "She was when a child much against the bishops, and prayed to God to take them to him. . . .

Sir Charles Cotterell, Philips's friend and literary adviser, to whom most of her surviving letters are addressed (portrait by William Dobson; from Philip Webster Souers, The Matchless Orinda, *1931)*

Prayed aloud, as the hypocriticall fashion then was."

As Claudia A. Limbert has recently noted (*Restoration,* Spring 1989), sometime in the mid 1640s John Fowler's widow married one George Henley. Whether the daughter went to live with the Henleys or stayed in Mrs. Salmon's school for a few more years is unknown, but it seems clear that when in late 1646 or early 1647 her mother married her third husband, Sir Richard Phillipps of Picton Castle in Pembrokeshire, the fifteen-year-old Katherine joined her in Wales. The earliest extant writing by the girl then named Katherine (sometimes spelled Catherine) Fowler is clearly connected with the area near Picton Castle.

Now in parcel 24 of the Orielton Collection of the National Library of Wales is a single sheet of paper signed "C Fowler" and dedicated to Anne

Barlow, daughter of Dorothy and John Barlow of Slebech, a town some two miles from Picton Castle. On one side of the paper, in the young poet's hand, is a sixteen-line poem arguing that "A marryd state affords but little ease / The best of husbands are so hard to please." The reader is urged to "be advised by me: / Turn, turn apostate to love's Levity." Following this witty antimarriage poem is a prose "recipt to cure a Love sick Person who cant obtain the Party desired." The latter urges one to combine "two oz: of the spirits of reason three oz: of the Powder of experiance five drams of the Juce of Discretion three oz: of the Powder of good advise, and a spoonfull of the Cooling watter of Consideration" to create pills which will save the head from "maggots and whimsies and you restored to your right sences." In a kind of postscript, the writer concludes, "if this wont do apply the plaister and if that

204

wont do itts out of my power to find out what will." On the opposite side of the paper is a poem in which the poet maintains that "If himans rites shall call me hence, / It shall be with some man of sence." The husband she seeks will be a man of Jonsonian moderation, "Nott with the great, but with a good estate," and he should be always "Ready to serve his friend, his country and his king." Although the phrase about a good husband serving friend, country, and king has a formulaic ring (and although one should of course be cautious about assuming that the speaker in the poem is Catherine Fowler herself), that phrase may suggest that its author was already bending away from Parliamentarian politics and toward a Royalist stance.

The man whom the poet married in August 1648, however, was not a Royalist but a Parliamentarian. James Philips was a relative of Sir Richard, their two families being descended from Sir Thomas Phillipps of Cylsant who lived early in the sixteenth century. Sir Richard was the direct descendant of Sir Thomas's heir; James was a descendant of a younger son, Owen. James Philips was also related by marriage to Sir Richard, for his first wife, Frances, was Sir Richard's daughter. Born in 1594, James was fifty-four years old when he married the sixteen-year-old Katherine Fowler.

The owner of property in both Cardiganshire and Pembrokeshire, James Philips of Cardigan Priory and nearby Tregibby was, by the 1640s, a person of some political significance – a member of Parliament and, in Philip Webster Souers's words, "a man of energetic character, who, throughout the period of the Commonwealth, enjoyed a degree of influence which was the portion of few men in all Wales." Though some have described him as a dedicated, even severe upholder of the Roundheads' cause, there is reason to believe that James Philips was instead a relatively apolitical man devoted more to the ideals of public service than to the nuances of partisan politics. In a seventeenth-century manuscript now in the National Library of Wales, he is described as one whose "genius is more to undertake public affaires, regarding sometim more the Employment then the Authority from whom he received the Same" and "One that had the fortune to be in with all Goverments, but thrived by none" (MS. Llanstephan 145, f. 70^v). It may be that Philips's assigning her husband the name "Antenor" in her poems is motivated partly by his age (Antenor was an elderly counselor in the *Iliad*). It may also be relevant, as Patrick Thomas suggests, that Antenor attempted to make peace between the Greeks and the Trojans. The name may thus designate James Philips as a man with a moderate temperament. It might even be a playful reminder to a beloved husband that he might be less partisan.

Neither Philips's poems nor her letters provide proof positive that Katherine and James Philips's marriage was a happy one. Nevertheless, as Orinda teases and cajoles Antenor, they image a relationship of easygoing respect. From the poetry can be drawn at least the outlines of one indicative episode in their political and personal lives. Sometime during the Protectorate (1653–1659), one J. Jones threatened to publish Philips's poem "Upon the double murther of K. Charles, in answer to a libellous rime made by V. P." Knowing how embarrassing the clearly Royalist publication of that poem would have been to her husband, Katherine Philips wrote "To Antenor, on a paper of mine which J. Jones threatens to publish to his prejudice." Her approach is a comic one in which she begins with the abrupt question, "Must then my crimes become thy scandall too? / Why sure the Devill hath not much to do." Rather than follow the common wisdom of the period that a man is responsible for his wife's actions, she asserts a separation of responsibilities by reminding Antenor that "Eve's rebellion did not Adam blast, / Untill himselfe forbidden fruit did tast."

On another occasion, Orinda bids Antenor, "give o'er, / For my sake talk of graves no more" in "To my Antenor, March 16. 1661/2." The date of the poem suggests that the situation in which it is written is intensely serious, for while in February 1662 James Philips had been found innocent of the charge that in 1654 he had sentenced the Royalist colonel John Gerard to death, in March he seems to have been in the midst of real financial difficulties. Nevertheless, Orinda's tetrameter lines are cheerful – as cheerful as Orinda is hoping Antenor will become. In "To my dearest Antenor on his parting," Orinda writes a poem whose paraphrasable content is not unlike poems of parting by her male contemporaries – John Donne, for example. In "A Valediction: forbidding Mourning" (1633) Donne employs his famous image of a compass to teach his lady that their parting is only physical; Philips uses the image of "watches, though we doe not know / When the hand moves, we find it still doth go, / So I, by secret sympathy inclin'd / Will absent meet, and understand thy mind." In both poems woman is the lesser partner: Antenor, Orinda says, is her "guide, life, object, friend, and destiny." And yet the very fact that a woman defines the relationship gives Philips's poem a different cast from Donne's lines.

As James Philips's wife, Katherine Philips lived from 1648 until her death in 1664 at his family home, Cardigan Priory. Cardigan is in the southwestern corner of Cardiganshire and thus only a short distance from Pembrokeshire, where many of her friends and relatives lived. Knowing that she also maintained many of her London friends throughout her adult life, one might speculate that Philips often, or at least sometimes, accompanied her husband when he went to London for meetings of Parliament. Certainly she was in London in the spring of 1655, for her only son, Hector, who died in infancy, was buried there in Saint Syth's Church. And from the title of the poem Philips wrote to mourn the death of her twelve-year-old stepdaughter, Frances Philips, we know that the girl died in 1660 in Acton – a London suburb where Katherine Philips's mother (by then married to a fourth husband, Maj. Philip Skippon) resided. Katherine and James Philips's only daughter (also a Katherine), born in Cardigan in April 1656, would live to marry Lewis Wogan of Boulston, Pembrokeshire, and to bear fifteen children – fourteen of whom lie buried with their parents in Boulston Church.

In the two poems Philips wrote on the death of her young son, she uses Judeo-Christian numerology to express the intense pain of a bereaved mother who, after seven years of marriage, bore a son who was "in less than six weeks, dead" ("Epitaph on Hector Philips"). She also uses the number forty, which is associated with periods of privation and pain – periods (such as the Israelites' forty years of wandering) followed by relief and joy. Moreover, forty is the number of days after childbirth when a mother is "churched," and Philips begins her poem "On the death of my first and dearest childe" with the stanza "Twice Forty moneths in wedlock I did stay, / Then had my vows crown'd with a lovely boy. / And yet in forty days he dropt away; / O! swift vicissitude of humane Joy!" Instead, then, of returning to the church to offer a monetary gift and prayers of thanksgiving for her son's birth, this mother can offer only poetry: "An Off'ring too for thy sad Tomb I have / Too just a tribute to thy early Herse, / Receive these gasping numbers to thy grave; / The last of thy unhappy Mothers Verse." As she puns on the word *numbers* in that poem, so Philips puns on the word *mourning* in the epitaph: "So the Sun, if it arise / Half so Glorious as his Ey's, / Like this Infant, takes a shroud, / Bury'd in a morning Cloud."

Among Philips's poems are many elegies and epitaphs, at least four of which were actually carved on church monuments. The only one known to survive is inscribed on John Lloyd's monument in Cilgerron Church, a few miles southeast of Cardigan. The others are the epitaph for young Hector Philips, who was buried in a church that a few years later burned in London's Great Fire of 1666, and two commemorating John Collier (described in John Fowler's will as his "servant and cozen") and Collier's daughter Regina, who were buried in Beddington, Surrey, in January 1650 and September 1649, respectively. Other poems occasioned by deaths of friends and relatives include verses in memory of Mrs. Mary Lloyd of Bodidrist in Denbighshire; a poem memorializing "the most Justly honour'd Mrs Owen of Orielton"; an epitaph on James Philips's mother; a poem on the death of Sir Walter Lloyd; and an "Epitaph on my truly honoured Publius Scipio," written in memory of her stepfather Philip Skippon. Philips also wrote two poems addressed to women who had lost their husbands – "To my dearest friend, on her greatest loss" and "To Mrs. Wogan . . . On the Death of her husband" – and she wrote two elegies on members of the royal family – "On the death of the Duke of Gloucester" and "On the Death of the Queen of Bohemia."

Interesting examples of the historical (and gender) specificity of Philips's poetry are to be found in her five epithalamia, all of which focus on the bride (rather than, as do the typical Renaissance epithalamia, on the groom) and which express hope that the marriage will be the kind of loving (albeit hierarchical) companionate marriage that seventeenth-century writers of marriage tracts and sermons recommended. In, for example, "To my deare Sister Mrs. C. P. on her nuptialls," addressed to her sister-in-law Cicily Philips, Orinda acknowledges the seventeenth-century reality of wives' marriage responsibilities with the line "May her content and duty be the same." But she also prays, "May his and her pleasure and Love be so / Involv'd and growing, that we may not know / Who most affection or most peace engross'd; / Whose Love is strongest, or whose bliss is most." That the poem's tone will be different from that of epithalamia such as Edmund Spenser's or Donne's is announced in the opening lines in which "wild toys" are rejected in favor of a different kind of "solemnitys." That the word *solemnities* is used in the Renaissance to refer to ceremonies such as marriage is especially relevant to a discussion of this poem because – as Patrick Thomas notes – Cicily Philips's wedding was the first to have been performed in Cardigan after the 1653 Barebones Parliament (of which James Philips was a part) had declared marriage a civil, rather than a religious, ceremony and required that it be performed by a justice of the peace. Indeed, the wedding in question was performed, the parish register indicates, "by James Phillips . . . one of the Justices of the peace of the said Countie of Cardigan." Just as this civil ceremony was performed in Saint Mary's Church rather than in a secular setting, so too are "Orinda's wishes for Cassandra's bliss" presented in a numerologically precise poem in which twenty-four lines (one for each hour of the day) close with the hope that the couple will "count the houres as they doe pass, / By their own Joys, and not by sun or glass; / While every day like this may sacred prove / To Friendship, duty, gratitude and Love."

Most, though not quite all, of Philips's poems are occasioned by specific events in the lives of relatives, friends, or members of the royal family. They include a variety of literary kinds: wooing poems and poems of parting; the epithalamia and the elegies and epitaphs previously mentioned; philosophical pieces on topics such as "The World," "Submission," and "Death"; verse letters to friends and relatives; pastoral dialogues; and even one pindaric ode, an ode on retirement (first published, as was Abraham Cowley's "On Orinda's Poems. Ode," in 1663 in *Poems, by Several Persons*). In addition to Cowley, Philips's acquaintances included many British writers. As early as 1651 Henry Vaughan printed in his *Olar Iscanus* the poem "To the most Excellently accomplish'd Mrs. K. Philips," in which he promises to "vow / "No *Lawrel* growes, but for your *Brow*." Two essays on the topic of friendship — one published by Francis Finch in 1654, the other by Jeremy Taylor in 1657 — were written for Philips. After Philips's death, James Tyrell, Thomas Flatman, Abraham Cowley, William Temple, and one J. C. wrote poems in her memory; and, as Allan Pritchard has noted, Marvell echoes several of Philips's lines in poems published in his posthumous volume of 1678.

Sixteen fifty-one, the same year that Vaughan praised his fellow Anglo-Welsh poet, marks Philips's earliest print publication. Her poem in praise of William Cartwright appeared as the first of fifty-four prefatory poems in the posthumous edition of his *Comedies, Tragi-Comedies, with Other Poems . . . The Ayres and Songs set by Mr Henry Lawes*. Several poets whose works appear there also appear in the next volume in which Philips's verses were printed: Henry Lawes's *Second Book of Ayres, and Dialogues* (1655). Dedicated to Mary Harvey, Philips's friend since their time together at Mrs. Salmon's school and by 1655 the wife of Sir Ed-

ward Dering, the 1655 book includes, as a prefatory poem, Philips's "To the much honoured Mr Henry Lawes, on his Excellent Compositions in Musick" and, with music by Lawes, her "Friendship's Mysterys" — called there "Mutuall Affection between Orinda and Lucatia."

The theme of friendship so apparent in her marriage poems is given a different spin in the poems for which Philips is best known: the poems in which she exploits the language and literary genres used by seventeenth-century love poets to treat Orinda's relationships with female friends such as Lucasia (Philips's name for Anne Owen, later Lady Dungannon), Rosania (Mary Aubrey), and Philoclea (Malet Stedman). If one were to substitute different names in some of the friendship poems, they might read like verses celebrating love between a Renaissance male poet and his lady. "Parting with a Friend," for example, which treats a leave-taking between Rosania and Lucasia, includes the lines "Although you lose each others Eyes, / You'l faster keep the Heart." In "Dialogue betwixt Lucasia and Rosania" (which eighteenth-century writers George Ballard and Elizabeth Elstob would later agree was one of Philips's best poems), Lucasia hopes that "when crumbled into dust / We shall meet and love forever." "Friendship in Emblem, or the Seale, to my dearest Lucasia" begins, "The hearts thus intermixed speak / A Love that no bold shock can break." The latter poem is one of several in which echo-allusions to poems by Donne help Orinda assert "Friendship's Mysterys." Whereas Donne's "The Canonization" (1633), for example, claims that poet and lady "prove / Mysterious by this love," Philips's "Friendship's Mysterys" calls to Lucasia, "let's prove / There's a religion in our Love."

Unlike Philips's marriage poems, which assume the hierarchical relationship between husband and wife implicit in seventeenth-century discussions of companionate marriage, the friendship poems stress the equality inherent in real friendship. Playing on "She's all States and all Princes I, / Nothing else is" in Donne's "The Sunne Rising" (1633), for instance, Orinda says, "All our titles [are] shuffled so, / Both Princes and both subjects too" in "Friendship's Mysterys." In another poem, "Friendship," Philips contrasts the two estates: "All Love is sacred, and the marriage ty / Hath much of Honour and divinity; / But Lust, design, or some unworthy ends / May mingle there, which are despis'd by friends."

Some critics have argued that the people to whom Philips gave coterie names formed a Society of Friendship. The title of the poem "To the excellent Mrs A. O. upon her receiving the name of Lucasia, and adoption into our society. 29 Decemb 1651" might help validate that idea, as indeed might "To my Lady M. Cavendish, chosing the name of Policrite." Moreover, "Friendship in Emblem, or the Seale, to my dearest Lucasia" can be read as a description of the society's actual insignia. Edmund Gosse describes Philips's society as an early salon: "It would appear that among her friends and associates in and near Cardigan she instituted a Society of Friendship, in which male and female members were admitted, and in which poetry, religion, and the human heart were to form the subjects of discussion." Souers's readings of the poems lead him to the conclusion that the society included only Orinda and her female friends, most likely only Lucasia and Rosania. Thomas quotes a letter from Sir Edward Dering to Lucasia to suggest that Gosse was closer to the truth than Souers. Thomas argues, however, that since many of Philips's connections, even those with Anglo-Welsh writers, were centered in London, any society that she might have headed must have been based there. It seems, however, that Philips uses the word *society* to refer to what twentieth-century writers might call a network of friends, what the *Oxford English Dictionary* refers to in definition I.1.a of "society": "Association with one's fellow men, esp. in a friendly or intimate manner; companionship or fellowship."

Be that as it may, there is no question that Philips's own contemporaries associated her name with the theme of friendship. The broadside written by one J. C. after her death, for example, includes these lines:

> She, who in Tragique buskins drest the Stage,
> Taught Honour, Love, and Friendship to this Age;
> Is gone to act her Part in bright attire,
> With Scenes of Glory, in th' Angelique Quire.
> She Taught the World the sweet and peaceful Arts
> Of blending Souls, and of compounding hearts;
> Without th' ingredients of reserv'd intents,
> Hypocrisies, and windy complements.

The theme of friendship was especially popular among seventeenth-century Royalist poets, who often used pastoral poetry to image court life as a place of polite civility in contrast to what they saw as the noisy barbarisms of their populist contemporaries. Philips's contribution to that tradition was to imagine the golden world as a female paradise in which Orinda and Ardelia could sit quietly and live "remov'd from noise of warres / In one another's hearts" ("A retir'd friendship, to Ardelia") or where

a poet could use the characteristically female activity, "to spin," in the assertion "But I, resolved from within, / Confirmed from without, / In privacie intend to spin / My future minuts out" ("A Countrey life").

As earlier noted, Philips's "Friendship's Mysterys" appeared with Lawes's music in his *Second Book of Ayres, and Dialogues*. Several other Philips poems suggest musical associations. Subtitles or side notes in Philips's own copies (in National Library of Wales MS. 775B) of three other poems ("A Dialogue between Lucasia and Orinda"; "To Mrs. M. A. upon absence. 12. December 1650"; and "On the death of my first and dearest childe, Hector Philipps") indicate that they were also set to music by Lawes (for the score of the elegy on Philips's son, see Joan Applegate's forthcoming article in volume four of *English Manuscript Studies*). Yet another, "Against Pleasure," was set by a Dr. Coleman, almost certainly Charles Coleman, doctor of music, who contributed to the *Second Book of Ayres, and Dialogues*. In addition, "Parting with Lucasia, 13th January 1657/8" is subtitled "A Song"; the poem beginning " 'Tis true, our life is but a long disease" is written "To my Lord Biron's tune of – Adieu Phillis" (an unidentified tune); and the one beginning "How prodigious is my Fate" is written to the tune of the French song "Sommes nous pas trop heureux," the latter to be published in an article Andrea Sununu and this writer have written for volume four of *English Manuscript Studies*. Whether other poems were intended as songs is unclear, but several were set to music and published in seventeenth-century songbooks. Two ("Upon the engraving. K:P: on a Tree . . . at Barn-Elms" and "On Solitude," Philips's translation of "La Solitude" by Marc-Antoine de Gérard Saint-Amant) were set to music by Henry Purcell. Philips wrote songs to be sung after each of the five acts of her translation (1663) of Corneille's *Pompey*. In a letter of 31 January 1663, she indicates that the first and last songs had been set by her friend Philaster (John Jeffries); the second by "a *Frenchman* of my Lord ORRERY's"; the third by Dr. Peter Pett (the advocate-general in Ireland); and the fourth by "one *Le* GRAND a *Frenchman,* belonging to the Dutchess of ORMOND." In the library of Christ Church College, Oxford, is a manuscript transcription of three of the songs for *Pompey,* but the music for the third song is ascribed there (and also in British Library Add. MS. 33234) to John Banister. As Curtis A. Price suggests, it may be that some or all of the Christ Church settings were composed for a later London performance of the play.

Letter from Philips to Dorothy Temple, wife of Sir William Temple, the diplomat, statesman, and essayist (from Philip Webster Souers,
The Matchless Orinda, *1931)*

Philips's poetry includes two Royalist poems written during the Civil War years, four celebrating the Restoration, and six occasional poems addressed in the early 1660s to members of the royal family. Among her poems on the Restoration are "On the numerous accesse of the English to waite upon the King in Holland," which portrays loyal Royalists going to Holland "to expresse their joy and reverence," and "Arion on a Dolphin to his Majestie in his passadge into England," which celebrates the sea journey by which Charles II returned to England in 1660. Both "On the faire weather at the Coronation" and "On the Coronation" present the crowning of Charles on 23 April 1661 as a sacred event "Since Kinges are Gods, and OURS of Kinges the best."

Most of Philips's extant letters were written between December 1661 and May 1664 to her friend and literary adviser Sir Charles Cotterell, then master of ceremonies in the court of Charles II (the exceptions are four letters to Berenice, one to Dorothy Temple, and a letter to Dering recently discovered by Peter Beal and scheduled for publication in volume four of *English Manuscript Studies*). Thus more is known about her life and work after the Restoration of the monarchy than before; and quite a bit is known about her interest in the court of Charles II. For example, on 3 May 1662 Orinda sent a poem, evidently "To her royall highnesse the Dutchesse of Yorke, on her command to send her some things I had wrote," to Poliarchus with the request that he "put it in a better Dress" so that she could insert his corrections before sending "the Dutchess another Copy, in obedience to the Commands she was pleas'd to lay upon me, that I should let her see all my Trifles of this nature." Orinda is clearly pleased to continue: "I have been told, that when her Highness saw my Elegy on the Queen of BOHEMIA, she graciously said, it surpriz'd her." On 4 June of the same year she thanked Poliarchus for sending from Portsmouth a "full Relation of the Queen's Arrival" – a topic Philips treated in "To the Queene on her arrivall at Portsmouth. May. 1662."

On 20 August 1662 Philips wrote from Dublin that she had met Roger Boyle, Earl of Orrery. Having read a scene Philips had translated from Corneille's *Mort de Pompée,* Orrery encouraged her to complete the work. By 3 December 1662 Philips had finished the translation, asking Cotterell to correct any errors he might find in it and agreeing that he should present a copy to Anne, Duchess of York. In early February 1663 Philips's *Pompey* was performed in Dublin's Smock Alley Theatre – Philips

thus becoming the first woman to have a drama produced in a British public theater. As Catherine Cole Mambretti points out, the play is also "the first clearly documented production of an heroic drama in English heroic couplets." Before 8 April 1663 John Crooke printed the translation in Dublin; later that year he published another edition in London. It may be that Philips's *Pompey* was played in London in July 1663, for it was parodied in William Davenant's *Play-house to be Let,* produced in August 1663.

During the winter of 1663–1664, Philips went on to translate most of Corneille's *Horace,* but the task was yet to be finished when she died in June 1664. First published in its unfinished state in the 1667 edition of her *Poems,* Philips's *Horace* was completed by John Denham in time for a February 1668 production at court. Denham's conclusion was also used for a winter 1668–1669 production at the Theatre Royal and for the 1669 and 1678 editions of Philips's *Poems.* When Jacob Tonson brought out an octavo edition of *Poems* in 1710, he replaced Denham's work with equivalent lines from Sir Charles Cotton's translation, first published in 1671.

Not long before she died, another publishing event captured Philips's attention – this having to do with her original poetry. As noted earlier, one of Philips's poems was printed in 1651; two, in 1655. As far as can now be determined, no other poems appeared in print until the publication of a 1663 collection (though an aside in one of Philips's letters may indicate that one poem was printed on a broadsheet earlier that year). On 15 May 1663 Philips wrote to Cotterell about "a Miscellaneous Collection of Poems, printed here; among which, to fill up the Number of his Sheets, and as a Foil to the others, the Printer has thought fit, tho' without my Consent or Privity, to publish two or three Poems of mine, that had been stollen from me." This collection is *Poems, by Several Persons,* printed in Dublin by John Crooke for Samuel Dancer in 1663, an apparently unique surviving copy of which has recently come to light at the Folger Shakespeare Library. Philips, it would seem, did not unduly mind that her poems had been "stollen" and printed, and she says she will send Cotterell a copy of the book "by the first Opportunity." Soon thereafter, however, Philips's letters tell of her severe distress over an unauthorized publication of her poems – this the volume titled *Poems. By the Incomparable Mrs. K. P.* printed by J. G. for Richard Marriott and advertised for sale in January 1664. Although a few twentieth-century readers have seen in Philips's distress a coy desire to obscure the fact that she herself had planned the volume's appearance, one might well believe that a seventeenth-century woman born into a merchant family and now a member of the gentry with many aristocratic friends would not have sought that kind of publicity. On 25 January 1664 Philips wrote to Dorothy Temple of her fear that "the most part of the worlde are apt to believe that I connived at this ugly accident. . . . I am soe innocent of this pittiful design of a knave to get a groat that I never was more vexed at anything."

A similar dismay informs Philips's other two letters about the book. Dated "Jan. 29 1663/4," one was for Cotterell's eyes alone, the other for him to circulate among their friends if he saw fit. In the private letter, Orinda asks her friend to "Let me know what they say of me at Court and everywhere else, upon this last Accident, and whether the exposing of all my Follies in this dreadful Shape has not frighted the whole World out of all their Esteem for me." The public letter is even more elaborate in its expression of Orinda's concern. In that letter, for example, one finds the complaint about the poet's being an "unfortunate Person that cannot so much as think in private, who must have all my Imaginations and idle Notions rifled and expos'd to play the Mountebanks and dance upon the Ropes to entertain the Rabble, to undergo all the Raillery of the Wits, and all the Severity of the Wise, and to be the Sport of some that can, and Derision of others that cannot read a Verse." Orinda regrets not only that her poems have been "collected," but also that they are "so abominably printed as I hear they are. I believe too there are some among them that are not mine." The poems in the 1664 volume are in fact Philips's, except that excerpts by Sir Edward Dering and Henry More preface two of her poems. The book does include some manifest errors, and three of Philips's lines are replaced by lines of asterisks.

Whether Poliarchus immediately showed the public letter to their mutual friends is unknown, but it is printed in the preface to the edition of Philips's works issued in 1667. The letter voices "how little she desired the fame of being in print, and how much she was troubled to be so exposed." Realizing the impossibility of completely suppressing a published book (indeed, many copies of the 1664 Poems survive even today), Cotterell advised Philips to issue a corrected version of the poems. It may be that her last poem, "To my Lord Arch: Bishop of Canterbury his Grace 1664," was written with that new volume in mind, for it treats the poet's wish that her "humble" muse, which had been "hurry'd

from her Cave with wild affright," might be protected by the archbishop. The poem concludes with the hope that the poet will then have the courage to speak in public:

> Your Life (my Lord) may, ev'n in me, produce
> Such Raptures, that, of their Rich Fury Proud,
> I may, perhaps, dare to repeat aloud;
> Assur'd the World that Ardour will excuse,
> Applaud the subject, and forgive the Muse.

Before, however, an authorized version of the poems was printed, Philips died of smallpox on 22 June 1664, at the age of thirty-two. Three years later the folio volume of her works was published by Henry Herringman – this book edited, it is often said, by Cotterell. Whereas the 1664 volume had comprised 75 poems, the 1667 edition prints 116 poems by Philips, 5 translations from French and Italian sources, and both Pompey and Horace. For the first part of the volume, the 1667 edition relied on the 1664 quarto, generally maintaining the order of poems but emending some words and whole lines. For example, line 4 of "On the numerous accesse of the English to waite upon the King in Holland" was changed from "As Pompey's residence made Africk Rome" to "As Pompey's Camp, where e're it mov'd, was Rome"; line 90 of "In memory of that excellent person Mrs. Mary Lloyd" was changed from "As ancient Lamps in some Egyptian Urn" to "As a bright Lamp shut in some Roman Urn." Although some of the 1667 variants match lines in autograph copies of Philips's poems, it is unknown whether the other variants introduced into the folio are by Philips, Cotterell, or a third hand. Nor is it known in what order Philips would have chosen to print her poems had she herself seen them through the press. Noting, first, that the custom of her age was to begin and end volumes of poetry with "serious" verse and, second, the enthusiastic tone of many of Philips's Royalist statements, one may speculate that she would have chosen to begin and end the 1667 volume with Royalist poems. It is possible that she wrote the poem to the archbishop of Canterbury because she wanted a poem to balance the first poem in the volume, for both the first and last poems in the 1667 folio employ the traditional humility topos to express the poet's reluctance to speak publicly about public events. Whereas "Upon the double murther of K. Charles" protests what Philips saw as the chaotic events of the civil wars, "To my Lord Arch: Bishop of Canterbury" expresses relief "after such a rough and tedious Storm / Had torn the Church, and done her so much harm."

Mezzotint of Philips by Isaac Becket

In 1697 Samuel Briscoe included four private letters from Philips in a volume entitled *Familiar Letters. Written by the Right Honourable John, late Earl of Rochester, and several other Persons of Honour and Quality.* Berenice, the woman to whom they were addressed, is as yet unidentified (Thomas suggests that she may have been Lady Elizabeth Ker). The story the letters tell is of a lost friendship. The first is dated "June the 25th," without a year; the second and third, 2 November and 30 December 1658. All three express Orinda's intense pleasure in her friendship with Berenice and conclude with some variation of the formula "Your Ladiships most Faithful, and most Passionate Friend and Servant, Orinda." In the fourth letter, which the editor observes "was wrote but a Month before Orinda died," the writer – who now signs herself "Your Ladiship's most affectionate humble Servant and

Friend, K. Phillips" – fervently hopes that Berenice will "once more receive me into your Friendship, and allow me to be that same *Orinda,* whom with so much goodness you were once pleased to own as most faithfully yours, and who have ever been, and ever will be so."

In 1705, three years after Sir Charles Cotterell's death, Bernard Lintott published a volume of letters chronicling a far more successful friendship. The preface to *Letters from Orinda to Poliarchus* validates the authenticity of the work by claiming that "Anyone who has a Nicety of Taste, or Judgment, may easily discern the following Papers to be the real Product of that Pen, which infinitely obliged us with so curious a Variety of Poems, that have procur'd themselves an universal Applause; and that her Writings in Prose deserve an equal Reputation, is no vain Conjecture." The preface then goes on to present the letters that follow as "worth the reading" on two counts. They offer, we are told, an excellent example of a prose style that avoids "the two Extremes, either of uncorrect Looseness in her Stile, or starch'd Affectation," and they "will sufficiently instruct us how an intercourse of writing, between Persons of different Sexes, ought to be managed, with Delight and Innocence." In this volume an Englishwoman has outdone French practitioners of the art of letter writing; indeed, " 'Tis very unaccountable, when we have such Examples of Excellency among our selves that the *French* writers, in the Epistolary Way, should be so frequently translated by us."

Lintott's collection begins with Orinda's letter of 6 December 1661, a letter that opens with an extended statement of her regard for Poliarchus. It ends on 17 May 1664, only a few weeks before Philips's death. Gossipy details about the royal family, rival poets, and rival wooers give the volume the piquancy of an epistolary novel. Several interwoven narratives present the story of Orinda's sorrow when her friend Calanthe (this code name for Lucasia, G. Blakemore Evans was the first to realize, was the name Cartwright first gave the character who would later become Lucasia in his play *The Lady Errant*) decides to marry Memnon (Marcus Trevor, later Lord Dungannon) instead of Poliarchus; the story of Philips's work on her translation of *Pompey* and of its success on the Dublin stage; the story of her distress over the publication of her poems; and the story of her intense desire to visit London and to see Poliarchus. The final letter apologizes to Poliarchus that his godson is to be named after his father, Hector Philips, rather than after Sir Charles. It ends with a perfect expression of friendship "between Persons of different Sexes . . . with Delight and Innocence": "If am not mistaken in your Goodness, be pleas'd to come hither this Afternoon a little before three, where it will be privately christen'd and where you shall find, &c. ORINDA." In 1729, when *Letters from Orinda to Poliarchus* was republished, it included one additional letter. The latter was then owned, as it is now, by Cotterell's family.

To Philips's canon, twentieth-century scholars have added a few poems not in the 1667 volume: the juvenilia described earlier; three poems in Cardiff City Library MS. 2 1073 ("To Sir Amorous La Foole," "On Argalus his vindication to Rosania," and "Juliana and Amaranta: A Dialogue"); "To the Lady Mary Butler at her marriage with the Lord

Cavendish, October 1662," which appears with Philips's poems in two manuscripts and in *Poems, by Several Persons*; "To Rosania and Lucasia: Articles of Friendship," in the Huntington Library; "On the Coronation" from MS. Locke e. 17 at the Bodleian Library; and the epitaph inscribed on John Lloyd's monument in Cilgerron (also in the Philips holograph, National Library of Wales, 775B). For various reasons, scholars have rejected "Upon his Majesties most happy restauration to his Royall Throne in Brittaine" and "Upon the Hollow Tree unto which his Majestie escaped after the unfortunate Battell at Worcester," both of which are ascribed "Cecinit Domina Phillips agro Pembrokiae" in the one known manuscript in which they appear (Bodleian br. bk. Firth b. 20).

The principal source for information about Philips's life and work remains Philip Webster Souers's biography (1931), refined and occasionally corrected by Patrick Thomas's edition of the poems (1990; as of this writing, an edition of the letters is forthcoming – as is a companion volume of the translations prepared by Ruth Little), and the articles by Lucy Brashear and Claudia A. Limbert. Much recent scholarship on Philips has focused on the means by which – in an age when women were urged to be "chaste, silent, and obedient" – she achieved acclaim as a poet to be read and emulated. Nevertheless, an increasing number of readers have turned to the works themselves to discover a writer whose talents were far from modest and whose recognition by seventeenth-century literati such as Abraham Cowley and John Dryden was well deserved.

Letters:

Julie G. Longe, ed., *Martha, Lady Gifford: Her Life and Correspondence (1664–1772): A Sequel to the Letters of Dorothy Osborne,* includes a letter by Philips to Dorothy Temple (London: George Allen, 1911).

Biographies:

Philip Webster Souers, *The Matchless Orinda* (Cambridge, Mass.: Harvard University Press, 1931);

Patrick Thomas, *Katherine Philips ("Orinda")* (Aberystwyth: University of Wales Press, 1988).

References:

Harriette Andreadis, "The Sapphic-Platonics of Katherine Philips, 1632–1664," *Signs,* 15 (Autumn 1989): 34–60;

Lucy Brashear, "Gleanings from the Orinda Holograph," *American Notes and Queries,* 23 (March/April 1985): 100-102;

Dorothy Frances Canfield, *Corneille and Racine in England* (New York: Columbia University Press, 1904);

Cyrus Lawrence Day and Eleanore Boswell Murrie, *English Song-Books, 1651-1702: A Bibliography with a First-Line Index of Songs* (London: Oxford University Press, 1940);

Celia A. Easton, "Excusing the Breach of Nature's Laws: The Discourse of Denial and Disguise in Katherine Philips' Friendship Poetry," *Restoration,* 14 (Spring 1990): 1-14;

G. Blakemore Evans, ed., *The Plays and Poems of William Cartwright* (Madison: University of Wisconsin Press, 1951);

Edmund Gosse, "The Matchless Orinda," in *Seventeenth-Century Studies* (London: K. Paul Trench, 1883), pp. 229-258;

Elizabeth H. Hageman, "Katherine Philips: The Matchless Orinda," in *Women Writers of the Renaissance and Reformation,* edited by Katharina M. Wilson (Athens & London: University of Georgia Press, 1987), pp. 566-608;

Hageman and Andrea Sununu, "New Manuscript Texts of Katherine Philips, 'the Matchless Orinda,' " *English Manuscript Studies,* 4 (forthcoming 1993);

Elaine Hobby, *Virtue of Necessity: English Women's Writing, 1649-88* (Ann Arbor: University of Michigan Press, 1989);

Hilton Kelliher, "Cowley and 'Orinda': Autograph Fair Copies," *British Library Journal,* 2 (Autumn 1976): 102-108;

William Van Lennep, *The London Stage, 1660-1800* (Carbondale: University of Illinois Press, 1965);

Claudia A. Limbert, "Katherine Philips: Another Step-Father and Another Sibling, 'Mrs. C. :P,' and 'Polex: ʳ,' " *Restoration,* 13 (Spring 1989): 2-6;

Limbert, "Two Poems and a Prose Receipt: The Unpublished Juvenilia of Katherine Philips," *English Literary Renaissance,* 16 (1986): 383-390; republished in *Women in the Renaissance and Reformation: Selections from "English Literary Renaissance,"* edited by Kirby Farrell, Hageman, and Arthur F. Kinney (Amherst: University of Massachusetts Press, 1990), pp. 179-186;

Catherine Cole Mambretti, " 'Fugitive Papers': A New Orinda Poem and Problems in her Canon," *Papers of the Bibliographical Society of America,* 71 (October–December 1977): 443-452;

Mambretti, "Orinda on the Restoration Stage," *Comparative Literature,* 37 (Summer 1985): 233-251;

Ellen Moody, "Orinda, Rosania, Lucasia *et aliae*: Towards a New Edition of the Works of Katherine Philips," *Philological Quarterly,* 66 (Summer 1987): 325-354;

Maureen E. Mulvihill, "A Feminist Link in the Old Boys' Network: The Cosseting of Katherine Philips," in *Curtain Calls: British and American Women in the Theater, 1660-1820,* edited by Mary Anne Schofield and Cecilia Macheski (Athens: University of Georgia Press, 1991);

John Pavin Phillips, "The 'Matchless Orinda,' and her Descendants," *Notes and Queries,* 5 (March 1858): 202-203;

Curtis A. Price, "The Songs for Katherine Philips' *Pompey* (1663)," *Theater Notebook,* 33 (1979): 61-66;

Allan Pritchard, "Marvell's 'The Garden': A Restoration Poem?," *Studies in English Literature,* 23 (Summer 1983): 371-388;

William Roberts, "Saint-Amant, Orinda and Dryden's Miscellany," *English Language Notes,* 1 (March 1964): 191-196;

Patrick Thomas, "Orinda, Vaughan and Watkyns: Anglo-Welsh Literary Relationships During the Interregnum," *Anglo-Welsh Review,* 26 (Autumn 1976): 96-102;

Marilyn L. Williamson, *Raising Their Voices: British Women Writers, 1650-1750* (Detroit: Wayne State University Press, 1990).

Papers:
Seventeenth- and early-eighteenth-century manuscript copies of Philips's works, some in her own hand, are to be found in the National Library of Wales; in the Harry Ransom Humanities Research Center at the University of Texas at Austin; at Oxford University; in the Cardiff City Library; in the British Library; in the Beinecke Library at Yale University; in the Folger Shakespeare Library; and in the Huntington Library. Manuscript letters are owned by Harvard University, the Cotterell-Dormer family, and the Center for Kentish Studies.

John Wilmot, Earl of Rochester
(1 April 1647 – 26 July 1680)

Graham Roebuck
McMaster University

BOOKS: *Corydon and Cloris or, The Wanton Sheepherdess* [broadside] (London, 1676?);

Artemisa to Cloe. A Letter from a Lady in the Town, to a Lady in the Country; Concerning The Loves of the Town: By a Person of Quality [broadside] (London, 1679);

A Letter from Artemiza in the Town, to Chloë in the Country. By a Person of Honour [broadside] (London, 1679);

A Satyr Against Mankind. Written by a Person of Honour [broadside] (London, 1679);

Upon Nothing. A Poem. By a Person of Honour [broadside] (London, 1679);

A Very Heroical Epistle from My Lord All-Pride to Dol-Common (London, 1679);

Poems on Several Occasions By the Right Honourable The E. of R-- (Antwerpen [i.e., London], 1680; facsimile, Menston: Scolar, 1971);

A Letter To Dr. Burnet, From the right Honourable the Earl of Rochester, As he lay on His Death-Bed, At His Honours Lodge In Woodstock-Park (London: Printed for Richard Bentley, 1680);

Poems on Several Occasions. Written by a late Person of Honour (London: Printed for A. Thorncome, 1685);

Valentinian: A Tragedy. As 'tis Alter'd by the late Earl of Rochester, And Acted at the Theatre-Royal, adaptation of John Fletcher's *Valentinian* (London: Printed for Timothy Goodwin, 1685);

Poems, &c. on Several Occasions: with Valentinian, a Tragedy (London: Printed for Jacob Tonson, 1691);

Poems, (&c.) On Several Occasions: with Valentinian; a Tragedy (London: Printed by Jacob Tonson, 1696);

Familiar Letters: Written by the Right Honourable John late Earl of Rochester. And several other Persons of Honour and Quality, 2 volumes (London: Printed by W. Onley for Sam Briscoe, 1697);

Poems on Several Occasions. By the R. H. the E. of R. (London: Printed for A. T., 1701);

Poems on Several Occasions; with Valentinian; a Tragedy (London: Printed for Jacob Tonson, 1705);

The Miscellaneous Works of the Right Honourable the Late Earls of Rochester And Roscommon. With The Memoirs of the Life and Character of the late Earl of Rochester, in a Letter to the Dutchess of Mazarine. By Mons. St. Evremont (London: Printed & sold by B. Bragge, 1707; second edition, London: Printed for Edmund Curll, 1707; third edition, 1709);

Poems on Several Occasions: with Valentinian; a Tragedy. To which is added, Advice to a Painter. Written by the Right Honourable John, late Earl of Rochester (London: Printed by H. Hills & sold by the booksellers of London & Westminster, 1710);

Poems on Several Occasions. By the R. H. the E. of R. (London, 1713);

The Works of John Earl of Rochester. Containing Poems, On Several Occasions: His Lordship's Letters To Mr. Savil and Mrs. ** with Valentinian, a Tragedy. Never before Publish'd together (London: Printed for Jacob Tonson, 1714);

Remains of the Right Honourable John, Earl of Rochester. Being Satyrs, Songs, and Poems; Never before Published. From a Manuscript found in a Gentleman's Library that was Cotemporary with him (London: Printed for Tho. Dryar & sold by T. Harbin, W. Chetwood & the booksellers of London & Westminster, 1718);

Poems on Several Occasions. By the R. H. the E. of R. (London, 1731);

The Poetical Works Of that Witty Lord John Earl of Rochester: Left in Ranger's Lodge in Woodstock Park, where his Lordship died, and never before Printed; with Some Account of the Life of that ingenious Nobleman. Extracted from Bishop Burnet, and other Eminent Writers (London, 1761).

Editions: *Rochester's Sodom Herausgegeben nach dem Hamburger Manuscript*, edited by L. S. A. M. von Römer (Paris: Welter, 1904);

Collected Works of John Wilmot, Earl of Rochester, edited by John Hayward (London: Nonesuch, 1926);

John Wilmot, second Earl of Rochester (portrait by Sir Peter Lely; Collection of Sir Edward Malet)

John Wilmot Earl of Rochester: His Life and Writings, edited by Johannes Prinz (Leipzig: Mayer & Müller, 1927);

Rochester's Poems on Several Occasions, edited by James Thorpe (Princeton: Princeton University Press, 1950);

Poems by John Wilmot, Earl of Rochester, edited by Vivian de Sola Pinto (London: Routledge & Kegan Paul, 1953; Cambridge, Mass.: Harvard University Press, 1953);

Sodom or the Quintessence of Debauchery. Written for the Royall Company of Whoremasters, possibly by Rochester (Paris: Olympia, 1957);

Sodom or the Quintessence of Debauchery by John Wilmot, Earl of Rochester, possibly by Rochester, edited by Albert Ellis (North Hollywood: Brandon, 1966);

The Gyldenstolpe Manuscript Miscellany of Poems by John Wilmot, Earl of Rochester, and Other Restoration Authors, edited by Bror Danielsson and David M. Vieth, Stockholm Studies in English, 17 (Stockholm: Almqvist & Wiksell, 1967);

The Complete Poems of John Wilmot, Earl of Rochester, edited by Vieth (New Haven: Yale University Press, 1968);

Lyrics and Satires of John Wilmot, Earl of Rochester, edited by David Brooks (Sydney: Hale & Iremonger, 1980);

John Wilmot, Earl of Rochester: Selected Poems, edited by Paul Hammond (Bristol: Bristol Classical Press, 1982);

The Poems of John Wilmot, Earl of Rochester, edited by Keith Walker (Oxford: Blackwell, 1984).

OTHER: "To His Sacred Majesty, on His Restoration in the Year 1660," possibly by Rochester, in *Britannia Rediviva* (Oxford: Excudebat A. & L. Lichfield, Acad. Typogr., 1660);

"In Obitum Serenissimae Mariæ Principis Arausionensis" and "To Her Sacred Majesty, the Queen Mother, on the Death of Mary, Princess of Orange," both possibly by Rochester, in *Epicedia Academiæ Oxoniensis, in Obitum Serenissimæ Mariæ Principis Arausionensis* (Oxford: Typis Lichfieldianis, 1660);

"Celia, the faithful servant you disown" and "All things submit themselves to your command," in *A Collection of Poems, Written upon several Occasions, By Several Persons. Never before in Print* (London: Hobart Kemp, 1672);

"The second Prologue at Court," in *The Empress of Morocco,* by Elkanah Settle (London: Printed for William Cademan, 1673);

"The Epilogue," in *Love in the Dark, or The Man of Bus'ness,* by Francis Fane (London: Printed by T. N. for Henry Herringman, 1675);

"While on those lovely looks I gaze," in *A New Collection of the Choicest Songs* (London, 1676);

"The Epilogue," in *Circe, a Tragedy,* by Charles D'Avenant (London: Printed for Richard Tonson, 1677);

"Give me leave to rail at you," lines 1–8 by Rochester, in *Songs for i 2 & 3 Voyces Composed by Henry Bowman* (1677).

John Wilmot, second Earl of Rochester and Baron of Adderbury in England, Viscount Athlone in Ireland, infamous in his time for his life and works and admired for his deathbed performance, was the cynosure of the libertine wits of Restoration England. He was anathematized as evil incarnate and simultaneously adored for his seraphic presence, beauty, and wit, even from his first appearance at the court of Charles II. This mercurial figure left a body of literary work the exact dimensions of which have provided an almost intractable puzzle. Whatever answer is provided for this conundrum of scholarship, the extent of his corpus will be small in comparison to his reputation. The oeuvre, not intended for publication as ordinarily understood, is that of an aristocratic courtier. The works are meant to be seen, perhaps, as ephemera, as bright filaments of the central work of art, the author himself, rather than as abiding literary monuments. It is not surprising, therefore, that Rochester served as a model for numerous depictions of rakish wits in the stage comedy of the period.

Yet Rochester's poetry, in his limpid love lyrics, lampoons, burlesques, and sharp satires, has an abiding presence. The philosophical and religious undertow – often detected in the deep disgust and misanthropic attitudes, the obverse of aristocratic insouciance – has especially fascinated modern readers. His poetic craftsmanship is repeatedly evident in the allusiveness and parodic facility he brings to his verse. That he was celebrated by contemporaries for his impromptu ripostes in verse will not seem, to readers who have tasted the fruits of his intellect, exaggerated praise, however remotely glittering and improbably theatrical his world must now appear. He was ranked as a poet second only to John Dryden, a judgment accorded as much to his genius as to his scandalous lewdness. Andrew Marvell's striking opinion, as recorded by John Aubrey in his *Brief Lives* (1813), is a sure guide to the heart of Rochester's appeal to the literate classes: "The Earle of Rochester was the only man in England that had the true veine of Satyre."

His private letters, more fully and accurately available now than ever before, have never lacked readers. He is a good correspondent – partly because of his seeming carelessness for effect and the attendant unguardedness of his person, and partly for the opposite reason, namely his studied formality of address (for instance, to a mistress) and amused indulgence in the pretenses and hypocrisies of social behavior. In all his writing, excepting the timeless love lyrics, he conveys the invigorating sense of an eye that has seen through the shabby veneer of human behavior, and yet he savors its ambivalences. That such a man alternately enthralled and provoked the anger of his master, Charles II, is not to be wondered at.

His reputation is similarly uneven. Sometimes moral concerns, sometimes aesthetic or philosophical ones, dominate in assessments of his place in literature. While Rochester's dissipation has led at times to revulsion and the near eclipse of his work, during his own lifetime it was his nihilistic atheism that most alarmed and disturbed. For this reason, Bishop Gilbert Burnet's report on Rochester's debate with him, *Some Passages* (1680), became a best-selling work. A later edition of Burnet's work is pointedly titled *The Libertine Overthrown; Or, A Mirror for Atheists* (1690). If one judges by the proliferation of printings, Rochester's own writings remained very popular throughout the first half of the eighteenth century. His reputation waxed to the point that Voltaire could write in his *Lettres philosophiques* (1734), "Tout le monde connoit de réputation le Comte de Rochester" (Everyone knows of the reputation of the earl of Rochester). Voltaire added that the gossip writers have pictured Rochester as a man of pleasure, but he would like to make known the genius, the great poet. The dissemination of the picture that Voltaire wanted to correct owes much to the *Mémoires de la Vie du Comte de Grammont* (1713; translated as *Memoirs of the Life of Count de Grammont*, 1714). Written by Philibert de Gramont's brother-in-law, Anthony Hamilton, possibly from Gramont's own dictation, these urbane and amusing anecdotes are employed in virtually every biographical notice of Rochester, although their reliability is suspect. Likewise a memoir of Rochester in the form of a letter from Seigneur de Saint-Evrémond to Hortense Mancini, Duchess of Mazarin, which appeared in the 1707 edition of Rochester's works, is now regarded as doubtful in attribution and, in some degree, misleading. (It is rejected by Saint-Evrémond's editor, Pierre Des Maizeaux.) Nevertheless, such near-contemporary portraits of the author in his social milieu provide valuable evocations of the age, including its delight in graceful exaggeration, the threshold of satire. How much in demand such anecdotes were among the spectating middle classes might be suggested by hastily compiled volumes such as *Pinkethman's JESTS: OR, Wit Refin'd. Being a New-Years-Gift for young Gentlemen and Ladies* (1721). This collection purported to be drawn from the writings of the greatest wits of the age, such as Ben Jonson, Rochester, and others, "adapted to the Conversation of People of the best taste." Along such lines as these – life versus work – Rochester's reputation is stretched or divided. The judicious account of Rochester in Samuel Johnson's *Lives of the Poets* (1779–1781) gives both disapproval of "the wild pranks," "the sallies of extravagance," and the "glare of his general character," as well as some praise for his works (especially where they imitate the classics to advantage), with restrained praise for "a mind, which study might have carried to excellence."

Alexander Pope detected in Rochester the intimations of a poetic practice of adapting classical and other (usually neoclassical) works with delicacy to the English heroic couplet, which Pope himself was to bring to final perfection. To people of the later eighteenth century and the first part of the next century, however, the kind of reprobation suggested in David Hume's *History of Great Britain* (1754–1757) held sway: "the very name of Rochester is offensive to modest ears." The subsequent neglect of Rochester's work was relieved only because of the late Romantic appropriation of his life. It is not unusual for comparisons to be drawn by nineteenth-century

commentators between George Gordon, Lord Byron, and Rochester, who came to be seen as a romantic figure and as a type of the outsider. In this context of romanticism, it is of great interest that Giuseppe Verdi (who would twice use Byron's work) selected Rochester as early as July 1835 as the subject of his first opera. But what was to have been his *Rocester* became his *Oberto* when the action was shifted from Restoration England to medieval Italy. The likely source of Verdi's inspiration is the French drama in three acts, *Rochester,* by Benjamin Antier and Théodore Nezel, published in Paris in 1829. This work epitomizes Rochester as a rake and seducer, and with lurid glamour traces his actions to a melodramatic denouement. An inventive touch is the creation of a character named Cowley (Rochester admired the poet Abraham Cowley in the highest degree), who, as officer in charge of a press gang, presses into Royal Navy service all Rochester's creditors. Although the quality of the play would hardly stimulate serious interest in Rochester, French literary criticism (taking its cue from Voltaire, perhaps) debated him seriously. In *La Revue de Deux Mondes* (August 1857), E. D. Forgues adopted a perspective that would be developed by twentieth-century biographers. Looking at Rochester's religious sensibilities, Forgues saw not a radical skeptic, but a despairing believer ("un croyant désesperé"), who therefore shouts bacchic refrains at the triumphal parade of the times. Hippolyte Taine, however, took a much more condemnatory line against Rochester's moral depravity in his *Histoire de la Littérature Anglaise* (1863).

In the later nineteenth century the project to recover, revise, and republish seventeenth-century poetry generally bypassed Rochester, although Sir Edmund Gosse in 1899 provided a selection in *The English Poets,* edited by T. H. Ward. Gosse judged Rochester as, in some respects, the last and best of the Cavalier poets, but he also added that Rochester was like a child who rolled in the mud, disgusting the wayfarer. Before World War I there were signs of the revival of a serious interest in Rochester. In *The Cambridge History of English Literature* (1912), Charles Whibley denied Johnson's opinion that Rochester's best poem was "On Nothing" and set firmly in the forefront the poem "A Satyr against Reason and Mankind," which many modern critics have agreed is his masterpiece.

David M. Vieth, widely regarded as having produced the most thorough investigation of the sources and the most reliable account of Rochester's canon, as well as much else of value in illuminating his work, expressed the dominant view of Roches-

Rochester's birthplace, Ditchley Park, circa 1674 (Collection of the Ditchley Foundation)

ter studies – that serious scholarly interest in the poet began in the 1920s. He added that the "impetus seems to have been profound disillusionment of the postwar generation, for whom Rochester spoke eloquently.... the 'lost' generation found Rochester." Vieth remarked that Whibley had at last separated morality from poetry, allowing scholarship to proceed according to more objective principles than hitherto; nevertheless, much of the scholarly interest and a great deal of the general reader's interest in Rochester is still very much fired by interest in the poet's thought, states of mind, and personality, even if it is much less attracted to anecdote than in earlier times. Even so, following John Hayward's edition (1926) and Johannes Prinz's books in 1926 and 1927, a great deal of the work of the 1930s was biographical. As with editions of Rochester, so the biographies were written and published with a wary eye for prosecution. Bowdlerization was common until almost the last quarter of the twentieth century, thus showing that, from at least one point of view, morality and poetry remained firmly intertwined. *Lord Rochester's Monkey,* written by Graham Greene in the early 1930s, was not published until 1974. Prinz wrote in his 1927 edition that Rochester was a "tabooed author," and so it proved. David M. Vieth, who recorded the rising tide of scholarly and critical attention up to 1982 in *Rochester Studies, 1925–1982: An Annotated Bibliogra-*

phy (1984), concluded that the poet composed some half-dozen satires and songs that are "beyond compare, radically unlike anything else ever written" and that though he wrote less than any other major poet, Rochester certainly is one.

John Wilmot was born on 1 April – All Fools' Day – 1647 to Anne and Henry Wilmot at Ditchley Park, Oxfordshire, near Woodstock. Ditchley Park was the family estate of Anne's first husband, Sir Francis Henry Lee, who had died in 1640. Henry Wilmot was created Baron Wilmot of Adderbury in June 1642 and became Lieutenant General of Horse in 1643 before his marriage to Anne the following year. Her family, St. John, was prominent in the parliamentary cause. During 1644 he commanded Royalist cavalry in a series of important battles. On 8 August he was removed from command, imprisoned, and then exiled for a period of time as punishment for his attempt to bring about a rapprochement between King Charles I and Parliament, a scheme that looked uncomfortably like treason to some senior Royalists. The judgment of Edward Hyde, first Earl of Clarendon, on a man "proud and ambitious, and incapable of being contented" rested on the recognition of Wilmot's almost complete lack of restraint. In his *History of the Rebellion and Civil Wars in England* (1702–1704), Hyde wrote that Wilmot "drank hard," "loved debauchery," and was even "inspired" in its exercise.

He also valued no "promises, professions, or friendships, according to any rules of honour or integrity." But he did experience "scruples from religion to startle him." This bacchic, mercurial figure – depicted in some accounts as a jolly, dashing cavalier – was, of necessity, not present at the birth of his son.

The poet's mother, all accounts agree, was pious, of Puritan leaning, of strong character, and tough-minded when it came to the protection of her property. In 1652 she was obliged to depart into exile with her children. Hyde (incidentally, her kinsman), managing the Royalist fortunes from his several stations abroad, wrote to Henry Wilmot, who was at the time in Germany on the king's business. Hyde remarked, in passing, that Wilmot's son was anxious for news of him. It is not likely that they ever saw much of each other, despite the imaginings of some romantic biographers about secret visits from Lord Wilmot on the run. Lady Anne returned with her sons to Ditchley in 1656 to contest the attempt by Parliament to sequester her estates. By this time her husband, using his experience with disguise, escaped from the aftermath of the totally unsuccessful attempt to foment a Royalist rising in the north of England. He died on the Continent on 19 February 1658, having been almost a total stranger to his son, yet setting a pattern of life for him marked by bravado, insecurity, debauchery, and, if Hyde is right, a tense relationship with religious thought. Given the unsettled times, however, John Wilmot's character might have arisen quite independently of his father's example.

John succeeded to his father's earldom – a powerless and impoverished title – in February 1658. One valuable property his father did leave to the young Rochester, however, could not have been foreseen at that time. In 1650 Henry Wilmot had accompanied the ill-fated expedition of Charles II to Scotland, which culminated in total defeat at the hands of Oliver Cromwell at Worcester the following year. The episode of Charles's escape, frequently recalled and embellished by him, credits Wilmot principally for saving his master in that extremity. So it was that Charles II entertained the second earl of Rochester with particular favor at his restored court and endured his subsequent outrages and extravagances with notable, and occasionally scandalous, restraint. Charles's court was to be the scene of Rochester's efflorescence. When the celebrated astrologer John Gadbury in his *Ephemeris* (1698) charted young John Wilmot's horoscope, he noted that the regnant planets disposed the child to poetry and a large stock of active spirits. What the

conjunction of his parents disposed him to was, perhaps, the more decisive.

The young earl of Rochester's education seems to have been in the hands of his able mother and her chaplain, Francis Giffard. The boy was sent later to attend Burford Grammar School nearby in Oxfordshire, where education centered on the Latin authors. This training was soon to show in his own works, especially in his ready ability to translate and adapt the classics to his own expression. Precisely what it was that Rochester drew from the Latin classics is a question of great interest to twentieth-century literary scholars, who are more concerned than their seventeenth-century counterparts with determining originality and genuineness of authorship. In Rochester's day events were interpreted according to the classical paradigms of political, social, and imaginative life as taught in the schools. His habit in his mature poetry of simultaneously alluding to his classical model and then immersing it in the corrosive of his contemporary cynicism makes fascinating reading in this century. In his time this habit was regarded as a component of wit. The same pattern holds for Rochester's use of religious and liturgical language, to which he frequently alludes.

By the standards of the previous generation, whose classrooms and lecture halls were untroubled by the upheavals of civil war, Rochester must have seemed distinctly underschooled. John F. Moehlmann terms him "half-educated." In September of 1661 Rochester graduated M.A. at Oxford (he was fourteen years old) at a formal ceremony where Edward Hyde, now Earl of Clarendon, Chancellor of the University, and Lord Chancellor of England, kissed him on the left cheek. Rochester's university career had been swift indeed. On 18 January 1660 he had been admitted a "fellow commoner" (that is, despite the phrase, as a nobleman) of Wadham College, founded in 1612. Wadham was particularly associated with the emerging experimental sciences, and it is sometimes thought that this academic setting affected him. Rochester entered the school under the tutorship of the mathematician Phineas Bury, but a more influential tutor was the physician Robert Whitehall of Merton College, who may have inducted him into the life of debauchery. It is said that Whitehall doted on him and taught him to drink deeply at the Oxford taverns, where he gained admittance in the disguise provided by a borrowed master's gown. This is unsubstantiated storytelling, though it gains credibility by the fact that Rochester left four silver pint pots to his college on going down from university. Such gifts, however, were common tokens of esteem from students to their colleges.

During his brief stay at the university, three poems attributed to Rochester appeared in two Oxford collections of encomium and consolation. *Epicedia Academiæ Oxoniensis* (1660) is a collection of poems condoling with the Queen Mother, Henrietta Maria, for the death by smallpox of her daughter Mary, the Princess Royal. Attributed to Rochester is a Latin poem, "In Obitum Serenissimae Mariae Principis Arausionensis," and an English poem, "To Her Sacred Majesty, the Queen Mother, on the Death of Mary, Princess of Orange." The former is striking for its reflection of medical opinion on the subject of lethal pustules on a woman's face. The poem then modulates to praise for a goddesslike beauty – "tota venustas" – total loveliness too fine for this mortal life. The latter poem, in elegant conceited couplets, rehearses the great misfortunes of Charles I's widow and urges her quite sternly to stay in England rather than return to France: "For we deprived, an equal damage have / When France doth ravish hence, as when the grave." But it is the poem in *Britannia Rediviva* (1660) celebrating the restored king, who is apostrophized as "Virtue's triumphant shrine," that is most striking for its ingenuity:

> Virtue's triumphant shrine! who dost engage
> At once three kingdoms in a pilgrimage;
> Which in ecstatic duty strive to come
> Out of themselves, as well as from their home.

Charles Williams observes that these opening lines have "something of the last mad metaphors of the metaphysical poets" and that Cowley might have penned them. Similarly, the dexterous handling of the oxymoron of the following couplet is worthy of note: "Forgive this distant homage, which doth meet / Your blest approach on sedentary feet." Yet, following Anthony Wood's assertion that Whitehall really wrote these verses, few commentators have been willing to attribute them wholly to Rochester. Rochester's age, thirteen, is the cause of incredulity. Some critics believe a degree of collaboration to be likely, and Vieth adds his view that at this time the major poetic possibilities of Rochester could not have been foreseen. On the other hand, the precocity of Rochester is to be reckoned with, and such precocity is not without a well-known precedent: Cowley composed "The Tragicall Historie of Pyramus and Thisbe" when he was ten and published his collected poems, *Poetical Blossomes,* in 1633 when scarcely older than Rochester. Dr. Johnson observed that Rochester's life was all over "before

the abilities of many other men began to be displayed."

Contradictory views of Rochester's life and works abound, even concerning his youth. Whereas Wood, for instance, does not credit Rochester's authorship of these poems, he held the view that Rochester was

> a person of most rare parts, and his natural talent was excellent, much improved by learning and industry, being thoroughly acquainted with all classick Authors, both Greek and Latine; a thing very rare (if not peculiar to him) among those of his quality.

Thomas Hearne reports that Rochester's private tutor, Giffard, said of his former pupil

> that my Lord understood very little or no Greek, and that he had but little Latin, and that therefore 'tis a great Mistake in making him (as Burnett and Wood have done) so great a Master of Classick Learning.

Giffard's testimony is perhaps to be weighed against the fact that he had hoped to come to Oxford with Rochester as his "Governor, but was supplanted." In addition to these details Giffard also gave Hearne an account of his good influence upon the young earl, implying that had it so continued, there would have been no debauchery.

The Royal Society, in which Wadham men were prominent, was founded in 1660. Whether or not Rochester received the imprint of the new experimental scientific learning during his time at Oxford is another question with no definitive answer. Certainly he later showed more than common interest in material and chemical phenomena and in the philosophy which nurtured such studies, namely that of Thomas Hobbes. To this rigorously skeptical, or atheistic, materialism he was strongly drawn, although it seems that he had little interest in Hobbes's far-reaching scheme of political relationships explored in *Leviathan* (1651).

After Oxford, in the charge of Dr. Andrew Balfour, a thirty-year-old Scottish physician and man of learning, Rochester set out on a grand tour of France and Italy on 21 November 1661. Little can be said with certainty of this period of Rochester's life and education, a period that was concluded in 1664, when he returned to England and presented himself at court. A distillation of the events of this ample tour was evidently given by Rochester on his deathbed to Burnet. Among the claims recorded are that he mastered French and Italian and that he owed more to Balfour, who encouraged his literary pursuits, than to anyone other than his parents. Later Balfour wrote about the grand tour in the form of a "Letter to a Friend," from which Rochester's typical itinerary might be reconstructed. Vivian de Sola Pinto does just that in *Enthusiast in Wit* (1962). It is documented that by October of 1664 Rochester and Balfour were at Venice and that later that month Rochester was enrolled as a student of "the English Nation" at Padua University, famous, among other things, for its anatomical and medical studies, as well as for the frequent unruliness of its students. Returning to England by the close of the year, he went to Whitehall Palace to present to Charles a letter from his sister, Henrietta, Duchess of Orleans, whose departure from Britain with her mother, Henrietta Maria, was bewailed in "To Her Sacred Majesty." Charles's reply to his sister indicates that he received the letter carried by Rochester on 25 December 1664.

It is not known whether Rochester wrote any poetry while on his tour. Here, as elsewhere, matching his literary work to his life is largely a matter of conjecture. Possibly some of the lyrical love poems written in conventional terms with pastoral names such as Strephon, Daphne, Olinda, Phyllis, and Alexis date from this period. In the most overworked of all lyric themes – disdained love – some of these poems impress by their craftsmanship and the implicit confidence of the poet, even as they justify Dr. Johnson's cool summary:

> His songs have no particular character: they tell, like other songs, in smooth and easy language of scorn and kindness, dismission and desertion, absence and inconstancy with the common places of artificial courtship. They are commonly smooth and easy; but have little nature, and little sentiment.

Perhaps these verses were part of the elegant art of aristocratic courtship, but just behind the hackneyed conventionality of a poem such as "A Dialogue between Strephon and Daphne" there may be detected an astringent whiff of Rochester's cynicism, which transforms the ordinary. Strephon, accused of perjury in love, slights Daphne's anguish with a glib superiority. As is often the case in the world of the Restoration wits and rakes, women turn out to have outmaneuvered men. At the conclusion of this poem, Daphne alarmingly whisks aside the mask of a conventional deserted shepherdess:

> DAPHNE.
> Silly swain, I'll have you know
> 'Twas my practice long ago.
> Whilst you vainly thought me true,

> I was false in scorn of you.
> By my tears, my heart's disguise,
> I thy love and thee despise.
> Womankind more joy discovers
> Making fools, than keeping lovers.

Possibly such subtle and beautifully managed insights derive from Rochester's experiences at Whitehall, which Prinz characterizes as "the notorious gynecocracy" of Charles's court. Some other lyrics, again of undetermined date, have been hailed as timeless and exquisite. One often held in that esteem is the song "Absent from thee, I languish still," with its nicely understated irony and plaintive modulations of the language of religious yearning.

The Saint-Evrémond letter describes Rochester on his first appearance at court:

> His person was graceful, tho' tall and slender, his mien and shape having something extremely engaging; and for his mind, it discover'd charms not to be withstood. His wit was strong, subtle, sublime, and sprightly; he was perfectly well-bred, and adorned with a natural modesty which extremely became him. He was master both of the ancient and modern authors, as well as of all those in the modern French and Italian, to say nothing of the English, which were worthy of the perusal of a man of fine sense. From all which he drew a conversation so engaging, that none could enjoy without admiration and delight, and few without love.

Beautiful, witty, and slender of means, Rochester had come to try his wits and to find a bride who might provide him with an adequate estate. While still at Oxford he had been granted a pension of five hundred pounds. The largesse of Charles II, however, came in incommensurate parts: the nominal amount of the pension and the uncertainty of the actual payment. Any attempt to understand Rochester and his works would be incomplete if it failed to recognize how central financial precariousness was to his life. In brief, he was always dependent, for he had a small estate, and, even though he succeeded in marrying an heiress, he had little access to her wealth. Rochester behaved toward Charles, at times, like a servant to a master and at others like a rebellious and unruly child to a father. He had no commanding stake in the politics of the nation. As Basil Greenslade has shown in his essay, "Affairs of State" (in Jeremy Treglown's *Spirit of Wit*, 1982), Rochester's father left him no political weight, no "interest." Henry Wilmot had been essentially a soldier, not a great landowner; his son, therefore, had to make the court and its satellite, the theater, his arenas. His writing reveals an intense interest in the power of influential women and, not infrequently, a contempt for the politics of the court. His main if not only source of independence, it might be concluded, was his own intellect. But he was also — given the times, the prevailing conventions of conduct, and his social caste — a man commanded by powerful imperatives of honor. From the tension between this view of the world and the Hobbesian view of the imperatives of self-interest, Rochester created his startling, amusing, and disgusting literary world.

From his first appearance at court to his spectacular abduction of the heiress, Elizabeth Malet, Rochester allowed little time to elapse. Samuel Pepys reported in his diary that on 26 May 1665, Miss Malet — a minor, as was Rochester — was returning to her lodgings with her grandfather Francis, Lord Hawley, when their coach was intercepted by Rochester and a body of armed men. Her abductors put her "into a coach with six horses and two women provided to receive her and carried her away" from Charing Cross. Rochester was captured at Uxbridge, on the road to Oxfordshire, and committed to the Tower of London on the king's orders, where Aubrey remembers seeing him. Miss Malet was soon restored to her family, and Rochester, after a short imprisonment, was conditionally discharged on 19 June in response to his petition, which urged, among other extenuations, "That Inadvertancy, Ignorance in ye Law, and Passion were ye occasions of his offence." Rochester temporarily thwarted, Miss Malet's many other suitors were thus fed more promise, believing that the king's great anger against Rochester would cancel his support for his suit. As late as 25 November 1666, however, the rich heiress — thought to be worth twenty-five hundred pounds per annum — was still unencumbered. Pepys reported her disdainful account of her suitors:

> my Lord Herbert would have had her – my Lord Hinchingbrooke was indifferent to have her – my Lord J. Butler might not have her – my Lord of Rochester would have forced her; and Sir [Francis] Popham (who nevertheless is likely to have her) would kiss her breech to have her.

On being temporarily thwarted, Rochester sought his fortune in the Second Dutch War. The king arranged for the admiral Edward Montagu, first Earl of Sandwich, to accommodate Rochester, and on 15 July 1665 he arrived on board the flagship *Revenge*. This is perhaps a sign that his beseeching the king "to pardon his first error, & not suffer one offence to bee his Ruine" had been answered. It is likewise a pattern of the future relationship between Charles and Rochester.

The ensuing expedition intended to surprise homeward-bound Dutch fleets in a neutral anchorage at Bergen, Norway, and to make off with the spoils has often been described. A long letter from Rochester survives, as do independent reports of his bravery. It is also clear that his inquiring skepticism about the claims of religion was engaged at this time, as is shown by his final talks with Burnet. But his hope of material rewards was not to be met.

Before the action began, Rochester and two other gentlemen volunteers, one of whom had intimations of his death, discussed the question of whether or not there is an afterlife, a question they proposed to solve in an experimental manner. Rochester and John Windham entered a formal pact that should either die, he would reappear to the survivor and give notice of the future state. Edward Montagu, whose presage of death was to prove true, refused to enter this pact. As it turned out, he and Windham were destroyed by a single cannonball during an enemy bombardment on 2 August. Windham died outright, the other an hour later, his belly ripped out by the missile. This story was told to Burnet by Rochester, who added that Windham's failure to reappear after death had been a "great snare" to him in his wrestling with the claims of religion, although his companion's presentiment of death impressed him with the view that the soul possessed a "natural sagacity."

Such thoughts as these are entirely omitted from the long letter written to his mother the following day. He provides her instead with a detailed account of the lead-up to the action devised by the commanding officer, Sir Thomas Teddeman, an account which includes expressions of thanks for "gods greate mercy" in not letting the ship founder on the rocky shoreline. The letter also describes the sailors' enthusiasm for booty, "some for diamonds some for spices others for rich silkes & I for shirts and gould wch I had most neede of." He concludes the account by remarking "Mr Mountegue & Thom: Windhams brother were both killed with one shott just by mee, but God Almyghty was pleased to preserve mee from any kind of hurt." He seems concerned to display conventional piety to his mother. He also abstains from mention of his own courage. Indeed, the letter suggests an almost self-effacing patriotic motivation. Burnet's account supports this "readiness to hazard his life in the defence and service of his country." There is no mention of debauchery. Perhaps Burnet is right in supposing an abatement of such tendencies until Rochester once again immersed himself in court life and gave himself over to

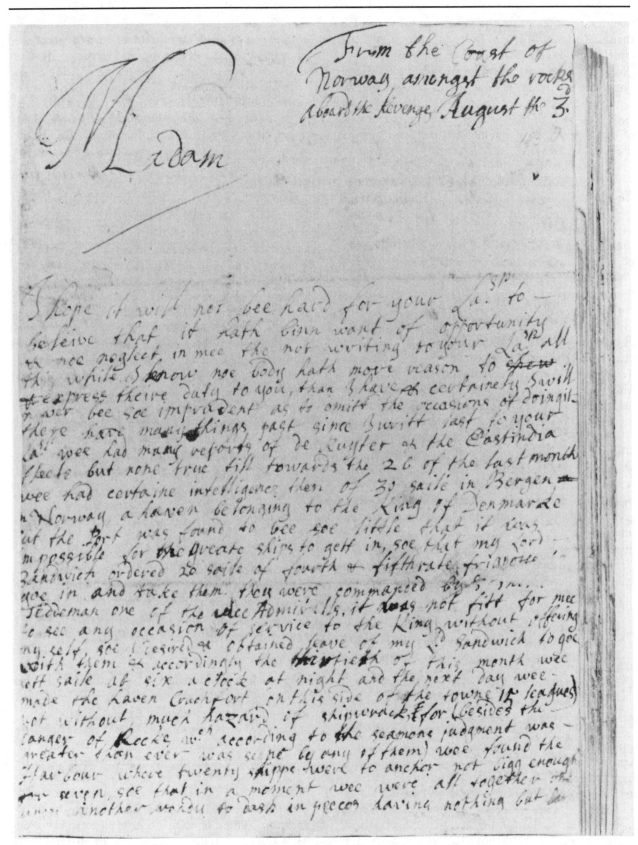

Page from a 1665 letter from Rochester to his mother, describing a battle in which he participated during the Second Dutch War (MS. Harleian 7003, f. 193, British Library)

a violent love of pleasure, and a disposition to extravagant mirth. The one involved him in great sensuality; the other led him into many adventures and frolics, in which he was often in hazard of his life.

This no doubt true depiction of his life interestingly suggests the habit of his mind – the dangerous brinkmanship that gives his mature poetry its edge.

The next notable hazard to his life was in June 1666. Again a volunteer, this time under the command of Sir Edward Spragge, Rochester took part in four days of ferocious battle in the English Channel. At one desperate juncture Spragge needed to send a message to one of his captains. Since most of the other volunteers aboard the ship had been killed, Rochester performed the task in an open boat under heavy fire. Instances of his notable courage are frequently invoked as contrasts to allegations of cowardice in his subsequent conduct at court, especially in connection with duels and the acts of drunken violence in which he and his friends indulged. Although there are some stories of cowardice that cannot be dismissed, not all of them are credible, whereas Rochester's courage and presence of mind are attested to by independent witnesses, in one case a rival for the hand of Miss Malet. In his edition of Rochester's letters (1980), Jeremy Treglown writes that the poet's life is one of "famous paradoxes." Indeed, the courage-cowardice paradox fascinated Rochester. He lived it to the extreme, and he situates it in a fundamental place in his mocking, Hobbesian, debunking of human pretension, "Satyr against Reason and Mankind":

Look to the bottom of his vast design,
Wherein man's wisdom, power, and glory join:
The good he acts, the ill he does endure,
' Tis all from fear, to make himself secure.
Merely for safety, after fame we thirst,
For all men would be cowards if they durst.

Whatever the impulses that moved him in the wars, it is certain that some tangible reward, or consolation, came his way. Between his first and second periods of naval service, he was granted £750 on 31 October 1665 and in March 1666 was appointed Gentleman of the Bedchamber at a salary of £1000 per annum, which was not, however, authorized until October – a presage of Charles's system of finance. Commissioned a captain in Prince Rupert's regiment of horseguards in June, he also prepared to take his seat in the House of Lords. Possibly the king wished to provide the now meritorious Rochester with tokens of favor sufficient for him to lure Malet, but this is only conjecture. In any event, they

married on 29 January 1667. On 4 February Pepys records that at the playhouse he saw

my Lord Rochester and his lady, Mrs. Mallett, who hath after all this ado married him; and, as I hear some say in the pit, it is a great act of charity for he hath no estate.

There has been a good deal of speculative and imaginative reconstruction of this marriage, tending to highlight its apparent success and its sustained mutual affection. There is warrant for this in the letters Rochester wrote to his wife and in her regrettably few surviving replies. Vieth is inclined to interpret the correspondence as "evidence that Rochester and his wife enjoyed an unusually happy marriage." Thus the paradox of his domestic amiability and his sexual depravity at court is more strikingly etched. Against this construction it might be urged that the marriage consisted rather more in separation than in union, and in frustration, often financial, rather than satisfaction; there are also many suggestions that Rochester maintained affectionate relationships with women in town. Indeed, a strand of recent criticism brings out a perceived protofeminism in the sexual politics of his poetry where it is interpreted as rejecting enslavement by sexual power. It may also be the case that all Rochester's experiences are subject to the fundamental skepticism he expressed to his wife in a late (1680?) letter. The first page of the letter is lost; the remaining page begins, "soe greate a disproportion t'wixt our desires & what it has ordained to content them." Treglown conjectures that the first part of the sentence must have concerned immortality and the idea that in the next world a benevolent deity makes up for the disappointments of this world. The passage suggests that Rochester found in sex, in love, and in all projects inevitable disappointment; yet an intense mutual sympathy of mind is powerfully delineated in this document. He adds that any benefit obtained by flattery, fear, or subservience is fit only for a dog and then cautions the countess not to lose this letter: "It is not fitt for every body to finde."

This is a picture of their marriage near the end. To its early stage belongs a pair of lyrics in the form of a complaint ("Give me leave to rail at you," in which the lover presents himself as a slave bound by a "servile chain") and a response to it. The latter is a witty rejection of the plea for kindness, which harnesses the language of sex and power quite directly at one point:

Think not, Thyrsis, I will e'er
By my love my empire lose.

perfect
How ..... 'tis, or how free
Won't these enjoyments proove,
But you wth formall jealouse
Are still tormenting live

Latt us (since witt instructs us how)
Raise pleasure to the topp,
If rivall bottle you't allow
Ile suffer rivall fopp,

Ther's not a brisk insipid sparke
That flutter in the Towne
But wth y[r] wanton eyes you marke
Him out to be y[r] owne

You never thinke it worth y[r] care
How empty nor how dull
The heads of y[r] admirers are,
Soe that their backs bee full.

Draft for a poem published in two different versions in 1676 and 1680 (University of Nottingham, Duke of Portland MS. PW V31)

All this you freely may confess
Yett wee'l not disagree
for did you love you pleasures less
You were not fitt for mee

Whilst I my passion to persue
Am whole nights taking in
The ~~Pine~~ lusty juice of grapes, take you
The juice of lusty Men —

Upbraid mee not that I designe
Tricks to delude yr charmes
When running after mirth & wine
I leave yr longing Armes

For wine (whose power Nine can raise
Our thoughts soe farr above)
Affords Ideo's fitt to praise
What wee thinke fitt to Love

You grow constant through despair:
  Kindness you would soon abuse.

This imperious tone then reveals itself as feigned, for "There remains no other art" by which to gain his love. A manuscript, one of seven in Lady Rochester's hand, supports the ascription of the poem to her. The glimpse this provides of a witty, mutually appreciative relationship is nowhere eclipsed in their correspondence. This view is even reinforced by the tone of the letter written by Lady Rochester from the country to the town that asks whether her uncertainty of seeing her husband "be to try my patience or obedyence." Should she, she asks, forget her hopes of seeing him and "in the memory only torment my selfe" rather than trouble him with the reminder that "thear liues such a creature" as she? At this stage she is still animated by the quality that a jilted suitor had described years earlier as "the vanity and liberty of her carriage."

Pinto suggested that in the early years of their marriage the Rochesters saw each other as "impassioned shepherd and the scornful shepherdess of the rococo Arcadia." From this relationship, rather than, say, Rochester's affair with the great actress Elizabeth Barry, come many love songs that make him, according to Pinto contra Dr. Johnson, "not merely one of the mob of gentlemen who wrote with ease" but rather "one of the great love poets of the world, worthy to rank with Catullus and Burns." Songs of this caliber include "My dear mistress has a heart," "While on those lovely looks I gaze," and the widely admired "Absent from thee, I languish still," which, among other things, has led to comparisons of Rochester with John Donne. Rochester's modern editor Paul Hammond, for instance, writes that Donne is the most significant influence on Rochester and regards Rochester as having brought back a Donnean strength to the English lyric. These poems expressing suave anguish are offset by poems of more playful eroticism such as "As Chloris full of harmless thought" (first published as *Corydon and Cloris* [1676?]). In this piece the shepherdess is wooed by a comely shepherd whom she faintly commands to desist. He does not.

Thus she, who princes had denied
  With all their pompous train,
Was in the lucky minute tried
  And yielded to the swain.

It is another Chloris, or the same one, come down a notch in the world, who features in "Fair Chloris in a pigsty lay," a poem in the territory of Rochester's more obscene humor. She dreams of an urgent warning from her swain that one of her "tender herd" is in peril near the mouth of Flora's cave. The swain's story is a ruse, for he follows her to the cave and rapes her. Then

Frighted she wakes, and waking frigs.
  Nature thus kindly eased
In dreams raised by her murmuring pigs
And her own thumb between her legs
  She's innocent and pleased.

Frequently these jovial, obscene lyrics bear a parodic relationship to more sober songs (such as those of Francis Quarles), or they indulge a jaundiced response to jollier views of the world (for example, Rochester's "Phyllis, be gentler, I advise" responds to Robert Herrick's "To the Virgins, To Make Much of Time"). Where Donne seems to be the source, it is noteworthy that his omnipresent cosmological awareness is discarded in favor of a world without a sense of a larger ordering, or even disordering, but rather one that is simply comprised of successive things tending in no direction. Rochester's ethos, if one can read it in his lyrical poetry, is essentially without rules, although it expresses itself in a spectrum of sentiment from benign amusement to deep disgust.

It is likely that the darker part of Rochester's spectrum — as well as the satires, the lampoons, and the dramatic pieces — belongs to the town side of his life. Lady Rochester spent most of her time at Adderbury and at her parents' estates in Somerset, although she had a court appointment to attend Anne, Duchess of York. In the course of these duties it seems that Lady Rochester was persuaded, with the approbation of her husband, to convert to the Roman religion. Possibly Rochester saw that she would be better placed to defend her interests in the crypto-Roman atmosphere prevailing at court and blatantly in the establishment of James, Duke of York. However that may be, she was by no means as bound to court and town as he. How the town-country dichotomy affected him is memorably expressed by Aubrey:

in the country he was generally civill enough. He was wont to say that when he came to Brentford [within sight of London] the Devill entred into him and never left him till he came into the Country again.

Their first child, Anne, was born and baptized in April 1669, when Rochester was in Paris, banished from the court for his involvement in a duel. This misdemeanor followed hard on the heels of his

Copy of Jacob Huysmans's portrait of Rochester (National Portrait Gallery, London). In a June 1678 letter to a friend, Rochester said he believed "it a fault to laugh at the monkey we have here when I compare his condition with mankind."

disgraceful outburst of petty violence at court in February. Pepys was shocked more by the seeming indifference of the king than by the action itself. He reports that the king and company were drinking at the Dutch ambassador's residence,

> and among the rest of the King's company, there was that worthy fellow my Lord Rochester and T. Killigrew, whose mirth and raillery offended the former so much, that he did give T. Killigrew a box on the ear in the King's presence; which doth much give offence to the people here at Court, to see how cheap the king makes himself.

The next day Pepys saw the king walking freely with Rochester, and he comments on the monarch's "everlasting shame to have so idle a rogue his companion." Pepys had earlier recorded his distaste for "the silly discourse of the king," when Charles told a story of Rochester's clothes and gold being stolen while he was with his whore. Sex and quarreling, one might conclude, were his pastimes. In fact, while in Paris he was involved in an affray at the opera. His quarrelsome nature, despite exaggeration in apocrypha, was very real. Hearne records a curious explanation he heard from Giffard concerning this trait of Rochester's:

> He says my Ld. had a natural distemper upon him which was extraordinary, and he thinks this might be one occasion of shortening his days, which was that sometimes he could not have a stool for 3 Weeks or a Month together. Which Distemper his Lordship told him was a very great occasion of that warmth and heat he always expressed, his Brain being heated by the

Fumes and Humours that ascended and evacuated themselves that way.

To his list of pastimes and cues for violence must also be added Rochester's predilection for drink. To Burnet he said that he had been drunk continually for five years, never in that time "cool enough to be perfectly Master of himself." This description is entirely credible from the supporting evidence of his conduct in the 1670s – his letters and poems – with their leitmotiv of drunkenness and nausea. No poet, even of that time, has outdone Rochester in this respect. His elegant "Upon His Drinking a Bowl," a reworking of Anacreon via Pierre de Ronsard and more explicit than either, may with some assurance be assigned to late 1673 because of references to military affairs of that year. The poem keeps copulation (nearly indifferent on whether it be with "lovely boys" or women) and drink in a kind of symbiotic balance: "Cupid and Bacchus my saints are / May drink and love still reign." Together these pursuits eclipse all other claims on life: the speaker disclaims any interest in military heroism (a nice self-deprecation, typical of Rochester) or the grander universe of stars and constellations.

"The Disabled Debauchee," written probably in 1675 according to a manuscript dating, brilliantly develops the comparison between a retired admiral of former wars watching the progress of a sea battle with empathetic enthusiasm and an about-to-be impotent debauchee:

> So, when my days of impotence approach,
>   And I'm by pox and wine's unlucky chance
> Forced from the pleasing billows of debauch
>   On the dull shore of lazy temperance[.]

Although hors de combat through drink, the speaker will counsel youth not to shrink from the noble vice. In a pair of famous heroic stanzas he recalls former glories fueled by wine, in terms inviting autobiographical interpretation:

> I'll tell of whores attacked, their lords at home;
>   Bawds' quarters beaten up, and fortress won;
> Windows demolished, watches overcome;
>   And handsome ills by my contrivance done.
>
> Nor shall our love-fits, Chloris, be forgot,
>   When each the well-looked linkboy strove t' enjoy,
> And the best kiss was the deciding lot
>   Whether the boy fucked you, or I the boy.

The savage daily round of dissipation is again depicted in "Regime d'viver" (possibly by Roches-

ter in Walker's view, spurious in Vieth's, but nonetheless apt), which is a wry mock-confession, a forensic account of how sex and drink occlude all else except, in the case of the whore, money.

> I Rise at Eleven, I Dine about Two,
> I get drunk before Seven, and the next thing I do,
> I send for my *Whore,* when for fear of a *Clap,*
> I spend in her hand, and I spew in her *Lap.*

Then she robs him and leaves him:

> I storm and I roar, and I fall in a rage,
> And missing my *Whore,* I bugger my *Page:*
> Then crop-sick, all *Morning,* I rail at my *Men,*
> And in Bed I lye Yawning, till Eleven again.

This self-mockery is in a minor key compared to what Treglown described as "the best poem ever written about premature ejaculation." "The Imperfect Enjoyment" arises from a genre established by Ovid and Petronius among the ancients and celebrated by Rochester's good friends George Etherege (in *The Man of Mode,* 1676) and Aphra Behn (in *The Rover,* 1677). Dorimant in the former play and Willmore in the latter are modeled on Rochester. In the poem the speaker outgoes the tradition for vehemence of invective against the offending member – "Thou treacherous, base deserter of my flame." In the final insult he hopes that "ten thousand abler pricks agree / To do the wronged Corinna right for thee." The violent denunciation of the quondam violent member ("The rakehell villain") is controlled by the good humor of the poem.

Whether the violence and vehemence of "A Ramble in St. James's Park" is likewise controlled is a debated question. The publishers of Pinto's edition suppressed it, and it has subsequently been judged unprintable. To an understanding of Rochester's sexual politics, it is central. In 1988 another consideration of the poem, by Marianne Thormählen, showed how distant is the prospect of consensus on Rochester and how exceedingly complicated are the critical and scholarly problems. The import of the violent second half of this poem depends on who the speaker is thought to be: Charles II, the clown hero, a jaded stallion, a satirized fop, the heroic self, or perhaps Rochester. The speaker, out to relieve drunkenness with a bout of lechery, enters a landscape that is a grotesque rendering of the *locus amoenas* (delightful place) trope, not just a garden conducive to love, but a scene of predatory copulation, where by "incestuous birth / Strange woods spring from the teeming earth" and where "mandrakes tall did rise / Whose lewd tops fucked the very skies." Here Corinna, who has disdained the speaker, is courted by fops and fools. At first he is amused, but then a storm of savage indignation against fools of all kinds erupts:

> Gods! that a thing admired by me
> Should fall to so much infamy.
> Had she picked out, to rub her arse on,
> Some stiff-pricked clown or well-hung parson,
> Each job of whose spermatic sluice
> Had filled her cunt with wholesome juice,
> I the proceeding should have praised
> In hope sh' had quenched a fire I raised.

The tirade continues for seventy more lines. It is not Corinna's infidelity which counts – fidelity in this world means nothing – but that she should choose such fools to satisfy her itch. Although Rochester's Corinnas have every right to rabid promiscuity, the fools put the speaker beyond measure. Lines such as these are responsible for Sir Sidney Lee's judgment, in the *Dictionary of National Biography,* of Rochester as "the writer of the filthiest verse in the language."

Rochester's literary production was in full spate in the 1670s, even as his life was increasingly punctuated by violent temper, flagrant indiscretions, and the almost routine banishments from court. Soon after John Dryden had dedicated to Rochester his *Marriage A-La-Mode* in 1673 and Elkanah Settle had dedicated to him his *Empress of Morocco,* Rochester offended the king by presenting to him a lampoon on his politics and his manners – "His scepter and his prick are of a length; / And she may sway the one who plays with th'other, / . . . / Restless he rolls about from whore to whore, / A merry monarch, scandalous and poor." The final couplet begins, "All monarchs I hate." What Rochester intended to give to Charles was his "Signior Dildo," a high-spirited work, which scandalously plays on the excitement of English ladies at the prospective arrival of the Italian dildo, much preferred to their spouses: "This signior is sound, safe, ready, and dumb / As ever was candle, carrot, or thumb."

On the occasion of the customs officers, or "farmers," seizing a consignment of leather dildos, Henry Savile, Rochester's constant friend, writes to him in the country that there

> has been lately unfortunately seized a box of those leather instruments y^r L^p carryed downe one of, but these barbarian Farmers prompted by ye villanous instigation of theire wives voted them prohibited goods soe that they were burnt without mercy.

Rochester is urged to think of his, as it were, religious and military duties:

> then pray consider whether it is fitt for you to bee blowing of coales in the country when there is a revenge due to ye ashes of these Martyrs. Y^{r}L^p is chosen Generall in this warr betwixt the Ballers & ye farmers.

Hayward described the Ballers as "the wildest and most mischievous set of young men and women that have ever met together." Pepys was thrilled by their company:

> And so to supper in an arbor; but Lord, their mad bawdy talk did make my heart ake. And here I first understood by their talk the meaning of the company that lately were called "Ballers," Harris telling how it was by a meeting of some young blades, where he was among them, and my Lady Bennet and her ladies, and there dancing naked, and all the roguish things in the world. But Lord, what loose cursed company was this that I was in tonight; though full of wit.

Pepys's reaction suggests how Rochester's reputation would develop in the final decade of his life. The town teemed with stories of his riotous escapades, even as his influence in the theater increased, as his poetry (especially his satire) was widely praised by qualified contemporaries, and as his family grew and prospered. His son Charles was born in January 1671, his second daughter, Elizabeth, in June 1674, and his third daughter, Malet, in January 1675. Another daughter was born to Elizabeth Barry in 1677 at the end of their protracted and passionate affair, during which he coached her talent for the stage.

After banishment for offense to the "merry monarch," Rochester was once again in favor, and a rise in his fortunes was signaled by the grant on 27 February 1674 of the Rangership of Woodstock Park and then on 2 May the Keepership, which allowed him to live at the fine lodge in the park. By late 1675, however, he had lost the reversion of this comfortable appointment – an indication of how badly he had again fallen into disfavor. One cause must have been his drunken destruction of the king's elaborate glass sundials on 25 June 1675, an escapade recorded by John Aubrey in his brief life of Linus. His giving offense to Louise Renée de Kéroualle, Duchess of Portsmouth, may also have contributed to his loss of favor (his correspondence shows that how he offended her was unclear to him). In a period of disgrace such as this he played out his famous masquerade as Dr. Bendo, the mountebank, on Tower Hill. This virtuoso display of deceit in action and its consequent demonstration of human gullibility has been compared by Anne Righter to the stage character of Volpone. In a nonextant broadside, "Dr. Bendo's Advertisement," Bendo asked, "Is it therefore, my fault if the cheat, by his wits and endeavours, makes himself so like me that consequently I cannot avoid resembling him?" As Righter points out, Bendo's wit, like his inventor's, depends on confounding antithesis in identity. It is also noteworthy that "Dr. Bendo's Advertisement" displays considerable knowledge of contemporary medicine, with especial interest in women's complaints, particularly disfigurements of facial beauty.

On the night of 17 June 1676, Rochester, in the company of other rakes at the village of Epsom, which they had visited for horse racing, initiated a brawl with first the local constable and then the watch called to his assistance. The fight culminated in the fatal wounding of Rochester's companion Captain Downs, who had interposed himself between Rochester's drawn sword and the constable. Downs was beaten to the ground by the watch; Rochester and the others fled, leaving him to his fate. Thus the naval hero now acquired a reputation for violent cowardice. On 4 June 1677, when a cook was stabbed to death at a tavern where Rochester was dining, instant rumor named him the killer. In a letter to Savile he refers to this and other apocryphal events, including alfresco debauches at Woodstock. Many years earlier, in 1669, he had been characterized as a coward for his conduct in a duel with John Sheffield, third Earl of Mulgrave. They remained lifelong enemies and fought repeated literary skirmishes. It might be judged that Rochester emerged victorious when he ridiculed Mulgrave as "My Lord All-Pride," published in a 1679 broadside, which begins, "Bursting with pride, the loathed impostume swells; / Prick him, he sheds his venom straight, and smells." Another victim of literary dueling was the rival wit Sir Carr Scroope, whom Rochester dispatched in the 1678 poem "On Poet Ninny." Scroope had earlier written of Rochester, "Thy Pen is full as harmlesse as thy Sword."

These were skirmishes in the larger literary war that developed between Rochester and Dryden. Earlier, of course, Rochester had been Dryden's patron, and many hyperbolic compliments passed between them. The reversal is seen in Rochester's "An Allusion to Horace," which starts,

> Well, sir, 'tis granted I said Dryden's rhymes
> Were stol'n, unequal, nay dull many times.
> What foolish patron is there found of his
> So blindly partial to deny me this?

The "foolish patron" is Mulgrave. By 1676 the world of the theater and the wits had taken sides in the quarrel. Thomas Otway, Elkanah Settle, Thomas Shadwell, George Villiers, second Duke of Buckingham, George Etherege, William Wycherley, John Crowne, and Francis Fane all at one time or another were on Rochester's side. Whether or not Rochester had any part in the brutal, cowardly beating of Dryden in Rose Alley on 18 December 1679, thought to be in response to his "Essay on Satire," is not resolved. It has been laid heavily to Rochester's discredit. Treglown includes a letter from Rochester to Savile on 21 November 1679 in which Dryden's poem is termed a libel, but the letter carrying a threat of physical violence – "leave the repartee to Black Will with a cudgel" – is from early 1676.

Rochester's theatrical work includes some prologues and epilogues, a scene for a play by Sir Robert Howard, and *Valentinian* (1685), an adaptation of John Fletcher's play of the same name. The manuscript copy of Rochester's version is titled "Lucina's Rape." Pinto regards Rochester's work as a transforming of a loosely structured melodrama into a "symbolic poem full of profound meaning." It may not have been performed until 1684, and it was not published until 1685.

Sodom was commonly ascribed to Rochester until recently, despite a poem attributed to him in the 1680 edition, "Upon the Author of the Play call'd Sodom," which vigorously denounces the work. The play has drawn extraordinarily vehement reactions and is still much in debate. Editions are very hard to come by. There is said to have been a 1684 edition, no longer extant, and J. W. Johnson reports a 1689 edition, the printers of which were prosecuted. L. S. A. M. von Römer's 1904 edition, the basis of modern ones, points out usefully the similarity in theme between this play and the passage in *Valentinian* in which Chylax characterizes women's love as usury, but boys' love as a "disinterested Flame."

Certainly *Sodom* examines the arena of sexual politics and "gynecocracy" and is not devoid of wit. Understanding the play and its relationship to Rochester, however, is a paradigm of the problem of Rochester scholarship. For example, although the poem of 1680 (one of several denouncing the play) has been cited as evidence that Rochester did not write *Sodom*, it has also been used as evidence that he did write the play on the ground that it shows a characteristic shift to an antithetical voice and posture. Dustin H. Griffin argues that the play is erotic and therefore not by Rochester, whereas Albert Ellis argues that it is a philosophical and moral

Frontispiece and title page for the bishop of Salisbury's account of the religious and moral debates that led to Rochester's deathbed conversion (Courtesy of the Special Collections Section of the Mills Memorial Library, McMaster University)

work and that it is by Rochester. It has also been argued that it is the work of John Oldham. A. S. G. Edwards, however, wisely cautions against the search for single authorship, advice that might be valuable in discussions of other works attributed to Rochester. The case for Rochester's authorship is argued at length by J. W. Johnson. However the case may be decided, Sir Sidney Lee's judgment that it is a play of "intolerable foulness" is not likely to deter readers in the light of modern mores.

Rochester's real reputation rests on the great satires that ask, in the words from "Tunbridge Wells," "what thing is man, that thus / In all his shapes, he is ridiculous?" The satires carry with them the paradoxically invigorating taste of what in "A Letter from Artemesia" he terms "the nauseous draught of life." On 29 February 1676 Rochester wrote, "This day I received the unhappy news of my own death and burial," adding that he will now live on out of "spite." That spite is the leaven of his satire. When Burnet objected to its malice, Rochester replied:

> a man could not write with life unless he were heated by revenge; for, to write satire, without resentment, upon the cold notions of philosophy, was as if a man would in cold blood cut men's throats who had never offended him.

Anything but coldly, Rochester gives to the nihilistic philosophy of the age its most incandescent, popular expression – especially in "On Nothing" and in "Satyr against Reason and Mankind," with its memorable figure of "reasonable" man falling from the mountain of his useless speculations (possibly a parody of Donne's "Satire III") into "doubt's boundless sea." The urbane self-mocking pose is beautifully rendered in the portrait of Rochester and his monkey (circa 1675; attributed to Jacob Huysmans).

As Rochester's health swiftly declined from multiple causes, including the effects of profligacy, the world awaited his death with eager anticipation. His discussions of theology and philosophy with the quartet of divines led by the indefatigable Bishop Burnet are minutely recorded by him, as is his repentance, which was broadcast as a triumph for the established faith. His death was celebrated by those with an interest in the morals of the nation and the efficacy of religion, as well as by the booksellers who ("merely for lucre sake," wrote Wood) rushed unauthorized editions of his poems and Burnet's *Some Passages* into print.

His death was mourned by the poets, however, who wrote many pastoral laments for "Strephon" (his name in Arcadia). These often elegant lamentations, such as the one by Thomas Flatman, provide distance from the ferocity of Rochester's own "To the Postboy." Although probably written some years before 1680, this poem is often taken as Rochester's epilogue:

> Son of a whore, God damn you! can you tell
> A peerless peer the readiest way to Hell?
> I've outswilled Bacchus, sworn of my own make
> Oaths would fright Furies, and make Pluto quake;
> I've swived more whores more ways than Sodom's walls
> E'er knew, or the College of Rome's Cardinals.
> Witness heroic scars — Look here, ne'er go! —
> Cerecloths and ulcers from top to toe!
> Frighted at my own mischiefs, I have fled
> And bravely left my life's defender dead;
> Broke houses to break chastity, and dyed
> That floor with murder which my lust denied.
> Pox on't, why do I speak of these poor things?
> I have blasphemed my God, and libeled Kings!
> The readiest way to Hell — Come, quick!
> *Boy:*   Ne'er stir:
> The readiest way, my Lord, 's by Rochester.

That there is any hell beyond this world, however, he denied, in what must be his last poetic effort, the elegant translation from Seneca's "Troades," starting "After death nothing is, and nothing, death," which he sent as part of a long correspondence to the deist philosopher Charles Blount. In his poem "On the Penitent Death of the Earle of Rochester," Sir Francis Fane wrote that this world itself was rendered a dark nothing after the departure of the flame of that "Seraphic Lord": "What words, what Sense, what Night-piece can express / The

worlds obscurity, and emptiness / Since Rochester withdrew his Vital Beams."

Letters:

The Rochester-Savile Letters 1671–1680, edited by John Harold Wilson (Columbus: Ohio State University Press, 1941);

The Letters of John Wilmot, Earl of Rochester, edited by Jeremy Treglown (Oxford: Blackwell, 1980).

Bibliographies:

Johannes Prinz, *John Wilmot Earl of Rochester, His Life and Writings With His Lordship's Private Correspondence, Various Other Documents, And A Bibliography Of His Works And Of The Literature On Him* (Leipzig: Mayer & Müller, 1927);

David M. Vieth, *Attribution in Restoration Poetry: A Study of Rochester's "Poems" of 1680* (New Haven & London: Yale University Press, 1963);

Vieth, *Rochester Studies, 1925–1982: An Annotated Bibliography* (New York & London: Garland, 1984).

Biographies:

Gilbert Burnet, *Some Passages Of The Life and Death of the Right Honourable John Earl of Rochester* (London: Printed for Richard Chiswell, 1680);

Anthony Wood, "John Wilmot," in his *Athenæ Oxonienses,* volume 3, edited by Philip Bliss (London: Printed for F. C. & J. Rivington & others, 1817), pp. 1228–1234;

Johannes Prinz, *Rochesteriana: Being Some Anecdotes Concerning John Wilmot, Earl of Rochester* (Leipzig: Privately printed, 1926);

Prinz, *John Wilmot Earl of Rochester* (Leipzig: Mayer & Müller, 1927);

Vivian de Sola Pinto, *Rochester: Portrait of a Restoration Poet* (London: John Lane, Bodley Head, 1935); revised as *Enthusiast in Wit: A Portrait of John Wilmot Earl of Rochester 1647–1680* (London: Routledge & Kegan Paul, 1962; Lincoln: University of Nebraska Press, 1962);

Charles Williams, *Rochester* (London: Arthur Barker, 1935);

Kenneth B. Murdock, " 'A Very Profane Wit': John Wilmot, Earl of Rochester, 1647–1680," in his *The Sun at Noon: Three Biographical Sketches* (New York: Macmillan, 1939);

John Harold Wilson, *The Court Wits of the Restoration: An Introduction* (Princeton: Princeton University Press, 1948);

Charles Norman, *Rake Rochester* (New York: Crown, 1954);

Samuel Johnson, "Rochester," in his *Lives of the English Poets,* volume 1, edited by George Birckbeck-Hill (New York: Octagon, 1967), pp. 219–228;

John Adlard, ed., *The Debt to Pleasure: John Wilmot, Earl of Rochester in the Eyes of His Contemporaries and in His Own Poetry and Prose* (Manchester: Carcanet, 1974);

Graham Greene, *Lord Rochester's Monkey being the Life of John Wilmot, Second Earl of Rochester* (London: Bodley Head, 1974; New York: Viking, 1974).

References:

W. J. Cameron, "A Late Seventeenth-Century Scriptorium," *Renaissance and Modern Studies,* 7 (1963): 25–52;

Larry Carver, "Rascal Before the Lord: Rochester's Religious Rhetoric," *Essays in Literature,* 9 (Fall 1982): 155–169;

A. S. G. Edwards, "The Authorship of *Sodom,*" *Papers of the Bibliographical Society of America,* 71 (Second Quarter 1977): 208–212;

David Farley-Hills, *Rochester: The Critical Heritage* (London: Routledge & Kegan Paul, 1972; New York: Barnes & Noble, 1972);

Farley-Hills, *Rochester's Poetry* (London: Bell & Hyman, 1978; Totowa, N. J.: Rowman & Littlefield, 1978);

Dustin H. Griffin, *Satires Against Man: The Poems of Rochester* (Berkeley & Los Angeles: University of California Press, 1973; London: University of California Press, 1973);

Thomas Hearne, *The Remains of Thomas Hearne: Reliquiæ Hearnianæ,* edited by John Buchanan-Brown (Fontwell & London: Centaur, 1966; Carbondale: Southern Illinois University Press, 1967);

J. W. Johnson, "Anthony à Wood and Rochester," *Restoration,* 12 (Fall 1988): 69–79;

Johnson, "Did Lord Rochester Write *Sodom?,*" *Papers of the Bibliographical Society of America,* 81 (June 1987): 119–153;

John F. Moehlmann, *A Concordance to the Complete Poems of John Wilmot, Earl of Rochester* (Troy, N.Y.: Whitston, 1979);

John D. Patterson, "Rochester's Second Bottle: Attitudes to Drink and Drinking in the Works of John Wilmot, Earl of Rochester," *Restoration: Studies in English Literary Culture, 1660–1700,* 5 (Spring 1981): 6–15;

Ronald Paulson, "Rochester: The Body Politic and the Body Private," in *The Author in His Work: Essays on a Problem in Criticism,* edited by Louis L. Martz and Aubrey Williams (New Haven & London: Yale University Press, 1978), pp. 103–121;

Anne Righter, "John Wilmot, Earl of Rochester," *Proceedings of the British Academy,* 53 (1967): 47–69;

Ken Robinson, "The Art of Violence in Rochester's Satire," in *English Satire and the Satiric Tradition,* edited by Claude Rawson (Oxford: Blackwell, 1984), pp. 93–108;

Robinson, "Rochester's Dilemma," *Durham University Journal,* new series 40 (June 1979): 223–231;

Marianne Thormählen, "Rochester and Jealousy: Consistent Inconsistencies," *Durham University Journal,* new series 49 (June 1988): 213–223;

Jeremy Treglown, ed., *Spirit of Wit: Reconsiderations of Rochester* (Oxford: Blackwell, 1982);

Francis Whitfield, *Beast in View: A Study of the Earl of Rochester's Poetry* (Cambridge, Mass.: Harvard University Press, 1936; London: Oxford University Press, 1936);

Reba Wilcoxon, "Rochester's Philosophical Premises: A Case for Consistency," *Eighteenth-Century Studies,* 8 (Winter 1974/75): 183–201;

Wilcoxon, "Rochester's Sexual Politics," *Studies in Eighteenth-Century Culture,* edited by Roseann Runte (Madison: University of Wisconsin Press, 1979), pp. 137–149.

Papers:

Manuscript versions of Rochester's poetry, and of poems attributed to him, are legion and widely dispersed. In many cases the manuscripts are copies of published versions of the poems, and frequently Rochester's work was copied into manuscript miscellanies by professional scribes ("factory" manuscripts) for the libraries of the aristocracy. An instance of the latter is the Gyldenstolpe miscellany in the Royal Library, Stockholm. Important manuscript collections are at Nottingham (the Portland MSS., which include some holographs), Yale University (Osborn MSS.), the Huntington Library (Ellesmere MSS.), the British Library (Harleian, Add., Sloane MSS.), the Bodleian Library (Add., Don., Douce, Eng. poet., Rawl. poet., etc. MSS.). Smaller collections in Great Britain relating to Rochester are at Lambeth Palace, the Victoria and Albert Museum, Cambridge University, Aberystwyth, Edinburgh, and Leeds. Rochester manuscripts in the United States are at the Folger Library, Harvard University, Princeton University, and the University of Illinois Library. There is also a manuscript at the Nationalbibliothek, Vienna. Rochester's letters are at the British Library (Harleian MS. 7003) and in the collection of the Marquess of Bath at Longleat (Portland II).

Sir Charles Sedley

(March 1639 – August 1701)

James E. Gill
University of Tennessee

BOOKS: *Pompey the Great: A Tragedy. As it was Acted by the Servants of His Royal Highness the Duke of York. Translated out of French by Certain Persons of Honour,* Pierre Corneille's *Mort de Pompée* translated by Sedley, Edmund Waller, Charles Sackville, Edward Filmer, and Sidney Godolphin (London: Printed for Henry Herringman, 1664);

The Mulberry-Garden, A Comedy. As it is Acted by His Majesties' Servants At the Theatre-Royal (London: Printed for Henry Herringman, 1668);

Antony and Cleopatra: A Tragedy. As it is Acted at the Duke's Theatre (London: Printed for Richard Tonson, 1677);

Bellamira, Or The Mistress, A Comedy: As it is Acted by Their Majesties Servants (London: Printed by D. Mallet for L. C. & Timothy Goodwin, 1687);

The Speech of Sir Charles Sidley in the House of Commons (London: Printed for L. C., 1691).

Editions: *Miscellaneous Works of Sir Charles Sedley,* edited by William Ayloffe (London: Printed & sold by John Nutt, 1702);

The Works of the Honourable Sir Charles Sedley, Bar^t, 2 volumes (London: Printed for S. Briscoe, sold by T. Bickerton, 1722);

The Poetical and Dramatic Works of Sir Charles Sedley Collected and Edited from the Old Editions, 2 volumes, edited by Vivian de Sola Pinto (London: Constable, 1928).

OTHER: *A Collection of Poems Written upon Several Occasions by Several Persons,* includes thirty poems attributed to Sedley (London: Printed for Hobart Kemp, 1672); revised as *A Collection of Poems By Several Hands. Most of them Written by Persons of Eminent Quality,* includes twenty poems attributed to Sedley (London: Printed by T. Warren for Francis Saunders, 1693);

The Fourth Book of Virgil, by a Person of Quality, translated by Sedley (London, 1692).

During the reign of Charles II, Sir Charles Sedley was known for his participation in the wild activities of the king's drinking companions, the "ministry of pleasure" – an irregular but influential group of men consisting of wits such as Charles Sackville, Lord Buckhurst; George Villiers, second Duke of Buckingham; John Wilmot, second Earl of Rochester; Sir George Etherege, and Henry Saville. Charles II was said to have delighted in Sedley's wit, and Sedley was affectionately known among his brother rakes as "Little Sid." Nearly all of these men participated in important ways in the literary and political life of their time, but, owing to an aristocratic prejudice against publishing poetry under their names, much of their verse circulated chiefly in manuscript or in unauthorized publications; as a consequence modern editors have only with great difficulty achieved fairly reliable texts of their work, and even then the authorship of many poems remains in doubt. Sedley is no exception to this rule.

Outside the "ministry of pleasure," Sedley came to be known for his wit, intelligence, and civility. John Dryden's dedication to Sedley of his comedy *The Assignation* (1673) and Thomas Shadwell's dedications of *A True Widow* (performed in 1678) and of his translation of *The Tenth Satire of Juvenal* (1687) show Sedley as a patron. Sedley also wrote plays and verse himself – his polished songs and lyrics, like those of other Restoration gentlemen and lords, circulated widely in manuscript – and he became involved in the literary alliances and quarrels of the time. Because of Sedley's collaboration in the translation of Pierre Corneille's *Mort de Pompée* (1642), Englished as *Pompey the Great* (1664), Dryden elegantly quarreled with him by modeling the

Sir Charles Sedley (portrait by an unknown artist; Collection of Lord Sackville of Knole)

Francophile Lisideius in the *Essay of Dramatic Poesie* (1668) after him. The issues in Corneille's *Mort de Pompée* – regicide, usurpation, and restoration of legitimate rule – were of the sort to appeal to Sedley and his Royalist companions. His first original drama, *The Mulberry-Garden,* modeled in part after Molière's *L'Ecole des maris* (1661), was produced and published in 1668. The play follows the peculiar form of early Restoration comedy developed by Dryden and Etherege in having a high plot mostly in rhymed verse and a low plot in witty prose. *The Mulberry-Garden* has a serious theme – that of honor and intelligent self-discipline and the kind of liberal governance which fosters them. In the high plot the attitudes and behavior of the puritanical Forecast and his daughters contrast with the liberal family regime of his brother Everyoung. In the low plot Forecast competes for the hand of a wealthy widow not for love but for money. In a very different form

analogous themes are apparent in Sedley's second drama, *Antony and Cleopatra* (1677; revised as *Beauty the Conqueror* in *Miscellaneous Works,* 1702). Sedley criticizes Charles II's policies and his chief minister Thomas Osborne, Earl of Danby, through Antony's enslavement to Cleopatra and his victimization by false advisers. In 1678 Dryden seems to have attacked Sedley again in the preface to *All for Love* and may have obliquely presented his own exculpation of the king through his version of the tragedy of these famous lovers. Many of Sedley's amorous songs and pastoral dialogues were probably written during the 1660s and 1670s, and they too reflect, in sometimes strange ways, Sedley's concern for control and liberal discipline.

Born in March 1639, Charles Sedley was the ninth child of Sir John Sedley (or Sidley), who had died the year before. Sir John Sedley had been a respected barrister and patron of learning, knighted and created baronet by James I. Charles's mother was a daughter of the great Elizabethan scholar Sir Henry Savile. Charles Sedley entered Wadham College, Oxford, as a fellow commoner on 22 March 1656, but he took no degrees. A few weeks after he entered Oxford, his brother Sir William died, and Sedley inherited his title and the extensive family estate. He married Katherine Savage, daughter of John Savage, Earl Rivers, on 9 February 1657. Their daughter Katherine, later a mistress of James II, was born in 1659. His wife gradually succumbed to serious emotional sickness, and, being Roman Catholic, she was eventually cared for in a convent on the Continent. After the Restoration Sedley achieved some notoriety (requiring royal intervention on his behalf) during a celebration in 1663 at the Cock Tavern, where, in a state of undress, he gave a drunken parody of a Puritan sermon and a mountebank's speech to an assembled mob of about one thousand scandalized citizens. Samuel Pepys wrote in his diary that in 1667 Sir Charles was "keeping merry house" with the actress Nell Gwyn and Lord Buckhurst. The diarist heard that during another period of debauch in 1668 Buckhurst and Sedley cavorted "up and down all night with their arses bare, through the streets; and at last fighting, and being beat by the watch," they were "clapped up all night." Presumably some of the pornographic poems attributed to Sedley by David M. Vieth in *The Gyldenstolpe Manuscript* (1967) date from this period, as well as many of Sedley's graceful love lyrics.

Sedley's political and literary interests in the late 1670s changed for two probable reasons. One was the gradual dissolution of King Charles's band of wits, in part caused by the disaffection or death of some of its members and in part by the ugly tone of the politics of the day, dominated as they came to be by the succession question, the Popish Plot, the king's French policy, his crypto-Catholicism, and the reactionary Oxford Parliament. Sedley began his parliamentary service as a supporter of the court, but by 1677 he began supporting the Whig cause, and by 1685 he was probably being deliberately and illegally excluded from the Parliament of James II. It is not surprising that Sedley, often critical of Charles, utterly opposed James and supported the cause of William of Orange both before the Glorious Revolution (1688–1689) and after, when he returned to Parliament. Like many of Charles's "ministers of pleasure," Sedley may have felt personal dislike for James II. Later referring to his daughter Katherine (whose services as one of his

mistresses James in January 1686 rewarded by making her countess of Dorchester and baroness Darlington) and to Queen Mary II (both the daughter of James and the wife of William III), Sedley was reported to have said after the revolution, "Well, I am even in point of civility with King James. For as he made my daughter a Countess, so I have helped to make his daughter a Queen" (from "Some Account of the Life of Sir Charles Sedley," in *Works*, 1722). As this witticism suggests, Sedley's later life was marked by some serious attention to politics, especially by his opposition to the Catholic monarch James and by his loyal service in Parliament to William III. It is from this period as well as the reign of James that many of Sedley's later satirical epigrams probably date, some of them written for the *Gentleman's Journal,* a new miscellany magazine.

Also to the end of James II's reign belongs Sedley's last play, *Bellamira, Or The Mistress, A Comedy* (1687), often said to be an adaptation of Terence's *Eunuch;* because of its cynicism and frank display of lust, sexual betrayal, and greed, this play, like many of its time, seems darker than the better-known comedies of the 1670s. Michael B. Hudnall, Jr., suggests that the theme of the play is moral and emotional impotence – it is about characters whose fatal need to manipulate others for profit or glory keeps them from living significant, fulfilled lives.

Besides age and the worsening political scene, another reason for Sedley's shift from amatory lyric and dialogue to satirical epigram is personal and doubtless owes to the settling of Sedley's love life. About 1670 Sedley met and fell in love with Ann Ayscough, the daughter of a Yorkshire gentleman. At first he apparently pursued her in the cavalier manner he used with all young women. According to Vivian de Sola Pinto, he ended "by making her his wife in every sense except a legal one," because he was of course still legally married to the mad Katherine Savage, cared for abroad. Though divorce was virtually unheard of, he apparently risked prosecution for the felony of bigamy by going through a form of marriage with Ann, and he remained her loving mate for as long as she lived. She bore him two sons, but only one lived to adulthood, and even he died before his father's death in 1701. This young man did, however, live long enough to run away with the daughter of a gentleman, and some of Sedley's most winning surviving letters deal with securing a reconciliation of the couple with his daughter-in-law's family. Sedley's song "Cloris, I justly am betray'd" and his later long

Katherine Sedley, Countess of Dorchester, daughter of the poet and a mistress of Charles II

poem "The Happy Pair," which satirizes mercenary, loveless marriages, are probably tributes to his genuinely happy relationship with Ann.

In Pinto's 1928 edition of Sedley's work, the "Poems and Translations" section in volume one follows the order of the first posthumous edition of the poetry, by William Ayloffe in 1702. "A Pastoral Dialogue between Thirsis and Strephon" is followed by over fifty poems that range from amatory songs, dialogues, advices, and complaints, to satirical pieces and epigrams; these are followed by an additional thirty satirical epigrams, or "Court Characters," imitating the Roman poet Martial's short biting poems and their English imitations by Ben Jonson (many of these were published first in the periodical press); next is "The Happy Pair" in elegiac couplets. Ayloffe's edition of the poems is concluded by translations from Virgil's fourth *Georgic* (there also exists a 1692 edition of this translation).

Pinto's edition added to these poems Sedley's translations of three elegies from Ovid's *Amores:* "He curses a Bawd, for going about to debauch his Mistress," "To his false Mistress," and "To A Man that lockt up his Wife."

In the introductory poem to Ayloffe's edition, "A Pastoral Dialogue Between Thirsis and Strephon," the interlocutor Thirsis successfully arouses the depressed swain Strephon (often the pastoral name given to Rochester) by urging him to compete in a wrestling match among shepherds for a coat spun by his beloved but cold nymph Galatea. The poem thus indirectly accounts for the poet's rousing himself to write the succeeding love poems. The first fifty or so of the poems in Ayloffe's edition can be seen mainly as the youthful poet's exploration of various amatory attitudes of swain and nymph. Most of the poems, however, celebrate a more detached and controlled attitude than one might expect from a poet of Sedley's reputation for wild behavior. The second poem of the series, for example, is very different in mode and message from its pastoral introduction. It is addressed to Phyllis, who with the speaker will "shun the common Fate, / And let our Love ne'r turn to Hate." The unconventional ideal in this poem is to accept gracefully the first flowering, the natural decay, and the inevitable death of passion and, if necessary, of affection too. The idea that parting well is an aspect or consequence of loving well appears very early in the series, and this is probably no accident, for the first lyrics forecast patterns and themes to come — the idea of a natural fidelity lasting only so long as genuine passion lasts, the economies or limits of despair in love, and the necessary (but short-lived) unity of desire, expression, and satisfaction in love. In "To Cloris," the poem that illustrates the last theme, one can see the usual strengths and weaknesses of the songs typical of Restoration wits such as Sedley. Such songs moderated the conceits and sophistic, logical play of earlier seventeenth-century lyrics such as those of John Donne, Thomas Carew, and Sir John Suckling and subjected them to the metrical polish of Cavalier lyrics such as those of William Cartwright, Richard Lovelace, and Edmund Waller.

> *Cloris,* I cannot say your Eyes
> Did my unwary Heart surprize;
> Nor will I swear it was your Face,
> Your Shape, or any nameless Grace:
> For you are so intirely Fair,
> To love a Part, Injustice were;
> No drowning Man can know which Drop
> Of Water his last Breath did stop;
> So when the Stars in Heaven appear,
> And joyn to make the Night look clear;
> The Light we no one's Bounty call,
> But the obliging Gift of all.
> He that does Lips or Hands adore,
> Deserves them only, and no more;
> But I love All, and every Part,
> And nothing less can ease my Heart.
> *Cupid,* that Lover, weakly strikes,
> Who can express what 'tis he likes.

This poem recapitulates in an easy, unforced way several common themes in seventeenth-century amatory verse. The themes of "all" and "nothing" in love appeared frequently after Donne's argumentative "Lovers infinitenesse" and "A Nocturnal upon S. Lucies day," and so did the theme of the inadequacy of language in love (see, for example, Donne's "The undertaking"). The mockery of inventories of the beloved's graces can be seen in William Shakespeare's anti-Petrarchan sonnet 130 ("My Mistress' eyes are nothing like the sun"), for example, and Suckling's "Deformed Mistress." The difference between "To Cloris" and its predecessors is that Sedley almost imperceptibly compresses his argument into a blandly conceited one about the impossibility of discriminating among the parts of virtual infinities. Just as the analogy ("So when the Stars . . . ") establishes a parity between the futility of micro- and macroscopic discrimination, so in the penultimate couplet the poem celebrates again antithetically ("All," "Heart") its desire for a totality of presence in language that cannot communicate it without its negatives ("Part," "nothing"); and, following this disjunctive or antithetical logic, the final lines almost deny a positive connection of feeling to speech. The problem here for the modern reader is that such a poem "undoes" itself by its procedures: its wit is all in negatives, and its art is muted and concealed (as George Williamson notes, the "wit of negation" was popular at the time). The modesty of the poem and its "good manners" — its avoidance of technical or learned terms — and its naturalness and understatement are supposed to be typical of what Alexander Pope termed the poetry of "the mob of gentlemen who wrote with ease." Sedley, however, more consistently than Rochester, Buckhurst, Etherege, or Buckingham, pursues these ideals in wedding theme and form in his amatory verse and as a result has been called by Pinto the "typical poet of this Utopia of gallantry. . . . He felt all the charm of the rococco pastoral and did not trouble to think about it too much" (*Restoration Carnival,* 1954). Such statements minimize the restraint and discipline implicit in much of Sedley's best verse, and they ignore entirely the tough-minded epigrams of his later years, but they do indicate his gentlemanly discipline. In "A Satire," the needy poet John Oldham wrote that Sedley, in contrast to the writer who lived by his pen, "may be content with Fame, / Nor care should an ill-judging Audience damn."

Such a stance and discipline may help to explain Rochester's feelings, expressed in "An Allusion to Horace," about the unforced ease and "cleanness" of Sedley's love poetry:

> For songs and verses mannerly obscene,
> That can stir nature up by springs unseen,
> And without forcing blushes, warme the Queene —
> Sedley has that prevailing gentle art,
> That can with a resistlesse charm impart

The loosest wishes to the chastest heart;
Raise such a conflict, kindle such a fire,
Betwixt declining virtue and desire,
Till the poor vanquished maid dissolves away
In dreames all night, in sighes, and tears all day.

Rochester exaggerates the understated pruriency of Sedley's poetry, however, and perhaps confuses his verse *about* women's amorous wishes with verse allegedly *arousing* such desire.

Sedley's next poem is "Indifference Excused," which follows up the theme of "To Cloris" by asserting that "Lovers should use their Love alone," and not verbal protestations or arguments, to seduce or "convince the cruel'st Maid"; for "Silence it self can Love proclaim." The movement in such verse is toward the utterly natural – toward validating the normal inability of the tongue-tied lover to hide his genuine feelings from his beloved. Such poetry seems in a way "self-denying" out of a distaste for display and a reluctance to obtrude (though the last lines may contain a hidden obscenity), for after all it is "a foolish Part, / To set to shew, what none can hide." Even when succeeding poems continue to vary the theme of the dangers of praising one's beloved or of the dangers of loving her, the modern reader may fail to see that the poet is again daringly flirting with understating or undermining his own poetic project. He is thereby paradoxically recommending to the reader his poetic control and reticence and his intellectual detachment in the face of an unstable world, even as he asserts his feelings.

Other themes are discernible in the remaining love poems: some deal with women who inspire love but resist yielding to it and sometimes even blame themselves for men's desiring them. In other poems the lover addresses the object of his attention and sometimes conventionally praises her beauty. Sometimes the poems consist of women's spirited replies to men who warmly press them for favors. The seventeenth poem in the series helps one to understand Sedley's efforts at detachment from involvement and passion, and interestingly, although the speaker is probably a young woman, it is not impossible to imagine a man expressing similar sentiments about the role of fancy or fantasy, and its dangers, in the growth of love:

Get you gone, you will undo me,
If you love me, don't pursue me,
Let that Inclination perish,
Which I dare no longer cherish;
With harmless Thoughts I did begin,

. . . .
At every Hour, in every Place,
I either saw or form'd your Face;
All that in Plays was finely writ,
Fancy for you, and me did fit.
My Dreams at Night were all of you,
Such as till then I never knew:
I sported thus with young Desire,
Never intending to go higher:
But now his Teeth and Claws are grown,
Let me the fatal Lion shun;
You found me harmless, leave me so;
For were I not, you'd leave me too.

Even if the poem seems to end rather lamely, it shows effectively Sedley's concern about the dangers of passions that begin innocently but eventually may come to feed on their power to devastate the beloved and annihilate themselves. The image of the lion suggests attributes of the monarchy, perhaps even of the monarch, but it also generally functions to suggest the projected triumph and subsequent destructive power of passion. Even if seen as inorganic, the image of passionate desire as the beast separable from innocent lovers and separating passionate ones functions well in a poem in which the speaker is struggling for detachment and control; this poem and others may show that, however one may come to judge Sedley's verse, he was no mindless hedonist nor, for that matter, a masochist in love. In "The Indifference," for example, he confesses, "I'm not of those who court their Pain, / And make an Idol of Disdain; / . . . / In Love Indifference is sure / The only sign of perfect Cure." Even when he sounds sincerely and entirely in love, as in the second poem "To Cloris," he incorporates a Jonsonian sense of justness into the verse:

Cloris, I justly am betray'd,
By a Design my self had laid;
Like an old Rook, whom in his Cheat,
A run of Fortune does defeat.
I thought at first with a small Sum
Of Love, thy heap to overcome;
Presuming on thy want of Art,
Thy gentle and unpractis'd Heart;
But naked Beauty can prevail,
Like open force, when all things fail.
Instead of that thou hast all mine
And I have not one Stake of thine;

. . . .
My hand, alas, is no more mine,
Else it had long ago been thine;
My Heart I give thee, and we call
No man unjust that parts with all.

241

Occasionally poems will again take the form of dialogues, as between Amintas and Celia or Mars and Cupid. The first of these rehearses all the arguments men use to urge women to make love and all the reasons women use to deny men, but the contention nevertheless ends with a vow and a kiss. In the second dialogue the god of war accuses Cupid of inventing new outlandish forms of courtship and making new wooers, but Cupid replies that love battles may be allowed to be as extravagant as military battles and campaigns: Sedley (like his companion Rochester) finds that both love and war, inevitably associated in the Restoration's sense of the heroic, have become stupidly extravagant and destructive crazes.

Although political panegyrics, prologues, and satirical poems appear occasionally among the first sixty or so poems in the Ayloffe edition, with the fifth-ninth poem songs and dialogues give way to "Epigrams: Or, Court Characters," and many of these are adaptations or "imitations" of the short stinging, satiric poems perfected by the Roman satirist Martial, who argued that when the learned condemn spite, fools flourish. Most of these poems are surely later productions of Sedley – several of them were published in the *Gentleman's Journal* in the 1690s, and the tone and subject matter of others place them in the 1680s and 1690s. Sedley's final explanation of his turning to satire in "To Nysus" maintains a shade of self-criticism and avoids the vanity of taking itself too seriously in its condemnation of its audience.

> How shall we please this Age? If in a Song
> We put above six Lines, they count it long;
> If we contract it to an Epigram,
> As deep the dwarfish Poetry they damn;
> If we write Plays, few see above an Act,
> And those lewd Masks, or noisie Fops distract:
> Let us write Satyr then, and at our ease
> Vex th' ill-natur'd Fools we cannot please.

Still, despite his implied self-deprecation, the epigrams can at times grow very dark, as in "A Ballad," which narrates how a young buck looking for excitement forces a quarrel on a sober gentleman and escapes punishment for what amounts to murder in a duel. Another example is "To Sextus," in which the speaker sarcastically asks Sextus why he has come to town when he cannot

> Pimp, nor Cheat, nor Swear, nor Lye?
> This Place will nourish no such idle Drone [as you];
> . . . .
> But thou hast Courage, Honesty, and Wit,

> And [believe] one, or all these three will give Thee
>   Bread:
> The Malice of this Town thou know'st not yet;
> . . . .
> Yet this [wit plus courage] is all thou hast to live
>   upon:
> . . . .
> Be wise, and e're th'art in a Jayl, be gone,
> Of all that starving Crew we saw to Day
> None but has kill'd his Man, or writ his Play.

Sextus in Sedley's version is not the dim-witted figure of Martial's poem, who, lacking quarrelsomeness and real courage, proposes only to write and cultivate rich patrons; Martial's Sextus faces only the humiliating neglect from patrons that every Roman client feared, whereas Sedley's brave young buck faces competition from a score of desperate and witty men who defend their pretensions in duels to the death. Here Sedley's London seems even grimmer than Martial's Rome.

The note of poised world-weariness and contemplative distance from one's active milieu (qualified by a masculine brusqueness) typifies the following lines of the fifty-second poem:

> Dear Friend, I fear my Heart will break;
> In t'other World I scarce believe,
> In this I little pleasure take:
> That my whole grief thou mays't conceive;
> Cou'd not I Drink more than I Whore,
> By Heaven, I wou'd not live an Hour.

Another of the epigrams, "To Quintus," provides insight into the mature poet's view of younger libertines who lack intellectual poise and who in fact become the slaves of their unconventional beliefs and their attendant vices. The poem seems to belong to the reign of the Catholic monarch James II and suggests that Sedley may have given up his earlier freethinking views. On the other hand, it is just as likely that he merely deplores the debasement of his own moderated libertinism and skepticism by an iconoclastic braggart who comes off worse in comparison to the conscientious man "enslaved" by religion.

> Thou art an Atheist, *Quintus,* and a Wit,
>   Thinkst all was of self-moving Atoms made,
> Religion only for the Vulgar fit,
>   Priests Rogues, and Preaching their deceitful Trade;
> Wilt drink, whore, blaspheme, damn, curse, and swear:
>   Why wilt thou swear, by G– , if there be none?
> . . . .
> ' Tis thou art free, Mankind besides a Slave,
>   And yet a Whore may lead the[e] by the Nose,
> A drunken Bottle, and a flatt'ring Knave,
>   A mighty Prince, Slave to thy dear Soul's Foes,

Thy Lust, thy Rage, Ambition and thy Pride;
He that serves G—, need nothing serve beside.

At the Glorious Revolution, Sedley, one of William III's earliest supporters, resumed his parliamentary career and for a time enjoyed the king's favor, his son being knighted in March 1689; but perhaps because of a speech in Parliament critical of William's "crafty courtiers," or possibly because of correspondence with "the King across the water," or because of his daughter Katherine's behavior displeasing Queen Mary, Sedley for a time fell under a shadow but emerged from it by 1694, perhaps because he supported William's call for a standing army. He may have devoted much of his time to his son, who in 1695 rewarded his father's care by running away and marrying the daughter of Sir Richard Newdigate without her father's permission. In letters which show him in his best light, Sedley supported his son's attempts to be reconciled with his father-in-law (and to gain his lady's dowry), who later forgave the couple.

Following Sedley's epigrams is the unusual and late poem "The Happy Pair," written circa 1700 according to Pinto. It celebrates in pentameter couplets the almost prelapsarian bliss of man and woman as they inhabit a sexual paradise free of struggle between the sexes: just as Adam was free of greed and "With heat of Love . . . flam'd upon his Mate," so she "lost the thoughts of Empire in his Love." The poem is virtually a satire, however, for in contrast with this original and entire commitment of primitive lovers, it deplores at length the debasement of modern love into a matter of business and self-aggrandizement: in modern society "Both Sexes now deprave their Noble Kind, / While sordid Avarice corrupts the Mind," and marriage as well as religion becomes a temporary escape or anodyne – "A meer Romance, and idle Dream of those, / Who wanting Wealth, think to disguise their Woes." It is interesting to observe how quasi-libertine sentiments – the critique of "customary" marriage, of ordinary religion, and a kind of false divertissement – are worked into this poem. The opening lines indeed imitate some of the themes, rhythms, and diction of Dryden's depiction in *Absalom and Achitophel* (1681) of the innocent sexual vigor and genuine (if short-lived) commitment of "pious times . . . before polygamy was made a sin." But Sedley's view of prelapsarian love is monogamous and lasting, and it doubtless reflects his deep and permanent relationship with Ann Ayscough. The critical de-

scription of religion as "a meer Romance" is attributed to the shallow and worldly who seek an easy refuge from their poverty and want of imagination. There is also an interesting and graphic depiction of the passionate but loveless rage of a modern love affair ("At most, they're but concatenated Beasts"); copulation in such a relationship gives no real satisfaction because it is essentially without true affection and a sense of loving interdependence. Thus the delights even of kings are likely to be false and their joys embittered. It may seem as though Sedley, from the perspective of the reigns of James II and William, was critically viewing all his past libertine views and his experiences as a wit and rakehell during the reign of Charles II. But one may see rather an interesting adaptation of libertine critiques of custom and conventional belief and libertine insistence on genuine (if sometimes short-lived) feeling than an outright repudiation of any earlier radical views. One must remember, moreover, that even in his early drama and poetry Sedley had revealed a surprising critical detachment and a concern for a natural, unforced discipline rather than the wild abandon which his youthful behavior and that of some of his companions suggests (for K. E. Robinson there is in Sedley sometimes a "courteous resignation only just short of existential endurance"). His concerns doubtless changed as he aged, but the economy of evidence indicates that, however he might later view his or other men's rambunctious youthful behavior, the self-critical terms of his thought, at least, did not drastically change, even if their application did; and this fact makes this late work, which otherwise might be easily obscured by the work of other, more brilliant satirists, interesting in any detailed attempt to trace shifting attitudes in the 1670s, 1680s, and 1690s, a period of serious political instability and significant intellectual change.

Biography:

Vivian de Sola Pinto, *Sir Charles Sedley 1639–1701: A Study in the Life and Literature of the Restoration* (London: Constable, 1927).

References:

N. J. Andrew, Introduction to John Dryden, *All for Love,* edited by Andrew (London: Benn, 1975), pp. xi–xxx;

Margaret P. Boddy, "The 1692 *Fourth Book of Virgil*," *Review of English Studies,* 15, no. 60 (1964): 364–380;

Bror Danielsson and David M. Vieth, eds., *The Gyldenstolpe Manuscript Miscellany of Poems by*

John Wilmot, Earl of Rochester, and other Restoration Authors. A Collection of English Poetry Principally Political &tc Satyrs from the Last Years of Charles II, Stockholm Studies in English, 17 (Stockholm: Almqvist & Wiksell, 1967);

Dustin Griffin, "Rochester and the Holiday Writers," in *Rochester and Court Poetry* (Los Angeles: William Andrews Clark Memorial Library, University of California, 1988), pp. 53–54;

Brice Harris, *Charles Sackville, Sixth Earl of Dorset: Patron and Poet of the Restoration,* Illinois Studies in Language and Literature, 26, nos. 3–4 (Urbana: University of Illinois Press, 1940);

Michael B. Hudnall, Jr., "Moral Design in the Plays of Sir Charles Sedley," Ph.D. dissertation, University of Tennessee at Knoxville, 1984;

Vivian de Sola Pinto, *Enthusiast in Wit: A Portrait of John Wilmot Earl of Rochester, 1647–1680* (Lincoln: University of Nebraska Press, 1962);

Pinto, *Restoration Carnival. Five Courtier Poets: Rochester, Dorset, Sedley, Etherege, and Sheffield* (London: Folio Society, 1954), pp. 27–70;

K. E. Robinson, "The Disenchanted Lyric in the Restoration Period," *Durham University Journal,* 73 (1980): 67–73;

Raman Selden, "Oldham's Versions of the Classics," in *Poetry and Drama, 1570–1700: Essays in Honour of Harold F. Brooks,* edited by Antony Coleman and Antony Hammond (London & New York: Methuen, 1981), pp. 110–135;

David M. Vieth, *Attribution in Restoration Poetry: A Study of Rochester's Poems of 1680* (New Haven & London: Yale University Press, 1963);

George Williamson, *The Proper Wit of Poetry* (Chicago: University of Chicago Press, 1962), pp. 125–127;

John Harold Wilson, *The Court Wits of the Restoration: An Introduction* (Princeton: Princeton University Press, 1948).

Edward Sherburne

(18 September 1616 – 4 November 1702)

Katherine M. Quinsey
University of Windsor

BOOKS: *Medea: a Tragedie. Written in Latine by Lucius Annæus Seneca. English'd by E. S. Esq; with Annotations* (London: Printed for Humphrey Moseley, 1648);

Seneca's Answer to Lvcilivs his Qvære; Why Good Men suffer Misfortunes seeing there is a Divine Providence? Written Originally in Latine Prose, and Now Translated into English Verse, By E.S. Esq. (London: Printed for Humphrey Moseley, 1648);

Poems and Translations amorous, lusory, morall, divine (London: Printed by William Hunt for Thomas Dring, 1651); republished as *Salmacis, Lyrian & Sylvia, Forsaken Lydia, The Rape of Helen, A Comment thereon, With Severall other Poems and Translations* (London: Printed by William Hunt for Thomas Dring, 1651);

The Sphere of Marcus Manilius Made an English Poem: With Annotations and an Astronomical Appendix. By Edward Sherburne, Esquire (London: Printed for Nathanael Brooke, 1675);

Troades, or, The Royal Captives. A Tragedy, written Originally in Latin by Lucius Annæus Seneca, the Philosopher. English'd by Edward Sherburne, Esq; with Annotations (London: Printed by Anne Godbid & John Playford for Samuel Carr, 1679);

The Comparison of Pindar and Horace, Written in French by Monsieur Blondel, Master in Mathematicks to the Dauphin, English'd By Sir Edward Sherburne, Kt. (London: Printed for Thomas Bennet, 1696);

The Tragedies of L. Annæus Seneca the Philosopher; viz. Medea, Phædra and Hippolytus, Troades, or the Royal Captives, and The Rape of Helen, out of the Greek of Coluthus; Translated into English Verse; with Annotations. To which is prefixed the Life and Death of Seneca the Philosopher; with a Vindication of the said Tragedies to Him, as their Proper Author. (London: Samuel Smith and Benjamin Walford, 1701; reprinted, 1702; facsimile of 1702 printing, New York: AMS, 1976).

Sir Edward Sherburne (location of original portrait unknown; from F. J. Van Beeck, ed., The Poems and Translations of Sir Edward Sherburne, *1961)*

Edition: *The Poems and Translations of Sir Edward Sherburne (1616–1702): Excluding Seneca and Manilius,* edited by Franz Josef Van Beeck (Assen: Van Gorcum, 1961).

OTHER: Charles Aleyn, *Historie of that wise and Fortunate Prince, Henry of that Name the Seventh,* includes a commendatory poem by Sherburne (London: Printed by T. Cotes for W. Cooke, 1638);

Ovid's Heroical Epistles, English'd by J. Sherburne, includes a commendatory poem by Sherburne (London: Printed by E. Griffin for W. Cooke, 1639);

Elegies Celebrating the Happy Memory of S[r] Horatio Veere, Baron of Tilbury, Collonell Generall of the English in the United Provinces, and M[r] of the Ordnance in England, includes an elegy by Sherburne (London: Printed by T. Badger for Christopher Meredith, 1642);

Thomas Stanley, *Poems and Translations,* includes commendatory poems by Sherburne (London: Printed for the Author and his Friends, 1647);

James Shirley, *Via ad Latinam Linguam Complenata, the Way Made Plain to the Latin Tongue. The Rules Composed in English and Latine Verse: For the greater Delight and Benefit of Learners,* includes English and Latin commendatory poems by Sherburne (London: Printed by R. W. for John Stephenson, 1649);

William Cartwright, *Comedies, Tragi-Comedies, with Other Poems,* includes a commendatory poem by Sherburne (London: Printed for Humphrey Moseley, 1651);

Claudius Aelianus His Various History, translated by Thomas Stanley, Jr., includes a commendatory poem by Sherburne (London: Printed for Thomas Dring, 1665);

"The Graces, or Hieron," translated by Sherburne from Theocritus' Idyl 16 (London, 1685).

Edward Sherburne exemplifies both the seventeenth-century mingling of humanistic and scientific disciplines and the changing practice of the poetics of translation. As a Royalist civil servant, scholar, and poet, he was at the center of the group of Cavalier poets surrounding Thomas Stanley, counting among his acquaintances Thomas Carew, Thomas May, Robert Herrick, Richard Lovelace, John Denham, and James Shirley; he also corresponded with a wide variety of scientists, scholars, and antiquarians, ranging from Isaac Vossius to Anthony Wood. In his own time Sherburne was respected not only for his learning but also for his poetic ability; in his dedication to *Theatrum Poetarum* (1675) Edward Phillips praises Sherburne's translations as discovering "a more pure Poetical Spirit and Fancy, then many others can justly pretend to in their original Works," and his Senecan translations were praised by Gerald Langbaine in *An Account of the English Dramatick Poets* (1691) as "the best Versions we have extant, of any of Seneca's; and show the Translator a Gentleman of Learning, and Judgment." As an exact poetic translator Sherburne has a significant place in the changing discourse of translation at the time, in which translation was increasingly seen as an original poetic effort comparable to imitation. In both his theorizing of translation

and his poetic practice, he is a notable proponent of close translation as a creative art in itself, one which can extend the boundaries of poetic definition. Those boundaries are also extended by the wide range of subjects and forms in which Sherburne works, from the refined amatory lyrics of the Cavaliers to the versified astronomy of Manilius.

Family tradition has it that Sherburne's grandfather Henry was related to the Sherburnes of Stonyhurst, and this relationship was recognized sufficiently for the wealthy Stonyhurst Sherburnes to help provide for Edward's needs in the final years of his life. Sherburne's father, Edward, held a variety of important positions in public service, which speaks for his talent, tact, and efficiency; he is remembered in literary history chiefly as the private agent of Sir Dudley Carleton, ambassador to the Hague, in which capacity he was involved (acting in Carleton's interests) in putting an end to Thomas Carew's career hopes under Carleton or anyone else. After some reversals of fortune (as Francis Bacon's secretary from 1617 he was involved in Bacon's downfall and lost everything, and yet four years later he was elected secretary of the East India Company) in 1635 he succeeded to the position of clerk of the office of the ordnance, granted to him in reversion in 1613. This position was inherited by his son. The chief clerk of the ordnance was responsible for the upkeep, storage, and deployment of military and naval supplies. As a perquisite, he and his family were given residence in the Tower of London.

In 1614 Sherburne senior had married Frances Stanley, daughter of John Stanley of Roydon Hall, Essex. According to Sherburne's autobiographical notes sent to Anthony Wood, many of which were published in Wood's *Fasti, or Annals* (1691, 1692), by 1616, the year of Edward's birth, the family was living in London at a "house in Goldsmyths Rents near Redcrosse street" in the parish of Saint Giles Cripplegate, where Sherburne spent his childhood and youth. Edward and his twin brother, John, were born on 18 September 1616, and baptized 27 September in the parish church of Saint Giles Cripplegate. It is noteworthy that of all his brothers and sisters his twin, John, was the one with literary inclinations; one of Edward Sherburne's first published works was a commendatory poem for John Sherburne's translation *Ovid's Heroical Epistles, English'd by J. Sherburne* in 1639.

Sherburne's classical groundwork was well laid. Both he and John had their early education under the eminent classicist and educationist Thomas Farnaby, who was a near neighbor; according to Sherburne, his father's house was "joyn'd to the backside of Mr. Farnabye's," and he himself "used to play amongst the Scollars in long coats." The school was a large (and profitable) affair drawing many aristocratic and wealthy pupils; it was surrounded by "handsome Houses, and great Accommodations for the young Noblemen," and divided into apartments for the different forms and classes. From the beginning, then, Sherburne had a sense of being in and yet not of a certain privileged world in educational and social institutions of his day; a pattern repeated later when, although he could not take an Oxford degree as a Catholic, he was stationed there and granted a degree in the king's service. One may speculate that this marginal position underlies his aspiring and self-conscious erudition. When Farnaby retired from his London school in 1634, Sherburne studied at home with a private tutor, Charles Aleyn, whose poetic *Historie of that wise and Fortunate Prince, Henry of that Name the Seventh* (1638) features another of Sherburne's earliest published pieces, in the commendatory poem, which engages in finely turned couplets the opposition of poetic and historic language in relation to truth, anticipating William Davenant:

No more, dull Chronicle thy worth shall hold [great
    Henry]
Or sullen prose thy Noble acts infold.
Behold! the shrine wherein they reverend story
Shall ever be preserved, and thy glory,
Fresh to all Ages[.]

In 1640–1641 Sherburne was sent to Europe ("my Father thought [it] fitt for my better Education"), traveling extensively in France until called back on account of his father's grave illness toward the end of 1641. With his father's death in December, Sherburne succeeded to the office of the ordnance, only to lose his position at the hands of the parliamentary regime. State papers show that the ordnance officers (Sherburne, Francis Coningsby, Richard March) resisted the commands of the House of Lords to deliver supplies, pleading royal command, and were briefly imprisoned, still pleading allegiance to King Charles I (and, as evidence of that allegiance, the fact that their salary as ordnance officers had not been paid for four and a half years), until apparently the doors were forced open and the supplies taken in their despite. Almost immediately after his release Sherburne was sent to Oxford with military supplies, where by his own account the king made him commissary general of artillery; he evidently performed well in that capacity, being one of those created M.A. (20 December 1642) in recog-

nition of his service to the king at the battle of Edgehill.

Not long after his imprisonment Sherburne had suffered the fate of sequestration allotted to those who adhered to the king's cause, losing "my House & all my Personal Estates & Household Goods among wch I lost a very good Study of Bookes as considerable as that I now have," indeed, "one of the most considerable belonging to any gent. in or near London." Considering that the later library referred to contained 831 titles, this was a heavy loss indeed. His four years of military service in Oxford, however, replaced the university career denied to Sherburne and so must to some extent have compensated for the loss of his library – "I did, at our draweing into Winter Quarters, indeavour to improve the little smattering I had in Bookes, gained under my old Master Mr Farnaby by reading of good Authors." Obviously the description of his "smattering" is rhetorical self-depreciation, over-emphasizing his marginality: given both Farnaby's training and the extent of his library, Sherburne was clearly widely read and well trained from early youth and must have felt very much at home in the academic environment.

On the rendition of Oxford in 1646, he moved to London, where he lived in the Middle Temple with his relative John Povey in the situation of enforced retirement and relative poverty common to many young Royalists of his generation. (He later describes himself as being "liable . . . to frequent midnight searches, & proclamation banishments out of the Lines of communication, as being a Cavalier, which the *godly party* then called *Malignant*.") Here he became intimate friends with the poet Thomas Stanley, perhaps initially with some reference to their distant blood relationship but more enduringly and deeply on the basis of shared interests and intellectual empathy (in Stanley's words, "the double Tye of Sympathy and Blood"). The friendship with Stanley appears to have lasted without diminution until Stanley's death in 1678, in spite of subsequent difference in occupations, and is eloquently set forth in Stanley's poem to Sherburne (effectively a versified critical biography) which appears in various forms over thirty years, to be completed as part of Stanley's "Register of Friends" shortly before his death. The two men cooperated closely in their literary endeavors as well as intellectual pursuits – quite closely indeed on their poems and translations, each publishing a collection in 1651, and in a more general way through Stanley's subsequent studies of ancient philosophy, which complemented Sherburne's astronomical studies.

In the Middle Temple Sherburne formed new acquaintances and strengthened old ones with "contemporary Witts," including Shirley, May, William Fairfax, William Hammond, John Hall, Lovelace, Herrick, and Denham. Most of these writers exemplified to some extent the pattern of literary activity sprung from enforced retirement from public life, but it is also true that in their literary activity they found a means of resisting an encompassing oppression and of publicly expressing an alternate framework of value. It is in this atmosphere that Sherburne produced his first substantial literary works, translations of two very different pieces from Seneca, the *Dialogus ad Lucilium de Providentia* and the tragedy of *Medea*. The first of these, with its central theme of integrity, or inner spiritual victory in the face of worldly defeat, is one of the purest expressions of the Stoic element in Cavalier ideals, both in its occasion and in its matter. Published by Humphrey Moseley in 1648, it is titled *Seneca's Answer to Lucilius his Quære; Why Good Men suffer Misfortunes seeing there is a Divine Providence?*, bearing the motto *Calamitatis, virtutis occasio* (Calamity is the opportunity of virtue) and Sherburne's signature as "E. S. Esq." Printed publicly with a title and motto so patently espousing the royal cause (note that "why good men suffer," boldly printed on Sherburne's title page, is not part of Seneca's title but rather occurs as a repeated rhetorical question in the text), it nicely points the conjunction of public and private both in Charles's situation and in the literary form, between the king as a public figure and the king as a private, moral self, and between literature as "diversion" and literature as a moral and political agent. In his dedicatory epistle to Charles, Sherburne represents himself as serving the king in a new capacity: "Sir, whilst the times are such, that they deny me according to my *particular Duty* to serve the just Commands of Your *Majesties Will,* I presume . . . to shew Your *Majesty* that yet I have a *Will* to serve You." The witty turn here pits the current political situation against itself, showing the power of will shifting from the royal will (public) to the individual will of the subject (private), a reciprocal relationship which underlies political ideals Sherburne later put down in an unpublished prose treatise. Writing "to the Reader," Sherburne again blurs private diversion with public benefit and in doing so reconstitutes his reading public: if this translation proves "not an unpleasing Diversion" to "divers good Men, honest and loyall Sufferers in these bad Times" then that approval shall "warrant the *Publi-*

cation above any Licence of an *Imprimatur*." The immediate political situation and the possibility of censorship transfer the classical *vir bonus* (good man) trope from the realm of idealism into that of practical reality.

The poetic translation closely follows Seneca's sense, in keeping with the principles to which Sherburne adhered throughout his life; in recasting running Latin prose into end-stopped English decasyllabic couplets, it sharpens oppositions and paradoxes. To illustrate, "cui non industrio otium poena est?" (To what industrious man is not idleness a punishment?) becomes

> And to a Soule industrious, what lesse
> Then a tormenting Paine, is Idlenesse?

The couplet structure balances "Soule industrious" with "tormenting Paine," thus activating the irony implicit in the latter, which is intensified through the long suspense before the final emphatic resolution in "Idlenesse." This work is perhaps the only one of Sherburne's Senecan translations which, while close, can be said to have political overtones in its diction and in its very few additions to the original. In one notable example Seneca's image of God as a father severely educating his children, who learn through imitating him, becomes tinged with the ideas of royal succession: "ille magnificus" (the great Parent) becomes specifically the "Royall Sire" whose "Legitimate Issue" are virtuous men, and the passage evokes the idea of divine right as based in a heavenly likeness, even a heavenly essence (comparable to the blood tie between parents and children). Elsewhere the same slight leaning in the diction appropriates Seneca's descriptions of general evils to the immediate British situation: "quamvis subita sunt" (no matter how sudden ills are) becomes "thought by some to be the Births of suddaine violence," language used by Sherburne elsewhere to describe the national upheaval.

Sherburne's translation of *Medea* (1648) has few if any of these political overtones. As a close translation which uses poetic technique to cut through to central dramatic issues, the play embodies Stanley's commendation – "Thy Version hath not borrow'd, but restor'd." This is particularly apparent in the final act, where Sherburne's talent for balance and paradox sharpens the psychological conflict with a precision not frequent in contemporary Senecan drama:

> Seek matter for thy Fury, for all harmes
> That brings a hand prepar'd. – Wrath whither, oh!
> Transported art thou? 'Gainst what trecherous Foe

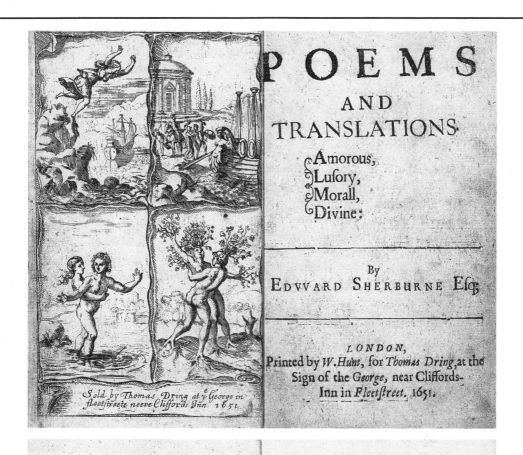

Frontispiece, title page, and dedication for the collection of his verse that Sherburne compiled while in forced seclusion at the home of his friend Thomas Stanley after the execution of Charles I (courtesy of the Henry E. Huntington Library and Art Gallery)

Intend'st these weapons? – Something my fierce mind,
But what I know not, hath within design'd,
Nor dares t'her self disclos't . – Fool I have been
Too fondly rash.

Like the Senecan original, Sherburne's *Medea* can be seen as subverting some of the Stoic formulas, seen when Medea justifies her desire for revenge by claiming Stoic integrity: "Fortune m'Estate may ravish from me, my / Minde she ne're can rob me of." Some of the narrative passages show consummate lyrical skill; in the story of Medea's witchcraft, for example, exquisitely tuned language and line structure oppose ideas and images in delicate, even amorous, balance:

These felt the Edge of Knife at Birth of day,
In dead of drousie Night, this slender spray
Was from his stalke cut downe. This ripened Blade
She did with her charme-tainted Naile invade.

During this period Sherburne also was writing various occasional and commendatory verses and possibly beginning the translations for his collection to appear in 1651. Of his occasional verse, however, the loveliest and most unexpected is the epithalamion on Stanley's marriage to Dorothy Enyon on 8 May 1648, printed among a group of epithalamia at the end of a very rare edition of Stanley's *Poems* of 1647. Sherburne writes in an elegant and balanced Pindaric, with graceful use of the variations in line length and repetition and with a rich yet restrained development of metaphor; particularly felicitous is the recurring pattern of the final line of each stanza, which places the "equal flames" of the lovers within the process of their marriage and finally resolves them into "equal ardour" in the transformed point of view of the final stanza. (Particularly striking, for a marriage poem, is the emphasis on mutual love and desire rather than on a fruitful line of succession.)

After the execution of the king in January 1649, Stanley took Sherburne to live with him at Cumberlow Green, which became a center of literary activity. Here the two friends worked in very close cooperation, Stanley on a new and expanded edition of his *Poems,* and Sherburne on his own collection of original and translated verse. The contents of the collections show this closeness, occasionally featuring poems based on the same models and in one instance confusing authorship. Both collections were published in 1651; Stanley's was published privately again, but Sherburne's *Poems and Translations* was publicly printed and sold by William Hunt and Thomas Dring. Sherburne's collection was republished later in the same year under the title *Salmacis, Lyrian & Sylvia, Forsaken Lydia.* Sherburne's dedication effusively declares the volume to be rooted in his friendship with Stanley – "nobilissimo amicissimo candidissimoque" (to the noblest, kindest, truest of friends) – consciously imitating the manner of a Latin monument; thus he grounds and validates both the poems and the friendship in enduring classical ideals.

This is Sherburne's only collection of nondramatic verse which was not reprinted in its entirety until Franz Josef Van Beeck's edition in 1961. In both its form and its content it closely follows the established models with which Sherburne's literary associates were working, primarily contemporary and near-contemporary French and Italian poets, who themselves imitated classical authors. The translations are divided in a manner imitating that of Giambattista Marino and others, based on classical ideas of decorum: "Erotica"; "Ludicra"; "Ethica"; "Sacra." These are given what amount to separate title pages, printed like an inscription in large Roman capitals on the verso of the page preceding the first poem in each section – like the dedication, a conscious visual imitation of Latin models. Sherburne's originals have been exhaustively documented by Mario Praz and Van Beeck; the amatory verse is dominated by Marino and Marc-Antoine de Gérard Saint-Amant (Sherburne has been called the major seventeenth-century English translator of Saint-Amant), and the sacred verse by Maciej Kazimierz Sarbiewski and Marino, while the ethical and satiric/comic directly translate classical models: Ausonius, Horace, Martial, Theocritus.

Sherburne translates closely in almost every instance, particularly when translating classical models directly; he takes more liberties with contemporary writers. His gift for close translation that re-creates the spirit of the original is most evident in the Theocritan idylls, which evoke the colloquial liveliness of the originals while closely imitating their sense:

Fetch me some water hither, *Eunoa:*
D'ee hear, *Joan Cleanly!* high you, make more haste;
Quick; *The Cat loves a Cushion:* see how fast
Shee comes with it! – pour forth: not so much (Drone!)
Yee idle slut, why hast thou wet my gown?

Here in idyll 15 Sherburne's contemporary references elide Theocritan Greek with something not unfit for the Restoration stage. In his translations of contemporary French and Italian poets, Sherburne tends to condense, to point oppositions, to sharpen turns of wit or unify them; he prunes excessive

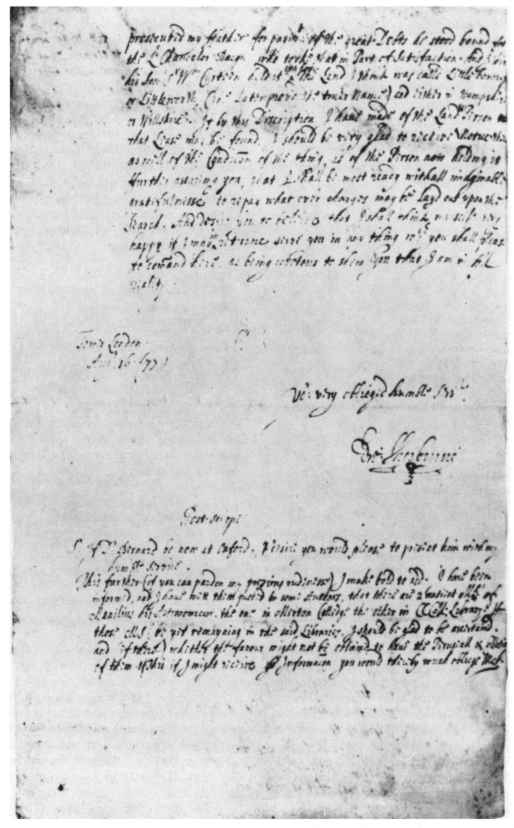

Page from Sherburne's 16 August 1677 letter to Anthony Wood (Bodleian Library, Oxford, Wood MS.
F44, f. 227ᵛ; cp. p. xxi)

metaphoric development and personal references, tending to universalize ideas and heighten thematic implications and questions. Where in the classical translation he more frequently imitates the meter of originals, with Marino and Saint-Amant he radically alters poetic units, transferring short stanzas or the variable lines of *madrigali* into longer verse paragraphs whose primary unit is the balanced decasyllabic couplet, thus allowing for more developed narrative and extended idea or argument. (In general, Sherburne has a flair for dramatic or narrative verse not found in Stanley.) Some of the shorter lyrics also show considerable technical skill, as in the following translation of Marino, in which the line structure re-creates the suspense and the movement of gaze:

> *Chloris!* on thine Eyes I gaz'd;
>   When amaz'd
>   At their brightnes,
> On thy Breasts I cast my Look;
>   No lesse took
>   With their whitenes:
> Both I justly did admire,
> These all Snow, and those all Fire.
>
> Whilst these Wonders I survay'd,
>   Thus I said
>   In suspence;
> Nature could have done no lesse
>   To expresse
>   Her Providence,
> Than that two such fair Worlds, might
> Have two Suns to give them Light.

One of very few poems in the collection to celebrate female physical beauty (as opposed to male), this lyric refines and tightens Marinistic wit while pursuing the implications of its artificiality: the cosmic doubling at the end completely obliterates the human woman (it would be distinctly odd if she had only one eye and one breast), the tenor disappears into the vehicle, and the external object looked on becomes an image in the gazer's mind. Sherburne's rare additions will occasionally question or alter the overall intent of an original, as seen in the following lines added to a translation of Giovanni Battista Guarini's "Celia Weeping": "What reall then in women can be known! / When nor their Joys, nor Sorrows are their Own?" This conventionally misogynistic lament can be read as cutting through to the heart of most amatory convention, exposing the falsity of its construction of feminine subjectivity.

The collection includes some possibly original poems under "Sacra," and under "Ethica" Sherburne includes his own commendatory poems

to Stanley and Shirley. This ordering, together with the overpowering classicism of the dedication to Stanley, joins Sherburne's immediate literary circle to the community of the past, giving it a validity transcending their present difficulties. Thus the collection, while it consists of "private exercises" as Sherburne claims, is given a redefined and idealized public meaning. A similar quiet politicizing can be found in Sherburne's version of Sarbiewski's *Amphion, seu Civitas bene ordinata,* titled "Amphion, or a City well ordered." Although it is a translation so close as to imitate the original sapphic meter, it embodies Sherburne's own positive political ideals as outlined in a manuscript prose treatise written between 1650 and 1660, which bases society on mutual help and friendship:

> Safer Course those Pilots run
> Who observe more Stars than One.
> Ships with double Anchors ty'd
>   Securer ride.
>
> Strength united firm doth stand
> Knit in an eternall Band:
> But proud Subjects private hate
>   Ruins a State.

The story of Amphion should be well noted – the poet has a prophetic voice, speaking a word of creative power – and creates the ideal community from nature, not art:

> Stones did leap about the Plains,
> Rocks did skip to hear his Strains,
> And the Groves the Hills did crown
>   Came dancing down.
>
> When he ceas'd, the Rocks and Wood
> Like a Wall about him stood;
> Whence fair *Thebes,* with seven Gates close
>   Of Brass, arose.

Shortly after the appearance of the two collections, Sherburne was called away from retirement with Stanley to enter the service of George Savile, later Marquis of Halifax, as his steward. In 1655, after possibly playing a part in the abortive uprising at Rufford, Sherburne was by the "good favour" of Lady Savile appointed tutor to her nephew Sir John Coventry, traveling through France, Italy, part of Germany, Holland, the Low Countries, and Flanders. As in his earlier European tour, Sherburne used this as an educational opportunity: "I did advance and promote my Bookish Inclination, by Conference with learned Persons, when I came to such Places as could afford Me their desired Con-

Frontispiece for Sherburne's translation of the first book of the Astronomica, *a Latin poem on astrology and astronomy (engraving by Wenceslas Hollar; courtesy of the Special Collections Library, University of Michigan). This engraving depicts Pan, the god of nature, Mercury, the god of interpretation and speech, with Urania, the goddess of astronomy.*

verse, rather than by any Academicall Course of Study." He began to pursue the mathematical and astronomical interests that bore fruit in the Marcus Manilius translation; he also started the correspondence with learned men that continued through the following decades and that was to include Elias Ashmole, Obadiah Walker, Edward Bernard (Savilian Professor of Astronomy at Oxford), and Isaac Vossius. (It was during the 1670s that he began a twenty-year correspondence with Anthony Wood, pursuing his own interest in the Sherburne family history and promoting Wood's interest in everybody else's.) During the tour Sherburne also probably began building up the library mentioned earlier, which by the 1670s contained a rich collec-

tion of classical and modern literature, dictionaries and grammars of various languages (including Arabic), scientific and mathematical books ranging from Euclid to Johannes Kepler, Robert Boyle, and William Harvey, and books on Catholic canon law and theology. According to Van Beeck, the library also included "a *Historia Byzantii* in twenty-one volumes, Grotius's works, and books, too numerous to mention, on numismatics, archaeology, legal science, heraldry, geography, biology, medicine, music, strategy, and philosophy."

After the Restoration of the monarchy in 1660 the restoration of Sherburne's position in the ordnance office did not come so easily; he returned to find someone else appointed to the place and had to petition to be reinstated. He brought with him claims for arrears going back to his father's time, and he received instead a retrenchment of his salary to one-fifth of its original amount. Although the arrears did not go away, the 1660s and 1670s were years of immensely productive activity for Sherburne in both the civil and literary spheres. The memoranda from the years of the Dutch war show Sherburne and the other officers working with great industry, efficiency, and meticulous attention to detail (and to protocol) — keeping lines of communication open and the supplies moving, often against high odds. Furthermore, Sherburne appears to have applied to his work as ordnance officer the same principles of scholarly ordering and research that formed an integral part of his literary achievement: a memoir of his life in *Gentleman's Magazine* (June 1796) accredits him with drawing up the "Rules, Orders, and Instructions' given to the Office of Ordnance in 1683; which, with very few alterations, have been confirmed at the beginning of every reign since, and are those by which the office is now governed."

Sherburne's intellectual activity during this period is given impressive witness by the Manilius volume, on which he was actively working during the 1660s and which was evidently in press with its commentary by 1669. When it did appear in its final form in January 1675, it was as a sumptuous folio edition with engravings by Wenceslaus Hollar (artist and cataloger to Charles I and for a time to Charles II), an apparatus of prose commentary unusually compendious even for the seventeenth century, various illustrated treatises on the nature and origin of astronomy and the different elements of the cosmos, and a descriptive "Catalogue of Astronomers" comprising over a thousand names, each with a vita. Both commentary and appendices reveal an impressive (if somewhat self-generating) knowledge of astronomy, astronomical history, and of comparative mythologies, religions, and philosophies, comparable to Ralph Cudworth's *True Intellectual System of the Universe* (1678). The battery of sources, careful comparison of texts, and weighing of different arguments show that Sherburne had read widely and long and that he was deeply grounded in and able to make his own judgments on historical and scientific matters.

The Sphere of Marcus Manilius was enthusiastically greeted by the Royal Society:

> The Learn'd and Intelligent Author of this Work, rightly considering the great importance of the mutual Helps, which the Knowledge of Antiquity and the Pur-

suit of New Discoveries of the Present Times may afford to one another, thought fit to imploy part of his ingenious Talent in rendring English this Ancient Poem . . . wherein divers Particulars do occur, touching the Nature of the Heavens and the Celestial Bodies, that agree with the Assertions of some of the most Eminent Modern Astronomers[.]

The review goes on to praise not only the compendious learning but also the technical knowledge evident in Sherburne's methods, evidence, and charts. Just as Manilius had set out to invent a new kind of poetry, so Sherburne explores the relation of the poem to its subject and of poetic tradition to empirical science. Indeed, poetry and science are almost identified in the act of knowledge and interpretation, bearing a similar relation to nature (their subject). This appears to be the import of the poem's magnificent frontispiece, whose "Mind" is explained in a verse on the opposite page:

> The Spheres (which ever moving are) imply
> That *Arts,* and *Learning,* if unactive, die.
> Our *Subject*'s Worth, is by *Urania* meant,
> Our Poet's, *PAN,* and *Mercury* present,
> Who sings *rough* Matter in *smooth* Verse, t'invite
> The *Ignorant* to Learn, the *Learn'd Delight.*

The frontispiece illustrates the invocation of the poem, made to both the god of nature and the god of interpretation and speech and linking the subject with the poetic form itself: Pan represents both the nature studied and the nature from which poetry springs; Mercury represents both the interpretative eloquence of poetry and the scientific act of knowledge and interpretation. Both poetry and science are linked as "human arts" which are themselves a part of the pattern embodied by the cosmos, the ultimate subject. (The presence of Urania as giving high worth to the subject is noteworthy, considering that *The Sphere of Marcus Manilius* was in press in 1669, two years after the first appearance of *Paradise Lost.*)

The poem translates the first book of the *Astronomica,* which describes various theories for the origin of the cosmos, followed by accounts of the rise of astronomy (in terms of the rise of all human culture and science), the nature of the cosmos (in particular the fixed stars in their constellations), the different ways of bounding and measuring the sphere, and finally the other heavenly bodies, sun and moon and comets. The interaction of poetry and science, and of poetry and classical learning, is embodied in both the subject and the form of the work, not only in the dense commentary which surrounds the lines on the page, but also in the numerous appendices that take up and expand the subjects of the poem in the order in which they appear. The notes are both knowledge and interpretation, just as poetry, like science, is an act of interpretation and discovery – a relationship which Stanley describes with a witty turn in his praise of *The Sphere of Marcus Manilius* in the "Register of Friends":

All who 'till now on the Smooth Surface saild
To fathom the vast Depth, despaird or faild.
This Thou hast done; Whose Notes like Seamarks stand
To guide us to the new-discovered Land.

("Notes," of course, can refer either to poetic song or to critical annotations.)

As with all Sherburne's translations of Latin, this one is very close to the original, but it succeeds to some extent in realizing the ideas outlined above, embodying the principles of physics in the sound and structure of couplet verse. The following passage, from the middle of the most mathematical section of the poem, which describes the different ways of measuring and viewing the sphere of the cosmos, is one of the happier examples of versified physics:

Look round about far as thy Sight will go,
What e're Earths Surface with Heavens Verge doth close,
And the divided Hemispheres compose; ...
....
... wheresoe're its wandring Course it steers,
As now to this, then to that Part it bears,
It changes still; a new Arch always making;
For leaving now this Heav'n, then that forsaking,
One half 'twill still disclose, or hide, or sign
With varying Limits which the Sight confine.
This is terrestrial, 'cause the Earth it rounds,
And call'd Horizon, 'cause the sight it bounds.

The swelling and movement of these lines re-create the infinite fluidity of perception, while at the same time they vividly convey the scientific and mathematical concept of the imaginary curve.

The publication of *The Sphere of Marcus Manilius* saw Sherburne at the height of public recognition, with a wide scholarly correspondence and various honors from fellow poets: he and Stanley were the dedicatees of Edward Phillips's *Theatrum Poetarum* (1675), in which Phillips describes Sherburne as "an intimate Friend and Acquaintance, as well of the ancient Greek and Latin, as of the choicest of Modern Poets." Sherburne was also given dedicatory mention in Thomas Roycroft's Virgil. It is after the appearance of *The Sphere of Marcus Manilius* that Stanley gives Sherburne the poet's laurel in his

poem in the "Register": "O my Defence and sweetest Ornament! / Whose Flame inspires Me, now my own is spent."

Sherburne's verse translation of *Troades, or, The Royal Captives* appeared in 1679. Here Sherburne has gained confidence and skill in the use of the couplet in dialogue, as demonstrated in the psychological immediacy of the scene where Ulysses manipulates Andromache into revealing the hiding place of Astyanax in Hector's tomb. Broken lines re-create the intense conflict and pressure:

Ulysses
The Prophet's Words shall be fulfill'd; the place
I will demolish.

Andromache
Which ye sold.

Ulysses
Deface
The Monument.

Troades is a play that itself deeply questions established order and tradition, exposing conflicting frameworks of value, criticising established heroic models (seen in the heroic deaths of women and children, and the curious abruptness of the ending, in which one poor old woman is left onstage lamenting her continued life as an undesired climax). It should be considered that *Troades* appeared at the height of public panic over the Popish Plot, a rumored Catholic conspiracy to assassinate Charles II (during which Sherburne himself was subjected to some harassment), and the play's questioning of innocent deaths and of public superstition would have been grimly apposite. In his annotations, moreover, Sherburne specifically points out Seneca's possible political motives in contrasting the moderation taught by Agamemnon with the brutality of Pyrrhus.

Being knighted by Charles II on 6 January 1683 may have seemed like the height of public honor, but it was also the beginning of Sherburne's downward trend. Something of this ambivalence appears in his description to Wood:

His Mat[y] in consideration of my many and great Sufferings & the long and faithfull Services by Me performed to his Royall Father of blessed Memory, and to himselfe was gratiously plesed to conferr the Honour of Knighthood upon Me in his private Bedchamber at Whitehall the 6th of January 1682 [1683] being 12th Day. This You will say cost Him not much, and gained me as little.

Whatever the reason, chronic arrears or the political climate, during the 1680s Sherburne appears to have been attempting to secure his financial position, seen in his (unsuccessful) efforts to secure a college lease from Oxford like those held by his father and grandfather. In 1688 Sherburne was doing his usual job making sure all the supplies were on hand to defend against the Dutch invasion, but by 4 December, one week before James's flight, he knew that his own position was in grave doubt. Referring to the replacement of Catholic officials by Protestant ones, he commented,

> We are like to fare yet worse, for Orange they say demands the Towre to be deliverd up to him, trusting in that more than a free Parliamnt wch they say he has no great Affection for, as not knowing how their Votes may answer his Designes.

On 13 December Sherburne was removed from his position and his home in the Tower of London with great suddenness. By the following August he had been replaced by John Swaddell, to whom his office had been granted in reversion, now "forfeited by Sir Edward Sherburne's declaring himself a Roman Catholic and not taking the oath and declaration" (*Calendar of Treasury Books,* 1689–1692). Although there is evidence that in 1673 he took the oaths and the Anglican Sacrament, shortly after the death of his mother and the passing of the Test Act, at all other times Sherburne seems to have adhered to Catholicism.

Sherburne's remaining years tell a rather grim tale. The romantic description in Wood's memoir describes him as spending his days in retirement, study, and prayer and exudes an image of cheerfully resigned piety and the comforts of learning. The reality, to judge from his manuscripts and other documentary records, is advanced age, illness, indigence, and a quantity of incomplete literary projects. He did not fail to publish altogether: a prose translation of Michel Blondel's *Comparison of Pindar and Horace* appeared in 1696, his first prose translation. He was probably working on another prose translation, "Tacitus His Morals, of flattery particularly towards princes, with remarques thereupon," from the French of Abraham Nicholas Amelot de la Houssaye, "English'd by a Person of quality, a lover of plaine dealing" which exists in manuscript in the commonplace book Sherburne kept from 1692 to 1698. In the final year of his life he brought out his collection of the Senecan tragedies, *The Tragedies of L. Annæus Seneca* (1701), which republished *Medea* (with a good many revisions and a virtually new set of annotations) and *Troades,* adding to the latter a reprint of his translation of Coluthus's *Rape of Helen,* which had appeared in the 1651 collection. *Phædra and Hippolytus* was his translation of *Phaedra* and was published for the first time in 1702, but Sherburne's translation of Seneca's play had existed in manuscript as early as 1679.

This collection was itself, however, simply the first volume of a projected *opera omnia,* or collected works (first mentioned in 1693), which never appeared. It is clear that Sherburne felt to some degree that his poetic flame was spent, and in some manuscript lines commenting on Wood's *Athenæ Oxonienses* he gives the work of creative transmission to antiquarians like Wood:

> Time who the Births of All Things brings to Light
> Devowres Them likewise with Saturnian Spight.
> . . . .
> Of what high Worth may be that worke esteemd
> Which Works of lost Creations hath redeemed.
> . . . .
> Which I would too; had I a Lute well-strung
> To sound the Places Praise from whence I sprung.
> But Phaebus warnes Me, tis in vaine to strive
> To play the Poet well at Eighty five.

By 1696 Sherburne's money problems were severe, and he spent the rest of his life petitioning the master general of ordnance and King William III (and later Queen Anne), first claiming the right of his patent to his position and the arrears due him, and finally asking for simple charity. These resulted in occasional gifts from royal bounty (in 1699 William refused to grant him a pension, "allowing the Lords to give him something, £50 or some such sum"); in one instance a petition seems to have gone unread for over a year before resulting in another gift of one hundred pounds. The last such gift (one hundred pounds from Queen Anne in July 1702) reached Sherburne not long before he died, "probably at his lodgings in Holborn," on 4 November 1702. He was buried in the Tower chapel. The draft of his Latin inscription emphasizes equally his service to three Stuart kings and his service to the republic of letters, applying the following adverbial characterization to both: "Summa Industria, Constantia Fideque Obsequentissima Inservissett" (He served devotedly, with the greatest industry, the most constant faith, and the most self-giving obedience).

Sherburne's knighthood has a certain moral and aesthetic appropriateness: he was a Cavalier all his life, both in his Royalist principles (in particular his loyalty to Charles I) and in his aesthetic achievement and ideals, which are based on a classical ideal of a moral and spiritual community that transcends time, distance, and difference of language. In the preface to the Senecan collection Sherburne vigorously defends his translation as

the genuine Sense of *Seneca* in these Tragedies intelligibly delivered, by a close Adherence to his Words as far as the Propriety of Language may fairly admit; in Expressions not unpoetical, and Numbers not unmusical. But representing, as in a Glass, his just Lineaments and Features, his true Air and Mien, in his own Native Colours, unfarded with adulterate Paint, and keeping up (at least aiming to do so) his distinguishing Character.

Here at the end of his life he had developed confidence in the ability of an exact translation to deliver that true poetic "spirit" central to Renaissance ideas of "imitation." At its best, his own poetry exhibits that ability not only to convey the literal meaning of the original (its "Mind," in Sherburne's habitual Latinate use of the term) but also to create a poetic sense and implications of its own – so that two minds meet to make a new one. He is thus a good exemplar of George Chapman's aim in his "Preface to Homer":

As well to reach the spirit that was spent
In his example, as with art to pierce
His Grammar, and etymologie of words.

Sherburne's classicism has its own revolutionary element. In claiming poetic value for those precise sciences of linguistic translation and astronomical observation, he helps alter and stretch the existing boundaries of poetic discipline. In this he shares in the dynamic flexibility of his time and in its own explosive questioning of long-held assumptions and categories in all areas of human experience.

References:

R. A. Beddard, "Two Letters from the Tower, 1688," *Notes and Queries,* 31 (September 1984): 347–352;

Gerald Eades Bentley, "James Shirley and a Group of Unnoted Poems on the Wedding of Thomas Stanley," *Huntington Library Quarterly,* 2 (January 1939): 219–234;

Galbraith M. Crump, "Edward Sherburne's Acquaintances," *Times Literary Supplement,* 14 March 1958, p. 139;

Theo Hermans, "Literary Translation: The Birth of a Concept," *New Comparison: A Journal of Comparative and General Literary Studies,* 1 (Summer 1986): 28–42;

Gentleman's Magazine, 66 (June 1796): 462–463;

Philosophical Transactions of the Royal Society, 110 (25 January 1675): 233–235;

Mario Praz, "Stanley, Sherburne and Ayres as Translators and Imitators of Italian, Spanish and French Poets," *Modern Language Review,* 20 (July 1925): 280–294; (October 1925): 419–431;

William Roberts, "Saint-Amant: Plaque Tournante de l'Europe au XVlle Siecle," in *Horizons europeens de la litterature francaise au XVlle siecle: L'Europe: lieu d'echanges culturels?,* edited by Wolfgang Leiner (Tübingen: Gunter, 1988);

"Sherburne (Sir Edward)," in *Biographia Britannica: or, the Lives of the Most Eminent Persons Who Have Flourished in Great Britain and Ireland, From the earliest Ages, down to the present Times,* volume 6, part 1 (London: Printed for J. Walthoe, T. Osborne, H. Whitridge, C. Hitch, L. Hawes & 13 others, 1763), pp. 3670–3676.

Papers:

Sherburne's principle manuscripts are found mainly in Britain. The British Library Sloane MSS. include among other things one notebook and five commonplace books kept from 1650 to 1701 and the catalogue of Sherburne's library. The Bodleian Library holds his correspondence with Anthony Wood, Elias Ashmole, and Edward Bernard. An interleaved and annotated copy of Joseph Justus Scaliger's 1600 edition of Manilius is in the University Library at Cambridge. Outside Britain a Latin letter to Isaac Vossius is in the University Library in Amsterdam.

Thomas Stanley

(September 1625 – 12 April 1678)

Reid Barbour

University of North Carolina at Chapel Hill

BOOKS: *Oronta, The Cyprian Virgin,* by Girolamo Preti, translated by Stanley (London: Printed for Humphrey Moseley, 1647);

Aurora, & The Prince, by Don Juan Perez de Montalvan, translated by Stanley (London: Printed for Humphrey Moseley, 1647);

Poems and Translations (London: Printed for the Author and his Friends, 1647 [i.e., 1648?]); revised as *Poems* (London, 1651);

Evropa. Cvpid Crucified. Venvs Vigils. With Annotations (London: Printed by W. W. for Humphrey Moseley, 1649);

The History of Philosophy, 3 volumes (London: Printed for Humphrey Moseley & Thomas Dring, 1655–1660);

Ayres and Dialogues, musical settings by John Gamble (London: Printed by William Godbid for the author, 1656; second edition, London: Printed by William Godbid for Humphry Moseley, 1657);

Psalterium Carolinum (London: Printed for John Martin & James Allestrey, 1657; second edition, London: Printed for John Martin, James Allestry & Thomas Dicas, 1660);

The History of the Chaldaick Philosophy (London: Printed for Thomas Dring, 1662);

Αἰσχυλου τραγωδιαι ἑπτα. *Aeschyli tragoediæ septem: Cum scholiis græcis omnibus: Deperditorum cum dramatum fragmentis. Versione & Commentario Thomæ Stanleii* (London: Typis Jacobi Flesher: Prostant vero apud Cornelium Bee, 1663).

Editions: *Poems,* edited by Egerton Brydges (London: Longman, Hurst, Rees, Orme & Brown, 1814);

Anacreon, Bion, and Moschus, with other translations, edited by Brydges (London: Longman, Hurst, Rees, Orme & Brown, 1815);

Anacreon, with Thomas Stanley's translation, edited by A. H. Bullen (London: Lawrence & Bullen, 1893);

Thomas Stanley: His Original Lyrics, edited by L. I. Guiney (Hull: Tutin, 1907);

A Platonick Discourse upon Love, edited by Edmund G. Gardner (London: Grant Richards, 1914; Boston: Merrymount, 1914);

Kisses, being the Basia of Iohannes Secundus, rendered into English by Thomas Stanley, 1647 (Soho: Nonesuch, 1923);

The Poems and Translations of Thomas Stanley, edited by Galbraith Miller Crump (Oxford: Clarendon Press, 1962).

Thomas Stanley was one of the most learned poets of the seventeenth century. In an age when poets from John Donne to John Milton were impressively educated, Stanley's devotion to classical studies reached beyond the scope of most of his peers. His *History of Philosophy* (1655–1660) and edition of Aeschylus (1663) were standards through the eighteenth and into the nineteenth century, while the composition of his love poems, often translations from Greek, Latin, French, Italian, and Spanish verse, was for Stanley a scholarly as well as artistic endeavor. Stanley may have felt some conflict between his lyrical flights of fancy and the serious endeavors of scholarship, but fellow poet James Shirley believed that, in the "learned loves" of Stanley's verse, the two – poesy and research – were married.

An early biographer of the poet (in the 1701 edition of *The History of Philosophy*) warns his reader not to expect from Stanley's life "a long Recital of Intrigues and Adventures." The scholar's days are lived out "in the Solitude of his Study: And as Mr. *Stanley's* Learning made up the brightest part of his Character, so an Account of his Life is but a Relation of his Achievements in the Learned World." It may be true that Stanley's life is no romantic tale, but the poet was hardly sequestered from the human comedy. One of the most important facets of his life is his association with family and friends. The Stanleys were a wealthy and propertied family; the poet was born to Thomas and Mary Stanley in September 1625 on one of the family estates,

Thomas Stanley (portrait by George Soest; National Portrait Gallery, London)

Cumberlow Green in Hertfordshire. His mother was related to several poets — George Sandys, Richard Lovelace, and William Hammond among them. Early in life Stanley received the best education from his private tutor, William Fairfax, who stayed with the poet through his years at Cambridge and beyond. From Fairfax (whose father, Thomas, was the well-known translator of Torquato Tasso) Stanley learned Greek and Latin in addition to the modern languages, Italian, French, and Spanish. After receiving his M.A. at Cambridge in March 1642, Stanley traveled on the Continent, mainly in France. His stay on the Continent most likely served two purposes for the poet: completing his education and protecting him from the dangers of the Civil War at home. In these troubled times Stanley was a Royalist whose devotion to the king may be witnessed in *Psalterium Carolinum* (1657), the poet's versification of the *Eikon Basilike* (1649), a book of meditations attributed at its publication to Charles I.

Midway through the 1640s Stanley returned to London, where he lived at the Middle Temple and gathered around him a group of poets including John Hall, James Shirley, Edward Sherburne, William Hammond, and Fairfax. Stanley played two roles in this circle: model poet and generous patron. Any account of Stanley's life must bear witness to the several works dedicated to him, a testament to Stanley's central position in this coterie of scholars and poets. There is some evidence, too, that he was their political leader, organizing a secret society of the "black band" in support of the king. Between 1647 and 1651 Stanley published most of his own verse and some prose translations; these books appear to have been private in their distribution, not exceeding fifty copies of any one edition. Whatever his audience, the poet tinkered with the constituents of his publications: for example, *Poems and Translations* (1648?) was printed piecemeal and in a variety of forms, while *Poems* (1651) omitted some of the poems found in the earlier collection but added

Page from the manuscript for Stanley's Poems and Translations, *written in the hand of a scribe, with additions and revisions made by Stanley when he was preparing the collection for publication (Cambridge University Library, Add. MS. 7514)* translations from Anacreon, Johannes Secundus, and others. Stanley may have envisioned a complete edition, but it never materialized. A few years later, in 1656, many of his poems were set to music by John Gamble in the *Ayres and Dialogues,* but others were left in manuscript.

For all his commitment to poetry, Stanley spent the rest of his life, from the early 1650s to his death in 1678, pursuing his scholarly interests in classical philosophy and literature. His first major project was the multivolume *History of Philosophy,* modeled on the works of Diogenes Laertius and Pierre Gassendi. Next Stanley focused on the tragedies of Aeschylus, and with the help of a community of scholars, especially the learned John Pearson, he produced an edition whose impressive critical apparatus was the subject of controversy in the nineteenth century and is still valued by Greek scholars. Some accuse Stanley of plagiarism while others praise his research for its sophistication and excuse his thefts as acceptable in the scholarly community of his day.

Outside the study Stanley had other concerns: he married Dorothy Enyon on 8 May 1648 and later became a member, then a fellow, of the Royal Society (1661, 1663). The early biographer protests that Stanley's marriage never impeded his scholarship; whatever the case, Stanley's father-in-law left debts that led the poet to ask Charles II for a special dispensation just after the Restoration. The family estates were always a refuge for Stanley and his circle of poets, scholars, and friends, and during the last years of his life the poet assumed the responsibilities of justice of the peace for Hertfordshire County. In the 1670s his sense of community is visible not just in the records of Hertfordshire, nor just in the dedications that continue to come his way as a patron of the arts, but also in a series of poems titled "A Register of Friends" that Stanley wrote two or three years before his death. On 12 April 1678, after bouts with what may have been diabetes, Stanley died in Suffolk Street, London, and was buried at Saint Martin-in-the-Fields.

From a sketch of his life, Stanley's main poetic subject, love, might be lost on the reader. But Stanley's lyrics are (unlike Ben Jonson's) all about love, kisses, cruel mistresses, and the wiles of Cupid. Shirley heralded Stanley as the new "Oracle of Love," one that would replace Thomas Carew. Indeed, Carew is a good place to start in assessing Stanley's relation to the poets of his age. Like Carew, Stanley polished his verse so that every syllable was securely in its place. A comparison between Stanley's manuscripts and the printed versions of his poems shows how hard he worked to perfect every word and cadence. The manuscript of "Chang'd, yet Constant" plods: "Wrong me no more in thy unjust complaint, / Nor falsely charge me with inconstancie; / I vowd affection to the fairest Saint, / Nor did I change my faith whilest thou wert she." In 1651 the same verses are music: "Wrong me no more / In thy complaint, / Blam'd for Inconstancy; / I vow'd t'adore / The fairest Saint, / Nor chang'd whilst thou wert she." In the words of his modern editor Galbraith Miller Crump, "the time and care Stanley spent in achieving the beauty of this lyric are displayed in [the manuscript's] many drafts and revisions."

Other poets write of both Carew and Stanley that their verse is "smooth" and "sweet," not elliptical or roughshod like much of Donne's verse. But, unlike Carew, Stanley rarely sounds like Donne. His syntax may at times become torturous or intricate in its inversion and suspensions, often depending on his model (Luis de Góngora y Argote, for instance). His images may indeed thrive on the strained conceits and paradoxes of such poets as Giambattista Marino, but the reader seldom if ever imagines that the poem is spoken extempore by a lover in the heat of the moment, even when a phrase strikes a Donnean chord. Stanley's muse is much more chaste than Carew's, often omitting erotic passages from his source; and Stanley is always the scholar, annotating poems with classical and modern analogues. In the eyes of his contemporaries, Stanley may be a Thomas Carew for his amorous subject or labored prosody, but he is a Hugh Grotius for his learning.

More often than not, for Stanley the composition of a poem involves translation, sometimes of more than one source per poem. In manuscript and print he renders into English many important classical and Renaissance poets, from Ausonius and Anacreon to Secundus and Battista Guarini. In general, Stanley works in two ways, either condensing the source or following its structure and language very closely. His reasons for omitting this or that passage are certainly aesthetic as well as moral; educators in Stanley's day heeded Plutarch's warning that a reader must be selective, imitating the bee that gathers sweetness from a variety of flowers. There was, furthermore, some controversy during Stanley's career over the word-for-word translation of a source. Poets distinguished between paraphrase, imitation, and translation, allowing for different relations to the original. But writers such as John Denham castigated the slavish translator who failed to capture the sense or spirit of the poet in an attempt to render every word as literally as possible. Such a translator, Denham complained, refuses to acknowledge changes in culture or language. Unlike Abraham Cowley, Stanley had little desire to take off in flights of paraphrase; but his fidelity to the texts of Anacreon and Ausonius seldom compromises the artistry with which he re-creates poem after poem.

Translations dominate most of the sections of Stanley's 1651 *Poems,* even the first, in which the reader also finds Stanley's original verses. These sections include the following: poems, mainly love lyrics but also commendatory verse and the didactic "Pythagoras his moral Rules"; translations, chiefly classical, from Anacreon, Bion, Moschus, Secundus, Ausonius, and anonymous; excitations, or notes on the translations, in the second section; translations from the modern languages, including works by Théophile de Viau, François Tristan L'Hermite, Mattia Preti, Marino, Juan Boscan, and Góngora; a rendering of Giovanni Pico della Mirandola's "Platonick Discourse upon Love," in prose and verse; and, in some printings, the translation of two novellas, *Aurora* and *The Prince,* by Don Juan Perez de Montalvan.

Even when he is not translating, Stanley's lyrics allude to other texts, in part because their images and conceits are commonplace. "To Love," the final poem of the first section of *Poems and Translations* but the dedication of the 1651 collection, cites in the margins of the former edition a host of classical analogues from Plato, Philo, and others. The message of the poem is that love is paradoxical and consuming. From Plato's *Symposium,* Stanley derives the idea that love is the youngest and oldest of the gods; indeed, love "all Passions doth comprize" and is powerful enough to alter the laws of nature. It compels the most rational creature to be a "willing Pris'ner" and forever yields the strange truth that lovers find their greatest liberty in the straightest confinement. Love itself is unconfined by reason or sense; in "Loves Innocence" it is said to imitate the plants and angels more than it does human beings and beasts. Yet love is so restrictive that Stanley's more libertine speakers get free of it only by deposing love ("Love Deposed") or by dispersing their desires among the widest variety of mistresses ("Loves Heretick").

In the lyrics of section 1, Stanley is an expert prosodist, a tireless inventor of stanza forms (like George Herbert), and a thorough student of the paradoxes and moods of love. Sometimes the same theme extends over a group of poems, either by design or chance. For instance, a group of songs and

POEMS
AND
TRANSLATIONS.

BY
THOMAS STANLEY
ESQVIRE.

*Quǎ mea culpa tamen, nisi si lusisse vocari
Culpa potest: nisi culpa potest & amasse, vocari?*

Tout vient a poinct qui peut attendre.

Printed for the Author,
and his Friends, 1647.

Title page for Stanley's first collection of verse, poems he had printed for circulation among his friends

lyrics centers on the cruel mistress who kills or sickens the hapless lover. The last of these, "The Tombe," imagines the guilty mistress at the speaker's funeral. "There is more liberty in Death then Love," he declares; yet, threatening the mistress with flames from the pyre or with oblivion in his marble tomb, he attempts to convince her that she will profit from burying him in her breast. Stanley's cruel fair ones – his Chariessa, Doris, and Celia – exact a variety of prices from their servants; in one case the cost is endless delay, but in another poem, from Marino, the unfortunate speaker is required to woo some other lover in the name of his mistress.

Just after this succession of cruel mistresses comes a group of poems in which a more mutual love is imagined. "The Enjoyment," translated from Marc-Antoine de Gérard Saint-Amant, finds the lovers far from the madding crowds of the court and city; their cottage is surrounded by woods and meadows in which the graces and satyrs delight and where Nature paints her most beautiful and innocent colors. But this is no philosopher's retreat, nor is it Horace's Sabine farm. Here the thirst of lovers is sated, their vows exchanged, and perfect ecstasy achieved, though Stanley does not translate the most erotic passages of the French. In the poems just after "The Enjoyment," the poet values "mutual" love, "equal" desire, and souls exchanged through kisses. Yet in all these poems mutuality is the projection of a speaker who can also imagine the demise of love. In one poem the mistress herself believes that she is unworthy; in another the speaker fears that the mistress will not exchange her heart for his – that the transaction of the kiss is one-sided. In "The Enjoyment" the speaker is afraid that his form is reflected in the mistress's eyes but not engraved in her heart.

If Stanley gathers like poems together, he also works by contrast. The cynical "Loves Heretick" is followed by "La belle Confidente," Stanley's contribution to the vogue of platonic-love poems. In the first poem, love is all flesh and blood; in the second, it is all soul and friendship. In the words of another poem ("The Snow-ball"), love is a "Strange Antiperistasis" or opposition of conditions. Stanley's stanza forms have as much variety as his lovers. There are several poems in couplets, pentameter and tetrameter alike. But the reader also encounters the following: *3a2b4a3b, 4a2b4a3b4c5c, 4a3b4a3b5c4c, 5a3b5a3b4c3d4d3c,* and *4a4b4b4a,* among others.

No matter what the stanza form, Stanley is often attracted to the intricate and surprising conceits of his model poets. In "The Gloworme," for instance, the mistress is asked to hold the "animated Gem" of the worm, which turns seriatim into a star, a galaxy, a cold flame, and a sacrifice on the altar of her hand. In "Desiring her to burn his Verses," his lines offend her ear with their sound, then rise in flame to become stars, then fall back to Earth as diamonds that once again trouble her ears, only now as ornaments. Elsewhere the speaker rhapsodizes over the voice or gaze of the mistress. His love for her always compels him into the strangest arguments or most vexing conundrums, here "wishing her lesse Fair," there deciding that "In Love uncertain to believe / I am deceiv'd, doth undeceive."

The first section of the 1651 edition concludes with a set of longer poems, some six in praise of authors and a translation of the didactic "Pythagoras his moral Rules." Verses by one poet commending the work of another were as conventional in the seventeenth century as love lyrics. From Stanley's com-mendatory verse one learns something of his views toward poetry, friendship, and their alliance. The first of these poems is the most impersonal. Praising the first folio (1647) of John Fletcher's works, Stanley emphasizes the passionate effects of the plays. No member of the audience leaves the theater unmoved by the "Counterfeit" passions of the drama, though the effects differ from soul to soul, with wild ones tamed and weak ones enlivened. Yet Stanley's verses applaud the folio itself as much as the works within. The publication of Fletcher's works in this form is considered especially significant in an age when the theaters have been closed.

The other commendatory poems are addressed to Stanley's literary friends and kinsmen. Shirley, who dedicated his poems to Stanley, is described as having the power to create and uncreate beauty with his art. In translating the tragedies of Seneca, Sherburne is like Fletcher or Shirley in representing passion for his readers; but his "vindication" of the Roman tragedian is also moral and scholarly, prompting Stanley to speak of translation itself as an act of recovery rather than an idle pastime. Other members of Stanley's coterie are praised: Hall, for instance, as the brilliant youth whose essays will never find a proper audience. A quarter century later Stanley reworked some of these verses into the more personal "Register of Friends"; indeed, throughout his life, these men were valued for their conjunction "of friendship, knowledge and of Art."

For Stanley, his uncle William Hammond was perhaps the greatest exemplar of this triangle of values. From Stanley's poem to this Greek scholar and poet, however, and from Hammond's several poems to Stanley, it appears that Hammond unsettled the ideal as well. On occasion the uncle makes it plain that he prizes Stanley's scholarship or "more serious labours" over his amorous poems. In other words, Hammond praises all of Stanley's work but elicits something of a tension between lyric fancy and learned judgment. In fact, the relation between the nugatory and weighty efforts of the artist persisted as an issue for Stanley; but, in the poem to his uncle, Stanley skirts the conflict by claiming that Hammond has saved him, not from love poetry but from the "female vanities" of falling in love. Even so, there is something literary in Stanley's account of his flirtation with love. The poet assumes the personae of the lovers in his poems, escaping (or at most feigning) love for so long, then coming under the tyrannical power of a mistress, only to be released by her cruelty. The poem concludes that friendship with such a scholar transcends love. No

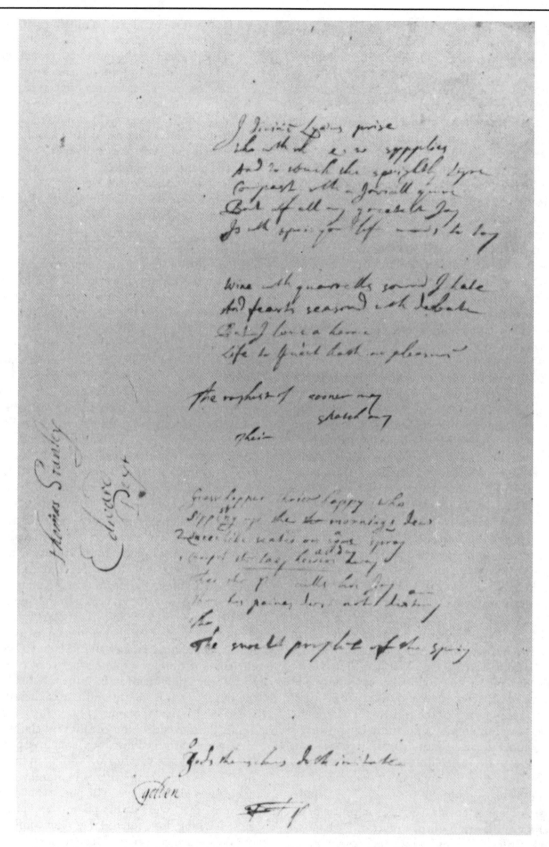

Stanley's signature and drafts for passages in his translation of the Anacreontea; *from the manuscript for* Poems and Translations *(Cambridge University Library, Add. MS. 7514)*

matter that Hammond is among the poets to praise Stanley's wedding and his wife a year or so later. In Stanley's coterie Greek and Latin scholarship remains the "male rite" described by Walter J. Ong in *Rhetoric, Romance, and Technology* (1971).

Stanley's verse translation of the ethical maxims, "Pythagoras his moral Rules," concludes the opening section of the volume as an example of the potential alliance between knowledge and poetry. These "rules," which instruct readers to love God and follow virtue, have their own scholarly appendix, with a commentary on authorship and with Greek analogues for a variety of phrases. What is more, Stanley inserts a revised version of the poem into *The History of Philosophy;* poetry, it appears, can approximate the "more serious labours" of the scholar.

In the next section of the 1651 *Poems,* Stanley collects his most famous translations, first and foremost from Anacreon but also from Bion, Moschus, Secundus, Ausonius, and the unknown author of *Pervigilium Veneris.* Each classic has its own set of "excitations," or scholarly notes, "to secure these Translations (which were never further intended then as private exercises of the Languages from which they are deduc'd) against the prejudice of such, as might perhaps apply the Copy to a different Original." Stanley's commentary examines textual variants, Greek and Latin analogues confirming the "genuine sence of [a] word," allusions to classical astronomy or customs, modern versions of the poem or idea, the decorum of a metaphor or meaning of a myth, questions of authorship, and the work of other scholars good and ill in transmitting the ancients to the modern world.

Anacreon, who flourished as a court poet around 530 B.C., was popular in the seventeenth century for his devotion to wine, love, and song. Very few of his poems have survived, but his followers over the centuries compiled what is known as the *Anacreontea,* a collection of some sixty poems. Among the Caroline poets, the pleasures of Anacreon are underwritten by the vision of England as an earthly paradise far from the tumult of the Continent; Carew, for instance, like Anacreon, refuses to sing of war and its heroes. The most somber Anacreontic theme is the brevity of life; but death, the poems insist, should not be feared provided that one drowns every moment in pleasure.

Stanley is perhaps the greatest translator of anacreontics into English. In *The Anacreontea and Principle Remains of Anacreon of Teos* (1915), Judson France Davidson praised Stanley's "perspicuity, simplicity, fidelity to the original, and . . . vigour re-

sulting from conciseness, precision and condensation." The very look of Stanley's anacreontics is concise. No poem is longer than thirty-two lines, and most are considerably shorter. As shown by the fourth poem in the Anacreon section, the verse is always the tetrameter couplet:

On this verdant *Lotus* laid,
Underneath the Myrtles shade,
Let us drink our sorrows dead,
Whilst Love plaies the Ganimed.
Life like to a wheel runs round;
And ere long, we underground
(Tane by Death asunder) must
Moulder in forgotten dust.
Why then graves should we bedew?
Why the ground with odours strew?
Better whil'st alive, prepare
Flowers and unguents for our hair:
    Come my fair One, come away;
All our cares behinde us lay;
That these pleasures we may know,
Ere we come to those below.

Some of the poems emphasize the tricks of Cupid, others the fruits of Bacchus. But in all they insist that, in a life so epigrammatically short as these verses, the poet should spend each night crowned in roses, locked in a kiss or dance, and blithely drunk among friends.

There is a pastoral side of the Anacreontic poems; in one, spring is described with its calm seas, birds, fruits, and "Plowmans labours"; in "The Grasshopper," a famous poem, the insect is said to reflect the careless state of the gods and to be loved by country folk for its harmless, happy singing. This interest in the pastoral might serve as one motive for Stanley's translation of Bion and Moschus, though several of their poems are scarcely pastoral at all. Certainly another motive is Stanley's interest in literary conventions, here the pastoral elegy. Still further, Stanley translates poems by the Greek bucolic poets that take love for their theme, including Bion's "Epitaph on Adonis" and Moschus's "Europa." Moschus's "Megara and Alcmena" is not so much about Hercules as it is about the women who love him.

In content and locution Stanley follows his originals closely; he seldom expands at any length in composing one couplet after another. But, for all his scholarly interest in the poems, Stanley has a poet's ear and re-creates the bucolic poets. "Europa" proves his facility in rendering not just the story of the myth but also its set speeches and blazons – for instance, Europa's golden basket or the Jovian "lovely Bull, whose divine smell / Doth far the

Meads perfumed breath excell." His version of Moschus's "Epitaph on Bion the Pastoral Poet" translates into English those conventions so dear to Milton's "Lycidas" (1638): nature and its gods in mourning, Arethusa and Orpheus, and the death of the shepherd poet. Here again is the brevity of life: "But Man, though ne're so great, so strong, so wise, / Once dead, inclos'd in hollow earth must keep / A long, obscure, inexcitable sleep."

In this section of *Poems,* Stanley Englishes two ancient Latin poems as well, Ausonius's *Cupido Cruciatur* and the anonymous *Pervigilium Veneris.* Stanley's version of Ausonius's fourth-century poem "Cupid Crucified" illustrates his devotion to the art of translation. As with "Europa," Stanley has left a different and earlier version of his Ausonius in manuscript. As always, he uses the best editions along with their emendations and notes. In this tale of Cupid's near demise at the hands of "Amorous Women," the seventeenth-century poet can be more literal than his modern counterpart Hugh G. Evelyn White. But Stanley's poetry must be supple enough to handle rapid-fire allusions to a variety of myths and to capture the suspensions of Latin syntax. For Stanley, translation requires, in theory at least, that the scholar and artist shake hands.

Stanley's care with the second poem, translated as "Venus Vigils," is even more remarkable. The poem presents the scholar with several puzzles: its authorship for one, its occasion for another. Stanley's notes on the poem consider the question of authorship in terms of style and conclude that "he was of the more modern time." The same attention is paid to the translation itself, of which there is another version in Stanley's manuscripts. The poem begins with its chorus in Latin thus: "cras amet qui numquam amavit, / quique amavit cras amet!" Stanley has this: "*Love he to morrow, who lov'd never; / To morrow, who hath lov'd persever.*" The morrow of the chorus is a festival for Venus marking the rebirth of spring. In rendering the poem's celebration of the season, Stanley is intent on keeping his version concise. Where the Latin has "ver novum, ver iam canorum, vere natus orbis est" (translated by J. W. Mackail as "Spring is young, spring now is singing, in the spring the world was born"), Stanley reduces the middle phrase to one word in the last: "The Spring appears, in which the Earth / Receives a new harmonious Birth." In this poem Stanley is less literal than Mackail, but he never strays far from his original: for "Cras Dione iura dicit fulta sublimi throno," readers of the English get "To morrow rais'd on a high throne, / *Dione* shall her Laws make known."

"Venus Vigils" proceeds with an account of the birth of Venus, with the dews in which Venus adorns the flowers of the morning, and with the story of the origin of roses. The poem ranges from an address to Diana (that she keep away from these rites) to a celebration of the life force in all things. At the center of all is the goddess who sets nature in motion, protects the Rome built by her Aeneas, and summons the maidens of the land to worship love. Even Philomela, who feels the absence of spring and the ill effects of love, sings so sweetly that her music inspires love.

Among these classical translations, Stanley includes one neo-Latin poet, Secundus, whose "Basia," or "Kisses," enjoyed a vogue in the Renaissance. As Crump notes, the English poet skips over those poems in the sequence that "were too sensuous for his liking"; Stanley prefers instead the mythos or nectar of the kiss over its flesh and blood, as shown by the twelfth poem in "Kisses by Secundus": "In such a Colour as the Morning Rose / Doth water'd with the Tears of Night disclose, / The blushing Kisses of *Neæra* shine / When they the humid Print retain of mine." In Stanley's version, one gets the origin of the kiss, the expiration of souls through a kiss, the sweetness and number of kisses, and even the scorching fire left by the kiss. But one does not find the tongue-centered "Basia VIII." There is some metrical variety in these translations, though with only two exceptions the rhymes are in couplets.

The next major section of translations in the 1651 edition forgoes Greek and Latin for the French, Italian, and Spanish poetry of Stanley's near contemporaries. There are six of these poems: "Sylvia's Park" (Théophile), "Acanthus Complaint" (Tristan), "Oronta: The Cyprian Virgin" (Preti), "Echo" (Marino), "Loves Embassy" (Boscan), and "The Solitude" (Góngora).

Stanley's translation of Théophile's *La Maison de Silvie* has its place among the country-house poems of the seventeenth century. Jonson, Carew, Robert Herrick, and Andrew Marvell lead the list of poets in this vein: a patron's estate is lauded as the new Eden securing virtue and prosperity for the world both inside and outside its walls. The French poem, written to the duchess of Montmorency, is much longer than Stanley's version; once again Stanley truncates rather than expands his original. In order to praise Sylvia, the poet casts her in the role of his muse. As the source of his inspiration, she silences the oracles of Apollo and replaces the god in much the same fashion that Christ does for Milton. Even if his poetry fails to survive, Sylvia's house and its gardens will honor her; it is therefore the poet's task to mythologize the stones, trees, rivers, and marbles.

Crump believes that the poem approaches the Marvellian wit of "Upon Appleton House." The reader might see some justice in this claim when the poet attaches his verses to the trees of the estate. The verses on the tree are reflected in nearby waters:

> These floating Mirrours, on whose Brow
>   Their various figures gently glide,
> For love of her shall gently grow,
>   In faithful Icy fetters ty'd.
> This cheerful Brooks unwrinkled face,
> Shall smile within its Christal case,
>   To see it self made permanent,
> And from Times rage secur'd, the deep
> Impression of my Cyphers keep,
>   And my fair Princess form present.

The beauty of Sylvia is not only preserved in verse and ice, it is written through all creation and will not be altered so long as the heavens keep their place. In such a time of civil war as the 1640s, this clever guarantee of permanence and beauty against the chaotic, "Stubborn," "senseless," and "obdurate" would obviously attract Stanley, whose own estates were a haven in the storm. As in Jonson's "To Penshurst," the fish are ready to sacrifice themselves for the owner; but Théophile's poem also paints an elaborate picture of Sylvia fishing. As she casts her line, all of nature grows silent and watches in amazement; her eyebeams pierce and tame the waters, then metamorphose the Tritons into deer. These new Actaeons, punished for looking at Sylvia through their "fluid windows," marvel "whence their young horns sprout, / Or how their rugged coat buds out, / Through the smooth hardness of their scales." The garden itself has peaceful isles and bowers, each of which (the poet concludes) deserves his praise, and all of which are glorified by the feet and eyes of Sylvia.

Of the other translations in this section, "Oronta" is the most impressive. Preti's poem is the most heightened that Stanley ever translated, its protagonist the most heroic. Oronta is a Cypriot captured by the Turks for the purpose of supplying the emperor with another virgin. But she saves her honor by setting fire to the ammunition on board the ship. Much of the poem is stereotypical: the Turk invader is crazed and savage against the Christians; Oronta is noble, virtuous, wise, and beautiful. Her Cyprus is devoted to love and beauty of which she is the very Idea. At the moment of her

suicidal triumph, Oronta speaks like Lovelace from his prison: "They have not robb'd me of my liberty; / Spight of these stubborn Bonds my soul is free." What follows in her escape from the barbarian is, according to the narrator, both gruesome and sublime:

> Her body by this sudden force is born
> Into the air, in thousand pieces torn:
> Her mangled limbs dispersed at their fall,
> In the kind Sea receive their burial.
> Thus she at once is burnt, is torn, is drownd,
> A glorious death, e're she perceiv'd, she found.

The plot of the poem is too simple perhaps for the stage; but its "high Theam" is precisely the kind of tragic subject that the Caroline and Restoration audiences admired. With the pastoral romance, the estate poem, the love lyric, the poem of praise, and the anacreontic, this type of heroic and orientalist romance shows how much Stanley's tastes agreed with those of his day. As Eduard Fraenkel has said of Stanley's major scholarly projects, Stanley's work had a "remarkable instinct for the needs and tastes of an educated public," combining "scholarship and deft popularization." Yet it is important to remember that Stanley produced his poetry for a small group of readers.

"Acanthus Complaint" and "Echo" are pastoral in setting, and both give voice to a devastated rural lover. These two poems suit the talents of Stanley more than Góngora's "The Solitude," in which the subject is a thwarted lover to whom goatherds offer the simple pleasures of their cottage. Even in the amorous paradise of "Loves Embassy" there is discontent and jealousy. Here Venus and Cupid strive to keep lovers happy in a land where all business is amorous: "Love is the subject all their talk implies; / Enamoured is the season of the Year: / Every thing kills with Love, or for Love dies: / Without Loves Pass, there is no coming near." The problems of rebellion, heresy, and rivalry are cured by love, making this "an easie people, vow'd to rest, / Who on Love onely all their hours bestow: / By no unwelcome Discontents opprest."

The next section escorts the reader into the arcane mysteries of love, for here Stanley places his translation of Pico's "Commento sopra una canzona de amore da H. Benivieni." As its Italian title suggests, "A Platonick Discourse Upon Love" is a prose meditation on a poem, both of which attempt to epitomize Marsilio Ficino's commentary on Plato's *Symposium*. The Caroline court spawned a vogue of platonic love, one both embraced and

Pſalterium Carolinum.

THE

DEVOTIONS

OF HIS

SACRED MAJESTY

CHARLES THE FIRST

IN HIS

SOLITUDES

AND

SUFFERINGS,

Rendred in Verſe by T. S. *Eſq;,*

And ſet to Muſick for three voices, an *Organ* or *Theorbo,*
by *John Wilſon,* D[r] and Muſick Profeſſor in
OXFORD.

LONDON;

Printed for *John Martin , James Alleſtry ,* and
Thomas Dicas, and are to be ſold at the Bell
in S[t]. *Paul's* Church-yard, 1660.

Title page for Stanley's versification of the prayers in the
Eikon Basilike *(1649)*

mocked by many poets, but Stanley's translation, not unlike the work of Henry More and
the Cambridge Platonists, demonstrates that beyond court fashion English writers in the second quarter of the century continued to admire
the occult truths and forms to which a heaven-
bound love can lead: "As from God Ideas descend into the Angelick Mind, by which the
Love of Intellectual Beauty is begot in her,
called *Divine Love;* so the same Ideas descend
from the Angelick Minde into the rational Soul,
so much the more imperfect in her, as she wants
of Angelicall Perfection: From these springs *Humane Love.*" Or to summarize the thrust of this
theosophy in simpler terms: "Celestial Love is
an Intellectual desire of Ideal Beauty."

This exercise in Neoplatonism shows how
closely poetry and learning mingle in Stanley's career; it appears both in *Poems* and in *The History of
Philosophy.* Even so, Stanley divides the weighty
from the nugatory. In *The History of Philosophy,* Pico's
commentary is lightweight: after the "serious" rehearsal of the life and doctrine of Plato, it is offered
as "a poetical entertainment" to recreate the weary
reader. In *Poems* the reverse is true: the commentary
is more difficult than the preceding poems about
sublunary love.

Yet another problem with Stanley's poetics
arises in this section. It is not altogether apparent
whether Pico's commentary, or just the sonnet that
it glosses, qualifies as poetry in Stanley's view. The
same question about the relative poetic merits of

prose and verse is even more vexing in the next section of *Poems,* which in some printings includes Stanley's rendering of two novellas by Don Juan Perez de Montalvan, *Aurora* and *The Prince.* Seventeenth-century England inherited its love of pastoral romance – prose narratives stippled with verse – from Sir Philip Sidney and Robert Greene. Whether Stanley (like Sidney before him) considered both the prose and verse of these novellas to be poetry is not certain; perhaps Stanley himself was uncertain, for the works do not appear consistently in copies of *Poems.* In "A Register of Friends," a poem written some twenty years later, Stanley prizes "Lyrick Poesy" over "rebellious Prose," but the point of this may be more political than literary.

Stanley's most significant poetry outside of *Poems* is his exercise at rendering prose into verse, the *Psalterium Carolinum,* written sometime between 1648 and its publication in 1657. Stanley's only explicitly political venture, it versifies prayers from the *Eikon Basilike,* thought by Stanley and his contemporaries to have been written by the royal martyr himself (Charles I) but in fact the work of his chaplain John Gauden. In 1649 Milton quipped in *Eikonoklastes* that the king's prose "wanted only Rime, and that, they say, is bestowed upon it lately." It is possible that Milton refers to Stanley's *Psalterium Carolinum.* The bulk of the original is a series of meditations on Civil War events: the Long Parliament; the death of Thomas Wentworth, first Earl of Strafford; the arrest of the five members of Parliament; and so forth. But Stanley skips over the longer commentaries of each chapter and concentrates on the final "psalm" in each. Accordingly, the persona of Charles is Davidic, repenting for whatever sins he has committed but fully trusting that God is on his side against the cruel and profane enemy.

Dedicated to Charles II, the *Psalterium Carolinum* was a labor of love for the executed monarch; Stanley worked as hard on this religious, political, and, for him, heroic subject as he ever did on the theme of love. Indeed, the series of poems appears in two major manuscripts with many variants and attempts with unfailing devotion to stay close to the "inaccessible perfection" of the original. A passage from *Eikon Basilike* –

For Thou, O Lord, hast made us see that resolutions of future reforming do not always satisfy Thy justice, nor prevent thy vengeance for former miscarriages. Our sins have overlaid our hopes; Thou hast taught us to depend on thy mercies to forgive

– is adapted by Stanley as –

Thou Lord, hast made us see, that pious thoughts
Of future reformation for past faults;
Nor satisfie thy justice; or prevent
Alwaies the strokes of thy dire punishment.
Our hopes, ore-laid by sin, on thee depend
For pardon[.]

Whatever the Royalist motives of this exercise, Stanley the poet must have profited too. Like the love lyrics or the paraphrases on two psalms, the poems of the *Psalterium Carolinum* have a variety of metrical and stanzaic forms. As Stanley may have recalled, even Jonson found it beneficial to compose his poetry first in prose.

In the 1650s and 1660s Stanley committed himself to scholarship, not poetry, but there does survive one last group of poems, "A Register of Friends," written late in his life (1675 or after). In this series of poems to Fairfax the tutor; Hammond the uncle, scholar, and poet; Shirley the playwright; Hall the prodigy; Lovelace the noble kinsman; Iseham the Royalist; Bowman the fellow exile; Sherburne the close associate; and Salmon the neighbor, Stanley underscores the irony of his career – that his labors of art and learning, so often devoid of any personal reference or anecdote, were inspired by a coterie of the most intimate friends. Stanley aimed *The History of Philosophy* and his Aeschylus at a wider audience than the fifty or fewer people for whom his poetry was printed in the earlier two collections; but as "A Register of Friends" makes clear, Stanley locates all things great and good within an inner sanctum sometimes imperiled by the debased world.

Fairfax is prized for the learning that has secluded the tutor from the chaotic world; he gets credit too for educating Stanley in the private (and safe) wars of philosophy: "The old Philosophers we did excite / To quarrell, whilst we smil'd to see the fight." Hammond is remembered for having grieved with Stanley over the loss of "halcion-days," while Hall is eulogized with the bitter remembrance that the youth compromised himself in "those Rebellious Epecurian Times." But Stanley has faith that even if the impieties and treasons of the day seduced Hall, the onetime essayist and poet was "Repentant, Loyall, pious, at [his] death."

For Stanley, "publick grief" motivates the retreat into an already attractive coterie of poetry, scholarship, and friendship. "A Register of Friends" rehearses what for this group of associates was a world run amok with Puritans and Levelers; but it is written after the Restoration, when Stanley can trust once again in the values embodied by "sacred friendship":

> then our sight
> More dear, and farr more cheerfull then the light;
> ....
> Though none I envy, all might envy mee,
> Who have so long, so happily possest
> The love of the most learned and the best.

If Stanley's friends provide his most cherished emblem of a Royalist culture, his colossal mind ensures for them the security of a cosmos ruled by God and king. As patron, scholar, and poet, Stanley guarantees for Hammond that the schismatics and skeptics of the world can never truly assail the order of things. According to his uncle in his *Poems* (1655), Stanley's learning extends beyond national boundaries and unites the world. Others (with Shirley) may value the Carew in Stanley, but Hammond elevates the scholar over the lyricist. His nephew may dally in the whims of "fancy," but the true depths of Thomas Stanley's learning preserve a world nearly lost in the flighty indecision that fancy loves: "Thus we poor sceptics in the region / Of Fancy float, foes to assertion; / But I will perch on thee, and make my stand / Of settled knowledge on thy steady hand." Without Stanley, philosophy faces an endless fragmentation: Hammond imagines a battle of the books in his library that only his nephew can "moderate." One senses that Hammond is not smiling at the fight: his Stanley keeps the world from chaos, even with a verse that, however fanciful, strikes Hammond as smooth and orderly.

Both creative and conservative in the eyes of his contemporaries, Stanley himself must have wondered what place his major projects might find in a Europe torn by civil strife and confronted by new theologies, radical politics, and rival philosophies. In his *History of the Chaldaick Philosophy* (1662), he writes that Eastern philosophies are less contentious, less bent on sectarianism, than Western, but even the Eastern ones are not free of division. What is more, *The History of Philosophy* also records the conflicting political values of the Western sages, some of whom wielded a monarch's powers, while others reformed the law and fought tyranny. With his edition of Aeschylus, Stanley gave the world its greatest dramatist of the momentous battle between kingship and democracy. One can assume that Stanley read Aeschylus's *The Persians* or *Prometheus Vinctus* with a political orientation contrary to the author of *Samson Agonistes* (1671), Milton. But even for so staunch a Royalist as Stanley the political scene of the 1650s was complex, with so many tyrants and liberators from which to choose. In Anacreon, Stanley found a court poet whose values were attractive to many a seventeenth-century lyricist and who flourished just prior to the age of Aeschylus and Athenian democracy. But in his excitations Stanley suggests that he was offended by the debauchery of anacreontics.

It is possible that Stanley believed in the ability of massive and painstaking scholarship to reconcile the factions of his day – the materialists and Platonists, for instance, or the Royalists and Parliamentarians. But one wonders if it occurred to Stanley that these great works might inflame the "wars of truth" even further, no matter what the scholar intended. It is possible, too, that Stanley focused almost entirely on what he felt were scholarly matters, a gloss here or an etymology there. Or perhaps he trusted that his "more serious labours" would teach universal truths no matter what their political context. On this score the prefatory material to *The History of Philosophy* moves back and forth between its commitment to general or exemplary truths and its obligation to every particularity neglected by the centuries of scholarship. With one eye on Diogenes Laertius and the other on Francis Bacon, Stanley remarks at the outset of his great history that the new ideas of his age will find both humility and encouragement in a study of the past. At some level Stanley appears to know that, whatever his exacting care, he must submit the rehearsal of philosophies and the edition of Greek tragedy to a world not registered among his friends. Indeed, most of Stanley's scholarly notes were left in manuscript, though almost certainly because scholars, especially those with the ill health of this one, run out of precious time.

In Thomas Stanley, mid-century Royalists among others throughout England and Europe applauded a quiet cultural hero, one who wrote and translated the kind of love lyric so favored in the seventeenth century, an expert linguist and prosodist and a classical scholar of the very first order. Seldom does his work directly respond to the controversies of his age, but it is always underwritten by the tastes and ideals of the mid seventeenth century. Each of his volumes, from the private editions of his poems to his Aeschylus, recuperates a past from Anacreon and the ancients to Marino, Joseph Justus Scaliger, and all the great poets and scholars of the Renaissance. Each volume foretells the future of neoclassicism, from the couplets that Stanley polished to the eventual debates over his plagiarisms.

These volumes also speak their own moment, when the people of England found themselves in a heated struggle over their ultimate values and national destiny.

References:

Ausonius, volume 1, translated by Hugh G. Evelyn White (New York: Putnam, 1919);

Gerald Eades Bentley, "James Shirley and a Group of Unnoted Poems on the Wedding of Thomas Stanley," *Huntington Library Quarterly,* 2 (January 1939): 219–232;

Margaret Flower, "Thomas Stanley (1625–1678): A Bibliography of his Writings in Prose and Verse (1647–1743)," *Transactions of the Cambridge Bibliographical Society,* 1, edited by Bruce Dickins and A. N. L. Munby (Cambridge: Bowes & Bowes, 1953), pp. 139–172;

Eduard Fraenkel, ed., *Agamemnon* (Oxford: Clarendon Press, 1950);

J. A. Gruys, *The Early Printed Editions (1518–1664) of Aeschylus: A Chapter in the History of Classical Scholarship* (Nieuwkoop: Graaf, 1981);

Philip A. Knachel, ed., *Eikon Basilike* (Ithaca, N.Y.: Cornell University Press, 1966);

Earl Miner, *The Cavalier Mode from Jonson to Cotton* (Princeton: Princeton University Press, 1971);

J. M. Osborn, "Thomas Stanley's Lost *Register of Friends,*" *Yale University Library Gazette,* 32 (1958): 1–26;

Pervigilium Veneris, translated by J. W. Mackail, second edition, revised by G. P. Goold (Cambridge, Mass.: Harvard University Press, 1988);

Mario Praz, "Stanley, Sherburne and Ayres as Translators and Imitators of Italian, Spanish and French Poets," *Modern Language Review,* 20 (July 1925): 280–294;

Edward M. Wilson and E. R. Vincent, "Thomas Stanley's Translations and Borrowings from Spanish and Italian Poems," *Revue de Littérature Comparée,* 32 (1958): 548–556.

Papers:
Stanley left numerous manuscripts comprising his poems and scholarly notes, both in his hand and in the hand of a scribe. The major manuscripts include Cambridge Add. MS. 7514; Trinity College, Cambridge R.3.54; and Bodleian Library MS. Mus.b.1. Galbraith Miller Crump and Margaret Flower give information about others.

Thomas Traherne

(1637? – 1674)

Stanley Stewart
University of California, Riverside

BOOKS: *Roman Forgeries, Or, A True Account of False Records Discovering the Impostures and Counterfeit Antiquities of the Church of Rome* (London: Printed by S. & B. Griffin for Jonathan Edwin, 1673);

Christian Ethicks: Or, Divine Morality. Opening the Way to Blessedness, By the Rules of Vertue and Reason (London: Printed for Jonathan Edwin, 1675);

A Serious and Pathetical Contemplation of the Mercies of God, In Several Most Devout and Sublime Thanksgivings for the same (London: Printed for Samuel Keble, 1699).

Editions: *The Poetical Works of Thomas Traherne 1636?–1674,* edited by Bertram Dobell (London: Dobell, 1903);

Centuries of Meditations, edited by Dobell (London: Dobell, 1908);

Traherne's Poems of Felicity, edited by H. I. Bell (Oxford: Clarendon Press, 1910);

The Poetical Works of Thomas Traherne, faithfully reprinted from the Author's Original Manuscript, together with Poems of Felicity, reprinted from the Burney manuscript, and Poems from Various Sources, edited by Gladys I. Wade (London: P. J. & A. E. Dobell, 1932);

A Serious and Pathetic Contemplation of the Mercies of God, In Several most Devout and Sublime Thanksgivings for the same, edited by Roy Daniells (Toronto: University of Toronto Press, 1941);

Centuries, Poems, and Thanksgivings, 2 volumes, edited by H. M. Margoliouth (Oxford: Clarendon Press, 1958);

Meditations on the Six Days of the Creation, edited by George Robert Guffey (Los Angeles: William Andrews Clark Memorial Library, University of California, 1966);

Poems, Centuries, and Three Thanksgivings, edited by Anne Ridler (London: Oxford University Press, 1966);

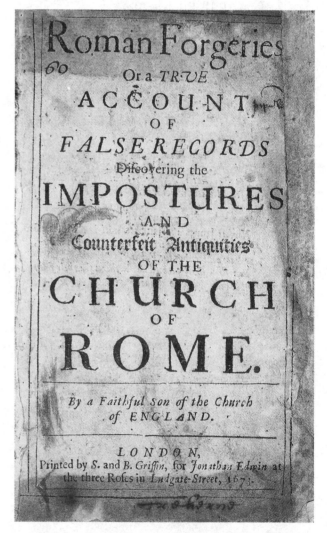

Title page for the only book by Traherne published during his lifetime (courtesy of the Henry E. Huntington Library and Art Gallery; R B 316370)

Christian Ethicks, edited by Carol L. Marks and Guffey (Ithaca: Cornell University Press, 1968);

Commentaries of Heaven: The Poems, edited by D. D. C. Chambers (Salzburg: Institut für Anglistik und Amerikanistik Universitat Salzburg, 1989).

OTHER: *Meditations on the Creation,* in *A Collection of Meditations and Devotions, in Three Parts* (London: Published by Nathaniel Spinkes. Printed for D. Midwinter, 1717).

Unlike the major figures of the "Metaphysical Revival," John Donne and George Herbert, whose works were widely known and discussed in the eighteenth and nineteenth centuries, Thomas Traherne is almost wholly a discovery of twentieth-century scholarship. In his own lifetime he published only one book, *Roman Forgeries* (1673), and, as a clergyman he did not rise to prominence. So obscure is his background, in fact, that scholars once argued about what family and even what part of the country he came from. Biographers have not gone far beyond Anthony Wood, who in *Athenæ Oxonienses* (1691, 1692) claimed that Traherne was of modest parentage from the Welsh border area, that he attended Brasenose College, Oxford, took an M. A. in 1661, and was soon assigned a living in a parish near Hereford. Later, he was made chaplain to Sir Orlando Bridgeman, Lord Keeper of the Great Seal, a connection which was to prove extremely important in identifying him as the author of some anonymous works thought of as indicative of the author of the *Centuries* and *Poems of Felicity.* Not long after Wood's account John Aubrey published in his *Miscellanies* (1696) a brief description of some visions related by Traherne, a basket floating in the air and an oddly attired apprentice, which presumably show his particular piety. If the few biographical remnants can be believed, he was a devoutly religious man, known for his charity to the poor and his rigorous devotional practices. As the anonymous author of the preface to *A Serious and Pathetical Contemplation* (1699) writes, "He never failed any one day either publickly or in his private closet, to make use of her [the church's] publick offices."

Even though much of the Traherne canon remains unpublished, the discovery of his work is one of the great stories of modern literary scholarship. In the winter of 1896–1897 William T. Brooke came across two manuscripts at a London bookstall. Thinking that they might be the work of Henry Vaughan, he showed them to Alexander Grosart. Convinced that they were Vaughan's, Grosart prepared to bring out a new edition of Vaughan, and, had he lived, it appears that he would have done so. After his death in 1899 the manuscripts found their way to Bertram Dobell, who decided they were the

work of someone other than Vaughan. Brooke's acquaintance with an anonymous work, *A Serious and Pathetical Contemplation,* part of which he had anthologized in *The Churchman's Manual of Private and Family Devotion* (1883), proved helpful to Dobell. After study he recognized that the author of the manuscripts and the author of *A Serious and Pathetical Contemplation* were one and the same; but who was that author? The preface to the latter work, hereafter referred to as the *Thanksgivings,* identified him as chaplain to "*the late Lord Keeper* Bridgman." Once Dobell consulted Wood, the connection between Bridgeman and Traherne was established. Traherne was known to have written *Christian Ethicks* (1675), and Dobell discovered that some verse in this work was almost identical with a passage in one of the manuscripts, thus confirming Traherne's authorship. This manuscript, called the "Centuries," was made up of short prose passages interspersed with a few poems. Half of the other manuscript comprised poetry; the rest was devoted to prose extracts and notes. Dobell brought out an edition of the poetry in 1903, and in 1908 he published the "Centuries" as *Centuries of Meditations.*

Yet there was little that could be added to Wood's biographical sketch. It is known that during Traherne's residence as a student at Brasenose, Oxford was an outpost of Royalist sentiment, and, in fact, the last military outpost of Charles I's forces. Even after the Royalist cause was lost, Oxford remained the center of Royalist publications. Traherne was there for the last eight years of the Protectorate; and, although the Puritans had power, student and faculty sentiment was never with them. The central issue for Traherne (and for many others at Oxford, no doubt) was ecclesiastical thought and practice. It was on the great issue of church government that Traherne wrote the only one of his works that would appear in his lifetime, *Roman Forgeries,* published anonymously in 1673. Traherne died the following year and was buried on 10 October in Teddington (near Hampton Court) under the reading desk of the church where he had preached. A disputatious essay, *Roman Forgeries* betrays its academic origins. Speaking in propia persona, Traherne claims that the work grew out of an argument that he had with a Roman Catholic. Having just emerged from the Bodleian Library, Traherne encountered a friend, who introduced him to his cousin, with whom Traherne was soon at loggerheads over the correct definition of a martyr to the Catholic church. Discussion turned, first, on what is unique to the Roman cause (as that would determine the numbers of martyrs Rome could legitimately claim), but it soon devolved into contention over the issue of the ancient documents on which church authority purportedly rested. According to Traherne's account, the other young man, apparently in frustration, denied that it made any difference whether or not contested documents were forgeries. Leaping on this statement as his point of departure, Traherne advanced his own thesis that the early church was uncorrupted by arbitrary power.

More than any of his other writings (except perhaps for certain entries in his unpublished "Commonplace Book"), *Roman Forgeries* exhibits Traherne's training as a scholar. It has been suggested that the work might have been Traherne's M. A. thesis. The work proceeds from the narrative of this heated exchange on various doctrinal issues (transubstantiation, papal authority, purgatory, the doctrine of merits, and so on) to the textual thesis of the volume, which Traherne presents dramatically. He braces his friend's cousin: "You met me this Evening at the *Library door;* if you please to meet me there to morrow morning at eight of the Clock, I will take you in; and we will go from Class to Class, from Book to Book, and there I will first shew you in *your own Authors,* that you publish such Instruments for good *Records;* and then prove, that those *Instruments* are downright frauds and *forgeries,* though cited by you upon all occasions." Traherne's interlocutor gives a flippant response, but agrees to continue the debate, and the thesis unfolds.

The tone of *Roman Forgeries* is at times so intemperate that some Traherne critics have felt obliged to apologize for it. This is a little bit like apologizing for an epic because there is violence in it; the flaw of intemperate diction in *Roman Forgeries,* if it is a flaw, is a shared feature of polemical treatises of the time. As modern readers look back at the issues involved in *Roman Forgeries,* they might be tempted to think of the participants as excessive or naive. But this may reflect a twentieth-century preference for such words as "xenophobia" to describe phenomena once delineated as "nationalism." One need only look at areas of controversy – economic, social, and military policies, for instance – to recognize how a tone of intemperance persists as part of polemical rhetoric, even though the subjects of controversy have changed considerably. Certainly *Roman Forgeries* exhibits erudition far in excess of most current doctoral dissertations in the humanities. Yet it must be admitted that Traherne stacks the deck by eliminating questions of doctrine. Furthermore, he insists that the only legitimate claims for Catholic authority date from before the year 420. Making

A

SERIOUS and PATHETICAL

CONTEMPLATION

Of the

Mercies of GOD,

IN SEVERAL

Most Devout and Sublime Thanksgivings for the same.

PUBLISHED

By the Reverend Doctor HICKS, At the request of a Friend of the Authors.

LONDON;

Printed for Samuel Keble, at the *Turks-head Fleet Street,* over against *Fetter-lane-end,* 1699.

Title page for the first edition of Traherne's Thanksgivings, *devotions echoing the rhythms of the English versions of the Psalms*

the pronouncements of the Nicene Council the virtual equivalent of Scripture, Traherne builds his case for the earliest practices as the only ground of ecclesiastical order. The fact that the Vatican housed most of the relevant manuscripts, then, "proves" Traherne's major thesis that the documents had been corrupted, misused, or suppressed. *Roman Forgeries* builds on a conspiratorial theory of history, which goes hand in hand with the abusive tone of the work – in this respect atypical of Traherne's poems and *Centuries.*

Christian Ethicks: Or, Divine Morality. Opening the Way to Blessedness, By the Rules of Vertue and Reason concerns many of the same issues, but the latter work is more concerned with the theological implications of Calvinist thought on freedom and necessity. Besides, this posthumous work is not at all polemical. On the contrary, parts of it are imbued with the themes and style of the *Centuries* and poems. With *Christian Ethicks,* Traherne comes as close as he gets to sustained theological discourse, and yet this work (as the subtitle suggests) is more ethical than religious in nature. Indeed, many features of the work can be construed as part of a reaction against the overheated, legalistic aspects of the controversy surrounding Calvinist thought on predestination. In this way, Traherne's work can be seen as a reaction against such thinkers as Thomas Hobbes; Traherne resists the tendency toward a conventional ethics. (History gave the victory to his adversaries in at least this matter.)

Yet, like Hobbes and Francis Bacon before him (in the unpublished "Early Notebook" Traherne includes a lengthy extract from Bacon's *De Augmentis Scentiarum,* 1623), Traherne was fascinated by the "new science," in particular, by its notion of infinite space, which he incorporates in some of his best writings. The interest in science of religious poets of the time is not sufficiently appreciated today; critics interested in "demystifying" the beliefs of poets like Herbert and Traherne are particularly inclined to ignore it in favor of an emphasis on their retrograde attachment to liturgical forms and the like. In any case, Traherne implicitly denies in *Christian Ethicks* the secular foundation of ethics by refusing to recognize any difference between justice and the other virtues. He stresses the individual's free and open access to the infinite enjoyment of "Felicity": "WHEN our own Actions are Regular, there is nothing in the World but may be made conducive to our highest Happiness." The only apparent obstacle to this enjoyment is a failure on man's part to exercise the God-given capacity of will: "This I would have you note well, for the intrinsick Goodness and Glory of the Soul consists in the Perfection of an excellent Will."

It may sound as if, in the end, Traherne succumbs to a Calvinist view of man's incapacity to preserve the innocent "seeing" of the infant, but nothing could be more remote from his thought on the subject. He recognizes human limitation, but he does not emphasize it, and he surely does not build a system of belief on it:

> IT is a great Error to mistake the *Vizor* for the *Face,* and no less to stick in the outward *Kind* and Appearance of things; mistaking the Alterations and Additions that are made upon the Fall of Man, for the whole Business of Religion. And yet this new Constellation of Vertues, that appeareth aboveboard, is almost the only thing talked of and understood in the World. Whence it is that the other Duties, which are the *Soul* of Piety, being unknown, and the *Reason* of these together with their Original and Occasion, unseen; Religion appears like a sour and ungratefull Thing to the World, impertinent to bliss, and void of Reason; Whereupon GOD is suspected and hated, Enmity against GOD and *Atheism,* being brought into, and entertained in the World.

The crucial word in this thoughtful passage is "bliss." If one knows oneself, one knows the infinite love of God, which is infinitely expressed:

> HE that would not be a stranger to the Universe, an Alien to Felicity, and a foreigner to himself, must Know GOD to be an infinite Benefactor, all Eternity, full of Treasures, the World it self, the Beginning of Gifts, and his own Soul the Possessor of all, in Communion with the Deity.

By a perhaps mysterious geometry of the cosmos, the soul is like a multifaced sand crystal, infinitely extended because of its connection – "Communion" – with God. Thus, one of the poems included in *Christian Ethicks* reads:

> In all Things, all Things service do to all:
> And thus a Sand is Endless, though most small.
> And every Thing is truly Infinite,
> In its Relation deep and exquisite.

The "*Sand is Endless*" because it presents the self with an occasion to see and know infinity. Traherne's expression here is not logical; nor do the chapters of *Christian Ethicks* proceed logically. The order of the cosmos – and of the work – may seem like disorder, but it is illuminated in the smallest segment: "*its Relation deep and exquisite.*"

The more one reads Traherne, the more one is struck by the incantatory effects of repetition. Traherne piles up words and phrases, proliferating synonyms, as if to suggest that individual segments, isolated by junctures in periodic sentences, might – or might not – suffice to convey a sense of the immensity of the infinite world:

> THE Sun is a glorious Creature, and its Beams extend to the utmost Stars, by shining on them it cloaths them with light, and by its Rayes exciteth all their influences. It enlightens the Eyes of all the Creatures: It shineth on forty Kingdomes at the same time, on Seas and Continents in a general manner; yet so particularly regardeth all, that every Mote in the Air, every Grain of Dust, every Sand, every Spire of Grass is wholly illuminated thereby, as if it did entirely shine upon that alone. Nor does it onely illuminate all these Objects in an idle manner, its Beams are Operative, enter in, fill the Pores of Things with Spirits, and impregnate them with Powers, cause all their Emanations, Odors, Vertues and Operations; Springs, Rivers, Minerals and Vegetables are all perfected by the Sun, all the Motion, Life and sense of Birds, Beasts and Fishes dependth on the same.

Passages like this, critics have argued, suggest a new attitude, associated with the romanticism that was to emerge a century later, concerning man's relationship with nature. Because of his themes of nature and of childhood innocence, Traherne is often compared to William Wordsworth. But his radically synecdochic style has more in common with William Blake or Walt Whitman. For them, the word is a miniature epiphany of divine love in the world; and it is this theme, which is poetic but which, for Traherne, bore important theological implications, that carries over from *Christian Ethicks* to his poems and *Centuries*.

As for Traherne's poetry, only the poems in *Christian Ethicks* and *Thanksgivings* appeared during the seventeenth century. The great critics of the Restoration and of the eighteenth and nineteenth centuries – Wordsworth, John Dryden, Alexander Pope, Joseph Addison, Samuel Johnson, Samuel Taylor Coleridge, Matthew Arnold, John Ruskin – had never heard of Traherne. It has been suggested that the famous opening of Blake's "Auguries of Innocence," "To see the World in a Grain of Sand / And a Heaven in a Wild Flower, / Hold Infinity in the palm of your hand / And Eternity in an hour," owes something to Traherne's *Centuries:* "You never Enjoy the world aright, till you see how a Sand Exhibtieth the Wisdom and Power of God." But there is no evidence that Blake ever saw the manuscript of the *Centuries,* which was not "discovered" until 1875, and not published until 1908.

Furthermore, even though several volumes of Traherne's writings appeared in the first half of the twentieth century, critical attention was slow in coming until the publication in 1958 of H. M. Margoliouth's two-volume, Clarendon Press edition of *Centuries, Poems, and Thanksgivings.* Other editions followed, and, from time to time, scholars announced discoveries of new manuscripts, including "Select Meditations," a volume highly reminiscent of the *Centuries,* and the manuscript D. D. C. Chambers published as *Commentaries of Heaven: The Poems* (1989). The latter volume represents the poetry extracted from a manuscript, which around 1967 was found on fire in a refuse dump in Lancashire by a man seeking spare auto parts. The length of this document (now in the British Library), along with volumes of manuscript material already known, suggests how prolific Traherne was. Thus, even if no other materials come to light, much of Traherne's work remains unpublished.

The only Traherne work other than *Roman Forgeries* and *Christian Ethicks* known to be published during the seventeenth century was the *Thanksgivings,* and it appeared anonymously. Largely a liturgical piece, the work was published by George Hickes, who claimed to have written the preface because he was a personal friend of the author. Hickes's preface, without clearly identifying the author, did hint at who he was, and for this modern scholarship is indebted. Although Hickes described the author as a "very devout Christian," he saw no need to personalize the matter of his identity: "To tell thee who he was, is I think, to no purpose: And therefore I will only tell thee what he was." It turns out that the author was a clergyman whose thoughts of "the Divine Image" were pursued with such fervor, "whether he had any sense of Religion or not," that he might have at times seemed "troublesome." Yet he was in fact no schismatic, but rather one "in love with the beautiful order and *Primitive* Devotions of" the Church of England. In other words, the primitivism that we find in Traherne's rather self-serving autobiographical account in *Roman Forgeries* persisted in his clerical and intellectual life. Known for his public and private keeping of the holy offices of the Church of England, Hickes continues, the author served as chaplain to "*the late Lord Keeper* Bridgman," in whose service "he died young."

In 1717 appeared Traherne's hexameron, *Meditations on the Six Days of the Creation,* and this was the last known publication of Traherne's works for almost two hundred years. Published in *A Collection of Meditations,* Traherne's hexameron bore no author's name (a full account of the work appears in George Robert Guffey's 1966 edition). Questions about the attribution arose, and the work was assigned to Traherne's friend, Mrs. Susanna Hopton. The attribution has since been resolved in Traherne's favor (this despite Margoliouth's unenthusiastic inclusion) based on scholarly research on the stylistic features of the work. Following the Genesis account, *Meditations on the Six Days of the Creation* devotes one segment to each day of creation; all but one of the entries is preceded by a verse from Psalm 49, and the work itself is fashioned in the tradition of the Psalms, which exercised great importance in all of Traherne's writings.

Until recently, critics regarded Traherne primarily as a prose writer who wrote poetry. His reputation rested largely on the *Centuries,* a long, somewhat repetitious series of meditations and reflections on a variety of social, religious, and spiritual topics. These pieces were numbered and divided into four sections, each comprising one hundred subsections or "centuries." An added "Fifth Centurie" comprised only a single "decade," followed by the number eleven. The striking quatrain with which the *Centuries* opens has been the focus of much critical comment:

This book unto the friend of my best friend
As of the Wisest Love a Mark I send
That she may write my Makers prais therin
And make her self therby a Cherubin.

Here, the speaker seems clearly to imply that "This book," the *Centuries,* will be completed by a female friend and coauthor. By receiving into her hands the unfinished meditations and adding to them, this collaborator will create "her self" anew, becoming "a Cherubin." A. Leigh DeNeef links this text and many of the devices throughout the *Centuries* with the "supplementarity" of interest in the post-structuralist thought of Jacques Derrida. Be that as it may, in the first meditation the author speaks of returning the notebook to his friend (probably Hopton) from whom he had received it as a gift, and to whom he provides the remaining empty pages as a figure of birth, a tabula rasa: "An Empty Book is like an Infants Soul, in which any Thing may be Written. It is Capable of all Things, but containeth Nothing." The paradoxical inclusion in the work of emptiness and "Profitable Wonders," of empty space and figures of generation, unfolds in a flood of nouns, which inevitably suggests plurality and plenitude: "Beauties," "Truths," "Things," "Hands," and "Wonders." Along with his female collaborator, the author "fills" the empty pages of the work, as God did the infinite void of space, with discrete acts of the word.

This figure of collaboration is more than an ornament of hyperbole. This shared authorship expresses a thematic interest represented throughout the work in the author's direct borrowing from biblical and other sources. It is God, not the isolated being of one mortal, who inscribes Himself – often in his own words from Scripture – in the text:

I will open my Mouth in Parables: I will utter Things that have been Kept Secret from the foundation of the World. Things Strange yet Common; Incredible, yet Known; Most High, yet Plain,; infinitly Profitable, but not Esteemed. Is it not a Great Thing, that you should be Heir of the World? Is it not a very Enriching Veritie? In which the Fellowship of the Mystery, which from the beginning of the World hath been hid in GOD, lies concealed!

Here is the vatic tone of the poet who is, in the language of Renaissance criticism, a poet because he is a prophet. Traherne's speaker is also a spiritual guide, addressing an auditor less traveled on the path. Here, the speaker declares his literary and spiritual lineage from Matthew, and, thence, from Christ as he addressed the multitude, who in turn intoned the familiar text from David's Psalms. So

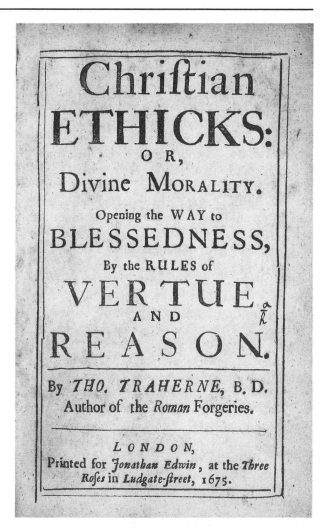

Title page for Traherne's discourse on the theological implications of Calvinist thought to the concepts of freedom and necessity (courtesy of the Henry E. Huntington Library and Art Gallery; R B 432911)

Traherne lays claim to the double heritage of the Law and the Gospel. But Traherne's speaker is first and foremost an imitator of Christ: "And I after his Similitude will lead you into Paths Plain and Familiar."

The *Centuries* has received considerable attention from critics, and parts of it, especially passages from the Third Century, are often anthologized. In fact, this segment is used by Gladys Wade and others as the sole basis of surmise regarding Traherne's life. Although lively and interesting, this section of the work is virtually lacking in any biographical details: one finds no names of parents, no particular locales, nothing that would differentiate this individual from his fellows growing up. Indeed, Traherne's theme is not that of one age as distinct from another, or of one person as different from another, but of recognition that such notions of boundaries must be overcome: "All Time was Eternity, and a Perpetual Sabbath. Is it not Strange, that an Infant should be Heir of the World, and see those Mysteries which the Books of the Learned never unfold?" Louis L. Martz sees in Traherne's unprogrammatic use of repetition, quotation, addition, and the like, a recurrence of ideas and practices ingrained in the writings of European religious devotions, some of which are typically described as "mystical." In this context, the "supplementarity," remarked upon by DeNeef, fits the desire of the finite being for immersion in or union with the eternal substance. It appears, then, that the Third Century subordinates biographical details to shared features of the Christian life, thus carrying on the theme of "Felicity" introduced in the Second Century. (The First Century elaborates the figures of the soul's "Wants" and God's "Love" seen in the gift of "the abyss of the Cross.") The author reiterates the act of giving in his relation to his audience. Hence, God's Love, recounted in the Old Testament, is recreated in the New (in Matthew), and then in turn inscribed again in the *Centuries,* as the two texts are melded into a new creation, which, at the time of Traherne's writing, is still in process.

This is the special thematic function of the opening quatrain and the blank leaves left at the end of the text. These pages remain for the original donor of the volume to fill. Presumably this friend, Hopton (to whom *Meditations on the Six Days of the Creation* was first ascribed), is to fill the empty pages with new wonders. The pages are a tabula rasa to be filled with "words," thus imitating the original "Creation" of the "Word." More than a hyperbolic statement of affection and trust, the collaboration is, in effect, a defining act of the speaker's character. In creating his "word," he creates the opening for "her" response ("I send / That she may write"). His love for the friend emerges as thematic and structural evidence of a will to accept – as his – her freedom to create *him* anew, and by this act, to create herself: "And make her self therby a Cherubin."

The notion, then, that the Third Century constitutes an autobiography may overestimate the historical content of a work explicitly fictive and unfinished. That is, its incompletion is a part of the fictional presentation of the character of the mentor who speaks, often in the language of others, throughout the work. Indeed, the literary progenitor of the speaker is the spiritual guide. Like Christ, the speaker is a teacher; but he is not so much a particular instructor as a type of prophet, or seer ("I will open my Mouth in Parables: I will utter Things

that have been Kept Secret from the foundation of the World. . ."). Here, as often in the *Centuries,* the rhetorical movement is from pedagogy to prophecy. Elaborating on Matthew 13, the speaker also echoes the words of Thomas à Kempis, thus creating a chorus of voices. In the here and now the speaker reinscribes Matthew's text of Christ's quotation from Psalms: The Word is a gift shared by "the Fellowship of the Mystery" of Christ's Sacrifice. Christ gave his body for man's sake in order to restore communion between God and man; but that gift was an eternal act, not of self-assertion, but of self-abnegation ("Thy will be done"). Hence, for Traherne, the Cross is a "Band." Conjunction is both cause and effect of man's "Wants" and God's "Love." This is the "Truth" "Kept Secret from the foundation of the World," and now taught to the "Friend," who will enter her own contribution, her own account of the appropriate experiences – what DeNeef calls the "supplement." Shared authorship is, then, a figurative representation of the plenitude of Grace, which is known in the abnegation of boundaries: between Father and Son, God and man, man and woman, flesh and spirit, word and act.

Similarly, the leitmotiv of dissolving boundaries has, in Traherne, typical stylistic features. He characteristically adds synonyms, phrases, sentences – whole meditations – meant to restate what has already been said, if perhaps in a somewhat different way, rather than to advance an "argument." Or, if one insists that there is an argument in the *Centuries,* then it proceeds not logically but by volume: the reader will be overwhelmed by myriad figures and flat assertions, by a veritable flood of synonymous or nearly synonymous utterances. The recurrent suggestion is that the particular formulation, once expressed, is therefore finite, and so infirm. By its very presence it cannot represent that plenitude which is infinite. The devices used lead away from particulars, which are always imbued with limitations of the concrete and finite. Autobiography, in this sense, is by definition limited – too limited a form to celebrate the being of "Felicity." So, in the Third Century, personal history gives way to allegory:

> I lived among Shadows, like a Prodigal Son feeding upon Husks with Swine. A Comfortless Wilderness full of Thorns and Troubles the World was, or wors: a Waste Place covered with Idleness and Play, and Shops and Markets and Taverns.

Buildings, people, places – these do not seem to matter. Traherne presents, instead, the tokens of unadorned existence in the form of abstract nouns: Thorns, Troubles, Wilderness, a Waste Place, Play, Shops, Markets, and Taverns. And overarching all of these is the narrative which Traherne knows the Prodigal Son will bring to mind. So, rather than the specific story of one childhood, Traherne presents a dreamlike landscape composed of abstractions and allegorical associations, which, taken together, suggest a motif of childhood alienation from the Father, and the setting aside of a rightful inheritance.

Indeed, the evidence indicates that so strong was Traherne's anti-autobiographical interest in the work that he, at one time, appears to have considered writing the entire work in the third person. Thus, in the Fourth Century, he writes of the protagonist in the third person, suggesting a marked distance between narrator and protagonist with respect to their spiritual development: Since the author in the preceding century has "spoken so much concerning his Enterance and Progress in Felicity," he writes, "I will in this Centurie speak of the Principles with which your friend endued Himself to enjoy it." Traherne means to draw attention to the limits of the speaker's earlier concern, "for besides Contemplativ," he insists, there is another, as yet unappreciated goal: "there is an Activ Happiness." What the earlier speaker has said pertains only to the "Contemplativ" part of Felicity. That perspective, by being partial, must be, with respect to Felicity, deficient, not because it propounds a falsehood, but because it leaves out something that is true. This fiction of a newly minted author may be easily penetrated, of course, but it is nevertheless indicative of the way in which, throughout the work, Traherne presents his speaker as shifting from one perspective to another, even changing identities by assuming those of others – by the use of quotation, or by soliciting another's entry in the text.

These shifts function in such a way as to challenge commonsense (in the sense of adult) perceptions, in effect to undermine ordinary ways of thinking about limits. This speaker is a sojourner in no particular time or country, but rather one who takes a moment as a flickering occasion to enter the timeless region of God's infinite love, which is expressed by no particular, but rather by what is comprehensive. The speaker's motive is often to suggest the nature of the union ("the Beatifick Vision") beyond the capacity of language to convey: "This Moment Exhibits infinit Space." Limitation in time and space is contrary to Traherne's theme of divine enjoyments to which he purports to introduce his au-

ditor. If he travels ("I saw my self like some Traveller"), it is not to any specific location: "Every Man is alone the Centre and Circumference" of his itinerary. For, like God, the self, when properly understood, is immense, indeed, comprehensive:

> Tho the Spirit of an Angel be limited and Circumscribed in it self, yet the Supreme Spirit, which is GOD, is uncircumscribed. He is evry where and wholy evry where: which makes their Knowledg to be Dilated evry where. for being wholy evry where They are immediatly present with his Omnipresence in evry place and wholy. It filleth them for ever.

Because of such thematic assurances, Traherne's expressions are often reminiscent of Giovanni Pico della Mirandola's "De dignitate hominis." The figure of creating one's auditor as a "Cherubin" implies that the mentor knows how to do that, and, what is more, has already done it for himself. And yet, in a sense, where Pico suggests that man might potentially rise to angelic status between God and Earth, Traherne suggests that man cannot be limited even to that exalted place, even though it is equidistant between Earth and empyrean. For man is "A seeming Intervall between Time and Eternity . . . the Golden link or Tie of the World, yea the Hymenaeus Marrying the Creator and his Creatures together."

Autobiography was a popular form in the seventeenth century. One thinks readily of Richard Baxter, George Fox, John Bunyan, Sir Thomas Browne, James Howell, John Milton, and, of course, Samuel Pepys. Yet when considering the related examples of spiritual autobiography, one should see how little interest Traherne exhibits in the temporal movement or development which is the defining feature of these forms. Indeed, Traherne's style militates against the notions of personal or spiritual history, for both forms overparticularize years and ages by conceding their claim on the soul. Traherne's speaker loves Scripture because its pages add "10000 Ages" to his life by making themselves eternally present to him. One of the poems in the *Centuries,* "On News," is representative of Traherne's treatment of this theme of temporal and spatial expansion. The speaker, presumably an adult, sees by no longer seeing as an adult, but as a child, that the figure of man as the "Crown of all" is not a figure at all, that man is in truth a little world:

> Yet thus it was. The Gem,
>   The Diadem,
> The Ring Enclosing all
> That Stood upon this Earthy Ball;

Title page for commonplace book in which Traherne wrote prose and verse during the last years of his life (British Library, Add. MS. 63054, f. 2). This bound manuscript of nearly four hundred pages was found on a trash heap in 1967.

The Heavenly Ey,
Much Wider then the Skie,
Wher in they all included were
The Glorious Soul that was the King
Made to possess them, did appear
A Small and little thing!

When René Descartes and Milton talk about education, they discuss their own experiences at school. Education is a matter of individual striving, struggle, and development. But this is not so with the learner in the *Centuries*. Here, education is an abstract concept represented, not by events and personal difficulties, but by a list of subjects. Indeed, it is as if those elements of the abstract institution of learning were themselves the parents that are somehow missing from this individual's life record:

There I saw into the Nature of the Sea, the Heavens, the Sun, the Moon and Stars, the Elements, Minerals and Vegetables All which appeared like the Kings Daughter, All Glorious within, and those Things which my Nurses and Parents should hav talkt of, there were taught unto Me.

Education gave "those Things" lacking in a life that, it is clear, is something of a collage of disparate thoughts, words, and feelings of people from many places and times. Unlike Heinrich Cornelius Agrippa, Michel Eyquem de Montaigne, Descartes, Sir Fulke Greville, and Milton, however, Traherne thinks that he, like David and Christ, has something of himself to add to every soul; for all souls are capable of expansion. Indeed, his critique of education – and it may be unique among such critiques in this – registers no resentment toward the curriculum or his mentors. The only thing wrong with the curriculum is that it does not provide for a proper study of one subject, albeit the most important one: "Felicity."

The theme of the soul as a wanderer in space and time suggests that man's essence does not exist in either domain, for if it did, his being would require separation from infinity and will. In Traherne's thought no less than in his style, the concept of infinity is important. Traherne will present an image, comparison, or description only to show how inadequate it is to express the truth of the Soul's unique status in the universe. This theme of unknowing is best seen, perhaps, in his frequent praise of infancy. It is as if man learns limitation through misunderstood experiences; or as if experience somehow separates consciousness into "seeming" and "knowing." The learned processes of the critical sense seem to undermine the child's aware-

ness of unity – what Sigmund Freud would later characterize as the "oceanic" feelings of the infant, who makes no distinction between the self and the mother; hence, Traherne's attachment to figures suggesting extension, expansion, flow, and stream. His diction tends to erode the idea of a set position in a set frame of space. God created the world with man in it because "He wanted the Communication of His Divine Essence, and Persons to Enjoy it." So the author recreates in the "Glass of Imagination" new worlds peopled by multitudes, as personalities and biographies shade into one another. Toward the close of the Fourth Century, Traherne introduces the theme that will carry through to the last decade: "Infinity." This region of the speaker's soul "is but one Object," a place that is no one place in which the voices of all ages exist at once, like objects on a painter's canvas.

This figurative sense of expansion, addition, and multiplicity merges with those of contraction and stasis. As in the famous Donne poem, "The Extasie," soul's mysteries are "unperplexed," but by an ecstatic experience that obliterates the incompleteness of all other, individuating acts. Hence, the Third Century, insofar as it is any kind of autobiography at all, is so in a drastically modulated sense. Autobiography of the seventeenth century tends to be univocal; in the *Centuries,* it becomes less and less so, and more and more like the psalmist's. For in Traherne's magisterial conception, here, above all others, one hears the celebratory and visionary account of the comprehensive soul, perceiving all time, all places, all occupations, "All":

A Shepherd, Soldier, and Divine,
A Judge, a Courtier, and a King,
Priest, Angel, Prophet, Oracle did shine
At once; when He did sing.
Philosopher and Poet too
Did in his Melodie appear;
All these in Him did pleas the View
Of Those that did his Heavenly musick hear
And evry Drop that from his flowing Quill
Came down, did all the World with Nectar fill.

From the august perspective of "Endless Intellect," the reader perceives the subject of the speaker's rapt contemplation in the Fifth Century. In an ecstatic sequence, which eludes biographical construction, one encounters a speaker/artist who sees without limits that the distinction between time and space is spurious:

This Moment Exhibits infinit Space, but there is a Space also wherin all Moments are infinitly Exhibited, and the Everlasting Duration of infinit Space is another Region and Room of Joys. Wherin all Ages appear together, all Occurrences stand up at once, and the innumerable and Endless Myriads of yeers that were before the Creation, and will be after the World is ended are Objected as a Clear and Stable Object, whose several Parts extended out at length, giv an inward Infinity to this Moment, and compose an Eternitie that is seen by all Comprehensors and Enjoyers.

Here, as elsewhere in his predominantly prose works – and in his poetry as well – Traherne imposes an erosive pattern. Divisions between parts are often as tenuous as the vague sense of difference among times. It is not just that objects give way before this rhetoric of erosion, but with it the logic of change – of progression, the staple configuration of the commonsense view of even spiritual biography – vanishes too.

This alogical characteristic may explain why Traherne's work is often compared unfavorably to that of Donne and Herbert. Trained to look for "logical" or "concrete" or "organic" systems of organization, critics find the absence of all of these offensive. (But by what rule did critics decide that continuity or particularity or univocality must be invoked as criterion – or, in tandem, as criteria – of excellence in every case?) At its best, Traherne's prose conveys a sense of onrush, as if the author would have the reader inundated – along with his speaker – by a tide of thoughts, which often overflow the limits of the normal English sentence. This strategy explains why so many periods occur in the *Centuries* where no sentences end, and why so many sentences end with no period at all, or with an inappropriate sign. That is the point, or, rather, that is the sense that Traherne's prose – as distinct, say, from Richard Hooker's or Bacon's or Hobbes's – conveys. For instance, in the following passage, the parenthetical utterances seem to suggest a separate strand of thought completely lost in the larger motion of ideas:

By this we may Discern what Strange Power GOD hath given to us by loving us infinitly. [Who more Prizeth our Naked Lov then Temples full of Gold: Whose Naked Lov is more Delightfull to us then all Worlds: And Whose Greatest Gifts and Treasures are Living Souls and Friends, and Lovers. Who as He hath Manifested His Lov by giving us His Son, hath Manifested it also by giving us all His Sons and Servants. Commanding them to lov us with that Precious Lov wherwith they do them selvs. but most] He giveth us a Power more to pleas him, then if we were able to Creat Worlds and present them unto Him.

Clearly, Traherne's diction and syntax are not like Donne's or Browne's; and to many readers, his prose will seem less appealing. His is a literary art of abstraction. It depends on a strategy which presupposes that one cannot think of the whole as apart from its smallest segment. In this way, Traherne's spiritual interest expresses itself in precisely the opposite way that Cardinal John Henry Newman's would. When Newman revised his *Apologia* (1864), he sought to make it more and more clear, more and more exact, more and more logical. For Traherne, such a strategy only compounded a common mistake. The idea was to feel, to see, to understand that in the smallest, unattached word – "Felicity" – there resided the numinous truth of "All." Such a perspective renders logical or temporal progression unnecessary.

Although much of what has been said about Traherne's prose applies also to his poetry, critics have not shown much interest in the latter. It has been said that Traherne's poetry is, in reality, little more than shortened versions of the prose, which, if true, would not explain why the verse is less worthy than the prose. But, in fact, several of Traherne's poems appear in his prose works, so, presumably, he thought they contributed something to those sequences. The poem on King David from the *Centuries* is a case in point. Here, the prophetic descendant of David asserts himself in the lyric mode in order, directly, to declare his literary heritage. Then, too, Traherne's paraphrases of the Song of Songs, which also announce their place in the biblical tradition, are, in a sense, even more tellingly brought into a Trahernean perspective. "Rise noble soule and come away" fuses the Canticles tradition (the poem is based on Canticles 2) with the popular carpe diem poem, which Traherne characterizes as the rapture of the mystic's spiritual union with God:

Come letts unite; and wee'l aspire
like brighter Flames of heavenly fire;
That with sweet Incense do ascend,
still purer to their Journeys End.
   Two – rising Flames – in one weel bee,
And with each other twining play,
And How, twill be a joy to see,
weel fold and mingle all the way.

Traherne's poetic range of expression is more vast than is often recognized, for, besides paraphrasing and imitating the Psalms and the Canticles, he wrote epigrams, apothegms, hymns, meditative verse, and long poems in heroic couplets. It could be argued that Traherne wrote some of the finest epitaphs of the seventeenth century. These disparate poetic ventures appear in various sources: segments distributed in such prose works (including those still in manuscript) as the *Centuries;* and in collections originating in two manuscripts of verse. The Dobell Folio manuscript is written in Thomas Traherne's hand, and a second volume, "Poems of Felicity: Divine Reflections on the Native Objects of An Infant Ey," is an arrangement by Traherne's brother, Philip, of the Dobell poems and another group of poems. In a carefully argued essay in *ELH* (June 1958), John Malcolm Wallace challenged this arrangement by treating the poems in the Dobell Folio as a coherent poetic sequence, which he thought accorded with the structure of the Ignatian meditation. Whether or not that particular paradigm holds, the argument that the Dobell poems must be separated from the sequence put together by Philip Traherne left another sequence of poems, namely, those in the Burney Manuscript – *Poems of Felicity* minus the poems that Thomas Traherne clearly put together as a coherent whole. To avoid ambiguity, this sequence will be referred to here as "Divine Reflections," from the subtitle of Philip's arrangement. This title parallels the newly discovered "Select Meditations," and is surely consonant with the poet's figurative interest in the Burney sequence in the figure of the water-mirror.

The poetic sequence of poems in the Burney Manuscript begins, in "The Author to the Critical Peruser," with something of a rejoinder to the Metaphysicals, who "Ransack all Nature's Rooms" in order to "amaze" their readers rather than to make them "wise." This poet/speaker would employ different means to a different end:

> No Curling Metaphors that gild the Sence,
> Nor Pictures here, nor painted Eloquence;
> No florid Streams of Superficial Gems,
> But real Crowns and Thrones and Diadems!
> That Gold on Gold should hiding shining ly
> May well be reckon'd baser Heraldry.

The emphasis here is on the contract between the real and the unreal, on the shining that is only on the surface, and on the deceptive ("Curling") aspect of "Metaphors that gild the Sence." That is, certain contemporary poetic practices – Herbert says much the same thing in his "Jordan" poems – only misdirect the reader's attention toward the trivially "seen." "Seeming" might be the truer experience, and this particular aspect of "seeing" Traherne associates with the unsophisticated apprehensions of the child.

Adulation of childhood – and Traherne's treatment of the water-mirror – is perhaps best seen in one of his most often anthologized poems, "Shadows in the Water," which appears in the Burney Manuscript but not in the Dobell, so it is possible that Philip made changes in the text. Thus, although there is no copy of this text in Thomas Traherne's hand, this poem is typical of Traherne's poetic achievement. In effect, the poem elaborates on an appropriate figure of "Self-Lov," namely that of the water-mirror. The locus classicus is, of course, found in the myth of Narcissus, who spurned the affections of others in favor of his own reflection, which Narcissus (with some justice, one is led to believe) found most beautiful. But Traherne's poem works by an ingenious reversal. The reflected image of the water fuses with the child's thought, and "a sweet Mistake" occurs. The child thinks "Another World" lies beneath the smooth surface. But it would be a mistake to think of the figure here as naive. Traherne is saying that experience can lead away from the insight of intuition: "A *Seeming* somwhat more than *View*." That is, in the original mistaken impression lies a profound insight:

> Beneath the Water Peeple drown'd.
> Yet with another Hev'n crown'd,
> In spacious Regions seem'd to go
> Freely moving to and fro:
>   In bright and open Space
>   I saw their very face;
> Eys, Hands, and Feet they had like mine;
> Another Sun did with them shine.

Common sense would say that, with their heads beneath the water, these creatures must be doomed to death by water. But the child's "seeming" adds something to "seeing" that an adult, critical understanding takes away. In this gestalt, the child observes that the others are "crown'd" by "another Hev'n." That is, in the world of this experience, a kind of royalty is bestowed that is otherworldly and splendid. The child's mind moves into the spacious regions beneath the surface of the water, and the chink expands into a cosmos; microcosm becomes macrocosm. As the poem unfolds, now, on mature reflection, the speaker sees what has been lost, and in this imaginative recuperation, regains the capacity to communicate with the other world:

> O ye that stand upon the Brink,
> Whom I so near me, throu the Chink,
> With Wonder see: What Faces there,
> Whose Feet, whose Bodies, do ye wear?
>   I my Companions see

25

Wn I heard any news I received it with Greediness & Delight, because my Expectation was awakend with som Hope that My Happiness & the Thing I wanted was concealed in it. Glad Tidings you know from a far Country brings us our Salvation. And I was not deceived. In Jury was Jesus killed, & from Jerusalem the Gospel came. Wch wn I once knew I was very Confident that evry Kingdom contained like Wonders & Causes of Joy, tho that was the fountain of them. Oll it was the first fruits so was it the pledg of wt I shall receiv in other Countries. They also wn any curious Cabinet, or secret in Chymistrie, Geometry or Physick was offerd to me, I diligently looked in it, but wn I saw it to the Bottom & not my Happiness I despised it. Thes Imaginations & thy Things of News occasiond thes Reflexions.

On News.

26.

1

News from a forrein Country came,
As if my Treasure & my Wealth lay there.
So much it did my Heart Enflame!
Twas wont to call my Soul into mine Ear.
Wch thither went to Meet
The Approaching Sweet.
And on the Thresh-hold stood,
To entertain the Unknown Good.
It Hoverd there,
As if twould leav mine Ear.
And was so Eager to Embrace
The Joyfull Tidings as they came,
Twould almost leav its Dwelling place,
To Entertain y'e same.

2

As if the Tidings were the Things,
My very Joys themselvs, my forrein Treasure,
Or els did bear them on their Wings;
Wth so much Joy they came, wth so much pleasure.
My Soul stood at the Gate
To recreat
It self wth Bliss. And to
Be pleasd wth Speed. A fuller view
It fain would take
Yet Journeys back would make
Unto my Heart: as if twould fain
Go out to meet, yet stay within
To fit a place, to Entertain,
And bring the Tidings in.

3

Part of the Third Century in Traherne's manuscript for the Centuries, *a work that was not attributed to him until the early years of the twentieth century (Bodleian Library, Oxford, MS. Eng. th. e. 50)*

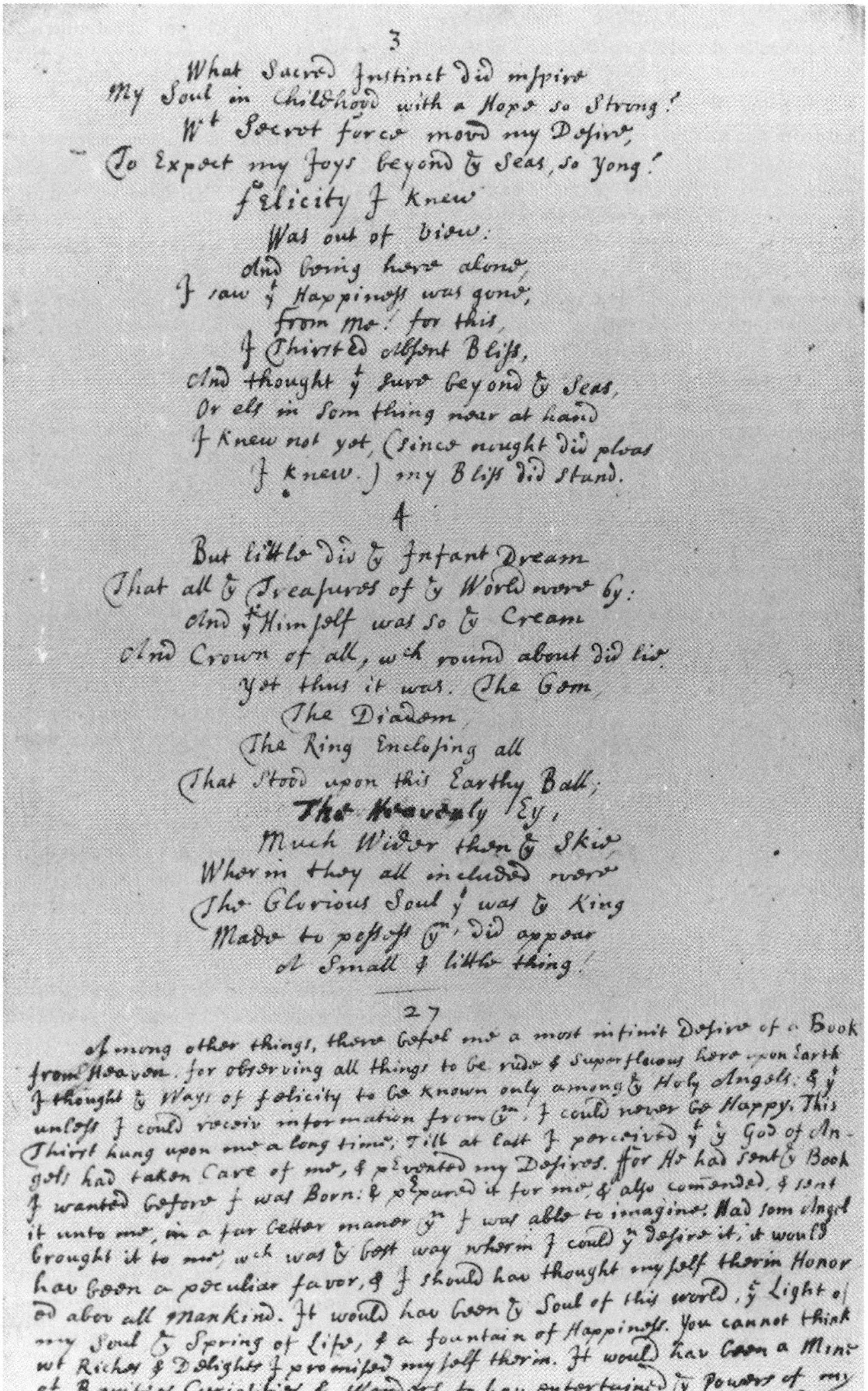

3

What Sacred Instinct did inspire
My Soul in Childhood with a Hope so Strong?
W.t Secret force movd my Desire,
To Expect my Joys beyond y.e Seas, so Yong?
Felicity I knew
Was out of View:
And being here alone,
I saw y.t Happiness was gone,
from me! for this,
I Thirsted Absent Bliss,
And thought y.t sure beyond y.e Seas,
Or els in Som thing near at hand
I knew not yet, (since nought did pleas
I knew.) my Bliss did stand.

4

But little did y.e Infant Dream
That all y.e Treasures of y.e World were by:
And y.t Himself was so y.e Cream
And Crown of all, w.ch round about did lie
Yet thus it was. The Gem,
The Diadem,
The Ring Enclosing all
That stood upon this Earthy Ball;
The Heavenly Ey,
Much Wider then y.e Skie
Wherin they all included were
The Glorious Soul y.t was y.e King
Made to possess (y.m) did appear
A Small & little thing!

––––––––––

27

Among other things, there befel me a most infinit Desire of a Book from Heaven. for observing all things to be rude & superfluous here upon Earth I thought y.e Ways of felicity to be known only among y.e Holy Angels: & y.t unless I could receiv information from y.m I could never be Happy. This Thirst hung upon me a long time; Till at last I perceived y.t y.e God of Angels had taken Care of me, & prevented my Desires. for He had sent y.e Book I wanted before I was Born: & prepared it for me, & also comended, & sent it unto me, in a far better maner y.n I was able to imagine. Had som Angel brought it to me, w.ch was y.e best way wherin I could y.e desire it, it would hav been a peculiar favor, & I should hav thought my self therin Honored abov all Mankind. It would hav been y.e Soul of this world, y.e Light of my Soul y.e Spring of Life, & a fountain of Happiness. You cannot think w.t Riches & Delights I promised my self therin. It would hav been a Mine of Rarities, Curiosities & Wonders, to hav entertained y.e Powers of my
Soul

In You, another Me.
They seemed Others, but are We;
Our second Selvs those Shadows be.

It is wrong to think that these "Shadows" are detritus dredged up from the memory of an early visual experience. The occasion makes sense only as the speaker understands the tactile aspects of the experience – the feel as well as the sight of the surface of the water: "Where Peeple's feet against Ours go." It is the tenuous, thin surface of the water that both conceals and reveals the nearness and splendor of the other world:

Of all the Play-mates which I knew
That here I do the Image view
In other Selvs; what can it mean?
But that below the purling Stream
    Som unknown Joys there be
    Laid up in Store for me;
To which I shall, when that thin Skin
Is broken, be admitted in.

The speaker sees that the adult correction of the child's mistake introduces an error of its own: a loss of sweetness, a loss of understanding. The adult tends to reduce everything to mere sense impression; thus, adult correction turns out to be overcorrection. The child sees that the wonder of creation is not available in a single, limited reaction to a sense impression. The child's "Mistake" is "sweet" because, as Traherne thinks, it brings in other times, all of them, and so relates the moment to infinity: or as Traherne would be more apt to say, to "Felicity."

Philip's additions to "Divine Reflections" suggest that he was aware of his brother's structural intentions for the poems in the Dobell Folio, for he includes all but one of the poems in the exact order in which they appear in Dobell. This fact alone would justify scrutiny of the Burney collection for those features associated with Traherne's method – or perhaps antimethod would be a more accurate term – of organization. Like the Dobell sequence (but after the prefatory "The Author to the Critical Peruser"), the Burney poems begin with a poetic treatment of childhood: "An Infant-Ey." A child is born, then learns about the other world ("The Return," "News") and, subsequently, of "Adam's Fall" from "uncorrupt Simplicity." In this preadult stage, the "I" perceives endless spaces filled with "Light and Lov" ("Felicity"). This is, of course, the antithesis of the surface glitter described in "The Author to the Critical Peruser." One might even characterize the opening sequence of "Divine Reflections" as a

meditation on the fault of Metaphysical ingenuity, for the speaker would put in the place of intellectualized comparisons a prolonged meditation on the experience of undifferentiated, "Simple Light."

From this creation, the soul in the form of the speaker's thoughts moves toward its destiny, which, paradoxically, is always present: the New Jerusalem ("The City"). In "The Review," unspeakable, unknowable qualities of experience are known, but known in part only by the unknown state of asking:

Did I grow, or did I stay?
Did I prosper or decay?
    When I so
From *Things* to *Thoughts* did go?

As in the *Centuries,* so in "Divine Reflections" the movement toward consummation is imperceptible, but nonetheless valued for being so:

The Thoughts of Men appear
Freely to mov within a Sphere
    Of endless Reach; and run,
Tho in the Soul, beyond the Sun.
The Ground on which they acted be
Is unobserv'd Infinity.

In this timeless moment, beginning, end, and present no longer oppress the speaker with their insistence on division and alienation.

Many of the themes found in the sequence extrapolated from the Burney Manuscript appear also in the Dobell poems; and, because of Philip's textual interventions in the former collection, it is probably on the latter sequence, written entirely in Thomas's scrupulous hand, that one finds the best evidence of the author's poetic practice. Yet the thematic movement of the Dobell poems begins, as did "Divine Reflections," with figures of birth, as represented in "The Salutation":

These little Limmes,
    These Eys and Hands which here I find,
These rosie Cheeks wherwith my Life begins,
    Where have ye been,? Behind
What Curtain were ye from me hid so long!
Where was? in what Abyss, my Speaking Tongue?

We know that Philip altered "Speaking" to "new-made Tongue," which shows that he did not always grasp his brother's point. Here, Traherne suggests that, paradoxically, prior to birth, the speaker owns his tongue, but owns it without knowing so. The original stanza has something surreal about it, in its bland assertion of consciousness before birth. Existence precedes what passes in adult conversation as cognition. It has been said that, like the Wordsworth of "Intimations of Immortality," Traherne believed in the preexistence of the soul; and yet what we see here is a more remarkable assertion of the preexistence of the body. Thus, the speaker salutes bodily members that "So many thousand thousand yeers, / Beneath the Dust did in a Chaos lie."

From this beginning as a stranger to his body, the speaker is born, soon to become a stranger to the world: "How like an Angel came I down" ("Wonder"). The soul descends from light into brightness of the child's growing awareness of the wonder of the world in which the "Soul did Walk." Everything is imbued with "SPIRIT," as the infant "I" sees "nothing in the World . . . But 'twas Divine." In the opening sequence characterizing childhood apprehensions ("The Salutation," "Wonder," "Eden," and "Innocence"), Traherne emphasizes the union between subject and object, between the self and the outside world. For Traherne, the ready reception of the child's senses marks a prelapsarian consciousness:

The Streets were pavd with Golden Stones,
    The Boys and Girles were mine,
Oh how did all their Lovly faces shine!
    The Sons of Men were Holy Ones.
Joy, Beauty, Welfare did appear to me,
    And evry Thing which here I found,
While like an Angel I did see,
    Adornd the Ground.

Traherne conveys a sense of the child's rapt attention as a wonderful inheritance of God's love; the very ground on which men walk is holy because they themselves are so. Later, in adult retrospection, the speaker recognizes that in the infant's uncritical perception lies an innocence and understanding which is later unlearned, as the self falls into the adult world. As in "Shadows in the Water," so in the Dobell poems, the speaker comes to know that one surrenders the child's feeling of oneness with the world at too great a cost. And yet, as in "The Approach," Traherne's meditator recognizes that a residue of truth lies even in bittersweet recollection:

But now with New and Open Eys,
    I see beneath as if above the Skies:
    And as I Backward look again,
See all his Thoughts and mine most Clear and Plain.
    He did Approach, He me did Woe.
    I wonder that my GOD this thing would doe.

In this recognition the adult tendency to dissect and to analyze gives way, and the soul is enlarged. Its

new mark, delineated in "Nature," is "Wide Infinitie." In "The Preparative" the child's immediate apprehension of a sense of unity is for Traherne the closest figurative representation of the soul's union with God:

I was an Inward *Sphere of Light,*
Or an Interminable Orb of *Sight,*
    An Endless and a Living Day,
A *vital Sun* that round about did *ray*
        All Life and Sence,
A Naked Simple Pure *Intelligence.*

Again, part of the adult's "Preparative" is the recognition that the child's misapprehension is not entirely wrong. Rather, the adult must reacquaint the soul with its true inheritance: "Get free, and so thou shalt even all Admire." "The Preparative," one of Traherne's finest poems, is almost lacking in verbs; the ideal of a renewal of the soul's relationship to all that is unfolds in a rush of adjectives and nouns, as if tensed verbs misdirect attention to a mistakenly understood and fractured time. It is a technique that occurs again and again in the sequence (for example, in "The Rapture" and "Dumnesse").

The desideratum of the speaker's growing awareness, and Traherne's constant theme in the prose as well as in the poetry, is attainment of a state of consciousness in which total "Dumnesse" is achieved. In this condition the soul achieves a Godlike sense in which opposites contain each other, and all that is true in human experience is seen as limiting and therefore false. Experience teaches that desire diminishes with possession; but the felicitous soul knows that wants and pleasures merge as one in divine Love, for in God, the apparent division between "Essence" and "Act" collapses, as shown in "The Anticipation":

His Essence is all Act: He did, that He
    All Act might always be.
    His Nature burns like fire;
His Goodness infinitly doth desire,
    To be by all possest;
    His Love makes others Blest.
Is it the Glory of his High Estate,
And that which I for ever more Admire,
He is an Act that doth Communicate.

Although the "Soul Walks," it does so by mysterious means; and yet the direction in the Dobell sequence is toward a state of transcendent awareness of paradisiacal wonders. The theme of the closing "Thoughts" suite of poems combines beginning with end by a fusion of the figures of Eden and the

New Jerusalem. In this closing segment, Traherne's theme is the total disintegration of the common-sense categories of time and space:

> The Ey's confind, the Body's pent
> In narrow Room: Lims are of small Extent.
>   But Thoughts are always free.
>   And as they're best,
>   So can they even in the Brest,
>   Rove ore the World with Libertie:
>   Can Enter Ages, Present be
> In any Kingdom, into Bosoms see.
>   Thoughts, Thoughts can come to Things, and view,
>   What Bodies cant approach unto.
> They know no Bar, Denial, Limit, Wall:
> But have a Liberty to Look on all.

An inner eye ("This Sight") perceives by an expansive process "Elements, and Time, and Space." Finitude is now recognized as an illusion. As in the *Centuries,* so here Traherne proceeds by rhetorical assertion of paradoxes to reconcile the irreconcilable. In "Thoughts. IV" the soul has discovered its response – in Being – to the words of the psalmist:

> Thoughts are the Wings on which the Soul doth flie,
> The Messengers which soar abov the Skie,
> Elijahs firey Charet, that conveys
> The Soul, even here, to those Eternal Joys.
> Thoughts are the privileged Posts that Soar
> Unto his Throne, and there appear before
> Our selvs approach. These may at any time
> Abov the Clouds, abov the Stars may clime.
> The Soul is present by a Thought; and sees
> The New Jerusalem[.]

The closing sequence of the Dobell poems, then, moves from verse paraphrase of the Psalms, in a manner reminiscent of *Meditations on the Six Days of the Creation,* to language as in "Goodnesse" (the final poem in the sequence) inviting visions of the Apocalypse, this accompanied by sounds of "A Quire of Blessed and Harmonious Songs."

   Appropriately, the Dobell sequence closes with a suite of poems that, drawing on the figure of the Wedding of the Lamb in the Apocalypse, is particularly sensuous and involves all of the five senses: "Thoughts. I," "Blisse," "Thoughts. II" "Ye hidden Nectars," "Thoughts. III," "Desire," "Thoughts. IV," and "Goodnesse." Besides figures of drinking and feasting, this closing sequence emphasizes figures of expansion and contraction, which, like the earlier figure of circulation, mark the same absorption of the many into One. In "Thoughts. II" the speaker declares, as an expression of the soul's freedom, the disintegration of the categories of time and space: "This Sight . . . / . . .

doth comprehend / Eternity, and Time, and Space." In "Thoughts. III," "Thoughts are the Angels which we send abroad" in just the same way that God sent the soul into the body ("How like an Angel came I down"). The mental process experienced at this stage of the development is characterized, again, by expansion, but an expansion which is literally infinite:

> They [Thoughts] bear the Image of their father's face,
> And Beautifie even all his Dwelling Place:
> So Nimble and Volatile, unconfind,
> Illimited, to which no Form's assignd,
> So Changeable, Capacious, Easy, free,
> That what it self doth pleas a Thought may be.
> From Nothing to Infinitie it turns[.]

This closing section of the sequence is marked by a hesitancy – a seeming discontinuity – not as evident in earlier passages. Themes from one poem emerge in the next, only to be dropped, and then to be picked up again, but again haltingly. "Thoughts. II" begins almost where "Thoughts. I" ends, but between the two poems one finds "Blisse," framed as if to hint at an underlying process at play in the ongoing sequence. But in the fourth and last of the "Thoughts" poems, the speaker offers his response to the psalmist, whose lines precede the poem, which draws together figures of prophetic ascent and the New Jerusalem. The soul in "Felicity" literally is Elijah and Elisha, and literally ascends ("Abov the Clouds, abov the Stars") beyond the limits of personal space: "The Soul is present by a Thought; and sees / The New Jerusalem."

   In this state the soul becomes, like God, able to love itself in others. This has been Traherne's insistent theme in *Christian Ethicks* and in the *Centuries.* God feels through human senses the soul's love of God; hence, the soul's love of God is an aspect of divine "Circulation," or "Self-Love." Likewise, the speaker, now, is in love with himself in others. At last, in the Wedding Supper of the Lamb, the speaker sees in the faces of others his own "Felicity." He sees divinity in them. "Goodnesse," the final poem in the Dobell sequence, is nothing short of Traherne's attempt to undo the Gordian knot of human existence. It shows, if the earlier poems have not made this clear, that Traherne sought through his poetic art to answer the philosophical questions, "Who are we? Why are we here? What is the good life?" "THIS *Divine* Goodness," one reads, "is . . . the efficient Cause of the Worlds Creation." God's "Essence," which is "Love," causes "being"; but the more faces that shine with "Felicity," the greater the evidence that the universe was created only for the speaker, who, in turn, sees in those many faces the shining light – reflected – of his own self-love. In this way, in every object, the love of God is "multiplied and magnified . . . as the same Object is in several Mirrors." By attending to the goodness in others, the initiated soul, now magnified, imitates God's self-love. God created more than one man, and more than one species, for just this reason: to experience their goodness, and so to magnify (by circulating) his "Self-Love." Were this not so, "Eternity and Immensity" would have been emptied of their manifold treasures. Thus, "Goodnesse" ends with emphasis on figures of ripeness and satiety:

> The Soft and Swelling Grapes that on their Vines
>   Receiv the Lively Warmth that Shines
>   Upon them, ripen there for me:
>   Or Drink they be
> Or Meat. The Stars salute my pleased Sence
> With a Derivd and borrowed Influence
>   But better Vines do Grow
>   And Better Wines do flow
>   Above, and while
>   The Sun doth Smile
> Upon the Lillies there, and all things warme
> Their pleasant Odors do my Spirit charm.

Traherne's contemporaries would have recognized the speaker's claim: the soul, transported in heavenly union, enjoys in the here and now the ultimate joys of the Wedding of the Lamb promised in Scripture. The speaker no longer discriminates between the psalmist and Saint John at Patmos. Present in his view is a new "Heaven and Earth," extending – like the world beyond the world that the child perceived in "Shadows in the Water" – beyond the skies. Mystical transport entails new blessings for the senses, as the speaker hears "A Quire of Blessed and Harmonious Songs." At the outset, the speaker asked: "Where was? in what Abyss, my Speaking Tongue?" Now the answer comes from the infinite cosmos in the perfect harmony of the angelic choir.

The Dobell poems as a sequence, which went unrecognized by Traherne's early editors, left the integrity of the poems in the manuscript in Philip Traherne's hand in doubt. As Thomas Traherne's earliest editor and critic, Philip failed to see that his brother meant to organize the volume that came to be known as the Dobell manuscript as a meditative sequence: a meditation on the soul's love from birth to the eternal present of matchless wonder. Yet some of Traherne's best poetry, though found in Philip's manuscript, does not appear in Dobell. This has led to the somewhat controversial anthologizing of poems such as "Shadows in the Water," arguably Traherne's most stunning individual poem. So

Philip's contribution remains substantial. For, barring discovery of another volume of poetry in Thomas Traherne's hand, Philip should be thanked for preserving the poetic sequence in the Burney Manuscript. Anne Ridler's Oxford edition (1966) provides a helpful perspective on the issue of Traherne's intentions, for she separates the poems into two groups: "Poems From Thomas Traherne's MS." and "Poems from Philip Traherne's MS." The later group differs from Margoliouth's arrangement by the telling deletion of all poems from Thomas Traherne's manuscript. The result is two sequences with close to the same number of poems (thirty-seven and thirty-nine, respectively), both beginning with a series of poems on childhood, and both progressing along lines of spiritual experiences to analogous insights into "Felicity." There are fifteen poems in the Dobell Manuscript not included in Philip's manuscript. Thus, either Philip had the Dobell Manuscript, or he had access to another manuscript that had the Dobell sequence in exactly the same order. It has been suggested that Philip intended to construct a second manuscript, this to be made up of the remaining fifteen poems from Dobell, and the poems (probably twelve to fifteen in number) with which Philip, not recognizing the "shape" of the manuscript in his brother's hand, had decided to form two sequences out of three.

When Wood wrote of Traherne's distinction as an Oxfordian, he did not mention his talent as a prose writer or poet. In the century since his "discovery," his reputation as an important minor author in a period of incredible literary riches has been well established. There are editions of his major works, including *Christian Ethicks,* the *Centuries,* the *Thanksgivings,* the poetry, and some of the minor works as well. His interest in childhood perceptions will probably invite further discussion by critics interested in romanticism or in psychological and psychoanalytic theories, and his writings have attracted critics interested in the history of mysticism. All of these perspectives will find much in the published and unpublished Traherne canon worthy of discussion, not only for its evidences of the precursor's thought, but also for its many interesting differences from that of poets and thinkers who would come later. Traherne's focus on the child's appreciative capacity was not merely a precursor of Freud's idea of infantile "oceanic" feelings toward the mother, though it may bear relation to it. Nor does Traherne's treatment of mystical themes necessarily entail the sort of unusual feelings and experiences that one associates with the writings of Saint Teresa and Saint John of the Cross. Rather,

Traherne's notion of "Felicity" concerns an aspect of nature which, he believed, had come to be ignored. Long before Freud or Carl Gustav Jung or Herbert Marcuse, Traherne sought to preserve something of value in the child's freedom and love of life which, through no particularly sinister mechanism of civilization, seems to be slowly extinguished by a "Fall" into growing up. Unlike many of the naysayers of the later periods, Traherne insists that such an extinction of "Joy" is neither inevitable nor irreversible. Appreciation of the here and now is not eternally lost merely by the acquisition of experience and judgment. For Traherne intellect and feeling are only apparent opposites. His theme is that God's love not only allows for but encourages and even insists on our enjoyment of the world. When the soul recognizes this, it becomes at one with prophets and angels, which explains why his theme is cast so often in paraphrase of Scripture, such as in "The Anticipation," drawn from Revelation 4: "And Holy, Holy, Holy, is his Name. / He is the Means both of Himself and all, / Whom we the Fountain Means and End do call."

References:

A. L. Clements, *The Mystical Poetry of Thomas Traherne* (Cambridge: Harvard University Press, 1969);

Malcolm Day, *Thomas Traherne* (Boston: Hall, 1982);

Jerome S. Dees, "Recent Studies in Traherne," *English Literary Renaissance,* 4 (Winter 1974): 189–196;

A. Leigh DeNeef, *Traherne in Dialogue: Heidegger, Lacan, and Derrida* (Durham & London: Duke University Press, 1988);

George Robert Guffey, *A Concordance to the Poetry of Thomas Traherne* (Berkeley: University of California Press, 1974);

Richard Douglas Jordan, *The Temple of Eternity: Thomas Traherne's Philosophy of Time* (Port Washington, N.Y.: Kennikat Press, 1972);

Louis L. Martz, *The Paradise Within: Studies in Vaughan, Traherne, and Milton* (New Haven: Yale University Press, 1964);

K. W. Salter, *Thomas Traherne: Mystic and Poet* (London: Arnold, 1964);

Stanley Stewart, *The Expanded Voice: The Art of Thomas Traherne* (San Marino: Huntington Library, 1970);

Gladys Wade, *Thomas Traherne: A Critical Biography* (Princeton: Princeton University Press, 1944).

Papers:

The manuscript for Traherne's "Centuries," the Dobell Folio (also called the "Commonplace Book"), "The Church's Year Book," and the "Early Notebook" (also called Philip Traherne's Notebook) are at the Bodleian Library, Oxford. The Burney Manuscript (also known as "Poems of Felicity") is at the British Library, London. The manuscript for Traherne's "Select Meditations" is in the Osborn Collection, Beinecke Library, New Haven.

Henry Vaughan
(1621 – 23 April 1695)

John N. Wall
North Carolina State University

BOOKS: *Poems, with the tenth Satyre of Ivvenal Englished* (London: Printed for G. Badger, 1646);

Silex Scintillans: or Sacred Poems and Private Ejaculations (London: Printed by T. W. for H. Blunden, 1650; second edition, enlarged, London: Printed for Henry Crips & Lodowick Lloyd, 1655);

Olor Iscanus: A Collection of Some Select Poems, and Translations (London: Printed by T. W. for Humphrey Moseley, 1651);

The Mount of Olives: Or, Solitary Devotions (London: Printed for William Leake, 1652);

Flores Solitudinis. Certaine Rare and Elegant Pieces (London: Printed for Humphrey Moseley, 1654);

Hermetical Physick: Or, The right way to preserve, and to restore Health. By That famous and faithfull Chymist, Henry Nollius. Englished by Henry Vaughan, Gent. (London: Printed for Humphrey Moseley, 1655);

The Chymists Key to shut, and to open: Or the True Doctrin of Corruption and Generation, Henry Nollius's *De Generatione Rerum naturalium,* translated by Vaughan (London: Printed by E. B. for L. Lloyd, 1657);

Thalia Rediviva: The Pass-Times and Diversions of a Country-Muse In Choice Poems On several Occasions (London: Printed for Robert Pawlet, 1678).

Editions: *Silex Scintillans,* edited by H. F. Lyte (London: William Pickering, 1847);

The Works in Verse and Prose Complete of Henry Vaughan, Silurist, edited by Alexander B. Grosart (Blackburn, Lancashire: C. Tiplady, 1871);

The Poems of Henry Vaughan, edited by E. K. Chambers (London: Lawrence & Bullen / New York: Scribners, 1896);

The Works of Henry Vaughan, edited by L. C. Martin (2 volumes, Oxford: Clarendon Press, 1914; second edition, 1 volume, 1957);

The Complete Poetry of Henry Vaughan, edited by French Fogel (Garden City, N.Y.: Doubleday / Anchor, 1964);

The Complete Poems, edited by Alan Rudrum (Harmondsworth, U.K. & Baltimore: Penguin, 1976);

George Herbert and Henry Vaughan, edited by Louis Martz (New York: Oxford University Press, 1986).

Henry Vaughan, the major English poet of the Commonwealth period, has been among the writers benefiting most from the twentieth-century revival of interest in the poetry of John Donne and his followers. Vaughan's early poems, notably those published in the *Poems* of 1646 and *Olor Iscanus* of 1651, place him among the "Sons of Ben," in the company of other imitators of Ben Jonson, such as the Cavalier poets Sir William Davenant and Thomas Carew. His poetry from the late 1640s and 1650s, however, published in the two editions of *Silex Scintillans* (1650, 1655), makes clear his extensive knowledge of the poetry of Donne and, especially, of George Herbert.

Even though Vaughan would publish a final collection of poems with the title *Thalia Rediviva* in 1678, his reputation rests primarily on the achievement of *Silex Scintillans.* In the preface to the 1655 edition Vaughan described Herbert as a "blessed man ... whose holy *life* and *verse* gained many pious *Converts* (of whom I am the least)." Vaughan's transition from the influence of the Jacobean neoclassical poets to the Metaphysicals was one manifestation of his reaction to the English Civil War. During the time the Church of England was outlawed and radical Protestantism was in ascendancy, Vaughan kept faith with Herbert's church through his poetic response to Herbert's *Temple* (1633).

Recent attention to Vaughan's poetic achievement is a new phenomenon. Even though he published many translations and four volumes of poetry during his lifetime, Vaughan seems to have attracted only a limited readership. The second edition of his major work, *Silex Scintillans,* included unsold pages of the first edition. When, in 1673, his cousin John Aubrey informed him that he had asked Anthony Wood to include information about Vaughan and his brother Thomas in a volume commemorating Oxford poets (later published as *Athenæ Oxonienses,* 1691, 1692) his response was enthusiastic. He thanked Aubrey in a 15 June letter for remembering "such low & forgotten things, as my brother and my selfe." In a letter to Aubrey dated 28 June, Vaughan confessed, "I never was of such a magnitude as could invite you to take notice of me, & therfore I must owe all these favours to the generous measures of yor free & excellent spirit."

In spite of Aubrey's kindness and Wood's resulting account of Vaughan, neglect of the Welsh poet would continue. Wood expanded his treatment of the Vaughans in the second edition of *Athenæ Oxonienses* (1721) to give Henry his own section distinct from the account of his brother, but Vaughan's work was ignored almost completely in the eighteenth century. Such attention as Vaughan was to receive early in the nineteenth century was hardly favorable: he was described in Thomas Campbell's *Specimens of the British Poets* (1819) as "one of the harshest even of the inferior order of conceit," worthy of notice only because of "some few scattered thoughts that meet our eye amidst his harsh pages like wild flowers on a barren heath."

Renewed appreciation of Vaughan came only at midcentury in the context of the Oxford Movement and the Anglo-Catholic revival of interest in the Caroline divines. Seeking a usable past for present-day experience of renewed spiritual devotion, Edward Farr included seven of Vaughan's poems in his anthology *Gems of Sacred Poetry* (1841). Awareness of Vaughan spurred by Farr's notice soon led to H. F. Lyte's edition of *Silex Scintillans* in 1847, the first since Vaughan's death. Yet wide appreciation of Vaughan as a poet was still to come.

Vaughan's *Complete Works* first appeared in Alexander B. Grosart's edition (1871), to be superseded by L. C. Martin's edition, which first appeared in 1914. Martin's 1957 revision of this edition remains the standard text. Together with F. E. Hutchinson's biography (1947) it constitutes the foundation of all more recent studies. Letters Vaughan wrote Aubrey and Wood supplying information for publication in *Athenæ Oxonienses* that are reprinted in Martin's edition remain the basic source for most of the specific information known about Vaughan's life and career.

In his letters to Aubrey, Henry Vaughan reported that he was the elder of twin sons born to Thomas and Denise Vaughan of Newton-by-Usk, in Saint Bridget's parish, Brecknockshire, Wales,

sometime in 1621. Seven years later, in 1628, a third son, William, was born. William died in 1648, an event that may have contributed to Vaughan's shift from secular to religious topics in his poetry. Henry and his twin, Thomas, grew up on a small estate in the parish of Llanssantffread, Brecknockshire, bequeathed to Vaughan's mother by her father, David Morgan. Denise and Thomas, Sr., were both Welsh; Thomas, Sr.'s home was at Tretower Court, a few miles from Newton, from which he moved to his wife's estate after their marriage in 1611. It is likely that Vaughan grew up bilingual, in English and Welsh.

Of Vaughan's early years little more is known beyond the information given in his letters to Aubrey and Wood. Images of childhood occur in his mature poetry, but their autobiographical value is unclear. "The Retreate," from the 1650 edition of *Silex Scintillans,* is representative; here Vaughan's speaker wishes for "backward steps" to return him to "those early dayes" when he "Shin'd in my Angell-infancy." As seen here, Vaughan's references to childhood are typically sweeping in their generalizations and are heavily idealized. Inevitably, they are colored by the speaker's lament for the interruptions in English religious life wrought by the Civil War. From the perspective of Vaughan's late twenties, when the Commonwealth party was in ascendancy and the Church of England abolished, the past of his youth seemed a time closer to God, during which "this fleshly dresse" could sense "Bright *shootes* of everlastingnesse."

In "Childe-hood," published in the 1655 edition of *Silex Scintillans,* Vaughan returns to this theme; here childhood is a time of "white designs," a "Dear, harmless age," an "age of mysteries," "the short, swift span, where weeping virtue parts with man; / Where love without lust dwells, and bends / What way we please, without self-ends." Now, in the early 1650s, a time even more dominated by the efforts of the Commonwealth to change habits of government, societal structure, and religion, Vaughan's speaker finds himself separated from the world of his youth, before these changes; "I cannot reach it," he claims, "and my striving eye / Dazles at it, as at eternity."

The question of whether William Wordsworth knew Vaughan's work before writing his ode "Intimations of Immortality from Recollections of Early Childhood" has puzzled and fascinated those seeking the origins of English romanticism. Both poems clearly draw on a common tradition of Neoplatonic imagery to heighten their speakers' presentations of the value of an earlier time and the losses experienced in reaching adulthood. Yet Vaughan's loss is grounded in the experience of social change, experienced as loss of earlier glory as much as in personal occurrence. A war to which he was opposed had changed the political and religious landscape and separated him from his youth; his idealizing language thus has its rhetorical as well as historical or philosophical import.

There is evidence that Vaughan's father and mother, although of the Welsh landed gentry, struggled financially. For the first sixteen years of their marriage, Thomas Vaughan, Sr., was frequently in court in an effort to secure his wife's inheritance. The home in which Vaughan grew up was relatively small, as were the homes of many Welsh gentry, and it produced a modest annual income. At Thomas Vaughan, Sr.'s death in 1658, the value of the property that Henry inherited was appraised at five pounds.

Nevertheless, there are other grounds for concluding that Vaughan looked back on his youth with some fondness. Vaughan's family has been aptly described as being of modest means but considerable antiquity, and Vaughan seems to have valued deeply his ancestry. With the world before him, he chose to spend his adult years in Wales, adopting the title "The Silurist," to claim for himself connection with an ancient tribe of Britons, the Silures, supposedly early inhabitants of southeastern Wales.

Vaughan would maintain his Welsh connection; except for his years of study in Oxford and London, he spent his entire adult life in Brecknockshire on the estate where he was born and which he inherited from his parents. In "The Praise and Happinesse of the Countrie-Life" (1651), Vaughan's translation of a Spanish work by Antonio de Grevara, he celebrates the rural as opposed to the courtly or urban life. Without the temptations to vanity and the inherent malice and cruelty of city or court, he argues, the one who dwells on his own estate experiences happiness, contentment, and the confidence that his heirs will grow up in the best of worlds.

This delight in the rural is also manifest in Vaughan's occasional use in his poetry of features of the Welsh landscape – the river Usk and the diversity of wildlife found in the dense woodlands, hills, and mountains of south Wales. Yet Vaughan's praise for the natural setting of Wales in *Olor Iscanus* is often as much an exercise in convention as it is an attempt at accurate description. Seeking in "To the River Isca" to "redeem" the river Usk from "*oblivious night,*" Vaughan compares it favorably to other literary rivers such as Petrarch's Tiber and Sir Philip Sidney's Thames. Proclaiming the quality of its "*green banks,*" "Mild, dewie *nights,* and Sun-shine *dayes,*" as well as its "gentle *Swains*" and "*beauteous Nymphs,*" Vaughan hopes that as a result of his praise "all *Bards* born after me" will "sing of thee," because the borders of the river form "*The Land redeem'd from all disorders!*"

Vaughan's life and that of his twin brother are intertwined in the historical record. Both grew up on the family estate; both were taught for six years as children by the Reverend Matthew Herbert, deemed by Vaughan in "Ad Posteros" as "the pride of our Latinity." Under Herbert's guidance in his "shaping season" Vaughan remembered that "Method and Love, and mind and hand conspired" to prepare him for university studies. Wood described Herbert as "a noted Schoolmaster of his time," who was serving as the rector of Llangattock, a parish adjacent to the one in which the Vaughan family lived.

As the eldest of the twins, Henry was his father's heir; following the conventional pattern, Henry inherited his father's estate when the elder Vaughan died in 1658. Eventually he would enter a learned profession; although he never earned an M.D., he wrote Aubrey on 15 June 1673 that he had been practicing medicine "for many yeares with good successe." His brother Thomas was ordained a priest of the Church of England sometime in the 1640s and was rector of Saint Bridget's Church, Llansantffread, until he was evicted by the Puritan forces in 1650. Their former teacher Herbert was also evicted from his living at this time yet persisted in functioning as a priest for his former parishioners.

There is no independent record of Henry's university education, but it is known that Thomas Vaughan, Jr., was admitted to Jesus College, Oxford, on 4 May 1638. Matriculating on 14 December 1638, Thomas was in residence there "ten or 12 years," achieving "no less" than an M.A. degree, Henry wrote to Aubrey. Concerning himself, Henry recorded that he "stayed not att Oxford to take any degree, butt was sent to London, beinge then designed by my father for the study of Law." As a result most biographers of Vaughan posit him as "going up" to Oxford with his brother Thomas in 1638 but leaving Oxford for London and the Inns of Court about 1640.

The easy allusions to "the Towne," amid the "noise / Of Drawers, Prentises, and boyes," in poems such as "To my Ingenuous Friend, R. W." are evidence of Vaughan's time in London. In "A Rhapsodie" he describes meeting friends at the

Globe Tavern for "rich Tobacco . . . / And royall, witty Sacke." There is no official record of his attendance at an Inn of Court, nor did he ever pursue law as a career. Instead the record suggests he had at this time other inns in mind. In his first published poetry Vaughan clearly seeks to evoke the world of Jonson's tavern society, the subject of much contemporary remembrance. Jonson had died in 1637; "Great BEN," as Vaughan recalled him, was much in the minds and verse of his "Sons" in the late 1630s. In his *Poems with the Muses Looking-Glasse* (1638) Thomas Randolph remembered his election as a Son of Ben; Carew's *Poems* (1640) and Sir John Suckling's *Fragmenta Aurea* (1646) also include evocations of the witty London tavern society to which Vaughan came late, yet with which he still aspired to associate himself throughout *Poems*.

Indeed the evidence provided by the forms, modes, and allusions in Vaughan's early *Poems* and later *Olor Iscanus* suggests that had he not shifted his sense of poetic heritage to Donne and Herbert, he would now be thought of as having many features in common with his older contemporary Robert Herrick. Another poet pleased to think of himself as a Son of Ben, Herrick in the 1640s brought the Jonsonian epigrammatic and lyric mode to bear on country life, transforming the Devonshire landscape through association with the world of the classical pastoral. His *Hesperides* (1648) thus represents one direction open to a poet still under the Jonsonian spell; his *Noble Numbers,* published with *Hesperides,* even reflects restrained echoes of Herbert.

In much the same mood, Vaughan's poems in *Olor Iscanus* celebrate the Welsh rural landscape yet evoke Jonsonian models of friendship and the roles of art, wit, and conversation in the cultivation of the good life. While Herrick exploited Jonson's epigrammatic wit, Vaughan was more drawn to the world of the odes "To Penhurst" and "On Inviting a Friend to Supper." Jonson's influence is apparent in Vaughan's poem "To his retired friend, an Invitation to Brecknock," in which a friend is requested to exchange "cares in *earnest* " for "care for a *Jest* " to join him for "a Cup / That were thy Muse stark dead, shall raise her up." Vaughan's own poetic effort (in "To The River Isca") will insure that his own rural landscape will be as valued for its inspirational power as the landscapes of Italy for classical or Renaissance poets, or the Thames in England for poets like Sidney.

Yet even in the midst of such celebration of sack and the country life – and of praise for poets such as John Fletcher or William Cartwright, also linked with the memory of Jonson – Vaughan introduces a more sober tone. The London that Vaughan had known in the early 1640s was as much the city of political controversy and gathering clouds of war as the city of taverns and good verses. *Olor Iscanus* also includes elegies on the deaths of two friends, one in the Royalist defeat at Routon Heath in 1645 and the other at the siege of Pontefract in 1649. Vaughan's return to the country from London, recorded in *Olor Iscanus* from the perspective of Jonsonian neoclassical celebration, also reflected a Royalist retreat from growing Puritan cultural and political domination.

The record is unclear as to whether or not Vaughan actually participated in the Civil War as a combatant, but there can be no doubt that the aftermath of the Puritan victory, especially as it reflected the Anglican church, had a profound impact on Vaughan's poetic efforts. His literary work in the 1640s and 1650s is in a distinctively new mode, at the service of the Anglican faithful, now barred from participating in public worship. In the preface to the second edition of *Silex Scintillans,* Vaughan announces that in publishing his poems he is communicating "this my poor Talent to the Church," but the church which Vaughan addresses is the church described in *The Mount of Olives* (1652) as "distressed Religion," whose "reverend and sacred buildings," still "the solemne and publike places of meeting" for "true Christians," are now "vilified and shut up."

Vaughan here describes a dramatically new situation in the life of the English church that would have powerful consequences not only for Vaughan but for his family and friends as well. In the mid 1640s the Church of England as Vaughan had known it ceased to exist. On 3 January 1645 Parliament declared the Book of Common Prayer illegal, and a week later William Laud, archbishop of Canterbury, was executed on Tower Hill. Four years later Charles I followed his archbishop to the scaffold.

Anglican worship was officially forbidden, and it appeared unlikely ever to be restored. Such records as exist imply that Anglican worship did continue, but infrequently, on a drastically reduced scale and in the secrecy of private homes. Penalties for noncompliance with the new order of worship were progressively increased until, after 15 December 1655, any member of the Church of England daring to preach or administer sacraments would be punished with imprisonment or exile. Many members of the clergy, including Vaughan's brother Thomas and their old tutor Herbert, were deprived of their livelihood because they refused to give up episcopacy, the Book of Common Prayer, and the old church. Throughout the late 1640s and 1650s, progressively more stringent legislation and enforcement sought to rid the community of practicing Anglican clergy.

Public use of the Anglican prayer book in any form, including its liturgical calendars and accompanying ceremonial, was abolished; the ongoing life of the Anglican church had come to an end, at least in the forms in which it had been known and experienced since 1559. In considering this stage of Vaughan's career, therefore, one must keep firmly in mind the situation of Anglicans after the Civil War. That community where a poet/priest like George Herbert could find his understanding of God through participation in the tradition of liturgical enactment enabled by the Book of Common Prayer was now absent. In the two editions of *Silex Scintillans,* Vaughan is the chronicler of the experience of that community when its source of Christian identity was no longer available.

Shifting his source for poetic models from Jonson and his followers to Donne and especially George Herbert, Vaughan sought to keep faith with the prewar church and with its poets, and his works teach and enable such a keeping of the faith in the midst of what was the most fundamental and radical of crises. Vaughan's concern was to maintain at least something of the Anglican experience as a part, although of necessity a private part, of English life in the 1640s and 1650s. In echoes of the language of the Book of Common Prayer, as well as in echoes of Herbert's meditations on its disciplines, Vaughan maintained the viability of that language for addressing and articulating the situation in which the Church of England now found itself. Vaughan's claim is that such efforts become one way of making the proclamation that even those events that deprive the writer and the reader of so much that is essential may in fact be God's actions to fulfill rather than to destroy what has been lost.

In Vaughan's view the task given those loyal to the old church was of faithfulness in adversity; his poetry in *Silex Scintillans* seeks to be flashes of light, or sparks struck in the darkness, seeking to enflame the faithful and give them a sense of hope even in the midst of such adversity. Vaughan's major prose work of this period, *The Mount of Olives,* is in fact a companion volume to the Book of Common Prayer and is a set of private prayers to accompany Anglican worship, a kind of primer for the new historical situation. There are prayers for going into church, for marking parts of the day (getting up, going from home, returning home), for ap-

proaching the Lord's table, and for receiving Holy Communion, meditations for use when leaving the table, as well as prayers for use in time of persecution and adversity.

Vaughan's model for this work was the official primer of the Church of England as well as such works as Lancelot Andrewes's *Preces Privatatae* (1615) and John Cosin's *Collection of Private Devotions* (1627). These books, written when the Book of Common Prayer was still in use, were intended to orient the lives of their users more fully to the corporate life enabled by the prayer book. Vaughan's version, by alluding to the daily offices and Holy Communion as though they had not been proscribed by the Commonwealth government, serves at once as a constant reminder of what is absent and as a means of living as though they were available.

Thus the "Meditation before the receiving of the holy Communion" begins with the phrase "*Holy, holy, holy,* is the Lord of God of Hosts, the whole earth is full of his glory," which is a close paraphrase of the Sanctus of the prayer book communion rite: "Holy, holy, holy, Lord God of hosts; heaven and earth are full of thy glory." The confession making up part of Vaughan's meditation echoes the language of the prayer that comes between the Sanctus and the prayer of consecration. The text from the Book of Common Prayer reads as follows: "We do not presume to come to this thy table (O merciful Lord) trusting in our own righteousness, but in thy manifold and great mercies. We be not worthy so much as to gather up the crumbs under thy table, but thou art the same Lord, whose property is always to have mercy." Vaughan's text enables the voicing of confession, even when the public opportunity is absent: "I confess, dear God, I confess with all my heart mine own extreme unworthyness, my most shameful and deplorable condition. But with thee, O Lord, there is mercy and plenteous redemption."

Later in the same meditation Vaughan quotes one of the "Comfortable words" that follows the absolution and also echoes the blessing of the priest after confession, his "O Lord be merciful unto me, forgive all my sins, and heal all my infirmities" echoing the request in the prayer book that God "Have mercy upon you, pardon and deliver you from all your sins, confirm and strengthen you in all goodness." Thus words of comfort once spoken by the priest to the congregation during the ordinary use of the prayer book would now facilitate the writing of a prayer asking that mercy, forgiveness, and healing be available although their old sources were not.

Such examples only suggest the copiousness of Vaughan's allusions to the prayer book in *The Mount of Olives*. What Vaughan offers in this work is a manual of devotion to a reader who is an Anglican "alone upon this Hill," one cut off from the ongoing community that once gave him his identity; the title makes this point. Vaughan's audacious claim is to align the disestablished Church of England, the Body of Christ now isolated from its community, with Christ on the Mount of Olives, isolated from his people who have turned against him and who will soon ask for his crucifixion. Because Vaughan can locate present experience in those terms, he can claim that to endure now is to look forward both to an execution and a resurrection; the times call for the living out of that dimension of the meaning of a desire to imitate Christ and give special understanding to the command to "take up thy cross and follow me."

Vaughan's work in this period is thus permeated with a sense of change – of loss yet of continued opportunity. The Puritan victory in the Civil War was not the only experience of change, of loss, and of new beginnings for Vaughan at this time. At the heart of the Anglicanism that was being disestablished was a verbal and ceremonial structure for taking public notice of private events. Henry married in 1646 a Welshwoman named Catherine Wise; they would have four children before her death in 1653. Shortly after the marriage Henry and Thomas were grieving the 1648 death of their younger brother, William. In addition Vaughan's father in this period had to defend himself against legal actions intended to demonstrate his carelessness with other people's money.

In this context Vaughan transmuted his Jonsonian affirmation of friendship into a deep and intricate conversation with the poetry of the Metaphysicals, especially of George Herbert. The shift in Vaughan's poetic attention from the secular to the sacred has often been deemed a conversion; such a view does not take seriously the pervasive character of religion in English national life of the seventeenth century. Religion was always an abiding aspect of daily life; Vaughan's addressing of it in his poetry written during his late twenties is at most a shift in, and focusing of, the poet's attention. The public, and perhaps to a degree the private, world seemed a difficult place: "And what else is the World but a Wildernesse," he would write in *The Mount of Olives,* "A darksome, intricate wood full of Ambushes and dangers; a Forrest where spiritual hunters, principalities and powers spread their nets, and compasse it about." Vaughan set out in the face of such a

world to remind his readers of what had been lost, to provide them with a source of echoes and allusions to keep memories alive, and, as well, to guide them in the conduct of life in this special sort of world, to make the time of Anglican suffering a redemptive rather than merely destructive time.

Vaughan was aware of the difference between his readers and Herbert's parishioners, who could, instead of withdrawing, go out to attend Herbert's reading of the daily offices or stop their work in the fields to join with him when the church bell rang, signaling his reading of the offices. In spite of the absence of public use of the prayer book, Vaughan sought to enable the continuation of a kind of Anglicanism, linking those who continued to use the prayer book in private and those who might have wished to use it through identification with each other in their common solitary circumstances. Vaughan's texts facilitate a working sense of Anglican community through the sharing of exile, connecting those who, although they probably were unknown to each other, had in common their sense of the absence of their normative, identity-giving community.

This essentially didactic enterprise – to teach his readers how to understand membership in a church whose body is absent and thus to keep faith with those who have gone before so that it will be possible for others to come after – is Vaughan's undertaking in *Silex Scintillans*. To achieve that intention he used the Anglican resources still available, viewing the Bible as a text for articulating present circumstances and believing that memories of prayer book rites still lingered or were still available either through private observation of the daily offices or occasional, clandestine sacramental use. At the same time he added yet another allusive process, this to George Herbert's *Temple* (1633). In the experience of reading *Silex Scintillans,* the context of *The Temple* functions in lieu of the absent Anglican services. Using *The Temple* as a frame of reference cannot take the place of participation in prayer book rites; it can only add to the sense of loss by reminding the reader of their absence. But it can serve as a way of evoking and defining that which cannot otherwise be known – the experience of ongoing public involvement in those rites – in a way that furthered Vaughan's desire to produce continued faithfulness to the community created by those rites.

Vaughan's extensive indebtedness to Herbert can be found in echoes and allusions as brief as a word or phrase or as extensive as a poem or group of poems. So thoroughly does Vaughan invoke

Herbert's text and allow it to speak from within his own that there is hardly a poem, or even a passage within a poem, in either the 1650 or the 1655 edition of *Silex Scintillans,* that does not exhibit some relationship to Herbert's work. Indeed this thorough evocation of the older poet's work begins with Vaughan at the dedication for the 1650 *Silex Scintillans,* which echoes Herbert's dedication to *The Temple:* Herbert's "first fruits" become Vaughan's "death fruits." These echoes continue in the expanded version of this verse printed in the 1655 edition, where Herbert's "present themselves to thee; / Yet not mine neither: for from thee they came, / And must return" becomes Vaughan's "he / That copied it, presents it thee. / 'Twas thine first, and to thee returns."

In addition, Herbert's "Avoid, Profanenesse; come not here" from "Superliminare" becomes Vaughan's "Vain Wits and eyes / Leave, and be wise" in the poems that come between the dedication and "Regeneration" in the 1655 edition. Vaughan also followed Herbert in addressing poems to various feasts of the Anglican liturgical calendar; indeed he goes beyond Herbert in the use of the calendar by using the list of saints to provide, as the subjects of poems, Saint Mary Magdalene and the Blessed Virgin Mary.

By using *The Temple* so extensively as a source for his poems, Vaughan sets up an intricate interplay, a deliberate strategy to provide for his work the rich and dense context Herbert had ready-made in the ongoing worship of the Church of England. Although the actual Anglican church buildings were "vilified and shut up," Vaughan found in Herbert's *Temple* a way to open the life of the Anglican worship community if only by allusion to what Herbert could assume as the context for his own work.

Vaughan's *Silex Scintillans* thus becomes a kind of "reading" of *The Temple,* reinterpreting Herbert's text to demonstrate that while Vaughan may be "the least" of Herbert's audience, he certainly is the one who gives *The Temple* whatever meaning it can have in the world of the 1650s. One may therefore see *Silex Scintillans* as resuming the work of *The Temple.* In this context *The Temple* serves as a textual manifestation of a "blessed Pattern of a holy life in the Brittish Church" now absent and libeled by the Puritans as having been the reverse of what it claimed to be. *Silex Scintillans* comes to be a resumption in poetry of Herbert's undertaking in *The Temple* as poetry – the teaching of "holy life" as it is lived in "the British Church" but now colored by the historical experience of that church in the midst of a rhetorical and verbal frame of assault. Even as

Engraved title page for Vaughan's best-known book, whose title may be translated as "Flashing Flint." The engraving is an emblem for the reawakening of religious feeling in the hardened human heart.

the life of that institution informs the activities of Herbert's speaker, so the desire for the restoration of those activities or at least the desire for the fulfillment of the promises that those activities make possible informs Vaughan's speaker.

Thus it is appropriate that while Herbert's *Temple* ends with an image of the sun as the guide to progress in time toward "time and place, where judgement shall appear," so Vaughan ends the second edition of *Silex Scintillans* with praise of "the worlds new, quickning Sun!," which promises to usher in "a state / For evermore immaculate"; until then, the speaker promises, "we shall gladly sit / Till all be ready." While Herbert's speaker can claim to participate in a historical process through the agency of the church's life, Vaughan's, in the absence of that life, can keep the faith by expectantly waiting for the time when the images of Christian community central to Herbert are finally fulfilled in those divine actions that will re-create Christian community.

For Vaughan's *Silex Scintillans,* Herbert's *Temple* functions as a source of reference, one which joins with the Bible and the prayer book to enable Vaughan's speaker to give voice to his situation. Ultimately Vaughan's speaker teaches his readers how to redeem the time by keeping faith with those who have gone before through orienting present experience in terms of the common future that Christian proclamation asserts they share. To use Herbert in this way is to claim for him a position in the line of priestly poets from David forward and to claim for Vaughan a place in that company as well, in terms of the didactic functioning of his Christian poetry. In Vaughan's day the activity of writing *Silex Scintillans* becomes a "reading" of *The Temple,* not in a static sense as a copying but in a truly imitative sense, with Vaughan's text revealing how *The Temple* had produced, in his case, an augmentation in the field of action in a way that could promote others to produce similar "fruit" through reading of Vaughan's "leaves."

Standing in relationship to *The Temple* as Vaughan would have his readers stand in relation to *Silex Scintillans,* Vaughan's poetry collection models the desired relationship between text and life both he and Herbert sought. Using the living text of the past to make communion with it, to keep faith with it, and to understand the present in terms of it, Vaughan "reads" Herbert to orient the present through working toward the restoration of community in their common future. Vaughan's audience did not have the church with them as it was in Herbert's day, but it had *The Temple;* together with *Silex Scintillans,* these works taught how to interpret the present through endurance, devotion, and faithful charity so that it could be made a path toward recovery at the last.

Silex Scintillans is much more about the possibility of searching than it is about finding. It is more about the possibility of living out Christian identity in an Anglican sense when the source of that identity is absent, except in the traces of the Bible, the prayer book, and *The Temple.* It is also more about anticipating God's new actions to come than it is about celebrating their present occurrence. The danger Vaughan faced is that the church Herbert knew would become merely a text, reduced to a prayer book unused on a shelf or a Bible read in private or *The Temple* itself.

If that happened, the Anglican moment would become fully past, known as an occasion for sorrow or affectionate memories, serving as a perspective from which to criticize the various Puritan alternatives, but not something to be lived in and through. Vaughan could then no longer claim to be "in the body," for Christ himself would be absent. Vaughan's challenge in *Silex Scintillans* was to teach how someone could experience the possibility of an opening in the present to the continuing activity of God, leading to the fulfillment of God's promises and thus to teach faithfulness to Anglicanism, making it still ongoing despite all appearances to the contrary.

Although most readers proceed as though the larger work of 1655 (*Silex II*) were the work itself, for which the earlier version (*Silex I*) is a preliminary with no claim to separate consideration, the text of *Silex Scintillans* Vaughan published in 1650 is worthy of examination as a work unto itself, written and published by a poet who did not know that five years later he would publish it again, with significant changes in the context of presentation and with significant additions in length. The title, *Silex Scintillans: or Sacred Poems and Private Ejaculations,* exists at once to distance Vaughan's work and his situation from Herbert's and to link them. Not merely acknowledging Vaughan's indebtedness to Herbert, his simultaneous echoing of Herbert's subtitle for *The Temple* (*Sacred Poems and Private Ejaculations*) and use of a very different title remind one that Vaughan writes constantly in the absence of that to which Herbert's title alludes.

Richard Crashaw could, of course, title his 1646 work *Steps to the Temple* because in 1645 he responded to the same events constraining Vaughan by changing what was for him the temple; by becoming a Roman Catholic, Crashaw could continue participation in a worshiping community but at the cost of flight from England and its church. Vaughan remained loyal to that English institution even in its absence by reminding the reader of what is now absent, or present only in a new kind of way in *The Temple* itself. Vaughan's goal for *Silex Scintillans* was to find ways of giving the experience of Anglicanism apart from Anglicanism, or to make possible the continued experience of being a part of the Body of Christ in Anglican terms in the absence of the ways in which those terms had their meaning prior to the 1640s.

Silex I thus begins with material that replicates the disjuncture between what Herbert built in *The Temple* and the situation Vaughan faced; again, it serves for Vaughan as a way of articulating a new religious situation. The Latin poem "Authoris (de se) Emblema" in the 1650 edition, together with its emblem, represents a reseparation of the emblematic and verbal elements in Herbert's poem "The Altar." While Herbert combined visual appearance with verbal construction, Vaughan put the language of "The Altar," about God's breaking the speaker's rocklike heart, into his poem and depicted in the emblem of a rocklike heart being struck so that it gives off fire and tears. In the prefatory poem the speaker accounts for what follows in terms of a new act of God, a changing of the method of divine acting from the agency of love to that of anger. Linking this with the bringing forth of water from the rock struck by Moses, the speaker finds, "I live again in dying, / And rich am I, now, amid ruins lying."

This poem and emblem, when set against Herbert's treatment of the same themes, display the new Anglican situation. The section in *The Temple* titled "The Church," from "The Altar" to "Love" (III), shifts in its reading of the Anglican Eucharist from a place where what God breaks is made whole to a place where God refuses, in love, to take the speaker's sense of inadequacy, or brokenness, for a final answer. In *Silex I* the altar shape is absent, even as the Anglican altar was absent; amid the ruins of that altar the speaker finds an act of God, enabling him to find and affirm life even in brokenness, "amid ruins lying." By placing his revision of the first poem in Herbert's "Church" at the beginning of *Silex I,* Vaughan asserted that one will find life amid the brokenness of Anglicanism when it can be brought into speech that at least raises the expectation that such life will come to be affirmed through brokenness itself.

So Herbert's *Temple* is broken here, a metaphor for the brokenness of Anglicanism, but broken open to find life, not the death of that institution Puritans hoped to destroy by forbidding use of the Book of Common Prayers. It is obviously not enough merely to juxtapose what was with what now is; if the Anglican way is to remain valid, there needs to be a means of affirming and involving oneself in that tradition even when it is no longer going on. Otherwise the Anglican enterprise is over and finished, and brokenness yields only "dust," not the possibility yet of water from rocks or life from ruins. Vaughan thus wrote of brokenness in a way that makes his poetry a sign that even in that brokenness there remains the possibility of finding and proclaiming divine activity and offering one's efforts with words to further it. In that light Vaughan can reaffirm Herbert's claim that to ask is to take part in the finding, arguing that to be able to ask and to seek is to take part in the divine activity that will make the brokenness of Anglican community not the end of the story but an essential part of the story itself, in spite of all evidence to the contrary.

If Vaughan can persuade his audience of that, then his work can become "Silex Scintillans," "flashing flint," stone become fire, in a way that will make it a functional substitute for *The Temple,* both as a title and as a poetic text. What Vaughan thus sought was a text that enacts a fundamental disorientation. What had become problematic is not Anglicanism as an answer or conclusion, since that is not what the Church of England sought to provide. What is at issue is a process of language that had traditionally served to incite and orient change and process. Now with such resources no longer available, Vaughan's speaker finds instead a lack of direction which raises fundamental questions about the enterprise in which he is engaged.

Rather than choose another version of Christian vocabulary or religious experience to overcome frustration, Vaughan remained true to an Anglicanism without its worship as a functional referent. If God moves "Where I please" ("Regeneration"), then Vaughan raises the possibility that the current Anglican situation is also at God's behest, so that remaining loyal to Anglican Christianity in such a situation is to seek from God an action that would make the old Anglican language of baptism again meaningful, albeit in a new way and in a new setting.

Vaughan thus constantly sought to find ways of understanding the present in terms that leave it open to future transformative action by God. "The Search" explores this dynamic from yet another perspective. In this poem the speaker engages in "a roving Extasie / To find my Saviour," again dramatizing divine absence in the absence of that earthly enterprise where he was to be found before the events of 1645. In language borrowed again from Herbert's "Church Militant," Vaughan sees the sun, the marker of time, as a "guide" to his way, yet the movement of the poem as a whole throws into question the terms in which the speaker asserts that he would recognize the Christ if he found him. Much of the poem is taken up with a description of the speaker's search through a biblical landscape defined by New Testament narrative, as his biblical search in "Religion" was through a landscape defined by Old Testament narrative. Yet, without the ongoing life of the church to enact those narratives in the present, what the poem reveals is their failure to point to Christ: "I met the *Wise-men,* askt them where / He might be found, or what starre can / Now point him out, grown up a Man."

In Vaughan's depiction of Anglican experience, brokenness is thus a structural experience as well as a verbal theme. While Herbert "breaks" words in the context of a consistent allusion to use of the Book of Common Prayer, Vaughan uses allusions to liturgical forms to reveal a brokenness of the relationships implicit in such allusions. For instance, early in *Silex Scintillans,* Vaughan starts a series of allusions to the events on the annual Anglican liturgical calendar of feasts: "The Incantation" is followed later with "The Passion," which naturally leads later to "Easter-day," "Ascension-day," "Ascension-Hymn," "White Sunday," and Trinity-Sunday." His insertion of "Christ Nativity" between "The Passion" and "Easter-day" interrupts this continuous allusion. He also avoids poems on Advent, Christmas, Epiphany, and Lent after "Trinity-Sunday" by skipping to "Palm Sunday" only six poems later. In addition, the break Vaughan put in the second edition between *Silex I* and *Silex II* obscures the fact that the first poem in *Silex II,* "Ascension-day," continues in order his allusion to the church calendar.

Because of his historical situation Vaughan had to resort to substitution. In "The Morning-watch," for example, "The great *Chime* / And *Symphony* of nature" must take the place of Anglican corporate prayer at the morning office. In "The Evening-watch" the hymn of Simeon, a corporate response to the reading of the New Testament lesson at evening prayer, becomes the voice of the soul to the body to "Goe, sleep in peace," instead of the church's prayer "Lord, now lettest thou thy servant depart in peace" or the voice of the second Collect, "Give unto thy servants that peace which the world cannot give." Vaughan thus finds ways of creating texts that accomplish the prayer-book task of acknowledging morning and evening in a disciplined way but also remind the informed reader of what is lost with the loss of that book.

Vaughan also created here a criticism of the Puritan communion and a praise of the Anglican Eucharist in the midst of a whole series of allusions to the specific lessons to be read on a specific celebration of Maundy Thursday, the "birthday" of the Eucharist. The result is the creation of a community whose members think about the Anglican Eucharist, whether or not his readers could actually participate in it. One can live in hope and pray that God give a "mysticall Communion" in place of the public one from which the speaker must be "absent"; as a result one can expect that God will grant "thy grace" so that "faith" can "make good." It is a plea as well that the community so created will be kept in grace and faith so that it will receive worthily when that reception is possible, whether at an actual celebration of the Anglican communion or at the heavenly banquet to which the Anglican Eucharist points and anticipates. As Vaughan has his speaker say in "Church Service," echoing Herbert's "The Altar," it is "Thy hand alone [that] doth tame / Those blasts [of 'busie thoughts'], and knit my frame" so that "in this thy Quire of Souls I stand." God's actions are required for two or three to gather, so "both stones, and dust, and all of me / Joyntly agree / To cry to thee" and continue the experience of corporate Anglican worship. Those members of Vaughan's intended audience who recognized these allusions and valued his attempt to continue within what had been lost without would have felt sustained in their isolation and in their refusal to compromise and accept the Puritan form of communion, all the while hoping for a restoration or fulfillment of Anglican worship.

The characteristics of Vaughan's didactic strategies come together in "The Brittish Church," which is a redoing of Herbert's "The British Church" by way of an extended allusion to the Song of Solomon, as well as to Hugh Latimer's sermon "Agaynst strife and contention" in the first Book of Homilies. In Herbert's poem the Church of England is a "deare Mother," in whose "mean," the middle way between Rome and Geneva, Herbert delights; he blesses God "whose love it was / To double-moat thee with his grace." In Vaughan's poem the speaker models his speech on Psalm 80, traditionally a prayer for the church in difficult times. The fact that Vaughan is still operating with allusions to the biblical literary forms suggests that the dynamics of biblical address are still functional. Like the speaker of Psalm 80, Vaughan's lamenter acts with the faith that God will respond in the end to the one who persists in his lament.

One of the stylistic characteristics of *Silex I,* therefore, is a functioning close to the biblical texts and their language. Weaving and reweaving biblical echoes, images, social structures, titles, and situations, Vaughan re-created an allusive web similar to that which exists in the enactment of prayer-book rites when the assigned readings combine and echo and reverberate with the set texts of the liturgies themselves. Without that network available in the experience of his readers, Vaughan provided it anew, claiming it always as the necessary source of informing his readers. This technique, however, gives to the tone of Vaughan's poems a particularly archaic or remote quality. His employment of a private or highly coded vocabulary has led some readers to link Vaughan to the traditions of world-transcending spirituality or to hermeticism, but Vaughan's intention is in no such place; instead he seeks to provide a formerly public experience, now lost.

Poems after "The Brittish Church" in *Silex I* focus on the central motif of that poem, that "he is fled," stressing the sense of divine absence and exploring strategies for evoking a faithful response to the promise of his eventual return. The rhetorical organization of "The Lampe," for example, develops an image of the faithful watcher for that return and concludes with a biblical injunction from Mark about the importance of such watchfulness. Vaughan develops his central image from another version of the parable, one found in Matthew concerning the wise and foolish virgins. The "lampe" of Vaughan's poem is the lamp of the wise virgin who took oil for her lamp to be ready when the bridegroom comes. In a world shrouded in "dead night," where "Horrour doth creepe / And move on with the shades," metaphors for the world bereft of Anglicanism, Vaughan uses language interpreting the speaker's situation in terms not unlike the eschatological language of Revelation, where the "stars of heaven fell to earth" because "the great day of his wrath is come."

In poems such as "Peace" and "The World" the images of "a Countrie / Far beyond the stars" and of "Eternity . . . Like a great *Ring* of pure and endless light" – images of God's promised future for his people – are articulated not as mystical, inner visions but as ways of positing a perspective from which to judge present conditions, so that human life can be interpreted as "foolish ranges," "sour delights," "silly snares of pleasure," "weights and woe," "feare," or *the lust of the flesh, the lust of the Eys, and the pride of life.* Vaughan's language is that of biblical calls to repentance, including Jesus' own injunction to repent for the kingdom is at hand. In that implied promise – that if the times call for repentance, the kingdom must be at hand – Vaughan could find occasion for hope and thus for perseverance. The act of repentance, or renunciation of the world's distractions, becomes the activity that enables endurance.

What Vaughan thus offered his Anglican readers is the incentive to endure present troubles by defining them as crossings related to Christ's Cross. Seen in this respect, these troubles make possible the return of the one who is now perceived as absent. Vaughan could still praise God for present action – "How rich, O Lord! how fresh thy visits are!" ("Unprofitableness") – but he emphasizes such visits as sustenance in the struggle to endure in anticipation of God's actions yet to come rather than as ongoing actions of God. Vaughan constructs for his reader a movement through *Silex I* from the difficulty in articulating and interpreting experience acted out in "Regeneration" toward an increasing ability to articulate and thus to endure, brought about by the growing emphasis on the present as preparation for what is to come. This is characterized by the speaker's self-dramatization in the traditional stances of confessional and intercessory prayer, lament, and joy found in expectation. Gradually, the interpretive difficulties of "Regeneration" are redefined as part of what must be offered to God in this time of waiting. Vaughan's "Vanity of Spirit" redoes the "reading" motif of Herbert's "Jesu"; instead of being able to construe the "peeces" to read either a comfortable message or "JESU," Vaughan's speaker can do no more than sense the separation that failure to interpret properly can create between God and his people, requiring that new act to come: *"in these veyls my Ecclips'd Eye / May not approach thee."* Only Christ's Passion, fulfilled when *"I'le disapparell, and / . . . / most gladly dye,"* can once more link heaven and earth. A similar inability to read or interpret correctly is the common failing of the Lover, the States-man, and the Miser in "The World"; here, too, the "Ring" of eternity is held out as a promise for those who keep faith with the church, for *This Ring the Bride-groome did for none provide / But for his bride.*

In his characterization of the Anglican situation in the 1640s in terms of loneliness and isolation and in his hopeful appeals to God to act once more to change this situation, Vaughan thus reached out to faithful Anglicans, giving them the language to articulate that situation in a redemptive way. "All the year I mourn," he wrote in "Misery," asking that God "bind me up, and let me lye / A Pris'ner to my libertie, / If such a state at all can be / As an Impris'ment serving thee." It is the oblation of self in enduring what is given to endure that Vaughan offers as solace in this situation, living in prayerful expectation of release: "from this Care, where dreams and sorrows raign / Lead me above / Where Light, Joy, Leisure, and true Comforts move / Without all pain" ("I walkt the other day").

Vaughan's intentions in *Silex I* thus become more clear gradually. His posing the problems of perception in the absence of Anglican worship early in the work leads to an exploration of what such a situation might mean in terms of preparation for the "last things." His taking on of Herbert's poet/priest role enables a recasting of the central acts of Anglican worship – Bible reading, preaching, prayer, and sacramental enactment – in new terms so that the old language can be used again. As a result, he seeks to create a community that is still in continuity with the community now lost because of the common future they share; he achieves this because he is able to articulate present experience in reference to the old terms, so that lament for their loss becomes the way to achieve a common future with them.

Joy for Vaughan is in anticipation of a release that makes further repentance and lament possible and that informs lament as the way toward release. In this light it is no accident that the last poem in *Silex I* is titled "Begging." The speaker, making a poem, asks since "it is thy only Art / To reduce a stubborn heart / . . . / let [mine] be thine!" Vaughan thus ends not far from where Herbert began "The Church," with a heart and a prayer for its transformation. Without the altar except in anticipation and memory, it is difficult for Vaughan to get much beyond that point, at least in the late 1640s. So the moment of expectation, understood in terms of past language and past events, becomes the moment to be defined as one that points toward future fulfillment and thus becomes the moment that must be lived out, as the scene of transformation as well as the process of transformation through divine "Art."

The publication of the 1650 edition of *Silex Scintillans* marked for Vaughan only the beginning of his most active period as a writer. Now in his early thirties, he devoted himself to a variety of literary and quasi-literary activities. There is some evidence that during this period he experienced an extended illness and recovery, perhaps sufficiently grave to promote serious reflection about the meaning of life but not so debilitating as to prevent major literary effort. *Olor Iscanus,* which had been ready for publication since the late 1640s, finally appeared in 1651. His prose devotional work *The Mount of Olives,* a kind of companion piece to *Silex Scintillans,* was published in 1652.

Vaughan also spent time in this period continuing a series of translations similar to that which he had already prepared for publication in *Olor Iscanus.* There he had offered a translation from the Latin of short works by Plutarch and Maximus Tirius, together with a translation from the Spanish of Antonio de Guevara, "The Praise and Happiness of the Countrie-Life." Now he prepared more translations from the Latin, concentrating on moral and ethical treatises, explorations of received wisdom about the meaning of life that he would publish in 1654 under

Engraved title page for Vaughan's 1651 collection of poems, advocating retirement to the country as a way to escape "the furious conflicts of Church and State"

the general title *Flores Solitudinis.* Emphasizing a stoic approach to the Christian life, they include translations of Johannes Nierembergius's essays on temperance, patience, and the meaning of life and death, together with a translation of an epistle by Eucherius of Lyons, "The World Contemned." To these translations Vaughan added a short biography of the fifth-century churchman Paulinus of Bordeaux, with the title "Primitive Holiness." A contemporary of Augustine and bishop of Nola from 410, Paulinus had embraced Christianity under the influence of Ambrose and renounced opportunity for court advancement to pursue his new faith. Vaughan may have been drawn to Paulinus because the latter was a poet; "Primitive Holiness" includes translations of many of Paulinus's poems.

Indicating his increasing interest in medicine, Vaughan published in 1655 a translation of Henry Nollius's *Hermetical Physick*. In this, Vaughan followed the guidance of his brother Thomas, who had studied the sciences at Oxford and resumed his interest after he was deprived of his church living in 1650. Thomas married in 1651 one Rebecca, perhaps of Bedfordshire, who helped him with his experiments until her death in 1658. Instead of resuming his clerical career after the Restoration of the Stuart monarchy, Thomas devoted the rest of his life to alchemical research. At the time of his death in 1666, he was employed as an assistant to Sir Robert Moray, an amateur scientist known to contemporaries as the "soul" of the Royal Society and supervisor of the king's laboratory.

Henry Vaughan's interest in medicine, especially from a hermetical perspective, would also lead him to a full-time career. Hermeticism for Vaughan was not primarily alchemical in emphasis but was concerned with observation and imitation of nature in order to cure the illnesses of the body. Vaughan was able to align this approach with his religious concerns, for fundamental to Vaughan's view of health is the pursuit of "a pious and an holy life," seeking to "love God with all our souls, and our Neighbors as our selves." Even though there is no evidence that he ever was awarded the M.D. by a university or other authorized body, by the 1670s he could look back on many presumably successful years of medical practice.

In the meantime, however, the Anglican community in England did survive Puritan efforts to suppress it. Increasingly rigorous efforts to stamp it out are effective testimony to that fact; while attendance at a prayer book service in 1645 was punished by a fine, by 1655 the penalty had been escalated to imprisonment or exile. Repeated efforts by Welsh clergy loyal to the Church of England to get permission to engage in active ministry were turned down by Puritan authorities. What role Vaughan's *Silex I* of 1650 may have played in supporting their persistence, and the persistence of their former parishioners, is unknown. It is certain that the *Silex Scintillans* of 1650 did produce in 1655 a very concrete response in Vaughan himself, a response in which the "awful roving" of *Silex I* is proclaimed to have found a sustaining response. Joining the poems from *Silex I* with a second group of poems approximately three-fourths as long as the first, Vaughan produced a new collection. *Silex II* makes the first group of poems a preliminary to a second group, which has a substantially different tone and mood.

His speaker is still very much alone in this second group of *Silex* poems ("They are all gone into the world of light! / And I alone sit lingring here"), perhaps reflecting Vaughan's loneliness at the death of his wife in 1653, but the sense of the experience of that absence of agony, even redemptive agony, is missing. Like so many poems in *Silex I*, this one ends in petition, but the tone of that petition is less anguished, less a leap into hope for renewed divine activity than a request articulated in confidence that such release will come: "Either disperse these mists, which blot and fill / My perspective (still) as they pass, / Or else remove me hence unto that hill, / Where I shall need no glass." In such a petition the problem of interpretation, or the struggle for meaning, is given up into petition itself, an intercessory plea that grows out of Paul's "dark glass" image of human knowing here and his promise of a knowing "face to face" yet to come and manifests contingency on divine action for clarity of insight – "disperse these mists" – or for bringing the speaker to "that hill, / Where I shall need no glass," yet that also replicates the confidence of Paul's assertion "then shall I know" (I Corinthians). In ceasing the struggle to understand how it has come to pass that "They are all gone into the world of light," a giving up articulated through the offering of the speaker's isolation in prayer, Vaughan's speaker achieves a sense of faithfulness in the reliability of divine activity. The quest for meaning here in terms of a future when all meaning will be fulfilled thus becomes a substitute for meaning itself. However dark the glass, affirming the promise of future clarity becomes a way of understanding the present that is sufficient and is also the way to that future clarity.

Vaughan's speaker does not stop asking for either present or future clarity; even though he is not to get the former, it is the articulation of the question that makes the ongoing search for understanding a way of getting to the point at which the future is present, and both requests will be answered at once in the same act of God. This relationship between present and future in terms of a quest for meaning that links the two is presented in this poem as an act of recollection – "Their very memory is fair and bright, / And my sad thoughts doth clear" – which is in turn projected into the speaker's conceptualization of their present state in "the world of light," so that their memory "glows and glitters in my cloudy breast." This juxtaposition of light and dark imagery as a way of articulating the speaker's situation becomes a contrast between the fulfillment of community imagined for those who have gone before and the speaker's own isolation.

Faith in the redemption of those who have gone before thus becomes an act of God, a "holy hope," which the speaker affirms as God's "walks" in which he has "shew'd . . . me / To kindle my cold love." Such a hope becomes "some strange thoughts" that enable the speaker to "into glory peep" and thus affirm death as the "Jewel of the Just," the encloser of light: "But when the hand that lockt her up, gives room / She'll shine through all the sphære." The ability to articulate present experience in these terms thus can yield to confident intercession that God act again to fulfill his promise: "O Father / . . . / Resume thy spirit from this world of thrall / Into true liberty."

This strongly affirmed expectation of the renewal of community after the grave with those who "are all gone into the world of light" is articulated from the beginning of *Silex II,* in the poem "Ascension-day," in which the speaker proclaims he feels himself "a sharer in thy victory," so that "I soar and rise / Up to the skies." Like "The Search" in *Silex I,* this poem centers on the absence of Christ, but the difference comes in this distance between the speaker of "The Search" and its biblical settings and the ease with which the speaker of "Ascension-day" moves within them. In this exuberant reenacting of Christ's Ascension, the speaker can place himself with Mary Magdalene and with "Saints and Angels" in their community: "I see them, hear them, mark their haste." He can also find in the Ascension a realization of the world-renewing and re-creating act of God promised to his people: "I walk the fields of *Bethani* which shine / All now as fresh as *Eden,* and as fine." What follows is an account of the Ascension itself, Christ leaving behind "his chosen Train, / All sad with tears" but now with eyes "Fix'd . . . on the skies" instead of "on the Cross." Having gone from them in just this way, "eternal Jesus" can be faithfully expected to return, and so the poem ends with an appeal for that return.

As a result "Ascension-day" represents a different strategy for encouraging fellow Anglicans to keep faith with the community that is lost and thus to establish a community here of those waiting for the renewal of community with those who have gone before. This shift in strategy amounts to a move from arguing for the sufficiency of lament in light of eschatological expectation to the encouragement offered by an exultant tone of experiencing the end to come through anticipating it. Vaughan prepared for the new strategy by changing the front matter of the 1650 edition for the augmented 1655 edition. Gone, first of all, are the emblem of the stony heart and its accompanying Latin verse,

which no longer serve to prepare the reader for the experience to follow. In their place comes a quotation from Job that rearticulates the searching motif of *Silex I* but puts it in the context of poetry and knowing: "*Where is God my Maker, who giveth Songs in the night? Who teacheth us more then the beasts of the earth, and maketh us wiser then the fowls of heaven?*" To these questions the volume that follows comes as one kind of answer. The God of Anglicans is known in the results of his actions; Vaughan presented his poems as the results of those divine actions, so that the poems themselves become a witness to the continuing activity of the God who might otherwise be seen as absent. *Silex II* thus demonstrates the effectiveness of articulating the Anglican experience of the 1640s and early 1650s in the terms Vaughan used in *Silex I,* showing how this process can be a source of Anglican identity and a support for faithfulness to Anglican expectations. If these poems are effective in teaching readers to sustain their faithful expectations, they may become occasions for hope in the efficacy of God's promises because they may be seen as evidence of the continuation of divine activity in human history in spite of all evidence to the contrary.

What Vaughan sought in this move is a role in which the presence of his poetic voice, in the time after the abolition of the Anglican church, is an effective witness that the promises of God still apply to those who keep the faith. That Vaughan can proclaim God at work in the events of his specific historic situation and describe them in the vocabulary of prophetic utterance becomes evidence in itself that God is not absent, that the old promises still hold. In the new poems of *Silex II,* there is a gathering sense that the time of release is near and that therefore the tone can lighten. The rhetorical approach encourages faith by means of evocation of what is to come and celebration of it in anticipation of its imminent arrival. Even as Job provides a biblical analogue for a religious text with a movement through the process of lament from a sense of God's absence to a sense of his presence, so Isaiah and some of the other prophetic books provide a similar model for a text that moves from the exploration of a difficult historic situation to a joyful anticipation of its resolution.

Vaughan's dedicatory verses of 1655 were added to the dedicatory verse of the 1650 *Silex Scintillans.* The earlier verse ends in begging "that thou wouldst take thy Tenants Rent." The later verses celebrate that " 'tis finished" and proclaim the text, in Herbert's language of dedication, as " 'Twas thine first, and to thee returns." Such language is available to him now because the speaker can see the events that destroyed the Anglican church as leading to the fulfillment of the promises made to that church. The speaker rehearses his life as filled with signs of divine "mercies" and "truth"; he speaks easily of God's "divinely" having "forgiven" his "relapse and wilful breach / . . . / While thy blood wash'd me white as heaven." With this confident reuse of biblical and prayer-book language, he says he has only in return this book to give: "this thy own gift, given to me. / Refuse it not!" Given the speaker's tone here, clearly he has no doubt concerning God's willingness to accept his offerings. Thus he ends, offering the book as a functional text to enable God to read the world: "for now thy Token / Can tell thee where a heart is broken." Quoting Revelation to the effect that as a result of what this text is about one can now confidently use the language of John the Divine that Christ "hath made us Kings and Priests unto God and his Father" as something that can be said in the past tense as a foregone conclusion, a past act, the speaker can confidently await his "coming with clouds" to reveal it to all.

Having thus redefined the function of *Silex I* and given it an even more dedicated public role as the site of a meeting between poet and reader that will lead to sight and *Silex II*, Vaughan then offered *Silex I*, essentially unchanged in text. When he begins the new poems of *Silex II*, it is with the decidedly more celebratory tone of "Ascension-day" already noted: "Lord Jesus! with what sweetness and delights, / Sure, holy hopes, high joys and quickning flights / Dost thou feed thine!"

In enacting his observance of the Anglican Feast of the Ascension in the terms that would have been appropriate if the Book of Common Prayer had been in use, Vaughan's speaker affirms that a kind of Easter has really occurred in the space between the Easter poems of *Silex I* and the beginning of *Silex II*. "Easter-day" in effect argues that if the reader will "Awake" and "Arise," then the "benefits of his passion" will be made available, for "his blood will cure thy mind." By "Ascension-day" and the beginning of *Silex II* his stance has shifted to suggest that such clarity of mind has been achieved, for it is now possible to proclaim that the world once more yields to articulation in terms of biblical narrative: "With these fair thoughts I move in this fair place, / And the last steps of my milde Master trace." Unlike the poems already examined in *Silex I* in which the journey motif leads through spaces impossible to interpret effectively, here because the speaker can "the last steps of my milde Master

trace," he can find the journey leading to places that yield readily to articulation in biblical terms, if not to clarity of understanding. Providing a typological language to describe this particular remembrance and reexperiencing of the Ascension, the biblical texts appointed for that day once more function to link past visits of God to people with the present in terms of their common future. Unlike similar episodes in *Silex I*, this speaker's journey through biblical "leaves" does not flounder over a sense of distance from those events or over the absence of a "cornerstone" in the tomb. Instead the post-Resurrection portion of the biblical narrative works to renew the world, to make "the fields of *Bethani* . . . shine / All now as fresh as *Eden*, and as fine." Performance thus functions to enable poetic resolution, Vaughan's text enacting what Herbert claimed for Anglican worship.

In the third poem of *Silex II*, "They are all gone into the world of light!," Vaughan's speaker affirms that "Their very memory / . . . / my sad thoughts doth clear." The ability to achieve an interpretation of Vaughan's historical situation in such positive terms, to see his situation in ways that promote effectiveness of interpretation, promotes and supports the tone of excited expectation that characterizes these poems. This is acted out in "White Sunday," a poem celebrating Pentecost itself in which Vaughan gives a full reading of his situation in biblical terms, claiming explicitly that "thy method with thy own, / Thy own dear people pens our times, / Our stories are in theirs set down / And penalties spread to our Crimes." Although such "Crimes" may be great, the very ability to "know which way to look" becomes evidence that enables the speaker to ask for a renewal of Pentecostal fire with an exuberance lacking in the petitions "Oh come! refine us with thy fire! / Refuse us! we are at a loss. / Let not thy stars for *Balaams* hire / Dissolve into the common dross!"

This ability to use biblical narrative to describe the present becomes in itself one sign of the presence of the "holy comfort" promised Christ's followers in the Pentecost event and thus a source of the speaker's confident ability to "discern Wolves from the Sheep." In Vaughan's reading of his situation on this Whitsunday, the distinctive note of Puritan claims – "some boast that fire each day, / And on Christ's coat pin all their shreds; / Not sparing openly to say, / His candle shines upon their heads" – is refuted by the evidence provided by a Bible that can once more be said to "Shine here below" so that "I will know which way to look." Vaughan's renewed sense of what God is doing in the critical events of Anglican history thus enables him to use biblical language to articulate the present with renewed confidence. Again, as in his earlier poems of *Silex I,* the experience of Anglicans is redeemed through association with the Cross. The aggressive confidence of such appeals, their insistent and urgent tone, again marks what Vaughan's speaker argues has been, and thus can be, achieved by the kind of faithfulness to Anglicanism enacted in *Silex I.*

This does not mean that Vaughan achieves the ability to articulate truth in the sense that his poems include a verbal equivalent of reality. Instead the radical future orientation of his speaker's anticipation indicates that what is claimed for *Silex II* is the achievement of a successful way of reaching that future, found through persisting in a mode of discourse. Use of language here continues to be functional rather than referential; Vaughan's claim is to be performing the language that is, or will be, successful in its functioning. Part of Vaughan's argument is thus that Anglicanism itself persists, even though it is hidden. In "The Palm-tree" traditional language for describing the Anglican church and the Christian life as a tree is evoked to depict the church in its present suppressed state. Although it is "prest and bow'd," it once "had equall liberty / With other trees"; now it "thrives no where." Yet that is not the end of the story, because "the more he's bent / The more he grows," since "Celestial natures still / Aspire for home." Indeed "This is the life which hid above with Christ / In God, doth always (hidden) multiply / . . . / A Tree, whose fruit is immortality." In this redoing of Herbert's "Colossians 3:3" it is the Church Triumphant, where "Spirits that have run their race / . . . / meet to receive their Crowns," but it is also the Church Militant in its current situation, made up of "the patience of the Saints / . . . / water'd by their tears" to whom Christ is still present, for "One you cannot see / Sits here and numbers all the tears they shed." In this image of the church in oppression, linked with its past and future, Vaughan evokes a sense of the ongoingness of Anglican insistence on the continued presence of Christ and, finally, invites the reader's participation. The private devotion forced on Anglicans by the abolition of their normative public worship achieves a kind of approval here, because through analogy with the weeping of the Magdalen it actually becomes public.

Vaughan's tone in *Silex II* is radically more confident and joyously expectant than in *Silex I.* This tone, part of Vaughan's rhetoric of persuasion to keep the faith, is achieved by asserting that old signs still reveal the faithfulness of God in his promises, as in "The Rain-bow," in which the ancient sign reveals "my God doth keep / His promise still, but we break ours and sleep." The lament of *Silex I* is evoked in the way "Fair and young light!" is transformed into a "holy Grief"; "How am I now in love," the speaker claims, "with all / That I term'd then meer bonds and thrall, And to thy name, which still I keep, / Like the surviving turtle, weep!" Yet such a change in tone functions as a divine answer to the lament of *Silex I,* a renewal of the promise that God will ultimately respond to the one who is faithful in his lament. What was then a sense of divine absence is now seen as a failure of interpretation; in "The dwelling-place," where God was when he was experienced as "shrowded" by the speaker, "I do not know / What lodgd thee then, nor where, nor how." But that does not matter anymore: "I am sure, thou dost now come / Oft to a narrow, homely room, / Where thou too hast but the least part, / My God, I mean *my sinful heart.*" In "The Men of War" the speaker interprets Luke to mean that "Thy Saints are not the Conquerors," another rejection of Puritan claims; what conquered Anglicans must do is be "patient, meek, and overcome / Like thee." Such a stance leads to a prayer for Jesus to "give me patience here, / And faith to see my Crown as near / And almost reach'd." The sufferings of isolated and outlawed Anglicans themselves become the signs of hope that their "Crown" is "near." Vaughan's ability to make faithful affirmations in *Silex II* now becomes proof that the faithfulness sought in *Silex I* is efficacious in surviving the interim time between Anglican abolition and restoration.

This is perhaps reflected in the fact that the syntax of *Silex II* lacks the convolutions of *Silex I.* In Vaughan's terms this is yet another way of pointing up the contrast between concern for divine absence in the former group, with the interpretive difficulties it brings, and the faith in the divine presence now and to come that promotes clarity of articulation in *Silex II.* This new sense of textual and interpretative clarity is made explicit in "The Agreement," in its contrast between a former state, in which the speaker's own writing was obscured so that "I read it sadly oft, but still / Simply believ'd, 'twas not my Quill," and the present state, in which "lifes kinde Angel came / . . . / Scatt'ring that cloud." If the book obscured is *Silex I,* and it might be since the speaker says that its subject was "my mid-day / Exterminating fears and night," then *Silex II* is the record of the result of the angelic visit, in which he was pointed "to a place / Which all the year sees the Suns face."

In bringing the Anglican calendar into *Silex II,* Vaughan resumed the progress to Easter and beyond that he halted at the end of *Silex I* by including the Ascension, Whitsunday, and Trinity Sunday poems. With "Palm-Sunday" he heralds the beginning of allusion to a new Holy Week, but he gives the reader no Easter poems. *Silex II* ends, in effect, in anticipation of the final Easter, its instigation to faithfulness residing in its claim to lead to that Easter. The last poems in *Silex II* Vaughan suggests were written while he feared he was near death — one sure way, in Vaughan's terms, to get to that final Easter. His emphasis here is on "False life" as both "foul deception" and also *"A quickness, which my God hath kist"* ("Quickness"). It is also on "that glad place, / Where cloudless Quires sing without tears, / Sing thy just praise, and see thy face" ("The Wreath"). What Vaughan has achieved in *Silex II* is a poetic strategy in which a renewed sense of divine activity is claimed through a mix of syntactic clarity, renewed typological relationship, and the speaker's own (claimed) awareness that God is at work in his experience of the absence of Anglican community. Coming after *Silex I,* it serves as a response to the struggles of that volume; yet *Silex II* still functions within the ongoing allusion to Anglican prayer-book experience, since the beginning "Ascension-day" resumes the allusion to the prayer-book calendar begun in *Silex I.* Vaughan, in these poems, casts the present in eschatological terms, enacting an articulation of the present lives in light of future promise. His discoveries are of the dimensions and complexities of that life (its terms of existence), describing how one can live by the Word without the ongoing mediation of that Word through liturgical enactment. This means that one's search must be for the Word outside that enactment, for signs of its presence confirming future promise, and in light of appeal for its coming soon. In terms of language the emphasis is on keeping language open so that the Word can be experienced, known, and recognized when it acts, when it breaks in. There must be a silencing, a breaking down of the clamor of human voices, a keeping open of human categories of knowing if the Word is to be heard when it comes, for "Thy . . . *Effects* no tongue can tell" ("To the Holy Bible"). Vaughan's echoes of the prayer book and its use finally reassure because they do not anticipate merely the restoration of that use but the fulfillment of the promises implicit in that use. The reader's experience of *Silex II* thus comes as an affirmative answer to the issues raised in *Silex I* and a further encouragement to keep faith with the community now broken and dispersed.

As a result it is appropriate that the final shaping of poetic experience in *Silex Scintillans* comes once more in terms of an allusion to Herbert. At the end of "To the Holy Bible" Vaughan repeats the opening words of the Gloria in Excelsis, as Herbert does at the end of "The Church." Vaughan follows this citation with a poem called "L'Envoy," just as Herbert does at the end of "The Church Militant." He then replicates Herbert's Trinitarian close. As Herbert's self-appointed successor to the role of poet/priest, Vaughan ends by again aligning his work with the work Herbert undertook, the moving of God's people through his empowering action toward participation in the fulfillment of God's promises: "Dear Lord . . . let grace / Descend, and hallow all the place. / Incline each hard heart to do good, / And cement us with thy sons blood, / That like true sheep, all in one fold / We may be fed, and one minde hold. / So shall we know in war and peace / Thy service to be our sole ease, / With prostrate souls adoring thee, / Who turn'd our sad captivity!"

There is more than a glance here at Puck's speech at the end of William Shakespeare's *Midsummer-Night's Dream* (1600), blessing and hallowing the lovers in their beds, and at the ending of Edmund Spenser's *Epithalamion* (1595), with its linking of the wedding night and the communion of saints. Now, however, the blessing desired is bestowed in that place to come, when the church as community is to be re-created, so "like true sheep, all in one fold, / We may be fed." This allusion to marriage may reflect Vaughan's looking forward to remarriage; in 1655, the year *Silex II* was published, he married Elizabeth Wise, his late wife's sister. But in terms of the argument of these poems, Vaughan is more likely demonstrating the strength of the Anglican poetic tradition in his ability to find in wedding hymns an appropriate way to conclude a poem about a search for a spouse who is yet to be found.

Yet there is a difference that is marked by the fact that when Vaughan here quotes the Gloria in Excelsis he does not quote the Book of Common Prayer version but the King James version of Luke, which differs slightly but significantly from the line at the beginning of the hymn in the prayer book; "Our sad captivity" had exacted a price; when use of the prayer book was restored in 1662, it would not immediately become again the normative source of Christian identity, "the means of grace and the hope of glory." In noting that subtle shift in Vaughan's allusion and by taking a closer look at one of the last poems in *Silex II,* one can begin to count the more subtle cost of that absence. Vaughan's final interpretation of the events of the

1640s and 1650s is that in them God is acting to bring about not a restoration of the pre–Civil War Anglican church but the future fulfillment of his promises made in the past to that church. In those terms the sufferings and deprivations of Anglicans in that time have meaning in biblical terms as the way of the cross they must walk in faithfulness to the God of those promises if they are to further their fulfillment and become citizens in the coming kingdom.

In light of the significance this proclamation gives to the situation of Anglicans in the Commonwealth period, Vaughan can find available the celebratory language of confident expectation he employed in *Silex II*. As a result, although the language familiar to Herbert about the church he knew is still available to Vaughan, it is now used to create images of the final end of things rather than to lament what is lost or to further the restoration of what is lost. Vaughan's "The Feast" is a poetic celebration of the Eucharist, but one that stresses its importance more in anticipation of being part of it than in actually being part of it. It thus stresses more the eschatological dimensions of the Eucharist than its worldly participation or community-building or identity-giving functions. In contrast to Herbert's "Love" (III), in which the speaker is called to the table to be served even though he feels unworthy, Vaughan's speaker calls the feast to come to him because he is now ready for it: "O come away, / Make no delay, / Come while my heart is clean & steddy!" The Eucharist in this world is defined in transitory terms ("No bliss here lent / Is permanent, / Such triumphs poor flesh cannot merit; / Short sips and sights / Endear delights, / Who seeks for more, he would inherit"), although the reception is defined here in classic Anglican terms as a conveyance of "all benefits of his passion": "O drink and bread / Which strikes death dead, / The food of mans immortal being! / Under veyls here / Thou art my chear, / Present and sure without my seeing."

Vaughan's images of the Eucharist derive from their situational context, as a culmination of a book-long search for a persuasive language and poetics of endurance, becoming now a preparation for fulfillment rather than restoration, in a situation in which that central Anglican act was absent, "without my seeing." What Vaughan provides here is an affirmation of his speaker's readiness for the Eucharist as well as of its importance even when not actually available. At this point in *Silex II* he anticipates the resumption of eucharistic reception in the terms used in the prayer book,

since all its language of the bread and wine as conveyance is displayed. In anticipation of such an event, "My soul and all, / Kneel down and fall / And sing his sad victorious story"; the poem is one of preparation for one who, in Vaughan's terms, must see his life of isolation from the eucharistic community as, finally, a preparation for fulfillment of that life.

Yet Vaughan was not sure that this fulfillment would ever happen on Earth; he had faith only that it would happen eventually: "Some toil and sow, / That wealth may flow, / And dress this earth for next years meat: But let me heed, / Why thou didst bleed, / And what in the next world to eat." Indeed the invitation to the Eucharist to come – to "Spring up, O wine, / And springing shine / With some glad message from his heart," in response to "the spilt dew, [which] / Like tears doth shew / The sad world wept to be releast" – suggests that the coming of the Eucharist once more is still far off, although it is richly anticipated. In contrast to Herbert's poem, "The Feast" speaks to a situation in which the only sure place of such experience is in the world to come, hence Vaughan's concluding quotation from Revelation: "*Blessed are they, which are called unto the marriage Supper of the Lamb!*" Preparation for the Eucharist thus makes one an invited guest at the eschatological banquet. The speaker has prepared; he is ready, and one sign of his readiness is his call for the banquet to come. Thus this poem is part of Vaughan's strategy toward the close of *Silex Scintillans* to celebrate the anticipated fulfillment of God's promises and encourage the faithfulness of his intended audience regardless of whether or not prayer-book worship is ever restored this side of the kingdom of God.

His great work over, and hopeful about the future, Vaughan essentially ended his poetic career at the age of thirty-five. Even though he lived forty more years, until 1695, nothing again in his life called forth an essentially literary response. Restoration of the monarchy and the Church of England in 1660 must, from Vaughan's perspective at least, have come as the fulfillment of his literary efforts. Remarriage in 1655 brought new responsibilities as well as four new children to join the four children from his first marriage; he plunged into his medical career and the life of a Welsh country gentleman, adopting the *silurist* title and the consequences of life far from the centers of art and culture. As the children of his second marriage grew older, Vaughan appears in the historic record more as a litigant in a series of legal actions taken by the children of one of his families against the children of the other. Defending himself against charges of favoritism in the dispersal of family property, Vaughan did not get the matter fully resolved until the year before his death, on Saint George's Day, 23 April 1695.

Biography:

F. E. Hutchinson, *Henry Vaughan: A Life and Interpretation* (Oxford: Clarendon Press, 1947).

References:

Joan Bennett, *Four Metaphysical Poets* (Cambridge: Cambridge University Press, 1934);

Thomas O. Calhoun, *Henry Vaughan: The Achievement of Silex Scintillans* (Newark: University of Delaware Press, 1981);

Arthur L. Clements, *Poetry of Contemplation: John Donne, George Herbert, Henry Vaughan, and the Modern Period* (Albany: State University of New York Press, 1990);

R. A. Durr, *On the Mystical Poetry of Henry Vaughan* (Cambridge, Mass.: Harvard University Press, 1962);

Ross Garner, *Henry Vaughan: Experience and the Tradition* (Chicago: University of Chicago Press, 1959);

M. M. Mahood, *Poetry and Humanism* (London: Cape, 1950; New York: Norton, 1970);

Louis A. Martz, *The Paradise Within: Studies in Vaughan, Traherne, and Milton* (New Haven: Yale University Press, 1964);

E. C. Pettet, *Of Paradise and Light: A Study of Vaughan's Silex Scintillans* (Cambridge: Cambridge University Press, 1960);

Jonathan F. S. Post, *Henry Vaughan: The Unfolding Vision* (Princeton: Princeton University Press, 1982);

Alan Rudrum, ed., *Essential Articles for the Study of Henry Vaughan* (Hamden, Conn.: Archon, 1987);

James D. Simmonds, *Masques of God: Form and Theme in the Poetry of Henry Vaughan* (Pittsburgh: University of Pittsburgh Press, 1972);

John N. Wall, *Transformations of the Word: Spenser, Herbert, Vaughan* (Athens: University of Georgia Press, 1988).

Thomas Vaughan

(1621 – 27 February 1666)

Donald R. Dickson
Texas A&M University

BOOKS: *Anthroposophia Theomagica; Or, A Discourse of the Nature of Man and his state after death,* as Eugenius Philalethes (London: Printed by T. W. for H. Blunden, 1650); published with *Anima Magica Abscondita; Or, A Discourse of the universall Spirit of Nature,* as Philalethes (London: Printed by T. W. for H. Blunden, 1650);

Magia Adamica: Or, The Antiquitie of Magic, and the Descent thereof from Adam downwards, proved. Whereunto is added a perfect, and full Discoverie of the true Coelum Terræ, or the Magician's Heavenly Chaos, and first Matter of all Things, as Philalethes (London: Printed by T. W. for H. Blunden, 1650); published with *The Man-Mouse Taken in a Trap, and tortur'd to death for gnawing the Margins of Eugenius Philalethes,* as Philalethes (London: Printed for H. Blunden, 1650);

Lumen De Lumine: Or, A new Magicall Light discovered, and Communicated to the World, as Philalethes (London: Printed for H. Blunden, 1651); published with *The Second Wash: Or, The Moore Scour'd once more,* as Philalethes (London: Printed by T. W., 1651);

Aula Lucis, Or, The House of Light, as S. N. (London: Printed for William Leake, 1652);

Euphrates, Or The Waters Of The East, as Philalethes (London: Printed for Humphrey Moseley, 1655).

Editions: *The Works of Thomas Vaughan: Mystic and Alchemist (Eugenius Philalethes),* edited by A. E. Waite (London: Theosophical Publishing, 1919);

The Works of Thomas Vaughan, edited by Alan Rudrum (Oxford: Clarendon Press, 1984).

OTHER: *The Fame and Confession of the Fraternity of R: C: Commonly, of the Rosie Cross,* preface by Vaughan as Eugenius Philalethes (London: Printed by J. M. for G. Calvert, 1652);

Eugenii Philalethis, Viri Insignissimi et Poetarum Sui Sæculi, meritò Principis: Vertumnus et Cynthia, &c., in Henry Vaughan, *Thalia Rediviva* (London: Printed for Robert Pawlet, 1678).

Thomas Vaughan was widely known in his time as a writer on occult topics, apologist for the Rosicrucian Brotherhood (a sect whose members claimed arcane and magical knowledge), and alchemical experimenter. Many readers today encounter him first as the twin brother of the poet Henry Vaughan. To appreciate Thomas Vaughan's intellectual contributions, one must have a clear picture of his role in the Samuel Hartlib and Sir Robert Moray circles, which included future founders of the Royal Society as members. By recognizing the consistency of his schema, by studying his Neoplatonic and hermetic sources, and by acknowledging the qualities of Vaughan's mythopoeic imagination, one can place him more accurately in the intellectually turbulent decades of the Interregnum – at a time when the boundaries between science and magic were not yet set.

Thomas Vaughan was a descendant of an ancient Welsh family, the Vaughans of Tretower Court. One ancestor was listed as among the vanquished at Agincourt; another played a significant role in the Wars of the Roses and is still kept in memory through William Shakespeare's *Richard III* (1597); through his maternal grandmother, Thomas was descended from the Somersets of Raglan, one of the most powerful families in Wales. The poet's grandfather William Vaughan had three children: Charles, Thomas (his father), and Margaret. As the elder son, Charles inherited the ancestral home at Tretower, situated about half a mile from the river Usk on the Brecon-Crickhowell Road. The great round tower of the castle keep (early thirteenth century) was fortified as late as 1403 during the Owen Glendower uprising, though by 1300 the lords had begun to build a fine house enclosing a courtyard, whose remains are still preserved. In 1611 the elder Thomas married Denise Morgan, heiress to her father's modest estate in Llansantffread parish, valued at four hundred pounds. At Trenewydd (Newton in English), a house in the hamlet and manor of Scethrog in the county of Brecon (or Brecknock), twin sons were born in 1621, Henry, the elder, and Thomas. The exact date of their birth is unknown. A younger son, William, was born in 1628, whose death on 14 July 1648 would be memorialized by both brothers. Little is known of the profession of Vaughan's father; he appears as justice of the peace in 1624 and as under sheriff in 1646. He was often before the law with petty suits – as was the case with many of the smaller gentry – and a distant kinsman, the Oxford antiquary John Aubrey, described him in *Brief Lives* (1813) as a "coxcombe and no honester than he should be – he cosened me of 50s. once."

Anthony Wood in *Athenæ Oxonienses* (1691, 1692) and Aubrey provide the few anecdotes and passing details about the Vaughans on which later biographers have relied. According to Wood both Henry and Thomas were "educated in Grammar Learning in his own Country for six Years under one *Matthew Herbert* a noted Schoolmaster of his time." Probably this tutelage took place from 1632 until 1638, when the brothers went down to Oxford. In his seventeenth year Thomas Vaughan was admitted to Jesus College (where fifty-nine of the ninety-nine men then on the college books were from Wales) on 4 May 1638 and was matriculated on 14 December 1638. Here, according to Wood, he "was put under the tuition of a noted tutor; by whose lectures profiting much, he took one degree in arts." A later poem shows that he also studied with William Cartwright, a reader in philosophy and a popular preacher. He proceeded to the B.A. degree on 18 February 1642. Though Henry wrote in a 15 June 1673 letter to Aubrey that Thomas stayed ten or twelve years and took the M.A. and Wood reported that Thomas was made a fellow of Jesus College, there are no records to support these claims.

As a younger brother, Thomas was destined for the church and may have begun to study divinity at Oxford after his arts course. Henry wrote Aubrey that Thomas "was ordayned minister by bishop Mainwaringe and presented to the Rectorie of St Brigets by his kinsman Sir George Vaughan." Since he attained the canonical age required for ordination as a priest in 1645, he was probably installed then as rector at Llansantffread, Saint Bride's (Bridget's in English). This parish church, only a few miles from his birthplace, came with a better-than-average stipend worth sixty pounds per annum. He lived here only a few years before evic-

tion under the "Act for better Propagation and Preaching the Gospel in Wales" in 1650. The document for his case reads as follows: "Tho: Vaughan out of Lansantfread for being a common drunkard, a common swearer, no preacher, a whoremast[r] & in armes personally against the Parliament." This last charge seems to be the motive force behind the others.

Vaughan was no doubt still at Oxford reading divinity and acquiring Oriental languages when King Charles I entered on 29 October 1642, after which time his studies were overtaken by the rush toward civil war. That he took up arms for the king is clear; to what extent he actively fought is largely unknown. After the Royalist defeat at Naseby in June 1645, King Charles himself had come to Brecon, lodging with Sir Herbert Price at Brecon Priory on 5 August, to raise support for a campaign to hold the north of Wales. Evidence suggests that Vaughan fought with Price's Breconshire regiment of horse at Rowton Heath near Chester, 24 September 1645, where the Royalists again suffered a great defeat. Among the list of captains from Price's company taken prisoner is the name "Tho. Vaughan." After the Restoration his name also appears on a claim made for the relief of the king's "truly loyal and indigent party" as captain of Price's company. Though he wrote five Latin poems on Col. John Morris's capture of Pontefract Castle (in 1648 during the last phase of the war), the poems do not necessarily reflect personal involvement in the fighting.

After his brief career as pastor to his native flock at Llansantffread (circa 1645–1648), Vaughan returned for a short time to Oxford for the "Acquisition of some naturall secrets, to which I had been disposed from my youth up." After the Restoration he never sought reinstatement once he discovered his true life's work in alchemical research. At Oxford, "in a sedate repose," according to Wood, he "prosecuted his medicinal geny, (in a manner natural to him) and at length became eminent in the chymical part thereof at Oxon, and afterwards at London." The dedication to his first book (published in 1650) is dated "Oxonii 48," so he may have returned as early as two years before his formal eviction. He stayed at Oxford for only a year or two, and most of his later addresses were in London. He married a woman named Rebecca (surname unknown) from Mappersall in Bedfordshire on 28 September 1651. There were no children. His notebook recording his alchemical experiments (British Library M.S. Sloan 1741) indicates she was an active partner; their combined initials are found under many entries. His touching remembrances of

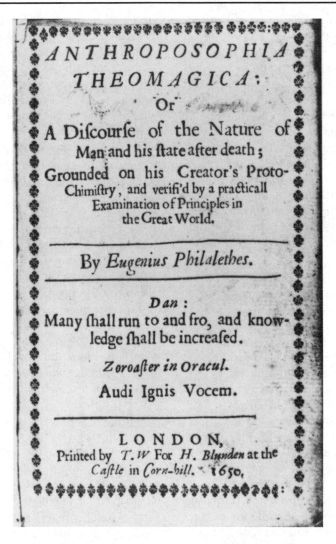

Thomas Vaughan's first published book, in which he described the basis for all his alchemical research

her show that theirs was a happy union. Soon after her death on 17 April 1658, having had a premonitory dream about his own death, he wrote that "most happy shall I bee in this Interpretation, If I may meete her again so soone, and beginn the heavenly and Æternall life with her, in the very same moenth, wherein wee began the Earthly."

Following his return to Oxford, Vaughan was closely associated with the eminent Samuel Hartlib, educational reformer and utopian idealist. In May 1650 Hartlib recorded in his notebook that "One Vaughan of Oxford is the author of Anthroposophia, who for some years hath tried Chymicall or Physical Conclusions. Hee now lives with Hinshaw at Kingsington [Kensington] where they lay their heads and hands together to see what they can produce." Thomas Henshaw (chosen fellow of the Royal Society at its first constitution in 1663) was Vaughan's closest friend. They could have met as early as 1638 at Oxford and may have been fellow prisoners after the Royalist defeat at Rowton Heath in September 1645. Hartlib also reports that a fellow experimenter, Dr. Robert Child, was "endeavouring to forme a chymical club with Hinshaw, Webbe, Vaughan, etc." whose purpose would be to make available manuscripts and translations of philosophical works and promote learning. Child later reported to Hartlib that Henshaw was about to establish "a model of [a] Christian Learned Society . . . that will have all in common, devoting thems[elves] wholly to devotion and studies, and separating thems[elves] from the world, by leading a severe life for diet, apparel, etc. They will have a Laboratorie and strive to do all the good they can to their neighbourhood." Thus during the early 1650s Vaughan was an active member of Hartlib's circle.

At what point Vaughan began his more important association with one of the principal architects of the Royal Society, Sir Robert Moray (president in 1661–1662), is not known. Wood described Moray as a "noted chymist" and Vaughan's patron; Aubrey reported that he was a "good Chymist and assisted his Majestie in his Chymicall operations" at the royal laboratory in Whitehall; Aubrey also recorded that Henry called Moray Thomas's "great friend . . . to whome he gave all his bookes and MSS." Thomas Willard has argued that Moray may have even provided Vaughan access to the translation of the Rosicrucian manifestos (published with a preface in 1652), thus placing their association in the early 1650s. Through Moray, Vaughan seems to have been employed with the Crown during the last five years of his life. When King Charles II left London for Oxford to escape the plague in 1665, Vaughan was evidently part of the entourage. He and Moray took lodging at the rectory in Albury (ten miles from Oxford), where they conducted experiments. According to Wood, it was during one of these experiments, "as it were suddenly, when he was operating strong mercury, some of which by chance getting up into his nose killed him." He died on 27 February 1666 and was buried in the village churchyard at Moray's expense. All his remaining manuscripts were left in Moray's hands (along with his library); only his notebook of experiments is now extant.

To appreciate Vaughan's writing fully, one needs to place it in its historical context. In the tumultuous decade of the 1640s, the world was being turned upside down: theological orthodoxy was being redefined; the prevailing Aristotelianism of the universities was under attack by the "new philosophy"; England was at war against itself; government was in a position to carry out radical reform in all areas of life; and the boundary between "magic" and "science" was being actively contested. Sir Isaac Newton's abiding interest in alchemy is a well-known instance. The underlying principle of Vaughan's worldview – a belief in the animism of the universe – gains ground when seen as a reaction to the threat posed by the emerging mechanistic view of the world. He devoted considerable effort in his writings to refuting the notion of an inert universe along Aristotelian or Cartesian lines. As a youth he was fascinated with the hidden forces of the natural world, which "(I know not how) surpris'd my first youth, long before I saw the University."

Perhaps the central idea to which he devoted his physical and intellectual energies is a belief in alchemical transformation. He describes his own treatises as "Judgements of *Philosophie*" rather than as works of alchemy, since the more common term suggests only the "*torture* of *Metalls*," which he claims never to have believed, much less studied. A good deal of confusion has reigned over the nature of Vaughan's alchemy (especially since he admits to having followed the chimera of metallurgical transmutation for three years). He was dismissed by many simply as a befuddled zealot; even his admirers in this century have sought to recuperate him by regarding his writings as an allegory for so-called spiritual alchemy. Vaughan was definitely an experimental alchemist who pursued an active research program. His notebooks recorded the experiments conducted with his wife in the 1650s; he continued his investigations in the 1660s with Moray; he died as a result of a laboratory accident. Despite what he said about the metaphysical side to alchemy, he was a chemist as well. He had nothing but contempt, however, for the "common illiterat Broyler" who "dreams of *Gold* and *Transmutations,* most noble and *Heavenly Effects,* but the *Means* whereby hee would *compasse* them, are worme-eaten, dustie, mustie *papers*." These common chemists did not fathom the philosophical foundations of the great work. Vaughan made it his task to set forth an elaborate, consistently maintained theory of elemental transformation.

Vaughan's alchemical research was characteristic of late Renaissance alchemy, whose practitioners were increasingly less interested in the transformation of metals and far more concerned with metaphysical speculations on the philosopher's stone. In *Anthroposophia Theomagica* (1650) he first established the basis of his schema, a conception of the threefold order of the cosmos, originating in the mystery of the Trinity, mirrored in the creation of the threefold universe and the "natural triplicity" of the elements. His universe – with its supercelestial, celestial, and sublunary realms – was essentially Neoplatonic. At the Creation, God, previously wrapped and contracted in himself, emanated divine light, the *Aleph Lucidum,* through the agency of the Holy Spirit; this light pierced the bosom of the first matter and the Idea of the world appeared in the primitive waters. After the "*primitive supernaturall part* of the *Creation*" had occurred, the work of the Creation involved separating different substances from this mass or *Limbus* into the elemental world perceivable to the outward senses. The elemental water and earth mentioned in Genesis were inferior principles, or secondary substances quite distinct from the *prima materia* (first matter). Since matter was separated from the original unity of the monad, it was subject to the confusion and duplicity of the lower world (the *Binarius* that had been subtracted from the monad). Crude metallurgical alchemists pursued these secondary substances whereas Vaughan pursued the "*Cælestiall hidden Natures* known only to absolute *Magicians,* whose eyes are in the *Center,* not in the *Circumference.*" Elements had a threefold nature, imaginable as concentric spheres with an occult center: The first was a "visible, *Tangible* substance, pure, *fixed,* and *Incorruptible.* . . . It answers to *God* the *Father,* being the *Naturall Foundation* of the *Creature,* as He is the *Supernaturall*: without this Nothing can be perfected in *Magick.* The Second Principle is the infallible *Magnet,* the *Mystery* of *Union.* . . . This answers to God the Son, for it is that which mediates between Extremes, and makes Inferiors and Superiors communicate. . . . The third Principle . . . answers to the *Holy Ghost,* for amongst Naturalls it is the onely Agent, and Artificer."

Anima Magica Abscondita (1650), published as a companion treatise bound with the first, was devoted to explaining generation and the motive forces in matter and the world in terms of the "universall *spirit* of Nature," which also operated through a threefold chain of descent and ascent. The process involved *anima mundi* (the divine spark of life principle that animates matter), *spiritus mundi* (the spiritual medium through which the *anima* was infused), and a "certaine oleous æthereall water" as the matrix of the spiritual in the sublunary realm. Vaughan thus promoted his beliefs in an animistic universe through the powerful analogies presented in the mystery of the Trinity.

Vaughan's major interest lay in observing the transformation of nature to its primal state, in essence a reenactment of the Creation. Most often he described this as a reduction of threefold elemental earth to its purity, *terra Adamica* (Adamic earth). *Euphrates* (1655), his final published treatise, outlined the meteorological cycles at the heart of the great work: water (fertilized "oleous humidity") served as the vehicle for earth (sublimated and resolved), and both were "perpetually *regenerated* by a circular *rarefaction,* and *condensation.*" As a result of this copulation or marriage, the "*seminall particle* . . . our onely *originall fundamentall Matter*" was produced. This *sperma* was also known as the *mercurius philosophorum* (philosophers' mercury) or as the "first *matter* of the *Philosophers stone.*" The privilege of removing the veil that occluded viewing of the regeneration of earth

before the Apocalypse was the goal of the adept. Vaughan explained that "We are all born like *Moses* with a Veil over the Face: This is it, which hinders the prospect of that Intellectuall shining light, which God had placed in us; And to tell a Trueth that concernes all Mankinde, the greatest Mystery both in *Divinity,* and *Philosophie* is, *How to remove it.*"

Vaughan's primary medium was prose; nonetheless he used poems effectively throughout his published treatises. His only published collection of poems was included in his brother's last collection as the "Learned *Remains.*" Henry's portion of *Thalia Rediviva* (1678) consists mostly of the aftergleanings for *Olor Iscanus* (1651) and *Silex Scintillans* (1650), according to F. E. Hutchinson. Given their subject matter, it is not unreasonable to assume that Thomas's poems were also early efforts. The two poems dedicating these "first fruits" to Matthew Herbert were signed with the initials "E. P." Since the first known occasion for styling himself Eugenius Philalethes was 1648 (in a commendatory poem to his brother's *Olar Iscanus*), these two poems offer evidence that he himself had plans for a volume of poems. The *Remains* closes with Henry's statement that many other poems were left at Oxford, including a heroic poem, *Alcippus et Jacintha.* Thus, only a fraction of Thomas's poetic output remains – and the early poems at that. In order to do justice to Vaughan, this should perhaps be seen as a first book.

Something of his reputation as a poet is known from the poems he dedicated to others. His first published work was a poem in *Horti Carolini Rosa Altera* (Oxford, 1640) celebrating the birth of the third son of Charles I. He later contributed "On the Death of Mr. William Cartwright" to Cartwright's *Comedies, Tragi-Comedies, and Other Poems* (1651). In addition were poems commending *Olor Iscanus* and his friend Thomas Powell's *Elementa Opticae* (1651). The title page of his *Remains* lists two poems, as if their titles were known well enough to induce further the purchase of the volume. Wood characterized him as a "tolerable good English and Latin poet" whose poems were "esteemed by many fit to be published." Along with this slender evidence for Vaughan's stature as a poet stand the poems themselves.

Vaughan's collection very much reflects the turmoil of the 1640s, the probable date of composition. "Vertumnus" and "Cynthia" are not only the longest poems, but they also present the major themes of the *Remains*: the wars of Mars and Venus. "Vertumnus" is a bitter invective delivered at the tomb of a fallen enemy. Vaughan's recent editor

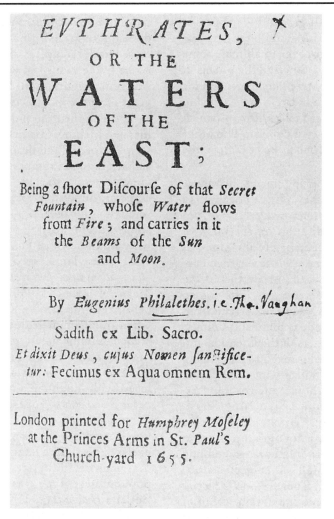

Vaughan's last published treatise, a description of how water and earth are "perpetually regenerated by a circular rarefaction, and condensation"

Alan Rudrum offers John Pym (1584–1643) as a possibility. The poem takes the form of an epitaph, though its purpose is to vent the spleen of the speaker; he uses many conventional devices ironically (for example, the *ubi sunt* formula and *memento mori*) to depict the woes of the kingdom as a result of those like Vertumnus who brought revolution to a peaceable land. In another key, five shorter poems celebrate the heroic exploits of Col. John Morris's capture of Pontefract Castle, the last hurrah for the Royalists in 1648. "Carolus *Primus*, Anglorum *Rex*," his poem on the martyrdom of Charles I in 1649, is one of his very best. Charles is made a type of Christ, and the intricate opening conceit is memorable: "Behold, the magnet of the gods, and the throne of God who has been drawn down below the sun: flint of heavenly fires, fretted by the steel and vanishing in flames!" The epitaph on William Laud is likewise polished. The three poems on Gustavus Adolphus are more than

likely schoolboy exercises that tell about the sensibilities of Protestant Britain during the Thirty Years' War. Gustav II of Sweden (1594–1632) was the hope of the Protestant cause against the Holy Roman Empire and the Counter-Reformation. The poems celebrate victories in 1631 and 1632. Aside from their somewhat stilted language and stale metaphors drawn from classical mythology, their subject matter would not have commended itself after so many new heroes emerged in the 1640s.

The other large group of poems consists of amatory verses in a classical vein. These poems to Cynthia, Chloe, and Stella are a bit too lush in their passion to be schoolboy exercises. Instead they are reminiscent of the works of other displaced Royalist poets who establish the values of love and friendship in the only realm they still control, their poems. Vaughan's amatory lyrics have polished surfaces with graceful wordplay in the manner of Catullus and Martial (and Ben Jonson); Vaughan manages moreover to animate some conceits typical of the genre. Since all the poems in *Remains* were in Latin, these were likely intended for a coterie audience – the kind of circle that existed in Brecon while he was vicar at Llansantffread (which would explain how Henry had copies). The other occasional poems suggest as much (for example, the poem on Thomas Powell).

Vaughan's most interesting poems, however, were published in his treatises. Of the dozen or so poems, three are especially noteworthy. "Lord God! This was a *stone*" is a meditation on the book of creatures (nature) – here specifically the stone of the philosophers, or the *prima materia* – which concludes a long description of the properties of the stone in *Anthroposophia Theomagica*. The poem illustrates the spiritual use Vaughan derived from his chemical studies. Its mode is biblical typology, employing images of the waters of the Creation and of baptism: the stone is transformed into a springing well, into a heart of flint, and finally into a perfected substance, suffused with light moving without "*Excentricity*" through the agency of the Holy Spirit. Vaughan's " 'Tis *Day*, my Chrystal *Usk*," from *Anima Magica Abscondita,* is a topographical poem and also a meditation on the creatures, resembling his brother's "The Water-fall" in subject matter. "*Pretty green* Bank *farewell!,*" from *Lumen De Lumine* (1651), was used to conclude the dream vision of Thalia. Vaughan's prose style, furthermore, is richly poetic in cast, a fit medium for his mythopoeic imaginings. His classical borrowings (from Virgil mostly) illustrate and embellish his texts quite appropriately. He might well have adopted Seneca's motto as his own – *tamquam explorator,* "always as a spy" into another's camp to explore new ideas.

Vaughan published most of his writing under the pseudonym Eugenius Philalethes, the well-born (that is, the noble) lover of wisdom. His pseudonym depicted him in the same vein as his hero Agrippa, a popularizer of Marsilio Ficino; all three saw themselves as disseminators of *prisca theologia* (ancient wisdom). In his first published work, Vaughan announced that Agrippa, whose portrait adorned the text, "is indeed my Author, and next to God I owe all that I have unto Him." In addition to *De occulta philosophia* (1533), Vaughan read deeply in the *Corpus Hermeticum* attributed to Hermes Trismegistus, *Novum lumen chemicum* (1607) of Michael Sendivogius, and *De arte cabalistica* (1517) of Johann Reuchlin (to name the most significant sources). As

did those before him, Vaughan hoped to preach the doctrine of transformation leading mankind to a closer understanding of God in the natural world. As he wrote in his last work, the mystery of generation and regeneration, "if rightly understood, is a great *Manuduction* to *Divinity.*"

It is difficult to judge Vaughan's reputation in his own lifetime. His first work circulated in manuscript before its publication in 1650, judging from a remark made in the preface to its companion tract. He also seems to have enjoyed the confidence of some of the founders of the Royal Society. But his reputation for posterity, much to his detriment, was shaped dramatically by a scurrilous pamphlet war with the Cambridge Platonist Henry More in 1650–1651. More launched a page-by-page attack in his *Observations upon Anthroposophia Theomagica and Anima Magica Abscondita* (1650), with his general charge being "enthusiasm" – a serious concern in an era when intellectual zealotry had endangered many. Vaughan immediately replied point for point in *The Man-Mouse Taken in a Trap* (1650); More's rebuttal, *The Second Lash of Alazonomastix* (1651), was countered with Vaughan's *Second Wash: Or, The Moore Scour'd once more* (1651). When Vaughan oversaw the publication of the first English translations of two Rosicrucian tracts and offered a long, rambling preface, his public image was set – despite the fact that he insisted that he was not a Rosicrucian. His popular stereotype was later exploited by Samuel Butler's *Hudibras* (1663–1678) and Jonathan Swift's *A Tale of a Tub* (1704).

His writings, however, were not ignored. Oliver Cromwell and Newton were known to have copies of his work; he served as a source for other writers, notably John Heydon. Unsold sheets of the first editions of *Magia Adamica* and *Euphrates* were republished in 1656 and 1671. His works were still read in Europe in the eighteenth century; all (except the pieces sparring with More) were translated into German between 1689 and 1789. Vaughan enjoyed a modest revival among occultists in the later nineteenth century through the efforts of A. E. Waite. Now that his works have been published in a critically edited, scholarly text by Alan Rudrum (1984), a more analytical appraisal of one of the best-known British occultists is possible.

References:

Noel L. Brann, "The Conflict between Reason and Magic in Seventeenth-Century England: A Case Study of the Vaughan-More Debate," *Huntington Library Quarterly,* 43 (Spring 1980): 103–126;

Frederic B. Burnham, "The More-Vaughan Controversy: The Revolt Against Philosophical Enthusiasm," *Journal of the History of Ideas,* 35 (January–March 1974): 33–49;

E. K. Chambers, "Thomas Vaughan," in *Poems of Henry Vaughan, Silurist,* 2 volumes, edited by Chambers (London: Routledge, 1896), II: xxxiii–lvi;

Arlene Miller Guinsberg, "Henry More, Thomas Vaughan and the Late Renaissance Magical Tradition," *Ambix,* 27 (1980): 36–58;

F. E. Hutchinson, *Henry Vaughan: A Life and Interpretation* (Oxford: Clarendon Press, 1947);

William Newman, "Thomas Vaughan as an Interpreter of Agrippa von Nettesheim," *Ambix,* 29 (1982): 125–140;

C. A. Ralegh Radford, *Tretower Court and Castle,* Welsh Office Publications (Cardiff: HMSO, 1969);

Alan Rudrum, "Biographical Introduction," in *The Works of Thomas Vaughan,* edited by Rudrum (Oxford: Clarendon Press, 1984), pp. 1–31;

Rudrum, "Thomas Vaughan's *Lumen De Lumine:* An Interpretation of Thalia," in *Literature and the Occult,* edited by Luanne Frank (Arlington: University of Texas at Arlington, 1977), pp. 234–243;

A. E. Waite, "Biographical Preface," in *The Works of Thomas Vaughan: Mystic and Alchemist (Eugenius Philalethes),* edited by Waite (London: Theosophical Publishing, 1919), pp. vii–xxiv;

Thomas Willard, "The Rosicrucian Manifestos in Britain," *Papers of the Bibliographical Society of America,* 77, no. 4 (1983): 489–495.

Papers:

Vaughan's notebook of alchemical experiments, "Aqua Vitæ: Non Vitis: Or, the Radical Humiditie of Nature," is at the British Library (MS. Sloane 1741). Most of the entries were written after the death of his wife, Rebecca, on 17 April 1658 and continued up to April 1659.

Appendix

Third-Generation Minor Poets of the Seventeenth Century

Third-Generation Minor Poets of the Seventeenth Century

Ernest W. Sullivan, II
Texas Tech University

The six poets discussed below represent only a few of the many lesser-known poets of their generation. All are "minor" in the sense that they have attracted little critical attention and are little read at present. Even so, a fuller understanding of seventeenth-century poetics will come about with further attention to such poets, because present scholarship focuses on lyric verse, often overlooking the diversity of seventeenth-century poetry and its cultural role. The particular authors selected have suffered the vagaries of twentieth-century critical prejudices: some are little thought of as poets because their other accomplishments overshadow their verse or because they wrote in genres (historical narrative, heroic romance, religious verse, epigram, verse translation, epitaph, verse letter) little valued today. There are no great individual talents among them, but these poets are working within the traditions that inform and shape the verse of their generation.

Robert Heath
(floruit circa 1650)

BOOKS: *Clarastella; together with Poems Occasional, Elegies, Epigrams, Satyrs* (London: Printed for Humphrey Moseley, 1650; facsimile, Gainesville, Fla.: Scholars' Facsimiles & Reprints, 1970);
Paradoxical Assertions and Philosophical Problems (London: Printed by R. W., sold by Charles Webb, 1659).
Edition: *Robert Heath: Poems and Songs,* edited by William G. Hutchinson (Hull: Tutin, 1905).

OTHER: Gabriel Dugrés, *Breve et Accuratum Grammaticae Gallicae Compendium,* Latin prefatory verses by Heath (Cambridge: Printers to the University, 1636).

The first part of Robert Heath's *Clarastella* (1650) consists of a series of love poems to the title character; among the "Poems occasional" are some verses headed "To a friend wishing peace," describing the Civil War and earnestly pleading for the establishment of peace; the third part of the work includes elegies on the deaths of Heath's friends (often casualties of the war), including Sir Bevil Grenville, William Lawes, four women identified only by their initials, as well as one lamenting three fingers lost by a musician during the Civil War; the fourth part is a collection of epigrams; and the volume concludes with four satires. The lyrics to Clarastella show the influence of Ben Jonson and Robert Herrick, as seen in the opening couplet of "Seeing Her Dancing": "RObes loosly flowing, and aspect as free, / A carelesse carriage deckt with modestie." Other poems, such as "The Quaere. What is Love?," in the "Clarastella" section reach for the wit of John Donne and George Herbert. Occasionally the epigrams resemble those of Donne: "To Madam Moyle on her Picture" has the same joke on the painted lady as Donne's "Phrine." The satires have some bite and concern the traditional topics of church and state.

Robert Heath the poet is probably the Robert Heath born in London, the fourth son of Sir Robert Heath. He entered Corpus Christi College, Cambridge, as a fellow commoner in 1634, was admitted to the Inner Temple in 1637, and made barrister in 1652. For a time he was an auditor in the Court of Wards.

References:
John P. Cutts, "Seventeenth-Century Lyrics," *Musica Disciplina,* 10 (1956): 142–209;

"Heath's *Clarastella,*" *Retrospective Review,* 2, part 2 (1820): 227–238;

R. G. Howarth, "Attributions to Herrick," *Notes and Queries,* 5 (June 1958): 249;

John and J. A. Venn, *Alumni Cantabrigienses,* volume 3 (Cambridge: Cambridge University Press, 1922).

Papers:
A Heath manuscript is at the Bodleian Library, Oxford (MS. Mus. b. 1).

Thomas Forde
(floruit circa 1660)

BOOKS: *The Times Anatomiz'd in Severall Characters, by T. F.* (London: Printed for W. L., 1647);

Lusus Fortunæ; The Play of Fortune; Continually Acted by the Severall Creatures on the Stage of the World (London: Printed for R. L., 1649);

A Theatre of Wits, Ancient and Modern. Attended with severall other ingenious Pieces from the same Pen. Viz. I. Fænestra in Pectore, or a Century of Familiar Letters. II. Loves Labyrinth: A Tragi-comedy. III. Fragmenta Poetica: Or Poetical Diversions. IV. Virtus Rediviva, a Panegyrick on our late King Charles of ever blessed Memory (London: Printed by R. & W. Leybourn for Thomas Basset, 1661);

Virtus Rediviva A Panegyrick On our late King Charles the I. &c. of ever blessed Memory. Attended, with severall other Pieces from the same Pen. Viz. I. A Theatre of Wits: Being a Collection of Apothegms. II. Fænestra in Pectore: or a Century of Familiar Letters. III. Loves Labyrinth: A Tragi-comedy. IV. Fragmenta Poetica: Or Poeticall Diversions. Concluding, with A Panegyrick on His Sacred Majesties most happy Return (London: Printed by R. & W. Leybourn for William Grantham & Thomas Basset, 1661).

Although the works in Thomas Forde's *Virtus Rediviva* (1661) have separate title pages and pagination, the sequence of signatures (*Virtus Rediviva* [A1–C3], *A Theatre of Wits* [C7–I6v], *Fænestra in Pectore* [I7–T8v], *Loves Labyrinth* [V1–2A7], and *Fragmenta Poetica* [2A8–2C4]) suggests that the volume was printed as a collection and not intended for piecemeal distribution. Forde's *Times Anatomiz'd* (1647) has been wrongly attributed to Thomas Fuller.

Quotations from Edmund Spenser, Abraham Cowley, John Donne, Charles Cornwallis, Francis Bacon, Thomas Fuller, Joseph Hall, Peter Heylyn, and Josuah Sylvester appear in the *Lusus Fortunæ* (1649); and a Latin prefatory poem is signed I. H., which may stand for James Howell. *Loves Labyrinth* includes a song from Robert Greene's *Menaphon* (1589). Forde's blank-verse play was never performed. The *Fænestra in Pectore* is a collection of Forde's letters, some to his father, a friend at Barbados, an E. B., Fuller, and others. Some of the verse in *Fragmenta Poetica* praises George Herbert and Thomas Bastard.

Virtus Rediviva: or, a Panegyrick on the late K. Charles the I is followed by *An Anniversary on Charles the First, &c. 1657* and *Second Anniversary on Charls the First, 1658.* The *Fragmenta Poetica* has appended to it *A Panegyrick upon His Sacred Majestie's Most Happy Return, on the 29. May, 1660.* The poems in this collection are often about biblical verses or are paraphrases of them. Several epigrams are translations of Martial or imitate him. Some of the longer epigrams, such as the concluding couplet of "Excuse for absence," show flashes of style and wit: "Planets are where they *worke,* not where they *move,* / I *am* not where I *live,* but where I *Love.*"

In *Fænestra in Pectore,* Forde describes himself as belonging to the neighborhood of Maldon, Essex, and as related to John Udall. A staunch Royalist, he was a friend of Howell. The dates and places of his birth and death are unknown.

Reference:
Bruce Redford, "Pope's Epistolary Theory and Practice: Two Probable Sources," *Notes and Queries,* 30 (December 1983): 500–502.

William Chamberlayne

(1619 – January 1689)

BOOKS: *Loves Victory: a Tragi-Comedy* (London: Printed by E. Cotes, sold by Robert Clavell, 1658); republished as *Wits Led by the Nose; or, a Poet's Revenge* (London: Printed For William Crook, 1678);

Pharonnida: a Heroick Poem (London: Printed for Robert Clavell, 1659);

Englands Jubile, or a Poem on the Happy Return of His Sacred Majesty Charles the Second (London: Printed for Robert Clavell, 1660);

Eromena: or, the Noble Stranger. A Novel (London: Printed for James Norris, 1683).

Editions: *Pharonnida* and *Englands Jubile,* in *Minor Poets of the Caroline Period,* edited by George Saintsbury (Oxford: Clarendon Press, 1905), I: 17–295; 297–303;

Love's Victory, edited by Charles K. Meschter (Bethlehem, Pa.: Bethlehem, 1914).

William Chamberlayne may have authored *The Cavaliers Letanie* (1648), and *A Puritane Set forth in His Lively Colours: or, K. James His Description of a Puritan. Whereunto is added, The Round-heads Character, with the Character of an Holy Sister* (1642) has also been attributed to him.

Pharonnida (1659) is dedicated to Sir William Portman, and in its epistle to the reader Chamberlayne complains that "*Fortune* had plac'd me in too low a *Sphear* to be happy in the Acquaintance of the Ages more *Celebrated Wits.*" Even so Chamberlayne had his admirers: in 1683 his romance *Eromena: or, the Noble Stranger* based on *Pharonnida* appeared; the poem was admired by Robert Southey, who, in a note to his "Vision of the Maid of Orleans," mentions Chamberlayne as a "poet to whom I am indebted for many hours of delight." Chamberlayne's *Wits Led by the Nose* was published and acted at the Theatre Royal in 1678.

Pharonnida is a poem in five books of five cantos each, and Arthur Henry Bullen in the *Dictionary of National Biography* compares it to a well-known poem by John Keats: "Both in its faults and its beauties 'Pharonnida' bears considerable resemblance to 'Endymion.'" In *Minor Poets of the Caroline Period* (1905), George Saintsbury wrote, "it is, with Davenant's much better known but far inferior *Gon-*

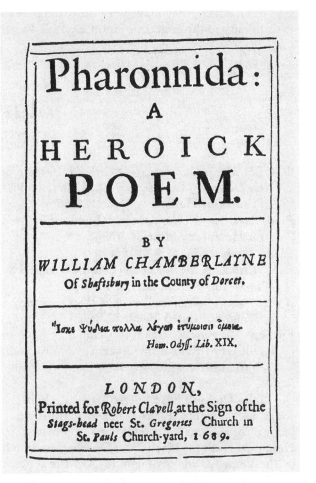

Title page for Chamberlayne's second book, a long poem that has been compared favorably to Sir William Davenant's Gondibert (1651) and John Keats's Endymion (1818)

dibert, the chief English example of that curious kind the 'Heroic poem' – the romanticized epic which, after the deliberations of the Italian critics and the example of Tasso, spread itself over Europe in the late sixteenth century and held the field for the greater part of the seventeenth. . . . The resemblance, indeed, between *Pharonnida* and the type of the Greek romance generally is very strong – in the prominence and persistent persecutions of the heroine, in the constant voyages and travels, alarums and excursions, ambushes and abductions, and, it may be added, in the very subordinate position of

Character. . . . Like the whole body of [Elizabethan] verse from Spenser downwards, it is of imagination (or at worst of fancy) all compact: the restraints of prose and common sense are utterly alien to it. Its author has passed from the merely 'conceited' to the 'metaphysical' stage; and if his excursions into the *au delà* [beyond] do not reach the sublimity or the subtlety of Donne, the flaming fantasy and passion of Crashaw, they leave very little to desire in their fidelity to the Gracianic motto *En Nada Vulgar* [in nothing vulgar]." Saintsbury declared *England's Jubile* (1660) "certainly the best of the poems on the Restoration next to Dryden's."

Chamberlayne was a physician at Shaftesbury in Dorsetshire. His strong Royalist sympathies evidently led to his participation in the Civil War, and details in *Pharonnida* suggest his involvement in the second battle of Newberry. His burial monument, erected by his son Valentine Chamberlayne, is at Shaftesbury in the churchyard of the Holy Trinity.

John Collop
(1625 – post 1676)

BOOKS: *Medici Catholicon; or A Catholick Medicine for the Diseases of Charitie,* by J. C., M.D. (London: Printed for Humphrey Moseley, 1656);
Poesis Rediviva: or, Poesie Reviv'd (London: Printed for Humphrey Moseley, 1656);
Charity Commended (London, 1658);
Itur Satyricum: in Loyall Stanzas (London: Printed by T. M. for William Shears, 1660);
A Letter with Animadversions upon the Animadverter (London: Printed for M. B., 1661).
Edition: *The Poems of John Collop,* edited by Conrad Hilberry (Madison: University of Wisconsin Press, 1962).

John Collop's lyrical verse, particularly in the songs, shows talent. *Poesis Rediviva* (1656) is a collection of poems and epigrams dedicated to Henry Pierrepont, Marquis of Dorchester. Much of the verse, as his prologue to "On the fencers for Religion" shows, satirizes Puritan sectaries: "THeir pens have swords bin which the Church did wound, / Whence all these scars are on her body found. / Polemicks of Religion sure have writ, / Not for the truth, but exercise of wit: / While Scriptures, Fathers, Councells, they do wrest. / As I name them, they use their names in jest." Other verses praise Collop's acquaintances such as Dr. Field, James Ussher, William Chillingworth, and Henry Hammond. His Royalist poems such as *Itur Satyricum* (1660) on political debate and the monarchy have both aesthetic and historical interest. "Writing at the highest moment of the Commonwealth, Collop historicizes the ideal world of the poet's imagination by comparing it with ideal political states, not with cities of God or arcadian fairylands in which Nature

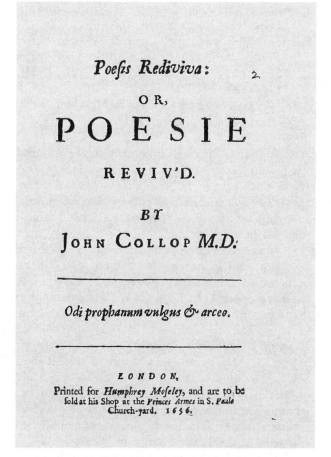

Poesis Rediviva: 2

OR,

POESIE

REVIV'D.

BY

JOHN COLLOP *M.D.*

Odi prophanum vulgus & arceo.

LONDON,
Printed for *Humphrey Moseley,* and are to be sold at his Shop at the *Princes Armes* in S. *Pauls* Church-yard. 1656.

Title page for Collop's first collection of verse, which includes poems satirizing Puritans

pours forth her bounty to a fortunate people," wrote Gerald M. MacLean. "The fictitious world of the poet's imagination still constitutes an ideal, but it has become a political ideal achieved through human contrivance rather than divine intervention; and it exists in the future, not the irrevocable past."

Collop's modern editor, Conrad Hilberry, notes the influence of John Donne: "Collop imitates the compression of some of Donne's arguments, the abrupt twisting and turning of logic. . . . Sometimes, as in the sun-shadow passage in 'The Church,' the imitation of Donne's tight logic serves Collop well." Collop's religious lyrics show the influence of George Herbert in the use of stanzaic shapes to effect meaning and in the use of the spiritual development of the narrator to structure the poem. Many of Collop's most interesting poems fall into the genre of the praise of the ugly or deformed mistress. This anti-Petrarchan subset of the paradox genre was practiced by better poets than Collop (such as William Shakespeare and Donne); however, the sexuality in poems such as "To a painted Lady, a Calf spotted, lusts Idol, like the Idol of the Egyptians" and "To a Lady of Pleasure" sets his "ugly mistress" poems apart.

John Collop, son of John Collop, was born at Flitwick, Bedfordshire, and was baptized on 4 July 1625. He was admitted as a pensioner on 14 October 1641 at age sixteen to Pembroke College, Cambridge, where he studied under William Quarles. As an M.D. in 1661 he appealed for arrears that had been withheld because he was a Royalist. He received eighty pounds. No record exists of his attendance at any medical school, though Hilberry suggests that he attended the Royal College of Physicians. Collop's first wife evidently died before he wrote *Poesis Rediviva,* and he married Anne Evington in 1676.

References:

Mary Ann Ida Gannon, "An Analysis of John Collop's *Poesis Rediviva,*" M.A. thesis, Loyola University of Chicago, 1948;

Gerald M. MacLean, *Time's Witness: Historical Representation in English Poetry, 1603–1660* (Madison: University of Wisconsin Press, 1990), pp. 213–308;

John and J. A. Venn, eds., *Alumni Cantabrigienses,* volume 3 (Cambridge: Cambridge University Press, 1922).

Papers:

A Collop manuscript is at the British Library (Add. Ms. 24492, f. 13^v).

John Hall

(August 1627 – 1 August 1656)

BOOKS: *Horæ Vacivæ, or, Essays. Some occasionall Considerations* (London: Printed by E. G. for J. Rothwell, 1646);

Poems (Cambridge: Printed by Roger Daniel, 1646 [i.e., 1647]) – includes *The Second Book of Divine Poems*;

A True Account and Character of the Times (London, 1647);

A Satire against Presbytery (London, 1648);

An Humble Motion to the Parliament of England Concerning the Advancement of Learning: and Reformation of the Universities (London: Printed by J. H. for John Walker, 1649);

The Grounds & Reasons of Monarchy Considered. In A Review of the Scotch Story (1650);

Paradoxes (London: Printed for John Walker, 1650; enlarged edition, London: Printed for Francis Eaglesfield, 1653);

Answer to the Grand Politick Informer (London, 1653);

A Letter Written to a Gentleman in the Country, Touching the Dissolution of the Late Parliament (London: Printed by F. Leach for Richard Baddeley, 1653);

Confusion Confounded; or, A Firm Way of Settlement Settled and confirmed (London: Printed by Henry Hills, 1654);

Emblems (London: Printed by Roger Daniel, 1658);

An Answer to Some Queries Propos'd by W. C. (Oxford: Printed by Leonard Lichfield for John Buckeridge, 1694).

Editions: *Poems,* edited by Samuel Egerton Brydges (London: Longman, 1816);

The Advancement of Learning (1649), edited by A. K. Croston (Liverpool: Liverpool University Press, 1953).

OTHER: Robert Hegg, *In aliquot Sacræ Paginæ loca Lectiones,* edited by Hall (London: Printed for Nathaniel Webb & J. Grantham, 1647);

A True Relation of the Unjust, Cruel, and Barbarous Proceedings against the English at Amboyna in the East Indies, by the Netherlandish Governour & Council

John Hall (engraving published as the frontispiece in Hall's first two books)

there, preface by Hall (London: Printed by Will. Bentley for Will. Hope, 1651; third edition, London: Tho. Mabb for William Hope, 1665);

Dionysius Cassius Longinus, *Longinus of the Height of Eloquence,* translated by Hall (London, 1652);

Michael Mayer, *Lusus Serius, or Serious Passe-Time. A Philosophicall Discourse concerning the Superiority of Creatures under Man,* translated by Hall as J. de La Salle (London: Printed for Humphrey Moseley & Tho: Heath, 1654);

Pythagoras, *Hierocles upon the Golden Verses of Pythagoras; Teaching a Vertuous and Worthy Life,* translated by Hall (London: Printed by John Streater for Francis Eaglesfield, 1657).

John Hinde's *A Gagg to Love's Advocate, or an Assertion of the Justice of the Parliament in the Execution of Mr. Love* (1650) is sometimes mistakenly attributed to John Hall. The *National Union Catalog Pre-1956 Imprints* assigns *An Humble Remonstrance to the High Court of Parliament* (1640) to Hall, but he would have been only thirteen years old when it was published. Anthony Wood in his *Athenæ Oxonienses* (1691, 1692) notes that Hall also wrote a romance titled "Lucenia," which was lost by a friend who borrowed the manuscript.

At age nineteen Hall published his *Horæ Vacivæ* (1646), dedicated to John Arrowsmith, the master of St. John's College, Cambridge. Thomas Stanley, William Hammond, and James Shirley wrote the commendatory verses; Dr. Henry More added Greek elegiacs; and Hall's tutor, John Pawson, contributed the preface. Hall presented a copy to James Howell, who acknowledged its receipt in *Epistolae Ho-Elianae* (1650). Henry More and others prefixed commendatory verses to Hall's *Poems* (1647), dedicated to Thomas Stanley. The general title page of *Poems* is dated 1646; included in the

SPARKLES
OF
DIVINE LOVE.

1

What am I without thee but one running
headlong? Aug. Conf. lib. 4. cap. 1.

Lord! send thine hand
Unto my rescue, or I shall
Into mine own ambushments fall,
  Which ready stand
  To d' execution All,
  Layd by self-love, O what
  Love of our selves is that
That breeds such uproares in our better state?

2

  I think I pass
A meadow guilt with Crimson showers,
Of the most rich and beauteous flowers,
  Yet Thou, alas!
  Espy'st what under lowers
  Tast them, they 're Poyson, lay
  Thy self to rest, there stray
Whole knots of Snakes that solely wait for prey.
    A 3   To

28   *Sparkles of*   Emb. 8.   Emb. 8.   *Divine love.*   29

The unlearned rise and take heaven by
violence; and we with our learning
without affection, behold! where we
wallow in flesh and bloud! Aug. Conf.
lib. 8. cap. 8.

Vain curiosity! yee lead
 The mind in mazes, make her tread
A-side, while that she toyles and is not fed.

 O empty searchings! do I care
 If I can slice yon burning sphere
To the least atoms, and yet near come there.

 Though I can number every flame
 That fleets within that glorious frame;
Yet do not look on him that can them name.

 Though I can in my travell'd mind
 The earth and all her treasures find
Yet leaving pride swolne into hills behind.

 Though I can plum the sea, and try
 What monsters in her womb do lie;
Yet n'ere a drop fall from my frozen eye.

 Am I the better, though I could
 All wisdome with a breath unfold,
And a heart boundless as the Ocean hold?

 No not a whit unless that he
 By whom these glorious wonders be
Lead me and teach mine eyes himself to see,
    B 5   Yet

Pages from Hall's Emblems *(1658), which he modeled on the better-known* Emblems *(1635) of Francis Quarles*

volume is *The Second Book of Divine Poems,* which has a 1647 title page.

As with most of the poets in this appendix, Hall shows the influences of the better poets of his time. Ben Jonson's classicism, Robert Herrick's love of beauty and sensitivity to its transcience, and John Donne's wit all inform Hall's work; unfortunately they sometimes all appear in the same poem, as shown in "The Morning Star":

> Still herald of the morn, whose ray
> Being page and usher to the day,
> Doth mourn behind the Sun, before him play;
> Who sets a golden signal, ere
> The bat retire, the lark appear,
> The early cocks cry comfort, screech-owls fear.
>
> Who wink'st while lovers plight their troth,
> Then falls asleep, while they are loath
> To part without a more engaging oath:
> Steal in a message to the eyes
> Of Julia, tell her that she lies
> Too long, thy Lord the Sun will quickly rise.
>
> Yet is it midnight still with me,
> Nay worse, unless that kinder she
> Smile day, and in my zenith seated be.
> But if she will obliquely run,
> I needs a calenture must shun,
> And like an Ethiopian hate my sun.

The Second Book of Divine Poems includes a variety of genres (odes, hymns, lyrics, epitaphs, even a pastoral hymn) in English and Latin, often on specific biblical passages. A few of the divine poems reappeared in Hall's posthumously published *Emblems* (1658), which includes a preface by John Quarles. The two books of Hall's *Emblems* have illustrations that resemble those (except for their greater detail and complexity) in Francis Quarles's *Emblems* (1635), though the poems are much superior to Quarles's. An epithalamion "Upon The Happy Nuptials of Jonathan Keile Esquire, And Mris. Susanna Hoo" is appended to his 1657 translation of Pythagoras's *Hierocles.*

John Hall, son of Michael Hall, was born in Durham and baptized on 20 August 1627. He attended Durham school and at age eighteen was admitted as a pensioner to St. John's College, Cambridge, on 26 February 1646. Hall left Cambridge in 1647 to enter Gray's Inn. He accompanied Oliver Cromwell to Scotland in 1650 and afterward began a career of political pamphleteering for which Cromwell awarded him a pension of one hundred pounds per year. At the time of his death he was translating Procopius. In his *Athenæ Oxonienses* (1691, 1692), Anthony Wood remarks how quickly Hall could translate: "Half of which [*Lusus,* 1654] almost was done in one afternoon, over a glass of wine in a tavern." According to John Davies of Kidwelly, in a memoir prefixed to *Hierocles,* Hall detested exercise to the point that in 1650 and 1651, he "being enclined to pursinesse and fatnesse, rather than he would use any great motion, he thought fitter to prevent it by frequent swallowing down of pebble-stones." Davies also notes Hall's mental agility: "I have diverse times writ down thirty or fourty words, and repeated them twice over leasurely, which done he gave them me in order forwards and backwards, and upon demand any particular number, as the 19th, 25th, 31th, or any other." Wood recorded Thomas Hobbes's opinion of Hall, which confirms Davies's account of the poet's physical weakness and mental potential: "had not his debauches and intemperance diverted him from the more serious studies, he had made an extraordinary person; for no man had ever done so great things at his age."

Daniel Baker

(circa 1650 – February 1723)

BOOKS: *Poems upon Several Occasions* (London: Printed for J. Jones, sold by Joseph Wilde, 1697);

The History of Job: a sacred poem in five books (London: Printed for Robert Clavel, 1706).

Daniel Baker's *Poems upon Several Occasions* (1697) is comprised of "Miscellanies and Translations," "Certain Copies of Love-Verses," "Pindarique Odes," and "Sacred Poems." After a poem praising Abraham Cowley, Baker offers translations from Horace, Moschus, Bion, and Virgil. Some of the amorous lyrics show the influence (and phrasing) of John Donne; the first four stanzas of "The Parting" closely parallel Donne's "Valdediction: Forbidding Mourning":

I.

AS virtuous Souls when they depart away,
  And leave their loved Bodies here alone,
In Rest abide, until the joyful day
  Appointed for their Resurrection:

II.

So now we're parting, let us make no noise,
  Nor beat the empty Air with fruitless cries,
Let us not make our cruel Foes rejoyce
  T' have griev'd our Heart, as well as vex'd our Eyes.

III.

Those Earth-born Souls, whose chiefest Good is Sense,
  Whose Joys are dirty, and their Love obscene,
Lament and howl when they are hurri'd hence,
  Because those Pleasures ne'er return again.

IV.

But we whose Love so spotless is and fine,
  Like that which Angels to each other bear,
Shall much disgrace our Souls, if we repine,
  and murmure when our Bodies absent are.

Other poems such as "The Rose" show the influence of Robert Herrick. Some of the "Sacred Poems" are on specific biblical verses, and a long poem "On Mr. George Herbert's Sacred Poems, called The Temple" identifies the major influence on these verses. Baker's *History of Job* (1706) is a combination of biblical epic and tragedy.

Daniel Baker, the son of John Baker of Godmanchester in Huntingdonshire, was born about 1650. His early schooling was at King's Lynn, and he was admitted as a sizar at age seventeen to Caius College, Cambridge, on 11 March 1671. He received the B.A. in 1675 and the M.A. in 1678. He became the chaplain of St. Margaret, Lynn, in Huntingdonshire in 1677 and was ordained a priest in February of 1681. He was chaplain of Tilney, Norfolk, in 1681 and spent the last forty years of his life as rector of Fincham. He married Anne Hebblethwaite, but she and their nine children died young. His second marriage, to Mary Francklin, was childless.

References:

Alun David, " 'A Tragick Scene of Endless Woe': Daniel Baker's *History of Job*," *Critical Survey*, 3, no. 2 (1991): 208–214;

John and J. A. Venn, *Alumni Cantabrigienses,* volume 1 (Cambridge: Cambridge University Press, 1922).

Papers:

Baker's manuscript for several of his unpublished poems is at the British Library (Add. Ms. 11723).

Checklist of Further Readings

Aers, David, Bob Hodge, and Gunther Kress. *Literature, Language and Society in England 1580–1680.* Dublin: Gill & Macmillan / Totowa, N.J.: Barnes & Noble, 1981.

Allen, Don Cameron. *Doubt's Boundless Sea: Skepticism and Faith in the Renaissance.* Baltimore: Johns Hopkins University Press, 1964.

Ashley, Maurice. *England in the Seventeenth Century,* revised. New York: Barnes & Noble, 1980.

Aubrey, John. *Aubrey's Brief Lives,* edited by Oliver Lawson Dick, third edition, revised. London: Secker & Warburg, 1958.

Baker, Herschel C. *The Wars of Truth: Studies in the Decay of Christian Humanism in the Earlier Seventeenth Century.* Cambridge, Mass.: Harvard University Press, 1952.

Bennett, Joan. *Five Metaphysical Poets: Donne, Herbert, Vaughan, Crashaw, Marvell,* third edition. Cambridge: Cambridge University Press, 1964.

Bethell, Samuel Leslie. *The Cultural Revolution of the 17th Century.* London: Dobson, 1951.

Bradbury, Malcolm, and David Palmer, eds. *Metaphysical Poetry.* London: Arnold, 1970.

Bredvold, Louis I. *The Literature of the Restoration and the Eighteenth Century: 1660–1798.* New York: Collier, 1962.

Bush, Douglas. *English Literature in the Earlier Seventeenth Century 1600–1660,* second edition, revised. Oxford: Clarendon Press, 1962.

Bush, *Science and English Poetry: A Historical Sketch, 1590–1950.* New York: Oxford University Press, 1950.

Cain, T. G. S., and Ken Robinson, eds. *"Into Another Mould": Change and Continuity in English Culture, 1625–1700.* London & New York: Routledge, 1992.

Canfield, J. Douglas. *Word as Bond in Literature from the Middle Ages to the Restoration.* Philadelphia: University of Pennsylvania Press, 1989.

Carlton, Charles. *Charles I, the Personal Monarch.* London & Boston: Routledge & Kegan Paul, 1983.

Chambers, A. B. *Transfigured Rites in Seventeenth-Century English Poetry.* Columbia: University of Missouri Press, 1992.

Clark, G. N. *Science and Social Welfare in the Age of Newton.* Oxford: Clarendon Press, 1937.

Colie, Rosalie L. *Paradoxia Epidemica: The Renaissance Tradition of Paradox.* Princeton: Princeton University Press, 1966.

Colie. *The Resources of Kind; Genre-Theory in the Renaissance,* edited by Barbara K. Lewalski. Berkeley: University of California Press, 1973.

Conlon, Michael J. "Politics and Providence: John Dryden's 'Absalom and Achitophel'." Ph.D. dissertation, University of Florida, 1969.

Cruttwell, Patrick. "The Metaphysical Poets and their Readers," *Humanities Association Review,* 28 (Winter 1977): 20–42.

Cruttwell. *The Shakespearean Moment and its Place in the Poetry of the 17th Century.* London: Chatto & Windus, 1954.

Davies, Horton. *Worship and Theology in England,* 5 volumes. Princeton: Princeton University Press, 1961–1975.

Eliot, T. S. "The Metaphysical Poets," in *Selected Essays,* third edition, enlarged. London: Faber & Faber, 1951, pp. 281–291.

Ellrodt, Robert. *L'Inspiration Personelle et l'Esprit du Temps chez Les poètes Métaphysiques Anglais,* 3 volumes. Paris: J. Corti, 1960–1973.

Ezell, Margaret J. M. *The Patriarch's Wife: Literary Evidence and the History of the Family.* Chapel Hill: University of North Carolina Press, 1987.

Feather, John. *A History of British Publishing.* London & New York: Croom Helm, 1988.

Fowler, Alastair. *A History of English Literature.* Cambridge, Mass.: Harvard University Press, 1987.

Fowler, ed. *The New Oxford Book of Seventeenth Century Verse.* Oxford & New York: Oxford University Press, 1991.

Freeman, Rosemary. *English Emblem Books.* London: Chatto & Windus, 1948.

Gordon, D. J. *The Renaissance Imagination: Essays and Lectures,* edited by Stephen Orgel. Berkeley: University of California Press, 1975.

Grant, Patrick. *The Transformation of Sin: Studies in Donne, Herbert, Vaughan and Traherne.* Montreal: McGill-Queen's University Press / Amherst: University of Massachusetts Press, 1974.

Green, I. M. *The Re-establishment of the Church of England 1660–1663.* Oxford & New York: Oxford University Press, 1978.

Grierson, H. J. C. *Cross Currents in English Literature of the XVIIth Century: or, the World, the Flesh, & the Spirit, Their Actions and Reactions.* London: Chatto & Windus, 1929.

Guibbory, Achsah. "Imitation and Originality: Cowley and Bacon's Vision of Progress," *Studies in English Literature,* 29 (Winter 1989): 99–120;

Guibbory. *The Map of Time: Seventeenth-Century English Literature and Ideas of Pattern in History.* Urbana: University of Illinois Press, 1986.

Halewood, William H. *The Poetry of Grace; Reformation Themes and Structures in English Seventeenth-Century Poetry.* New Haven: Yale University Press, 1970.

Haller, William. *The Rise of Puritanism*. New York: Columbia University Press, 1938.

Hammond, Gerald. *Fleeting Things: English Poets and Poems, 1616–1660*. Cambridge, Mass.: Harvard University Press, 1990.

Hammond, Paul. *John Dryden: A Literary Life*. New York: St. Martin's Press, 1991.

Harris, Victor. *All Coherence Gone*. Chicago: University of Chicago Press, 1949.

Haselkorn, Anne M., and Betty S. Travitsky, eds. *The Renaissance Englishwoman in Print: Counterbalancing the Canon*. Amherst: University of Massachusetts Press, 1990.

Haydn, Hiram C. *The Counter-Renaissance*. New York: Scribners, 1950.

Hester, M. Thomas, " 'broken letters scarce remembred': Herbert's *Childhood* in Vaughan," *Christianity and Literature,* 40 (Spring 1991): 209–222;

Hill, Christopher. *The Century of Revolution 1603–1714*. New York: Norton, 1961.

Hill. *Puritans and Revolution: Studies in Interpretation of the English Revolution of the 17th Century,* edited by Donald Pennington and Keith Thomas. Oxford: Clarendon Press, 1978.

Hill. *Society and Puritanism in Pre-Revolutionary England*. London: Secker & Warburg, 1964.

Hobby, Elaine. *Virtue of Necessity: English Women's Writing 1649–88*. London: Virago, 1988; Ann Arbor: University of Michigan Press, 1989.

Holden, William P. *Anti-Puritan Satire, 1572–1642*. New Haven: Yale University Press, 1954.

Hollander, John. *The Untuning of the Sky: Ideas of Music in English Poetry 1500–1700*. Princeton: Princeton University Press, 1961.

Hughes, Ann. *The Causes of the English Civil War*. New York: St. Martin's Press, 1991; London: Macmillan, 1991.

Hutton, Ronald. *The British Republic, 1649–1660*. New York: St. Martin's Press, 1990.

Jones, James Rees. *Country and Court: England, 1658–1714*. London: Arnold, 1978; Cambridge, Mass.: Harvard University Press, 1978.

Jose, Nicholas. *Ideas of the Restoration in English Literature 1660–71*. Cambridge, Mass.: Harvard University Press, 1984.

Kahn, Victoria. *Rhetoric, Prudence, and Skepticism in the Renaissance*. Ithaca, N.Y.: Cornell University Press, 1985.

Kay, Dennis. *Melodious Tears: The English Funeral Elegy from Spenser to Milton*. Oxford: Clarendon Press / New York: Oxford University Press, 1990.

Keast, William R., ed. *Seventeenth-Century English Poetry; Modern Essays in Criticism*. New York: Oxford University Press, 1962.

Keller, Evelyn Fox. *Reflections on Gender and Science*. New Haven: Yale University Press, 1985.

Kernan, Alvin B. *The Cankered Muse: Satire of the English Renaissance*. New Haven: Yale University Press, 1959.

Lamont, William M. *Godly Rule: Politics and Religion, 1603–60*. London: Macmillan / New York: St. Martin's Press, 1969.

Laslett, Peter. *The World We Have Lost*. London: Methuen, 1965; New York: Scribners, 1966.

Leishman, J. B. *The Metaphysical Poets: Donne, Herbert, Vaughan, Traherne*. Oxford: Clarendon Press, 1934.

Lewalski, Barbara K. *Protestant Poetics and the Seventeenth-Century Religious Lyric*. Princeton: Princeton University Press, 1979.

Lewis, C. S. *The Abolition of Man*. New York: Macmillan, 1947.

Lovejoy, Arthur O. *The Great Chain of Being; A Study of the History of an Idea*. Cambridge, Mass.: Harvard University Press, 1936.

Low, Anthony. *Love's Architecture: Devotional Modes in Seventeenth-Century English Poetry*. New York: New York University Press, 1978.

Lyons, Bridget Gellert. *Voices of Melancholy: Studies in Literary Treatments of Melancholy in Renaissance England*. London: Routledge & Kegan Paul, 1971.

Lyons, John D., and Stephen G. Nichols, Jr., eds. *Mimesis, from Mirror to Method, Augustine to Descartes*. Hanover, N.H.: University Press of New England, 1982.

MacCulloch, Diarmaid. *The Later Reformation in England, 1547–1603*. New York: St. Martin's Press, 1990; Basingstoke, Hampshire: Macmillan, 1990.

Manley, Lawrence. *Convention, 1500–1750*. Cambridge, Mass.: Harvard University Press, 1980.

Martines, Lauro. *Society and History in English Renaissance Verse*. Oxford: Blackwell, 1985.

Martz, Louis L. *The Paradise Within: Studies in Vaughan, Traherne, and Milton*. New Haven: Yale University Press, 1964.

Martz. *Poet of Exile: A Study of Milton's Poetry*. New Haven: Yale University Press, 1980.

Martz. *The Poetry of Meditation: A Study in English Religious Literature of the Seventeenth Century*. New Haven: Yale University Press, 1954.

Mazzeo, Joseph A. *Renaissance and Revolution: Backgrounds to Seventeenth-Century English Literature*. New York: Pantheon, 1967.

Mazzeo. *Renaissance and Seventeenth-Century Studies*. New York: Columbia University Press, 1964.

Merchant, Carolyn. *The Death of Nature: Women, Ecology and the Scientific Revolution*. San Francisco: Harper & Row, 1980; London: Wildwood, 1982.

Merton, Robert King. *Science, Technology and Society in Seventeenth-Century England*. Bruges, Belgium: Saint Catherine, 1938; New York: Harper & Row, 1970.

Miner, Earl. *The Cavalier Mode From Jonson to Cotton*. Princeton: Princeton University Press, 1971.

Miner. *The Metaphysical Mode from Donne to Cowley*. Princeton: Princeton University Press, 1969.

Miner. *The Restoration Mode from Milton to Dryden*. Princeton: Princeton University Press, 1974.

Mulder, John R. *The Temple of the Mind: Education and Literary Taste in Seventeenth-Century England*. New York: Pegasus, 1969.

Nevo, Ruth. *The Dial of Virtue: A Study of Poems on Affairs of State in the Seventeenth Century*. Princeton: Princeton University Press, 1963.

Nicolson, Marjorie Hope. *The Breaking of the Circle: Studies in the Effect of the "New Science" upon Seventeenth-Century Poetry,* revised edition. New York: Columbia University Press, 1962.

Owens, W. R., ed. *Seventeenth-Century England: A Changing Culture,* volume 2. London: Ward Lock Educational, in association with the Open University Press, 1980.

Parfitt, George. *English Poetry of the Seventeenth Century*. London & New York: Longman, 1985.

Parry, Graham. *The Seventeenth Century: The Intellectual and Cultural Context of English Literature, 1603–1700*. London & New York: Longman, 1989.

Patrides, C. A., and Raymond B. Waddington, eds. *The Age of Milton: Backgrounds to Seventeenth-Century Literature*. Manchester: Manchester University Press / Totowa, N. J.: Barnes & Noble, 1980.

Patterson, Annabel. *Censorship and Interpretation: The Conditions of Writing and Reading in Early Modern England*. Madison: University of Wisconsin Press, 1984.

Post, Jonathan F. S. *Henry Vaughan: The Unfolding Vision*. Princeton: Princeton University Press, 1982.

Praz, Mario. *Studies in Seventeenth-Century Imagery,* 2 volumes, second edition, enlarged. Rome: Edizioni di storia e letteratura, 1964, 1974.

Radzinowicz, Mary Ann. *Toward Samson Agonistes: The Growth of Milton's Mind*. Princeton: Princeton University Press, 1978.

Ricks, Christopher, ed. *English Poetry and Prose, 1540–1674*. London: Barrie & Jenkins, 1970.

Rivers, Isabel. *Classical and Christian Ideas in English Renaissance Poetry: A Students' Guide*. London & Boston: Allen & Unwin, 1979.

Roberts, Clayton. *The Growth of Responsible Government in Stuart England*. Cambridge: Cambridge University Press, 1966.

Ross, Malcolm M. *Poetry and Dogma: The Transfiguration of Eucharist Symbols in Seventeenth Century English Poetry*. New Brunswick: Rutgers University Press, 1954.

Røstvig, Maren-Sofie. *The Happy Man: Studies in the Metamorphoses of a Classical Ideal,* 2 volumes, revised. Oslo: Norwegian Universities Press, 1962, 1971.

Sampson, George. *Concise Cambridge History of English Literature*. Cambridge: Cambridge University Press / New York: Macmillan, 1941.

Seaward, Paul. *The Restoration, 1660–1688*. New York: St. Martin's Press, 1991.

Selden, Raman. *English Verse Satire, 1590–1765*. London & Boston: Allen & Unwin, 1978.

Sharp, Robert L. *From Donne to Dryden: The Revolt Against Metaphysical Poetry*. Chapel Hill: University of North Carolina Press, 1940.

Sharpe, Kevin, and Steven N. Zwicker, eds. *Politics of Discourse; The Literature and History of Seventeenth-Century England*. Berkeley: University of California Press, 1987.

Shaw, Robert B. *The Call of God: The Theme of Vocation in the Poetry of Donne and Herbert*. Cambridge, Mass.: Cowley, 1981.

Shawcross, John T. *Paradise Regain'd: "worthy t'have not remain'd so long unsung."* Pittsburgh: Duquesne University Press, 1988.

Shawcross. *With Mortal Voice: The Creation of Paradise Lost*. Lexington: University Press of Kentucky, 1982.

Smith, A. J. *The Metaphysics of Love: Studies in Renaissance Love Poetry from Dante to Milton*. Cambridge & New York: Cambridge University Press, 1985.

Spingarn, J. E., ed. *Critical Essays of the Seventeenth Century,* 3 volumes. Bloomington: Indiana University Press, 1957.

Staves, Susan. *Players' Scepters: Fictions of Authority in the Restoration*. Lincoln: University of Nebraska Press, 1979.

Stewart, Stanley. *The Enclosed Garden; The Tradition and the Image in Seventeenth-Century Poetry*. Madison: University of Wisconsin Press, 1966.

Stone, Lawrence. *The Causes of the English Revolution, 1529–1642*. New York: Harper & Row, 1972.

Stone. *The Family, Sex and Marriage in England, 1500–1800*. New York: Harper & Row, 1977.

Summers, Claude, and Ted-Larry Pebworth, eds. *"Bright Shootes of Everlastingnesse": The Seventeenth-Century Religious Lyric*. Columbia: University of Missouri Press, 1987.

Summers and Pebworth, eds. *"The Muses Common-Weale": Poetry and Politics in the Seventeenth Century*. Columbia: University of Missouri Press, 1988.

Summers, Joseph H. *The Heirs of Donne and Jonson*. New York: Oxford University Press, 1970.

Sutherland, James. *English Literature of the Late Seventeenth Century*. Oxford: Clarendon Press, 1969.

Swardson, H. R. *Poetry and the Fountain of Light: Observations on the Conflict Between Christian and Classical Traditions in Seventeenth-Century Poetry*. London: Allen & Unwin, 1962.

Tawney, R. H. *Religion and the Rise of Capitalism*. New York: Harcourt, Brace, 1926; London: Murray, 1936.

Tayler, Edward William. *Nature and Art in Renaissance Literature*. New York: Columbia University Press, 1964.

Tuveson, Ernest Lee. *Millennium and Utopia: A Study in the Background of the Idea of Progress*. Berkeley: University of California Press, 1949.

Underdown, David. *Royalist Conspiracy in England, 1649–1660*. New Haven: Yale University Press, 1960.

Vickers, Brian. *Classical Rhetoric in English Poetry*. London: Macmillan / New York: St. Martin's Press, 1970.

Wall, John N. *Transformations of the Word: Spenser, Herbert, Vaughan.* Athens: University of Georgia Press, 1988.

Wallerstein, Ruth C. *Studies in Seventeenth-Century Poetic.* Madison: University of Wisconsin Press, 1950.

Wedgwood, C. V. *Poetry and Politics Under the Stuarts.* Cambridge: Cambridge University Press, 1960.

Wedgwood. *Seventeenth-Century English Literature,* second edition. London: Oxford University Press, 1950.

Willey, Basil. *The Seventeenth-Century Background; Studies in the Thought of the Age in Relation to Poetry and Religion.* London: Chatto & Windus, 1934.

Williamson, George. *The Donne Tradition; A Study in English Poetry from Donne to the Death of Cowley.* Cambridge, Mass.: Harvard University Press, 1930.

Wilson, F. P. *Elizabethan and Jacobean.* Oxford: Clarendon Press, 1945.

Wilson, Katharina M., and Frank J. Warnke, eds. *Women Writers of the Seventeenth Century.* Athens: University of Georgia Press, 1989.

Wood, Anthony. *Athenæ Oxonienses,* 5 volumes, edited by Philip Bliss. London: Printed for F. C. & J. Rivington, 1813–1820.

Wrightson, Keith. *English Society, 1580–1680.* London: Hutchinson, 1982; New Brunswick, N. J.: Rutgers University Press, 1984.

Contributors

Reid Barbour..*University of North Carolina at Chapel Hill*

Thomas O. Calhoun...*University of Delaware*

J. Douglas Canfield ....*University of Arizona*

Eugene R. Cunnar...*New Mexico State University*

Donald R. Dickson...*Texas A&M University*

Jean Gagen..*University of Kansas*

Anne Barbeau Gardiner ....*John Jay College of Criminal Justice*

James E. Gill...*University of Tennessee*

Elizabeth H. Hageman ....*University of New Hampshire*

Ann Hurley...*Skidmore College*

Albert C. Labriola ....*Duquesne University*

Steven Max Miller.......................................*Millersville University of Pennsylvania*

Katherine M. Quinsey...*University of Windsor*

Graham Roebuck...*McMaster University*

Sharon Cadman Seelig ....*Smith College*

John T. Shawcross..*University of Kentucky*

Louise Simons ....*Boston University*

Stanley Stewart ....*University of California, Riverside*

Arlene Stiebel ....*California State University, Northridge*

Ernest W. Sullivan, II...*Texas Tech University*

John N. Wall ....*North Carolina State University*

Deborah Wyrick...*North Carolina State University*

R. V. Young ....*Franciscan University of Steubenville*

Cumulative Index

Dictionary of Literary Biography, Volumes 1-131
Dictionary of Literary Biography Yearbook, 1980-1992
Dictionary of Literary Biography Documentary Series, Volumes 1-10

Cumulative Index

DLB before number: *Dictionary of Literary Biography*, Volumes 1-131
Y before number: *Dictionary of Literary Biography Yearbook*, 1980-1992
DS before number: *Dictionary of Literary Biography Documentary Series*, Volumes 1-10

A

D

G

H

M

N

O

406

Y

Z

ISBN 0-8103-5390-3

9 780810 353909

Documentary Series

Yearbooks